The Reformation and the Book

St Andrews Studies in Reformation History

Editorial Board:

Titles in this series include:

The Reformation and the Book

Edited by JEAN-FRANÇOIS GILMONT

English edition and translation by
KARIN MAAG

Ashgate

Aldershot • Brookfield USA • Singapore • Sydney

First published as *La Réforme et le livre: L'Europe de l'imprimé (1517–v.1570)*, edited by Jean-François Gilmont © Les Editions du Cerf, 1990.
This English translation and new edition © Karin Maag and the contributors, 1998.
By kind permission of Les Editions du Cerf.

Published by
Ashgate Publishing Limited
Gower House
Croft Road
Aldershot
Hants
GU11 3HR
England

Ashgate Publishing Company
Old Post Road
Brookfield
Vermont 05036–9704
USA

British Library Cataloguing in Publication Data

The Reformation and the Book.
  (St Andrews Studies in Reformation History)
  1. Reformation. 2. Book—History—1400–1600.
  I. Gilmont, Jean-François. II. Maag, Karin.
  270.6

Library of Congress Cataloging-in-Publication Data

Réforme et le livre. English.
    The Reformation and the book/edited by Jean-François Gilmont:
  English edition and translation by Karin Maag.
      p.   cm. (St Andrews Studies in Reformation History)
    Includes bibliographical references and index.
    ISBN 1–85928–448–5 (hb)
    1. Printing—Europe—History—16th century. 2. Christian
  literature—Publication and distribution—Europe—History—16th
  century. 3. Reformation. 4. Books and reading—Europe—
  History—16th century. I. Gilmont, Jean-François. II. Maag,
  Karin. III. Title. IV. Series.
  Z124.R42313   1998
  686.2'094'09031—dc21   97–34903
                                                         CIP

ISBN 1 85928 448 5

This book is printed on acid free paper

Typeset in Sabon by Manton Typesetters, 5–7 Eastfield Road, Louth, Lincolnshire, LN11 7AJ and printed in Great Britain by

Printed in Great Britain by Galliard (Printers) Ltd, Great Yarmouth

Contents

vi   CONTENTS

List of illustrations

List of figures

Notes on contributors

Peter G. Bietenholz
Born in 1933, he received his PhD from the University of Basle in 1958, and became professor of history at the University of Saskatchewan (Canada) in 1963, where he received a D.Litt. He specializes in the history of the Renaissance and Reformation and his works include *Der italienische Humanismus und die Blüterzeit des Buchdrucks in Basle* (Basle, 1959), *Pietro Della Valle, 1586–1642* (Basle, 1962), *History and Biography in the Work of Erasmus of Rotterdam* (Geneva, 1966), *Basle and France in the Sixteenth Century* (Geneva, 1971) and *Historia and Fabula. Myths and Legends in Historical Thought from Antiquity to the Modern Age* (Leiden, 1994). He edited Mino Celsi's *In haereticis coërcendis quatenus progedi liceat* (Naples, Chicago, 1982), *Contemporaries of Erasmus: A biographical register of the Renaissance and Reformation* (Toronto, 1985–87) and Erasmus' *Collected Works* (Toronto, 1985–87).

Mirjam Bohatcová
Born Mirjam Daňková in 1919, she completed her doctorate in auxiliary historical sciences at the Charles University in Prague, specializing in the history of the book and printing in the sixteenth to eighteenth centuries. She was head of the department of printed works from the fifteenth to eighteenth centuries in the library of the National Museum in Prague. She worked for 19 years in the Czechoslovak Academy of Sciences, and finally as an editor for the ARTIA publishing house. Her list of publications up to 1990 has been published in the year-book of the Historical Institute of the Czechoslovak Academy of Sciences, *Folia Historica Bohemica* 13 (1990), pp. 511–23. She regularly publishes abroad, including German articles in the *Gutenberg-Jahrbuch*.

Gedeon Borsa
Born in Budapest in 1923, he worked for three decades in the Hungarian National Library. The main focus of his research has been the establishment of a Hungarian national bibliography for the period prior to 1801. The section on the fifteenth and sixteenth centuries appeared in Budapest in 1971: *Régi Magyarországi Nyomtatványok 1473–1600 = Res litteraria Hungariae vetus operum impressorum 1473–1600*. In his studies on the history of the book, he concentrates primarily on the history of printing, the focus of many of his articles. He is Senior Research Fellow of the National Széchényi Library of Hungary in Buda-

pest. His research has not, however, focused on Hungary alone, as he published a valuable *Clavis typographorum librariorumque Italiae 1465–1600* (2 vols, Baden Baden, 1980).

Miriam Usher Chrisman

Born in 1920, she trained at Yale University, where she received her doctorate in 1962. She taught at the University of Massachusetts, Amherst from 1962 until becoming emeritus in 1987. She published *Strasbourg and the Reform: A Study in the Process of Change* (Yale, 1967), *Lay Culture, Learned Culture: Books and Social Change in Strasbourg, 1480–1599* and *Bibliography of Strasbourg Imprints, 1480–1599* (New Haven, 1982), *Conflicting Visions of Reform: German Lay Propaganda Pamphlets, 1519–1530* (Atlantic Highlands, 1996). Her work attempted to establish the intellectual and social context in which the Reformation occurred. She was president of the American Society for Reformation Research (1975–77) and the American editor of the *Archive for Reformation Research/Archiv für Reformationsgeschichte* (1982–87). She received the Wilbur Cross Medal from the Yale Graduate School in 1996 for 'scholarship transforming the history of Reformation Europe'.

John L. Flood

John Flood is Professor of German in the University of London and Deputy Director of the University of London Institute of Germanic Studies. He has written extensively on the history of the book and on medieval and early modern German literature. His most recent works include *The German Book 1450–1750* (with W. A. Kelly) (London, 1995) and *Johannes Sinapius (1505–1560), Hellenist and Physician in Germany and Italy* (with D. J. Shaw) (Geneva, forthcoming, 1997).

Jean-François Gilmont

Born in 1934, he is Curator and Professor at the Catholic University of Louvain (Louvain-la-Neuve). His research stands at the crossroads of the history of the book and that of the Reformation in the sixteenth century, with a particular focus on Calvin. His works include *Jean Crespin: Un éditeur réformé du xvie siècle* (Geneva, 1981), *Bibliographie des éditions de Jean Crespin, 1550–1572* (2 vols, Verviers, 1981) and *Le livre, du manuscrit à l'ère électronique: Notes de bibliologie* (Liège, 1989), the two first volumes of the *Bibliotheca calviniana* begun by Rodolphe Peter (Geneva, 1991–94) and *Jean Calvin et le livre* (Geneva, 1997). Apart from numerous articles, dictionary entries and reviews, he edited *Palaestra typographica: Aspects de la production du livre humaniste et religieux au xvie siècle* (Aubel, 1984).

Francis M. Higman

Born in 1935, he studied in Oxford under W. G. Moore. He taught French language and literature at Bristol University, at Trinity College (Dublin) and at Nottingham University. Since 1988, he has been the director of the Institut d'Histoire de la Réformation in Geneva. While his earlier research focused on Calvin's style, he has broadened his work to include the impact of Calvinist Reform in French-speaking lands. His many works include *The Style of John Calvin in his French Polemical Treatises* (Oxford, 1967), *Three French Treatises* by Calvin (London, 1970), *Censorship and the Sorbonne: A Bibliographical Study of Books in French Censured by the Faculty of Theology of the University of Paris, 1520–1551* (Geneva, 1979), *Le Pater Noster et le credo en françoys* by Guillaume Farel (Geneva, 1982), and *Piety and the People: Religious Printing in French, 1511–1551* (Aldershot, 1996). He jointly edited the *Index de l'Université de Paris* (Sherbrooke, Geneva, 1986), and has also written many articles.

Andrew G. Johnston

Andrew Johnston completed a PhD at the University of Southampton in 1986 on the relationship between printing and the Reformation in the Netherlands. Since then, he has taught History both in Southampton and, more recently, in Eastbourne, where he is Head of History at Eastbourne College. He has continued to research and write on various aspects of the Reformation.

Alodia Kawecka-Gryczowa (1903–90)

She was chief curator of the Rare Books department in the National Library of Warsaw. She studied at the Jagiellonian University of Cracow under the direction of Stanisław Kot, the eminent historian of the Renaissance and Reformation. Her doctoral thesis dealt with Polish Protestant hymn-books in the sixteenth century. She was appointed professor in 1954, and directed major collective bibliographical and historical projects on older books (fifteenth to eighteenth centuries), both in the National Library and in the Institute of Literary Research of the Polish Academy of Sciences. She published more than 180 works dealing with the history of rare books, the Renaissance and the Reformation. Among these is her bilingual Polish–French work, *Les imprimeurs des antitrinitaires polonais Rodecki et Sternacki. Histoire et bibliographie* (Geneva, 1974).

Remi Kick

Born in Strasbourg in 1960, he studied in the city, obtaining his masters' in Protestant theology in 1983, for work on the three confessions of faith of Upper Hungary, directed by Professor Marc Lienhard. In 1984, Kick obtained the Diploma of in-depth studies in Protestant theology. He has written a thesis on the ecclesiology of Laurentius Petri, the first evangelical archbishop of Uppsala, which should be published in the course of 1997. He is currently pursuing his research on the Swedish Reformation. His most recent works include, 'L'Héritage de Bucer en Suède', in Christian Krieger and Marc Lienhard (eds) *Martin Bucer and Sixteenth Century Europe: Actes du Colloque de Strasbourg 28–31 August 1991* (Leiden, 1993), pp. 533–45 (Studies in Medieval and Reformation Thought, 53).

A. Gordon Kinder
Born in 1927, he studied at the University of Sheffield from 1947 to 1951. Between 1951 and 1981 he taught in grammar schools, obtaining a PhD from Sheffield University in 1971, helped by a Schoolmaster Studentship at Corpus Christi College, Oxford, in 1970. In 1981, he took early retirement and joined the Department of Spanish and Portuguese Studies in the University of Manchester, where he is now Honorary Senior Research Fellow. In addition to more than 45 articles, he has published *Casiodoro de Reina, Spanish Reformer of the Sixteenth Century* (London, 1975), *Spanish Protestants and Reformers: A Bibliography* (London, 1983) with a first supplement in 1994, *La Confesion de fe espanola de Londres, 1560/61* (Exeter, 1988) and *Servetus* (Baden-Baden, 1989). Many of his articles have been republished in Spanish translation.

David Loades
Born in Cambridge in 1934, he attended the Perse School. Following his military service in the Royal Air Force, he returned to Cambridge to teach history at Emmanuel College. Having obtained his doctorate in 1961, he continued his research in Cambridge under the direction of G. R. Elton. From 1961 to 1963 he was an honorary lecturer in political science at the University of St Andrews. He then went to Durham, where he taught history as lecturer, senior lecturer (1971) and then reader (1977). In 1980, he was appointed to the chair of history at the North Wales University College in Bangor. He became Director of the British Academy John Foxe Project in 1993, and retired from Bangor in 1996. He is currently honorary Research Professor at the University of Sheffield (where the John Foxe Project is based) and Emeritus Professor of the University of Wales. Alongside numerous articles, he has published *Two Tudor Conspiracies* (Cambridge, 1965), *The Oxford Martyrs* (London, 1970), *Politics and the Nation, 1450–1660. Obedience, Resistance and Public Order* (London, 1974), *The Reign of Mary*

Tudor (New York, 1979) (translated into German, Munich, 1982), *The Tudor Court* (London, 1986), *The Tudor Navy* (Aldershot, 1992) and *John Dudley, Duke of Northumberland* (Oxford, 1996).

Anne Riising

Born in 1926. Following her studies in history at the University of Aarhus (MA 1951), she became an archivist in 1952, and was chief archivist in Funen in 1972, retiring in 1985. In 1950, she won the Essay Prize (for a work on the thesis of Pirenne) and obtained her doctorate (with a dissertation on preaching in medieval Denmark). From 1968 to 1973, she was honorary lecturer in Medieval History at the University of Odense. She has written numerous works on medieval history, local history, and the history of the Danish administration.

Ugo Rozzo

Born in 1940. After having been director of the Biblioteca Civica de Tortona for 20 years, he is currently associate professor of the history of libraries in the Faculty of Arts and Philosophy of the University of Udine. Among other works, he published *Stampa e cultura a Tortona nel xvi–xvii secolo* (Tortona, 1972) and edited *I 'Dialogi Sette' e altri scritti del tempo della fuga* by Bernardino Ochino (Torino, 1985). He has also published *Linee per una storia dell'editoria religiosa in Italia (1465–1600)* (Udine, 1993) and *Biblioteche italiane del Cinquecento tra Riforma e Controriforma* (Udine, 1994). In 1994, he contributed to the ninth volume of *Index des livres interdits* by providing the *Index de Parme 1580*, pp. 17–185.

Silvana Seidel Menchi

Born in 1938, she studied Modern History in Florence with Delio Cantimori, in Basle with Werner Kaegi and Medieval Latin philology in Munich with Bernhard Bischoff. She is a former fellow of the Harvard University Center for Italian Renaissance Studies. She has been a contributor to the international edition of the complete works of Erasmus. She republished a version of Francesco Guicciardini's *Storia d'Italia* with a critical apparatus (Turin, 1970), and a critical version with translation and commentary of the full-length version of Erasmus's *Adagia* (Turin, 1980). She has also published a monograph *Erasmo in Italia 1520–1580* (Turin, 1987) as well as many articles on the spread of Reformation ideas in Italy.

Janusz Tazbir

Born in 1927, he is professor of the Historical Institute of the Polish Academy of Sciences. He is the editor-in-chief of *Odrodzenie i Reformacja w Polsce* [Renaissance and Reformation in Poland]. He received his degree from the University of Warsaw, where he began his academic career. The main focus of his works is the Renaissance and Reformation period from the standpoint of cultural history. He has written more than 160 articles in Polish and foreign languages, and has published around 20 books, including *A State without Stakes: Polish Religious Tolerance in the Sixteenth and Seventeenth Centuries* (New York, 1973), *Geschichte der polnischen Toleranz* (Warsaw, 1977), *La République nobiliaire et le monde. Etudes sur l'histoire de la culture polonaise à l'époque du baroque* (Wroclaw, 1986), *Polskie przedmurze chrzescijańskiej Europy. Mity a rzeczywistość hist.* [Poland as the Rampart of Christian Europe. Myths and Historical Reality] (Warsaw, 1987).

Preface to the English edition and translator's note

The publication of *The Reformation and the Book* in its English version is the result of close collaboration between the original editor, Jean-François Gilmont, the contributors, and members of the St Andrews Reformation Studies Institute. I wish to thank Jean-François Gilmont especially for supporting the idea of an English edition, and for encouraging the project every step of the way. The English version owes much to his careful editing of the French text. I also wish to express my thanks to Professor Andrew Pettegree for entrusting the English editorial work and translation to me, and to the editorial board of the St Andrews Studies in Reformation History for agreeing to publish the book in its series. Thanks also to my colleagues in the Reformation Studies Institute and in other departments, who provided suggestions and comments on various translated passages, especially Augustine Kelly and Dr Susanna Phillippo.

My particular thanks go to Anne Chalmers, secretary of the Reformation Studies Institute, for her patient and accurate typing of the translated chapters.

I translated the introduction, chapters 1, 4–6, 11–16 and the conclusion. The other chapters were provided in an English version.

The editors note with sadness the sudden death of Dr Gordon Kinder on 13 August 1997, prior to this book going to press. His work on Spain in the sixteenth century was highly regarded, and he will be missed by scholars both in Britain and across Europe. The proofs for his chapter were revised by Karin Maag.

Karin Maag
St Andrews

Abbreviations

AA	Archivio Arcivescovile
AGB	*Archiv für Geschichte des Buchwesens* (Frankfurt am Main, 1959–)
AGS	Simancas, Archivo General
AHN	Madrid, Archivo Histórico Nacional
ARG	*Archiv für Reformationsgeschichte* (Gütersloh, 1903–)
AS	Archivio di Stato
BHR	*Bibliothèque d'Humanisme et Renaissance* (Geneva, 1941–)
BRN	*Bibliotheca reformatioria neerlandica* S. Cramer and F. Pijper (eds) (The Hague, 1903–14)
BSHPF	*Bulletin de la Société d'Histoire du Protestantisme français* (Paris, 1852–)
BSSV	*Bollettino della Società di Studi Valdesi* (Torre Pellice, 1934–)
CD	*Corpus documentorum inquisitionis haereticae pravitatis Neerlandicae* P. Fredericq (ed.) (Ghent, 1889–1916)
Claus/Pegg	H. Claus and M. A. Pegg, *Ergänzungen zur Bibliographie der zeitgenössichen Lutherdrucke* (Gotha, 1982) (Veröffentlichungen der Forschungsbibliothek Gotha, 20)
CODOIN	*Colección de documentos inéditos para la historia de España* (112 volumes, Madrid, 1842–95)
CR	*Corpus reformatorum* (Berlin, 1834– ; Leipzig, 1906–)
Febvre/Martin	L. Febvre and H.-J. Martin, *L'apparition du livre* (Paris, 1958, reprint Paris, 1971)
GJ	*Gutenberg Jahrbuch* (Mayence, 1926–)
GW	*Gesamtkatalog der Wiegendrucke* (Leipzig, Berlin, 1925–)
HÉF	*Histoire de l'édition française* R. Chartier and H.-J. Martin (eds) (Paris, 1982) vol. 1
Index 1	*Index de l'Université de Paris* J. M. de Bujanda, F. M. Higman and J. K. Farge (eds) (Sherbrooke, Geneva, 1985) (Index des livres interdits, 1)
Index 2	*Index de l'Université de Louvain, 1546, 1550, 1558* J. M. de Bujanda, L.-E. Halkin, P. Pasture, and G.

Glorieux (eds) (Sherbrooke, Geneva, 1986) (Index des livres interdits, 2)

Index 3   *Index de Venise 1549, Venise et Milan 1554* J. M. de Bujanda (ed.) (Sherbrooke, Geneva, 1987) (Index des livres interdits, 3)

Index 5   *Index de l'Inquisition espagnole 1551, 1554, 1559* J. M. de Bujanda (ed.) (Geneva, Sherbrooke, 1984) (Index des livres interdits, 5)

LB   J. Benzing, *Lutherbibliographie. Verzeichnis der gedruckten Schriften Martin Luthers bis zu dessen Tod* (Baden Baden, 1966) (Bibliotheca Bibliographica Aureliana, 10, 16, 19)

NK   W. Nijhoff and M. E. Kronenberg, *Nederlandsche bibliographie van 1500 tot 1540* (The Hague, 1923–1971)

Reusch   *Die Indices librorum prohibitorum des sechzehnten Jahrhunderts* F. H. Reusch (Tübingen, 1886) (Bibliothek des Litterarischen Vereins in Stuttgart, 176)

RMNy   *Régi Magyaroszáki Nyomtatványok 1473–1600 = Res litteraria Hungariae vetus operum impressorum 1473–1600* G. Borsa et al. (eds) (Budapest, 1971)

ROPB2   *Recueil des ordonnances des Pays-Bas* Ch. Laurent, J. Lameere, H. Simont (eds) (8 vols, Brussels, 1893–1978)

SB   Staatsbibliothek

STC   *A Short Title Catalogue of Books Printed in England ... and of English Books Abroad, 1475–1640* A. W. Pollard and G. R. Redgrave (1st edn eds); W. A. Jackson, F. S. Ferguson and K. F. Pantzer (2nd edn eds) (2 vols, London, 1976–1983)

SU   Santo Ufficio

VD 16   *Verzeichnis der im deutschen Sprachgebiet erschienen Drucke des XVI. Jahrhunderts VD 16* (Stuttgart, 1983–)

WA   M. Luther, *Werke, Kritische Gesamtausgabe* (Weimar, 1883–)

WA Br.   *Briefwechsel* (Weimar, 1930–)

WA DB   *Die Deutsche Bibel*

WA Tisch.   *Tischreden*

Introduction

Jean-François Gilmont

The Bibles printed in Antwerp by Martin Lempereur and Willem Vorsterman beginning in 1530 show the writers of the various New Testament books composing their text with the help of divine inspiration. This traditional representation is significantly altered in the case of Saint Matthew. Indeed, he does not write by taking dictation from one of God's envoys, but he transcribes the text of an open book presented to him by an angel.[1] We have moved from dictation to transcription, from reception through hearing to reception through sight. This engraving appears on the front cover of this work. By symbolizing the evolution towards a world where written communication is increasingly significant, it provides a perfect introduction to the theme of this research.

What impact did printed books have on the early spread of the Reformation, and vice versa, what effect did the Reformation have on the development of printing? This double question, almost as old as the Reformation itself, is today more central than ever following recent developments in the history of the book.

Already in the sixteenth century, certain participants in the Reformation movement were keenly aware of the fundamental role of printing in the spread of Luther's ideas. Following in their footsteps, historians have repeated from generation to generation that the Reformation is Gutenberg's child. In most cases, these historians base themselves on a few key references. Luther's comment in his Table Talk has been quoted often, though mainly at second-hand:

> Printing is God's ultimate and greatest gift. Indeed through printing God wants the whole world, to the ends of the earth, to know the roots of true religion and wants to transmit it in every language. Printing is the last flicker of the flame which glows before the end of this world.[2]

The same holds true for the description of printing as 'a divine and miraculous invention' by John Foxe, the writer of the English martyrol-

---

[1] This image had appeared already in 1522 in Amsterdam. See B. Rosier, 'De illustraties in Doen Pieterszoons uitgave van het Evangelie naar Mattheus (Amsterdam, 1522)', *Nederlands Archief voor kerkgeschiedenis*, 74 (1994), 22–3.

[2] W. A. Tisch., vol. 1, p. 523, no. 1038; see also vol. 4, pp. 436–7, no. 4697.

ogy.[3] Praise for the new invention and for its role in the Reformation is not hard to find. A systematic search would bring many more enthusiastic reactions to light, such as those of François Lambert of Avignon or of Melanchthon.[4]

Yet for those who attempt to move away from uncritical commonplaces on the subject, is this influence of printing on the Reformation as obvious as all that? Luther and many of his contemporaries had several reservations regarding the rapid multiplication of printed books. In fact, apart from Luther's comment quoted above, he made few favourable remarks about printing. More often than not, he held a negative view of the new invention. In his eyes, there was an abundance of useless or even harmful books. 'There have never been sufficient numbers of good books, and even today these are in short supply.'[5] Luther therefore advised choosing books with care, and even wished for a reduction in the number of works on theology.[6] This pessimistic outlook was shared by Conrad Gesner, author of the first universal bibliography: 'Even though printing seems designed for the preservation of books, most of the published works are frivolities written by our contemporaries, or entirely useless works, while the ancient and better works are left aside.'[7] In 1566, Matthaeus Judex, one of the Centuriators of Magdeburg wrote De typographica inventione – a source for John Foxe in his praise of printing. Judex's views on the subject were mixed. Indeed, he was firmly convinced that printing 'has greatly advanced the restoration of doctrinal purity and the revelation of the Antichrist'.[8] But

---

[3] J. Foxe, *Acts and Monuments*, G. Townsend and S. R. Cattley (eds), (London, 1837–41) vol. 3, p. 720.

[4] Fr. Lambert, *Commentarii de prophetia, eruditione et linguis*, 1526 (cited in J. Lebeau and J.-M. Valentin (eds), *L'Alsace au siècle de la Réforme, 1482–1621: Textes et documents* (Nancy, 1985) p. 218). For Melanchthon, see below, p. 25.

[5] WA, vol. 54, p. 3. See also WA, vol. 6, p. 458; vol. 15, p. 50; vol. 53, pp. 217–18; W. A. Tisch., vol. 4, no. 4012, p. 75; no. 4025, pp. 84–5; no. 4691, pp. 432–3; no. 4763, pp. 476–8; vol. 5, no. 6442, pp. 662–5. See also H. Flachmann, *Martin Luther und das Buch* (Tübingen, 1996).

[6] WA, vol. 6, p. 461. See also vol. 15, pp. 51–2; W. A. Tisch., vol. 3, no. 2881, p. 48; no. 2894a, p. 57. Luther's wish was for few books apart from scripture (WA, vol. 10/1–1, p. 627). He went as far as rejoicing in the disappearance of many books by the Church Fathers and the Councils (WA, vol. 10/1–1, p. 728; vol. 38, pp. 133–4; vol. 43, pp. 93–4; vol. 50, p. 657; WA Br., vol. 2, p. 191) because all books should lead to scripture (WA, vol. 1/1–1, pp. 627, 728; vol. 6, p. 461, vol. 10/3, p. 176; vol. 43, p. 94; vol. 48, p. 218; vol. 50, pp. 657–8). See also O. Clemen, *Luthers Lob der Buchdruckerkunst* (Zwickau, 1939), repeated in Clemen, *Kleine Schriften zur Reformationsgeschichte, 1897–1944*, E. Koch (ed.), (Leipzig, 1985), vol. 7, pp. 429–50.

[7] C. Gesner, *Bibliotheca universalis* (Zurich, 1545), fol. 3ʳ.

[8] M. Judex, *De typographia inventione* (Copenhagen, 1566), p. 4.

the main focus of his work was his denunciation of the corruption of this divine gift, not only by the papists, but also by the chancelleries and consistories of the Empire. In short, he concentrated more on the control of books by civil and religious authorities than on an unreserved paean of praise to 'divine' typography. In the end, his views match the combination of enthusiasm and reservations expressed in Roman circles from the end of the fifteenth century onwards, from the Constitution of Innocent VIII in 1487 to the decree of the fifth Lateran Council in 1515.[9]

The actual evolution of printing in Reformation Europe calls for a certain distance from A. G. Dickens's humorous tag: 'Doctrine of Justification by Print Alone'.[10] In the context of printing R. Engelsing's

0.1   Saint Matthew, from the Antwerp Bible of Martin Lempereur, 1530

---

[9] C.-J. Pinto de Oliveira, 'Le premier document pontifical sur la presse: la Constitution "Inter Multiplices" d'Innocent VIII', *Revue des sciences philosophiques et théologiques*, 50 (1966), 628–43 (with a transcription of the document, its French translation, as well as the mention of a few changes made to this constitution by Alexander VI in 1501). The text of the conciliar constitution 'Inter sollicitudines' of 1515 is in G. Alberigo, P.-P. Joannou, C. Leonardi, and P. Prodi, *Conciliorum oecumenicorum decreta* (Freiburg im Breisgau, 1962), pp. 608–9; 3rd edition (Bologna, 1973), pp. 632–3. Commentary and French translation in O. de la Brosse, J. Lecter, H. Holstein and C. Lefebvre, *Latran V* (Paris, 1975), pp. 83–5, 425–6. See also below, p. 92.

[10] A. G. Dickens, *The German Nation and Luther* (London, 1974), p. 103.

statement regarding popular reading of the German Bible is worth repeating: it is 'a myth and a fable'.[11] The situation of printed books during the entire century is certainly a varied one. The 'pamphlet war' that took place in Germany between 1520 and 1525, and which made Luther a household name[12] was striking, as much to sixteenth century minds as to later ones, but it was a temporally and spatially limited phenomenon. What was the situation of books elsewhere and at other times? What role did printing play in the service of liturgy, catechisms, theology and especially in the dissemination of Scripture? These questions arise not only in Germany but also for the rest of Europe, from England to Hungary and from Finland to Spain.

These classical questions have now been reinforced by new perspectives. The core interest in the history of the book has moved gradually from the text to the reader. It is no longer enough to build as precise a picture as possible of the body of work published in a certain period, as one must also determine how this body of work was read. These are unquestionably delicate explorations in an area where historical traces are few and far between. It is in fact somewhat contradictory to attempt to write a history of individual experiences which by their nature cannot be drawn into a single entity. But this approach to history has made progress in the last few years, largely by being undertaken from different angles.[13] The implicit assumption that reading remained static and monolithic throughout the ages has been usefully challenged.

---

[11] R. Engelsing, *Der Bürger als Leser: Lesergeschichte in Deutschland, 1500–1800* (Stuttgart, 1974), p. 37.

[12] On this central event for our subject, see the fundamental work by M. Gravier, *Luther et l'opinion publique* (Paris, 1942). See also the research being carried out under the direction of H.-J. Köhler (below, pp. 77, note 86), and G. Cavallo and R. Chartier (eds), *Histoire de la lecture dans le monde occidental* (Paris, 1997).

[13] See W. J. Ong, *The Presence of the Word* (New Haven, London, 1967); J. Goody (ed.), *Literacy in Traditional Societies* (Cambridge, 1968); R. Engelsing, *Der Bürger als Leser*; A. Petrucci (ed.), *Libri, scrittura e pubblico nel Rinascimento: Guida storica e critica* (Bari, 1979); P. Saenger, 'Silent reading: its impact on late medieval script and society', in *Viator: Medieval and Renaissance Studies*, 13 (1982), 367–414; A. Petrucci, 'Lire au moyen âge' in *Mélanges de l'École française de Rome. Moyen âge et temps modernes*, 96 (1984), 603–16; R. Chartier (ed.), *Pratiques de la lecture* (Paris, 1985), especially R. Chartier, 'Du livre au lire', pp. 61–88; R. Chartier (ed.), *Les usages de l'imprimé* (Paris, 1987). One should also read the methodological remarks of N. Z. Davis at the start of her article 'Printing and the people' (in N. Z. Davis, *Society and Culture in Early Modern France* (Stanford, 1975), pp. 189–226).

A collective and comparative work

Original research on sixteenth-century books is being carried out throughout the western world. These highly skilled monographs deserve to be compared and contrasted with one another in the European context. Thus research had to be undertaken on the book in Reformation Europe, with a specific scheme enabling comparisons to be made between countries.

This ambitious project could only be carried out by an international and interdisciplinary team. From the start, the contributors agreed that individual essays could not be presented merely as units independent from one another. Our intention was to carry out a joint inquiry, going beyond national boundaries and borders between fields of research in particular. A single outline was thus proposed to each contributor, yet this was not sufficient. The results of individual research were examined by the group during a residential conference at Froidmont, near Brussels, on 3 and 4 December 1987. The reactions of the group to individual presentations led to the final versions of each contribution as it appears in this volume.

In each case, the analysis follows the same path:

1. The production conditions of the books.
2. An analysis of their contents.
3. A study of their reception.

The first point deals with the world of the printers and publishers who joined the Reformation camp. Who prints 'Lutheran' books, and in which cities did the printers and publishers establish their workshops? Which printing features do the publishers prefer in terms of format, page settings, print characters, illustrations, etc? Finally what distribution network do the booksellers use? The second point focuses on authors and their texts. Who wrote the works available for sale? How does one classify the texts, both in terms of their doctrinal content and their literary genre? The final point deals with the relatively recent domain of reading practices. This theme is at the heart of our project, since one has to determine how much impact printed books had on a largely illiterate population. Following an examination of literacy rates among the population, the contributors bring together clues as to the publishers' target audience, and the readers' reactions, including the response of the authorities who exercised the right of censorship. Catholic responses to Protestant writings also provide a means of assessing the latter's impact on public opinion.

For the purposes of this study, Europe has been divided along linguistic, rather than political lines. The role of language seemed crucial in the study of printing as a means of communication. In the sixteenth century, just as today, linguistic frontiers did not always match the political borders of individual states. Minority viewpoints disseminated through printed works often originated in more tolerant neighbouring states. Border crossings which make traffickers rich also played a role in the distribution of printed works.

Our approach takes both the development of the Reformation and that of printing into account. Thus, the survey begins with an analysis of the main areas involved in the production of Protestant works, namely the German Empire, France and The Netherlands. This first group is complemented by three chapters dedicated to cities on the border between the German and Romance worlds, Antwerp, Strasbourg and Basle. These examples help to remedy any rigidity in the linguistic distribution. The rest of Europe is then analysed counterclockwise, from Great Britain to the Iberian Peninsula, represented by Spain, Italy, Central Europe, with studies on Hungary, Bohemia, Moravia, and Poland, and finally to the Nordic lands.

Establishing the chronological limits for the early stages of the Reformation across the whole of Europe is no easy task. Therefore contributors were given a certain amount of leeway in terms of the time-scale of their studies. The theoretical starting point was 1517, the traditional beginning of the Reformation, but in many cases contributors had to go back in time in order to bring to light both continuity and the break caused by the Reformation. The end date was set as 1560. In the German world, 1555 and the Peace of Augsburg is a useful marker, without necessarily bringing about a radical shift. In the Calvinist world, 1560 marks the appearance of several confessions of faith, signalling the creation of national churches. It is also the end of the Council of Trent, and the growing politicizing of religious conflict, leading to the wars of religion. In Central Europe, however, religious change occured at a different tempo, and its impact lasted until a correspondingly later date. In fact, establishing starting and closing dates is not vital, since the main concern is above all to define general trends as regards the implantation of the Reformation.

Because of its complexity, a study of the book requires a multidisciplinary approach. Our contributors include scholars from many fields: historians, literature scholars, bibliographers and theologians. Even though each chapter may not necessarily reflect all these approaches, the overall work is largely an accurate representation of new currents of research.

In spite of the aim of a common approach throughout the book, we did not wish to impose a strait-jacket on individual contributors. Our intention was to bring a collective work to press, but still left each contributor free to stress specific questions and address issues which each considered central. The end result is one of cheerful diversity, reflecting both the varied situations of books in sixteenth-century Europe and the sensitivities of each author. Two different approaches to the question of early printing confront one another in this book. One view favours a bibliographical study, focusing primarily on the printing and circulation of books, while the other advocates a focus on the literary side of printed books, examining the texts and the ideas contained therein. In a nutshell, some look at books without reading them while others read them without looking at them.

A tentative synthesis

By proposing a multi-faceted approach to the effects of books on the early Reformation, and by providing the grounds for comparison across Europe, this study is breaking new and fertile ground. A work of this size cannot hope to be based entirely on primary sources, but can only draw conclusions from the work already carried out. Clearly, by asking certain questions, some of our contributors will have explored previously uncharted areas. They will have had the opportunity to publish the results of primary research, and will have been able to suggest new paths of inquiry. In principle the aim of each contribution is to reflect the state of research on the topic.

This work makes no claim, therefore, to be the definitive volume on this topic, and does not consider itself as the 'Bible' on this matter. The lack of original research has in fact made certain contributions more limited than would otherwise be the case. Evidence of this lies in the lack of complete inventories of works published in the sixteenth century in certain areas, which then precludes an overall assessment of printing production. Our contributors repeatedly remind us of these gaps and emphasize the difficulties of tracing books due to camouflage of clandestine editions and the book-burnings of the Inquisition. In spite of these difficulties, our study is based on sufficiently rich sources to engage in international comparisons. Our hope is that this work will stimulate thoughts on Reformation historiography and will lead to new paths of inquiry.

Problems of exactitude

Following the Reformers, who invited their hearers to verify theological doctrines solely on the basis of Scripture, we suggest that our readers examine this work without abandoning their critical faculties. Due to certain problems encountered in the course of this research, our attention has been drawn to the precarious nature of any scholarly undertaking.

Contributors discussing the use of statistical tables have shown once again the weaknesses inherent in numerical data. Counting editions remains a task fraught with difficulties. As regards general estimates of the number of books, there is sometimes little agreement as to the specifications of a book as a countable unit, and matters are further complicated by doubts as to the identity of the publishers of certain works. It is unclear whether one should simply count titles, in which case small pamphlets and large folio volumes hold the same status. Several contributors offer statistical analyses on the basis of the books' volume, by counting the number of sheets.[14] In fact, in terms of cultural history, numbers only provide indications: they lay the foundation for further thought and suggest interpretative hypotheses.

In joint sessions, another problem surfaced, namely confessional designation. Should one use sixteenth-century vocabulary, or current names for each church or Christian sect of the sixteenth-century? In each case, lack of precision is inevitable, and furthermore the situation changes from country to country. In the end, each contributor was left free to choose appropriate categories, and as the Italian contribution points out, the very definition of Protestantism must be re-evaluated regularly.

In spite of collective efforts to reduce the number of material errors, the following pages are meant for critical readers. As in all good historical work, disparate elements are brought together in a more or less harmonious construction. First, one can draw general conclusions based on well-established series of facts. These are the surest foundations, and one would always prefer to be able to build on such bases. In cases where exhaustive data is lacking, the starting-point is the establishment of isolated but verified facts, used as examples. In such instances, one moves into the realm of tentative hypotheses, pending inventories of books in that area and period. Apart from these two paths of research, there is a third approach, which is, however, more tricky to elucidate and interpret. Indeed any synthesis calls for a more general conception of humanity and society. In this case, one runs a great risk of anachro-

---

[14] Below, there is a section on production statistics based on the number of sheets. See p. 18.

nism, even though the theory may be a sensible one. Reading practices provide a good example: until recently the common understanding of literacy in the sixteenth century was that the literate could also read silently to themselves, but this is a dangerous assumption. Any analysis of the motivations of printers and publishers is another area in which one must proceed with caution, and where great care is needed. Readers of this work must therefore decide for themselves how to use this book.

We are delighted to be able to thank the numerous friends who have encouraged our team of contributors. From the very start, certain friends have provided valuable support. Recruiting authors was a delicate task, calling for searches in different directions to locate scholars who were both up to the task and available for it. First, we wish to thank Philippe Denis and Hugh R. Boudin, faithful companions for this project. We would also like to acknowledge our debt of gratitude to Elly Cockx-Indesteege, Jean-Pierre Massaut, Clive Griffin, Bernard Roussel, André Seguény, Louis-Marie Dewailly, Ingun Montgomery and Johannes Trapman. Our project was initially generously funded by the University Faculty of Protestant Theology of Brussels and the National Fund of Scientific Research.

CHAPTER ONE

Printing at the dawn of the sixteenth century

Jean-François Gilmont

What was the situation of printed books when the Reformation began?
Printing technology and the religious movement centred on Luther met
at the precise moment when after decades of fine tuning, the new

1.1 Discussion during a Protestant sermon. Cicero, *De Officiis* (Augsburg:
Heinrich Steiner, 1530)

invention gained its independence from manuscripts. Thus the first paragraphs of this chapter describe the early stages of printing. But the history of the book is also tied to that of reading, and therefore the development of reading practices at the dawn of the Reformation constitutes another major theme of this analysis. The final sections of this chapter examine the actual technical constraints imposed on the book, on publishing and on printing.

The first tentative steps: incunabula

When Luther first appeared at the forefront of the European stage, printing was a relatively recent phenomenon, less than 70 years old, and beginning to leave its cradle. This image is reinforced by the name given to fifteenth-century imprints. However, the end-date of incunabula, traditionally set around 1500, is unfortunate, since the real transition period for printing occured between 1520 and 1540.[1]

At the beginning, the *ars artificialiter scribendi* was firmly based on the manuscript. As time went on, printers discovered the possibilities inherent in the new technology, giving imprints their own identity. The timing of this new mastery of printing techniques coincided approximately with Luther's attack on the preaching of Indulgences.

Due to daily contact with manuscripts from the early Middle Ages and incunabula, the first decades of printing showed more signs of continuity than of change. The external appearance of books remained the same. Pagination, division into sections, and the set-up of the entire work copied the format of manuscripts. Signalling and reference devices were based on manuscript practices, in terms of the organization of sections through signatures and announcements, to help in reading (foliation, pagination, illuminated initials, marginalia) or in reference work (alphabetical indices, concordances). Slowly, over the course of 80 years, printers discovered that the repeated reproduction of a text led to new commercial constraints, particularly as regards the external aspect of the book. A mass-produced book needed individual features, to distinguish it from the other works on the market. Little by little, printers realized the need for a title-page specifying the contents of the book and its place of origin, by indicating the name of the author and title of the book, and the name of the publisher, together with the date and place of publication. The use of printers' marks provided an added decorative feature.

---

[1] In his exemplary study of Aldus Manutius, M. Lowry showed clearly how this humanist printer carved a path for himself in a world in rapid transition: *The World of Aldus Manutius* (Oxford, 1979).

At the same time, typesetters moved away from the models provided by manuscript calligraphy. Around 1540, making print characters became an independent and specialized industry.[2] The first fifteenth-century fonts contained multiple ligatures, which were easily drawn by hand, but which needlessly complicated typesetters' work. In the first decades of the sixteenth century, fonts were simplified, and the number of characters with ligatures was considerably reduced.[3]

Slowly, the choice of texts to be published also evolved. Understandably enough, the first printers chose their works from the *scriptoria*. Only as time went on did they realize that a more widespread distribution of texts changed the patterns of reading, that the growing numbers of readers meant that new works were needed, that medieval best sellers needed to be replaced by other works and that contemporary writers' works also had a place in the books to be published.[4]

The geographical map of European printing needed, therefore, more than 50 years before achieving a measure of stability. The first spread of printing was due to travelling printers guided more by chance than by any assessment of profitable centres in which to establish themselves. Starting from the German lands, they migrated first into Italy and then across Europe. This ceaseless anarchic development continued for a number of decades. Estimates of the number of cities which housed printing presses at the dawn of the sixteenth century vary between 240 and 270 cities.[5] A slow filtering process enabled a few printing centres to emerge as leaders in the following centuries. A classification of cities based on the earliest evidence of printing occuring there does not, therefore, match the list of cities which later controlled the book trade. In France, Paris and Lyon held a monopoly on new inventions, while in Italy, more than half of all books produced came from Venice alone, and in The Netherlands, Antwerp became the centre of printing *par excellence*. There were no such clear winners in the cities of the German Empire. More peripheral lands took longer to gain their independence in terms of printing, as in the case of England, still reliant on foreign imports at the beginning of the sixteenth century.

---

[2] Lowry, *The World*, p. 11.

[3] W. J. Ong, 'Oral residue in Tudor prose style', *PMLA* (*Proceedings of the Modern Language Association*), 80 (1965), 146. Indeed, this is the reason for criticism of the Greek characters used by Aldus Manutius: as they imitate manuscript writing, they use a large number of ligatures and decorative flourishes (see Lowry, *The World*, pp. 129–35).

[4] Several contributions underline this. See pp. 66–8 and 285. For France, see H.-J. Martin and J.-M. Dureau, 'Années de transition, 1500–1530', *HÉF*, 217–25; H.-J. Martin, 'Classements et conjonctures', *HÉF*, 429–57.

[5] See Febvre/Martin, pp. 275–81; J. M. Lenhart, *Pre-Reformation Printed Books* (New York, 1935).

Indeed the map of printing centres does not match that of the most densely populated European cities.[6] Although printing was indeed a primarily urban activity, every large European city did not automatically house a flourishing printing industry. In southern Europe several cities of more than 100 000 inhabitants by 1500, such as Milan or Naples, were not major typographical centres. Other cities containing populations of 60 000 to 100 000 like Seville, Cordova, Granada, Florence and Genoa played only modest roles in the printing world. In contrast, more northern cities with between 40 000 and 60 000 inhabitants like Lyon, Antwerp, Augsburg and Cologne had flourishing printing presses. Even cities of 10 000 inhabitants, like Basle, played a major role in the international book trade.

The establishment of printing in specific cities was tied to the development of trade routes. While small-scale printers provided books for local consumption, large printing firms looked to wider markets. From the fifteenth century onwards, booksellers built links with colleagues in other cities to sell their stock. The fairs, with roots in the early Middle Ages, were the ideal location to exchange printed works, to announce new publications, to purchase typographical material, to hire workers, and to settle bills. From the first years of the sixteenth century, all the features of the international book trade were in place. Besides the Lyon and Leipzig fairs, those of Frankfurt am Main drew the leading European publishers.

Varied reading practices

In *The Printing Press as an Agent of Change*, E. Eisenstein attempts to prove that the introduction of printing led to deep divisions in the history of western culture. This viewpoint is not shared by all. Other scholars argue the opposite; that Gutenberg's invention, in the course of the long history of the book, was much less revolutionary than it might seem at first. Changes like the move from the *rotulus* to the *codex* or the more scientific approach to learning in medieval universities made a much greater impact on reading and the book. This view is upheld by R. Hirsch and R. Chartier, to name but two scholars.[7] This perspective

---

[6] For the publishing centres, see *HÉF*, 442. For the size of cities, see R. Mols, 'Population in Europe 1500–1700', in C. M. Cipolla (ed.), *The Fontana Economic History of Europe: The Sixteenth and Seventeenth Centuries* (London, 1974), p. 41.

[7] R. Hirsch, *Printing, Selling and Reading, 1450–1550* (Wiesbaden, 1967), p. 2; R. Chartier, 'De l'histoire du livre à l'histoire de la lecture: les trajectoires françaises', *Archives et Bibliothèques de Belgique*, 60 (1989), 161–89.

does not see the Reformation bursting on the scene at a key point in the history of reading practices. The large-scale changes which brought Europe from an oral society to a literate one began in the Middle Ages, and their final impact only became clear in the eighteenth and nineteenth centuries.

Several ways of reading have coexisted since ancient times. Silent reading to oneself may have occurred, but was uncommon, and rare during the high Middle Ages. Reading softly to oneself, by murmuring or ruminating, or by speaking out loud were the norm.[8] Until the development of the first universities in the twelfth and thirteenth centuries, to read a book meant to enter into a text slowly and to explore it from start to finish. The growth of canon law and scholasticism led to a new use of the written word, namely as a reference tool. Reading practices moved from gaining knowledge of the whole work to rapid searching for quotations as 'authorities'. This new approach led to the creation of techniques for easier access to texts, namely indices and concordances, and redeveloped the format characteristics of the book.

The university textbook in the thirteenth and fourteenth centuries with its compact pages and overuse of abbreviations was not yet a model of clarity. Furthermore it is possible that at the time sight reading was a specialist task, as individuals were only able to read fluently in their heads in the limited areas of their own studies.[9] Armando Petrucci highlighted the revolutionary changes brought about in the world of the book and of reading by 'a band of arrogant young Florentines' in the late fourteenth and early fifteenth centuries. Following Niccolò Niccoli's lead, they fundamentally reshaped the book, abandoning traditional Gothic script in favour of a new font borrowed from Carolingian models. They transcribed texts into small-sized books, eliminating many abbreviations, and making the text less cluttered by refusing to include invasive commentaries, preferring to be in direct contact with the text itself. A. Petrucci refers to these transformations as the introduction of bourgeois reading. Thanks to the innovations of Italian humanists, printed texts which were created in the German Empire following the model of university manuscripts found a new format in Italy. Aldus

---

[8] P. Saenger's chronology may be too rigid and systematic ('Silent reading: its impact on late medieval script and society', *Viator: Medieval and Renaissance Studies*, 13 (1982), 367–414; Saenger, 'Manières de lire médiévales', *HÉF*, 131–41). A. Petrucci takes a more nuanced approach ('Lire au moyen âge', *Mélanges de l'École française de Rome. Moyen âge et temps modernes*, 96 (1984), 603–16). For manuscript books, see J. Glénisson (ed.), *Le livre au moyen âge* (Paris, 1988), a very thorough book which unfortunately makes little mention of reading practices.

[9] This is a perceptive suggestion of H.-J. Martin, *Histoire et pouvoirs de l'écrit* (Paris, 1988), p. 152.

Manutius is the symbol of this rebirth of the printed book. In the long run, these changes favoured silent reading thanks to a better balance between print and blank space on the page.[10]

Preceding the development of printing, the *Devotio Moderna* based itself firmly on silent sight reading. The importance given to individual contact with the text led to a policy encouraging the transcription of manuscripts and the development of education.[11] The Brethren of the Common Life adopted the *ars artificialiter scribendi* without difficulty, opening several printing shops from the end of the fifteenth century onwards. Evidence of the mastery of silent reading before Gutenberg can easily be gathered from elsewhere in Europe in the late Middle Ages.

Furthermore, the sudden appearance of reading in the context of piety opens up a secondary debate on the nature of prayer. Was prayer a collective ritual act, often described as a magical practice by its opponents, or was it meant to be a private, interior dialogue? This debate first surfaced in the fifteenth century. 'The contrast [between the partisans of each of these two views] appeared first and foremost between those who can be broadly categorized as the representatives of book culture and those who followed the practices of oral culture'.[12]

The study of reading practices is essential, for the progressive transition from an oral to a written society involves changes which are both far-reaching and profound. One of the main consequences of silent reading is certainly the increasing privacy of actions and thoughts. Was the Reformation, through its systematic encouragement of reading, really responsible for this evolution?

However, this central question runs into numerous unknown factors, particularly as regards the nearly insoluble question of the number of literate people in sixteenth-century Europe. R. Chartier believes that due to the lack of information, one can only measure this rate at the very end of the sixteenth century.[13] The situation is even more unclear if one wishes to examine the levels of literacy. The main historical evi-

---

[10] See Petrucci, 'Lire' pp. 613–14; Petrucci, 'Typologie du livre et de la lecture dans l'Italie de la Renaissance: de Pétrarque à Politien', in *From Script to Book: A Symposium* (Odense, 1986), pp. 127–39; M. Lowry, *The World*, pp. 135–44.

[11] There are some very significant quotations in Saenger, 'Manières', pp. 136–7. On the printing done by the Brethren of the Common Life, see R. R. Post, *The Modern Devotion: Confrontation with Reformation and Humanism* (Leiden, 1968), pp. 346–9. See also Saenger, 'Silent reading', pp. 396–8.

[12] A. Prosperi, 'Les commentaires du Pater Noster entre XVe et XVIe siècles', in P. Colin et al. (eds), *Aux origines du catéchisme en France* (Paris, 1989), pp. 89–90.

[13] R. Chartier, 'Les pratiques de l'écrit', in Ph. Ariès and G. Duby (eds), *Histoire de la vie privée*, vol. 3: *De la Renaissance aux Lumières* (Paris, 1986), p. 122.

dence is provided by the ability to sign one's name. But on the one hand, the link between signing and writing is not a constant, and on the other, the connection between writing and reading is not straightforward.[14]

Therefore, one must gather together all the clues about the contacts between the people of the Reformation period and the printed book. All external facets of the life of the book deserve analysis, whether from above or from below. In the context of the use of printed books, the study of book collections has now been given a role in its own right. Lists of books owned by specific individuals provide fascinating insights as to the readership of specific works, but it would be wrong to assume that book owners read all the books on their shelves, and furthermore, 'that the readers necessarily agreed with the ideas expressed in the books they read'.[15] As the repeated rereading of a book in the end leaves traces in the most literal sense, examining the copies which have survived can also provide certain information.

At the same time, one must go back to the conception of the book, and examine the intentions of its creators. The external features of the book – format, set-up of the pages, illustration, etc. – provide crucial evidence as to the kind of reading which the publisher suggested. A. Petrucci expresses this aptly in his distinction between *libri da banco, libri da bisaccia, libretti da mano*, books to go on bookrests, books to go in bags, and booklets to be carried by hand.[16] The relative weight of the book automatically specified the type of reading which would be done. The folio size needs a bookrest, while as Jean Crespin said at the beginning of an edition of the *Iliad*, and in sexto-decimo 'can be carried around at home, is not cumbersome outside, and still allows one to stroll through the countryside without encumbrance'.[17]

However, one must not be taken in entirely by the preoccupations of publishers. As N. Z. Davis points out, one must make a clear distinction

---

[14] See R. S. Schofield, 'The measurement of literacy in pre-industrial England', in J. Goody (ed.), *Literacy in Traditional Societies* (Cambridge, 1975), pp. 311–25; M. de Certeau, *L'invention du quotidien*, vol. 1: *Arts de faire* (Paris, 1980), pp. 283–5; R. Chartier, 'Du livre au lire', in R. Chartier (ed.), *Pratiques de la lecture* (Paris, 1985), pp. 61–88. Precise information regarding the distinct learning processes of reading and writing are available for the seventeenth century in D. Julia, 'La leçon de catéchisme dans l'*Escole paroissiale* (1654)', in Colin et al. (eds), *Aux origines*, pp. 164, 166.

[15] N. Z. Davis, 'Printing and the people', in N. Z. Davis, *Society and Culture in Early Modern France* (Stanford, 1975), p. 191.

[16] A. Petrucci, 'Alle origini del libro moderno: libri da banco, libri da bisaccia, libretti da mano', *Italia medioevale e umanistica*, 12 (1969), 295–313.

[17] Homer, *The Iliad*, Geneva, J. Crespin, 1559, fol. a ii^r. See J.-Fr. Gilmont, *Bibliographie des éditions de Jean Crespin* (Verviers, 1981), vol. 1, p. 117.

'between the readership of books, those who actually read them – and their audience – those to whom authors and publishers direct their works'.[18] One must therefore distinguish clearly between indications of the authors' and publishers' intentions, and evidence of actual reactions from readers. Both are linked, since a publisher cannot bring out books for long if he has absolutely no interest in his readership.

Technical problems in manual typography

Across sixteenth-century Europe, the daily use of typography was a constant feature.[19] The first point to bear in mind is that the printed text is made up of independent sheets. To make the book into a unit, sheets are assembled in order, having been printed recto–verso and then folded and bound. In discussions of price and length of production, one must base oneself on a measure of the book in terms of its number of sheets. This measuring system goes back to former practices, as specified in contracts between publishers and printers,[20] and in the inventories of booksellers' stocks.[21] Although it may seem odd today, the

---

[18] Davis, 'Printing', pp. 192–3.

[19] The best general survey of these problems is that of Ph. Gaskell, *A New Introduction to Bibliography* (Oxford, 1972). J. Veyrin-Forrer offers a good synthesis in 'Fabriquer un livre au XVIe siècle', in *HÉF*, 279–301. The information gathered from the Plantin archives is priceless, even though one should always bear in mind that Plantin exemplified exceptional success in the field. (L. Voet, *The Golden Compasses: A History and Evaluation of the Printing and Publishing Activities of the Officina Plantiniana at Antwerp*, vol. 2: *The Management of a Printing and Publishing House in Renaissance and Baroque* (Amsterdam, 1972)). Crucial data taken from notary records in particular in A. Parent, *Les métiers du livre à Paris au XVIe siècle (1535–1560)* (Geneva, Paris, 1974); and H.-J. Bremme, *Buchhändler zur Zeit der Glaubenskämpfe: Studien zur Genfer Druckgeschichte, 1565–1580* (Geneva, 1969). These studies enabled me to establish Crespin's working conditions (J.-Fr. Gilmont, *Jean Crespin, un éditeur réformé du XVIe siècle* (Geneva, 1981), ch. II). Conditions were generally similar in Spain (Cl. Griffin, *The Crombergers of Seville: the History of a Printing and Merchant Dynasty* (Oxford, 1988) especially ch. V).

[20] For example, see Parent *Les métiers du livre*, especially the table inserted between pp. 136 and 137. This was also Lazarus Spengler's calculation method when deciding the price of the *Kirchenordnung* of Brandenburg–Nuremberg: 1 denier per ordinary sheet, 1.5 deniers for sheets printed in red and black. (H.-O. Keunecke, 'Die Drucklegung der Brandenburg–Nürnbergischen Kirchenordnung' *AGB*, 21 (1980), col. 786–7; see also pp. 49–50.

[21] This was the case for the posthumous inventory of the Genevan bookseller Laurent de Normandie (Bremme, *Buchhändler*, pp. 42–3, 31). I am now less certain about this measuring system following my analysis of the inventory of Laurent de Normandie: 'L'imprimerie réformée à Genève au temps de Laurent de Normandie (1570)', *Bulletin du bibliophile* (1995) no. 2, 262–78.

production cost of four in folio pages printed in large type was approximately the same as that of 32 pages in sexto-decimo in small type. The notion of the sheet, printed on the basis of two forms, is a direct consequence of the work of the printing press. There was very little difference in terms of book format in the eyes of the printing workers, as the same effort was required each time in applying the pressure of the plate on to the forme. The historian analysing the rhythm of book production must counterbalance the data provided by the number of book titles by calculating the number of formes needed.[22]

From this starting-point one should also emphasize certain economic constraints; first, the economic links between the printer who made the books and the bookseller who financed their production. Setting up a printing press did not require vast sums of money. The major expense lay in the purchase of fonts. By the 1550s, while one needed 20 to 40 *livres tournois* to buy a printing press and associated material, purchasing a font cost between 250 and 600 *livres*. In this light, the investment needed to bring out a book was very large: in the same period, an in-octavo of 800 pages with a print-run of 1 400 copies cost at least 450 *livres tournois*, for a book containing only 50 sheets.[23] In other words the costs of producing a book of this format for a bookseller were about the same as the expense of setting up a press.

An analysis of the average cost of a printed sheet is equally revealing of work practices in the period. The greatest expense was that of paper. As an approximate generalization, the minimum cost of paper was between 40 and 50 per cent of the production costs, and this percentage varied enormously depending on the quality of the paper.[24] The printing costs themselves, including the salaries of the typesetters and the pressmen as well as the profit of the master printer came to approximately 50 per cent of the total. A maximum of 10 per cent remained, covering any additional production or administrative expenses.[25] This very rough estimate shows that large print-runs held little benefit. There were no savings in terms of paper costs, nor in terms of the workers' salaries.

---

[22] See the contributions of M. U. Chrisman, Al. Kawecka-Gryczowa and R. Kick, pp. 216, 411 and 452.

[23] Gilmont, *J. Crespin* pp. 49–50; 53–4.

[24] L. Voet's calculations based on Plantin's accounts put the price of paper at between 60 and 65 per cent, or even 75 per cent of the production cost. However, unlike the pattern described above, Plantin was not a publisher dealing with a printer, and having to take the latter's profit margins into account. Instead, Plantin's internal accounting only mentions the cost of paper, the workers' salaries and potential reproduction costs (paying the author, translation costs, etc.); see Voet, *The Golden Compasses*, vol. 2, pp. 379–86.

[25] Gilmont, *J. Crespin*, p. 54.

Both the costs of paper and wages were directly linked to the size of the print-run. Any profit was measured against the composition costs, around 15 to 20 per cent of the total outlay. This minimal profit was also put at risk by the danger of unsold copies, immobilizing printed paper with its associated high cost.[26]

The retail sales price of books was obviously affected by other expenses, principally the bookseller's profit and transportation costs. A book could easily be sold for twice the cost-price paid by the bookseller.[27] Transportation costs, including the risks of losses, explain why works which could easily be sold were re-edited. Works attracting a broad readership were best printed near their sale locations, rather than being brought there from afar.

Therefore it is understandable that print-runs remained small until the nineteenth century. The size of print-runs is a much researched topic. Several scholars have attempted estimates of the number of works for sale at various times. In fact, the only certainty is the link between the print-run and the production capacity of a printing press in a day.[28] Depending on the area, this meant a daily print-run of 1 300 to 1 500 sheets printed on both sides. This norm, set out by the ancient printing ordinances, forms the basis of debates on the printing profession, although the norm may not always have been respected. An analysis of the actual print-runs in Paris or at Plantin's in Antwerp highlights large variations, going from 250 to 2 600 copies in Paris and from 100 to 5 000 copies at Plantin's presses. Furthermore these variations are not arbitrary, as they correspond to workdays based on certain simple formulas: 1, 1.5, 2, 3, or 4 formes were printed daily. The Parisian average for 33 books is 940 copies of each, while Plantin and his son-in-law Moretus produced an average of 1 300 to 1 550 copies of more than 400 works. A reasonable estimate of the average print-run in the sixteenth century is between 1 000 and 1 350 copies.

Too often, certain basic consequences of the set-up of printed texts for the transmission of books are ignored. The major expense of print fonts, and perhaps also printers' lack of imagination meant that in most cases sixteenth-century print shops operated continuously. A team of workers, often two typesetters and two pressworkers were given a 'task'. As the formes were typeset, pages were printed, and once the printing work was done, the formes were returned to the typesetter in

---

[26] In establishing this data, one must avoid any confusion between the number of sheets and the number of formes needed to produce a book, which would otherwise double the figures.

[27] Bremme, *Buchhändler*, pp. 42–3.

[28] J.-Fr. Gilmont, 'Printers by the rules', *The Library*, 6th series, 2 (1980) 143–8.

order to reuse the fonts. Correcting proofs was both a rushed and a slow task. The rush was caused by the fact that the typesetter often only had half a day to correct a forme. The slow-down was due to the fact that corrections were done gradually, forme by forme. In the case of large folio volumes, this could take months if not an entire year.[29] Present-day correction of proofs is very different.

---

[29] Gilmont, 'Printers', pp. 129–55.

CHAPTER TWO

The book in Reformation Germany[1]

John L. Flood

Germany was the cradle both of printing and of the Reformation. It has often been claimed that the Reformation would never have succeeded without printing. While its importance should not be exaggerated – A. G. Dickens has rightly warned against the notion of 'Justification by Print Alone' – it is certainly undeniable that the availability of printing technology was a significant factor in its success. It is equally certain that printing, especially in the vernacular, would not have grown so rapidly without the stimulus of the Reformation. This mutual interaction is the subject of this chapter. But printing in the service of the evangelical movement, though overwhelmingly important in the period 1517–55 (and beyond) is only part of the picture: we must consider the relationship between printing and the Church of Rome, too, nor can we ignore the continuing role of printers and publishers as purveyors of secular writing of all kinds. The scope of the subject is, therefore, clearly immense: many types of books dealing with a multiplicity of individual subjects, printed and published by a huge number of individuals in a large number of towns, each with its own peculiar circumstances over a period of half a century which witnessed some of the most far-reaching events in the whole course of German history. Inevitably the picture we shall convey will be selective. It will also have to be impressionistic, for – despite some two centuries of effort – the present state of research does not yet permit a comprehensive view to be given. There have been in-depth studies of many individual printers, of printing in particular towns, of the bibliography of many individual writers (especially Luther) and of types of book (notably the German Bible), but these are only individual pieces in a large and complex jigsaw puzzle; the general outlines of the whole picture are only now gradually emerging.

One of the major problems militating against a comprehensive survey is, of course, the fact that the situation with regard to bibliographies of

---

[1] The text is substantially the same as that which was prepared for the original French version of this book, though it has been brought up to date where this was essential. In particular, the notes and bibliography have been amended to reflect more recent scholarship, though it has not been possible to revise them as fully as I should have liked.

the period is, despite much endeavour, still woefully inadequate. The *Index Aureliensis. Catalogus librorum sedecimo saeculo impressorum*, even some 35 years after beginning publication (1962), has not progressed very far, and although the first phase of the invaluable *Verzeichnis der im deutschen Sprachgebiet erschienenen Drucke des XVI. Jahrhunderts. VD 16* (Stuttgart, 1983–) has now been completed, much remains to be done before it can be regarded as providing a comprehensive picture of sixteenth-century German book production. The first phase of the project, covering about 90 000 items, is chiefly based on the holdings of only two major libraries, the Bavarian State Library at Munich and the Herzog August Bibliothek at Wolfenbüttel. Even when the second phase, taking the holdings of a handful of other major libraries into account and bringing the total number of items listed to an estimated 150 000 (excluding broadsheets), has been completed, it is thought that only about 80 per cent of German book production of the sixteenth century will have been covered. In the introduction to his Huberinus bibliography, we may note, Gunther Franz has shown that of 158 attested editions of the texts in which he is interested fewer than half are to be found in Munich or Wolfenbüttel and even all the libraries which will eventually be covered by the second phase of the *VD 16* project hold only 70 per cent of the relevant editions; 12 of the 158 are known only from copies held in libraries outside the German-speaking countries.[2]

Some other open questions regarding the book in the Reformation period have been addressed by Erdmann Weyrauch.[3] He questions, for instance, the wisdom of restricting an enquiry to the period up to 1555, given that the religious situation in cities and territories was then still far from settled. In any case, 1555 does not represent a particularly significant date in the history of printing or of the German book trade generally. There is no denying the validity of this. Accordingly, though this study will concentrate on the period 1517–55, the Peace of Augsburg will not mark a rigid cut-off point. Yet another question is the extent to which the supply of books stimulated demand and the extent to which

---

[2] G. Franz, *Huberinus – Rhegius – Holbein. Bibliographische und druckgeschichtliche Untersuchung der verbreitesten Trost- und Erbauungsschriften des 16. Jahrhunderts* (Bibliotheca Humanistica et Reformatorica, 7) (Nieuwkoop, 1973), p. 221.

[3] E. Weyrauch, 'Überlegungen zur Bedeutung des Buches im Jahrhundert der Reformation', in H.-J. Köhler (ed.), *Flugschriften als Massenmedium der Reformationszeit. Beiträge zum Tübinger Symposium 1980* (Spätmittelalter und frühe Neuzeit, 13) (Stuttgart, 1981), pp. 243–59. A major contribution to discussion of the impact of printing on early modern society has been made by M. Giesecke, *Der Buchdruck in der frühen Neuzeit. Eine historische Fallstudie über die Durchsetzung neuer Informations- und Kommunikationstechnologien* (Frankfurt am Main, 1991).

demand stimulated the Reformation movement itself. This chapter, indeed this book, will attempt to supply some of the answers.

Printing, towns and religious movements

Printing was from the start an urban industry. After its experimental stage in Strasbourg around 1440 and the outstandingly successful trial period in Mainz in the 1450s, it spread rapidly to other towns large and small, so that by 1500 printing had been attempted in some 60 towns in German-speaking countries and was well established in most of them. By then, too, the technological development of printing was largely complete in all its essentials. Thus well before the Reformation the technology had become widely available, and printing had developed into a sizeable industry, in terms both of the labour force and of the capital invested. Whereas in the fifteenth century printing was chiefly – though by no means exclusively – confined to the larger commercial, episcopal and Imperial cities, in the sixteenth century (and especially with the growth of pamphlet printing after 1517) the industry spread to a multitude of small, relatively unimportant towns. In Cole's words, 'decentralized printing coupled with the fact that pamphlet printers strongly identified with the Reformation created a web of print that became inexorably connected with the fate of Protestantism'.[4]

The evangelical movement, too, was primarily an urban phenomenon, with northern Germany and Franconia inclining towards the Wittenberg Reformation and the Swabian–Alemannic area (with the initial exception of Reutlingen) tending to follow Zwingli and Bucer.[5]

---

[4] R. G. Cole, 'The Reformation pamphlet and communication processes', in Köhler, *Flugschriften*, pp. 139–161, here p. 150.

[5] See A. G. Dickens, *The German Nation and Martin Luther*, (London, 1974), p. 182 f. There is an extensive literature on the subject of the penetration of the Reformation into the towns; see Kaspar von Greyerz, 'Stadt und Reformation. Stand und Aufgaben der Forschung', *ARG*, 76 (1985), 6–63. See also B. Moeller, *Reichsstadt und Reformation* (revised edition, Berlin, 1987). Useful studies of specific towns include M. U. Chrisman, *Strasbourg and the Reform* (New Haven, 1967); M. U. Chrisman, *Lay Culture, Learned Culture, Books and Social Change in Strasbourg, 1480–1599* (New Haven, 1982); B. Moeller, *Johannes Zwick und die Reformation in Konstanz* (Gütersloh, 1961); G. Strauss, *Nuremberg in the Sixteenth Century* (New York, 1966); G. Seebaß, 'The Reformation in Nuremberg', in L. P. Buck and J. W. Zophy (eds), *The Social History of the Reformation* (Columbus, 1972), pp. 17–40; R. W. Scribner, 'Why was there no Reformation in Cologne?', *Bulletin of the Institute of Historical Research*, 49 (1976), 217–41; H. Schwarz (ed.), *Reformation und Reichsstadt. Protestantisches Leben in Regensburg* (Schriften der Universität Regensburg, N.F. 20), (Regensburg, 1994); W. Eger (ed.), *Reformation und Protestation in Speyer* (Veröffentlichungen des Vereins für

The foundations of the Reformation were laid in the free cities, and it was there that it was first put into practice, and there too that the Evangelical cause was transformed from a provincial issue into a mighty German movement. Here also were to be found not only the authors, editors and printers, but a very high proportion of the literate public as well.

Printing, available for several decades before the Reformation, had already ensured that the Renaissance became an influential cultural force. As Dickens has put it, 'thanks to printing, Erasmus had become an international legend, while on the eve of Luther's appearance the world of humanism seemed to have achieved through printing a new cohesion, a strange hold upon Europe's lay and ecclesiastical leaders'.[6] The magic of Gutenberg's 42–line Bible was already apparent to Enea Silvio Piccolomini in 1454: in a letter of 12 March 1455 to Cardinal Carvajal he told of a 'vir mirabilis' at the Diet of Frankfurt in October the previous year who had been able to supply a Bible which might be read without spectacles and in 158 identical copies![7] But while Werner Rolevinck had as early as 1470 observed that there was no easier way than printing to communicate his sermons to a greater number of people,[8] the Roman Church – with rare exceptions such as Johann Cochlaeus, Johann Eck and Johann Fabri – was slow, because of its allegiance to Latin, to realize its potential as a tool for the diffusion of the faith and as a weapon of propaganda.[9] In his *Brevis descriptio*

---

pfälzische Kirchengeschichte, 16) (Speyer, 1991). W. Hubatsch (ed.), *Wirkungen der deutschen Reformation bis 1555*, (Darmstadt, 1967), and T. A. Brady Jr, *Turning Swiss. Cities and Empire, 1450–1550* (Cambridge Studies in Early Modern History) (Cambridge, 1985) are also valuable.

[6] Dickens, *The German Nation*, p. 104 f. On the reception of printing by the humanists see H. Widmann, 'Die Wirkung des Buchdrucks auf die humanistischen Zeitgenossen und Nachfahren des Erfinders', in F. Krafft and D. Wuttke (eds), *Das Verhältnis der Humanisten zum Buch* (Deutsche Forschungsgemeinschaft: Kommission für Humanismusforschung, 4) (Bonn, 1977), pp. 63–88. On the exploitation of the medium by Erasmus see L. Jardine, *Erasmus, Man of Letters. The Construction of Charisma in Print* (Princeton, 1993).

[7] See E. Meuthen, 'Ein frühes Quellenzeugnis (zu Oktober 1454?) für den ältesten Buchdruck', *GJ*, 57 (1982), 108–18. Meuthen's opinion that the 'vir mirabilis' was Gutenberg himself has been contested by E. König, in H. Limburg, H. Lohse and W. Schmitz (eds.), *Ars impressoria. Entstehung und Entwicklung des Buchdrucks. Eine internationale Festgabe für Severin Corsten zum 65. Geburtstag* (Munich, 1986), p. 290; König considers it more likely that Johannes Fust was the man in question.

[8] See R. Hirsch, *Printing, Selling and Reading, 1450–1550* (Wiesbaden, 1967), p. 8.

[9] Cole 'The Reformation pamphlet' p. 139, attributes this to the fact that, having been 'long accustomed to power and authority' they 'felt little need to experiment with radically new methods of mass communication'. He notes that as late as 1590 handwritten liturgical books were still in demand for use in Catholic churches and that some Catholic clergy would not pray from a printed book.

Germaniae (Nuremberg, 1512), cap. III, 5, Cochlaeus called printing the most beneficial thing any mortal had invented. (The reason he cites in support of this opinion is interesting, however: it has nothing to do with the faith, rather he sees the importance of printing as lying in the fact that it enabled the forgotten literature of Rome and Greece to be revived.) It should not be overlooked, however, that, once sides had been joined, a Catholic response to Lutheran polemics was effectively stifled in some areas by a complex of local ordinances, designed to protect local printers and the Lutheran position. For instance, the press of the Brothers of the Common Life at Rostock was closed down by Lutherans in 1530.

The Reformers, by contrast, quickly seized upon printing to further their ends, recognizing how it made rapid dissemination possible. As Bernhart Hertzog later put it, 'viel zeit mag ersparet werden / vnd in einem tag mehr durch zwo Personen gesetzt vnnd getrucket wurde / dann zuvor zwentzig oder mehr inn etlich Jaren erschreiben könden' ('much time can be saved, and in a single day two men can set and print off more than 20 or more were previously able to write in several years').[10] Hardly ever can a technological breakthrough have come about at a more opportune moment. Printing was 'God's highest and extremest act of Grace,' said Luther, 'for by this means God desires to drive forward the cause of true religion to the ends of the earth and to make it available in all languages'.[11] This opinion was echoed by the English martyrologist John Foxe in 1572–73 when he offered thanks 'to the high providence of almighty God for the excellent art of printing, most happily of late found out, and now commonly practised everywhere to the singular benefit of Christ's Church'.[12] Similiarly Melanchthon said 'Printing is truly an art communicated by God to mankind'.[13] Even 80 years after the invention of printing it must indeed have seemed a miracle, a kind of divine gift, to the contemporaries. Given the poor communications of the period, the speed with which their ideas, their sermons, the new Bible translations were disseminated must have been astonishing. It must be realized, however, that the acceptance of printing in part was a matter of the generations: in 1517 Luther was only 34 and many of his supporters and fellow

---

[10] In the preface to his *Chronicon Alsatiae. Edelsasser Cronick* (Strasbourg: B. Jobin, 1592), quoted by J. Lebeau and J.-M. Valentin, *L'Alsace au siècle de la Réforme 1482–1621. Textes et documents* (Nancy, 1985), p. 219.

[11] WA Tisch. vol. 1, p. 523, no. 1038; see also vol. 4, p. 436 f., no. 4697.

[12] Quoted by Dickens, *The German Nation*, p. 110.

[13] H. Wendland, 'Martin Luther – seine Buchdrucker und Verleger', in H. G. Göpfert, P. Vodosek, E. Weyrauch and R. Wittmann (eds), *Beiträge zur Geschichte des Buchwesens im konfessionellen Zeitalter* (Wolfenbütteler Schriften zur Geschichte des Buchwesens, 11) (Wiesbaden, 1985), pp. 11–35, here p. 13.

pamphleteers were still under 30. Cole draws attention to an Erfurt pamphlet of 1523, *Eynn Dialogus ader gesprech zwischen einem Vatter unnd Sun dye Lere Martini Luthers und sunst andere sachen des Cristlichen glaubens belangende*, which neatly illustrates in a dialogue between father and son the different uses of oral and printed culture as seen from the two sides of the generation gap.[14]

How successfully the Reformers employed printing is demonstrated by the large number and rapid succession of editions some of their writings enjoyed. Four thousand copies of the pamphlet *An den Christlichen Adel deutscher Nation von des Christlichen Standes Besserung*, issued on 15 August 1520, sold so quickly that a second edition was required within five days – only to be followed by 15 more. The pamphlet *Von der Freiheit eines Christenmenschen* underwent 18 editions in a single year. Johannes Froben's first Latin edition of Luther's writings (Basle, October 1518) was sold out in a few months, and the second edition, of February 1519, went just as quickly. The books had been in demand not only in Germany but also in France, Spain, Italy, Holland, and England. Froben himself said that he had never had another success like it. Luther's *Ein Sermon von Ablaß und Gnade* (WA, 1, pp. 240 ff.), a German résumé of the most important arguments put forward in the Ninety-Five Theses, first published by Rhau-Grunenberg in the spring of 1518, went through 25 editions by 1520. Luther's writings were not the only ones which proved attractive: the dialogue *Karsthans* went through ten editions in a year. Martin Bucer's *Gespräch zwischen einem Schultheiß und einem Pfarrer* went through 13 editions in a year, and the *Zwölff Artickel der Bauern* (1525) saw 25 editions in six months.

The Reformation was precipitated by Pope Leo X's institution, in the Bull *Sacrosanctis salvatoris et redemptoris* of 31 March 1515, of an indulgence for use in the provinces of Mainz and Magdeburg, intended to promote the construction of the new St Peter's at Rome. (In fact half the proceeds were destined to help the Archbishop of Mainz, Albrecht von Brandenburg (elected 9 March 1514) repay a large loan of 21 000 ducats to the Augsburg bankers, the Fuggers.) It was this indulgence which provoked Luther to issue his 95 theses against the practice of indulgences.[15] In a letter to Christoph Scheurl of 5 March 1518 (WA,

---

[14] Cole, 'The Reformation pamphlet', p. 141. See C. S. Meyer (ed.), *Luther for an Ecumenical Age* (St Louis, 1967), pp. 82–107.

[15] H. Volz, 'Der St. Peters-Ablass und das deutsche Druckgewerbe', *GJ*, 41 (1966) 156–72, gives a comprehensive account of the various items of printed matter generated by the indulgence: the text of the Bull, vernacular summaries, printed instructions for the administration of the indulgence, and blank certificates. On the publication and printing of the 95 theses see H. Grimm, 'Luthers "Ablassthesen" und die Gegenthesen von Tetzel-Wimpina in der Sicht der Druck- und Buchgeschichte', *GJ*, 43 (1968), 139–50.

2.1 Indulgence granted to the Dominicans of Mühlhausen by Albrecht,
     Archbishop of Magdeburg and Mainz, benefiting St Peter's in Rome,
     dated 12 June 1517 in Mühlhausen

Br., 1, p. 152) Luther expressed his regret at the fact that, through
printing, the theses had been so widely disseminated.

Printing, or rather a printer, was in at the birth of the Reformation in
Zurich too. The Reformation may be said to have begun there on Ash
Wednesday 1522 when the printer Christoph Froschauer invited a
number of guests, including Huldrych Zwingli (1484–1531), to a modest repast at which some sausages were served, in contravention of the
regulations on fasting. When called to account, Froschauer declared

On Aplas von Rom
kan man wol selig werden
durch anzaigung der götlichen
hailigen geschrifft.

2.2   The sale of indulgences as portrayed on the title-page of a pamphlet
(Augsburg: Melchior Ramminger, 1520)

that he had to have such substantial sustenance to give him the strength needed to carry out the hard work involved in printing the Pauline epistles which he wanted to get ready in time for the Frankfurt Fair. Though Zwingli himself had refrained from consuming the sausages he came out in defence of his fellow citizens, publishing to this end his tract *Von Erkiesen und Freiheit der Speisen*, a milestone in a chain of events which was to lead to Zurich's becoming a Protestant city in 1525.[16]

The close link between the Reformation and printing is shown by the fact that there were many towns where a marked feature of the first printer's output was publication of Lutheran – or indeed anti-Lutheran – books. Though the press may not in all these cases have been specifically set up to produce such literature, works of this kind certainly figured prominently and at an early stage in the prototypographer's output. To judge from Benzing's *Die Buchdrucker des 16. und 17. Jahrhunderts im deutschen Sprachgebiet*, this appears to have been the case in the following towns:[17] Ingolstadt and Schlettstadt (Sélestat) (1519); Halberstadt (1520); Stuttgart (1521); Coburg, Eilenburg, Grimma, Regensburg (1522); Altenburg, Jena (1523); Allstedt, Dresden, Königsberg, Wertheim (1524); Halle, Lucerne, Zwickau (1525); Nikolsburg (1526); Marburg (1527); Kiel (1528); Ettlingen (1530); Schwäbisch Hall (1536); Berne (1537); Nördlingen (1538); Annaberg (c.1540); Berlin (1540); Bonn, Hanover, Hildesheim (1543); Neuburg on the Danube (1544); Parchim (1547); Dillingen (1550); Schleusingen (1555); Oberursel (1557).

Some particularly interesting cases deserve closer inspection. The first printer in Landshut, Johann Weissenburger, who established himself

---

[16] See E. Egli (ed.), *Aktensammlung zur Geschichte der Zürcher Reformation in den Jahren 1519–1533* (Zurich, 1879), no. 233 and 234.

[17] J. Benzing, *Die Buchdrucker des 16. und 17. Jahrhunderts im deutschen Sprachgebiet* (2nd edn, Wiesbaden, 1982). The dates in parentheses are those at which printing was introduced or revived. References to individual writings by Luther are to: J. Benzing, *Lutherbibliographie. Verzeichnis der gedruckten Schriften Martin Luthers bis zu dessen Tod* (Bibliotheca Bibliographica Aureliana, X, XVI, XIX) (Baden-Baden, 1966) [cited as *LB*], or to the supplement: Helmut Claus and Michael A. Pegg, *Ergänzungen zur Bibliographie der zeitgenössischen Lutherdrucke* (Veröffentlichungen der Forschungsbibliothek Gotha, 20), (Gotha, 1982). The addenda have meanwhile been consolidated in J. Benzing/H. Claus, *Lutherbibliographie*, Bd 2 (Bibliotheca Bibliographica Aureliana, CXLIII), (Baden-Baden, 1994). These bibliographies, though excellent, are doubtless incomplete: M. Santoro, in his review of G. Mazzetti, *Le prime edizioni di Lutero (1518–1546) nelle biblioteche italiane* (Florence, 1984), in *Esperienze Letterarie* 10 (1985), 201–3, observes (p. 202) that, of 378 books listed by Mazzetti, as many as 95 are allegedly not in Benzing. See also my review of M. A. Pegg, *A Catalogue of German Reformation Pamphlets (1516–1550) in Swedish Libraries* (Bibliotheca Bibliographica Aureliana, 150). Valentin Koerner, (Baden-Baden, 1995), in *The Library*, 6th series, **18** (1996), 76.

2.3 Luther's 95 theses against indulgences (Nuremberg: Hieronymus Höltzel, 1517)

there in 1513, was a priest and in the 1520s he brought out reprints of both Lutheran and Catholic works. And in Dresden Wolfgang Stöckel printed for the anti-Lutheran party until 1539 when the Reformation was introduced there; thereafter he printed for the Protestants. By contrast, Johann Grüninger at Strasbourg continued to print only Catholic works after the Reformation there and got into trouble for it with the city authorities. Also in Strasbourg, Wolfgang Köpfel, Capito's nephew, was a convinced Protestant from the start of his career, the first book he printed being a polemical letter from Luther to Hartmut von Cronberg. When the question of whether the clergy should be permitted to marry raged between the bishop and the Reformers in 1523–24, Köpfel helped to gain support for the married pastors by printing their treatises on marriage. In the university town of Ingolstadt, Alexander Weissenhorn established himself as a printer in 1539, having left Augsburg to print books for Johann Eck. His was the only sizeable Catholic press in southern Germany. In Augsburg he had printed Reformation texts, including Urbanus Rhegius's *Seelenarznei* and Caspar Huberinus's *Tröstung aus göttlicher Schrift* in 1537 and two pieces by Luther (*LB*, 3287 and 3294) in 1538, and even in 1548 books by Melanchthon and Agrippa were found among his stock and confiscated. When Eck died in 1543 Weissenhorn faced ruin and contemplated returning to Ausgsburg. Cochlaeus, who happened to be in Ingolstadt, feared that, in order to get work in Augsburg, Weissenhorn might print Protestant books, so he arranged to provide him with Catholic works to print, himself penning 29 tracts between 1543 and 1546 to keep Weissenhorn in business and in Ingolstadt. At Dillingen printing was re-established in 1550 not only to serve the newly established university (1549) which was intended to be a bulwark of the Counter-Reformation but specifically to help in a situation when there was a dearth of presses committed to the Catholic cause. The aim was to publish distinguished Catholic writers who had had difficulty in finding a printer willing to accept their works. Sebald Mayer was appointed by Cardinal Otto Truchsess von Waldburg, Bishop of Augsburg. He published many works by Johannes Fabri, Bishop of Vienna, (who was himself a firm advocate of the use of printing to counter the Protestants) and a good deal by Juan Luis Vives, Pedro de Soto, Sebastianus Solidus, Marcus von Weyda, Jean Gerson, Thomas à Kempis and many others. At Oberursel Nikolaus Henricus (Heinrich) was invited to set up his press here by Count Ludwig von Stolberg und Königstein who had introduced the Reform in the town. He printed many polemical tracts against Melanchthon and his supporters, against the Calvinists, the Zwinglians, and the Catholics. It is also interesting to note that the last Grand Master of the Order of Teutonic Knights, Albrecht von Brandenburg, had the Lutheran catechisms printed as the first books ever printed in Prussian (in 1545) and Lithuanian (1547); these are the first substantial monuments surviving in either language. Similarly, the Croatian magnate Johann Ungnad established a printing shop at Urach, near Tübingen, in 1561 which, between then and 1564, produced, at his expense, 25 Protestant books in Croatian.

It is instructive also to see where and when works by Luther were first printed:[18]

1513	Wittenberg
1517	Basle, Landshut, Leipzig, Nuremberg
1518	Augsburg, Braunschweig
1519	Breslau, Erfurt, Mainz, Munich, Strasbourg, Vienna
1520	Cologne, Danzig, Hagenau, Halberstadt, Lübeck, Schlettstadt (Sélestat), Zürich
1521	Konstanz, Speyer, Worms
1522	Bamberg, Coburg, Grimma, Hamburg, Regensburg, Stuttgart
1523	Colmar, Zwickau
1524	Altenberg, Eilenburg, Jena, Königsberg, Magdeburg, Tübingen, Wertheim, Würzburg
1525	Dresden, Lippstadt, Reutlingen, Rostock
1527	Ingolstadt, Marburg
1529	Ulm
1535	Frankfurt am Main, Neuenburg (Neuchâtel)
1536	Schwäbisch Hall
1539	Berne, Geneva
1542	Halle
1543	Wesel
1544	Hanover
1545	Neuburg (Danube), Nördlingen
1546	Berlin, Bonn

Printers who supported one faction or the other risked their livelihoods for their religious ideas. And those who printed the works of the Spiritualists and the Anabaptists risked even more. In Strasbourg Martin Flach II and Johann Prüss the Younger were in the forefront, printing Karlstadt's work as early as 1520, and Prüss continued to publish him even after he had become unpopular with the Strasbourg reformers, issuing four of his treatises in 1524 alone. Prüss's brother-in-law Johann Schwann followed his lead, and Balthasar Beck printed treatises of Caspar Schwenckfeld, Melchior Hoffmann, as well as Sebastian Franck's scandal-provoking chronicle. The support of these Strasbourg printers was vital for the diffusion of Anabaptist and Spiritualist theology. The dangers that a printer could face are memorably exemplified by the case of the Nuremberg printer Hans Hergot who was executed in Leipzig on 20 May 1527 for having published the pamphlet *Von der*

---

[18] The list has been compiled on the basis of the information contained in the index of printers and publishers in Claus/Pegg.

newen wandlung eynes Christlichen Lebens which envisioned a utopian state based on common ownership and a communist agrarian system.[19]

German printers and the Reformation

The general situation in the German printing trade

Despite the German origin of European printing and in spite of the fact that printing was well established in very many German towns in the sixteenth century, even the largest centres there were modest in comparison with places like Paris, Lyon and Rouen. Calculations based on Benzing's *Die Buchdrucker des 16. und 17. Jahrhunderts im deutschen Sprachgebiet* show that the German cities with the largest numbers of printers in the sixteenth century were Cologne with 93, Nuremberg with 62, Strasbourg 57, Basle 54, Wittenberg 38, Frankfurt am Main 37, Augsburg 32, Leipzig 29, Erfurt 28 and Vienna 22, though of course the important question is how many were printing in a given place at any one time: normally it was not many. The individual busi-

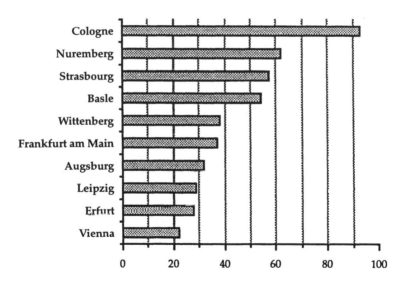

Figure 2.1 The leading German printing centres: numbers of printers active in the sixteenth century

---

[19] See M. Steinmetz and H. Claus, *Hans Hergot und die Flugschrift 'Von der newen wandlung eynes Christlichen Lebens'* (Leipzig 1977). This pamphlet appeared in two editions, not one, as is generally thought; see F. Ganseuer in *AGB*, 21 (1980), cols 1541–2.

nesses were generally of modest scale too. While the Kobergers of Nuremberg in their heyday may have had as many as 100 men working for them directly or indirectly, the individual printing shop was, by modern standards, very small. While a large-scale enterprise, working at full capacity, might employ as many as 10 to 12 men, including the master-owner, a medium-sized shop – the backbone of the industry – probably had about half a dozen employees including a two-man team of compositors and two pressmen, with the master-owner perhaps doing some of the composition and presswork himself. The smallest businesses probably consisted of the master-owner and an apprentice only.

The early history of the printing industry is marked by a high degree of mobility amongst the personnel. Not least perhaps because of the apprenticeship system, few printers actually worked in the place of their birth. Chrisman states that of the 77 Strasbourg printers falling within the scope of her study, only ten can be identified as having been born there. The overwhelming majority were immigrants, as indeed were many other craftsmen, the high mortality rate in that period, especially during outbreaks of plague, leaving the city no alternative but to regenerate itself from outside.[20] A glance at Benzing shows that, of 46 printers identified as working in Nuremberg before 1555, at least 14 definitely came from outside, five were definitely born in Nuremberg, while for the remainder Benzing at least does not give the relevant information. Of 19 printers active in Vienna before 1582 only one was born there.

As for the social standing of the printers, there were several crafts which provided easy entry to printing because many of the skills required were the same or because the trade was congenial to entrepreneurs. Thus one finds goldsmiths (e.g. Georg Husner, Christian Döring, though the latter was probably only a financier), engravers (e.g. Jakob Cammerlander) and painters (e.g. Lucas Cranach, Bartholomäus Kistler). Scholars were another group of recruits; many printers had studied at university. Printing was also a family business; family ties and marriages between printers and printers' widows were important as a means of giving security and ensuring continuity, though perhaps the main reason for marrying a printer's widow was to obtain not only the printing equipment but especially the privileges she had inherited in respect of books printed by her late spouse.

The early stages of printing at Wittenberg

According to Steinberg, Wittenberg owed its fame as a printing centre partly to the one blunder the shrewd Nuremberg printer Anton Koberger

---

[20] M. U. Chrisman, *Lay Culture*, p. 13.

ever committed when he turned down Luther's offer to become his publisher.[21] The early history of printing in Wittenberg and Luther's dealings with printers there, which are unusually well documented, well illustrate many of the conditions obtaining in the period and deserve to be treated more fully not only for that reason but also because of the central importance of Wittenberg in the Reformation.[22]

On 26 August 1485, Ernst, Elector of Saxony (1484–86), divided his territories into two: the 'Ernestine' Electorate (*Kurfürstentum*) and the 'Albertine' Duchy of Saxony. As a result, the only Saxon university, Leipzig, fell to the duchy, and with it went the only printing shop, that of Konrad Kachelofen who, arriving from Lorraine, had set up a press there the previous year, in competition with Markus Brandis who had been there since 1481 but left soon after 1485. In order to have a university in his land, Ernst's successor, his eldest son, Frederick the Wise, founded one at Wittenberg, a town of little more than 2 000 inhabitants, in 1502; the influx of students soon doubled the population. Already in the fifteenth century every German university town[23] – with the sole exception of Greifswald – had had at least one printing house, so it was natural for a press to be set up in Wittenberg too.

As a small community of craftsmen and smallholders, the town hardly provided the climate for strong growth of printing such as one might expect to find in big commercial centres like Augsburg, Nuremberg, Strasbourg, Cologne or Lübeck.[24] Accordingly, the beginnings were modest: Wolfgang Stöckel came from Leipzig in 1504 for a brief period, followed by a couple of equally short-lived private presses, of Nikolaus Marschalk, the first teacher of Greek in Wittenberg, and Hermann Trebelius, *poeta laureatus*, who acquired some of Marschalk's equip-

---

[21] S. H. Steinberg, *Five Hundred Years of Printing* (2nd edn, Harmondsworth, 1961), p. 45.

[22] The very full information we have about Luther and his printers contrasts, for instance, with the marked paucity of information about other leading figures of the Reformation and their dealings with printers. See for example Gottfried Seebaß, 'Andreas Osiander und seine Drucker', in Göpfert et al., *Beiträge zur Geschichte*, pp. 133–45. The following account of Wittenberg is substantially indebted to H. Volz, 'Die Arbeitsteilung der Wittenberger Drucker zu Luthers Lebzeiten', *GJ*, 32 (1957), 146–54, and to Wendland, 'Martin Luther', pp. 11–35.

[23] As one example, for an account of the situation in Cologne see S. Corsten, 'Universität und Buchdruck in Köln', in L. Hellinga and H. Härtel (eds), *Buch und Text im 15. Jahrhundert. Book and Text in the Fifteenth Century* (Wolfenbütteler Abhandlungen zur Renaissanceforschung, 2) (Hamburg, 1981), pp. 189–201; and W. Schmitz, 'Buchdruck und Reformation in Köln', *Jahrbuch des Kölnischen Geschichtsvereins*, 55 (1984), 117–54.

[24] On the intellectual life of Wittenberg see M. Grossmann, *Humanism in Wittenberg 1485–1517* (Bibliotheca Humanistica et Reformatorica, 11) (Nieuwkoop, 1975).

ment. Printing came to be firmly established in Wittenberg only with the arrival of Johann Rhau-Grunenberg in 1508. Rhau-Grunenberg, who remained until 1525, was the first printer of Luther's works.

Rhau-Grunenberg's first publications were for use in the university, texts printed with ample margins and plenty of space between the lines for the students to enter notes from their teachers' dictation. One such was the Latin psalter he printed for Luther in 1513, intended for use in his lectures.[25] At the end of 1516 he printed Luther's first vernacular book: *Eyn geystlich edles Buchleynn von rechter underscheyd vnd vorstand, was der alt vnd new mensche sey* (*LB*, 69), which was shortly to be followed by Luther's German translation and exposition of the seven pentitential psalms (*LB*, 74 and 75).

In 1518 Rhau-Grunenberg printed a number of tracts for Luther (*LB*, 90, 91, 92, 125, 127, 135, 160, 181, 182, 183, 192, 205, 206, 210, 212, 234, 235, 240, 249; Claus/Pegg 91a, 114a), but it seems that it was already becoming apparent that Rhau-Grunenberg's enterprise could not meet the demands being placed upon it. In a letter to Georg Spalatin, written on 15 August 1521, Luther complained about Rhau-Grunenberg:

> You would not believe how I regret and how I am disgusted by his work. If only I had never sent him anything in the vernacular! He has printed these things so shoddily, so carelessly, so confusedly that I keep these scruffy types and paper hidden away. Johann the printer never gets any better! (WA Br., 2, p. 379, no. 427)

In the summer of that year Luther made contact with Melchior Lotter the Elder in Leipzig and a close relationship developed between them. (Luther actually lodged with Lotter during the Leipzig disputation with Eck in 1519.) At first the printing of Luther's smaller pieces seems to have been shared by Rhau-Grunenberg and Lotter, but when it came to larger-scale works such as the Latin commentary on Galatians of 1519 it was entrusted to the more competitive Lotter in Leipzig (*LB*, 416–20). Together with a number of other professors and the rector of the university, Luther appealed to the Elector to invite Melchior Lotter to set up a business in Wittenberg itself. So productive was Luther as a writer that Melchior Lotter deemed it a worthwhile opportunity and he set up a branch of his firm under his son Melchior the Younger in Wittenberg; for a time it was located in Lucas Cranach's house. Among the first products of the press were two of Luther's major pamphlets of 1520, *An den christlichen Adel deutscher Nation* (*LB*, 683–5) and *De captivitate Babylonica ecclesiae* (*LB*, 704, 705), while the third great programmatic

---

[25] This survives in a unique copy, with manuscript annotations by Luther himself. See E. Roach and R. Schwarz (eds), *Wolfenbütteler Psalter 1513–1515. Faksimile und Kommentar mit Umschrift des Manuskriptes* (Frankfurt am Main, 1983).

tract, *Von der Freiheit eines Christenmenschen*, was printed by Rhau-Grunenberg (*LB*, 734). There seems to have been no particular pattern as to whether Luther's writings were published by Rhau-Grunenberg or Lotter, though Melanchthon preferred the latter because he was well equipped with Greek types. When in the spring of 1522 a decision had to be taken as to who should print Luther's translation of the New Testament, it was clear that it had to be entrusted to Melchior Lotter the Younger, not least perhaps because of his father's firm's many years' experience of printing missals, breviaries, liturgical psalters and similar works. The 'September Testament', the 'December Testament', both of 1522, the Low German version of 1523, and the High German and Low German versions of the Pentateuch all bear eloquent testimony to the skill and high technical standards of Lotter's press.

But meanwhile there were problems. Rhau-Grunenberg[26] and Melchior Lotter the Younger (who was joined by his brother Michael in 1523) now had competitors to contend with. Nikolaus Schirlentz had arrived in 1521 and set up a press in the house of Andreas Karlstadt. In 1523 Hans Lufft[27] came from Leipzig, and the same year Lucas Cranach and the goldsmith Christian Döring, who hitherto had acted only as publishers of the books printed by Lotter, set up a press of their own under the technical supervision of Josef Klug, possibly as a result of the envy of Lotter who after all was able to see what great profits his labours earned for his publisher partners.[28] This press not only issued the second and third parts of Luther's Old Testament translation but for a time it published first editions of most of Luther's writings as well as the first separate edition of his German psalter. Cranach and Döring had the capital to strengthen their position, and the other Wittenberg presses came to be largely dependent on reprints of Luther's works. In 1528 Michael Lotter deemed it wiser to quit the town and seek his fortune in Magdeburg. There he became the most important printer of Lutheran works, with several hundred titles to his credit. His brother Melchior had already left Wittenberg in 1525 after apparently falling out with

---

[26] On the later history of Rhau-Grunenberg's press see H. Claus, 'Zur Tätigkeit der Presse Johann Rhau-Grunenbergs in den Jahren 1524/25', *GJ*, 39 (1964), 155–63.

[27] On Lufft see W. Meier, *Der Buchdrucker Hans Lufft zu Wittenberg* (2nd enlarged edn, Leipzig, 1923; reprint Nieuwkoop, 1965).

[28] See H. Kühne, 'Lukas Cranach d. Ä. als Verleger, Drucker und Buchhändler', *Marginalien*, 47 (1972), pp. 59–73, and now also J. L. Flood, 'Lucas Cranach as publisher', *German Life and Letters*, n.s., 48 (1995), 241–63. Cranach's main business was that of court painter of course, but he also had many other interests: he was a large property owner, he ran the apothecary's, was a wine dealer, dealt in paper and owned a quarry. He also had municipal duties as councillor and mayor. Döring, for his part, also ran a carrier's business and an inn, was a councillor and a church treasurer.

Cranach and Döring and specifically following a quarrel with a local bookbinder which cost him a heavy fine, the protection of the Elector, and the favour of Luther. For some reason which is not clear,[29] the Cranach–Döring press ceased in 1526 too, and for the last 20 years down to Luther's death in 1546 Wittenberg printing lay chiefly in the hands of four firms: Hans Lufft, Nikolaus Schirlentz, Josef Klug (who had worked for Cranach and Döring and had already during that period printed a few things on his own account), and Georg Rhau who had come from Eisleben as a music teacher in 1520 but set himself up as a printer, notably of music, in 1525.[30]

Because of his many other commitments, Luther's pen, though always busy, was less productive from the late 1520s onwards. This exacerbated the problem for the printing firms that were competing with one another. Fortunately, however, there were a number of works – Luther's Bible, prayer books, his *Kirchenpostille* (*Auslegung der Episteln und Evangelien*), *Großer* and *Kleiner Katechismus*, and hymns, Melanchthon's *Confessio Augustana*[31] and his *Loci communes* – for which there was necessarily a constant demand. In the late 1520s the Wittenberg printers seem to have reached an agreement as to who should concentrate on what. After the closure of the Cranach and Döring press in 1526 Hans Lufft was entrusted with printing virtually all the German Bibles, his first work being a revised New Testament. He produced all the remaining parts of the Old Testament, the first complete Bible (1534), as well as further editions of the psalter and the New Testament. He was to dominate this field until 1572. Until 1546 he also produced Low German editions of the psalter, New Testament and the complete Bible. Lufft also printed Luther's *Betbüchlein* (first edition 1522)[32] and, from 1528 onwards, the *Kirchenpostille*. He enjoyed the benefit of the Elector's privilege in respect of all these works. So competitive and efficient was he that he printed all but four volumes of the Wittenberg edition of Luther's collected works, in 12 German and seven Latin volumes (1539–59; *LB*, 1 and 2).[33] Lufft's

[29] Wendland, 'Martin Luther' p. 24, also p. 30, speaks of Döring having got into debt.

[30] It is generally assumed that Georg Rhau was a relative of Johann Rhau-Grunenberg, but see M. Geck in *Die Musik in Geschichte und Gegenwart* vol. 11 (Kassel, 1963), col. 372.

[31] See W. H. Neuser, *Bibliographie der Confessio Augustana und Apologie 1530–1580* (Bibliotheca Humanistica et Reformatorica, 37) (Nieuwkoop, 1987).

[32] There is a facsimile of the 1529 edition, with an afterword by Frieder Schulz, *Martin Luther, Ein Betbüchlein mit Kalender und Passional* (Kassel, 1982).

[33] On this enterprise see E. Wolgast, *Die Wittenberger Luther-Ausgabe. Zur Überlieferungsgeschichte der Werke Luthers im 16. Jahrhundert* (Nieuwkoop, 1971). The publishing of the 1534 Bible and of Luther's collected works was entrusted to a company comprising the booksellers Moritz Goltz, Christoph Schramm and Bartholomäus Vogel in which Goltz was the senior partner (see Wendland, 'Martin Luther', p. 30).

work was one of the chief reasons why Wittenberg grew to such importance in the history of printing, yet his beginnings had been quite inauspi-
cious: one of his earliest books was an octavo Pentateuch (unique copy in
Hamburg State and University Library) in which no typographical distinction was made between text and notes and in which spaces were left
for initials to be inserted by hand.[34] Even later he had to borrow woodcut
blocks and ornaments from Michael Lotter. This nicely illustrates the
difficulties with which Wittenberg printers had to contend, and the fact
that Lufft emerged as leader of the pack is not only a reflection of the
quality of his work but also shows that he must have had both business
acumen and a measure of luck.

2.4   Georg Rhau, printer and publisher in Wittenberg, 1542

For Georg Rhau there were few crumbs of the great Bible-printing
industry left. Instead he concentrated on printing the *Großer Katechismus*
(from 1529 onwards) of which he produced 13 (mostly octavo) High
German and five Low German editions by 1546 (*LB*, 2548, 2552–4,
2556–7, 2560, 2563–7, 2569; 2571–3, 2575, 2578). He alone printed
both Latin and German editions of Melanchthon's *Confessio Augustana*
and *Apologia*. Rhau also printed proclamations and official publications
for the government, Wittenberg being the only printing centre in Ernestine
Saxony. He even supplied a field press and men to operate it when Elector
Johann Friedrich embarked on military campaigns in 1542 and 1546.[35]

---

[34] See Wendland 'Martin Luther', p. 24.
[35] See H. Volz, 'Zur Geschichte des Wittenberger Buchdrucks 1544–47', *GJ*, 38 (1963),
113–19, here pp. 116 f.

The other Wittenberg printers had a relatively thin time. Nikolaus Schirlentz published two editions of Ecclesiasticus and of the books of Solomon between 1535 and 1546. In 1529 he published Luther's revision of the Latin Bible which the brothers Lotter were originally to have printed. He did specialize, however, in publishing Luther's *Kleiner Katechismus*, in High German and Low German. Josef Klug did not have a share in printing the Bible at all; his speciality was Luther's hymn-books and to some extent also Hebrew printing. Peter Seitz the Elder, who arrived in Wittenberg in 1534, printed Ecclesiasticus and the books of Solomon but his importance rests on his editions of Melanchthon's *Loci communes* (four octavos of the revised edition from 1536 to 1541 and two of the third revised edition between 1543 and 1545).[36]

Luther's writings were of course widely printed throughout Germany, but editions published outside Wittenberg were seldom authorized. Luther rarely made direct use of printers outside Wittenberg, though when he was staying in Coburg in 1530 he did have contact with Hans Bär from Coburg and the publisher Georg Rottenmaier from Nuremberg,[37] and the *Sendbrief von Dolmetschen* (1530), for instance, was first printed in Nuremberg and only subsequently in Wittenberg.

The kind of specialization we have observed in Wittenberg of course came to be practised elsewhere too, though naturally the reasons for it may have been rather different. The situation in Strasbourg has been well described by Chrisman.[38] Here, after the Reformation, the only printer to continue to publish Catholic books was Johann Grüninger; they represented 44 per cent of his output. Protestant books were a major feature of the output of Wolfgang Köpfel (62 per cent), Matthias Apiarius (Biener) (50 per cent) and Johannes Schwan (74 per cent). Forty-eight per cent of Matthias Schürer's output were humanist works, while scientific and medical works formed a substantial proportion of the books printed by Balthasar Beck (40 per cent), Jakob Cammerlander (54 per cent), Christian Egenolff (51 per cent) and Heinrich Seybold (89 per cent).[39] Thiebolt Berger specialized in music. The steady growth in

---

[36] For a provisional bibliography of editions of Melanchthon's works see R. Keen, *A Checklist of Melanchthon Imprints through 1560* (Sixteenth Century Bibliography, 27) (St Louis, 1988). A more authoritative bibliography is currently being prepared by Dr Helmut Claus (Gotha).

[37] On Luther and Bär see J. Erdmann, 'Luther in einer Bibliothek. Luther im Spiegel der Coburger Büchersammlungen', in Göpfert et al., *Beiträge zur Geschichte*, pp. 37–55, here pp. 40–41. The books previously assigned to Rottmaier are now believed actually to have been printed by Johann Petreius; see Benzing/Claus, *LB*, II, p. 8.

[38] Chrisman, *Lay Culture*, p. 35.

[39] Chrisman, *Lay Culture*, p. 36, suggests that Beck and Cammerlander may have published such works as a cover for their religious activities or to subsidize their religious publications.

the market for vernacular books is indicated by the high proportion they represented in the publishing programme of printers like Bernhard Jobin (40 per cent), Bartholomäus Grüninger (54 per cent), Paul Messerschmidt (53 per cent), Bartholomäus Kistler (47 per cent) and Jakob Frölich (89 per cent). Early in the century Heinrich Knoblochtzer had pioneered the illustrated popular book. Others, like Peter Hugg and Nikolaus Faber, worked as jobbers, concentrating on broadsheets, songs, legal documents and the like.

One of the most important printing houses of the Reformation and of early Protestantism was that of Peter Braubach at Frankfurt am Main. Braubach had learned printing with Wolfgang Köpfel at Strasbourg from about 1525 to 1528. On 26 December 1528 he registered at the University of Wittenberg, but already in 1529 he entered the business of Johann Setzer at Hagenau where works by Luther, Melanchthon and Bugenhagen were printed. In 1536 he moved to Schwäbisch Hall where he was the first printer. Here he published in particular works by the Württemberg Reformer Johannes Brenz and by Melanchthon, as well as Luther, Urbanus Rhegius and Anton Corvinus, and classics too such as Xenophon, Ovid, Cicero and Pliny. When he moved to Frankfurt in 1540 he continued to specialize in Luther, Melanchthon and particularly Brenz, but many other Protestant authors were added to his list, including Johannes Aepin (d. 1553), Matthias Flacius Illyricus (d. 1575), Paul von Eitzen (d. 1598), Erasmus Alberus (d. 1553), Christoph Hofmann (d. c.1576), Joachim Westphal (d. 1574), Johannes Magdeburg (d. 1565, author of *Der Psalter Dauids Gesangsweise* (1565)), Hartmann Beyer (d. 1577), Basilius Monner (d. 1566), Johann Freder (d. 1562) and Johann Wigand (d. 1587). He printed mainly in Latin but there were some German titles too. He also continued to bring out editions of classical authors: Aristophanes, Euripides, Demosthenes, Sophocles, Aristotle, Hesiod, Pindar, Tacitus, and others. Contemporaries praised the clarity and accuracy of his Greek and Hebrew editions. (None of his Hebrew works has been identified.)[40]

Who printed for the Catholics?

Despite Cochlaeus's famous complaint that the printers would only print Lutheran books, it was of course possible to get Catholic books published, though as we have seen, it was often necessary for specific inducements – such as the provision of a fully-equipped press – to be provided. There were some printers who, when they printed religious

---

[40] See H. von Schade, 'Peter Braubach in Frankfurt (1540–1567). Ein Werkverzeichnis', *AGB*, 21 (1980), cols 849–964.

material, printed exclusively or virtually exclusively Catholic material, and there were many who seem to have been happy to print anything that came their way, whether Catholic or Protestant. The first category included for instance:

- at Augsburg: Johann Miller, a native of the city, (active 1514–28?), who also printed grammars and editions of the classics
- at Cologne: Peter Quentel (1520–46)
- at Ingolstadt: Alexander Weissenhorn (1539–49); his heirs published many Jesuit works
- at Leipzig: Nikolaus Wolrab (1536–47 and 1551) who acted as distributor for the works of his wife's uncle Johann Cochlaeus who, with the support of Johann Fabri, Bishop of Vienna, set up a press for him in 1536
- at Lucerne: Thomas Murner (1525–29), mainly printing his own works
- at Oppenheim: Jakob Köbel (1499–1532)
- at Strasbourg: Johann Grüninger (1482–1531)
- at Vienna: Johann Singriener the Elder (1510–45) who was on good terms with the Catholic bishops Johann Fabri and Friedrich Nausea.

Later on, the publishing of Counter-Reformation works lay in the hands of men like Adam Berg the Elder at Munich (1564–1610) and Martin Böckler at Freiburg im Breisgau (1592–1615). Among printers who printed Catholic books side-by-side with Protestant ones were:

- at Erfurt: Hans Knappe the Elder (1508–1523) though most of his religious books were Catholic
- at Freiburg im Breisgau: Johann Faber (1529–42)
- at Leipzig: Nickel Schmidt (1521–ca. 1545), and Valentin Schumann (1513–42) who printed Lutheran material from 1518 to 1521 and Catholic books from 1521 onwards; it was possibly Schumann who worked the Emser press at Dresden in 1524–25
- at Mainz: Johann Schöffer (1503–31)
- at Landshut Johann Weissenburger (1513–33)
- at Munich: Hans Schobsser (1500–30) who published not only Lutheran material but the anti-Lutheran polemics of Kaspar Schatzger
- at Tübingen: Ulrich Morhart the Elder (1523–54), who, despite his own Lutheran sympathies, found himself printing pamphlets by Cochlaeus, Eck, Dietenberger, Fabri, and the Franciscan Schatzger.

The growth of German book production

In this period the bulk of German books were of course in Latin – as late as 1570 Latin still accounted for some 70 per cent of all publications – but one of the most important effects of the Reformation was that it occasioned unprecedented growth in vernacular book production. Figures assembled a century ago by Friedrich Kapp are still a useful indicator.[41] Basing himself on earlier figures (of Panzer, Weller and Kuczynski), he established the number of books printed in German, as displayed in Figure 2.2. (He notes that of the 3 113 items printed between 1518 and 1523 approximately 600 were published in Wittenberg.) Between 1517 and 1523, then, there was a tenfold increase. Though it would be possible now to compute more accurate figures, they would only confirm this general trend. Cole speaks of an

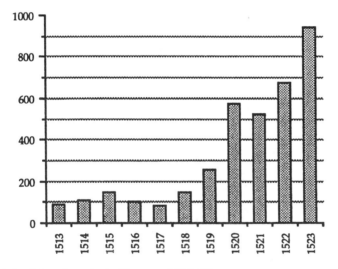

Figure 2.2   Printed works in German, 1513–23

41 F. Kapp, *Geschichte des deutschen Buchhandels bis in das siebzehnte Jahrhundert* (Geschichte des deutschen Buchhandels, 1) (Leipzig, 1886; reprint Leipzig, 1970), pp. 407–8. In *Lay Culture*, Chrisman has examined the changing relationship between Latin and German books for Strasbourg in great detail, on the basis of her *Bibliography of Strasbourg Imprints 1480–1599*, (New Haven, 1982). Though the study has numerous shortcomings, not the least of which is the unreliability of the bibliographical base (see in particular the reviews by M. Pegg in *The Library* 6th series, 6 (1984), 85–6; T. Scott in *ARG*, 75 (1984), 309–14 (with a response by the author, pp. 314–16); and J.-D. Müller in *Arbitrium* (1985), pp. 147–59), such analyses are extremely instructive and need to be undertaken in respect of other major printing centres, particularly Nuremberg and Leipzig and, for the second half of the sixteenth century, Frankfurt am Main.

increase in the order of 2 300 per cent in the number of pamphlets published, from 13 in 1517 to 299 in 1524.[42] Johannes Schwitalla quotes Walther Gose as speaking of a tenfold increase in the general book market (i.e. presumably the market for Latin books as well as vernacular ones) between 1500 and 1519 while the production of small quartos (as an indicator of pamphlet production) increased twentyfold over the same period.[43] Schwitalla himself reckons that at least 3 million copies of pamphlets were in circulation between 1518 and 1525, with the German population standing at approximately 13 million.[44] But at least as far as the number of pamphlets was concerned the boom did not last. After 1525 it declined rapidly, doubtless bringing financial ruin to many small printers, but the output of pamphlets increased again in the 1530s, reaching a high point in 1546 at the time of the Schmalkaldic War, and the number remained at a fairly high level until the Peace of Augsburg in 1555. A factor which was conducive to growth in book production and sales was, of course, the falling book prices. Pamphlets were relatively inexpensive anyway, but larger books were cheaper too: Hans Lufft's 1534 first edition of Luther's complete Bible translation cost 2 gulden 8 groschen, whereas the earliest printed German Bible (Strasbourg: Johann Mentelin, before 27 June 1466, GW, 4295) had cost 12 gulden, and Koberger's Bible of 1483 (GW, 4303) was worth 6 gulden. Luther's 'September Testament' of 1522 is thought to have cost 10.5 groschen in loose sheets, while a bound copy is estimated to have cost 1 gulden, the value of a pig ready for slaughter.

---

[42] R. G. Cole, 'The Reformation in print: German pamphlets and propaganda', ARG, 66 (1975), 93–103.

[43] J. Schwitalla, Deutsche Flugschriften 1460–1525, (Tübingen, 1983), p. 6, note 2.

[44] Little is known about the size of editions and actual sales, but W. Krieg, Materialien zu einer Entwicklungsgeschichte der Bücher-Preise und des Autoren-Honorars vom 15. bis zum 20. Jahrhundert (Vienna, 1953), pp. 226–7, gives some useful pointers. Of the account of Luther's disputation with Eck, 1 400 copies were sold at the autumn fair at Frankfurt in 1518, so that Froben could claim: 'haud feliciorem venditionem in aliquo libro sumus unquam experti' (WA Br., 1, p. 333). Luther's An den christlichen Adel of 18 August 1520 (LB, 683) sold 4 000 copies immediately, so that Melchior Lotter had to prepare a new edition for 23 August. In 1525 Adam Petri in Basle printed 3 000 copies of Bugenhagen's commentary on the psalter. According to Cochlaeus, Nikolaus Wolrab of Leipzig generally printed works by Georg Witzel, Johann Fabri, Friedrich Nausea, and Cochlaeus himself in editions of 1 000 to 1 500 copies. Konrad Pellikan's commentary on the Book of Ruth (Zurich: Froschauer, 1531) had a run of 800 copies and was sold out in a matter of weeks. The small Nuremberg printer Hans Hergot printed 500 copies of Thomas Müntzer's tract Ausgetrückte Emplößung des falschen Glaubens (29 October 1524); 400 copies were confiscated by the Nuremberg council, the remainder having already been taken off to Augsburg. (Of these 100, 12 survive today!) In a letter to Wenceslaus Linck of 29 December 1541, Luther mentioned that Hans Lufft's folio edition of the Bible of that year had been printed in 1 500 copies.

The bibliographical problems presented by the pamphlet literature of the period in particular are immense. Their chances of survival were rather more slender than other books, so we cannot be certain that those which have survived necessarily give a complete picture of the range that once existed. Throughout the centuries cultural prejudices have helped determine which relics of the past should be preserved, so certain items have found their way into libraries while others have been lost because of negligence, lack of interest or because they were despised. Consequently, a pamphlet bearing Luther's prestigious name had a much better chance of survival than an anonymous tract.[45] The number of separate items printed will never be known. Many of those which survive have come down to us in a single copy, so there must have been many more which have disappeared entirely. A representative collection of what survives is now available on microfiches.[46] One problem presented by the pamphlets is that the majority of them appeared without any specific indication of their printer, place or date of publication. To illustrate this with a random sample, analysis of the contents of the series of pamphlets issued as part of the Tübingen project in 1978, 1982 and 1985 showed that some 71 per cent bear no indication of place of printing. The others came principally from Wittenberg, Augsburg, Strasbourg, Leipzig, Basle, Nuremberg, Zurich, Cologne, Zwickau, Vienna, Erfurt and Hagenau, with a couple of dozen other towns being represented by a handful of items. Dating the pamphlets is almost as problematic. In the same sample, 797 items bear a date or could be readily dated on the basis of their contents by the Tübingen editors; 703 (nearly 47 per cent) remained to be dated largely on the basis of bibliographical evidence.

---

[45] On the importance of this consideration see J.-F. Gilmont, 'Pour une typologie du "Flugschrift" des débuts de la Réforme', *Revue d'Histoire Ecclésiastique*, 78 (1983), 788–809, here 803 f.

[46] The original microfiche project, published by Inter Documentation Company, Zug, between 1978 and 1988 under the title *Flugschriften des frühen 16. Jahrhunderts* directed and edited by H.-J. Köhler, H. Hebenstreit-Wilfert and C. Weismann, is now available from Inter Documentation Company, Leiden, under the title *Sixteenth Century Pamphlets in German and Latin*. It comprises reproductions of 5 000 pamphlets, mainly of the period 1517 to 1530. A descriptive bibliography of these pamphlets is found in H.-J. Köhler, *Bibliographie der Flugschriften des 16. Jahrhunderts. Teil I: Das frühe 16. Jahrhundert (1501–1530)* (6 vols, Tübingen, 1991–). A second series of reproductions on microfiches, *Pamphlets of the Later Part of the Sixteenth Century, 1531–1600*, edited by H.-J. Köhler, comprising at least ten annual instalments of 190 fiches carrying 350–500 pamphlets, has been in progress since 1990.

Printing in the vernaculars: High German and Low German

The linguistic situation in Germany was characterized by the dichotomy of High German (in the southern and central regions) and Low German (in the north). But the books which appeared in High German were by no means linguistically uniform. Books from different parts of the German-speaking area showed considerable diversity in respect of orthography and morphology. The linguistic character of a particular book was determined by a number of factors such as the nature of the author's copy, the compositor's habits, a particular house style (Hans Lufft at Wittenberg promoted a highly regular orthography in his editions of Luther's works), and not least consideration for the intended public. For instance, some Swiss printers would employ conservative Swiss orthography and morphology in books intended for local consumption but a more progressive form of German in those intended for a wider market. Generally, however, one can observe a gradual but distinct development towards a more unified form of German during the sixteenth century. Cologne was something of an exception: here the change from the local Ripuarian dialect in favour of High German was effected comparatively rapidly in the late 1520s.

In the north, Low German was still a language of some significance in the Reformation period. Its decline had, however, already begun: during the sixteenth century many north German chanceries went over to keeping their records and conducting their correspondence in High German, the majority of them making the change between the period 1540 and 1560. In most cases the change was a gradual process usually taking some 30 years or even much longer to complete. Interestingly, school books in High German do not appear in the north until the early years of the seventeenth century.

Up to 1520 the most important centre of Low German printing had been Lübeck, with Magdeburg and Rostock some way behind. Braunschweig, Hamburg, Stendhal and Halberstadt were of no importance, and Lüneburg, Münster and Danzig produced virtually nothing. Some Low German books were published in Cologne and Deventer, and even in some towns in the High German-speaking area such as Mainz and Strasbourg. During the Reformation period itself Lübeck ceded its pre-eminent position as the main centre of Low German printing to Magdeburg. Hamburg and Halberstadt grew to importance, as indeed did Wittenberg and Erfurt in the High German-speaking area. From 1533 to 1535 the Anabaptists gave a strong stimulus to printing in Münster,[47]

---

[47] See the literature cited by G. Vogler, 'Das Täuferreich zu Münster im Spiegel der Flugschriften', in Köhler, *Flugschriften*, pp. 309–51.

and after 1530 a number of Low German Counter-Reformation tracts were issued from Cologne. By the end of the sixteenth century Hamburg became the principal centre for Low German books.

Analysis of the items recorded in the *Niederdeutsche Bibliographie* of Conrad Borchling and Bruno Claussen reveals the picture, in Figure 2.3, of the number of Low German books published each decade from 1471 to 1580. Apart from a short-lived decline in the first decade of the sixteenth century, there was steady growth until 1530, but thereafter the trend was equally steadily downward. By 1631–40, in fact, the number had fallen to 82. From the outset most of the Low German books were of a religious nature – there were four pre-Lutheran Bibles (two published in Cologne in 1478, one in Lübeck (1494) and one in Halberstadt (1522)). Psalters, plenaries, and prayer-books were frequently issued in the early period, along with some popular literature, almanacs, and handbooks of various kinds, including some medical works and herbals. The Reformation made full use of the language. Testaments, Bibles, prayer-books, postils, and church ordinances were printed in large numbers. Bugenhagen's first complete Low German Luther Bible was published by Ludwig Dietz at Lübeck in 1534 (several months before Luther's own original complete High German translation appeared) and ran through more than 20 editions before its final appearance in 1623. Of the approximately 425 Low German books issued between 1521 and 1530 about a quarter represented the writings of Luther, Bugenhagen and Melanchthon. The first Low German Lutheran tract, the *Sermon van dem Aflath und genade* (*LB*, 113) appeared

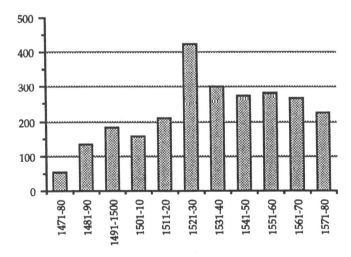

Figure 2.3   Printed works in Low German, 1471–1580

already in 1518. Slüter's translation of Luther's hymn-book was published in Rostock in 1525, further editions following at Erfurt in 1527, Magdeburg in 1534 and Hamburg in 1558. By 1600, 55 Low German hymn-books had been published. The strong emphasis on religious and devotional works indicates that the Reformation itself was not a factor which hastened the decline of Low German.[48]

The quality of German book production

A few general points need to be made about the quality and appearance of German books in the sixteenth century.

It was already the practice to use 'broken' black letter types (Upper Rhenish bastarda, Schwabacher, Wittenberger Schrift, Fraktur) for German works. With the massive increase in vernacular printing in the Reformation these became the norm, roman types being reserved for books in Latin and other foreign languages.[49] (This remained the essential pattern of use of gothic and roman types in Germany right down until 1941). However, roman was used for some of the Swiss Reformed Bibles, including a 1523 edition of Luther's New Testament and the 1527 and 1530 editions of the Froschauer Bible. Roman was also used by Paul Schede Melissus for his Calvinist translation of the first 50 Psalms (Heidelberg, 1572), a fact which has been held to be one of the factors that contributed to the book's failure to become popular.[50]

In an age when there was no effective protection against piracy a rapid rate of production was generally essential. In particular cases there will have been other reasons for speed too. A famous instance is that of the first edition of Luther's New Testament, the 'September Testament' of 1522, which took five months to print. Working for the Cranach–Döring publishing partnership, Melchior Lotter started setting up the type on 5 May 1522 and the whole enterprise was kept secret. Three presses had to be used and overtime and even night shifts were

---

[48] On Low German see M. Gesenhoff and M. Reck, 'Die mittelniederdeutsche Kanzleisprache und die Rolle des Buchdruckes in der mittelniederdeutschen Sprachgeschichte', in W. Besch, O. Reichmann, S. Sonderegger (eds), *Sprachgeschichte. Ein Handbuch zur Geschichte der deutschen Sprache und ihrer Erforschung*, 2 Halbband (Handbücher zur Sprach- und Kommunikationswissenschaft, Bd. 2.2) (Berlin, 1985), pp. 1279–89, and T. Sodmann, 'Der Rückgang des Mittelniederdeutschen als Schreib- und Druckersprache', in ibid., pp. 1289–94.

[49] See now J. L. Flood, 'Nationalistic currents in early German typography', *The Library* 6th series, 15 (1993), 125–41.

[50] M. H. Jellinek (ed.), *Die Psalmenübersetzung des Paul Schede Melissus (1572)*, (Neudrucke deutscher Literaturwerke des XVI. und XVII. Jahrhunderts, 144–8), (Halle an der Saale, 1896).

necessary to ensure that the book was ready by 21 September 1522 for the start of the Leipzig autumn fair. Estimates of the number of copies printed vary: Kühne speaks of 5 000, Volz of 3 000.[51] Three months later, in December 1522, Luther and Lotter were already able to produce a revised edition.

A particularly instructive illustration is that of the printing of the *Brandenburg–Nürnbergische Kirchenordnung* of 1533.[52] The city of Nuremberg and Margrave Georg as ruler of the two Franconian principalities of Ansbach and Kulmbach collaborated closely when the Reformation was being introduced. One fruit of this was the *Brandenburg–Nürnbergische Kirchenordnung*, a book which subsequently became of general importance for the Reformation. Correspondence and accounts relating to it have been edited with a commentary by Hans-Otto Keunecke. Between 800 and 1 000 folio copies on good paper were ordered by the Margrave for distribution to the clergy. Copies in a smaller format were to be printed for sale, but the printer in fact succeeded in selling 700 copies of the folio edition within a week before the smaller edition was produced. Since production of the book was a matter of some urgency, two printers were involved: Jobst Gutknecht, who printed the *Kirchenordnung* proper, and Johann Petreius who printed Andreas Osiander's catechism sermons; both parts form a single bibliographical unit, appearing under a joint title page. Printing had already started by 5 December 1532 and in order to make as rapid progress as possible with the work, both printers took on extra staff, operated night shifts and even worked on Sundays and holidays. By 20 December the end was in sight. Gutknecht invoiced the Margrave 42 pfennigs a copy for the *Kirchenordnung* and Petreius 56 pfennigs for the sermons, making 98 pfennigs a copy for the whole book, unbound and exclusive of carriage charges. This was a considerable sum, corresponding to four days' wages for an unskilled labourer or the price of two pairs of high-class shoes. For the four barrels used to transport the books Gutknecht charged 210 pfennigs, Petreius for three barrels 252

---

[51] H. Kühne, in *Marginalien*, 47 (1972), 63; H. Volz, *Hundert Jahre Wittenberger Bibeldruck 1522–1626*, (Göttingen, 1954).

[52] *Kirchen Ordnung In meiner gnedigen herrn der Marggrauen zu Brandenburg Vnd eins Erbern Rats der Stat Nürnberg Oberkeyt vnd gepieten wie man sich bayde mit der Leer vnd Ceremonien halten solle* (Nuremberg: [Jobst Gutknecht], 1533), with *Catechismus oder Kinderpredig* ([Nuremberg:] Johann Petreius, 1533). A modern edition of the text in E. Sehling (ed.), *Die evangelischen Kirchenordnungen des XVI. Jahrhunderts* Bd. 11 Bayern, Teil 1: (Franken, 1961), pp. 135–283. On the origins of the *Kirchenordnung*, see ibid., pp. 113–22. On the printing see H.-O. Keunecke, 'Die Drucklegung der Brandenburg-Nürnbergischen Kirchenordnung', *AGB*, 21 (1980), 769–90.

pfennigs. The Margrave's government officials in Ansbach considered the price too high, saying not only that the work could have been done better at Wittenberg but that the printers did not need to charge extra on the grounds that it was a rush job because, having finished so quickly, they were going to get their money quickly too! They wanted to pay only 36 Pfennigs for the *Kirchenordnung* and 42 pfennigs for the sermons, a total of 78 pfennigs a copy instead of the 98 Pfennigs asked. Eventually they compromised on 39 pfennigs for the *Kirchenordnung* and 50 pfennigs for the sermons, a total of 89 pfennigs a copy. The printers' men, who were said 'to have many children', were paid a little extra for night shifts but double rates on Sundays and holidays, this last being explained by the fact that such work involved breaking the Fourth Commandment. The book was printed in black and red; the extra work involved in putting the sheets through the press twice added two weeks to the production time and represented about 20 per cent of the total cost. In addition to the more than 800 copies provided for the Margrave, Gutknecht sold 700 copies of the *Kirchenordnung* at not less than 42 pfennigs each, so at least 1 500 copies of the folio edition were printed. The quarto edition that followed would have been cheaper.

The need to undercut one's rivals explains in part the low standards of accuracy found in much run-of-the-mill printing in Germany in the sixteenth century (though there was of course much fine printing too). Misprints, errors in pagination, wrong running headings and the like abound. Whereas the tasks of typefounders, compositors and pressmen soon emerged as separate trades in the printing industry, that of professional proofreader did not develop until about 1540.[53] One reason for this was that the compositors resented and resisted any interference with their work, another that the general run of authors and publishers tended to attach little importance to proofreading – not everyone subscribed to Henri Estienne's view that 'proof-reading is to printing what the soul is to the body'. Proofreading added to the cost of production and could only be reduced in relative terms when larger editions were produced. Georg Rörer, the Wittenberg deacon who worked for local printers, charged two groschen a sheet for proofreading. Only a few large and financially strong firms employed correctors. It was more usual for them to recruit qualified scholars from the relevant discipline to help with any large or important book. Just as Beatus Rhenanus served Johannes Froben at Basle, so Matthias Ringmann served as reader and scholarly adviser to the Strasbourg printers Johann Prüss and Johann Grüninger. Grüninger also had Gervasius Sopher working

---

[53] See H. Grimm, 'Von dem Aufkommen eines eigenen Berufszweiges "Korrektor" und seinem Berufsbild im Buchdruck des XVI. Jahrhunderts', *GJ*, 39 (1964), 185–90.

for him, and Matthias Schürer was assisted by Nikolaus Gerbel. Johann Adelphus Müling translated a variety of medical and literary works for printing by Strasbourg printers and worked as a proofreader for Grüninger and Prüss. Peter Braubach, who trained as a printer with Wolfgang Köpfel at Strasbourg, also worked for him checking Greek texts. Johann Fischart worked for many years as a proofreader for Bernhard Jobin. In Tübingen Melanchthon was a corrector for Thomas Anselm in 1514–16. Yet despite the assistance of reputable scholars, the completed volumes were often slipshod and indeed were recognized to be such even in their own day. Thus Johannes Gallinarius's comment that Grüninger's edition of Henry VIII's *Assertio septem sacramentorum* (9 August 1522) was 'unworthy' (Erasmus, *Epistolae*, 1307) was typical. Often enough a specialist adviser was not considered necessary, particularly seeing that so many of the books produced were straight reprints.

The problem of unauthorized reprints

In this period *Nachdruck*, the publication of unauthorized editions, was simply a fact of life in any case, but Luther's writings were particularly prone to it, not just because of the interest the writings themselves engendered but also because of the fact that the Wittenberg printers had not been particularly successful in building up a widespread network of important business connections. In the early period especially, unauthorized editions of Luther's writings frequently far outnumbered the Wittenberg editions: Hans Widmann has estimated that between 1522 and 1526 there were five for every Wittenberg original.[54] For instance, in the case of the *Sermon von Ablaß und Gnade* 1517 Benzing records three Wittenberg editions dating from 1518 (*LB*, 90–92; Claus/Pegg also list no. 91a as a *Zwitterdruck* (composite edition) of no. 91) with, in the same year, four from Leipzig (*LB*, 93–6), two from Nuremberg (97–8), two from Augsburg (99–100), two from Basle (101–2) and one whose place of publication has not been identified (103); 1519 saw three more from Leipzig and one each from Basle and Breslau, and 1520 another from Leipzig, two more from Augsburg and at least one other from Wittenberg (*LB*, 112). Or take one of the great tracts of 1520, *An den christlichen Adel deutscher Nation von des christlichen Standes Besserung*: Melchior Lotter the Younger brought out three editions in 1520 (*LB*, 683–5), yet in the same year seven more editions appeared: two in Leipzig, four in Augsburg, one in Basle, two in Strasbourg, and one in Halberstadt. As for the New Testament, the Basle

---

[54] H. Widmann, *Geschichte des Buchhandels*, I (Wiesbaden, 1975), p. 66.

printer Adam Petri brought out a reprint of the September 1522 edition in December of that year – at the same time as Luther's authorized revised edition appeared. Further ones were issued by the Augsburg printers Silvan Otmar and Hans Schönsperger in the spring of 1523.

Luther himself did not object to *Nachdruck* in principle – after all, the practice assisted in the dissemination of God's Word. But he did condemn reprints produced solely out of greed, with errors and corruptions of the text. Protesting in September 1525, he enquired of printers whether they had turned into robbers seeing that they were stealing his property:

> I started work on the postils from Epiphany to Easter, and then some rogue steps in, a compositor who lives off the sweat of our brow, steals my manuscript before I have finished it, takes it away and has it printed somewhere else, ignoring our expenditure and our labour. [...] Now we could tolerate the harm they do us if they would not print my books so inaccurately and disgracefully. But as it is, they print them and they do it so hastily that when they reach me I do not even recognize my own books. They leave things out, they put things in the wrong order, or they falsify the text or fail to correct it. They have even learnt the trick of putting Wittenberg at the beginning of some books which have never been in Wittenberg or printed there. These are simply tricks to deceive ordinary people because by the grace of God we have the reputation of being able to turn out well-produced, serious books. Thus greed and envy drive them to deceive people by appropriating our name and to the ruination of our [Wittenberg] printers. It is very unfair that we toil away and have all the expense while others reap the profit and we suffer loss.[55]

Luther felt that, out of Christian charity, printers should wait a month or two before reprinting a work.

The considerable demand for Luther's writings meant that the pirates had a rewarding and safe business. But because it was important to get a reprint out quickly before a rival could get in first, speedy production was essential, and inevitably this tended to mean that quality left something to be desired.[56] The printers often unwittingly corrupted the text, and sometimes deliberate alterations were made. Thus Karlstadt complained that whole columns of text were disregarded and sentences muddled by those who printed him,[57] and in a letter to Spalatin of 15

---

[55] Preface to the *Fastenpostille*, WA 17/2, p. 3 and following.

[56] For an illuminating illustration of the methods employed in printing houses in order to optimize the rate of production see M. Boghardt, 'Partial duplicate setting: Means of rationalization or complicating factor in textual transmission?', *The Library* 6th series, 15 (1993), 306–31.

[57] See Gordon Rupp, *Patterns of Reformation*, (Philadelphia, 1960), p. 121.

August 1521 Luther expressed his concern that errors introduced by printers would be perpetuated in subsequent editions. Johann Eberlin's answer to the dangers inherent in printing was to find a printer of integrity (few though they were, he admitted) who carefully proofread and used good type and good quality paper: 'I praise a printer who produces books properly corrected with elegant type on good paper. People like that will earn praise and profit thereby, and one can now find such printers here and there, few though they are.'[58]

On several occasions, Luther had reason to voice his grievances. For instance, on 26 September 1525, in the complaint to the city council of Nuremberg that part of the manuscript of his postil had been stolen during printing, he was incensed, he said, because the book had been issued there before the Wittenberg original had even been completed (WA Br., 3, p. 577 f.). (In fact Luther was wrong: the manuscript had been taken to Regensburg and printed there.) Similarly, in his 'warning' to the printers in 1541, he says:

> Because they [i.e. the rival printers] are only interested in money, they do not bother about whether they print well or badly, and it has often been the case that when reading these pirated editions I have found them to be so corrupt that I have sometimes not recognized my own work and have had to improve it again. (WA DB, 8, pp. 8–9)

As a result of his bad experiences Luther gave some thought to measures that might be taken to protect what he wrote. Thus, unwittingly, he was one of the earliest proponents of the idea of the protection of intellectual property. Above all, he wanted God's Word to reach the reader in accurate and uncorrupted form. In order to try to guarantee this he arranged for two 'marks of quality' to be printed in authorized editions of his works. Appearing for the first time in the Third Part of the Old Testament 1524, they comprised (1) the Lamb with chalice and flag with the device of the cross as a symbol of the sacrifice of Christ, and (2) the 'Luther rose', an armorial device inherited from his father, flanked by the letters M L, below which was written: 'Dis zeichen sey zeuge / das solche bucher durch meine hand gangen sind / den des falsche druckes vnd bucher verderbens / vleyssigen sich ytzt viel' ['Let this sign be a guarantee that these books have passed through my hands for wrong printing and corrupt books now abound'].

In 1533 Elector Johann Friedrich, at Luther's suggestion, granted the publisher of the first complete edition of the Bible translation in 1534 a

---

[58] J. Eberlin von Günzburg, *Sämtliche Werke*, edited by L. Enders, (vol. 3, Halle an der Saale, 1902), p. 162.

Dis zeichen sey zeuge / das solche bucher durch
meine hand gangen sind/den des falsche druckes
vnd bucher verderbens/vleyssigen sich ytzt viel

Gedruckt zu Wittemberg.

2.5   The 'seal of quality' marks indicating editions authorized by Luther

permanent privilege, protecting Lufft from unauthorized reprints within Saxony and from competition from Bibles imported from elsewhere.

The distribution of books

Whereas Luther often commented on printing and printers he seems to have had nothing to say on publishing and distribution. Wendland concludes from this that the distribution of Wittenberg books was carried out away from the town itself,[59] which may indeed well have been the case. At this time the German book trade was dominated by the printer-publisher selling direct to the consumer and by the itinerant dealer, sometimes the printer himself, visiting the great fair towns like Frankfurt am Main, Leipzig, Nuremberg, Strasbourg, Basle, Augsburg, Nördlingen, Naumburg, Erfurt and Breslau and turning up at church festivals and similar events. Only after about 1560 did the wholesale dealer come to predominate, the period until the eighteenth century being marked by the so-called exchange trade and by the personal visits of publishers to the great fairs.

---

[59] Wendland 'Martin Luther', p. 13.

As one of the major trade fairs of the time, Frankfurt – an important city centrally situated at the cross-ways of many water and land trade routes and not far from Mainz, the cradle of printing – was a natural place for books to be marketed. The autumn fair itself had originated at least by 1240 and the spring fair was established in 1330. Books had been traded there since at least 1485. Printers, publishers and booksellers had their traditional stands in the Buchgasse, near St Leonard's church, during the fair. (At Leipzig books were sold near the Nikolaskirche.) Guarantees of safe passage to the fairs and conditions of security when there provided the basis for an influence which soon extended beyond the borders of Germany. Thanks to the predominance of Latin as the language of scholarship, Frankfurt made a significant contribution to the European book trade and to intellectual life generally. During its greatest period, 1550 to 1630, this book fair attracted most of the great names in the trade – one only has to think of Amerbach, Froben, Herwagen, Oporinus of Basle, of Birckmann and Hittorp of Cologne, Koberger of Nuremberg, Anshelm of Tübingen, of Froschauer from Zurich, Wechel from Paris, Gryphius from Lyons, the Elzevirs from Holland, and many others from Leipzig, Nuremberg, Erfurt, Wittenberg, Venice and Rome, to realize the international standing of the fair. Peter Braubach, who came to establish himself as a major printer in Frankfurt in 1540, had had a stall at the Frankfurt fair while he was still a printer in Hagenau (1529–36).[60]

The first Frankfurt fair catalogue was compiled by the Augsburg bookseller Georg Willer in 1564 and appeared regularly twice a year. It comprised, first, a list of Latin books, then a list of German books and, from 1568, a list of books in other languages too.[61]

Outside the towns where the books were printed or which were main centres of the burgeoning book trade the public were dependent on what itinerant traders offered them and on word of mouth. The correspondence of Beatus Rhenanus is illuminating in this regard. On 26 December 1518 Beatus, writing from Basle to Zwingli in Zurich, mentions that a bookseller had come from Berne on 24 December to purchase a pile of books by Luther (CR, 94, p. 123). And in another letter to Zwingli, on 24 May 1519 he mentioned that the Basle printer Adam Petri was printing a number of German writings by Luther and suggested that if Zwingli recommended them 'from the pulpit, i.e. if you advise the people to buy them' he would find that his own work

---

[60] See von Schade, 'Peter Braubach', col. 851.

[61] On the Frankfurt fair see the introduction to H. Estienne, *The Frankfurt Book Fair* ..., edited by J. W. Thompson (Amsterdam, 1969). The early catalogues have been edited in facsimile by B. Fabian.

would prosper (*CR*, 94, p. 175). Beatus sent him Luther's theses against Eck and the *Auslegung des Vaterunsers* and advised him to tell other priests to commend them to the people. Again, in July 1519 Beatus recommended to Zwingli a certain itinerant bookseller who went from town to town and village to village, door to door, offering nothing but Luther's writings for sale. 'This', added the humanist, 'will virtually compel the people to buy them, which would not be the case if he offered them a wide choice.'[62] Another important form of distribution was the passing of copies from hand to hand; an excellent instance of this is found in the case of the Kitzbühel miner Hans Steinberger who was a popular preacher in the years 1569–71 and who used an inconspicuous woman to pass Lutheran tracts from one group of his adherents to another in the Kitzbühel, Röhrerbichl and Kirchberg area.[63]

The authors and their works

In her analysis of the intellectual community at Strasbourg Chrisman distinguishes four major groups – theologians, scholars and teachers, men of science, and vernacular writers – each with several subdivisions and with much overlap between them.[64] Intellectual variety, though perhaps not always of the same range or calibre as Strasbourg's, was found in other cities too, Basle, Augsburg and Nuremberg being obvious examples. Nuremberg had Hartmann Schedel, Willibald Pirckheimer and Christoph Scheurl (the man who, in a speech at the University of Bologna, could exclaim 'God be thanked that I was born a man, not a woman, a citizen of Nuremberg and not an Italian') and artists of the calibre of Albrecht Dürer, Adam Krafft, Veit Stoss and Peter Fischer, while the shoemaker and poet Hans Sachs was busy popularizing many themes from Renaissance literature through his prodigious output of verse. Many German humanists had travelled and studied in Italy, and Germany itself already had an impressive number of universities of its own. One pointer to the degree of intellectual vigour that could be found is given by Scribner's investigation of 176 preachers active in Germany between 1520 and 1550. He found that 135 (77 per cent) definitely had a university training while only eight (4.5 per cent) definitely did not; the background of the remaining 33 could not be estab-

[62] Cited by A. G. Dickens, *The German Nation*, p. 111.
[63] See J. L. Flood, 'Subversion in the Alps: books and readers in the Austrian Counter-Reformation', *The Library*, 6th series, 12 (1990), 185–211.
[64] Chrisman, *Lay Culture*, pp. 37–58.

lished. Over half the total took or at least started a second university qualification.[65]

Of particular importance in the context of the book trade is the question of the relationship between Latin and German in this period. The humanists conducted their correspondence, private and official business largely in Latin. The poets and orators saw it as their duty to preserve and encourage Latin. Many writers of the younger generation, such as Bebel, Hutten and Murner, saw the use of the vernacular (though they employed it themselves) as a 'descent' to a lower linguistic level. (Aventinus was an important exception here.) It is not totally clear in every particular case why the humanists promoted German translations so strongly, though in general the answer is to be found in their pronounced didactic intention, their propagandistic aims, commissions received from patrons or printers, or a desire to improve the vernacular. We know of 100 or more humanists writing in German, penning didactic and satirical poems, propagandistic treatises, works on historical subjects and handbooks on technical subjects, but above all producing translations of the classics, of medieval authors and of their own contemporaries. As Worstbrock points out, in this period translations were not regarded as inferior to indigenous original works (though the target language itself might have been regarded as inferior to the original).[66] The high regard in which the foreign authors were held is evident from the laudatory epithets scattered liberally on the title-pages: *berümpt, hochberümpt, hochberümptest, aller hochberümptest, kunstreich, hochweyse, aller sinnreichest*, etc. The translators and publishers were proud of their achievements: thus Matthias Ringmann's Caesar (Strasbourg, 1507) proudly proclaims 'erstmals vß dem Latin in Tütsch bracht' ['brought from Latin into German for the first time'], Walther Ryff's *Vitruvius Teutsch* (Nuremberg, 1548) 'erstmals verteutscht / vnd in Truck verordnet' ['translated into German and printed for the first time'] and 'Vormals in Teutsche sprach zu transferiren / noch von niemand sonst vnderstanden / sondern fur vnmüglichen geachtet worden' ['No translation into German has previously been attempted, but has been considered an impossibility']. And Thomas Murner (1475–1537) dedicates his translation of the *Aeneid* (1515) to Emperor Maximilian I with the remark that he has brought it from death in Latin to life in German ('von latynschem todt in tütsches leben ... erquicket').

---

[65] See R. W. Scribner, 'Practice and principle in the German towns: preachers and people', in P. N. Brooks (ed.), *Reformation Principle and Practice: Essays in Honour of A. G. Dickens*, (London, 1980), pp. 97–117, especially pp. 103–4.

[66] On this see F. J. Worstbrock, *Deutsche Antikerezeption 1450–1550. Teil 1: Verzeichnis der deutschen Übersetzungen antiker Autoren. Mit einer Bibliographie der Übersetzer* (Veröffentlichungen zur Humanismusforschung, 1) (Boppard, 1976), p. 1.

The range of these translations covers not only literary works but also and especially Roman law, history, medical and technical works (Vitruvius, Vegetius, Frontinus). Johann Eberlin von Günzburg (c.1470–1532) translated Tacitus's *Germania*. Johann Agricola (c.1494–1566) did a translation of Terence's *Andria*, published at Berlin in 1544. Hieronymus Boner (d. 1555/56) translated Herodotus, Justinus, Plutarch and Xenophon. The historian Nikolaus Fabri Carbach (c.1485–c.1534), who worked for the Mainz printer Johann Schöffer as a proofreader, translated parts of Livy's history of Rome from a manuscript he had discovered in Mainz. Dietrich von Pleningen (c.1450/55–1520) translated Seneca's *De ira* (Landshut, 1515), as well as his *De clementia* and other pieces (though these are known only in manuscript). Johann Reuchlin (1455–1522) translated Lucian and Demosthenes. Simon Schaidenreisser (c.1505–c.1573) is renowned as translator of Homer's *Odyssey*. Johann von Schwarzenberg (1465–1528) translated Cicero's *De officiis*. In 1544 Jörg Wickram (c.1505– before 1562) edited Albrecht von Halberstadt's Middle High German rendering of Ovid's *Metamorphoses*. Worstbrock records sixteenth-century printed editions of translations from classical authors from Augsburg, Basle, Berlin, Colmar, Dresden, Esslingen, Frankfurt am Main, Freiburg, Ingolstadt, Landshut, Leipzig, Magdeburg, Mainz, Marburg, Nuremberg, Strasbourg, Tübingen, Vienna, Wittenberg, Worms and Zurich. The principal figure was Heinrich Steiner at Augsburg who, between 1531 and 1545, published well over 40 editions of translations of works by Vegetius, Cicero, Herodian, Justinus, Thucydides, Plutarch, Plato, Plautus, Xenophon, Demosthenes, Lucian and others. Also in Augsburg Alexander Weissenborn published two editions of Murner's translation of the *Institutiones* of Justinian in 1536, Schaidenreisser's Homer translation in 1537 and 1538, Schaidenreisser's version of Cicero's *Paradoxa stoicorum* and Johann Sieder's translation of the *Metamorphoses* of Apuleius in 1538. At Mainz Johann Schöffer published translations of Livy, Caesar and Plutarch between 1505 and 1533 and his nephew Ivo Schöffer did the same for Caesar, Livy (four editions), Tacitus and Ovid between 1532 and 1546. At Strasbourg Balthasar Beck published Caspar Hedio's translations of Josephus and Hegesippus as well as Michael Herr's translation of selected writings of Seneca between 1531 and 1545, and Jakob Cammerlander published Valerius Maximus, Sallust, Suetonius, Cicero and Lucian in German over the same period, while Johann Schott was doing Plutarch and Pliny. At Tübingen Ulrich Morhart issued three editions of Albrecht von Eyb's translation of the comedies of Terence in 1540, 1544 and 1546. Virgil's *Aeneid* was issued in German by Johann Grüninger at Strasbourg in 1515, and it was reissued twice by Gregor Hofmann at Worms in 1543 and 1545.

A plethora of pamphleteers

Within the narrower sphere of religious and social controversy there was also an extensive and diverse list of writers. The pamphlet authors alone are legion, including Johann Agricola, Erasmus Alberus, Nikolaus Amsdorf, Johannes Brenz, Martin Bucer, Johannes Bugenhagen, Heinrich Bullinger, Johannes Cochlaeus, Veit Dietrich, Johann Eberlin, Johannes Eck, Hieronymus Emser, Erasmus, Johannes Fabri, Matthias Flacius Illyricus, Pamphilus Gengenbach, Ludwig Hätzer, Valentin Ickelsamer, Justus Jonas, Andreas Karlstadt, Wenceslaus Linck, Martin Luther, Philipp Melanchthon, Thomas Murner, Johann Oecolampadius, Andreas Osiander, Urbanus Rhegius, Hans Sachs, Kaspar Schatzger, Kaspar Schwenckfeld, Jakob Wimpheling, and Huldrych Zwingli. Best known among the few women among the pamphleteers was Argula von Grumbach.[67] In order to flesh out a few of the major figures, especially some who are of interest in connection with printing, we will focus briefly on a small and random selection to demonstrate the wide range in intellectual interests, sociological background and status, and religious persuasion. Of Luther himself, of course, nothing need be said. Emser, Eck and Cochlaeus will represent the Catholics; Ulrich von Hutten takes up an anti-Catholic position; Bugenhagen and Melanchthon represent the Lutherans, with Caspar Hedio serving as an example of a writer from the Strasbourg reform group, while Sebastian Franck represents the Spiritualists and Balthasar Hubmaier the Anabaptists.[68]

Hieronymus Emser (1479–1527) studied at Tübingen and Basle and became tutor to the sons of Johann Amerbach in 1500 but was forced to leave the city in 1502 for having written some abusive verses about the Swiss victory over Maximilian I in 1499. In 1504 he joined Wimpheling in Strasbourg and there edited the works of Giovanni Pico della Mirandola (Strasbourg: Johann Prüss, 15 March 1504). After further studies in Erfurt and Leipzig he was appointed secretary and chaplain to Duke George of Saxony. Emser was not at first opposed to calls for reform of the Church. In July 1518 he even received Luther as a guest in his house at Dresden, but a rift between them developed at the Leipzig disputation with Eck in 1519, and from that time on Emser was tireless in writing pamphlets, letters and epigrams attacking Luther

---

[67] On von Grumbach see R. H. Bainton, *Women of the Reformation*, (Minneapolis, 1971), pp. 98–109; I. Bezzel, in *GJ*, 62 (1987), 166–73; and P. Matheson (ed.), *Argula von Grumbach. A Woman's Voice in the Reformation* (Edinburgh, 1995).

[68] For up-to-date information on these writers, P. G. Bietenholz and T. B. Deutscher (eds), *Contemporaries of Erasmus*, (3 vols, Toronto, 1985–87), will be found particularly helpful.

and other Reformers, for example in *An den Stier zu Wiettenberg* (Leipzig: M. Landsberg, 1521) against Luther, *Annotationes Hieronymi Emser vber Luthers Naw Testament gebessert vnd emendirt* (Dresden, on his own press, 1524) criticizing Luther's New Testament translation for its '1400 heretical errors', *Das man der Heyligen Bilder ... nit abthon noch unehren sol* (Dresden, on his own press, 1524?) against Karlstadt's inconoclasm, and his *Apologeticon* (n.p., 1525) against Zwingli's *Antibolon*. He published several translations, including one of King Henry VIII's book on the sacraments, under the title *Schutz und Handthabung der siben Sacrament* (Augsburg: J. Schönsperger 1522),[69] and Erasmus's *Hyperaspistes* (Leipzig: M. Lotter, 1526), but most importantly a German New Testament which followed Luther's translation as far as it was compatible with Catholic theology. This first appeared in 1527, under the title *Das naw testament nach lawt der Christlichen kirchen bewerten text / corrigirt / vnd widerumb zu recht gebracht*, printed by Wolfgang Stöckel at Dresden (*VD 16*, B 4374). It is prefaced by Duke George's privilege forbidding the distribution or possession of Luther's Bible in his territory and threatening offenders with a fine of 200 Rhenish gulden.[70] What is particularly interesting about Emser is that whereas he reveals in an afterword that he harbours doubts 'ob es gut odder bös sey das man die Bibel verdewtschet vnd dem gemeynen vngelarten man fürlegt' ['whether it is a good or a bad thing that the Bible is translated into German and made available to the common, untutored man'], the very fact that he did produce this translation reveals how far he had already been influenced by the Reformation, despite his hostility towards it. The following list of further editions of his New Testament eloquently demonstrates where and with whom Catholic support could be found:

Cologne: Peter Quentell, 1528, *VD 16*, B 4382
[Cologne: P. Quentell] 1528, *VD 16*, B 4383
Leipzig: Valentin Schumann, 1528, *VD 16*, B 4384. With Emser's *Anotationes über Luthers New Testament*. The colophon gives the place of sale: 'Wirt verkaufft / in Johann Haßfurts haws zu Leyptzig in der Ritter strassenn'.

---

[69] On this and other contemporary pamphlets on the controversy between Henry VIII and Luther see J. L. Flood, 'Heinrich VIII. und Martin Luther. Ein europäischer Streit und dessen Niederschlag in Literatur und Publizistik', in K. Gärtner, I. Kasten and F. Shaw (eds), *Spannungen und Konflikte menschlichen Zusammenlebens in der deutschen Literatur des Mittelalters* (Tübingen, 1996), pp. 3–32.

[70] On this see O. Vossler, 'Herzog Georg der Bärtige und seine Ablehnung Luthers', *Historische Zeitschrift*, 184 (1957), 272–91.

Augsburg: A. Weissenhorn the Elder, 1529, *VD 16*, B 4389
Freiburg/Br.: J. Faber, 1529, *VD 16*, B 4390
Cologne: H. Fuchs for P. Quentell, 23.8.1529, *VD 16*, B 4391
Leipzig: V. Schumann, 1529, *VD 16*, B 4392
Tübingen: [U. Morhart the Elder] for P. Quentel, 31.8.1532, *VD 16*,
    B 4406
Freiburg/Br.: J. Faber, 1534, *VD 16*, B 4411
Freiburg/Br.: J. Faber, 1539, *VD 16*, B 4424
Freiburg/Br.: J. Faber, 1539, *VD 16*, B 4425
Freiburg/Br.: Stephan Graff, 1551, *VD 16*, B 4446
Cologne, 1562, *VD 16*, B 4457
Cologne: Maternus Cholinus, 1568, *VD 16*, B 4465
Neisse: Johann Creutziger, 1571, *VD 16*, B 4470
Cologne: M. Cholinus, 1573, *VD 16*, B 4472
Cologne: J. von Waldorff, 1577, *VD 16*, B 4478
Cologne: G. Grevenbroich, 1587, *VD 16*, B 4485
Cologne: J. Waldorff, 1587, *VD 16*, B 4486

There was also a Low German translation of Emser's New Testament:

Cologne: H. Voss (= Hero Fuchs), 1528, *VD 16*, B 4510
[Rostock: Brothers of the Common Life] 1530, *VD 16*, B 4515
Bonn: Laurenz van der Müllen, 1547, *VD 16*, B 4529

Johann Eck (Johann Maier) 1486–1543, born in the village of Egg near
Ottobeuren, was the son of a farmer and magistrate. He studied at
Heidelberg, Tübingen, Cologne and Freiburg and became Professor of
Theology at Ingolstadt in 1510. The details of Eck's lifelong campaign
against Luther are well known. He wrote some 100 works during his
career. His pre-Reformation theological views are stated in *Chrysopassus
praedestinationis* (Augsburg: J. Miller, November 1514) and *Disputatio
Viennae Pannoniae habita* (Augsburg: J. Miller, February 1517). There
are three works which are important in connection with the Leipzig
disputation with Luther in 1519 and the build-up to it: his *Obelisci*,
written in 1518 and published only after his death by Luther among his
Latin works; the *Defensio contra amarulentas D. Andreae Bodenstein
Carolstatini invectiones* (Augsburg: S. Grimm and M. Wirsung, 1518),
and his own account of the event: *Disputatio Iohannis Eccii et Andreae
Carolstadii et Martini Lutheri* (Erfurt: M. Maler, July 1519). His more
noteworthy polemical writings include *De primatu Petri adversus
Ludderum* (Ingolstadt: [Andreas Lutz] 1520), *De poenitentia et
confessione contra Lutherum* (Tübingen: Ulrich Morhart, November
1522), *De purgatorio contra Ludderum* (Rome: J. Mazzocchi, June

1523), and *Enchiridion locorum communium adversus Lutteranos* (Landshut: J. Weissenburger, April 1525), a work which went through at least 91 editions and translations. Though he disapproved of vernacular Bibles he published one of his own, at the insistence of Dukes Wilhelm and Ludwig of Bavaria. For the New Testament he used Emser's text, and the Old Testament was based on the Vulgate. It was published by Georg Krapf at Ingolstadt in 1537 and was protected by an imperial privilege. It was not as popular as another Catholic Bible, that of the Dominican Johann Dietenberger (1475–1537) which was first printed by Peter Jordan at Mainz for Peter Quentel of Cologne in 1534 and went through 41 editions by 1776. Among Eck's exegetical works are *Christenliche Ausslegung der Evangelienn vonn der Zeit, durch das gantz Jar* (Ingolstadt: G. Krapf and J. Vogker, January 1530) and *Explanatio psalmi vigesimi* (Augsburg: A. Weissenhorn, March 1538). His intellectual autobiography was edited after his death by his half-brother Simon Thaddeus Eck and printed by Alexander Weissenhorn at Ingolstadt in 1543. Weissenhorn also published his funeral eulogies: *Tres orationes funebres in exequiis Ioannis Eckii habitae* (Ingolstadt, 1543).

Johannes Cochlaeus (*c*.1485/90–1552), the son of a Franconian peasant, attended school in Nuremberg and studied at Cologne. Here he published a textbook, *Musica* ([Cologne]: J. Landen, 1507). After being appointed rector of the Latin school at St Lorenz at Nuremberg in 1510, he published a Latin grammar, *Quadrivium grammatices* (Strasbourg, 1511), another textbook on music, *Tetrachordum Musicae* (Nuremberg: J. Weissenburger, 1511; ninth edition, 1526), and an edition of the *Cosmographia* of Pomponius Mela (Nuremberg: J. Weissenburger, 1512). In 1515 he was appointed tutor to three nephews of Willibald Pirckheimer and went with them to Italy. He studied law at Bologna, took a doctorate in theology at Ferrara in 1517, and spent the next two years in Rome where he was ordained, taking up a benefice in Frankfurt am Main. In 1520 he read Luther's *An den christlichen Adel* and *De captivitate Babylonica* and planned a refutation which, however, was never printed for lack of funds. Meetings with Luther in 1521 led Cochlaeus to conclude that it was his duty to attack the Reformers in his writings. But he often had difficulty in finding publishers. His *Assertio pro Emsero*, for instance, written in 1521 was not printed for more than 20 years, eventually appearing in *In causa religionis miscellaneorum libri tres* (Ingolstadt: A. Weissenhorn, 1545). In the 1520s Cochlaeus moved a great deal: from Frankfurt to Nuremberg, Stuttgart, Regensburg, Mainz, Frankfurt again, then Cologne, until in 1528 he succeeded Hieronymus Emser as secretary and chaplain to Duke George of Saxony. In this post he continued his attacks on Luther, finding it increasingly difficult to fund the printing of his polemics. In 1535 he became a canon at Meissen and in 1536 financed the press of his niece's husband Nikolaus Wolrab at Leipzig. Cochlaeus eventually became a canon at Breslau (Wrocław) where he died. His writings exceed 200 pieces, including *Philippicae quattuor* (Leipzig: N. Schmidt, 1534), an attack on Melanchthon, and *Antiqua et insignis epistola Nicolai Papae I* (Leipzig: M. Lotter, 1536) which included a vitriolic attack on King Henry VIII for the execution of his friends John Fisher and Thomas More.

The case of Ulrich von Hutten (1488–1523) is an interesting example of a writer in this period. His works fall into two quite distinct phases, before and after the autumn of 1519. In the first phase nearly all his works appear with an indication of printer and place of publication; in the second they rarely do. In the earlier period 23 items were published by Johann Schöffer at Mainz, but his involvement came to a rapid end after Pope Leo X had written to Cardinal Albrecht on 12 July 1520 to complain about Hutten's anti-Catholic writings. For a short period Schöffer was under arrest. Hutten himself left Mainz in August 1520 and, becoming ever more polemical, he found printers wherever he happened to be. The works of this second phase are emphatic in their attacks on the Catholic hierarchy (but the Worms Carthusians at least knew how to defend themselves: they used his writings as lavatory paper!), and the printers clearly thought it prudent to refrain from identifying themselves. Hutten's preferred printer for the rest of his life was Johann Schott in Strasbourg who brought out 17 editions for him (though, interestingly, these did not include his *Invectivae* directed against leading participants in the Diet of Worms; they were printed by Pierre Vidoue at Paris (after 27 March 1521)). Further editions, authorized or otherwise, appeared with a number of Strasbourg printers, but all told his works were printed not only in all the major German centres but also abroad: Antwerp, London, Lyon, Milan, Paris and Venice.

Johannes Bugenhagen (1485–1558), described by Cochlaeus as one of the 'four apostles of the new teachings' (Luther, Melanchthon, Justus Jonas and Bugenhagen), was the son of an alderman in Wolin, Pomerania. He studied at Greifswald from 1502 to 1504 and took holy orders in 1509. After reading Luther's *De captivitate Babylonica* he went to Wittenberg in 1521, to become pastor there in 1525. (He officiated at Luther's marriage and his funeral). He wrote church ordinances for Hamburg, Lübeck, Pomerania, Minden, Osnabrück, Soest, Bremen and Brunswick, many pamphlets, including *De coniugio episcoporum et diaconorum* (Nuremberg: J. Petri, 1525) and *Von dem christlichen Glauben und rechten guten Wercken* (Wittenberg: G. Rhau, 1527), Bible commentaries such as *In librum Psalmorum interpretatio* (Basle: A. Petri, 1524) and *Annotationes ... in Deuteronomium* (Nuremberg: J. Petri, 1524), helped with the translation of the New Testament into

Low German and assisted Luther and Melanchthon with the revision of the German Bible in 1539.

Philipp Melanchthon (1497–1560), who began his studies at the University of Heidelberg at age 12, graduating in 1511 and taking his Master's degree at Tübingen in 1514, was appointed Professor of Greek at Wittenberg at age 21. Here he soon became deeply involved with Luther's cause and applied himself to the interpretation of St Paul's Epistle to the Romans, eventually expanding his analysis of its basic ideas into a summary account of the opinions of the Reformers. This work, his *Loci communes*, ran through 18 editions in four years; it came to be recognized as a major statement of the principles of the Reformation. At the request of the territorial princes who supported Luther he also composed the *Confessio Augustana* in 1530.[71] In addition to composing these two major theological documents, Melanchthon, a fervent advocate of education who played a major role in the establishment of schools (at Magdeburg and Nuremberg) and universities (at Marburg, Jena and Königsberg), was tireless in writing textbooks on a wide range of subjects, his Greek and Latin grammars becoming standard handbooks.

Caspar Hedio (1494–1552), the son of a rope-maker from Ettlingen in Baden, studied in Basle and got to know Erasmus, the Amerbachs, Oecolampadius, Beatus Rhenanus and others. A protégé of Wolfgang Capito, he became a preacher at Strasbourg Minster where he supported the efforts of Martin Bucer and Matthias Zell to reform the Strasbourg church. His scholarly endeavours were mainly devoted to history. His publications include *Chronica der alten Christlichen Kirchen ausz Eusebio, Ruffino, Sozomeno, Theodoreto, Tertulliano, Justino, Cypriano, und Plinio* (Strasbourg: G. Ulricher, 1530, W. Köpfel 1545, 1558), *Ein auszerlesne Chronik von anfang der Welt bis auf das jar nach Christi unsers eynigen Heylands geburt MDXXXIX* (Strasbourg: C. Mylius, 1539), and German translations of Johannes Cuspinianus: *Chronika von C. Julio Cesare dem ersten, bisz auff Carolum quintum diser zeit Rhömischen Keyser, auch von allen orientischen oder Griechischen und Türckischen Keysern* (Strasbourg: C. Mylius, 1541), and of Baptista Platina: *Historia von der Bäbst und Keiser Leben* (Strasbourg: W. Rihel, 1546; J. Rihel, 1565). He also translated works of Juan Luis Vives, such as *Von Almuosen geben zwey Büchlin* ([Strasbourg? 1533?]).

Sebastian Franck (1499–1542/3), born in Donauwörth, studied at Ingolstadt and Heidelberg, took holy orders in the diocese of Augsburg, then became a Lutheran pastor in Nuremberg. Later, influenced by the

---

[71] See note 31 above.

ideas of Denck, Karlstadt and Müntzer and by Luther's attitude to the peasants, the suppression of the Anabaptists in Nuremberg area and a conviction that emphasis on Justification by Faith alone would lead to the moral degeneration of the peasants, he broke with the Reformers and moved to Strasbourg in 1529. There, he tried to settle down as a private scholar and came to adopt a fully spiritualist position, becoming a convinced opponent of any organized religion. When in the third part of his *Chronica, Zeytbuch vnd Geschichtbybell* (Strasbourg: Balthasar Beck, 1531) he listed Arius, Hus, Wyclif, Luther, Erasmus, Augustine, Ambrose and others as men persecuted for striving after truth, he offended everyone: Erasmus lodged a complaint, and Albrecht of Mainz and Duke George of Saxony outlawed it. Franck was arrested, the sale of his books was forbidden, and he was expelled, moving to Esslingen where he tried to make a living as a soap-boiler, then in 1532 went to Ulm where, having worked for a while with Hans Varnier the Elder (who printed his *Paradoxa* in 1534 and his *Chronica* in 1536), he set up his own printing press on which he printed mainly his own writings, only to fall foul of the authorities, escaping expulsion only by agreeing to submit whatever he printed to the Council's prior censorship. To evade this he had *Die guldin Arch*, the most important statement of his beliefs, printed by Heinrich Steiner at Augsburg in 1538 and his *Germaniae Chronicon* by Christian Egenolff at Frankfurt am Main in the same year. This brought him fresh trouble, and the Council, with the support of Luther himself, forced him to leave in 1539. He went to Basle and collaborated with the printer Nikolaus Brylinger but refrained from printing his own works – his great collection of German proverbs was printed in Frankfurt in 1541. After that he disappears. He may have died in Basle, but curiously enough his last works appear only in Dutch. Even his *Chronica, Zeytbuch vnd Geschichtbybell* appeared in a Dutch translation in 1558.[72]

Balthasar Hubmaier (d. 1528) studied at Freiburg and Ingolstadt as a pupil of Johann Eck and was appointed chaplain at Regensburg cathedral before becoming a parish priest at Waldshut, then under Austrian administration. He studied the ideas of Luther and Zwingli and introduced German into the services at Waldshut. He began to show sympathy with the growing Anabaptist movement there and in 1524 was forced to flee. Eventually he went to Nikolsburg (Mikulov) in Moravia and there became the leader of a large Anabaptist community. The Austrian government had him extradited because of his political in-

---

[72] For a recent reassessment of Franck see B. Quast, *Sebastian Francks 'Kriegbüchlin des Frides'. Studien zum radikalreformatorischen Spiritualismus* (Bibliotheca Germanica, 31) (Tübingen, 1993).

volvement in Waldshut and he was burnt at the stake in Vienna on 10 March 1528. He had written a number of pamphlets, including *Achtzehn Schlussreden so betreffende eyn ganz christlich Leben* (Waldshut, 1524), *Von Ketzern und ihren Verbrennern* (1524), *Vom christlichen Tauf der Gläubigen* (1525), *Eine christliche Lehrtafel* (Nikolsburg, 1526/27), *Von der Freiheit des Willens* (Nikolsburg, c.1527), and *Von dem Schwert* (Nikolsburg, c.1527). The Nikolsburg books were printed by Simprecht Froschauer, son of the Augsburg printer Johann Froschauer whose press and types he had inherited. He had intended to establish himself in Vienna but, having learned that all Protestant printers in Vienna were thrown into prison, he first went to Nördlingen but then followed Hubmaier's suggestion to set up his press in Nikolsburg.

This small selection illustrates the immense diversity of serious writers in the earlier part of the sixteenth century. And the cases of Melanchthon and Hedio, for instance, show clearly how humanism and religious controversy overlap.[73] The humanist authors represented the intellectual elite of Germany and provided a considerable amount of work for the German book trade. The earliest phases of German humanism – from 1450 to 1480, with the Swabian and Franconian writers like Albrecht von Eyb, 'Arigo', Heinrich Steinhöwel, Konrad Humery, Hans Neidhart and Niklas von Wyle, or that from 1480 to 1500, represented by the Heidelberg circle (Rudolf Agricola, Johann Reuchlin and others) or the 'Alsatian school' (Sebastian Brant, Geiler von Kaisersberg and Jakob Wimpheling) – will not concern us here, but the third phase, that of 'High Humanism', including people like Johann Adelphus, Johannes Aventinus, Heinrich Bebel, Johann Eberlin, Hieronymus Emser, Ulrich von Hutten, Thomas Murner, Willibald Pirckheimer and Albrecht Dürer, is important. In the early years of the Reformation, the aims of humanism and of the Reformation itself become inextricably intertwined, with many of these writers (and others) taking sides in the religious debate.

New types of vernacular books

Latin gained new strength through humanism, but the vernacular achieved literary status above all through the Reformation movement.

---

[73] See for example J. Livet, 'Humanisme allemand, Réforme et Civilisation européenne', in J. Lefebvre and J.-C. Margolin (eds), *L'Humanisme allemand (1480–1540) XVIIIe Colloque International de Tours*. (Humanistische Bibliothek, Reihe I: Abhandlungen, Bd. 38), (Munich, 1979), pp. 7–30; also, in the same volume, H. O. Burger, 'Martin Luther und der Humanismus', pp. 357–69; further: E. Bernstein, *German Humanism* (Twayne's World Authors Series, 690) (Boston, 1983), pp. 129–40.

German was vital if the Reformers were to win over the masses. Hutten was one who recognized the importance of German as a weapon of propaganda:

> Latein ich vor geschrieben hab
> das war eim jeden nit bekannt,
> jetzt schrei ich an das vaterland
> deutsch Nation in ihrer sprach
> zu bringen diesen Dingen Rach ...[74]
> [Not everybody knew that I used to write in Latin,
> but now I appeal to the fatherland,
> the German nation in its own tongue,
> to set these things aright.]

But even Luther's opponents, like Murner, Emser and others, realized the importance of the vernacular, so they too wrote in German and made use of printing in an attempt to catch a wide public – but some publishers had difficulty in disposing of such writings. Thus Wolfgang Stöckel in Leipzig, compelled by the authorities to print anti-Lutheran books, complained about his business declining; only Lutheran works found a ready sale. In many cases Catholic authors had to bear the printing costs themselves.[75]

The year 1521, with the Diet of Worms and the Edict, was not only a milestone in the history of the church in Germany. It was something of a watershed too in the history of vernacular publishing. Not only did printers, particularly in the imperial cities, turn increasingly to the writings of the Reformers, they began to turn away from the traditional staple fare of the book trade. Thus works like *Der Heiligen Leben* (the German version of the *Legenda aurea*), *Tnugdalus*, *Brandan* (which went through more than 20 editions between about 1476 and 1521) and other religious narratives appear to have been printed for the last time that year.[76] In due course the new outlook was to give rise to new subjects for popular narrative too. Thus humanism encouraged an interest in the heroes of antiquity and mythological figures, and the 'discovery' of the Bible enriched vernacular literature with subjects such

---

[74] *Gesprächsbüchlein Ulrichs von Hutten*, edited by K. Kleinschmidt (Leipzig, n.d.), Introduction, p. 7.

[75] See Kapp, *Geschichte des deutschen Buchhandels*, vol. 1, pp. 410 ff.

[76] See for instance N. F. Palmer, 'Visio Tnugdali'. *The German and Dutch Translations and their Circulation in the Later Middle Ages*. (Münchener Texte und Untersuchungen, 76), (Munich, 1982). Also: W. Williams-Krapp, *Die deutschen und niederdeutschen Legendare des Mittelalters. Studien zu ihrer Überlieferungs-, Text- und Wirkungsgeschichte* (Tübingen, 1986), p. 313, and now also M. Brand, K. Freienhagen-Baumgardt, R. Meyer and W. Williams-Krapp (eds), *Der Heiligen Leben* (Texte und Textgeschichte, 44) (Tübingen, 1996).

as David, Judith and Susanna, and made stories such as that of the Prodigal Son popular, both in prose and drama.

To ensure that the Bible and other basic religious texts (catechisms, etc.) really got into the hands of as many people as possible it was necessary to encourage literacy, and this resulted in publication of primers and manuals on spelling and on grammar, such as Valentin Ickelsamer's *Die rechte weis aufs kürtzist lesen zu lernen* (Erfurt: Johannes Loersfeld, 1527). While in the Middle Ages schools had predominantly served to train men for the priesthood, Luther in *An die Ratsherren aller Städte deutschen Lands, daß sie christliche Schulen aufrichten und halten sollen* (1524) declared it to be the duty of the secular authorities to establish and maintain schools to instruct and educate the citizens. This necessarily encouraged the production and distribution of books, the establishment of printing shops and the translation of useful books. Here space permits consideration of only a few manifestations of this phenomenon. We will look briefly at the Bible, Luther's catechisms, collections of hymns, consolatory literature, and pamphlets.

The Bible

Although there had been 14 printed Bibles in High German and four in Low German before Luther embarked upon his undertaking the Reformers recognized that the provision of a generally accessible, good German translation of the Scriptures was a task of supreme importance.[77] It was an essential corollary of Luther's insistence that the Scriptures were the ultimate authority.

Though the Wittenberg friends first conceived the plan for a translation in November 1520 it was only early in December 1521 that Melanchthon persuaded Luther to translate the New Testament. The principal reason for starting with the New Testament was that considerable importance was attached to a reliable and intelligible translation of the Pauline Epistles. In addition, of course, the New Testament was less difficult to translate than the Hebrew Old Testament for which Luther would need to invoke the assistance of his scholarly friends.

In the space of 11 weeks, by the end of February 1522, the New Testament translation had been completed. Luther had sent the first half of the manuscript from the Wartburg to Wittenberg around 20 February and he travelled to Wittenberg in person on 4 March to deliver the rest for discussion and final revision before it was handed

---

[77] See W. Eichenberger and H. Wendland, *Deutsche Bibeln vor Luther* (Hamburg, 1977).

over to Melchior Lotter the Younger who printed it for the publishers Lucas Cranach and Christian Döring. The work was carried out in strict secrecy to avoid the risk of theft and of piracy. The first proofs were ready at the beginning of May. Printing took five and a half months in all. Initially a single press was used, but – mindful of the need to have the book (222 folios) available in time for the Leipzig autumn fair which would run from 29 September to 6 October 1522 – from the end of May two presses were employed and in the latter stages even three. It seems to have been ready shortly before 21 September. It bears no indication of the name of the translator or of the printer or publisher. (It was not until later, when the Book of Job was published with a 'Preface of Dr Martin Luther', that the translator's name actually appeared in association with the translation). The title-page carries only the simple xylographic legend: *Das Newe Testament / Deutzsch* and the place of publication, *Wittenberg*.

It was decided that the New Testament should contain a number of pictures, though it can hardly be called an illustrated Bible. Some of the pre-Lutheran printed German Bibles contained illustrations, in the Old Testament rather than in the New Testament. In Luther's 'September Testament' the Gospels and Epistles are introduced with an ornamental initial showing the author concerned in the pose of a writer. The only part of the New Testament to be given a cycle of illustrations was Revelation. This consisted of 21 full-page woodcuts, carried out by Cranach and his assistants known only by their monograms HB and MB. The illustrations, deriving from the 15 pictures in Dürer's *Apocalypse* and constituting one of the book's chief glories, are noted for their anti-Papal features, particularly (in Rev. 17) the picture of the Whore of Babylon wearing the Papal tiara.[78]

The publishers rightly foresaw that the 'September Testament' would be a great success. It was completely sold out by early December, but precautions had been taken to prepare a second, revised edition, which was ready at least by 19 December 1522, the 'December Testament'. It has been estimated that during Luther's lifetime 100 000 copies of the New Testament were printed in Wittenberg alone. Another measure of its popularity was the fact that by the end of the year 1522 a dozen reprints had appeared, seven of them in Basle, three in Augsburg, one in Grimma and one in Leipzig.

If translation of the New Testament from Erasmus's Greek text occupied Luther for 11 weeks, translating the Old Testament from the

---

[78] On the illustrations see P. Martin, *Martin Luther und die Bilder zur Apokalypse. Die Ikonographie der Illustrationen zur Offenbarung des Johannes in der Lutherbibel 1522 bis 1546.* (Vestigia Bibliae, 5) (Hamburg, 1983).

2.6   The first page of St Matthew's Gospel (woodcuts by Urs Graf) Erasmus, *Novum Instrumentum* (Basle: Johannes Froben, 1516)

Hebrew kept him busy for 12 years. From the outset Luther was acutely aware not only of the immensity of the task but also of the desirability of not publishing such a large and necessarily expensive work as a single volume. Accordingly he announced on 3 November 1522 that he would begin by translating the Pentateuch, which would then be followed by the historical books and finally by the Prophets and the poetical books. The translation of the Pentateuch and of the historical and poetical books was ready by October 1524, but the remainder was to take ten years, not least because of the extreme difficulty of translating the Book of Job. The Pentateuch was published around July 1523 (and the Augsburg printer Silvan Otmar published a reprint on 24 October 1523). The second part of the Old Testament, comprising the historical books from Joshua to Esther, was out in 1524, and again Otmar produced a reprint within three or four months. The third part, comprising some of the prophets and the poetical books, appeared in 1524 with the symbols devised by Luther as a mark of authenticity as discussed above. Almost simultaneously there appeared a separate edition of the Psalter, with a number of textual improvements. Thereafter, until 1532, Luther had little time for his translating; over that whole period there were separate editions of six individual books. 1528 saw a revised translation of the Psalter and in 1529/30 a new edition of the New Testament. The books of Jonah, Habakkuk and Zechariah came out between 1526 and 1528. Isaiah followed in 1528, Wisdom in 1529, and Daniel in 1530. Luther hoped that, just as he had found the leisure in the Wartburg to translate the New Testament, he would use his sojourn at the castle of Coburg during the Diet of Augsburg in 1530 to complete the Old Testament: Jeremiah, Ezekiel, and the remaining minor prophets. Illness prevented him from achieving this goal, but nevertheless the fourth and final part of the Old Testament, *Die Propheten alle Deudsch*, did appear in the spring of 1532.

Luther's slow progress with the Prophets only served to encourage others to try to expedite matters. Thus the Spiritualists Ludwig Hetzer (d. 1529) and Hans Denck (d. 1527) published their very successful translation of the Prophets, at Worms in 1527. A plagiarized edition came out in Zurich in 1529. In the same year the Zurich theologian Leo Jud published his translation of the Apocrypha. This meant that it was now possible to put together translations of the whole of the Scriptures, and this was precisely what the Worms printer Peter Schöffer (younger son of Peter Schöffer of Mainz) did: his 'combined' Bible of 1529 comprised the first three parts of Luther's translation of the Old Testament, Hetzer and Denck's Prophets, Jud's Apocrypha, and Luther's New Testament. Froschauer's Zurich Bible of 1530 and Wolfgang Köpfel's Strasbourg one of 1529/30 were of a similar nature.

Competition such as this made it imperative for Luther to complete his prophets and the Apocrypha. He had Philipp Melanchthon, Caspar Cruciger and Justus Jonas help him with the latter, and the manuscript, complete with Luther's prefaces, was ready in the spring of 1534. At last the Wittenberg Bible was finished, though before it appeared in print the Apocrypha, recast in Low German by Bugenhagen, was first published on 1 April 1534 by the Lübeck printer Ludwig Dietz.

Luther's catechisms

Luther's *Deutsch Catechismus*, the *Großer Catechismus* as it was called from 1542, was prepared in 1529. Luther completed the manuscript at the end of March and it was published by Georg Rhau on 23 April 1529.[79] Two separate Low German versions and two separate Latin translations appeared. In the second High German edition (1529) Luther expanded the Lord's Prayer commentary and made a number of other small changes. This edition and the first edition of the Low German text and succeeding ones also contained woodcuts by Lucas Cranach the Elder; these had originally been prepared for Melanchthon's 1527 commentary on the catechism. Luther approved of illustrated books because children and simple folk 'durch Bildnis und Gleichnis besser bewegt werden, die Göttlichen geschicht zu behalten, denn durch blosse Wort odder lere' ['can be more effectively motivated through pictures and images than through mere words or teaching to remember the course of divine history'] (*Betbüchlein*, 1529, fol. V4[r], WA, 10, 2, p. 453). The third High German edition (1530) has a longer preface.

As for the *Kleiner Catechismus*, before it appeared in the familiar book form, it had its antecedents in individual cards or sheets for hanging on the wall; these contained the Ten Commandments, the Creed, the Lord's Prayer, etc. The first edition in book form was published by Nickel Schirlentz at Wittenberg in May 1529 under the title *Enchiridion. Der kleine Katechismus für die gemeinen Pfarherrn und Prediger.*[80]

The Low German translations were intended for the rural population of central and northern Germany. By 1600 13 Low German editions of the *Großer Catechismus* and 20 of the *Kleiner Catechismus* had appeared. There were 18 editions of the Latin–Low German version which the Magdeburg schoolmaster Georg Major had produced for his school in 1532.

---

[79] On the catechisms see C. Weismann, *Eine kleine Biblia. Die Katechismen von Luther und Brenz. Einführung und Texte* (Stuttgart, 1985). Also G. Strauss, *Luther's House of Learning. Indoctrination of the Young in the German Reformation*, (Baltimore, 1978). For a bibliography of editions to 1600, including *Nachdrucke*: WA, 30/1, pp. 499–521; to 1546 only *LB*, 2548–88.

[80] Bibliography of editions to 1600, including *Nachdrucke*: WA, 30/1, pp. 666–807; to 1546 *LB*, 2589–666. For a map showing the places in which the *Kleiner Katechismus* was printed up to 1600 see G. Lüdtke and L. Mackensen (eds), *Deutscher Kulturatlas*, vol. 3, (Berlin, 1928–37), Tafel 214c (prepared by H. Volz).

IMAGO MARTINI LVTHERI EO HABITV
PRESSA, QVO REVERSVS EST EX PATHMO WITTE·
BERGAM ANNO DOMINI 1522.

Quæsiros toties, toties tibi Roma petitus,
En ego per Chriſtum uiuo Lutherus adhuc,
Vna mihi ſpes eſt, quo non fraudabor, Iesus,
Hunc mihi dum teneam, perfida Roma uale.

ANNVS CONFESSIONIS WOR-   ANNVS PATHMI   ANNVS REDITVS EX
MACIÆ 1521.   1521.   PATHMO 1522.

2.7   'Junker Jörg': Luther at the Wartburg, 1522. Woodcut by Lucas Cranach
the Elder

Of the Latin versions of the *Kleiner Catechismus* the most important was that by Johann Sauermann, probably made at Luther's request and first published by Georg Rhau in September 1529. As the title indicates, it was specifically intended for use in Latin schools: *Parvus Catechismus pro pueris in schola*. By 1600 more than 60 editions had appeared, in 17 versions.

Hymn-books

Following the sporadic introduction of services in the vernacular – by Karlstadt at Wittenberg in 1521, by Kaspar Katz at Nördlingen, Wolfgang Wissenburger in Basle and Johann Schwebel in Pforzheim in 1522 – and Thomas Müntzer's publication of his *Deutsches Kirchenampt*[81] around Easter 1523, Luther came under increasing pressure to spell out his liturgical ideas, especially since there was a real danger that Müntzer's order of service would be adopted by evangelical congregations. The result was Luther's *Formula missae et communionis* (WA, 12, pp. 205–20), written in November 1523. Though a somewhat cautious document, one innovation proposed was that the people should join in the singing of hymns in German, thus establishing congregational praise in the vernacular as a legitimate part of the Lutheran church service, a development which ran counter to the medieval church which laid down that only the choir should sing, in Latin, in the main masses, and that vernacular hymns, if tolerated at all, should be limited to certain subordinate offices and to extra-liturgical use, for instance to accompany processions or on pilgrimages.[82] So successful was the innovation that, in the *Deutsche Messe und ordnung Gottis diensts* (WA, 19, pp. 72–113) of 1525, the scope for use of the vernacular was increased.

The problem was that, initially, there was a lack of suitable texts – 'poetae nobis desunt, aut nondum cogniti sunt, qui pias et spirituales cantilenas (ut Paulus vocat) nobis concinnent, quae dignae sint in Ecclesia dei frequentari' ['we lack the poets, or they are as yet unknown, who can sing pious and spiritual songs (as St Paul calls them) which are suitable to be used in the church of God'] (*Formula missae et communionis*, WA, 12, p. 218). This concern surfaces again in the celebrated letter to Spalatin (WA, Br., 3, p. 220) of December 1523, telling him of the need for vernacular hymns and inviting him to contribute a version of either Psalm 6 or Psalm 143. Luther himself gave the lead with his version of Psalm 130, the famous 'Aus tieffer not', a

---

[81] Text in T. Müntzer, *Schriften und Briefe*, ed. G. Franz, (Gütersloh, 1968), pp. 25–155.
[82] See J. Janota, *Studien zu Funktion und Typus des deutschen geistlichen Liedes im Mittelalter* (Munich, 1968).

hymn later given pride of place in Klug's *Christlich Geseng zum Begrebnis* (1542) and sung at the funerals not only of Frederick the Wise on 7 May 1525 and John of Saxony in August 1532 but also of Luther himself on 24 February 1546. During 1523–24 Luther wrote 24 hymns to serve as an inspiration and stimulus to others. Around mid-January 1524 the Nuremberg printer Jobst Gutknecht put together a small hymn-book, the 'Achtliederbuch', containing Luther's versions of Psalms 12, 14 and 130, with the assertion on the title-page that they were in part already in regular use at Wittenberg: *Etlich Cristlich lider Lobgesang / vñ Psalm / dem rainen wort Gottes gemess / auss der heyligē schrifft / durch mancherley hochgelerter gemacht / in der Kirchen zu singen / wie es dann [z]um tayl berayt zu Wittenberg in übung ist.* Gutknecht's 'Achtliederbuch' was a purely private venture, without any ecclesiatical standing. A more substantial collection of 38 German and five Latin compositions was put together by Luther's musician friend Johann Walter under the title *Geystliche gesangk Buchleyn* (Wittenberg, 1524). This had polyphonic settings for choral use. Hymn-books were primarily intended for choirs, choirmasters, organists and schoolmasters. The choirs were expected to teach the congregations the hymns, and when the second edition came out two years later, by which time congregations might reasonably be expected to have learned them, the compositions were arranged monophonically.[83]

By way of a footnote it may be added that of course Jobst Gutknecht's idea of publishing collections of songs was not new. The late Middle Ages had seen many manuscript collections of songs, ranging from manuscripts of courtly lyric poetry, such as the famous Manesse manuscript in Heidelberg, to such compilations as Klara Hätzlerin's, made in Augsburg in 1471. Some vernacular secular song collections had al-

---

[83] There is an extensive literature on German hymn-books. The following is a small selection: W. Lipphardt, *Gesangbuchdrucke in Frankfurt am Main vor 1569,* (Frankfurt am Main, 1974); O. Bill, *Das Frankfurter Gesangbuch von 1569 und seine späteren Ausgaben,* (Marburg, 1969); W. Hollweg, *Geschichte der evangelischen Gesangbücher vom Niederrhein im 16.–18. Jahrhundert,* (Gütersloh, 1923); J. Smend, *Das evangelische Lied von 1524. Festschrift zum 400-jährigen Jubiläum,* (Leipzig, 1924); F. Hubert, *Die Strassburger liturgischen Ordnungen im Zeitalter der Reformation,* (Göttingen, 1900); M. Jenny, *Geschichte des deutsch-schweizerischen evangelischen Gesangbuches im 16. Jahrhundert,* (Basle, 1962); A. Dürr and W. Killy (eds), *Das protestantische Kirchenlied im 16. und 17. Jahrhundert* (Wolfenbütteler Forschungen, 31), (Wiesbaden, 1986). The handiest discussion of Luther's hymns and the circumstances of their composition is M. Luther, *Die deutschen geistlichen Lieder,* edited by G. Hahn (Neudrucke deutscher Literaturwerke, N.F. 20) (Tübingen, 1967); see also G. Hahn, 'Luthers Lieder. Einheit und Vielfalt', in H. Bungert (ed.), *Martin Luther. Eine Spiritualität und ihre Folgen. Vortragsreihe der Universität Regensburg zum Luther-Jahr 1983* (Schriftenreihe der Universität Regensburg, 9) (Regensburg, 1983), pp. 73–87.

ready appeared in print, such as those by Öglin (Augsburg, 1512), Schöffer (Mainz, 1513), Arnt von Aich (Cologne, c.1515), which in due course were to be followed by Johann Ott's collection (Nuremberg, 1534), the anonymous *Grassliedlin* (Nuremberg, 1534), Egenolff's *Gassenhawerlein* (Frankfurt, 1535), Matthias Apiarius's *Fünff vnd sechzig teütscher Lieder* (Strasbourg, 1536), and Georg Forster's *Frische Teutsche Liedlein* (Nuremberg, 1539–40). These comprise drinking songs, bawdy street ballads, humorous ditties, historical folksongs and vulgarized love songs, many of which were by no means necessarily sixteenth-century compositions, though the circumstances of their transmission may initially suggest this.

Consolatory works

Versehung von Leib, Seel, Ehre und Gut, first published by Peter Wagner at Nuremberg in 1489 (subsequent editions: Augsburg: H. Schobser, 1490; Augsburg: Hans Schönsperger, 1493; Nuremberg: W. Huber, 1509; Strasbourg: J. Knoblouch, 1518) has been considered the only medieval consolatory book for the dying which survived the advent of the Reformation. In fact, however, only the medical portion of the work remained essentially unchanged; the religious, consolatory part was replaced by the *Tröstung aus göttlicher Schrift* by Caspar Huberinus. Huberinus (Huber), born near Ausgburg in 1500, was a follower of Luther, opposing the Zwinglians and Anabaptists at Augsburg from 1525 to 1544 and playing a major role in the 1535 concordat between Luther and the Augsburg clergy. From then until 1553 he was the first Protestant preacher in Hohenlohe in north Württemberg. He became one of the favourite authors of devotional literature in the sixteenth century. In the space of 50 years his *Wie man den Sterbenden trösten und ihm zusprechen soll*, appeared in 125 editions, usually as an accompaniment to larger works, in almost a dozen languages. The combination of *Vom Zorn und der Güte Gottes* and *Wie man den Sterbenden trösten und ihm zusprechen soll*, first published by Philipp Ulhart at Augsburg in 1529, is known in 23 High German editions, some of them with a preface by Luther, and 15 Low German editions, as well as two Danish and two or three Icelandic ones. Eventually *Wie man dem Sterbenden trösten und ihm zusprechen soll* became as well known internationally as the *Seelenarznei (Medicina animae)* of Urbanus Rhegius, together with which it was also published in 1536; there were at least 13 High German editions, six Low German, as well as Dutch, Latin and Polish versions of this combination.[84] Rhegius

---

[84] The bibliography of the works of Huberinus and Rhegius has been excellently studied by G. Franz, *Huberinus – Rhegius – Holbein* (note 2 above).

(Rieger) (1489–1541), a former pupil of Johann Eck at Ingolstadt and crowned *poeta laureatus* by Emperor Maximilian I in 1517, was the principal mouthpiece for Luther in Augsburg (though for a time he sided with Zwingli over the issue of the Eucharist), a city which he left in 1540 to become Superintendent at Celle in 1534. He was the author of more than 100 works.

Pamphlets

The growth of pamphlet literature seems to be a phenomenon specially characteristic of the German-speaking lands.[85] While prior to the Reformation there were few signs of pamphlet activity, by 1524 it had grown into a flood which ebbed and flowed for the next 20 years. Pamphlet production may, then, be regarded as a barometer of religious and social tension.

What is a pamphlet? Hans-Joachim Köhler has proposed defining it as an unbound printed brochure consisting of more than a single leaf, published separately and not in a regular series or at regular intervals and which is directed at the general public with the aim of influencing their actions or their opinions.[86] This is a fair statement of the common denominators but it scarcely conveys an impression of the variety of pamphlets known to us in the early sixteenth century.

Aesthetically the pamphlets were seldom attractive. They generally give the impression of having been printed quickly and cheaply, and as such are indicative of a shift in the use of the new technology. To some extent the printers were testing the market for what would sell, both with regard to quality of the product itself and the quality of the content – how polemical and libellous could one be and still get away with it? In his famous pamphlet *Mich wundert, daß kein Geld im Land ist* (Eilenburg: J. Stöckel, 1524) Eberlin von Günzburg (1483–1532)

---

[85] The literature on Reformation pamphlets is vast. A brief but good and clear survey of the the the state of research to 1982 is given by Schwitalla, *Deutsche Flugschriften*, pp. 7–11. In the present context the papers by R. G. Cole mentioned in notes 4 and 42 above have been found particularly useful.

[86] H.-J. Köhler, 'Die Flugschriften. Versuch der Präzisierung eines geläufigen Begriffs', in H. Rabe, H. Molitor and H.-C. Rublack (eds), *Festgabe für Ernst Walter Zeeden zum 60. Geburtstag* (Münster, 1976), pp. 36–61, here p. 50: 'Eine Flugschrift ist eine aus mehr als einem Blatt bestehende, selbständige, nichtperiodische und nicht gebundene Druckschrift, die sich mit dem Ziel der Agitation (d.h. der Beeinflussung des Handelns) und/oder der Propaganda (d.h. der Beeinflussung der Überzeugung) an die gesamte Öffentlichkeit wendet'. See also Köhler's paper 'Fragestellungen und Methoden zur Interpretation frühneuzeitlicher Flugschriften', in Köhler, *Flugschriften als Massenmedium*, pp. 1–27, here p. 3, n. 5, and H. Walz, *Deutsche Literatur der Reformationszeit* (Darmstadt, 1988), pp. 62–4.

urged printers to exercise discrimination when considering what to print; they should not print second-rate stuff just for quick sales and good profit. Eberlin had an unusually early and clear conception of the value of printing as a medium for polemics and for instruction. He recognized that the medium itself lent authority to a statement: 'if you have questions on the sacraments, read a pamphlet by Dr Martin Luther,' he once wrote.[87] The 'brief, blunt, vulgar'[88] Reformation pamphlet intended for a wide but often unsophisticated and sometimes confused readership became a major tool of those who sought to change the religious loyalties of large numbers of people.

Stylistically many Reformation pamphlets are, in Cole's words, 'disorganized, repetitive, forming a mosaic of information quite unappealing to the modern mind' (p. 145). This he ascribes to the fact that 'many of the written statements of the Reformation were published in the nascent period of the typographical age during which the rules for linear consistency were not fully laid down' (ibid.) and draws attention to the preface to the reader in *Disputatio excellentium D. doctorum Iohannis Eccij* ... , (Erfurt: Matthes Maler, 1519), a pamphlet giving an account of the Leipzig disputation between Luther and Eck, in which the author remarks that the debate seemed 'a chaotic sea of words', an admission which implies that the medieval mode of oral disputation did not lend itself to reproduction in the medium of the printed pamphlet.

Despite the stylistic shortcomings, it is nevertheless apparent that the authors were mostly educated folk. This is evident from their use of literary forms which are characteristic of the universities and the church – sermon, commentary, thesis, treatise. The most important genres used are the sermon, the dialogue and the letter.[89] As we have seen, among the authors of pamphlets are all the major figures of the period, as well as a host of minor ones. In some cases the authors will have written their pieces specifically for publication in pamphlet form, in others publication will have taken place at the initiative of the printer/publisher. For instance, Pope Adrian VI is unlikely to have been consulted

---

[87] For the writings of Eberlin see L. Enders (ed.), *Johann Eberlin von Günzburg, Ausgewählte Schriften* (Neudrucke deutscher Litteraturwerke des XVI. und XVII. Jahrhunderts, Bd. 139–41, 170–172, 183–88) (3 vols, Halle an der Saale, 1896–1902). The passage relevant here is from vol. 3, p. 161.

[88] Cole, 'The Reformation pamphlet', p. 139.

[89] See Schwitalla, *Deutsche Flugschriften* pp. 89–92 (on the sermon), pp. 92–97 (on the dialogue) and pp. 97–103 (on the letter). Gottfried Seebaß has drawn attention to the important interaction of sermons and pamphlets in Nuremberg, in his paper 'Stadt und Kirche in Nürnberg im Zeitalter der Reformation', in B. Moeller (ed.), *Stadt und Kirche im 16. Jahrhundert* (Schriften des Vereins für Reformationsgeschichte, 190) (Gütersloh, 1978), pp. 66–86, here p. 71.

about pamphlets nos 3528 and 3668 in the Tübingen microfiche project, let alone John of Damascus (no. 3678) or the Venerable Bede (no. 3965)! Luther, Heinrich von Kettenbach, Urbanus Rhegius, Johann Eberlin and others often had their sermons printed in pamphlet form, but these were then sometimes reprinted in unauthorized editions. When dedicating his sermon *Von den guten Werken* (1520) to Duke John of Saxony Luther remarked that, though he could write long and learned tomes, God's purposes would be better served by little sermons directed to the common man (WA, 6, p. 203). (Benzing's *Lutherbibliographie* lists well over 150 sermons by him, many of which appeared in several editions.) It is perhaps likely too that some of the sermons printed were written up by someone other than the preacher.

In subject matter the pamphlets covered a vast range. Broadly speaking, they discuss the interconnections between religious reform and traditional social and economic issues, and the repercussions of changes in religious practice on society at large. Many of them reflect the psycho-social grievances of people who left the old religion for the new and the psycho-social needs of those who remained loyal to the old church, while others make a self-conscious social commentary by identifying social and economic ills and proposing constructive solutions.[90] The changes brought about by the Reformation in popular religious practice represented for the contemporaries a major upheaval in the world as they knew it. The Reformation was to sweep away or at least have a lasting effect on many traditional practices. The veneration of saints, penance, relics, indulgences, pilgrimages, masses for the dead, the Latin mass and liturgy, belief in purgatory, clerical celibacy, monastic vows, clerical immunity from civil taxes and laws, traditional ceremonies and festivals, mendicant orders – these and other issues were addressed over and over again in the pamphlets (as indeed also in open debate and from the pulpit). A recurrent theme also was the insistence that the 'old' religion (the medieval church) was really a 'new' religion and that the alleged 'new' religion (the Reformation), based on scriptural authority, was really the 'old' religion.[91]

---

[90] See S. Ozment, 'The social history of the Reformation: what can we learn from pamphlets?', in Köhler, *Flugschriften*, pp. 171–203. Of particular interest as an example of a tract discussing the problems of people who tried to remain loyal to the old church is Eberlin's *Syben frumm aber trostloss pfaffen klagen ire not* ... (Basle, 1521), Enders (ed.), *Johann Eberlin*, vol. 2, pp. 57–77.

[91] See especially H.-G. Hofacker, '*Vom alten und nüen Gott, Glauben und Ler.* Untersuchungen zum Geschichtsverständnis und Epochenbewußtsein einer anonymen reformatorischen Flugschrift', in J. Nolte et al. (eds), *Kontinuität und Umbruch. Theologie und Frömmigkeit in Flugschriften und Kleinliteratur an der Wende vom 15. zum 16. Jahrhundert* (Stuttgart, 1978), pp. 145–77. The theme also occurs in U. Rhegius's *Novae*

A recent approach to pamphlets has been to consider them from the point of view of communication theory. Schwitalla, for instance, distinguishes 21 types of pamphlets according to their communicative emphasis.[92] As Schwitalla himself admits, some pamphlets may seem to fall into more than one category; an element of subjective judgement may therefore be required. On the whole his classification by *Textsorten* does seem helpful. He shows that the eight most frequently found types, which include appeals of various kinds, reasoned statements, persuasive instructional texts, treatises, debates, complaints, polemics, between them account for some 76 per cent of the pamphlets. The types purveying basic information represent only 10 per cent of the total, and it is particularly noteworthy that the outright defamatory or eulogizing texts make up a mere five per cent.

Among the pamphlets the prose dialogues form a particularly interesting subgroup. The form of the dialogue had been revived by the humanists, and in the struggle against the Roman Church it was first used by Ulrich von Hutten who was to play a decisive role in the war of the pamphlets, despite the fact that his contribution was initially in Latin. Eight of his dozen dialogues are directed against the Church.[93] But more than that, already in the *Gesprächsbüchlein* (begun in the autumn of 1518 but published in January 1521) one can see how the function of the dialogue changes from satire to being a weapon of propaganda, a means of mobilizing and manipulating public opinion. Direct polemic is dominant in *Vadiscus* which, even before the publication of Luther's *An den christlichen Adel*, inaugurates the real pamphlet offensive against the Church of Rome. This process is completed in the carefully constructed *Dialogi novi* (written in the winter of 1520) in which Hutten fully commits himself to the 'Pfaffenkrieg', the struggle against the clergy.[94] In his *Bulla* Hutten sets himself up as the champion of German liberty.

---

doctrinae ad veterem collatio (1522) and in H. von Kettenbach's *Eyn gesprech bruder Hainrichs von Kettenbach mit aim frommen altmüterlin von Ulm von etlichen zufeln und anfechtung des altmütterlin* … (n. pl. 1523) (Oxford, Bodl.: Tractt. Luth. 26.75); see also O. Clemen, *Flugschriften der ersten Jahre der Reformation*, (vol. 2, reprint, Nieuwkoop, 1967), pp. 52–75.

[92] Schwitalla, *Deutsche Flugschriften*.

[93] The eight are *Febris prima, Febris secunda, Vadiscus sive Trias Romana, Inspicientes* (all printed in April 1520 and published in German in the *Gesprächsbüchlein*) and the Latin *Dialogi novi (Bulla vel Bullicida, Monitor primus, Monitor secundus* and *Praedones*), published more or less at the same time as the *Gesprächsbüchlein*.

[94] See B. Könneker, 'Vom "Poeta laureatus" zum Propagandisten. Die Entwicklung Huttens als Schriftsteller in seinen Dialogen von 1518 bis 1521' in *L'Humanisme allemand*, pp. 303–19 (see note 73); and Walz, *Deutsche Literatur*, pp. 85–93.

By 1524/25 the prose dialogue had become a popular form. At least 50 dialogues had already appeared, several of them in a number of editions, authorized or otherwise. The majority are of anonymous authorship, but recent research has thrown light on the identity of some. At least one dialogue is the work of two authors, which of course exacerbates the problem. The authors were Lutheran theologians (Urbanus Rhegius, Martin Bucer, Johann Eberlin, Erasmus Alberus), former monks, theologians and preachers who sympathized with the aspirations of the 'common man' and spoke his language.

In response to Luther's tract *An den Christlichen Adel deutscher Nation* (1520) Thomas Murner had accused Luther of conspiracy to cause unrest, saying it was wrong 'hanß karsten vnd die vnuerstendigen gemain so bald zu boesen als guotem anzuzünden vnd in schellige flammen zu bewegen' [to incite the *Karsthans* and others among the common people to do wrong under pretence of doing good and to cast themselves into the fire].[95] 'Karsthans' was the Swabian–Alemannic name for a peasant who worked with a field hoe (*Karst*). This was answered by the publication of the *Karsthans* dialogue of January 1521 (Strasbourg: J. Prüss) in which 'Karsthans' becomes a name of honour, a positive figure. Authorship has been attributed to various people, including the Strasbourg reformer Matthias Zell, the Strasbourg humanist Nikolaus Gerbel, Martin Bucer, and the St Gallen Reformer Joachim von Watt.[96] Within a year at least ten editions had appeared, including three in Strasbourg, three in Basle and four in Augsburg. The dialogues *Neu-Karsthans* [Strasbourg: M. Schürer, 1521] and *Pfarrer und Schultheiß* [Augsburg: M. Ramminger, 1521] are very probably the work of Martin Bucer.[97]

Books and their readers

> 'Il n'y a de livre complet que de livre lu.'
> (Albert Labarre)

So far this study has been concerned with authors and with printers, publishers and booksellers, about whom, relatively speaking, we know a good deal. When we consider the *traditio passiva*, the reception of books by consumers, the picture is much more sketchy. We have little

---

[95] T. Murner, *Deutsche Schriften*, F. Schultz et al. (eds), VII, (Berlin, 1928, reprint, 1990), p. 63.

[96] See W. Lenk (ed.), *Die Reformation im zeitgenössischen Dialog* (Berlin, 1968), p. 254.

[97] See Lenk, *Die Reformation*, p. 263.

detailed knowledge of which books reached particular kinds of readers and in what period. Though we know something about the reading habits of the political and intellectual élites – princes, noblemen, patricians, priests, lawyers, teachers – what books 'the common man' owned and read (which are not necessarily the same thing) is largely shrouded in mystery.

Before looking into these matters, we should explicitly point out that of course a study of reading habits will not provide an adequate explanation of how Reformation ideas or other contemporary notions were disseminated among the population at large. Though printing was undeniably a major factor in the success of the Reformation and though Bernd Moeller is right to see German book production as a barometer of the Reformation movement,[98] the diffusion of Reformation ideas cannot be explained by reference to printing and the book trade alone. One must resist the temptation to read history backwards in terms of the inevitable triumph of the printed word. The printed word was just *one* of the ways in which the Reformation message was transmitted. The role of the illiterate population must not be discounted.[99] While there is a certain merit in comparing the dissemination process with the ripples caused by throwing a stone into a mill-pond – the greatest stir is at the centre, the Reformation beginning with the élite, those able to read in the cities, and spreading from there to those less well able to read, from large towns to smaller ones, from town to country, that is, from centre to periphery and from top to bottom – this is by no means the whole story, for such a model, implying a one-way process, fails to do justice to the complicated relationship between the culture of the élite and popular culture or between town and country. Scribner rightly stresses the need to examine the interdependence of different modes of communication in the sixteenth century. The pamphlet itself was part of a complex, total picture of communicative experiences involving not just reading but hearing, seeing, discussing, and performing too.

Scribner distinguishes oral communication, visual communication, and action as communication. Oral communication took place through the pulpit, the town hall, the market-place, in inns and taverns and in the home. Reading aloud was the norm, and public readings were

---

[98] B. Moeller, 'Stadt und Buch. Bemerkungen zur Struktur der reformatorischen Bewegung in Deutschland', in W. J. Mommsen (ed.), *Stadtbürgertum und Adel in der Reformation* (Stuttgart, 1979), p. 31: 'Die Massenhaftigkeit der Reformationsbewegung wird gerade an der Massenhaftigkeit der Buchproduktion greifbar'.

[99] R. W. Scribner, 'Flugblatt und Analphabetentum. Wie kam der gemeine Mann zu reformatorischen Ideen?' in Köhler, *Flugschriften*, pp. 65–76, and especially Scribner's book, *For the Sake of Simple Folk. Popular propaganda for the German Reformation* (Cambridge Studies in Oral and Literate Culture, 2), (Cambridge, 1981).

common. Scribner cites the case of the scribe Erasmus Wisperger who was arrested in 1534 for giving a public reading of a work by Karlstadt on the market-place in Nuremberg. Discussion and talk of what one had heard or read were important too. The pamphlet *Diss biechlein zaygt an die weyssagung von zukunfftiger betrubnuss* (Augsburg: Hans Schönsperger, 1522; Munich, Bavarian State Library, P. lat. 251d, fol. a2^r) urges the reader not only to pass the booklet on to a friend but also to discuss it with him. Regular discussion groups might result: precisely such activities were condemned by the authorities at Ulm in 1523/24 and Regensburg in 1535 after public discussion of religious topics had been expressly forbidden. This vital link between printed text and oral culture is best demonstrated by the many songs produced. The pedlar himself might advertise his wares by singing the versified title or the text of the song itself. Scribner ('Flugblatt and Analphabetentum', p. 69) cites the cases of a poor clothmaker who sang Luther's hymns which he was selling on the market-place in Magdeburg, a blind beggar singing them as he went from door to door in Lübeck in 1529, and journeymen singing them to travellers in inns in Brandenburg in 1524. Songs were a vehicle for imparting news of the latest developments, for pouring scorn on the Catholic clergy, for poking fun at church music and the liturgy, and for professing the new faith.

Then there was visual communication. As the passionate debates over images show, this was an age which made considerable use of visual imagery: pictures and other artefacts, processions, ceremonies, etc., and the printers only reinforced this with the mass-production of woodcuts and engravings: devotional pictures, picture-sheets, illustrated broadsheets, brochures and books. From the very outset, the picture – which could appeal to the illiterate as easily as to the literate – had been an important element in the Lutheran propagandistic armoury: already in 1520 and 1521 Luther pictures had been widely available, showing him as a champion of Christian liberty, as saint with a nimbus, as a man divinely inspired, with the Holy Spirit hovering over his head, as prophet and as Father of the Church. His enemies, by contrast, were ridiculed in offensive pictures, showing for instance Cardinal Aleander hanging from the gallows by his feet. Particular mention must be made here too of picture books like the *Passional Christi et Antichristi* (WA, 9, 677–715), printed by Cranach in 1521, and the *Abbildung des Papsttums* of 1545 (WA, 54, 346–73).[100] In his book *For the Sake of Simple Folk*, Scribner demonstrates that, whereas the equivocalness of the language

---

[100] On the former see G. Fleming, 'On the origin of the *Passional Christi and Anti-Christi* and Lucas Cranach the Elder's contribution to Reformation polemics in the iconography of the Passional', *GJ*, **48** (1973), p. 352 f.

of pictures militated against its effective use for the transmission of precise theological points, it did serve to evoke hostility towards the old faith and to foster an emotional attachment to the new. This was achieved by the use of a number of basic images: Luther as saint, man of God or prophet; the Pope as antichrist or apocalyptic beast, and the like. Pictures were the object of censorship as often as were texts.[101]

Finally, there was communication through action. Besides religious drama and shrovetide plays, this includes such symbolic actions as the public burning of Luther's books or Luther's own public, solemn, almost ritual burning of the Bull *Exsurge Domine*. Reports of such events in printed form could give rise to similar happenings elsewhere.

Thus we have to ask not just what people read but how they read, and also what other cultural experiences they brought to their reading. As Scribner observes, whereas the claim is often made that the greatest consequence of printing was that the reader's enthusiasm for the new medium made him receptive to new ideas, this will have been counterbalanced by the conservative effect of the traditional media with which he was familiar. What results this could have is shown by what happened with Luther's concept of Christian liberty at the time of the Peasants' Wars: it was not so much that the peasants read Luther wrongly as that they read him differently. There was always a risk that the printed pages would be read in a manner quite at variance with the author's original intention.[102]

Who read books? In his classic study *Medieval Texts and their First Appearance in Print*, E. P. Goldschmidt painted a broad picture of the public for printed books in the fifteenth and the first half of the sixteenth century:[103] the members of universities, the higher and lower clergy, monasteries and convents with large and small libraries, officials in the service of princes, prelates and municipalities, the nobility, lawyers and physicians, schoolboys and their teachers. Such general statements, while true, lack the essential detail which illuminates the real situation and brings the period to life. A good example of the kind of study needed is provided in a paper by Ursula Altmann, which goes a long way towards explaining the policy of early printers to publish for a less sophisticated stratum of society.[104]

---

[101] See T. Hampe, *Nürnberger Ratsverlässe über Kunst und Künstler im Zeitalter der Spätgotik und Renaissance*, (Vienna, 1904), nos 1378, 1380, 1381, 1444, 1446, 1454. 1455, 1459 from the years 1522 to 1524 alone.

[102] A good example is given by Cole, 'The Reformation pamphlet', p. 144 f.

[103] E. P. Goldschmidt, *Medieval Texts and Their First Appearance in Print*, (London, 1943), here p. 14 f.

[104] U. Altmann, 'Leserkreise zur Inkunabelzeit', in Hellinga and Härtel, *Buch und Text*, pp. 203–17.

The crisis in the printing industry, resulting from the fall in book prices towards the end of the fifteenth century, had forced printers to seek out new texts and new markets to survive. Hence the growth of publication in print of vernacular works, of religious and of secular content. Just as authors too, after the introduction of printing, found themselves writing for a wider, largely unknown public whose tastes they had to try to take into account, so printers too had to experiment with length (abridged texts), formats, language, illustration and ornament and so on to find the right formula for the target public for vernacular books. The practice of illustrating such works with woodcuts, sometimes abundantly, clearly indicates that they were not intended for the traditional types of readers but for a new breed of customer: people in the towns above all, and not necessarily only the well-to-do (but hardly for Scribner's 'simple folk').

Even without the excitement engendered by the Reformation there would almost certainly have been a substantial increase in the number of people able to read in the sixteenth century, for the population of Germany doubled to some 20 million between 1470 and 1600. According to Engelsing, at the beginning of that century about 3 to 4 per cent of the German population, perhaps 400 000 people, could read.[105] By the end of that century there must have been at least 1 million readers, still of course concentrated in the urban areas. ('Urban' is of course a relative term: on the eve of the Reformation 90 per cent of German towns had fewer than 2 000 inhabitants, and there were only 25 cities in the Empire with more than 10 000). While Kamann claimed that a large proportion of the lower classes in sixteenth-century Nuremberg could read and write,[106] perhaps a third to a half would be a more sober estimate, yet the opinion of the mastersinger Daniel Holzmann is worth noting: 'Dieser ist nur ein halber man / Der nicht lesen und schreiben kann.'[107]

'Reading' did not of course mean reading silently to oneself. Virtually everyone who read read aloud, and this inevitably meant that reading became a voluntary or involuntary group activity. Hearing others read was a most important means of gathering information for a large pro-

---

[105] R. Engelsing, *Analphabetentum und Lektüre*, (Stuttgart, 1973), p. 20. Engelsing has used the case of Bremen to exemplify the reading habits of the bourgeoisie in particular in the Protestant north, in his book *Der Bürger als Leser. Lesergeschichte in Deutschland 1500–1800* (Stuttgart, 1974). See also the review by R. König, in *Internationales Archiv für Sozialgeschichte der deutschen Literatur*, 2 (1977), 140–43.

[106] J. Kamann, 'Altnürnberger Gesindewesen', *Mitteilungen des Vereins für Geschichte der Stadt Nürnberg*, 14 (1901), 124. See Engelsing, *Analphabetentum*, p. 32.

[107] 'Anybody who cannot read and write is only half a man.' See R. Hirsch, 'Two Meisterlieder on the art of writing', *GJ*, 33 (1958), 178–82.

portion of the population. Authors had to take the different kinds of readers into account – those who read for themselves and those who listened. How one author, Johann Eberlin, shaped his material stylistically and syntactically to take account of listeners has been analysed by Monika Rössing-Hager in her study of his *Ein vermanung aller christen das sie sich erbarmen vber die klosterfrawen.*[108]

A good instance of group reading was found in the 1560s in the mining communities of Tyrol. Many people from Kitzbühel, for example, came together in private houses or inns to hear evangelical books read, particularly by the popular preacher Hans Steinberger. Sometimes 30 or 40 miners and their wives would go from the parish of St Johann to Kirchberg to hear Steinberger read from his books. On one occasion 60 or 70 people heard him preach from his books in the open air, and on Sundays some 200 might hear his sermons.[109]

It is amazing what books were to be found in these remote communities of silver and copper miners. We are so well informed about them because in 1569 Archduke Ferdinand of Tyrol ordered commissioners to go and make inventories of the books to be found there. There was no intention of confiscating the books for fear of causing unrest, even strikes, among the miners, as the economy of the area largely depended on the fruits of their labours. The intention was to encourage people to buy good Catholic books (specially bought in from the Augsburg bookseller Georg Willer) instead, but this scheme failed so dismally that most of the books had to be given away. The surviving inventories are so detailed that in many cases they record even the printers and places and dates of publication of the books. We learn what a good cross-section of the community owned in the way of books, from the local clergy, the town clerk and mine official down to the humble miner, innkeeper, butcher, miller and apprentice. Some of the collections are impressive, such as that of the 'froner und pergkhgerichtschreiber' Basileus Praun who owned 326 volumes with many Latin works including Cicero, Terence and Catullus. At the other end of the scale were people like Christen Kirckh of Kufstein who had only two heroic poems, *Dietrich von Bern* and *Der Hürne Sewfrid*, and Hans Capeller, miller in Kössen, who possessed only an arithmetic book of some kind. All told, religious books formed a significant proportion of the books listed: prayer-books, saints' legends (particularly *Der Heiligen leben*), Bibles, Testaments, postils, gospels and epistles, theological works both Catholic and Protestant. The remainder comprised chronicles and news-

---

[108] M. Rössing-Hager, 'Wie stark findet der nicht-lesekundige Rezipient Berücksichtigung in den Flugschriften?', in Köhler, *Flugschriften*, pp. 77–137.

[109] On this and what follows see Flood, 'Subversion', note 63 above.

sheets ('Newe Zeitungen'), all kinds of practical handbooks: arithmetic books, cookery books, lawbooks (the *Bayrisches Landrecht* and the *Sachsenspiegel*), books on names and titles, agricultural guides, weather books, herbals, books on distilling, Latin dictionaries. Many Latin authors were represented, as were many German ones: Luther, Eck, Brant's *Narrenschiff*, Pauli's *Schimpff und Ernst*. There were comedies of Hans Sachs, *Till Eulenspiegel, Fortunatus, Tristrant, Kaiser Octavian* and several other romances and popular novels, heroic poems, and many more. If these were the kinds of books found in remote mining communities in Tyrol, what would the picture have been if we had similarly detailed information about book ownership among the burghers in such sophisticated cities as Frankfurt, Nuremberg, Augsburg, Strasbourg and Basle?

Luther believed one should rely on a few good books.[110] In *An die Ratsherren aller städte deutsches Lands, daß sie christliche Schulen aufrichten und halten sollen* (Wittenberg: Cranach and Döring, 1524) (WA, 15, pp. 9–53), he set forth his views on what constitutes a sound collection: the Bible and the best commentaries on it; books useful for the study of languages irrespective of whether the authors were classical or Christian; books on the liberal arts and a careful selection of legal and medical works; and chronicles and histories. Luther's conception of a good library was influential, as is evidenced by its repetition in all its essential features in Cyriakus Spangenberg's *Adelspiegel* (Schmalkalden, 1591–94).[111] He is simply more specific with regard to authors. He recommends:

1. the Bible, in Hebrew, Greek and Latin, and in Luther's translation; Luther's works in Latin and German, including the *Kirchen-* and *Hauspostille*, the *Tischreden* and his letters
2. the Church fathers: Augustine, Basil, Jerome, Chrysostom, and others
3. other theologians: Georg von Anhalt, Brenz, Rhegius, Flacius Illyricus, Andreas Lang, Bartholomeus Westheimer, and the postils of Corvinus, Johann Spangenberg, Caspar Huberinus and Simon Musaeus
4. historical works by Johann Balaeus, Sixtus of Siena, Ludwig Rabus,

---

[110] WA Tisch. 3, pp. 57–8, no. 2094.

[111] See Richard Kolb, '"A beautiful, delightful jewel." Cyriakus Spangenberg's plan for a sixteenth century noble's library', *Journal of Library History*, 14/2 (1979), 129–59. Also Weyrauch 'Überlegungen', pp. 255–9. In this context a study of what books were available at Wittenberg University at this time is illuminating; see S. Kusukawa, *Wittenberg University Library Catalogue of 1536*. (Libri Pertinentes, 3) (Cambridge, 1995).

Herodotus, Thucydides, Tacitus, Krantz, Sleidanus, also Strabo, Pliny and Sebastian Münster

5. books on the liberal arts, law, medicine, and other useful things, including Cicero, Melanchthon's *Declamationes*, Gessner's books on animals, Tragius's herbal, Baudouin's commentaries on civil law, and Lazius's books on the Roman Republic.

The only major difference between Spangenberg and Luther is that Spangenberg does not include the books on language and literature. Nevertheless, the *Adelspiegel* does afford a good idea of what the contemporaries deemed salutary and useful, especially when it is clear that Spangenberg informed himself of the details using some important collections such as those of Duke Johann Friedrich of Saxony, the Fuggers in Augsburg, and others.

The reception of Luther's Bible

Space permits discussion of the reception of only one book, Luther's Bible. Antonius Corvinus (Rabe, 1501–53), the Reformer of Lower Saxony, wrote to the translator on 24 November 1534 to congratulate him on the completion of the Bible translation: 'Quod tandem sacra Biblia felitius quam vnquam antehac versa tuo auspicio in publicum prodierunt, Lutere omnium, qui viuunt, charissime, dictu mirum, quam me exhilararit, imo omnium bonorum centurias' [It is marvellous to tell you, Luther, you who are beloved among all, how delighted I was, and hundreds of good men with me, at the publication of the Holy Bible under your direction, in the best translation ever] (WA, Br., 7, p. 119, no. 2148). There seems to have been a general climate of enthusiasm to embrace any vernacular Bible, for even before Luther's New Testament appeared Hartmuth von Cronberg (1488–1549) wrote to Luther on 14 April 1522:

> Gott hat uns teütschen sein göttlichs wort vnd die unwidersprech-leich warheit vor andern Nacionen geoffenbaret, die kunst des Truckens, darauß der gantzen wellt trost vnnd seligkeyt komen mag, yst in teütschem lanndt erstlich erfunden, dar zu mögen wir nit leücknen, wir haben die hymmellische schrifft vnd warheyt yn gutem clarem teütsch, darauß der aller armest sein heyl als wol hören vnnd verstehen mag, als der aller reichest. [It is to us Germans rather than to other nations that God has given his Divine Word and revealed his ineffable truth, and the art of printing, which will afford the whole world consolation and bliss, was first invented in Germany, nor may we deny that we possess the heavenly scriptures and truth in good, clear German, from which the poorest as well as the richest may hear and understand his salvation.] (WA Br., 2, p. 500).

𝔍𝔬𝔟𝔞𝔫𝔫𝔦𝔰.

2.8   The Whore of Babylon as depicted by Lucas Cranach the Elder in Luther's
Das Newe Testament/Deutzsch (Wittenberg, September 1522)

Though Cronberg knew of Luther's plan to translate the New Testament (WA, 10/2, p. 60), at this date he could only be referring either to
the German version of the Gospels by Johann Lang (*c.*1488–1548) and
Nikolaus Krumpach, published in 1522, or to one of the complete

pre-Lutheran German Bible translations. The eagerness with which Luther's translation of the New Testament had been received by the reading public was described by Johannes Cochlaeus:

> Eh dann aber Embsers arbeit an tag gegeben / war Luthers new Testament durch die Buchtrucker dermassen gemehrt / vñ in so grosser Anzahl außgesprengt / Also / daß auch Schneider vnd Schuster / Ja auch Weiber vnd andere einfältige Idioten / souil deren diß new Lutherisch Euangelium angenommen / die auch nur etwas wenigs Teutsch auff ein Lebzeiten lesen gelehrnt / dieselbe gleich als ein Bronnen aller warheit mit höchster begird lasen / Etliche trugen dasselbe mit sich im Busen herumb / vnd lehrnten es außwendig. [But before Emser's version came out, so many copies of Luther's New Testament had been brought out and distributed by the printers that even tailors and shoemakers, even women and other simple folk who had ever learnt to read a bit of German, read it with great eagerness as though it were a fount of all truth. Some clutched it to their breasts and learnt it by heart.][112]

The vehemence of this criticism demonstrates the significance of Luther's Bible translation. It represented a danger to the classes that had traditionally reserved the privilege of education and the monopoly of knowledge for themselves, it breached a closed society which did not recognize its own limits and was not able to see its own limitations. But there is no more eloquent testimony to the success of Luther's translation than the many reprints. Whatever Luther and the Wittenberg printers may have thought, there is no doubt that the translation could not have become so widely known so quickly had it not been for printers elsewhere. Roughly speaking, for every Wittenberg edition three more appeared elsewhere. Often enough the speed with which these editions were published led to the introduction of textual corruptions, but some of the rival printers promoted the reception of the translation, and bore witness to its linguistic excellence, by supplementing their editions with glossaries. Adam Petri's Basle New Testament of March 1523 is the best known example.[113]

---

[112] J. Cochlaeus, *Historia Martini Lutheri ... jetzo auß dem Latein ins Teutsch gebracht Durch Johann Christoff Hueber ...*, (Ingolstadt: David Sartorius, 1582), p. 121; cited after Heimo Reinitzer, *Biblia deutsch*, (Wolfenbüttel, 1983), p. 193. The Latin original, *Commentaria de actis et scriptis M. Lutheri Saxonis*, was published in 1549.

[113] For this and similar glossaries see D. M. Luther, *Die gantze Heilige Schrifft Deudsch. Wittenberg 1545* edited by H. Volz (Munich, 1972), vol. 3: *Anhang und Dokumente*, pp. 259–69.

Censorship

In view of the success Luther and his supporters were enjoying the authorities had to step in quickly to try to suppress the reading of their books. (But intolerance was not the preserve of the Catholic side only: on 10 December 1520 Luther and the Wittenberg students responded to the Papal Bull *Exsurge Domine* and to the burnings of Lutheran tracts in Liège and Louvain, Cologne and Mainz with a bonfire of their own outside the Elstertor.) Though the Catholic Church's official *Index* was not issued until 1559, censorship was

2.9   The 'Exsurge Domine' Bull (Rome: Giacomo Mazzochi, 1520)

nothing new.[114] As far as the Bible was concerned, as long ago as 1229 the Council of Toulouse had proscribed translations of the Vulgate or of parts thereof, and this decision had been confirmed by a number of Popes in succeeding ages. On 22 March 1485 Berthold von Henneberg, Archbishop of Mainz, forbade clerical and lay persons alike in Mainz's jurisdiction to translate any books from Greek, Latin or any other tongue into the vernacular or to disseminate or buy works so translated. The prevailing climate emerges from a document in the hand of Hartmann Schedel headed 'Avisamentum Salubre, quantum ad exercicium artis impressorie literarum', dating probably from between 1480 and 1490 and possibly linked with Anton Koberger's plan to bring out a German Bible. The document seems to be a kind of expert opinion on whether it was advisable to proceed. It states that although printing can be of use to the Church, it can also be harmful to it if the printers misuse it. In particular, it was harmful to the Church if theological works were translated into the vernacular and translations of the Bible got into the hands of uneducated and inquisitive laymen. This was so much the more dangerous, the document continues, because such inquisitive and uneducated people do not listen to the Word when they hear it from the priest but prefer to discuss the interpretation of the Scriptures with other people and hold themselves to be cleverer than the clergy.[115] Despite such strictures, however, the German authorities in general seem to have had a much more liberal attitude towards vernacular Bibles than was the case in Romance countries.

Nevertheless, it was presumably because of the threat of censorship and political circumspection that Luther's 1522 Testaments appeared anonymously, both in respect of the translator and the printer, though the authorship was evident to friend and foe alike, especially given that the programmatic word *Wittenberg* appeared on the title-page. Scarcely had the 'September Testament' been published, Duke George of Saxony (1471–1539, Duke since 1500) ordered his subjects to hand in every available copy in exchange for payment so that they might be destroyed. Though the plan met with little success, it did result in the

[114] In Germany, G. Rabe published *Postremus catalogus haereticorum Romae conflatus 1559* (Pforzheim, 1560) with the commentary by P. P. Vergerio, and the important Tridentine *Index librorum prohibitorum cum regulis confectis per patres à Tridentina Synodo delectos* was published by Maternus Cholin at Cologne in 1564 and 1568 (both octavos) and in 1576 and 1597 as duodecimos.

[115] F. Geldner, 'Ein in einem Sammelband Hartmann Schedels (Clm 901) überliefertes Gutachten über den Druck deutschsprachiger Bibeln', *GJ*, 47 (1972), 86–9. See also H. Gelhaus, *Der Streit um Luthers Bibelverdeutschung im 16. und 17. Jahrhundert* (Tübingen, 1989), especially vol. 1, pp. 2–5, and vol. 2, pp. 1–6.

toning down of some of the most vehemently criticized features, specifically the depiction of the Whore of Babylon wearing the Papal tiara. But the Duke was not satisfied merely by banning the translation: he commissioned his secretary and chaplain Hieronymus Emser to undertake a critical examination of the 'heretical' translation and then to prepare an acceptable Catholic version. Luther defended himself in the preface to the Old Testament, the first part of which, bearing his name, appeared in 1523, and in the *Sendbrief von Dolmetschen* (1530) and the *Summarien über die Psalmen und Ursachen des Dolmetschens* (1531).

While preachers and orators could quite readily be gagged by rulers and magistrates, the pamphlet was more difficult to stop. In 1523 Pope Adrian VI complained to Emperor Charles V about the cities of Augsburg, Strasbourg and Nuremberg where the authorities allowed Lutheran pamphlets to be printed and sold rather than having them burned. Aware that the imperial authorities themselves were too remote to take effective action, the Imperial Diet at Nuremberg in 1524 authorized the various governments in Germany to enforce censorship in their respective territories, while the imperial commission was to form only a court of appeal. This provision proved unsatisfactory both to the Church and the Empire because many of the princes of north Germany turned Protestant, and the final decree of the Imperial Diet of Speyer of 1529 and that of Augsburg in 1530 instituted in principle censorship by the Empire again. The decree of 1530 was directed particularly against the spread of satirical and slanderous literature, the authors, printers and sellers of which were to be prosecuted. This was ineffectual. A decree of 30 June 1548 reasserted the claims of the Empire to complete control of the press, instituting strict police supervision directed against satirical and heretical literature throughout the Empire, and at the same time making provision for a system of imperial privilege, intended to check piracy and to protect authors and publishers. The Erfurt diet of 1567 again had to legislate against libellous literature, and the decree of Speyer of 1570 restricted the establishment of printing presses to capitals, university towns, and important imperial cities. In 1569 the Emperor ordered the city council of Frankfurt to examine the privileges of all booksellers visiting the fair to see what they had printed during the previous five years and to send an inspection copy of each work to the Reichshofratskanzlei.[116] When the council had to admit its inability to

---

[116] See Kapp, *Geschichte des deutschen Buchhandels*, vol. 1, pp. 608–12. For a more recent summary of the situation in Germany see U. Eisenhardt, 'Staatliche und kirchliche Einflußnahmen auf den deutschen Buchhandel im 16. Jahrhundert', in Göpfert et al., *Beiträge zur Geschichte*, pp. 295–313, and particularly his book *Die kaiserliche Aufsicht über Buchdruck, Buchhandel und Presse im Heiligen Römischen Reich Deutscher Nation*

deal with the situation and sought help in the execution of their duties the Emperor responded by establishing the Imperial Book Commission in Frankfurt in 1579.[117]

A good insight into the measures the authorities attempted to take against the dissemination of undesirable books is given by the leaflet *Catalogus der Büecher vnnd Schrifften, vnser Heilige Religion vnnd Geistliche sachen belangendt, welche im Landt zu Bayrn, offentlich fayl zuhaben vnd zuuerkauffen, erlaubt seindt*, published by Adam Berg at Munich in 1566.[118] It confirms the 1565 ordinance of Duke Albrecht V of Bavaria forbidding booksellers, both local and foreign, to sell any religious works, in Latin or in German, except those printed in Munich, Ingolstadt, Dillingen, Mainz, Cologne, Freiburg im Breisgau, Innsbruck, Paris, Lyon, Venice, Rome, Florence, Bologna, Antwerp, Louvain, and Spain. The only Bibles permitted were those of Eck and Dietenberger and Emser's New Testament. The Psalms of Ottmar Nachtigall (Luscinius) (1524) and Georg Gienger were allowed, as were the postils of Eck, Nausea, Wild, Hoffmaister, Dietenberger and Witzel. The catechisms of the Bishop of Merseburg and of Canisius were approved, as were the prayer-books of Fabri, Nausea, Wild, Canisius and others, printed at Dillingen and Ingolstadt. The pamphlet concludes with a warning against historical works, including John Foxe ('Johannes Foxius Anglicus'), Sebastian Franck, Matthias Flacius Illyricus and others and with a condemnation of the 'devil books' that were popular at the time, the *Eheteufel, Spielteufel*, etc.[119] Another booklet, in Latin, printed by Adam Berg in 1569, not only lists banned books but also includes an 'Index selectissimorum auctorum, ex quibus integra bibliotheca catholica institui recte possit',[120] a list rather different from Spangenberg's concept of an ideal library, needless to say. A third document issued by Berg, also in

---

(1496–1806), (Karlsruhe, 1970). The matter is placed in a broader European context by E. Weyrauch, 'Leges librorum. Kirchen- und profanrechtliche Reglementierungen des Buchhandels in Europa', in Göpfert et al., *Beiträge zur Geschichte*, pp. 315–35.

[117] To take this further see G. Richter, 'Die Sammlung von Drucker-, Verleger- und Buchführerkatalogen in den Akten der Kaiserlichen Bücherkommission', in E. Geck and G. Pressler (eds), *Festschrift für Josef Benzing zum sechzigsten Geburtstag 4. Februar 1964*, (Wiesbaden, 1964), pp. 317–72.

[118] Reprinted in F. H. Reusch (ed.), *Die Indices librorum prohibitorum des 16. Jahrhunderts* (Bibliothek des Litterarischen Vereins in Stuttgart, 176), (Tübingen, 1886), pp. 324–8.

[119] On these see H. Grimm, 'Die deutschen "Teufelbücher" des 16. Jahrhunderts', in *AGB*, 2 (1960), cols. 513–570; and R. Stambaugh (ed.), *Teufelbücher in Auswahl* (5 vols, Berlin, 1970–80). According to Walz, *Deutsche Literatur*, p. 157, there were more than 140 editions of 38 separate works of this kind between 1552 and 1604, representing some 235 000 copies.

[120] Reusch, *Die Indices*, pp. 329–37.

1569, is the *Schul Ordnung der Fürstentumb Obern vnnd Nidern Bayerlands* which prescribes what might be read in schools. [121]

In Nuremberg it was with an eye to possible external political repercussions that the Council, about whose policy we are well informed,[122] prohibited the printing of 'Schmachbüchlein' against the Pope, the Emperor, the King of England, bishops, and other political figures in the Empire. It is not likely that the local printers felt themselves seriously constrained. The same applies to Strasbourg. There were always ways around prohibition. The simplest course was to publish anonymously, but the authorities tried to prevent this: on 7 March 1523 eight Augsburg printers were summoned to the Rathaus to swear not to publish anything anonymously.[123] Alternatively, a publisher could arrange for a book to be printed in another town. Thus Peter Braubach had books prohibited or disapproved of by the Frankfurt authorities printed by Nikolaus Henricus at Oberursel.[124] False imprints were commonly employed, 'Rome' being a favourite.[125] Serious actions against printers, such as the execution of the Nuremberg printer Hans Hergot at Leipzig on 20 May 1527 at the behest of Duke Georg of Saxony for having published *Von der newen wandlung eynes Christlichen lebens*, were rare. The Strasbourg authorities confiscated copies of Grüninger's 1522 edition of Murner's *Von dem grossen Lutherischen Narren*. Grüninger, convinced that it was no worse than any Protestant polemic, retained some of the stock and issued it again, adding an apology for Murner's work. But the council stepped in again and this time confiscated everything. Grüninger was shattered and withdrew from active work at the press, leaving it in the hands of his son Bartholomäus. Interestingly, when Murner visited England in 1523 Henry VIII instructed him to castigate the Strasbourg magistrates for taking a Lutheran stand. Another Strasbourg printer affected by confiscation was Balthasar Beck: it happened in 1531 when Erasmus complained to the council about Sebastian Franck's *Chronick*, and Beck also lost his copies of Melchior Hoffmann's *Prophesy oder weyssagung* and *Prophetisch gesicht*.

---

[121] Ibid., pp. 337–41.

[122] See A. Engelhardt, *Die Reformation in Nürnberg* (Mitteilungen des Vereins für Geschichte der Stadt Nürnberg, 33, 34, 36), (Nuremberg, 1936–39).

[123] On the other hand, K. Schottenloher, *Philipp Ulhart*, (Munich, 1921), p. 10, quotes a case when the council of Augsburg expressly permitted printers to publish their wares – 'schmach schand vnd lesterschriften' – without an impressum.

[124] See H. von Schade, 'Peter Braubach', col. 852.

[125] On the devices employed by booksellers to evade censorship see H. Schnabel, 'Zur historischen Beurteilung der Flugschriftenhändler in der Zeit der frühen Reformation und des Bauernkrieges', *Wissenschaftliche Zeitschrift der Humboldt-Universität Berlin*, **14** (1965), 869–81.

Apart from formal censorship, there were of course unofficial, informal warnings against reading 'erroneous' works. One relatively early example is the anonymous octavo brochure *Ain klarer / vast nützlicher vnterricht / wider ettliche Trück / vnd schleichendt Geyster / so jetz in verborgener weiß außgeen / dadurch viel frommer hertzen verirrt vnd verfürt werden / kürtzlich / getrewer warnungsweiß herfür gebracht*, (n. pr., n. pl., 1523; British Library: C.125.dd.23), which, however, fails to specify which authors and works the author objects to.

Despite all restrictions and constraints, knowledge and new ideas found their way to the reading public. Printers and publishers are perhaps the unsung heroes of the Reformation. They witnessed and often stimulated intellectual life, but sometimes too they were its victims. By taking risks – financial and political – by taking decisions to publish particular works printers helped to determine the course of events.

Select bibliography

This list comprises chiefly bibliographies of the works of the principal writers mentioned and works on printing, publishing and the book trade in sixteenth-century Germany. Other titles are mentioned in the notes.

Amelung, P., 'Humanisten als Mitarbeiter der Drucker', in F. Krafft and D. Wuttke (eds), *Das Verhältnis der Humanisten zum Buch* (Boppard, 1977) pp. 129–44 (Deutsche Forschungsgemeinschaft. Kommission für Humanismusforschung. Mitteilung IV).

Balzer, H. R., *Reformatoren in Niedersachsen. Luthers Anhänger im 16. Jahrhundert* (Wolfenbüttel, 1983) (Wolfenbütteler Schriften zum Lutherjahr 1983 in Niedersachsen, 1).

Baring, G., *Bibliographie der Ausgaben der 'Theologia Deutsch', 1516–1961. Ein Beitrag zur Lutherbibliographie* (Baden-Baden, 1963) (Bibliotheca Bibliographica Aureliana, 8).

Benzing, J., *Lutherbibliographie. Verzeichnis der gedruckten Schriften Martin Luthers bis zu dessen Tod* (Baden-Baden, 1966) (Bibliotheca Bibliographica Aureliana, X, XVI, XIX) (=LB). Second, revised edition, in two volumes, by Helmut Claus (Bibliotheca Bibliographica Aureliana, X and CXLIII) (= Claus, *LB*) (Baden-Baden, 1989 and 1994).

Benzing, J., *Die Buchdrucker des 16. und 17. Jahrhunderts im deutschen Sprachgebiet* (2nd edn, Wiesbaden, 1982) (Beiträge zum Buch- und Bibliothekswesen, 12).

Bezzel, I., 'Das humanistische Frühwerk Friedrich Nauseas (1496–1552)', *Archiv für Geschichte des Buchwesens*, 26 (1986), 217–37.

Bibel und Gesangbuch im Zeitalter der Reformation. Ausstellung zur Erinnerung an die 95 Thesen Martin Luthers vom Jahre 1517 (7. Juli–27. August 1967), Germanisches Nationalmuseum Nürnberg (Nuremberg, 1967).

Bibliographie de la Réforme 1450–1648, published under the auspices of the Commission Internationale d'Histoire Ecclésiastique Comparée, part of the Comité International des Sciences Historiques. Vol. 1: G. Franz, 'Allemagne'; J. N. Bakhuizen, 'Pays-Bas' (3rd edn, Leiden, 1964). Vol. 6: G. Rill, 'Autriche' (Leiden, 1967).

Bietenholz, P. G. and Deutscher, I. B. (eds), *Contemporaries of Erasmus* (3 vols, Toronto, 1985–87).

Black, M. H., 'The printed Bible', in *Cambridge History of the Bible*, vol. 3: S. L. Greenslade (ed.) *The West from the Reformation to the Present Day* (Cambridge, 1963), pp. 408–75.

Black, M. H., 'The typography of Luther's Bible and its influence', *Gutenberg-Jahrbuch*, 44 (1969), 110–13.

Bott, G. (ed.), *Martin Luther und die Reformation in Deutschland. Ausstellung zum 500. Geburtstag Martin Luthers. Veranstaltet vom Germanischen Nationalmuseum Nürnberg in Zusammenarbeit mit dem Verein für Reformationsgeschichte* (Frankfurt am Main, 1983).

Breitenbruch, B., *Predigt, Traktat und Flugschrift im Dienste der Ulmer Reformation. Ausstellung zur 450. Wiederkehr ihrer Durchführung im Jahre 1531. Katalog* (Weissenhorn, 1981). (Veröffentlichungen der Stadtbibliothek Ulm, 1).

Buchwald, G., 'Stadtschreiber M. Stephan Roth in Zwickau in seiner literarisch-buchhändlerischen Bedeutung für die Reformationszeit', *Archiv für die Geschichte des deutschen Buchhandels*, 16 (1893), 6–246.

Chrisman, M. U., *Lay Culture, Learned Culture. Books and Social Change in Strasbourg, 1480–1599* (New Haven, 1982).

Chrisman, M. U., *Bibliography of Strasbourg Imprints 1480–1599* (New Haven, 1982).

Clemen, O., *Die lutherische Reformation und der Buchdruck* (Leipzig, 1939).

Cole, R. G., 'The dynamics of printing in the sixteenth century', in L. P. Buck and J. W. Zophy (eds), *The Social History of the Reformation* (Columbus, 1972), pp. 93 ff.

Cole, R. G., 'Reformation printers – unsung heroes', *Sixteenth Century Journal*, 15 (1984), 326–39.

Crofts, R. A., 'Printing, reform, and the Catholic Reformation in Germany (1521–1549)', *Sixteenth Century Journal*, 16 (1985), 369–81.

Davies, C. S. L., *Peace, Print and Protestantism, 1450–1558* (London, 1975).

Dickens, A. G., *The German Nation and Martin Luther* (London, 1974).

Diehl, E., 'Herstellung und Verbreitung der Lutherbibel im Wandel der Jahrhunderte', in *Die Lutherbibel. Festschrift* (Stuttgart, 1934), pp. 89–115.

Edwards Jr, M. U., 'Catholic controversial literature, 1518–1555: some statistics', *Archiv für Reformationsgeschichte*, **79** (1988), 189–205.

Eisenstein, E. L., 'The advent of printing and the Protestant revolt', in R. M. Kingdon (ed.), *Transition and Revolution. Problems and Issues of European Renaissance and Reformation History* (Minneapolis, 1974) pp. 235–70.

Eisenstein, E. L., *The Printing Press as an Agent of Change. Communications and cultural transformations in Early Modern Europe* (2 vols, Cambridge, 1979).

Eisenstein, E. L., *The Printing Revolution in Early Modern Europe* (Cambridge, 1983).

Engelsing, R., *Der Bürger als Leser. Lesergeschichte in Deutschland 1500–1800* (Stuttgart, 1974).

Finsler, G., *Zwingli-Bibliographie. Verzeichnis der gedruckten Schriften von und über Zwingli* (Zurich, 1897; reprint Nieuwkoop, 1968).

Franz, G., 'Bibliographie der Schriften Thomas Müntzers', *Zeitschrift des Vereins für thüringische Geschichte*, **42** (1940), 161–73.

Freys, E. and Barge, H., 'Verzeichnis der gedruckten Schriften des Andreas Bodenstein von Karlstadt', *Zentralblatt für Bibliothekswesen*, **21** (1904) 153–331, (Reprint Nieuwkoop, 1965).

Geisenhof, G., *Bibliotheca Bugenhagiana. Bibliographie der Druckschriften des D. Joh. Bugenhagen* (Leipzig, 1908, reprint Nieuwkoop, 1963). (Quellen und Darstellungen aus der Geschichte des Reformationsjahrhunderts, 6).

Gollob, H., *Bischof Friedrich Nausea (1496–1552). Probleme der Gegenreformation* (2nd enlarged edn, Nieuwkoop, 1967).

Götze, A., *Die hochdeutschen Drucker der Reformationszeit* (2nd edn with a preface by Martin von Hase, Berlin, 1963).

Grossmann, M., *Wittenberger Drucke 1502–1517: ein bibliographischer Beitrag zur Geschichte des Humanismus in Deutschland* (Vienna, 1971).

Gruber, L. F., 'The Wittenberg originals of the Luther Bible', *Papers of the Bibliographical Society of America*, **12** (1918), 1–33.

Haller, B., *Der Buchdruck Münsters, 1485 bis 1583: eine Bibliographie* (Münster, 1986).

Hillerbrand, H. J., *Bibliographie des Täufertums 1520–1630* (Gütersloh, 1962).

Hohenemser, P., *Flugschriften-Sammlung Gustav Freytag* (Frankfurt am Main, 1925, reprint Nieuwkoop, 1955).

Index Aureliensis. Catalogus librorum sedecimo saeculo impressorum (Baden-Baden, 1965–).

Joachim, J., 'Die Drucker Johannes Grunenberg und Georg Rhau in Wittenberg', *Zentralblatt für Bibliothekswesen*, 21 (1905), 433–9.

Kaczerowsky, K., *Sebastian Franck. Bibliographie* (Wiesbaden, 1976).

Kapp, F., *Geschichte des Deutschen Buchhandels bis in das siebzehnte Jahrhundert*. (= F. Kapp and J. Goldfriedrich, *Geschichte des Deutschen Buchhandels*, 1) (Leipzig, 1886), especially pp. 405–47.

Kawerau, G., *Hieronymus Emser. Ein Lebensbild aus der Reformationsgeschichte* (Halle, 1898) (Schriften des Vereins für Reformationsgeschichte, 61).

Keen, R., *A Checklist of Melanchthon Imprints through 1560* (St Louis, 1988) (Sixteenth Century Bibliography, 27).

Keunecke, H. O., 'Die Drucklegung der Brandenburg-Nürnbergischen Kirchenordnung. Kosten, Preise und Mengenrabatt im Jahre 1533', *Archiv für Geschichte des Buchwesens*, 21 (1980), cols 769–90.

Kittelson, J. M., *Wolfgang Capito. From Humanist to Reformer* (Leiden, 1975) (Studies in Medieval and Reformation Thought, 17).

Klaiber, W. (ed.), *Katholische Kontroverstheologen und Reformer des 16. Jahunderts* (Münster, 1978) (Reformationsgeschichtliche Studien und Texte, 116).

Knepper, J., *Jakob Wimpfeling (1450–1528). Sein Leben und seine Werke nach den Quellen dargestellt* (Freiburg im Breisgau, 1902, reprint Nieuwkoop, 1965).

Köhler, H. J. (ed.), *Flugschriften als Massenmedium der Reformationszeit. Beiträge zum Tübinger Symposium* (Stuttgart, 1981) (Spätmittelalter und Frühe Neuzeit. Tübinger Beiträge zur Geschichtsforschung, 13).

Köhler, W., *Bibliographia Brentiana. Bibliographisches Verzeichnis der gedruckten und ungedruckten Schriften und Briefe des Reformators Johannes Brenz* (Berlin, 1904; reprint Nieuwkoop, 1963).

Kolb, R., *Nikolaus von Amsdorf (1483–1565). Popular Polemics in the Preservation of Luther's Legacy* (Nieuwkoop, 1978) (Bibliotheca Humanistica et Reformatorica, 24).

Krüger, G., *Hans Lufft und die Anfänge des Wittenberger Buchdrucks* (Wittenberg, 1936).

Kuczynski, A., *Thesaurus libellorum historiam Reformationis illustrantium. Verzeichnis einer Sammlung von nahezu 3000 Flugschriften Luthers und seiner Zeitgenossen* (Leipzig, 1870–74; reprint Nieuwkoop, 1969).

Künast, H.-J., 'Getrucht zu Augspurg': *Buchdruck und Buchhandel in Augsburg zwischen 1468 und 1555* (Tübingen, 1997) (Studia Augustana, 8).

Liebmann, M., *Urbanus Rhegius und die Anfänge der Reformation. Beiträge zu seinem Leben, seiner Lehre und seinem Wirken bis zum Augsburger Reichstag von 1530 mit einer Bibliographie seiner Schriften* (Münster, 1980) (Reformationsgeschichtliche Studien und Texte, 117).

Loesche, G., *Johannes Mathesius. Ein Lebens- und Sittenbild aus der Reformationszeit* (Gotha, 1895; reprint Nieuwkoop, 1971).

Lorz, J., *Bibliographia Linckiana. Bibliographie der gedruckten Schriften Dr. Wenzeslaus Lincks (1483–1547)* (Bibliotheca humanistica et reformatorica, 18) (Nieuwkoop, 1977).

Lülfing, H., 'Universität, Buchdruck und Buchhandel in Wittenberg, vornehmlich im 16. Jahrhundert', in *450 Jahre Martin Luther-Universität Halle-Wittenberg*, vol. 1: *Wittenberg 1502–1817* (Halle, 1952), pp. 377–418.

Luther, J., 'Aus der Druckerpraxis der Reforamtionszeit (1)', *Zentralblatt für Bibliothekswesen* 27 (1910), 237–64.

Luther, J., 'Die Schnellarbeit der Wittenberger Buchdruckerpressen in der Reformationszeit', *Zentralblatt für Bibliothekswesen* 31 (1914), 244–64.

Luther, J., 'Der Wittenberger Buchdruck in seinem Übergang zur Reformationspresse', in *Lutherstudien zur vierten Jahrhundertfeier der Reformation veröffentlicht von den Mitarbeitern der Weimarer Lutherausgabe* (Weimar, 1917), pp. 261–82.

Luther, J., 'Drucker- und Verlegernöte in Wittenberg zur Zeit des Schmalkaldischen Krieges', in G. Leyh (ed.), *Aufsätze, Fritz Milkau gewidmet* (Leipzig, 1921), pp. 229–43.

Luther, J., 'Luthers Bibel und die Buchdruckerkunst', *Die Wartburg*, 33 (1934), 333–40.

[Luther] *D. Martin Luthers Werke. Kritische Gesamtausgabe* (Weimar, 1883–1987) Weimarer Ausgabe (= WA).

[Luther] *D. Martin Luthers Werke. Kritische Gesamtausgabe. Briefwechsel* (Weimar, 1930–) Weimarer Ausgabe (= WA Br.).

Mejer, W., *Der Buchdrucker Hans Lufft zu Wittenberg* (2nd edn, Leipzig, 1923).

[Melanchthon] C. G. Bretschneider (ed.) *Philippi Melanchthonis opera quae supersunt omnia*, (Corpus Reformatorum, 1–28) (Halle, 1836–60; with supplement (5 vols) Leipzig, 1910–29; reprint 1968).

Mentz, F., 'Bibliographische Zusammenstellung der gedruckten Schriften Butzers' in *Zur 400-jährigen Geburtsfeier Martin Butzers* (Strasbourg, 1891), pp. 99–163.

Metzler, J., 'Verzeichnis der Schriften Ecks', in *Tres orationes funebres in exequiis Joannis Eckii habitae* (Münster, 1930) pp. lxvii–cxxxii (Corpus Catholicorum, 16).

Moeller, B., 'Stadt und Buch. Bemerkungen zur Struktur der reformatorischen Bewegung in Deutschland', in W. J. Mommsen (ed.), *Stadtbürgertum und Adel in der Reformation. Studien zur Sozialgeschichte der Reformation in England und Deutschland* (Veröffentlichungen des Deutschen Historischen Instituts London, 5) (Stuttgart, 1979), pp. 25–39.

Mullett, M., *Popular Culture and Popular Protest in Late Medieval and Early Modern Europe* (New York, 1988).

Newman, J. O., 'The Word made print: Luther's 1522 New Testament in an age of mechanical reproduction', *Representations*, 11 (1985), 95–133.

Holger, N., 'Stephan Roths Buchhandel', in H. G. Göpfert, P. Vodosek, E. Weyrauch and R. Wittmann (eds), *Beiträge zur Geschichte des Buchwesens im konfessionellen Zeitalter* (Wiesbaden, 1985), pp. 241–50 (Wolfenbütteler Schriften zur Geschichte des Buchwesens, 11).

Packull, W. O., 'The image of the "Common Man" in the early pamphlets of the Reformation (1520–1525)', *Historical Reflections*, 12 (1985), 253–77.

Reinitzer, H., *Biblia deutsch. Luthers Bibelübersetzung und ihre Tradition* (Wolfenbüttel, 1983).

Richter, G., *Die Schriften Georg Witzels bibliographisch bearbeitet* (Fulda, 1913; reprint Nieuwkoop, 1963) (Veröffentlichung des Fuldaer Geschichtsvereins, 10).

Robinson-Hammerstein, H. (ed.), *The Transmission of Ideas in the Lutheran Reformation* (Dublin, 1989).

Roth, F. W. E., 'Die Schriften des Otto Brunfels 1519–1536', *Jahrbuch für Geschichte, Sprache und Literatur Elsaß-Lothringens*, 16 (1900), 257–88.

Russell, P. A., *Lay Theology in the Reformation. Popular Pamphleteers in South-West Germany 1521–1525* (Cambridge, 1986).

Schade, H. von, 'Luther und die Folgen für das Bibliothekswesen', *Auskunft* (1984) no. 2, pp. 72–91.

Schmidt, J., *Lestern, lesen und lesen hören. Kommunikationsstudien zur deutschen Prosasatire der Reformationszeit* (Berne, 1977) (Europäische Hochschulschriften. Reihe I. Deutsche Literatur und Germanistik, 179).

Schmitz, W., 'Buchdruck und Reformation in Köln', *Jahrbuch des Kölnischen Geschichtsvereins*, 55 (1984), 117–54.

Schottenloher, K., 'Buchdrucker und Buchführer im Dienste der Reformation', *Realencyklopädie für protestantische Theologie*, 23 (1913) 270–74.

Schottenloher, K., 'Die Druckauflagen der päpstlichen Lutherbulle "Exsurge Domine"', *Zeitschrift für Bücherfreunde* N.F., 9, 2 (1917),

197–208.

Schottenloher, K., *Philipp Ulhart. Ein Augsburger Winkeldrucker und Helfershelfer der 'Schwärmer' und Wiedertäufer', 1523–1529* (Munich, 1921; reprint Nieuwkoop, 1967) (Historische Forschungen und Quellen, **4**).

Schottenloher, K., *Das alte Buch* (3rd edn, Braunschweig, 1956) (Bibliothek für Kunst- und Antiquitätenfreunde, **14**), especially 'Martin Luthers deutsche Bibelübersetzung' (pp. 167–85).

Schottenloher, K., *Bibliographie zur deutschen Geschichte im Zeitalter der Glaubensspaltung, 1517–1585* (Stuttgart, 1956–66).

Scribner, R. W., *For the Sake of Simple Folk. Popular Propaganda for the German Reformation* (Cambridge, 1981).

Scribner, R. W., *Popular Culture and Popular Movements in Reformation Germany* (London, 1988).

Seebaß, G., *Bibliographica Osiandrica. Bibliographie der gedruckten Schriften Andreas Osianders d. Ä. (1496–1552)* (Nieuwkoop, 1971).

Sehling, E. (ed.), *Die evangelischen Kirchenordnungen des 16. Jahrhunderts*, (vols 1–5, Leipzig, 1902–13; vols 6–15 Tübingen, 1955–77).

Spahn, M., *Johannes Cochläus. Ein Lebensbild aus der Zeit der Kirchenspaltung* (Berlin, 1898, reprint Nieuwkoop, 1964).

Spitz, L., *The Religious Renaissance of the German Humanists* (Cambridge, Mass., 1963).

Staedtke, J., *Heinrich Bullinger. Bibliographie. Bd. 1: Beschreibendes Verzeichnis der gedruckten Werke von Heinrich Bullinger* (Zurich, 1972).

Staehelin, E., 'Oekolampad-Bibliographie. Verzeichnis der im 16. Jahrhundert erschienenen Oekolampaddrucke', *Basler Zeitschrift für Geschichte und Altertumskunde*, **17** (1918), 1–119. (Reprint, with the supplement of 1928, Nieuwkoop, 1963).

Stiegler, E., 'Die Durchsetzung des Buchverlages in Wittenberg (1522 bis 1533)', *Marginalien*, **111** (1988), 39–48.

Stopp, H., 'Verbreitung und Zentren des Buchdrucks auf hochdeutschem Sprachgebiet im 16. und 17. Jahrhundert', *Sprachwissenschaft*, **3** (1978), 237–61.

Strauss, G., *Nuremberg in the Sixteenth Century: City Life and Politics between the Middle Ages and Modern Times* (revised edn, Bloomington, 1976).

Strauss, G., *Luther's House of Learning. Indoctrination of the Young in the German Reformation* (Baltimore, 1978).

Strohm, S. and Zwink, E. (eds), *Ursprung der Biblia Deutsch von Martin Luther. Ausstellung in der Württembergischen Landesbibliothek Stuttgart ... 1983* (Stuttgart, 1983).

Swanson, R. G., 'The changing word. A media analysis of the writings of Martin Luther' (PhD thesis, University of Pittsburg, 1972).

Ullmann, E. (ed.), *Kunst und Reformation* (Leipzig, 1982).

Verzeichnis der im deutschen Sprachbereich erschienenen Drucke des 16. Jahrhunderts (VD 16) (Stuttgart, 1983–).

Vogel, P. H., 'Luthers deutsche Bibel sowie römisch-katholische deutsche Bibeldrucke im 16. Jahrhundert', *Libri. International Library Review*, 8 (1958), 49–66.

Vogel, P. H., *Europäische Bibeldrucke des 15. und 16. Jahrhunderts in den Volkssprachen. Ein Beitrag zur Bibliographie des Bibeldrucks* (Baden-Baden, 1962) (Bibliotheca bibliographica aureliana, 5).

Volz, H., *Bibel und Bibeldruck in Deutschland im 15. und 16. Jahrhundert* (Mainz, 1960) (Kleiner Druck der Gutenberg-Gesellschaft, 70).

Volz, H., 'Aus der Wittenberger Druckpraxis der Lutherbibel (1522–46)', *Gutenberg-Jahrbuch*, 36 (1961), 142–55.

Volz, H., 'Zur Geschichte des Wittenberg Buchdrucks 1544–47', *Gutenberg-Jahrbuch*, 38 (1963), 113–19.

Volz, H., 'Die Lutherbibliographie im Lichte der Geschichte', *Gutenberg-Jahrbuch*, 44 (1969), 313–30.

Volz, H., 'Martin Luthers Schriften und ihre Druckgeschichte', in J. Möckelmann (ed.), *Sprache und Sprachhandeln. Festschrift für Gustav Bebermeyer zum 80. Geburtstag am 16. 10. 1970* (Hildesheim, 1974), pp. 1–25.

Volz, H., 'Verlag und Absatz von Lutherbriefausgaben – ein verlegerisch-buchhändlerisches Problem', *Gutenberg-Jahrbuch*, 47 (1972), 237–43.

Volz, H., *Martin Luthers deutsche Bibel* (Hamburg 1978).

Wedewer, H., *Johannes Dietenberger 1475–1537. Sein Leben und Wirken* (Freiburg in Breisgau, 1888; reprint Nieuwkoop, 1967).

Weismann, C., *Eine kleine Biblia. Die Katechismen von Luther und Brenz. Einführung und Texte* (Stuttgart, 1985).

Whaley, J., *Religious Toleration and Social Change in Hamburg 1529–1819* (Cambridge, 1985).

Wiedemann, T., *Dr Johann Eck. Eine Monographie* (Regensburg, 1865).

Williams, G. H., *The Radical Reformation* (Philadelphia, 1962).

Wolf, H., *Martin Luther. Eine Einführung in germanistische Luther-Studien* (Stuttgart, 1980). (Sammlung Metzler, M 193).

Wolf, H., *Germanistische Luther-Bibliographie. Martin Luthers deutsches Sprachschaffen im Spiegel des internationalen Schrifttums der Jahre 1880–1980* (Heidelberg, 1985).

Wolgast, E., *Die Wittenberger Luther-Ausgabe. Zur Überlieferungsgeschichte der Werke Luthers im 16. Jahrhundert* (Nieuwkoop, 1971).

CHAPTER THREE

French-speaking regions, 1520–62

Francis M. Higman

The geographical limits of this survey are inevitably somewhat impre-
cise. 'French' refers not to a political but to a linguistic entity. 'France'
and 'the francophone area' were different in the sixteenth century, just
as they are today. In this essay, we shall take into account all the
French-speaking regions of Europe, and all editions in French, since in
many cases a major role was played by publications produced outside
the sphere of control of the French authorities, at first in the Low
Countries, later in Geneva.

The (approximate) chronological limits we have suggested are easily
explained. Luther's writings begin their first penetration into France
around 1520 (see Johann Froben's letter to Luther dated 14 February
1519, in which the printer claims to have sold 600 copies of Luther's
works in France; he adds that the Paris theologians are particularly
interested in them). The year 1562 marks a brutal turning point in the
history of France, with the outbreak of the civil wars, the so-called wars
of religion; they inaugurated a period radically different from the early
days.

The first printing press in Paris, indeed in France, was set up by
theologians, in the Collège de Sorbonne, in 1470. The origins of the
French printed book are thus found under the twin patronage of education and religion.

In fact, alongside editions of grammatical and rhetorical school-books,
classical authors and scholastic theology, and, of course, alongside novels and other literary texts, the first Parisian printers turned out a
considerable number of works of piety in French: the Bible in Jean de
Rély's translation, lives of saints, liturgies and books of hours, instructional manuals for nuns, for curates and for 'the simple' (of particular
note are the little treatises of Jean Charlier de Gerson, pioneer of the use
of the written word for religious education), brief explanations of the
faith, dialogues, meditations, poetry – French religious literature is
abundant before the end of the fifteenth century.[1]

---

[1] Febvre/Martin, pp. 400 and following. See also Dominique Coq, 'Les Incunables:
textes anciens, textes nouveaux', *HÉF* 1, 177–93.

Given that the religious book was far from being an innovation, what impact did the Reformation have on the history of the book? First, and most obviously, the Reformation offered a 'new' doctrine (rather, from the Reformers' point of view, a doctrine restored to its original purity). That doctrine was based on the authority of scripture, not on a magisterial Church. The text thus took on a primary importance: an author had to justify his arguments by biblical references, without resorting (as does the Bishop and Doctor Guillaume Petit, in the *Viat de salut*) to the crushing argument: 'If you have some doubt, or temptation in your faith ... leave it all to God and the Church, saying: *Credo in Deum, Credo sanctam ecclesiam*. And ask no further.' Thirdly, the Reformation book did not treat doctrine as taken for granted, but as problematic and requiring discussion. It was thus a new form of literature, not concerned only with the transmission of an agreed doctrine, but with debate, argument, battle.

Of course there was not a total break. Works of piety continued to appear in the sixteenth century as before – the library of the son of Christopher Columbus contains numerous examples.[2] Moreover, some new texts became absorbed into earlier genres: the new message was communicated in orthodox disguise.

The book as an industrial product

When one writes about the French Reformation book, one must necessarily concentrate on books in the French language, with only minor references to productions in Latin. The lists of works censured by the Paris Faculty of Theology published between 1544 and 1556[3] illustrate why. In all, 250 books in French were condemned. The proportion of these books printed in France – some 40 titles – was relatively small; but clearly, all 250 titles were destined for a French-language public. As regards books in Latin, 278 titles featured in the 'catalogues' of condemned books; but 251 were printed outside France, and were destined for a Europe-wide market, not only for France. Only 27 Latin titles were printed within the kingdom (eight in Lyon, 19 in Paris, including 12 editions of Robert Estienne's Bibles), and may thus be regarded as specifically 'French'. This extraordinarily small proportion of Reformation works in Latin printed in France deserves comment, and we shall return later to the subject.

---

[2] J. Babelon, *La Bibliothèque française de Fernand Colomb* (Paris, 1913).
[3] See *Index 1*.

The modest and dispersed beginnings of production (1523–33)

There were two places where the French Reformation book appeared simultaneously – Paris and Basle – and a point of contact between the two: the Basle bookseller Conrad Resch, owner of the bookshop *A l'écu de Bâle* in Paris.[4] We find here an intellectual circle in which the works of Erasmus and of Luther were equally appreciated, and printed side by side. In 1524–25, the Basle branch of the firm belonging to Resch and to his relatives Jean Vaugris and Conrad Wattenschnee published Farel's *Pater noster*, which includes Luther's commentary on the Creed, Claude Chansonnette's translation of a work by Erasmus, and a New Testament copied from a Parisian edition brought to Basle by Resch.[5] But in Erasmus's city, which moreover lacked a French-speaking community, there were only a few isolated editions thereafter until almost 1550.

It was probably the same Conrad Resch who brought to Paris a copy of Farel's *Pater noster*, for a second edition printed with the material of Simon de Colines, the printer of the Meaux group.[6] This was the first active circle of writers determined on the reform of the Church: Lefèvre d'Étaples, Louis de Berquin, Pierre Caroli. They were supported by two printers, Simon de Colines and Simon Du Bois. From this centre came:

Le Nouveau Testament translated by Lefèvre d'Étaples (Simon de Colines, 1523 and 1524, and Simon Du Bois, 1525, plus a possibly pirated edition by Antoine Couteau in 1524).[7]

Les Epistres et evangiles des cinquante et deux dimanches de l'an by Lefèvre d'Étaples and his disciples (Simon Du Bois, 1525; possibly an earlier edition, now lost, in 1523).[8]

L'Oraison de Jesuchrist [by Farel and Luther] (Simon de Colines, c.1525; subsequently adapted for inclusion in the *Livre de vraye et parfaicte oraison*, Simon Du Bois, 1528).[9]

---

[4] On the relation between Conrad Resch and France see P. Bietenholz, *Basle and France in the Sixteenth Century* (Geneva, 1971), pp. 27–43. Cf. also G. Farel, *Le Pater noster et le Credo en françoys*, F. M. Higman (ed.), (Geneva, 1982), pp. 19–20.

[5] A.-L.- Herminjard, *Correspondance des Réformateurs dans les pays de langue française* (Geneva, 1866–97), vol. 1, p. 306.

[6] F. M. Higman, 'Les traductions françaises de Luther, 1524–1550', in J.-Fr. Gilmont (ed.), *Palaestra typographica: aspects de la production du livre humaniste et religieux au XVIe siècle* (Aubel, 1984), pp. 15–27.

[7] Facsimile reproduction of the 1523 Simon de Colines edition, by M. A. Screech, (New York, 1970).

[8] Facsimile reproduction of the 1525 edition, by M. A. Screech, (Geneva, 1963).

[9] On the *Livre de vraye et parfaicte oraison*, see F. M. Higman, 'Luther et la piété de l'église gallicane', *Revue d'Histoire et de Philosophie religieuses*, 63 (1983), 91–111.

Brief Recueil de la substance et principal fondement de la doctrine Evangelique (anonymous text variously attributed to François Lambert or to Nicolas Le Sueur of Meaux; printed by Simon Du Bois, *c.*1525).

Erasmus, *Le Symbole des apostres* [translated by Louis de Berquin], (Simon Du Bois, 1525).

Erasmus, *Brefve Admonition de la maniere de prier* [translated by Louis de Berquin], (Simon Du Bois, 1525).

Erasmus, *Declamation des louanges de mariage* [translated by Louis de Berquin], (Simon Du Bois, 1525).[10]

The five last editions are undated, and the place of printing and name of printer are not mentioned; in the whole list, Erasmus is the only author named.

During the capitivity of Francis I in Madrid (1525–26) the combined efforts of the Faculty of Theology and the Parlement led to the dispersal of the Meaux group and to the condemnation, in August 1525, of all Bible translations.[11] Simon de Colines lost interest in this trade in more or less dangerous publications; subsequently his stepson Robert Estienne became involved in the production of Latin Bibles, which landed him in deep trouble with the theologians. In 1525–29, Simon Du Bois limited himself to printing humanist and medical texts, and some apparently orthodox religious works; then, in 1529, he moved his press to Alençon where, under the protection of Marguerite de Navarre, he produced – alongside the Queen's *Miroir de l'âme pécheresse* – a series of short books, almost all without the printer's address, and of a much tougher nature: translations from Luther, Farel's *Sommaire*, the *Combat chrestien*.[12] In Paris the production of Reformation or reforming books ceased almost entirely after 1526. An occasional daring spirit may have slipped a few dubious passages into his Latin editions, for example Chrétien Wechel (Conrad Resch's successor at the *Écu de Bâle*), who inserted two treatises by Luther in his edition of Otto Brunfels's *Precationes Biblicae* in 1530, or the courageous Robert Estienne, who devoted his philological learning to the textual study of the Bible and who, a quarter of a century later,

---

[10] The three Erasmus texts edited in facsimile by E. V Telle, (Geneva, 1976, 1979).

[11] See J. K. Farge, *Orthodoxy and Reform in Early Reformation France: The Faculty of Theology of Paris, 1500–1543* (Leiden, 1985), pp. 177–9; F. M. Higman, *Censorship and the Sorbonne* (Geneva, 1979), pp. 24–7, 77–80.

[12] On Simon Du Bois see G. Clutton, 'Simon Du Bois of Paris and Alençon', *GJ* (1937), 124–30; A. Tricard, 'La propagande évangélique en France: l'imprimeur Simon Du Bois (1525–1534)', in G. Berthoud et al. (eds), *Aspects de la propagande religieuse* (Geneva, 1957), pp. 1–37.

Summaire a Bri-
efue declaration
daufcuns lieux fort
neceffaites a bng chaf-
cun chreftien/ pour mettre
fa confiance en dieu/et
apber fon pro-
chain.

Jaques Chap.i

En manfuetube et doulceur
recepuez fa parolfe de dieu / fa-
quelle eft puiffante de fauluer
noz ames.

¶ Imprime a Turin Lan de
grace 1525

3.1 Guillaume Farel, *Summaire et brieve declaration* Printed in Turin [Alençon]: [Simon du Bois], 1525 [c.1533]

ended up by emigrating to Geneva.[13] It is significant that no edition of the Bible in French appeared in Paris between 1527 and 1565.[14] Where, then, were the printers to come from for this new religious literature? Lyon? One would have expected a considerable amount of activity in the second-largest city in the kingdom, the only important printing centre outside Paris, and without direct supervision either by a Parlement or by a university. Yet, despite the contacts between Basle and Lyon established by the Resch/Wattenschnee clan, Lyon printers seem to have contributed little to the early history of the Reformation

---

[13] See A. E. Armstrong, *Robert Estienne, Royal Printer* (Cambridge, 1954; revised edn, Appleford, 1986).

[14] B. T. Chambers, *Bibliography of French Bibles: Fifteenth- and Sixteenth-Century French-Language Editions of the Scriptures* (Geneva, 1983), p. 356.

book. It was only around 1529 that Pierre de Vingle, son-in-law of Claude Nourry (who printed the first editions of Rabelais's novels in 1532), launched a series of editions which rapidly led to his exile: Farel's *Sommaire* alongside an Erasmian commentary on the Lord's Prayer, the *Complainte de la Paix* by Erasmus himself, Lefèvre's *Epistres et evangiles*, Brunfels's *Prieres et oraisons de la Bible* in French, and several editions of the *Nouveau Testament*.[15] But Vingle was 'thrown out of Lyon because of his New Testaments', as he put it in 1532; the city's religious printing returned to the traditional path – the *Imitation de Jésus Christ*, Guillaume Petit's *Viat de salut*.

So where to print? There remained locations outside the kingdom but with the possibility of distributing material in France. Two cities stand out, Antwerp and Strasbourg.[16] In Antwerp, the printer Martin Lempereur (De Keysere), at first aided by Guillaume Vorsterman, took over from the Paris presses the task of completing Lefèvre's Bible (1530), and also produced a series of translations from Luther, Brunfels and Erasmus in the period 1525–35 (date of Lempereur's death).[17] Strasbourg was a 'free' city, had turned Protestant in 1523, and in 1525 received some of the refugees from Meaux: Lefèvre and Girard Roussel stayed in the city, along with François Lambert and Guillaume Farel, who had definitively separated from the Roman Church. The Strasbourg printer Johann Herwagen Sr had found his speciality in producing Latin translations of Luther's works – and since the German language was almost unknown in France, these Latin translations formed an essential link in the transmission of Lutheran texts in France. The printers Johann Prüss Jr and Johann Schott (the latter working for the bookseller Wolfgang Köpfel, uncle of the Reformer Wolfgang Capito), were producing French translations of Luther (including the *Liberté chrétienne*, *c.*1525, the first French printing known in Strasbourg), and works by local authors, Wolfgang Schuch and Guillaume Dumolin.[18] Strasbourg thus contributed much to the dissemination of Reformation thought in France, by the Latin editions of the German Reformers (the first edition of the *Precationes Biblicae* came from here, in 1528); but, as concerns printing in French, Strasbourg does not seem to have joined the network of

---

[15] E. Droz, 'Pierre de Vingle, l'imprimeur de Farel', in Berthoud et al., *Aspects*, pp. 38–78.

[16] The most important study on the spread of Reformation literature is still W. G. Moore, *La Réforme allemande et la littérature française. Recherches sur la notoriété de Luther en France* (Strasbourg, 1930).

[17] See p. 199.

[18] R. Peter, 'Les premiers ouvrages français imprimés à Strasbourg', *L'Annuaire des amis du vieux-Strasbourg*, 4 (1974), 73–108; 8 (1978), 11–75; 10 (1980), 35–46; 14 (1984) 17–28. On the texts by Schuch and Dumolin, see 4 (1974), 74–9, and also p. 218.

connections which linked Lyon, Paris, Alençon and Antwerp, and thanks to which we find the *Prieres et oraisons de la Bible* or Erasmus's *Enchiridion* in Lyon and in Antwerp, the *Livre de vraye et parfaicte oraison* in Paris and Antwerp, Luther's *Exposition sur le Magnificat* in Alençon and Antwerp, the *Sommaire* in Alençon and Lyon, and the *Nouveau Testament* in all four cities.

Certain features characterized the centres of production of this first period of the Reformation: rather than writing of cities, one should rather consider isolated printers working to spread this new literature. They were individuals, even if often with family connections, like the Resch clan; and they were not normally among the leaders of the profession: we do not find Josse Badius or Jean Petit among the printers, nor Galliot du Pré among the booksellers. The speciality of the press in which Pierre de Vingle worked in Lyon was the popular novel; in Paris, Simon Du Bois printed to order for some of the most influential booksellers, but with relatively modest equipment.

Moreover, in all cases except Strasbourg, which focused chiefly on publications composed locally, the printers did not differentiate clearly between non-schismatic reform and definitive Reformation: the works of Erasmus or Lefèvre appeared alongside those of Farel or Luther in the output of Simon Du Bois, Martin Lempereur and Pierre de Vingle.

Finally, until 1533 there was no printing house dedicated to the Reformation cause and established in a French-speaking area definitely won over to the Reformation – and therefore free to express a new thought. In this first period of the Reformation, its literature is characterized by clandestinity and marginality.

The heroic period of the Reformation book (1533–50)

A second period begins around 1533, marked by the establishment of the Reformation in French-speaking Switzerland and almost simultaneously by the setting up of a book industry there. The same Pierre de Vingle who was expelled from Lyon in 1532 worked temporarily in Geneva in 1533, and settled in Neuchâtel the following year.[19] Between 1533 and 1535 he printed some 20 books, but died after producing his masterpiece, the Bible in the French translation by Olivétan. Geneva accepted the Reformation in May 1536, and only a few months later the Vaudois printer Jean Girard arrived in the city. In both cases, the invitation came from the same man, Guillaume Farel. Farel was acutely

---

[19] See Droz, 'P. de Vingle'; Th. Dufour, *Notice bibliographique sur le Catéchisme et la Confession de foi de Calvin (1537) et sur les autres livres imprimés à Genève et à Neuchâtel dans les premiers temps de la Réforme (1533–1540)* (Geneva, 1878).

conscious of the importance of printing to the Reformation movement, and in particular of the need to install presses in localities firmly won over to the Reformation. When Farel met the Piedmont Vaudois at the Synod of Chanforan, he succeeded in obtaining from them 800 écus to pay for the translation and printing of the Olivétan Bible. The size of this donation suggests that it was intended not only to finance the edition itself, but more generally to fit out Pierre de Vingle's press and to finance other publications. These Provençal-speaking Vaudois can only have had a minor interest in a French-language Bible; one has the impression that Farel, obsessed by the need to install an evangelical press, obtained the money while thinking more of the French public than of the Vaudois.[20]

Between 1536 and 1550, Girard was responsible for the great majority of Genevan editions: this was the heroic period of Reformed printing, with the rise of Calvin, the establishment of the Reformed book trade, and the introduction of a censorship system in France. During this period of struggle, there were only three printers working in Geneva – not counting Wigand Koeln, who kept his distance from the new theological orientation of the city: Jean Michel, who inherited Vingle's material (1538–44),[21] Michel Du Bois (1540–41),[22] and Girard, the only Reformed printer in the city after 1544. We shall see below the extraordinary impact achieved by this isolated workshop.

One result of the establishment of the Reformation in Geneva was the almost total concentration of Reformation printing in that city during the 1540s. In Strasbourg, the organization of a community of French refugees (of which Calvin was the first pastor, in 1538) led to an increase in activity by printers such as J. Knobloch Jr and, after 1546, Rémy Guédon; but they printed mainly for the local market: liturgies, hymn-books, catechisms.[23] On the other hand, the Strasbourg tradition of printing in Latin was maintained: Calvin preferred to have his Latin works (1539 *Institutio*, commentaries on Paul) printed in Strasbourg,

---

[20] G. Berthoud, 'Le solde des livres imprimés par Pierre de Vingle et les Vaudois du Piémont', *Musée neuchâtelois*, (1980), 74–9; J.-Fr. Gilmont, 'La fabrication et la vente de la Bible d'Olivétan', *Musée neuchâtelois*, (1985), 216–18; G. Casalis and B. Roussel (eds), *Olivétan, traducteur de la Bible: Actes du colloque Olivétan, Noyon, mai 1985* (Paris, 1987).

[21] See G. Berthoud, 'Les impressions genevoises de Jean Michel (1538–1544)', in J.-D. Candaux and B. Lescaze (eds), *Cinq Siècles d'imprimerie genevoise: Actes du Colloque international sur l'histoire de l'imprimerie et du livre à Genève, 27–30 avril 1978* (Geneva, 1980), vol. 1, pp. 55–88.

[22] See R. Peter, 'Un imprimeur de Calvin: Michel Du Bois', in *Bulletin de la Société d'histoire et d'archéologie de Genève*, 16 (1978), 285–335.

[23] Peter, 'Premiers ouvrages'.

until the risk of losing a manuscript in transit led him to have them printed in Geneva.[24]

In Antwerp the successor to Martin Lempereur, Antoine Des Gois, went on printing the Bible and some editions of the Psalms; but the printers no longer involved themselves in the theological questions of the period, since the pressure of censorship, until then only discreet, became increasingly heavy in the great metropolis around 1545.[25]

Finally in Lyon, a number of major printers and booksellers made their appearance in the 1540s (the Frellon brothers, and above all Jean de Tournes)[26] who began to produce books on the borders of orthodoxy (and sometimes beyond); but the example of Étienne Dolet, humanist printer turned evangelical propagandist in 1542, burnt at the stake in Paris in 1546, was there to discourage any excessively bold spirits.[27] But the whole of this production in other centres pales into insignificance beside the 196 editions of Reformation texts printed in Geneva between 1540 and 1549 (162 of them by Jean Girard).[28]

Consolidation and diversification (1550–62)

A third period, from 1550 to 1562, is characterized by the enormous expansion of the Genevan printing industry, and by an ever closer relationship between Geneva and certain Lyonnais printers and booksellers (leading to an increase in Reformation book production in Lyon). These years also saw the spread of secondary, more or less clandestine, printing operations within France (Orléans, Caen, Rouen), and a marked increase in the production, especially in Paris, of Roman Catholic responses to the rising tide of propaganda coming from Geneva.

The Genevan industry   In 1550 Jean Girard lost his monopoly of Reformation printing in Geneva. Jean Crespin[29] and Conrad Badius

---

[24] See T. H. L. Parker, *Calvin's New Testament Commentaries* (London, 1971), pp. 13–16.

[25] See pp. 155, 194–6, and 210.

[26] A. Cartier, *Bibliographie des éditions des de Tournes, imprimeurs lyonnais* (2 vols, Paris, 1937–1938).

[27] L. Febvre, 'Dolet propagateur de l'évangile', *BHR*, 6 (1945), 98–170. For Dolet's editions, Cl. Longeon, *Bibliographie des oeuvres d'Étienne Dolet, écrivain, éditeur et imprimeur* (Geneva, 1980).

[28] J.-Fr. Gilmont, 'Bibliotheca Gebennensis: les livres imprimés à Genève de 1535 à 1549', in *Genava*, 28 (1980), 229–51.

[29] J.-Fr. Gilmont, *Jean Crespin, un éditeur réformé du XVIe siècle* (Geneva, 1981); J.-Fr.Gilmont, *Bibliographie des éditions de Jean Crespin, 1550–1572* (2 vols, Verviers, 1981).

(son of the famous Parisian printer Josse Badius), refugees in Geneva, set up a printing press; the great Robert Estienne followed them one year later. In 1551, the Edict of Châteaubriant, by which the French authorities hoped at last to establish a proper control of the book trade, provoked a massive emigration of printers and booksellers to Geneva: more than 130 of them settled in the city between 1550 and 1560.[30] According to Chaix's (incomplete) figures, book production rose from 193 for the period 1541–50 to 527 between 1551 and 1564.[31]

Various factors led the Genevan authorities, in 1563, to limit the number of printing presses in the city. The government was concerned by the effervescent editorial activities in the city, and by the increasingly tough competition between printers; but it also foresaw a looming crisis in the foundation of Huguenot printing houses in France itself, and in the onset of the wars of religion. Nineteen printers were licensed to print in the city. Only Jean Crespin and Henri Estienne were permitted to work four presses each (and more by subcontracting to certain other printers); other printers were limited to one, occasionally two, presses. Although the bookseller Antoine Vincent was only 'habitant', not 'bourgeois' of Geneva, he also was granted the right to operate four presses. The same right was granted, on appeal, to the bookseller Laurent de Normandie.[32]

Following a capitalist structure also found in the major French centres, the Genevan book trade was dominated by a few large-scale printers or booksellers, who farmed out work to the numerous jobbing printers. Apart from Crespin and Estienne, there was the bookseller Laurent de Normandie, Calvin's compatriot, who arrived in the city in 1548;[33] from 1550 until his death in 1569, he was one of the major organizers of book exports from Geneva to France. We shall return later to his activities as bookseller; for the moment we note that he had the right to operate four presses and owned his own printing material; but no book carries his address, and he did not even own a printer's mark. Antoine Vincent, an important Lyon merchant resident in Geneva from 1559 onwards, was in the position to order enormous editions from the small Genevan printers, as we shall see in the case of the psalter. It appears that Calvin's brother Antoine was also involved in

---

[30] P. Chaix, *Recherches sur l'imprimerie à Genève de 1550 à 1564: Étude bibliographique, économique et littéraire* (Geneva, 1954), p. 48.

[31] P. Chaix, A. Dufour and G. Moeckli, *Les Livres imprimés à Genève de 1550 à 1600* (revised edn, Geneva, 1966).

[32] Chaix, *Recherches*, p. 32.

[33] H.-L. Schlaepfer, 'Laurent de Normandie', in G. Berthoud et al., *Aspects*, pp. 176–230; H. Bremme, *Buchdrucker und Buchhändler zur Zeit der Glaubenskämpfe* (Geneva, 1969), pp. 17–27, 212.

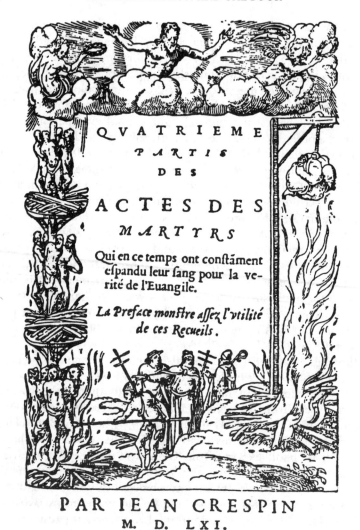

QVATRIEME
PARTIS
DES
ACTES DES
MARTYRS
Qui en ce temps ont conſtáment
eſpandu leur ſang pour la ve-
rité de l'Euangile.

La Preface monſtre aſſez l'vtilité
de ces Recueils.

PAR IEAN CRESPIN
M. D. LXI.

3.2   Jean Crespin, *Quatrième partie des Actes des Martyrs* (Geneva: Jean
Crespin, 1561)

the book trade: he saw the definitive editions of the *Institutio* (in Latin
from Robert Estienne in 1559, in French from Jean Crespin in 1560)
through the press, and subsequently oversaw several editions of his
brother's works. But neither he nor Laurent de Normandie ever had
their name printed on a title-page. The great Genevan editors are famous for their discretion. As J.-Fr. Gilmont writes:

The majority of expensive editions seems to have been underwritten by financiers like Laurent de Normandie, Antoine Vincent, Antoine Calvin or Philibert Grené, without any trace of their involvement surviving in the bibliographical addresses, or even in the registers of the City Council. A close study of the world of Genevan printing gives the impression of looking at an iceberg: the major part of the phenomenon, financially speaking, is hidden.[34]

The Lyon–Geneva axis   The example of Antoine Vincent leads us to the second characteristic of the period 1550–62: the ever closer links between Geneva and Lyon. Naturally, the Genevan output was almost entirely concerned with religious propaganda, while the Lyon printers handled a far wider range of texts; but some major figures in Lyon, such as Jean de Tournes, had embraced the new doctrines, and sought to communicate their beliefs in a fundamentally hostile environment. De Tournes, for example, produced a whole series of Bibles with the two prefaces by St Jerome (therefore apparently quite orthodox); but the text is that of the Genevan Bibles, and therefore heretical.[35] In the ever more tense and uncontrollable atmosphere of the late 1550s, other Lyon printers began producing openly Calvinist editions, in particular Sebastien Honorati and above all Jean Saugrain. As N. Z. Davis puts it, 'Protestantism took hold early [in Lyon] and by the mid-1550s had won the commitment of the large majority of men in the printing industry'. She adds later: 'so many heretical editions came out of Lyon in the 1550s, despite periodic investigations of the printing shops by Catholic authorities, that the canon-counts feared that "all Christianity is going to think that Lyon lives like Geneva"'.[36] To complete this survey, let us add that in 1562 the Huguenots took over the city, and for the following three years the production of some of the Lyon printers is identical with that of Geneva: Bibles, catechisms, polemical tracts.[37] When the city was recaptured by the Catholics in 1565, this second centre of Calvinism rapidly returned to obedience. The great majority of the printing workers reverted to Catholicism, while the major editors remained faithful to the Reformation, in some cases by emigrating to Geneva.[38]

---

[34] *J. Crespin*, p. 49. On Antoine Vincent, see E. Droz, 'Antoine Vincent. La Propagande protestante par le Psautier', in G. Berthoud et al., *Aspects*, pp. 276–93; Bremme, pp. 240–41. On Antoine Calvin's activities as editor, see Bremme, p. 125.

[35] Chambers, p. 202.

[36] N. Z. Davis, 'Strikes and Salvation at Lyons', *ARG*, 56 (1965), 49 and 54 note 23; reprinted in N. Z. Davis, *Society and Culture in early modern France* (Stanford, 1975), p. 2 and p. 273 note 22.

[37] For example, see the list of Jean Saugrain's publications in H.-L. Baudrier, *Bibliographie lyonnaise* (Lyon, Paris, 1895–1921), vol. 4, pp. 317–46.

[38] Davis, 'Strikes', p. 49; Davis, *Society*, p. 2.

Centres of book production in France   In the feverish atmosphere of the years preceding the outbreak of the so-called wars of religion, several more or less clandestine centres of book production appeared in France and on its borders. In Caen, Martin and Pierre Philippe reprinted the *Bref Discours de la république française* produced by Dolet in 1542;[39] the same Pierre Philippe re-edited works of Genevan origin in 1560–63, along with other Caen and Rouen printers.[40] In Rouen, Orléans and La Rochelle, clandestine publications made their appearance right at the end of our period (Abel Clémence in Rouen in 1561; Éloi Gibier in Orléans in 1562; Louis Rabier in Orléans and Barthélemy Berton in La Rochelle in 1563).[41] A new period was taking shape, but one which extends beyond our chronological limits.

Outside France, printers restarted the production of books in French. Apart from the case of Strasbourg, already mentioned, we again find titles in French coming from Basle. This is a rather special case: for the most part the authors are dissidents from the Genevan Reformation, seeking a freer air on the banks of the Rhine – Castellio, Bernardino Ochino and Pietro Paulo Vergerio – who find printers, or at least a printer, Jacques Estauge (or Kündig), to answer their needs.[42] But in all these cases we are dealing with individual editions, at most with a

---

[39] Cl. Longeon, 'Sur la trace d'une édition perdue d'Étienne Dolet', in P. M. Smith and I. D. McFarlane (eds), *Literature and the Arts in the Reign of Francis I: Essays Presented to C. A. Mayer* (Lexington, 1985), pp. 89–102.

[40] The pirate editions attributed to a 'Norman forger' by J.-Fr. Gilmont (*J. Crespin* [quoted note 30], pp. 102–5) were produced in several workshops. For the productions of Pierre Philippe (1560–69) and Pierre le Chandelier (1562–98?), see P. Aquilon and A. Girard (eds), *Bibliographie normande: bibliographie des ouvrages imprimés à Caen et à Rouen au seizième siècle*, fasc. 7. (Baden Baden, 1989). For other editions probably from Rouen, some first indications are given in Aquilon and Girard as 'éditions de provenance incertaine'.

[41] On Abel Clémence, see G. Clutton, '"Abel Clémence" of "Rouen": a sixteenth-century secret press', *The Library*, 20 (1939–40), 136–53; H. de la Fontaine Verwey, 'Une presse secrète au XVIe siècle: Abel Clémence imprimeur à Rouen', in *Mélanges F. Calot* (Paris, 1965), pp. 81–9; J.-Fr. Gilmont, 'Premières éditions françaises de la "Confessio belgica"', *Quaerendo*, 3 (1972), 173–81. On Éloi Gibier, see L. Desgraves, *Éloi Gibier, imprimeur à Orléans (1536–1588)* (Geneva, 1966); L. Desgraves, 'Supplément à la bibliographie des ouvrages imprimés par Éloi Gibier à Orléans', *BHR*, 32 (1970), 127–31; J.-Fr. Gilmont, 'Éloi Gibier, éditeur de théologie réformée: nouveau complément à la bibliographie de ses éditions', *BHR*, 47 (1985), 395–403. On Louis Rabier, see P. Aquilon, 'Pierre Haultin et Louis Rabier, co-éditeurs de la Bible française', *GJ* (1975), 142–9. On Barthélemy Berton, see E. Droz, *Barthélemy Berton, 1536–1573* (Geneva, 1960).

[42] On Kündig, or Estauge, see A. Cartier, 'Les dixains catholiques et Jacques Estauge imprimeur à Bâle', in *Mélanges É. Picot* (Paris, 1913), vol. 1, pp. 307–13. More generally, see P. Bietenholz, *Basle and France in the Sixteenth Century* (Geneva, 1971), and his chapter below (p. 235–63).

dozen or so, never with printing on a large scale. Apart from the special case of Geneva, Reformation printing in French remained a very limited phenomenon.

The Catholic response   The Reformation book was a dangerous product, as is shown by the fate of Antoine Augereau, Étienne Dolet, and of numerous book salesmen in the 1550s: only printers with strongly held beliefs became involved. On the other hand, religious books clearly sold well. The production of religious books untainted by heresy was good business. Books of Hours, liturgical works, pious treatises continued to appear copiously in France, as if to show that the Reformation was not happening. But at the same time, and from early on, a new wave of Catholic writings appeared: replies to Reformation publications. The *Determinatio* of the Faculty of Theology (1521) condemning Luther's works began a series of refutations: treatises in Latin by Béda, Clichtove, Jérôme de Hangest, Robert Ceneau maintained the output. More interesting, and less well known, was the involvement of Roman Catholic theologians in the battles surrounding 'popular' publications in French. The friar Jean de Gacy, Bishop Guillaume Petit, doctor of theology Pierre Doré and several others undertook the refutation of Reformation publications, as early as the 1520s. Until 1550 the struggle was very unequal: Reformation editions were available by the hundred, while Catholic replies were isolated cases. But after 1550, and especially in the decade of the 1560s, theological refutations of Reformation writings became very common (René Benoist, Gentian Hervet, Émond Auger, Antoine Mouchy, Antoine Du Val ...).[43] Naturally this production was centred on Paris, where several printers specialized in Catholic pamphlets – and after 1560 they were to become major suppliers of the political pamphlets of the so-called wars of religion. This was a large-scale phenomenon which played a major role in adapting French to the needs of abstract debate.

Before embarking on the study of the physical characteristics of the Reformation book, it is worth underlining the essential role played by the Reformation in the evolution of the French language. Prior to the

---

[43] F. M. Higman, 'Premières réponses catholiques aux écrits de la Réforme en France, 1525–c.1540', in *Le Livre dans l'Europe de la Renaissance: Actes du XXVIIIe Colloque international d'Études humanistes de Tours* (Paris, 1988), pp. 361–77; F. M. Higman, 'Theology in French: religious pamphlets from the Counter-Reformation', in *Renaissance and Modern Studies*, 23 (1979), 128–46; M.-M. de La Garanderie, 'La Réponse catholique aux placards de 1534: La "Contre les tenebrions lumiere evangelicque" de Jérôme d'Hangest, "marteau des hérétiques"', in M. Péronnet (ed.) *La Controverse religieuse (XVIe-XIXe siècles): Actes du 1er colloque Jean Boisset, 6e colloque du Centre d'histoire de la Réforme et du protestantisme* (Montpellier, 1980), vol. 1, pp. 1–6.

Reformation there was indeed a beautiful French language, admirably adapted to the needs of narration, of meditation, of poetry; but that language had rarely been used to communicate abstract thought or closely argued dialectic. During the 1530s there are several indications of a growing interest in the vernacular: developments in typography (the use of roman and italics for works in French instead of black letter or 'lettres bâtardes', introduction of accents and other diacritical signs); the imposition, by the Edict of Villers-Cotterêts (1539), of the French language in all legal texts; the appearance of the first grammars of French. We return later to questions of spelling and typography; but the clear connection between Reformation and literacy is suggested by the common phenomenon of school readers which also communicated religious doctrines, for example the *Instruction des enfans* by Olivétan, translator of the Bible.[44] The translations of scripture by Olivétan (1535) and Lefèvre d'Étaples (1523–30) played the same role in French as did Luther's German version (1523), and Tyndale's English one (1525), for their respective languages. Equally important in the case of French was the French translation of Calvin's *Institution* (1541), and the series of theological and polemical works by the same author spread over the following 20 years: in these writings Calvin created a simple, disciplined, linear, strongly structured language, which was admired not only by his friends (Farel or Pierre Viret, for example), but also by his enemies (René Benoist, Antoine Du Val). These latter writers undertook the refutation of Calvin's ideas; by dint of quoting the Reformer before refuting him, they frequently absorbed his linguistic techniques.[45] Calvin's· linguistic influence thus spread far beyond the circle of his disciples and admirers.

The physical make-up of the Reformation book: format

There is a striking contrast with Germany here: I know of no French book produced by the Reformation which resembles those quarto pamphlets of eight or 12 leaves which spread Martin Luther's thought in Germany during the 1520s. For the doctrinal treatises as for the polemical writings of the French Reformation, by far the most popular format was the octavo of 50, or even 100 pages – in any case an object which looks like a proper little book, not a pamphlet.

---

[44] G. Berthoud, 'L'Edition originale de l'"Instruction des enfans" par Olivétan', *Musée Neuchâtelois* (1937) 1–10. See also R. Peter, 'L'Abécédaire genevois ou catéchisme élémentaire de Calvin', *Revue d'Histoire et de Philosophie religieuses*, 45 (1965), 11–65.
[45] See Higman, 'Theology'.

Two reasons may be suggested for this characteristic of the French Reformation book. On the one hand, it clearly mirrored the pious publications of the previous period (the *Livre de vraye et parfaicte oraison*, for example, could easily be taken for an orthodox book of instruction and prayers). The Reformers adopted what was already the norm for religious texts. On the other hand, and more simply, these little books, often no larger than 8 × 10 cms, could easily be concealed in a bundle of other goods, or in some modest hiding place.[46] Here, for example, is how the anonymous printer of an edition of Viret's *Exposition du symbole des Apostres*, in 1557, explained his choice of a small format (in this case an octavo): on the one hand the edition was cheaper, therefore accessible to 'the ignorant and to those who have few goods', and on the other,

> the smaller the pages are of a book, the easier it is to carry, and the less dangerous – a point well worth considering when there are so many and so vicious enemies of God and of the spread of His word; so much so that someone who could scarcely carry [the previous editions] anywhere at all, can now do so easily and securely.[47]

More important works, like Calvin's *Institution* and his commentaries, were often quartos. The folio format was rare, except in the case of the Bible.[48]

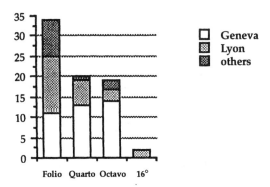

Figure 3.1   Format of French Bibles (1530–70)

---

[46] See for example F. M. Higman, 'A heretic's library: the Drilhon inventory, 1545', in A. L. Lepschy, J. Took and D. E. Rhodes (eds), *Book Production and Letters in the Western European Renaissance: Essays in Honour of Conor Fahy* (London, 1986), pp. 184–209.

[47] Copy, without title-page, in Glasgow U.L., Bh.y.1.13.

[48] According to the information in Chambers, *Bibliography*.

Bearing in mind these two criteria which favoured the small format (lower price, ease of concealment), we may conclude that the Genevan industry, with its preference for the quarto and above all for the octavo, was particularly geared to large-scale distribution.

Illustrations in French Reformation books

Here we find another contrast, perhaps even more striking, with the German scene. With the exception of certain Antwerp Bibles produced by Martin Lempereur, illustrations were extremely rare in French Reformation printing, in particular in its dominant, Genevan, form. The only outstanding exception, the *Faictz de Jesus Christ et du pape* [Neuchâtel, Pierre de Vingle, c.1534], proves the rule: it was based on a German publication, the *Passional Christi et Antichristi* of 1521, with a text derived from Luther and woodcuts by Cranach.[49] The book was reprinted in Geneva by Jean Michel, c.1544, and again, probably in Lyon, in 1555–60, each time with the same woodcuts or copies of them.

In 1557, Jean Crespin produced two engravings of monsters, the pope-ass and the monk-calf, with explanatory notes translated from Melanchthon and Luther. Otherwise, one would look in vain for the portraits which decorate the title-pages of some sermons by Luther, or the many satirical engravings circulating in Germany. The only variety beyond the austere sequence of alphabetical characters which the Genevan printers allowed themselves was their printer's mark, musical notation – and they were slow in acquiring the material even for that[50] – an occasional geographical map, and 'scientific' illustrations representing, in Genevan Bibles in the 1550s and 1560s, certain buildings and temple furniture described in the Old Testament – illustrations copied from those of Robert Estienne in his Latin *Biblia*. One may finally mention the *Mappemonde nouvelle papistique* attributed to Conrad Badius, a satirical map of the Pope's kingdom, probably published c.1566. Even here the visual element was secondary: the full meaning of the map could only be grasped by studying the solid, 190-page quarto *Histoire de la Mappemonde Papistique* which accompanied the map.

How do we explain this almost total lack of pictures in French Reformation printing? Was there a desire to underline the difference from the pious books of the beginning of the century? It does not seem so. Was it the difficulty of obtaining the necessary equipment? The

---

[49] Berthoud, 'Les impressions', pp. 62–7.

[50] P. Pidoux, 'Les Origines de l'impression de musique à Genève' in J.-D. Candaux and B. Lescaze (eds), *Cinq Siècles*, vol. 1, pp. 97–108.

¶Les faitz de Jesus Christ t du Pape/
par lesquelz chascun pourra facilement congnoistre la grande differëce dëtre eulx : nouuellemët reueuz/corrigez/
¶augmëtez/selon la Berite de la saincte Escri-
pture/¶ des droictz canôs/p le lecteur
du sainct Palais.

Cum priuilegio Apostolico.

3.3   *Les faitz de Jesus Christ et du Pape* (Geneva: Jean Michel, 1538/44)

hypothesis seems improbable: since Genevan printers were supplied from Lyon with typographical material in general, there is no reason why they should not also have acquired woodcuts from the same source. The most likely explanation seems to me to be a theological one. The

LE PARVIS.

3.4   The Court of the Temple (from the Book of Exodus) in François Estienne's Geneva Bible of 1567

Genevan Church stressed particularly the prohibition of images of the Divinity, witness their adoption of the division of the Ten Commandments which makes the forbidding of graven images into the Second Commandment, where Luther, like the Roman Catholics, made it part of the First. This was the specific ground on which the censors of the Sorbonne condemned certain commentaries on the Ten Commandments coming from Geneva. This hostility towards images seems to have been extended beyond representations of the Divinity, to include images of all sorts. Against pictures and statues, 'Bibles for the unlettered', Calvin contrasted the Word which invites the reader to 'lift up your hearts', rather than remaining bound to the physical world. This attitude seems to have had its influence on the physical appearance of the French Reformation book.[51]

Choice of typefaces

The norm, at the beginning of the century, was to use so-called 'bâtarde' letters for printing works in French. The first French texts printed in roman characters appeared *c*.1520 (by Pierre Vidoue, followed around 1530 by Geoffroy Tory); but the usage spread only slowly. Roman Catholic works of piety continued to appear in 'bâtardes' until mid-century. The earliest Reformation books (New Testaments and other editions by the printers Simon de Colines, Simon Du Bois, Pierre de Vingle) likewise followed this tradition. The only exception was Farel's first treatise, dated 1524, and printed in roman because the Basle printer Cratander did not have the preferred material for an edition in French).[52] A rapid change took place before 1540. In Paris, the *Livre de vraye et parfaicte oraison*, printed in 'bâtardes' in 1528, 1529 and 1530, appeared in roman in 1539. In Geneva, the printer Jean Girard, who moved there in 1536, equipped himself only with roman and italic type. From then on, the work of printers like Jean Michel of Geneva, who clung to 'bâtardes', took on an obsolete appearance. Similarly in Lyon, by 1540 most printed texts in French were appearing in roman characters (Dolet, the Trechsel brothers; a little later, Jean de Tournes), while a few printers (like Olivier Arnoullet) continued to use their old equipment.

Did the Reformation have an influence on French spelling and on typographical practices? One should not be too categorical. It is certainly true that the Reformers, with their affirmation of the primacy of the Word, were particularly concerned to foster literacy and education. It is noticeable that the great majority of those who, in the 1530s and 1540s, were involved in spelling reform were, to say the least, touched by a spirit of religious reform: Marot and Marguerite de Navarre (in the *Briefve Doctrine pour deuement escripre selon la propriete du langaige francoys*, printed with the *Miroir de l'ame pecheresse* by Antoine Augereau in 1533), Olivétan (*Instruction des enfans*, 1533), Dolet (in

---

[51] See Carlos M. N. Eire, *War Against the Idols: the Reformation of Worship from Erasmus to Calvin* (Cambridge, 1986); Ph. Denis, *Le Christ étendard* (Paris, 1987).

[52] See Farel, *Le Pater*, introduction, p. 14.

his *Maniere de bien traduire*, 1540), the anonymous *Instruction et creance des Chrestiens* of 1546 (and maybe already before 1542). But in choosing roman characters for printing French texts, Girard only joined a more general movement; as regards innovations in spelling, the Reformation dissociated itself from the quest for a fundamental modernization (by Meigret, Pelletier, Ramus), at the point where such a development threatened to act as a barrier to the easy comprehension of the text (see Bèze's preface to the *Abraham sacrifiant*, 1550).[53]

Distribution networks

From the beginning of the Reformation one finds two parallel systems: booksellers, and peddlers. It seems that, during the 1520s, booksellers were able to operate without serious obstacles: the edict of 5 February 1526, for example, forbidding scripture translations, is directed at 'those who *own*' condemned books. But from 1531, life became more difficult for French booksellers. The Parlement established an inspection system, the Faculty condemned a collection of books confiscated from a Paris bookseller, and several printers and booksellers were hunted in the aftermath of the Affair of the Placards (1534).[54] The edict of 1 July 1542 imposed stricter control of printers (no more anonymous editions) and booksellers (inspection by the authorities prior to putting books on sale).[55] It took a long time before the sale of 'dangerous' books by booksellers was effectively controlled. However, from 1551, the contribution of booksellers to the spread of Reformation books was significantly reduced. The Edict of Châteaubriant, 26 June 1551, reaffirmed the edict of 1542 and others, explicitly condemned all books coming from Geneva, forbade the sale of any book listed in the 'catalogue' of censored books, refined the system of visitation of bookshops (two visits a year in Paris, three in Lyon), and attempted to establish a special control of imported books. And finally, as if to foresee the future, the sale of books by peddlers was forbidden.[56]

---

[53] On the subject of orthography in general, see N. Catach, *L'Orthographe française à l'époque de la Renaissance* (Geneva, 1968); on the Reformation and spelling reform, S. Baddeley, *L'Orthographe française au temps de la réforme* (Geneva, 1993). Also worthy of note is Robert Granjon of Lyons, who (from 1557 onwards) created a new typeface imitating contemporary handwriting: the so-called 'lettres françaises', better known as 'caractères de civilité'. The choice of typeface is not a proof of religious convictions; it is none the less noteworthy that most of the printers who imitated Granjon's characters were Huguenots. See H. Carter and H. D. L. Vervliet, *Civility Types* (Oxford, 1966).

[54] Higman, *Censorship*, pp. 80, 82–5.

[55] N. Weiss, 'Un Arrêt inédit du parlement de Paris contre l'"Institution chrestienne", 1er juillet 1542', *BSHPF*, 33 (1884), 16–21.

[56] Higman, *Censorship*, pp. 64–6; Farge, *Orthodoxy and Reform*, pp. 218–19.

Until this date, booksellers sold their wares as much due to commercial motives as because of religious conviction. After the Edict of Châteaubriant, only the committed believer dared to make Reformation literature available to the faithful.[57] On the other hand, an alternative distibution network, via peddlers, was expanded.

The itinerant vendor, selling ribbons, trinkets, pictures, pamphlets, and objects of all sorts, was already well known throughout Europe. The idea of exploiting this practically uncontrollable sales network came very early to the promoters of the new doctrine. Take Jean Vaugris, bookseller, giving advice in 1524 to Guillaume Farel on how to distribute his *Pater noster*: 'But give them to some mercer, so that he gets into the habit of selling books'.[58] Tribunal records give some insight into the activities of peddlers in the 1530s; but this clandestine trade became organized on a large scale from 1550. It is by definition difficult to form a complete picture of a secret enterprise; but such evidence as survives enables us to pick out certain characteristics.

On the one hand, the registers of provincial courts recorded numerous cases of travellers arrested for carrying heretical books in their baggage: in Dijon in 1549, 1556, 1557, and three separate cases in 1561; at the fair in Givrey in 1560 (involving a re-edition of the 1534 placards), in Tournai in 1563, between Tournai and Valenciennes in 1564, to mention just a few examples.[59] Books were usually transported in small quantities; there are, however, cases of large-scale traffic: in 1562 a barge loaded with books from Geneva was seized on the Seine; eight booksellers took several days to draw up an inventory.[60]

On the other hand, documents concerning Laurent de Normandie, Genevan publisher and bookseller from his arrival in the city in 1548 to his death in 1569, reveal an organized book-distribution system di-

---

[57] See for example the raid of Pierre Haultin's shop in Paris in October 1570: H. Stein, 'Une saisie de livres protestants en 1570', in *Mélanges de bibliographie*, 1e série (Paris, 1893), pp. 10–13; reproduced by I. Desgraves, *Les Haultins* (Geneva, 1960), pp. x–xii. In 1571, an inventory of the possessions of Richard Breton, Parisian printer and bookseller, revealed an amazing stock of 'some 1 200 items, representing more than 100 different editions, almost all imported from Geneva (and some from Normandy), and smuggled in by pedlars in small quantities': see G. Wildenstein, 'L'imprimeur-libraire Richard Breton et son inventaire après décès, 1571', *BHR*, 21 (1959), 364–79.

[58] Herminjard, *Correspondance des Réformateurs*, vol. 1, p. 279.

[59] E. Belle, 'Les libraires dijonnais et les débuts de la réforme à Dijon', *BSHPF*, 59 (1910), 481–95; on the Givrey (or Guibray) fair, see R. Hari, 'Les placards de 1534', in G. Berthoud et al., *Aspects*, pp. 112–13; on Tournai, see G. Moreau, 'Un colporteur calviniste en 1563', *BSHPF*, 118 (1972), 1–31; J.-Fr. Gilmont, 'Une édition inconnue du martyrologe de Jean Crespin', *BHR*, 30 (1968), 363.

[60] E. Maugis, *Histoire du parlement de Paris de l'avènement des rois Valois à la mort d'Henri IV* (Paris, 1913–1916), vol. 2, p. 343.

rected at France in mid-century.[61] De Normandie provided a stock of books to merchants and peddlers, undertaking to underwrite the cost if the merchandise was 'seized from the purchaser by the enemies of the gospel' within two or three months of the date of the contract. The risks were high: a list has been established of 21 of de Normandie's clients who were persecuted or put to death.[62] At the same period Geneva was training, and sending into France, a considerable number of pastors,[63] a programme which facilitated the setting up of a book distribution network. By identifying the place of origin of de Normandie's clients as listed in the inventory of his inheritance, H.-L. Schlaepfer drew up the following list of regions of France and beyond where his agents were active: Albigeois, Anjou, Artois, Auvergne, Bazadois (Guyenne), Béarn, Beauce, Berry, Bourbonnais, Bourgogne, Bretagne, Brie, Champagne, Dauphiné, Gascogne, Gévaudan, Ile-de-France, Languedoc, Lyonnais, Nivernais, Normandie, Orléanais, Périgord, Picardie, Poitou, Provence, Quercy, Touraine, Alsace, Lorraine, Savoie, Vaud, Frankfurt and Poland.[64]

Since the Frankfurt book fairs played a central role in the book trade throughout the sixteenth century, they deserve to be mentioned. In fact certain Genevan printers and publishers were regular attenders at the fairs (which took place annually before Easter and in September), at least from 1557 on. Catalogues of the books on sale exist only from 1564, and we do not know what was available earlier. The most active Genevans during the 1560s seem to have been Jean Crespin and Henri Estienne (33 titles from Crespin, 25 from Estienne between 1564 and 1572). But it does not seem that the Frankfurt book fairs played any great part in the spread of French Reformation thought, with the exception of Genevan polemics against the Lutherans; Crespin sold mainly works in Greek or in Latin, and non-religious literature in particular. The theological works which he offered were editions of German-language authors rather than of Calvin.[65]

Sources of finance

Whether a book was freely displayed on a bookseller's stand or smuggled in to the area, there remains a fundamental question, namely the

---

[61] Schlaepfer, 'Laurent de Normandie'.

[62] Schlaepfer, 'Laurent de Normandie', pp. 181–2.

[63] R. M. Kingdon, *Geneva and the Coming of the Wars of Religion in France, 1555–1563* (Geneva, 1956).

[64] Schlaepfer, 'Laurent de Normandie', p. 182.

[65] Gilmont, *J. Crespin*, p. 201 ff., gives the details. See also Chaix, *Recherches*, pp. 56–7.

financing of publications. The production of a book, especially a large volume like a Bible, implies a huge capital investment which could only be recovered slowly by means of sales. What were the financial arrangements for the Reformation book, an object with both commercial and spiritual, indeed 'missionary' features, and a dangerous object involving many risks (seizure) over and above the normal problems of transport in the sixteenth century?

The input of capital which enabled a printer to undertake an edition came from various sources. We have already mentioned the financing of Olivétan's Bible. More usually, the great merchant-editors would order an edition from a printer, provide the necessary funds as an advance, maybe lend him printing materials, and take the profits from the distribution of the resulting edition. Sometimes several editors co-financed an edition; or a printer would take on a share of the cost of the edition, in exchange for sales rights to part of the edition – this particularly in the case of texts which were easy to sell, New Testaments, psalters or catechisms. In other cases, notably for works of erudition for which the market was more limited, a benefactor was needed: thus, in a period slightly later than ours, Henri Estienne was able to finance many of his Greek editions thanks to the support of Ulrich Fugger.[66]

Once the edition was financed and complete, it had to be sold. What did books cost in the period? Apart from the indications given in Chaix, *Recherches*, some precious clues are found in Laurent de Normandie's inventory; the information dates from 1569, but one may presume that inflation had not totally altered the situation. From the inventory it appears that the cost of a printed sheet was relatively constant, between 1.0 and 1.5 deniers per sheet.[67] But, since folios required more sheets than smaller formats for the same text, prices varied considerably according to format:

	sheets	price per volume	price per sheet
folio Bible			
R. Estienne, 1553	254	30s.	1.42d.
F. Jaquy, 1562	278	22s. 6d.	0.97d.
H. Estienne, 1565	346	35s.	1.21d.
quarto Bible			
J. Crespin, 1564	126	16s.	1.52d.

---

[66] Detailed examples of these financial methods in Chaix, *Recherches*, and especially in R. M. Kingdon, 'The business activities of printers Henri and François Estienne', in G. Berthoud et al., *Aspects*, pp. 258–75.

[67] This matches the prices, 1.4 to 1.7 deniers, proposed by H. J. Bremme, *Buchdrucker*, pp. 31–2, who adds to the indications in Chaix, *Recherches*, pp. 53–4.

	sheets	price per volume	price per sheet
octavo Bible			
J. de Laon, 1570	75	7s.	1.12d.
octavo Psalter			
J. Crespin, 1563	27	2s.	0.89d.
Psalms (trans. L. Budé)			
J. Crespin, 1551	24	2s.	1.00d.
16° Psalter			
A. Davodeau, 1562	34	1s. 6d.	0.53d.

These prices corresponded to the costs of production, and must be doubled or even trebled to ascertain the retail price;[68] and, naturally, the quality of the paper and of the binding also affected the price. According to P. Chaix, the maximum salary of a mason or a carpenter was fixed in 1559 at 6 sols per day. It is clear that small-format books were accessibly priced for a workman, while the large formats were beyond their reach.

One final aspect of book financing concerns the author's rights. Throughout the *ancien régime* editors and printers owned the rights to the text (as can be seen from privileges, almost always granted to an editor or a printer, not to an author). In the most favourable case, the author could sell his manuscript to the editor, but derived no other profit from it.[69] At the end of our period there were occasional cases in which the author had a share in the financial rewards for the success of his work. For the publication of the Marot-Bèze *Psautier* in 1561, the agreement stipulated that the printers would give an account of the production costs of their editions, and that they would pay 8 per cent of this sum to the Poor Fund (of Paris or Geneva according to the place of printing).[70] The same system was later applied to other Genevan productions, including Bibles and some of Calvin's sermons.

Discreet editorial practices

Under the heading 'distribution networks', one final characteristic of the Reformation book deserves mention: its anonymity. We shall return later to the anonymity of authors, but let us deal first with books printed without address or printer's name, or with a false address. The edict of 1 July 1542 forbade all clandestine or anonymous printing: the

---

[68] Bremme, *Buchdrucker*, pp. 42–3.

[69] A. Charon-Parent, 'Le monde de l'imprimerie humaniste: Paris', *HÉF*, 241–2; J. Lough, *L'Écrivain et son public* (Paris, 1987), pp. 43–9.

[70] Droz, 'A. Vincent', pp. 281–3. For the later extension of the system, see Droz, *B. Berton*, pp. 50–52.

printer's mark and his address had to appear on the title-page. Thus it became all the easier to identify suspect editions, especially since (apart from Pierre de Vingle) false addresses were relatively rare. One quite common feature of Genevan printing was the existence of twin issues of the same edition, one with the name and address of the printer, the other without. Since, from 1547 on, any book emanating from Geneva was automatically condemned, and often the owner along with it, a fair proportion of Reformation editions adopted the solution of anonymity. We have already mentioned the self-effacement of the great Genevan merchants, Laurent de Normandie or Antoine Calvin for example. Even more notable is the observation of G. Guilleminot with reference to French book production in 1561: 'anonymous Catholic texts being exceptional, more or less any edition without printer's address belonged to Protestant propaganda, or at least to unorthodox currents'.[71]

The vulnerability of these anonymous publications, the increasing severity of censorship, and the preponderance of small formats all help to explain why most French Reformation publications are extremely rare. Many editions survive only in single copies, and a considerable proportion only in two or three copies. This is a salutary reminder that our knowledge of the subject is fragmentary, and possibly a significant proportion of Reformation books is definitively lost.

Authors and texts

We have just mentioned anonymous editions; we should add that authors, in the French Reformation, are equally anonymous. The last and most complete version of the *Index* of the university of Paris, in 1556, listed 253 works in Latin attributed (sometimes erroneously) to a named author, and 25 anonymous texts. For French works, the same catalogue provided the names of 84 titles attributed (sometimes erroneously) to a named author, and 166 anonymous works. Moreover, most of the Latin titles in the catalogue came from abroad. The majority of French-language Reformation publications did not carry the author's name on the title-page.

The sixteenth century notion of 'authorship' was different from our own. Many writers incorporated into their works texts from other pens of which they approve: Farel did so in his *Pater noster*, Pierre Doré in his *Dyalogue instructoire* (1538), as did the anonymous translator or adaptor (Antoine Du Pinet?) of the commentaries on Revelation by

---

[71] G. Guilleminot, 'Religion et politique à la veille des guerres civiles. Recherches sur les impressions françaises de l'année 1561' (Paris, École des Chartes thesis, 1977), p. 96.

François Lambert and Sebastien Meyer.[72] We find collective works, like the *Epistres et evangiles* of Lefèvre and his disciples,[73] and compilations like the *Livre de vraye et parfaicte oraison*.

In the hostile climate of France at the beginning of the Reformation, it was certainly not the name of the author which made a book successful. Among all the editions from Paris, Antwerp or Strasbourg in the 1520s only one author is named: Guillaume Dumolin of Strasbourg. Translations from Luther and Brunfels, Farel's treatises, the little manuals distributed by Simon Du Bois, were all anonymous. Similarly, after the establishment of a printing centre in Neuchâtel, and later in Geneva, the earliest works appeared without the author's name: Antoine Marcourt's first treatises, Farel again, and the *De la tressaincte cene* which may well be by Farel and Viret.[74] From about 1540, however, a change set in: translations from Zwingli and from Bucer, treatises by Calvin and Viret, were signed – sometimes with an anonymous printing for export. And re-editions of Farel or Marcourt in the 1540s often named the author for the first time.

Not surprisingly, the German Reformation provided a considerable proportion of authors published in French especially in the early days: Luther, Brunfels, Sebaldus Heyden, Urbanus Rhegius and Johannes Brenz had appeared in French before 1535, Megander in 1538 and Zwingli in the following year. This list grew rapidly around 1540 – Calvin was in exile in Strasbourg, and the Genevan printers undertook an important programme of translations: Oecolampadius, Bullinger, Bucer, Sebastien Meyer; the first French translation of an important work by Melanchthon dates from 1542, *De l'authorité de l'Eglise*.

As regards editions in Latin of German authors, one can find only a single edition of Luther in Geneva: the *Praefatio methodica*, published by Crespin in 1550.

Let us add a word on Latin texts which come within the purview of the French Reformation. The list of French authors publishing in France is brief indeed. Lefèvre d'Étaples and Claude Guillaud proposed sufficiently heterodox doctrines as to attract the attention of the Sorbonne censors. Robert Estienne was by far the most frequently targeted individual in the censorship process: apart from his numerous annotated editions of the Bible, the New Testament and the Psalter, he also edited school texts by Melanchthon, Hegendorf and Brunfels, and other works,

---

[72] On this last case see *Index 1*, p. 318; E. Droz, *Chemins de l'hérésie* (Geneva, 1970–76), vol. 2, pp. 56–60.

[73] See in particular the enlarged edition of *Epistres et evangiles*, G. Bedouelle and F. Giacone (eds) (Leiden, 1976).

[74] F. M. Higman, 'Les débuts de la polémique contre la Messe: "De la tressaincte Cene ... "', *Revue française d'histoire du livre*, 50 (1986), 35–92.

condemned in 1540 and subsequently transcribed into the *Catalogues*. In Lyon, Étienne Dolet produced two Latin texts, the *Fata Regis* (also published in French), and the *Cato christianus*, which turned out to be a paraphrase of Megander's catechism.[75]

As already mentioned, the majority of Latin editions in the early period came from Strasbourg and Basle, and originally the Genevan Reformers looked to Strasbourg for editions of their works in Latin, as did Calvin in 1539 for his *Institutio*, for example, and for his commentary on Romans in 1540. In Geneva itself production was mainly in French. But from 1543 on we find Latin editions of Calvin's works printed in Geneva, in particular ephemeral pieces attacking a person or an event beyond the francophone world, as in the case of the *Supplex exhortatio* to the Emperor, and Calvin's reply to Albert Pighius. But in 1548 Calvin began to publish in Geneva both the Latin and French editions of his commentaries and treatises. The following figure shows, however, that printing in Latin remained distinctly in the minority.[76]

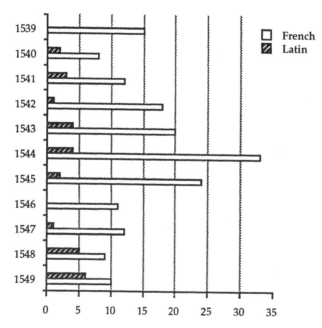

Figure 3.2   Genevan printing by language, 1539–49

[75] Cl. Longeon, 'Dolet et les Zwingliens', in *Prose et prosateurs de la Renaissance: Mélanges offerts à R. Aulotte* (Paris, 1988), pp. 57–64.

[76] Figures based on J.-Fr. Gilmont, 'Bibliotheca Gebennensis'. The data only goes to 1549, the end of the period covered by that survey; for the following years no comparable evidence is available.

The years around 1530 saw the appearance of thoroughgoing Reformed writers. The first of these was Guillaume Farel (1489–1565): a
former member of the Meaux group, he preached the Reformation in
Basle in 1524, then in Montbéliard, Aigle, Neuchâtel (1530), Geneva
(1532–35) and Lausanne (1536): Farel was without doubt the pioneer
of the French-language Reformation.[77] He wrote the first exposition of
Reformation faith (the *Pater noster*, 1524), the first doctrinal summary
(the *Sommaire et briefve declaration*, 1529), the first liturgy (*Maniere et
fasson*, 1533, perhaps preceded by an earlier version, *c*.1528–29).

In Neuchâtel, Farel joined forces with the young Pierre Viret and with
Antoine Marcourt. Marcourt, originally from Lyon and the first pastor
of Neuchâtel, is noted as the author of two treatises on the Mass and
the 1534 *placards*, as well as the satirical *Livre des marchans* (1533).[78]
No works can be unequivocally ascribed to Pierre Viret (1511–71)[79]
during the 1530s, although he probably contributed to Marcourt's Declaration de la Messe, and also to the anonymous *De la tressaincte Cene
de nostre seigneur* (*c*.1532); but in 1542 he established himself as the
writer with the most popular appeal of the French Reformation, with
*De la difference qui est entre les superstitions et idolatries des anciens
...* . He is particularly noted for his use of dialogue, which enabled him
to expound Reformation doctrines in a relaxed and amusing way, as for
example in the *Disputations chrestiennes* (1544).

But these writers of the early period, writing almost exclusively in
French, became very secondary – as they themselves admitted – with the
appearance on stage of Jean Calvin (1509–64).[80] His training in logic,
in law, in classical literature, acquired before he left France in 1535,

---

[77] For biographical questions, the basic study of Farel remains *Guillaume Farel 1489–
1565. Biographie nouvelle* (Neuchâtel, 1930). Complementary information in P. Barthel,
R. Scheurer and R. Stauffer (eds), *Actes du Colloque Guillaume Farel, Neuchâtel, 29
septembre – 1er octobre 1980* (Geneva, 1983) (*Cahiers de la Revue de Théologie et de
Philosophie, 9*). For the bibliography of Farel's works, J.-Fr. Gilmont, 'L'Oeuvre imprimée
de Guillaume Farel', in *Actes du Colloque Guillaume Farel, Neuchâtel, 29 septembre –
1er octobre 1980*, vol. 2, pp. 108–45.

[78] G. Berthoud, *Antoine Marcourt, réformateur et pamphlétaire du Livre des Marchans
aux Placards de 1534* (Geneva, 1973).

[79] On Pierre Viret, see J. Barnaud, *Pierre Viret, sa vie et son oeuvre (1511–1571)*
(Saint-Amans, 1911); G. Busino and P. Fraenkel, 'Rediscovering the minor Reformers.
Towards a reappraisal of Viret?', *BHR*, 24 (1962), 611–19; G. Bavaud, *Le Réformateur
Pierre Viret (1511–1571): sa théologie* (Geneva, 1986).

[80] The literature on Calvin is of course immense. Among the best biographies are B.
Cottret, *Calvin. Biographie* (Paris, 1995); T. H. L. Parker, *John Calvin: a Biography*
(London, 1975). For his thought, see F. Wendel, *Calvin: the Origins and Development of
his Religious Thought* (London, 1963); T. H. L. Parker, *Calvin: An Introduction to his
Thought* (London, 1995).

prepared him admirably for the complex responsibilities of his life in Geneva. His Latin *Institutio* (1536) does not seem to have been widely noticed; and the *Instruction et confession de la foy* drawn up in conjunction with Farel in 1537 so displeased the Genevans that they expelled both pastors. But the appearance of the French translation of the *Institutio* in Geneva in 1541, the year of his return to the city, marked a turning-point in the French Reformation. The French authorities reacted by the edict of 1 July 1542 which named the *Institution* specifically; Farel told his readers they would do better to study the *Institution* than his own *Sommaire*.[81] Once re-established in Geneva, Calvin devoted himself to the huge task of thoroughly reforming the city itself, spreading the Gospel message throughout Europe by his works in Latin (thanks to the successive editions of the *Institutio* and his biblical commentaries in particular), and in French for the local and, especially, the French market: the *Petit Traité de la saincte cene* (1541), the *Traité des reliques* (1543), the *Excuse aux Nicodemites* (1544). He wrote treatises against the Anabaptists, against the Spiritualists, against astrology. Through his copious correspondence, he kept in touch with the great and the simple, from Poland to England, from the Queen of Navarre to captives in the Lyon prison.

Farel and Viret had written popular expositions of the outlines of Reformation teaching; Calvin gave that teaching a systematic, theological framework which has been compared to that of St Thomas Aquinas's *Summa*. Farel and Viret addressed themselves particularly to a French-speaking, therefore limited, audience; Calvin broadened the Genevan Reformation into a European phenomenon by producing his works in parallel in French and Latin. Farel and Viret have certain stylistic qualities – Farel's verve and energy, the urbanity and wit of Viret. But Calvin created a new French idiom, incisive, clear, transparent, which drew the praise not only of his friends but also of his enemies, and which contributed powerfully to the evolution of the modern French language.

Most of these French Reformation writers were pastors, or 'ministers' as they were called; the leaders – Calvin, Farel, Viret, Bèze, by far the most prolific writers – had all been educated in Paris. Only Viret was Swiss by birth, the others were all refugees from France. Some of them, like François Lambert, Jean Ménard or Barthélemy Causse, had begun

---

[81] In the postface which he added to a new edition of the *Sommaire* in 1542, Farel wrote: 'Jean Calvin [...] has, in his *Institution*, treated so amply all the points mentioned in this booklet that it has taken away from me and from others the desire or the need to write more fully of them, or to try to produce a more extensive work; so I think it unnecessary to do anything other than refer everyone to this excellent work.' (1542 edition, fol. T 2ᵛ-3ʳ)

their careers as monks. It is quite rare to find a layman who took up his pen to compose a work on religion: one example is Benoist Textor, Calvin's doctor. Only at the very end of our period, around 1560, did Frenchmen living in France dare to put pen to paper, in the exchange of pamphlets preceding the wars of religion; Antoine de La Roche-Chandieu and Augustin Marlorat, pastors in Paris and Rouen respectively, are cases in point.

Paul Chaix lists 59 authors of theological or polemical works published in Geneva in the period 1551–64. Having remarked that all except two of these authors were contemporaries, he adds:

> We have here a striking summary of the Reformation movement shown through the printing houses of Calvin's city. During these few years, all the great names of the Reformation feature on Genevan editions. Each country provides its contingent of theologians or polemicists. The most important contribution comes from France; Strasbourg has an influential theological circle; the German-language Reformation is well represented with translations from Bullinger. England sends Knox, Gilby and Goodman during Mary Tudor's reign. Italy stands out with Bernardino Ochino, Vicar-General of the Capuchins, and the noble Balbani. Even Spain is represented by Juan de Valdès.[82]

Doctrines

A perceptible change of direction occurred during the 1530s. Before that period two characteristics stood out: on the one hand the overwhelming predominance of Lutheran rather than Zwinglian influences; on the other, in this period marked by a certain doctrinal variety, the attitudes of Luther and Erasmus – Reformer and Reformist – frequently overlapped. Thus, it is from Luther that Farel borrowed the commentary on the Creed in his *Pater noster*; and both the Antwerp printers and the French refugees in Strasbourg devoted themselves to spreading Luther's thought in France.[83] Zwingli was not mentioned. As regards the blend of reformist tendencies – criticism of Church abuses, aspiration towards a more spiritual, biblical religion, doctrinally relieved of the ballast of 'human inventions', a simplified and comprehensible liturgy – and Lutheran positions – faith as the sole basis of justification, the primacy of divine grace in the work of salvation, and consequently the questioning of the reality of human freedom; the break with Rome and the denunciation of its Church as false – the most eloquent evidence is perhaps the *Livre de vraye et parfaicte oraison*. Since their first

---

[82] Chaix, *Recherches*, pp. 90–91.
[83] See especially Moore, *La Réforme allemande*.

appearance in French in Farel's *Pater noster* and in the thoroughly Lutheran *Oraison de Jesuchrist* (1525), Luther's commentaries on the Creed and the Lord's Prayer underwent textual modifications – for example, the word 'only' was suppressed in formulations like '*only* by faith are we saved', thus changing its import – and making the *Livre* acceptable to the Gallican Church, all the more so since Luther's writings were accompanied by other tracts of far less radical origins.[84]

This tendency to mix orthodox and heretical strands, particularly noticeable before 1530, could still be found in France much later: in Paris, in the 1540s, the Parisian priest François Landry had reprinted an *Introduction pour les enfans* which had originated in Antwerp and which contained unorthodox ideas on confession and absolution; in the same circles we find a Gallican *Exposition de l'oraison de nostre Seigneur Jesus [...] avec l'exposition du Symbole Apostolique*, half of which is taken from Calvin's *Instruction et confession de la foy*; while the *Consolation en adversité*, published under his own name by the Paris Doctor Claude d'Espence in 1547, turns out to be an unacknowledged translation from Luther.[85]

But with the implantation of the Reformation in French-speaking Switzerland, at the beginning of the decade 1530–40, a different, and definitive, direction was adopted: the French Reformation became intransigent, and it turned towards Zurich rather than Wittenberg. The treatise *De la tressaincte cene*, Marcourt's pamphlets and the 1534 placards, the positions adopted by Farel and Viret in the disputations in Geneva in 1535 and Lausanne in 1536 – in all these cases, the central concern was the confrontation of the Mass and the Lord's Supper, and in all these cases a Zwinglian doctrine, rather than a Lutheran one, was promoted: the bread remained bread and the wine remained wine, the Supper was above all a *sign* and a *commemoration* of the unique sacrifice on the Cross. From 1536 on, the doctrine of the French Reformation was no longer either Lutheran or Zwinglian, but that of Calvin who, in his *Petit Traité de la saincte Cene* (1541), tried to formulate a doctrine on the Lord's Supper which could reconcile Luther and Zwingli.

After 1541 the doctrines of the French Reformation were more or less exclusively identified with the doctrines of Geneva. Farel, Viret and Calvin spoke with one voice, and the French church in Strasbourg adopted their liturgy and their doctrine. When, later, Lyon 'went Reformed', that move-

---

[84] Higman, 'Luther'.

[85] On François Landry, see E. Droz, 'Le Curé Landry et les frères Langelier', in *Chemins*, vol. 1, pp. 273–391; on the *Exposition* and the *Consolation en adversité*, see F. M. Higman, 'Farel, Calvin et Olivétan, sources de la spiritualité gallicane', in *Actes du Colloque G. Farel*, vol. 1, p. 45–61.

ment was defined in terms of Geneva: the authorities feared that 'all Christianity is going to think that Lyon lives like Geneva'.[86]

It was to Basle that the dissidents of the Reformation were drawn in mid-century. Sebastian Castellio, the Italians Ochino and Vergerio printed texts there which dared to offer divergent views from Genevan orthodoxy, in particular concerning toleration (Castellio) and predestination.[87]

Finally, the French-language radical Reformation should not be forgotten. It is all the easier to overlook the Anabaptists and the Spiritualists since no text presenting the radical Reformation appears to have survived from the period under review. The Anabaptists seem to have spread their message by the spoken word, by sermons or discussions, rather than by writings. But in his treatises against the Anabaptists, the 'Libertins spirituels', and 'a certain Dutchman' (Dirck Coornhert),[88] Calvin said that he was writing in order to refute written texts: the Schleitheim Articles (1527) for the Anabaptists, and some tracts by Antoine Pocques or Pocquet for the spiritualists. But apart from the quotations from a text by Pocques which Calvin gives in *Contre les libertins*, no samples of radical writings survive earlier than the end of the century.[89] It is also noticeable that these radical writings did not attract the attention of the censorship authorities.

Literary genres

Which literary genres were preferred by Reformation writers? The works censored by the Paris Faculty of Theology give a first, approximate reply. Figure 3.3 is based on an analysis of the 1556 *Catalogue des livres censurez*, the most complete of the indexes.[90] Two figures are particularly striking in this figure: the preponderance of biblical commentaries in Latin compared to the relatively modest production in French, and conversely the important place taken by polemics in French, a relatively unimportant category in Latin. In both cases the explana-

---

[86] Text quoted above, p. 115.

[87] See below, pp. 255–9.

[88] On the radical Reformation, see especially G. H. Williams, *The Radical Reformation* (London, 1962), in particular pp. 580–614 on Calvin's controversies with the spiritualists.

[89] The 'libertine' treatises which G. Jaujard attributed to Jean Girard's press, *c.*1548 (*Essai sur les libertins spirituels de Genève* (Paris, 1890)) were actually printed in the 1580s, and were composed by David Joris: see E. Droz, 'Sur quelques traductions françaises d'écrits de David Joris, Rotterdam, Dierck Mullem, vers 1580', in *Het Boek*, 37 (1965), 152–62.

[90] *Index 1*, pp. 92, 110. The figures are approximations, since the categories are not identical in the analysis of Latin and of French titles; moreover, it is sometimes impossible to distinguish between doctrinal and polemical works.

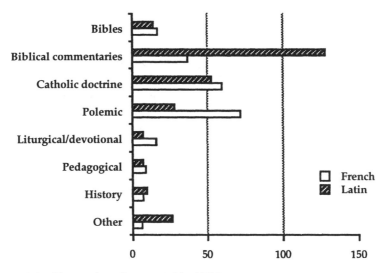

Figure 3.3   Types of work censored in 1556

tion is simple. The Latin commentaries include the major writings of all the leading German-language Reformers (Luther, Melanchthon, Bullinger, Zwingli and Bucer), as well as some publications by French-language authors; moreover, the publication of a commentary in Latin was no innovation, but a continuation of the tradition of the past. Conversely, what is striking in French is the very existence of this category. Prior to the Reformation, only a single systematic commentary of a biblical text was available (the *Epistres sainct Pol glosees*, 1507); but the new importance attributed to the Word of God and its understanding naturally led the Reformers to devote themselves to the systematic explanation of the Bible in a language accessible to the faithful.

The field of polemics naturally offered a concentration of compositions in the 'vulgar tongue' intended to appeal to the 'simple and unlettered'. In this somewhat elastic category some special forms may be noted including attacks on specific subjects – the Mass in Marcourt's writings; in Calvin, relics, 'Nicodemites' (compromisers with Rome), the Anabaptists; and purgatory in an anonymous 1534 pamphlet. Polemical forms included Viret's dialogues, which enabled him to raise a whole range of controversial questions entertainingly but unsystematically; satirical or spiritual songs, theatre – farce, morality, comedy, and, thanks to the Greek specialist Théodore de Bèze, the first tragedy in French, *Abraham sacrifiant* (1550).[91]

---

[91] F. M. Higman, 'Les genres de la littérature calviniste du seizième siècle', in *Prose*, pp. 123–34.

During a short period in 1533–35, Marcourt and his entourage adopted a specific genre of propaganda for use in a hostile environment: the treatise with an ambiguous title.[92] We find (and, exceptionally, I give these titles in translation): *The book of Merchants, very profitable to all folks to know of what wares they ought to beware of, for the beguiling of them* (title of the 1547 English translation); *Very useful and salutary treatise on the Holy Eucharist of our Lord Jesus Christ; A declaration of the mass, the fruit thereof, the cause and the means wherefore and how it ought to be maintained* (title of the 1547 English translation); the *Confession and reason of the faith of Master Noel Beda, Doctor of Theology and Syndic of the holy University of Paris, sent to the Very Christian King of France*, all printed by Pierre de Vingle in Neuchâtel in 1533–34. The last-mentioned text was formulated with sufficient as-

3.5 *La Confession et rayson de la foy de maistre Noel Beda* ([Neuchâtel]: [Pierre de Vingle], 1533)

---

[92] G. Berthoud, 'Livres pseudo-catholiques de contenu protestant', in G. Berthoud et al., *Aspects*, pp. 143–54.

tuteness to oblige the famous Syndic of the Sorbonne to return from his exile in order to establish his innocence before the royal officials.

Subsequently, however, these ambiguous titles are rarely found, except for Calvin's most popular treatise, the *Very profitable treatise declaring what great profit might come to all Christendom, if there were a register made of all Saints' bodies and other relics, which are as well in Italy as in France, Dutchland, Spain, and other kingdoms and countries* (1543, title here of the 1561 English translation). Otherwise, titles were almost always explicit. One genre which continued to appear was the parodied edict, proclamation of a pardon or a jubilee, which rephrased official texts to give them an evangelical message: *Royal edicts and ordinances of the high, supreme and sovereign Court of the Kingdom of Heaven* ... , known in a 1550 edition; or the *General Pardon of total forgiveness to all persons to all eternity*, also dated 1550.

The *Psautier* by Marot and Bèze constitutes a special case among genres. The versified translations of the Psalms undertaken by Clément Marot – the first sample, Psalm VI, first appeared in pamphlet form, then as an appendix to Marguerite de Navarre's *Miroir de l'ame pecheresse* in 1533 – were in no sense seen at first as contributing to the Reformation as such. But the Psalms were adopted in Geneva as a hymn-book (*Aucuns pseaulmes*, Strasbourg, 1539; *Trente Pseaumes* in 1542, 50 in 1543), provided with very sober musical settings and printed in several Genevan and Lyon editions; from then on they became heretical in the eyes of the Sorbonne. However, successive condemnations by the theologians failed to prevent the text from circulating – it appears to be the only case of a censored text continuing to appear in Parisian editions with impunity. Marot died in 1544; from 1551 to 1561, Théodore de Bèze continued the work. The complete *Psautier*, finished at the time of the Colloquy of Poissy, was the subject of the biggest publishing deal involving Geneva in the century. In the climate of toleration surrounding the Colloquy, Beza managed to obtain a certificate of orthodoxy from two Doctors of the Sorbonne, a royal privilege, and a contract with 19 Parisian printers and publishers. As a result of the failure of the Colloquy of Poissy, the contract was annulled, and only seven Parisian editions are known. On the other hand, Genevan and Lyon publishers produced at least 30 000 copies of the *Psautier* in 1562 and 1563.[93]

The Psalter, conceived as poetry and adopted as church hymnal, became one of the most powerful propaganda weapons of the whole

---

[93] Chaix, *Recherches*, p. 52; Droz, 'A. Vincent'; P. Pidoux (ed.), *Les Psaumes en vers français* (Geneva, 1986), pp. 26–8; *Le Psautier de Genève, 1562–1865* (Geneva, 1986).

century.[94] The community singing of psalms enabled the faithful to manifest their identity and their adherence to the Reformed faith. The unlettered could participate as well as the educated. In clandestine meetings, in public worship, in the family and on the battlefields of the civil wars, the Psalms became a central factor in Calvinist spirituality.

The style of polemical writings is varied, but within a limited range. In particular among the Italian refugees in Geneva or Basle, one finds violent denunciations, such as this attack by Piero Paolo Vergerio against a Jubilee proclaimed for 1550, which was translated into French and published in Basle the same year:

> But first let me tell you what sort of man was this Boniface. He was hugely ambitious, cruel, avaricious, seditious and full of deceit, to put it shortly, a thorough villain: just read his life. This was the lad who set up the subtle trick and deception of a voice which, one night, seemed to come from heaven, and told Celestin to renounce the papacy, which he did; Boniface took his place, and promptly had the poor man thrown in prison, where he died of ill treatment. Now let's listen to this holy pope inventing a Jubilee ...[95]

But this energetic and choleric style already practised by Marcourt and sometimes by Farel, was not found uniformly elsewhere. Viret preferred a more relaxed style imitating conversation, even when the text was not in dialogue form, for example in asking questions of the reader. His comic vein was unleashed particularly when he wrote of the Mass:

> Now what would St Paul say today if he went into a church, and heard people singing in a language no one among the people could understand; [...] if he saw this mummer dancing around a wafer like a cat with a mouse, pretending to be afflicted like a crocodile, which cries when it's about to eat a man, then gobbles him up; taking this bread, beating on his breast as if he was really upset; calling it Lamb of God, then eating it, and helping himself to a drink afterwards. What could anyone say who had never seen such pirouettes, such contortions, such a farce? Wouldn't he have to say, 'That poor Lamb never had a chance to become a sheep, since this wolf ate him'?[96]

One of the qualities of Viret's style is the alternation of various tones he can use, from the comic to the furious. Calvin stands out even more in this respect. For example, in the *Excuse aux Nicodemites*, he used vulgar imagery:

---

[94] In Richard Breton's inventory in 1571, the *Psaumes* made up by far the most important item in the stock.

[95] *La Declaration du Jubilé qui doit etre à Rome l'an M.D.L.*, fol. A 2ᵛ (Vienna, Österreichische Nationalbibliothek, 79.Ee.175).

[96] *Des Actes des vrays successeurs de Jesus Christ*, 1554, pp. 32–3.

> I find no more appropriate comparison than to associate them [the
> Nicodemites] with lavatory cleaners. Just as a latrine cleaner, who
> has spent a long time in his profession of shovelling excrement, no
> longer smells the bad odour, [...] so also these people have
> become so habituated to living in their excrement that they imag-
> ine they are among roses.

He parodied the playboys of the court:

> I seem to hear them: 'Don't talk to us of Calvin, he's far too
> inhuman. What? if we were to believe him, he wouldn't just reduce
> us to beggars, but he would lead us straight to the stake. What's
> the hurry? If he wants everyone to be like him, and if he's upset
> that we're better off than he is, what's that to us? We're fine here;
> let him stay where he is, and leave everyone alone'.

He adopted a lawyer's tone:

> I beg them: if they are advocates, let them not take on a case so
> impossible to defend, and which can lead to no other result than
> their confusion. If they are judges, let them not undertake to pass
> sentence on the word of God, which is not subject to their jurisdic-
> tion; indeed, distrusting themselves, and regarding themselves as
> suspect in their own case, let them abstain from judging.

Or the tone could be dramatic: '[when Nicodemus asked Pilate for the
body of Jesus], he did not fear shame and contempt. He did not fear
being hated. He did not fear disorder. He did not fear persecution. That
is to "Nicodemize" ... '. Calvin also added a more sympathetic note for
those who did not reject the doctrine he was expounding – 'Now I will
address myself to those who, in papist countries, fearfully and with
humility recognize their wretched state, and find themselves unwillingly
among the abominations they are forced to witness there, and in which
it even happens that they pollute themselves by their weakness. I well
recognize that they are terribly perplexed ... ' – and he concluded with a
solemn exhortation:

> Let the preachers pay less attention to their own security than to
> what their vocation demands of them, and what they promised
> when they entered the pulpit of truth, when they undertook to
> speak in the name of our Lord Jesus. Let the people treasure the
> doctrine they have received, and may all make it fruitful by pub-
> lishing it from hand to hand. For the rest, since David, wanting to
> bear testimony on behalf of all the faithful, said that he would not
> take part in the sacrifice of idols, and would not allow their name
> in his mouth, then at least let those who fall away from this purity
> recognize their fault, and pray unceasingly to God both to pardon
> them and to bring them back to the straight path.

French Reformation writing generally maintained a stylistic level which,
though not pretentious, was not particularly lowbrow either. The *Ex-*

cuse aux Nicodemites was addressed to clerics, to courtiers, to writers and, lastly, to merchants and the common people. Only the songs and the stage plays were really addressed to the people; and these genres were not the most common in the French Reformation.

Two gaps in the range of genres confirm this 'bourgeois' tendency: the almost total absence of propaganda through images which we have already mentioned, and the rarity of printed sermons. Two of Luther's sermons were translated early into French, and Aimé Meigret's 1524 sermon which caused one of the first scandals of the Reformation in France was published; a few of Calvin's sermons were edited in Geneva in specific contexts. But thousands of sermons preached by Calvin and taken down as they were preached by Denis Raguenier were not printed in the sixteenth century, and some still await a first edition. Among all the sermons which must have been composed by Farel, Viret and Bèze, scarcely a dozen seem to have found their way into print.

Reception

We shall focus on three questions: who could read? What was the intended public for the Reformation book? What reactions were there from the authorities in France?

Literacy rates

We have no direct evidence regarding literacy rates in the sixteenth century. We shall try to bring together some scattered clues which seem to point, despite some inconsistencies, to a certain pattern. In his *Viat de salut*, Guillaume Petit, confessor to Francis I, orders 'all curates, chaplains, vicars and schoolmasters to own the present book, to read it or to have it read in the services on Sundays and feast days, and in the schools, to those children who are capable of understanding it', with the promise of 'forty days' pardon every time they read it or hear it read'. This expression 'read it or hear it read' serves to draw attention to a major feature of the time: reading aloud for the benefit of the illiterate. Petit's text, which is the first French Roman Catholic response to a Reformation book, gives us a general context for the question of reading in the sixteenth century.

The earliest meetings of French 'Lutherans' took place in private homes, where a few people would meet to pray, to listen to the reading of scripture, and to talk about the 'new' teaching. One can well imagine the earliest printed tracts and treatises circulating in such a context, the clandestinity of which matches well the anonymity of the works. 'To read or to hear it read ... ': the same principle can be extended to the early Reformation context.

But later, the book seems to have become a propaganda medium without going through the stage of reading aloud. A splendid ordinance from the city of Laon, in 1565, ordered that all ventilation shafts from basements giving on to the street should be sealed off:

> The reason for this order was that there came into the city men secretly sent from the city of Geneva, carrying little books. [...] These men threw these books secretly and by night into the cellars and basements through the air vents, with the result that, shortly after, a fair number of inhabitants who were avid for novelties abandoned the Roman Catholic religion and adopted the new one, which was then called Lutheran, and all because of these little books.[97]

Was it the servants and the women who first read these 'little books'?

That literacy was far from universal is suggested by the fact that, as late as 1580, out of 115 companion printers who signed a document in Lyon, 43 were unable to write their names. This in a group which in principle should have had a much higher than average literacy rate.[98] We shall come back later to the even lower literacy rates among women, in particular the wives of artisans and workmen.

On the other hand, it is noteworthy that, in Geneva, the whole population was supposed to be able to read from 1542 on: the order of worship in *La Forme des prieres et chants ecclesiastiques* involved participation by the whole congregation in the singing of the Psalms. Was this, however, an ideal rather than reality?

The intended public

At first, Reformation books in French, whether they came from Antwerp, Strasbourg, Alençon, Lyon or from Paris, were mainly aimed at a public within the kingdom of France. Once the 'Swiss' base of the Reformation was affirmed, there were two publics: the convinced faithful in Geneva, Lausanne or Neuchâtel; and the French, in missionary territory.

As regards the first group, the word 'Swiss' is in inverted commas, since it is a glaring anachronism. Neuchâtel, an independent county with allegiance to Berne, became solidly reformed in 1530; but, after the death of Pierre de Vingle in 1535, there was no printing house

---

[97] A. Richart, *Mémoires sur la Ligue dans le Laonnais* (Laon, 1869), p. 492.

[98] Baudrier, vol. 3, p. 1–4, reproduced in N. Z. Davis, 'The printing workers of Lyons in 1551', in G. Berthoud et al., *Aspects*, pp. 256–7.

62 PSEAVME XXII.

Et tes faicts racontans.

PSEAVME XXII. CL. MA.

Prophetie de Iesus Christ, en laquelle Dauid chante d'entree
la baſſe & honteuſe deiection:puis l'exaltation & l'eſtendue
de ſon royaume iuſques aux fins de la terre, & la perpetuelle
duree d'iceiuy.

On Dieu, mô Dieu, pourquoy

m'as tu laiſ ſé Loin de ſecours, d'ennuy

tant op preſ ſé; Et loin du cri que ie

t'ay a dreſ ſé, En ma complainte?

De iour, mô Dieu, ie t'in uo que ſans fein

te, Et tou tes fois ne reſpond ta voix
fam-

3.6 *Les Pseaumes mis en rime francoise* ([Geneva]: Michel Blanchier, 1562).
Note the double marking: the name of each note appears alongside it in
the music

PSEAVME XXII.   63

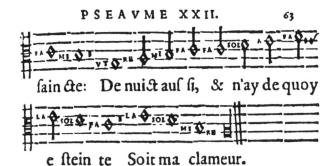

fain &te: De nui&t auſ ſi, & n'ay de quoy

e ſtein te   Soit ma clameur.

Helas, tu es le fain&t & la tremeur,
   Et d'Iſrael le reſident bon-heur,
   Là où t'a pleu que ton los & honneur
      On chante & priſe.
   Nos peres ont leur fiance en toy miſe,
   Leur confiance ils ont ſur toy aſſiſe,
   Et tu les as de captifs en franchiſe
      Touſiours boutez.

A toy crians, d'ennuy furent oſtez,
   Eſperé ont en tes fain&tes bontez,
   Et ont receu ſans eſtre rèboutez,
      Ta grace prompte.
   Mais moy, ie ſuis vn ver qui rien ne monte,
   Et nõ plus hõme, ains des hõmes la honte:
   Et plus ne ſers que de fable & de conte
      Au peuple bas.

            ⁎   *⁎*   *⁎*

through which the pastors and writers of Neuchâtel could spread new texts. Lausanne, a Bernese colony, seems to have had the persistent feeling that the Reformation was imposed on the city by its German-speaking conquerors; in any case, no printer was established in the city before the 1550s, and the leading writers of Lausanne – Viret and Beza – took their manuscripts to Geneva.

In Geneva itself a sizeable proportion of book production was intended for the export market rather than for local consumption. Especially after 1550, the centre of gravity of the Reformation movement in the city was represented by the French refugees rather than by the established Genevan families – a fact which the latter bitterly resented. For those who lived in the city, the evangelical message was above all communicated by sermons: one should bear in mind some 2 300 sermons by Calvin alone recorded by Denis Raguenier, not to speak of those which were preached before this 'stenographer' began work, nor those of all the other pastors in the city. Of course some of the Reformers' writings were aimed at the local population: Calvin's commentaries and other educational works for the Academy, warnings to the faithful against the Anabaptists, the Spiritualists, the astrologers; catechisms and psalters for the life of the Church. But in each case the text was also destined for a wider public, beyond the city limits. Essentially, the Genevan book served the function of long-distance education.

So it is mainly the French public that needs to be studied. What was the target readership, in France or elsewhere? As we have already noted, the Frankfurt fairs provided an important centre for the distribution of works in Latin. Calvin's theology, and his confrontation with strict Lutherans like Westphal, were spread through these fairs towards Germany, Poland, the Low Countries and England.

As regards works in French, we may first note the analysis Calvin himself gave of people who were interested in the new ideas. In the *Excuse aux Nicodemites*, he addressed four categories of people: first churchmen, priests or monks; then courtiers; a third category consisted of 'men of letters', including members of the liberal professions, doctors and lawyers; and finally, the merchants and the common people.

These were represented as potential 'Nicodemites', that is to say people who sought a compromise, who did not want to declare themselves fully for the Reformation. But we know from other sources that the Reformation recruited many of its leaders, and a number of its martyrs, from these social classes: the former monks turned pastors whom we mentioned as authors; Antoine Fumée, councillor in the Paris Parlement; Jean Crespin, lawyer; Laurent de Normandie, royal lieutenant in Noyon; Robert Estienne, scholar and printer; Estienne de La Forge, merchant.

As regards the nobility, several nobles, and in particular noblewomen, took a lively interest in the Reformation from an early stage, including Marguerite de Navarre and Renée de Ferrare. But otherwise, the aristocracy seems to have been little affected in the early period. There was a marked change in the 1550s: Reformed communities in need of protection were more and more placed under the leadership of noblemen, and in the same period, a considerable proportion of noblemen had been noted among the missionaries sent from Geneva to France.[99]

Most attention is usually paid to the names of noblemen, of the wealthier bourgeois, of more or less eminent personalities. But to concentrate on these classes alone would give an entirely false global picture of the Reformation. Imbart de La Tour analysed the victims of persecution in France in the 1540s:

> carpenters, barrel-makers, weavers, tailors, nail-makers, porters, pewter-workers, leather workers, furriers … all the trades appear before the tribunal. Sometimes it is small shopkeepers, well-established, well-known people with a respectable address; at other times journeymen or apprentices, a nomadic population which wanders from town to town, or even from country to country, seeking work and bringing back new ideas.

And later:

> curates, monks, students, tutors, schoolmasters, medical workers, journeymen, and with them the wives, the sisters, the daughters of these artisans who follow them to their secret meetings, to the tribunal, and even to the stake: these are the believers in the new faith … A religion of little people, as the King and his councillors were to put it.[100]

These lists of artisans match the constant preoccupation of Reformation writers to communicate mainly with 'the simple and the unlettered', with the 'little folk', with the 'simple people'. The considerable proportion of artisans is confirmed by the statistics of refugees in Geneva after 1550. For the period 1555–60, two thirds of those who stated their profession when registering their arrival in Geneva were artisans, including weavers, tailors, and goldsmiths.[101] In Lyon, where the Reformation was always a minority phenomenon, converts came 'especially from the newer or more skilled occupations, occupations where the literacy rate was higher'.

---

[99] Kingdon, *Geneva*, pp. 6, 138–9.

[100] P. Imbart de La Tour, *Les Origines de la Réforme* (Paris, 1909–35), vol. 4, pp. 255, 264. On the sociological distribution of the Reformation, see also the important study by H. Heller, *The Conquest of Poverty. The Calvinist Revolt in Sixteenth-Century France* (Leiden, 1986).

[101] Imbart de La Tour, vol. 4, pp. 435–6.

Similarly, 'at the top of urban society, it is the new élite rather than the more established élite that tends to produce Protestants'.[102] Was there any link between this preponderance of the more literate classes and the types of Reformation literature coming from Geneva (more intellectual, more abstract than the German equivalent)?

Finally, among the observations of Imbart de La Tour quoted above, one highly significant allusion should be noted, to women. From Erasmus's hopes that 'even' women should study scripture (*Novum Instrumentum*, 1516) to Florimond de Raemond's denunciation of the fact that women were involving themselves with theology,[103] from the noble ladies such as Renée de Ferrare to the cobbler's wife burnt alive on 22 January 1535 or the five 'Lutheran women' banished on 6 March 1535, the Reformation gave women an autonomous status. Other examples include Marie Dentière, wife of the Geneva pastor Antoine Froment and, it seems, practically the only woman writer of the French Reformation. All these women played a role in Protestant life and worship – 'hence Chrysostome exhorts both men and women and little children to learn to sing them [the Psalms]'[104] – which contrasted with the religious subordination of Roman Catholic women. There was no Reformed literature directed exclusively to women, whereas in Catholicism there was an abundance of books composed specifically for nuns, in which the burning questions of the day were carefully avoided.[105] For the Reformers, the lessons of the faith were directed indiscriminately to both sexes.

Access to books does, however, seem to have been more difficult for women. Among the wives in the better-off social groups – merchants, lawyers, doctors – an education at least in their mother tongue seems to have been the norm. On the other hand, among artisans, where men already had a low literacy rate, almost all their wives appear to have been illiterate.[106]

---

[102] N. Z. Davis, 'The rites of violence: religious riot in sixteenth-century France', *Past and Present*, 59 (1973), 80–81; reprinted in Davis, *Society*, p. 178.

[103] *Histoire de la naissance, progrez et decadence de l'heresie de ce siecle*, Book 7, ch. 7, para. 5 (Paris, 1605), vol. 1, fol. 171ᵛ: 'Even silly little women wanted to pass judgement [on the Bible] as they might on their needle and thread.' On the place of women in the Reformation, see N. L. Roelker, 'The Appeal of Calvinism to French Noblewomen in the Sixteenth Century', in *Journal of Interdisciplinary History*, 2 (1979), 391–418; and especially N. Z. Davis, 'City women and religious change in sixteenth-century France', in D. G. McGuigan (ed.) *A Sampler of Women's Studies* (Ann Arbor, 1973), pp. 17–45; reprinted in N. Z. Davis, *Society*, pp. 65–95.

[104] Foreword to the Geneva *Psautier*.

[105] The *Quenouille spirituelle*, the *Fagot de Myrrhe*, the *Sentier et adresse de devotion*, for example.

[106] Davis, 'City Women', pp. 22–3; Davis, *Society*, pp. 72–3.

There is one almost total gap in the sociological survey of readers: one finds little trace among the refugees, or among the martyrs, of members of the rural population. Right at the end of our period, in the South especially, one finds peasants following their leaders in the Reformation movement; but, illiterate and conservative, they showed a certain degree of hostility to doctrines which offended them 'in the deepest, most intimate fibre of their souls: the cult of saints and the cult of the dead'.[107]

It seems then that in general the Reformation book was aimed more at the city than at the countryside. Within the urban population, almost all classes were affected, but to different extents: the artisans and the 'little folk' received the new faith warmly, the richer classes were very interested, but much tempted by 'Nicodemism'; on the whole the nobles were little affected before the middle of the century, and their motives were often other than religious.

Censorship

One measure of the impact of the Reformation book may be the energy which was deployed in the attempt to suppress it. In France the monarch was referred to as the 'Most Christian King', and the capital housed one of the oldest faculties of theology of Europe; as of April 1521, date of the faculty's *Determinatio* against Luther, there was a rejection in principle of 'heretical' doctrines. However, the definition of 'heresy' was not always entirely clear: while the faculty – or 'the Sorbonne', to those who did not like it – insisted on condemning the works of Erasmus, associating him explicitly with Luther, the king was trying to attract this same Erasmus to a teaching position in France (1523–26). In fact the king, probably highly influenced in his religious policy by his sister Marguerite de Navarre, was long attracted to the 'evangelical' tendency of reformers within the Gallican Church, hostile to the traditionalist theologians grouped around Noël Béda, Syndic of the Sorbonne. Moreover, Francis I needed allies against Charles V, Emperor and King of Spain: it was thus not in his interest to offend Henry VIII of England or the Protestant princes in Germany. One may recall the unedifying spectacle of the royal arm-twisting, exercised via the Du Bellay brothers, and applied to the faculty of theology in order to obtain a vote favourable to Henry VIII's divorce.[108] There was thus

---

[107] Imbart de La Tour, *Les Origines de la Réforme*, vol. 4, p. 263.

[108] See J. S. Brewer, J. Gairdner, R. H. Brodie (eds), *Letters and Papers Foreign and Domestic of the Reign of Henry VIII* (London, 1862–1910), vol. 4/3; for a study of the period, see J. Le Grand, *Histoire du divorce de Henry VIII, roy d'Angleterre, et de Catherine d'Aragon* (Paris, 1688), vol. 3; see also G. Bedouelle and P. LeGal, *Le 'Divorce' d'Henry VIII d'Angleterre* (Geneva, 1987); Farge, *Orthodoxy and Reform*, pp. 135–43.

plenty of potential for conflict between the king and faculty. The third important factor was the Parlements, magistrates responsible for registering the edicts of the royal administration, and equipped with the physical means – officers, prisons, torture chambers – for the imposition of the law. At the time there were seven regional Parlements in France; but only the Parlement of Paris, with its close proximity to the faculty of theology, seems to have played an active role in the censorship process. The faculty could not act on its own, but was dependent on the co-operation of the secular powers in order to apply a censorship policy.

During the 1520s this co-operation was not always forthcoming. Lefèvre d'Étaples and Louis de Berquin benefited from royal protection when the Sorbonne sought to condemn their translations; when Noël Béda published his censures of the writings of Lefèvre and of Erasmus in 1526, the Parlement, on the instructions of the King, forced him to justify himself, and compelled him to recover, as far as possible, the copies which had been put on sale.[109] On the other hand, during the king's imprisonment in Madrid in 1525–26, faculty and Parlement came together in a concerted condemnation of French translations of the Bible and Lefèvre's *Epistres et evangiles*; as has already been noted, no Parisian edition of the Bible in French appeared between 1527 and 1565. In 1529, while the king was away from Paris, Berquin was hastily condemned and executed.

But these were specific events; moreover, the very modest scale of the trade in 'heretical' books did not demand a huge repressive mechanism. Censorship proper did not appear until the three power bases – the king, Parlement and faculty – acted in unison, and until the problem grew in size. A first example of united action was the aftermath of the *Affaire des placards* (1534–35):[110] executions of heretics, including two printers and a bookseller; book condemnations (but without any examination which would have left clues as to what books were condemned); a list of wanted persons, including three printers, two bookbinders and a peddler; and the notorious royal edict forbidding any printing at all in the kingdom until further order (13 January 1535). But once the crisis was past, the edicts of July 1535 and May 1536 reinstated a relative toleration, discussions with Melanchthon resumed, and the printers continued to work. Since there was a sort of hiatus throughout the francophone world in the production of Reformation books in the period 1535–40, the problem lost its urgency.

---

[109] Farge, *Orthodoxy and Reform*, p. 193; Higman, *Censorship*, p. 27.

[110] R. Hari, 'Les placards de 1534', in G. Berthoud et al., *Aspects*, pp. 79–142; the list of 'wanted persons', pp. 104–6.

There was a radical change after 1540, thanks mainly to the installation in Geneva of a sizeable printing industry directed primarily towards France. In 1542, Calvin's *Institution* was condemned. In 1543, a first list of works condemned by the Faculty appeared, no longer focusing solely on individual items: 63 titles were listed, of which 27 were from Geneva. This first list was not published; but the 1544 *Catalogue des livres censurez* was published by the faculty, and thus became the earliest manifestation of the Roman Catholic *Index des livres interdits*. In 1545 this same list reappeared, this time with the authority of the Paris Parlement. The reaction of the accredited booksellers of the University of Paris to this 1545 edict is eloquent concerning the respective authority of the faculty and the Parlement: the 24 *libraires jurés* complained to the Parlement that 'these books, or many of them, have always been freely on sale, without their being condemned or forbidden by anyone', and that 'no order had ever been made to them forbidding the printing, purchase from foreigners, or putting on sale of the same'. Since three-quarters of the French-language books which were thus 'condemned or forbidden' came from Geneva, this affirmation is somewhat surprising.[111] It seems that it was possible to ignore a list published by the faculty of theology; but that a condemnation backed by the authority of the Parlement was another matter. Since censorship was henceforth official, however, the trade in Reformation books definitively became clandestine.

But it did not cease. A succession of edicts concentrated ever more specifically on imported books, notably from Geneva, since the Parisian censorship had succeeded in more or less suppressing the production of Reformation books in Paris. The 1551 Edict of Châteaubriant attempted to control once and for all book production and trade: no anonymous printing, no importation of books without inspection, searches of bookshops, display of a list of books on sale side by side with a copy of the *Catalogue des livres censurez*. The 1551 edition of the *Catalogue* bears the clearest witness to the extraordinary influence which could be exerted by a single printshop. Of the 16 French texts condemned for the first time and for which the origin can be identified, 11 came from Geneva; and among them, eight were printed by Jean Girard, the only printer active in the city between 1544 and 1550.

During the decade after the Edict of Châteaubriant, the lists of refugees in Geneva include more than 130 booksellers and printers: the polarization of the world of books between Reformation and ortho-

---

111 N. Weiss, 'La Sorbonne et la librairie parisienne: requête des vingt-quatre libraires jurés de l'université au Parlement, 29–30 juin 1545', *BSHPF*, 40 (1891), 634–8; Higman, *Censorship*, p. 62.

doxy was complete, and the Genevan printing industry was launched on a period of expansion which continued until the outbreak of the wars of religion.[112] A final list of condemned books, in 1556, continued the concentration of previous lists on Genevan titles, with this time an important contribution from printers recently established in the city, such as Jean Crespin, Robert Estienne and Philibert Hamelin; but this was the last published list from Paris, and book censorship became thereafter a responsibility of Rome.

The responses

Censorship may have made the trade in forbidden books dangerous; but it could not suppress that trade. The only valid response to a bad book is a good book. This was one of the most important influences of the Reformation: the French language was adapted for the communication of theological thought, in the Roman Catholic Church as well as in Protestantism. We have already mentioned the development of the Catholic polemical book:[113] Catholic replies to Reformation treatises appeared from 1526 on and, after a period of considerable hesitation until 1550, certain theologians applied themselves energetically to the explanation of the Roman Catholic faith in French. True, they were not on the whole great writers – for that one must await Jacques Davy Du Perron or St François de Sales – but none the less, men like Gentian Hervet, René Benoist, Antoine Du Val, and Émond Auger contributed powerfully to one of the most durable effects of the Reformation in France: the forging of the French language as a weapon for abstract argument, first in the field of theology, then, after 1560, in politics.

Summary bibliography

Berthoud, G., et al., *Aspects de la propagande religieuse*, (Geneva, 1957) (Travaux d'Humanisme et Renaissance, 28).

Bujanda, J. M. de, Higman, F. M. and Farge, J. K., (eds), *Index de l'Université de Paris* (Sherbrooke, 1985) (Index des livres interdits, 1).

Droz, E., *Chemins de l'hérésie. Textes et documents* (4 vols, Geneva, 1970–76).

---

[112] On the successive edicts concerning the book trade, see Higman, *Censorship*, pp. 50, 64–6. For the refugees in Geneva, see Chaix, *Recherches*, pp. 48–51.
[113] See above, pp. 117–18.

Martin, H.-J. and Chartier, R. (eds), *Histoire de l'édition française*, vol. 1: *Le Livre conquérant. Du Moyen Age au milieu du XVIIe siècle* (Paris, 1982).

Moore, W. G., *La Réforme allemande et la littérature française: Recherches sur la notoriété de Luther en France* (Strasbourg, 1930)

Complementary bibliography

Since the publication of the French original of this book, a number of works have advanced our knowledge of the field of French Reformation printing. Of particular note are the following:

Baddeley, S., *L'Orthographe française au temps de la Réforme* (Geneva, 1993).

Cottret, B., *Calvin. Biographie* (Paris, 1995).

Higman, F., *La Diffusion de la Réforme en France* (Geneva, 1992).

Higman, F., *Piety and the People. Religious Printing in French, 1511–1551* (Aldershot, 1996).

Peter, R. and Gilmont, J.-F., *Bibliotheca Calviniana. Les oeuvres de Jean Calvin publiées au XVIe siècle*, vol. I: *Écrits théologiques, littéraires et juridiques, 1532–1554* (Geneva, 1991), vol. II: *Écrits théologiques, littéraires et juridiques, 1555–1564* (Geneva, 1994).

These publications fill out various aspects of the picture presented in the original text; but the general outlines remain unchanged.

CHAPTER FOUR

Printing and the Reformation in the Low Countries, 1520–*c*.1555

Andrew G. Johnston

The printing output of the Low Countries was insignificant compared with the 10 000 Protestant pamphlets printed in German in the first half of the sixteenth century.[1] Between 1520 and 1540, only 170 Protestant works appeared in Dutch.[2] But if one considers the areas in which civil powers opposed the Reformation, this figure is astonishingly high. More than 40 different works by Luther were translated into Dutch between 1520 and 1540, while only 16 translations into French and eight into English appeared in the same time span.[3]

The production of Catholic works in the Low Countries in the early sixteenth century provides another barometer of the Reformation's impact on printing. After reaching their zenith in 1518, vernacular Catholic works (books of hours, lives of Christ, etc.) rapidly diminished in number in the 1520s, and only rose slightly in the 1530s. This evolution was similar to that encountered in a city like Strasbourg, where the Reformation received official support.[4] In Strasbourg, the drop in the number of Catholic works was sharper, and there was no revival in the 1530s, unlike in the Low Countries, but both areas experienced the same decrease in the 1520s.

All these indications point to the major influence of the new theology on the literate population of the Low Countries. Some 202 Catholic

---

[1] S. Ozment, 'Pamphlet literature of the German reformation' in S. E. Ozment (ed.) *Reformation Europe: A Guide to Research* (St Louis, 1982), p. 85.

[2] This figure excludes Bibles and works published in Latin and French, but includes Anabaptist writings and texts which have been lost. In general, Anabaptist works are not dealt with, as they were mainly printed outside the Low Countries.

[3] M. E. Kronenberg, 'Uitgaven van Luther in de Nederlanden verschenen tot 1541', in *Nederlands archief voor kerkgeschiedenis*, 40 (1954), 6–15; 49 (1968/69), 102. F. M. Higman, 'Les traductions françaises de Luther, 1524–1550', in J.-Fr. Gilmont (ed.) *Palaestra typographica: aspects de la production du livre humaniste et religieux au XVIe siècle* (Aubel, 1984), pp. 11–13. For English works see *STC*, nos 16962, 16979.7, 16988, 16999, 10493, 11394, 13086, 20193.

[4] See M. U. Chrisman's chapter on Strasbourg and her work, *Lay Culture, Learned Culture: Books and Social Change in Strasbourg, 1480–1599* (New Haven, London, 1982), p. 288.

works compare with 170 Protestant ones printed between 1520 and 1540. In a society in which the Reformation was fiercely attacked by the civil and religious authorities, the fact that the evangelical works made up half of the total number of religious books was astounding.

Book production

The production centres

Beginning in 1473 in Alost and Utrecht, printing spread rapidly in many cities of the Low Countries.[5] After a slow start, Antwerp became the most important printing centre in the sixteenth century. Indeed, for 25 years, Antwerp retained its role as a centre of Protestant book printing, and its influence in this field spread far beyond the borders of the Netherlands.[6]

Antwerp's domination continued until around 1545. However, other cities in the Low Countries also printed Protestant works: Zwolle (Simon Corver), Amsterdam (Doen Pietersz), Delft (Cornelis Henricz. Lettersnijder), Leiden (Jan Seversz and Peter Jansz), Ghent (Joos Lambrecht Lettersnijder) and elsewhere. However, of the two dozen printers of evangelical works in these years, more than half were based in Antwerp.

By the mid-1540s Antwerp, for several reasons, ceased to be the hub of the Protestant book trade in the Low Countries. First, the effectiveness of persecution and repression meant that some of the main Antwerp printing houses were closed down. Second, the confessional stance of the Low Countries changed from Lutheran to Calvinist.

John Calvin's influence began to be felt in the Low Countries over the set-up of a church structure independent from that of the Roman church. Naturally enough, his views entered the Netherlands through French-speaking areas. In 1543, 200 copies of his *Petit traicté monstrant que c'est que doit faire un homme fidele congnoissant la verité de l'evangile: quant il est entre les papistes* were handed out in Tournai. Because of the objections of certain members of the Protestant community against Calvin's rigid views, the Genevan reformer answered them in an even harsher pamphlet, *L'Excuse à messieurs les Nicodemites sur la complainte*

---

[5] P. R. J. Obbema and A. Derolez, 'De productie en verspreiding van het boek 1300–1500', in *Algemene geschiedenis der Nederlanden* (Haarlem, 1980) vol. 4, p. 351; *Le cinquième centenaire de l'imprimerie dans les anciens Pays-Bas: Catalogue* (Brussels, 1973).

[6] See Chapter on Antwerp in this volume.

qu'ils font de sa trop grande rigueur (1544).[7] These two anti-Nicodemite pamphlets were the first of Calvin's writings to be translated into Dutch: both were printed in Emden in 1554.[8]

In spite of his initial lack of appeal, Calvin's position grew steadily stronger. Around 1550, a full-fledged Protestant church was set up in London led by Martin Micron.[9] In 1553, Mary Tudor's accession led to the restoration of Catholicism in England and to the exile of most Dutch Protestants. The exiles established Flemish communities in Frankfurt and Emden, and their importance cannot be underestimated. First, these stranger churches provided organizational and structural models for the establishment of Reformed congregations in the Low Countries. Second, these churches provided a general oversight of the congregations in their homeland. The Reformed community in Antwerp, for instance, asked for advice and directions from the Emden church because of a conflict over the role of their minister, Adriaen van Haemstede.[10]

Thus, after 1545, many of the Protestant printers left the Low Countries, to settle in cities outwith the political control of Charles V, and then of his successor, Philip II.[11] Setting up print-shops in other areas had clear advantages over clandestine printing, as it offered much more freedom to a heterodox printer. But this was only a minor advantage, as the main reason for leaving the Low Countries was the growing success of repression of the heretical booktrade.[12]

---

[7] A. Erichson, *Bibliographia Calviniana* (Berlin, 1900), p. 4; J.-Fr. Gilmont, 'Bibliotheca gebennensis: les livres imprimés à Genève de 1535 à 1549', *Genava*, 28 (1980), 237, 239. These texts have been reprinted in J. Calvin, *Opera quae supersunt omnia*, G. Baum, E. Cunitz and E. Reuss (eds), (Brunschwig, Berlin, 1863–1900) vol. 6, cols 537– 614. On this episode, see G. Moreau, *Histoire du protestantisme à Tournai jusqu'à la veille de la Révolution des Pays-Bas* (Paris, 1962), p. 90.

[8] *Van dat schuwer der afgoderie valschen godsdients, ende gheveynstheyt* (Amsterdam, VU, XC 05517) and *Excuse tot mijn heeren die nicodemiten* (ibid., XC 05516).

[9] For a detailed study of the London refugee churches see A. Pettegree, *Foreign Protestant Communities in Sixteenth Century London* (Oxford, 1986).

[10] H. Q. Janssen and J. J. van Toorenenbergen, 'Brieven uit onderscheine kerkelijke archieven' in *Werken der Marnix-vereeniging*, 3rd series, vol. 11/1 (Utrecht, 1877), pp. 53, 72. See also Ph. Denis, *Les Eglises d'étrangers en pays rhénans (1538–1564)* (Paris, 1984).

[11] The clandestine work of several printers has been investigated by P. Valkema Blouw, 'Printers to Hendrik Niclaes: Plantin and Augustijn van Hasselt', *Quaerendo*, 14 (1984), 247–72; *idem*, 'Augustijn van Hasselt as a printer in Vianen and Wesel', *Quaerendo*, 16 (1986), 83–109, 163–90; *idem*, 'The secret background of Lenaert der Kinderen's activities, 1562–1567', *Quaerendo*, 17 (1987), 83–127.

[12] The gradual decline of Emden as a printing centre after 1572 and the rising importance of Reformed printing presses in Holland and Zeeland suggest that the Dutch printers preferred to work in their homeland, as soon as this was possible.

In the 1540s, many Flemish printers left Antwerp for London, where they produced Reformed works in their native language. In 1553, they were forced to go into exile once more, following the accession of Mary Tudor. The printers settled in Emden, where they began to publish works in the following year. Emden thus became a highly productive printing centre, and even the most important one for Dutch Protestantism. Between 1554 and 1569, 230 works were published there. Two rival firms carried out most of the printing: the firm first owned by van der Erven and van den Berghe, and that of Gaillairt and Mierdmans.

Emden's book production differed from that of the Antwerp presses. In the 1520s, 1530s and 1540s, the latter published evangelical non-confessional works, strongly influenced by Lutheranism. In the 1550s, partly due to their experiences in London, the Emden printers produced Reformed works: catechisms, Bibles, and writings by Bullinger, Beza, Melanchthon, de Brès and Calvin.[13] Following the same confessional line, numerous pamphlets were also published in Vianen beginning in 1563, thanks to the hospitality of the sovereign powers of the Brederode family.[14]

As the Reformed Protestants' influence grew over evangelicals in the Low Countries, the Lutherans tried belatedly and unsuccessfully to bring the Dutch Reformation on their side, through a series of works printed by Hans de Braecker at Wesel.[15] Encouraged by a certain H. de Bert, these were clearly confessional publications: the *Augsburg Confession*, for instance, was translated and printed in 1558. This type of work marked a clear contrast with the broadly evangelical Lutheran writings published in the previous decades.

By this stage, not all Protestant print-shops were polarized by the confessional conflict between the Reformed and the Lutherans. Peter Warnersz in Kampen pursued the tradition of a more general evangelism in the 1550s and 1560s,[16] in particular with *Der christen reghel*, a

---

[13] A. Pettegree, 'The exile churches and the churches "under the cross": Antwerp and Emden during the Dutch Revolt', *Journal of Ecclesiastical History*, 38 (1987), 196–7. See also J. Decavele, 'Enkele gegevens betreffende de relaties tussen het drukkerscentrum Emden et het gebied Gent-Oudenaarde tijdens het "Wonderjaar", in *Liber amicorum Dr. J. Scheerder* (Louvain, 1987), pp. 17–28.

[14] H. de la Fontaine Verwey, 'Hendrik van Brederode en de drukkerijen van Vianen', *Het boek*, 39 (1949/51), 3–41.

[15] For a list of these works, see J. W. Pont, *Geschiedenis van het Lutheranisme in de Nederlanden tot 1618* (Haarlem, 1911), pp. 55–9.

[16] G. H. A. Krans, 'Peter Warnersen, drukker en uitgever te Kampen', *Het boek*, 24 (1936/37), 147–86.

reprint of the catechism first printed by Crom in 1543,[17] *Van dye bruyt Christi, een devote contemplacie*, a partial reprint of the semi-mystical work *Profitelic ende troostelic bockxken van der ghelovve ende hoope*[18] and Matthijs Lenaerts's *Sterfboexken*.[19]

Between 1520 and 1566, around 40 printers of Protestant works were active in the Low Countries, making up about a fifth of the total number of printers. Most of these only produced one or two pamphlets, a Bible or a New Testament. The highly productive printers only numbered a half-dozen, most based in Antwerp.[20] However, there were others, like Simon Corver, one of the very first evangelical printers. A priest from Amsterdam, he was rapidly part of the Reformation movement in his native city. In an ordinance dated 13 June 1536, he was described as 'the first to have established Luther's sect in Amsterdam'.[21] Corver pioneered the printing and distribution of evangelical pamphlets in the Low Countries. Between 1519 and 1522, he printed a total of 14 Lutheran pamphlets in Zwolle.[22] Corver returned to Amsterdam at the end of 1522 or early in 1523, according to the testimony of a priest who claimed that in June 1523, Corver was in jail in Amsterdam.[23] The priest asked for Corver to be kept there, as he was under suspicion of heresy. It seems that Corver's presses were then taken over by his brother Wilhelm, who left Amsterdam for Hamburg in 1522. Between 1522 and 1523, Wilhelm Corver printed 15 other pamphlets, 11 by Luther but only one of these in Dutch. The others were in German. Corver's presses shut down abruptly in 1523; his presses and founts were bought by the Antwerp printer Johannes Hillenius.[24]

---

[17] For Crom's edition see J. Machiels (ed.) *Catalogus van de boeken gedruckt voor 1600 aanwezig op de centrale bibliotheek van de rijksuniversiteit Gent* (Ghent, 1979) R 85; Warnersz's edition is kept in The Hague, KB, 1708 D 34(5).

[18] The Hague, KB, 1708 D 34(4). Re-edition in *BRN*, 5, pp. 521–92.

[19] London, BL 4401. aa. 6. This is not Warnersz' edition, but the 1570 Index notes an edition which states 'Ghedruckt te Campen. In die Broederstrate bij mij Peter Waermersoene' (Reusch, p. 316).

[20] For a description of these printers, see the chapter on Antwerp.

[21] M. E. Kronenberg, 'Simon Corver in de gevangenis (1536)', *Het boek*, 30 (1949–51), 315.

[22] C. Ch. G. Visser, *Luther's geschriften in de Nederlanden tot 1546* (Assen, 1969), p. 150.

[23] J. G. C. Joosting and S. Müller (eds) *Bronnen voor de geschiedenis der kerkelijke rechtspraak in Utrecht* (The Hague, 1906–24) vol. 3, p. 404.

[24] Visser, *Luthers geschriften*, p. 150. M. E. Kronenberg, 'S. Corver', p. 314. The source of heretical works appearing in Hamburg in 1522–23 remains unclear: were they produced by Wilhelm Corver or Johannes Hillenius? The typographical equipment went from the one to the other, but when? J. Benzing, *Die Buchdrucker des 16. und 17. Jahrhunderts im deutschen Sprachgebiet* (Wiesbaden, 1982), pp. 179–80.

Hillenius, who printed in Antwerp from 1525 to 1530 and 1535 to 1543, also spent time in Lübeck in 1531–32, and in Malmö between 1533 and 1535.[25] His foreign stays enabled him to publish Protestant works for Pedersen, both in Hamburg and in Malmö.

Steven Mierdmans, who was forced into exile around 1546, spent seven years in London, where he printed a few Dutch works. After Mary's accession to the throne, he emigrated to Emden, where he printed under his own name and under the pseudonym of Magnus vanden Merberghe van Oesterhout. He often worked with Willem Gaillart, competing with the rival firm of Gillis van der Erven (Ctematius) and Niclaes van den Berghe.[26]

More than half of the evangelical texts and Dutch Bibles printed between 1520 and 1565 were the work of Simon Corver and the Antwerp printers Johannes Hillenius van Hoochstraten, Adriaen van Berghen, Jacob van Liesvelt, Matthias Crom, Steven Mierdmans (and the mysterious Nicolas van Oldenborch). Of these six printers, one was jailed at least twice (Simon Corver), one was exiled twice (Steven Mierdmans), while two or perhaps three others were executed for heterodox activities (Adriaen van Berghen, Jacob van Liesvelt, and perhaps Nicolas van Oldenborch). This result makes one wonder whether these printers were fully aware of the risks they took. Alternatively, it can be argued that these prosecutions demonstrate the printers' commitment to the evangelical cause.

As for the 30 or so other printers responsible for the rest of the heterodox editions, their main motivations may well have been opportunism and the search for profits. After all, the printers' aim was to make money, and evangelical books represented a growing market. Some printers were happy to print both orthodox Catholic works and evangelical ones simultaneously. Willem Vorsterman was the most typical of these printers.[27] Whatever the motivations of that group, it is more difficult to believe that men like van Berghen and Liesvelt printed evangelical works solely for profit. The leading Reformation printers seemed to be deeply involved in the Protestant cause, an involvement which did not, however, exclude the occasional printing of a few Catholic works. Liesvelt printed a decree against heresy, probably hoping to deflect the authorities' suspicions. However, the number of evangelical publications printed by these men, and their continuing work following

---

[25] Benzing, *Die Buchdrucker*, p. 302.

[26] H. F. Wijnman, 'The mysterious sixteenth-century printer Niclaes van Oldenborch: Antwerp or Emden?' in S. van der Woude (ed.) *Studia bibliographica in honorem Herman de la Fontaine Verwey* (Amsterdam, 1968), pp. 463–72.

[27] See p. 200–201.

persecution, suggest that there were more than financial interests at stake.

The importance of repressive legislation meant that evangelical printers and publishers had to work under conditions of absolute secrecy, thus making it difficult to identify their presses. The printers produced many anonymous works, so that bibliographers were forced to use typographical clues to determine who printed the works. Furthermore, these printers deliberately misled their readers by using fake addresses to avoid detection. M. E. Kronenberg identified around 40 books printed in the Low Countries between 1520 and 1540 bearing false addresses.[28] Most of these were in English and in Latin; 12 were published in Dutch. In essence, there are two types of fictional addresses. One set could be described as extravagant and absurd, and are clearly false. These were the first to be used by Dutch printers, appearing in Latin publications beginning around 1521.[29] Two Dutch pamphlets bear this kind of address. An anti-papal tract entitled *De daden werken ende leringhe ons Heeren Ihesu Christi ende des Paus* (c.1525)[30] had as colophon 'Buyten Rome in S. Pieters Hof'.[31] The address provided for the *Gulden opschrift in der Minrebroeders reghel* by François Lambert (1526) was 'In Eutopia bij Resam Mondorf'.[32] In both cases, the printer was poking fun at the authorities while at the same time avoiding detection; in the first case, the address added another element of anti-papal satire.

A more subtle strategy offered a more plausible address in order to appear authentic. The past master of these counterfeit addresses was

4.1   Colophon from *De daden werken ende leringhe ons heeren* (c.1525)

---

[28] M. E. Kronenberg, 'Forged addresses in Low Country books, in the period of Reformation', *The Library*, 5, II (1947) 81.

[29] See NK 2227, 3998, 4154.

[30] NK 675.

[31] This satirical colophon was not unique. Another antipapal pamphlet, probably published for the first time in the 1560s had as colophon 'Buyten Roomen'. See W. P. C. Knuttel, *Catalogus van de pamfletten-verzameling berustende in de Koninklijke Bibliotheek* (The Hague, 1889–1916) p. 549.

[32] NK 1310

℃ Gbebⱬuct te Baſel/by mi Adam Anonymus
Jnt laer ono Beeren.M.CCCCC.ᵣᵣviᶝ.

4.2   Colophon from Luther's *Postillen* (Antwerp: Hillenius, 1528)

Johannes Hillenius van Hoochstraten, the printer and publisher:[33] he used a variety of pseudonyms for a large number of English works and four Dutch ones. Highly ingenious, Hillenius used the colophon 'Gedruckt te Basel bi mi Adam Anonymus' twice in Dutch works: in Johannes Bugenhagen's *Souter* (1536)[34] and Luther's *Postillen* (1528).[35] Furthermore, Hoochstraten used the address 'Gedruckt te Marborch bi mi Steffen Rodt' for Luther's *Vermaninge aen de gheestelike op de rijcsdach te Ausborch vergadert* (1530)[36] and 'Gedruct te Marburg in Hessen bi Hans … ' for the *Articulen te Marburg geaccordeert* (1529).[37] These more complicated addresses had two main advantages over the more absurd ones. First, not only did they distract the attention of the authorities, but they pointed to a foreign place of printing. As regards the names mentioned above, Stephan Rodt was rector and secretary in Zwickau, where he played a major role in the distribution of Luther's works, while Hans Luft was an evangelical printer in Wittenberg, who sometimes worked in a Marburg branch of the presses.[38] Second, this type of address increased the evangelical readers' interest in these works. The printers of Protestant pamphlets could have used colophons indicating that these were orthodox works, by adopting the name and address of a Catholic printer in Louvain, for instance. However, this would then have discouraged potential Protestant buyers. By using the addresses of well-known Protestant centres, the works were unmistakably Protestant. This scheme was clearly successful, for no Dutch printer was attacked for printing heretical works with a false address.

The printed format

As regards the format, the majority of Protestant works followed a simple model. They were printed in gothic type, in octavo, on poor quality paper. In the sixteenth century, there were essentially only two

---

[33] See pp. 198–9.
[34] NK 508. M. E. Kronenberg, 'De geheimzinnige drukkers Adam Anonymus te Bazel en Hans Luft te Marburg ontmaskerd', *Het boek*, 8 (1919), 241–80.
[35] NK 3464.
[36] NK 4163.
[37] NK 2314.
[38] M. E. Kronenberg, *Verboden boeken en opstandige drukken in de hervormingstijd* (Amsterdam, 1948), pp. 78–9.

fonts: gothic and roman.[39] Roman fonts, made fashionable by Petrarch and his disciples, were used in general for Latin texts and for humanist works in particular, while gothic fonts were the traditional choice for vernacular works and theological writings. In the Low Countries, as in Germany, Scandinavia and the Slavic lands, gothic fonts remained dominant. It seems that the Dutch found it difficult to read their own language in roman font. In the preface of *Refereynen int vroede, int sotte, int amoureuze* (1539),[40] printed in roman font, the editor, Joos Lambrecht from Ghent wrote, 'I am ashamed of the rustic nature of so many people in our lands, who are unable to read Dutch or Flemish printed in Roman characters, and who say that they do not know these letters, but imagine that they are Latin or Greek'.[41] The gothic font seems to have been more accessible to the literate public of the Low Countries who did not know Latin. Although the Antwerp printer Pieter Coecke published the French and German versions of Sebastiano Serlio's work on architecture in roman font, Coecke returned to the gothic font for the Dutch text, 'so that the common man may read it more easily'.[42]

From time to time, printers of Protestant works used characters other than gothic. Lenaert der Kinderen published a Protestant Bible in 1563 entirely in cursive,[43] but this attempt was only partially successful.[44] The only notable exception to the use of gothic font in Flemish texts was in the work of certain printers who used script type in the 1560s. Script type, known in Dutch as *geschreven letter* and in French as *caractère de civilité* was an adaptation of manual gothic cursive, and was used for the first time by the French printer Robert Granjon in Lyon in Innocenzio Ringhieri's *Dialogue de la vie et de la mort* (1557).[45] As script type was used in many French catechisms and school-books with Calvinist tendencies, it is often linked to heterodoxy.[46] However, these catechisms were not purely Calvinist, but instead were part of an evangelical, humanist and Christian tendency. But it is still possible that

---

[39] There were three types of gothic characters: the accounting character, the breviary character, and the bastard (Febvre/Martin, p. 109).

[40] NK 1785.

[41] H. de la Fontaine Verwey, *Uit de wereld van het boek. I. Humanisten, dwepers en rebellen in de zestiende eeuw* (Amsterdam, 1975), p. 135.

[42] Fontaine Verwey, *Uit de wereld* pp. 64, 135.

[43] Cursive or chancellery characters were tied to Roman writings, and were the origin of italic (Febvre/Martin, p. 109).

[44] Fontaine Verwey, *Uit de wereld* p. 20.

[45] H. Carter and H. D. L. Vervliet, *Civilité types* (Oxford, 1966), p. 11.

[46] Fontaine Verwey, *Uit de wereld*, pp. 139–41. For the similar situation in France, see Chapter 3, footnote 53 in this volume.

the script type was used by the Christian humanists when they wrote in the vernacular because they felt that the gothic font was unpleasant and barbaric. The only Dutch evangelical works to be printed in script type were the *Gheestelijcken ABC ghelegen wt den psalm van David*, by the Antwerp rhetorician Cornelis Crul (Antwerp, Willem Silvius, 1564)[47] and two short anonymous treatises printed by Ameet Tavernier from Antwerp, the *Fonteyne des levens* (1564 and 1567)[48] and *Een corte onderwijsinghe wter heyliger schriftueren* (1562 and 1567).[49] There are few other exceptions to the use of gothic. As the vast majority of Dutch works appeared in gothic font, one must conclude that they were aimed at a less well-educated readership.

In the same way as most of these works are in gothic font, all but a small minority are in octavo format. Obviously there are a few exceptions, as in the case of the fonts. The anti-papal satire, *Die daden werken ende leerijnghe ons heeren Ihesu Christi ende des Paus* was published in quarto, as was the Dutch translation of Bugenhagen's commentary on the Psalms, *Die souter Verclaringhe des ghehellen psalters*.[50]

The books printed in larger formats were generally longer works. Bugenhagen's *Souter* has 316 sheets, whereas Luther's folio volume *Postillen op die epistelen ende evangelien* (1528) is 600 sheets long. Because of the small number of characters printed on an octavo page, a larger format for very long works is more practical: as the book is thinner, it is easier to bind and handle. However, the vast majority of evangelical works are in octavo. This reflects the general tendency of sixteenth-century printing: approximately half the books published by Christopher Plantin were in octavo.[51] But there were other practical reasons for printing heterodox works in a smaller format, since they could easily be concealed if necessary. A Protestant from Bruges, the carpenter Dierik van Eeno, hid his copy of the *Fonteyne des levens* up his sleeve.[52] Similarly, when Jan Schats from Louvain handed Urbanus Rhegius's *Dialogus van de prekinghe die Christus den tween discipelen dede tot Emaus* (1538) to an evangelical disciple, Jan van Ousberghen, he carried the book in his sleeve.[53]

---

[47] Carter and Vervliet, *Civilité types*, p. 95, number 81.

[48] Ibid., pp. 95–6, nos 82, 107.

[49] Ibid., pp. 95–6, nos 58, 91.

[50] NK 508.

[51] L. Voet, *The Golden Compasses* (Amsterdam, 1969) vol. 2, p. 167.

[52] J. Decavele, *De dageraad van de reformatie in Vlaanderen (1520–1565)* (Brussels, 1975) vol. 1, p. 259.

[53] NK 1789. Francisco de Enzinas, *Mémoires*, Ch. Al. Campan (ed.), (Brussels, 1862) vol. 1, p. 362 (Collection de mémoires relatifs à l'histoire de Belgique, 13).

In general, Protestant works were published on poor quality paper, reflecting the need to reduce costs, for paper was one of the most expensive factors in book production. L. Voet estimates that in Plantin's firm, paper made up 60 to 70 per cent of the printing cost of the book, and this figure could rise to 75 per cent for very large print runs.[54] Plantin specialized in printing missals and breviaries. In these cases, very high quality paper was required, while costs played a more minor role. Thus, paper costs for Plantin were probably higher than the norm. Furthermore, Reformation books were aimed at a very wide public, and therefore, costs were kept down in order to end up with reasonably priced books.[55]

The absence of woodcuts in the first years of the Reformation in the Low Countries is striking.[56] Some trials did mention heretical illustrations. In 1527, a goldsmith belonging to the evangelical circle of Nicolas van der Elst in Brussels owned a lampoon against the clergy.[57] In Amsterdam in 1534, the painter Peter Rippensz was condemned to a pilgrimage to Rome because of one of his paintings, showing monks as demons, chasing money, cheeses and other goods.[58] Certain books, especially Luther's *Postillen op die epistelen ende evangelien* and Cornelis vander Heyden's *Corte instruccye* (1543) contained engravings depicting biblical scenes.

However, in general engravings did not play a prominent role in the Dutch Reformation. There are three possible reasons for this. As we shall see, literacy rates in the Low Countries were higher than in Germany. If illustrations were intended primarily as a means of communicating the Reformation to the illiterate population, one can suggest that there were fewer reasons to print illustrations if the reading public was more numerous in the Low Countries. However, this hypothesis is open to question, as it cannot explain the many satirical engravings which were distributed in the 1560s and 1570s, after the explosion of the Revolt.[59] A more plausible explanation for the absence of engravings during the first years of the Dutch Reformation can be found in the

[54] Voet, *The Golden Compasses*, p. 19. See additional remarks p. 18.

[55] In the sixteenth century, printed books were usually sold in loose sheets, which also reduced costs.

[56] F. Higman noticed the same lack of illustrations in the French Reformation: 'Le levain de l'Evangile', *HÉF*, p. 313, and in this volume, pp. 120–23.

[57] J. Duverger, 'Lutherse predicatie te Brussel en het proces tegen een aantal kunstenaars (april–juni 1527)', *Wetenschappelijke tijdingen*, 36 (1977), col. 225.

[58] I. H. van Eeghen, 'Een kettersche schilderij in 1534', *Oud-Holland*, 57 (1940), 108.

[59] For examples of these illustrations, see S. Groenvelt, H. L. Ph. Leeuwenberg etc., *De kogel door de kerk* (Zutphen, 1979); J. Decavele, *Eenheid en scheiding in de Nederlanden 1555–1585* (Ghent, 1976); Decavele, *Opstand en onafhankelijkheid* (Dordrecht, 1972).

nature of evangelical religion in the Low Countries. The German Reformation engravings were almost always polemical. In the Low Countries, however, the relatively late confessional divide between Protestants and Catholics resulted in a more minor role for polemic in Reformation writings. A more irenic Reformation would thus lead to fewer satirical illustrations. Once a clearly confessional Reformation was established by the Calvinists in the 1560s and 1570s, polemical works were frequently illustrated. Finally, the clandestine nature of evangelical books in the Low Countries could lead to the lack of engravings for financial reasons. *Die daden wercken ende leerijnghe ons heeren Ihesu Christi ende Paus*, for instance, a translation of the highly polemical *Passional Christi und Antichristi* (1521) was not illustrated, whereas the German original had 36 illustrations, contrasting Christ and the Pope. Indeed, it is difficult to explain this presentation other than on economic grounds, as the German original linked text and image closely together.

Print-runs and sale prices

Because the Protestant book trade in the Low Countries was clandestine, there is very little information available on print-runs. One can cite a few isolated examples. Among the largest print-runs were the 2 500 copies of the Dutch translation of the New Testament by Jan Utenhove, printed by Gillis van der Erven in 1556.[60] Other works where the print-run is known include the translation of a Calvinist remonstrance to Philip II (2 000 copies)[61] and the songs of the Gueux printed in Kampen in 1567 (1 000 copies).[62] Among the shorter print-runs were the 500 copies of a pamphlet against Luther, sponsored by the cathedral chapter of Utrecht and printed in 1522–23,[63] and the 500 copies of a pamphlet celebrating Luther's death, *Vander doot ende overlijdene van Maertin Luther*, printed in Bruges by Erasmus Querceus in 1547. The shortest known print-run of an evangelical work is that of the 100 copies of *Half blat pampiers met epistele up de name van sinte Pauwels ghezonden an die an Lardiceen* printed by Querceus in Bruges, also in 1547.[64]

---

[60] J. H. Hessels, *Ecclesiae Londino-Bataviae archivum* (Cambridge, 1889–97), vol. 2, p. 63.

[61] Moreau, *Histoire du protestantisme*, p. 165, n. 4.

[62] S. Elte, 'De rechtzaak tegen Peter Warners, boekdrukker te Kampen (1566–1567)', *Kamper Almanak* (1951/52), 162.

[63] W. J. Alberts (ed.) *Bronnen tot de bowgeschiedenis van het dom te Utrecht* (The Hague, 1976), p. 582. (Rijks geschiedkundige publicatien, 155).

[64] A. Dewitte, 'Chronologie van de reformatie te Brugge en in het Brugse vrije (1485–1593)' in *Brugge in de geuzentijd. Bijdragen tot de geschiedenis van de hervorming te Brugge et in het Brugse vrije tijdens de 16de eeuw* (Bruges, 1982), p. 36.

Although it would be wrong to establish an average based on such a limited sample, these examples mark the upper and lower limits of the print-runs of Protestant books. It is generally accepted that 4 000 copies of the first edition of Luther's *An den christlichen adel deutscher nation* were printed in 1520,[65] and that Luther's German Bible was printed for the first time in 3 000 copies,[66] but these were exceptional cases. Conversely, few works were printed in less than 500 copies, which would not have been cost-effective. Jean Moretus, Christopher Plantin's son-in-law, pointed out that printing 12 copies of De Kerle's music was not viable in financial terms.[67] In all likelihood, print-runs of 1 500 and 1 000 were nearer to the norm. Indeed, Lucien Febvre and Henri-Jean Martin placed early sixteenth century print-runs at this level.[68]

What about prices? There is little doubt that book prices dropped at the end of the fifteenth century and beginning of the sixteenth. In part, this was the result of better organization of the production process and of an improvement in commercial practices. In 1466, a printed German Bible cost 12 florins. In 1470, this price dropped to 9 florins, and around 1483, it cost 6 florins.[69] Once the Reformation began, prices dropped even lower. A looseleaf copy of Luther's first complete German Bible only cost 2 florins 8 pence; in 1541, however, the price rose slightly to 3 florins.[70] From then on, Bibles were printed on lower-quality paper, and with larger print-runs, leading to a drop in prices.

However, the price of a Luther Bible as compared with daily salaries was not cheap. A Saxon stonemason or carpenter earned an average of half a florin for three days' labour; thus the most affordable Bible represented three weeks' work.[71] In the Low Countries as well, a complete Bible was still an expensive acquisition. The inventory of a Leiden bookseller showed that a Bible retailed for one florin two deniers and, around 1540, a Louvain townsman bought a Bible from a student for 30 stuivers

---

[65] Febvre/Martin, p. 438.

[66] C. C. de Bruin, *De Statenbijbel en zijn voorgangers* (Leiden, 1937), p. 118. See also Chapter 2 above, footnote 44.

[67] Voet, *The Golden Compasses*, p. 169. The Basle printer Johannes Bebel also thought that a print-run of three copies was not financially viable. C. A. Pater, *Karlstadt as the Father of the Baptist Movements: The Emergence of Lay Protestantism* (Toronto, 1984), p. 291.

[68] Febvre/Martin, p. 330. See also above, p. 19.

[69] De Bruin, *De Statenbijbel*, p. 89.

[70] R. Gawthrop and G. Strauss, 'Protestantism and literacy in early modern Germany', *Past and Present*, 104, (1984), 40, n. 41.

[71] Gawthrop and Strauss, 'Protestantism and literacy' p. 113.

and two tankards of beer.[72] In 1548, Thierry d'Ubach, the future master-general of the Croisiers bought a Vorsterman Bible of 1533–34 for 38 patards and resold it in 1556 to the Huy convent for 33 stuivers.[73] Between 1540 and 1549, the highest daily salary for the work of a qualified master stonemason in the city of Aalst was 12 groats.[74] As a stuiver is equivalent to two groats,[75] the cost of a Bible represented at least a week's wages, and much more than that for many artisans.

Short pamphlets obviously cost less than Bibles. During his travels in the Low Countries in 1520–21, Albrecht Dürer bought the *Condemnatio doctrinalis librorum Martini Lutheri* (1520) for only 1 denier.[76] In all likelihood, he purchased the 12–page edition published by Claes de Grave in Antwerp in June 1520.[77] *De val de roomscher kercken* (1553), a strident attack of around 44 pages against the doctrine of transubstantiation, cost 2 deniers when purchased in 1555 by an Anabaptist, Jan de Monick.[78]

More significant works were obviously more expensive. Niclaes Peeters' *Sermonen* (c.1540, two volumes of 288 and 392 pages)[79] were sold for 12 deniers in Louvain in 1543,[80] while Urbanus Rhegius's *Dialogus van*

---

[72] De Bruin, *De Statenbijbel* p. 186. Any comparison between German and Dutch prices is a delicate one. A German florin was not the same as a Dutch florin, in spite of the similar names.

[73] This information is taken from two handwritten notes on the cover page of the copy held by the Grand Séminaire in Liège. 'Comparata sunt hec biblia per R. P. fratrem Theodoricum ab Ubach, anno domini 1548 pretio xxxviij stuivers brabantiae' – 'Liber fratrum Sancte Crucis conventus Huyensis diocesis leodiensis ab eodem R. P. F. Theodorico ab Ubach per fratrem Paulum Proveners 33 stuivers brabantiae redemptus anno domini 1556'. See *Ex libris, livres rares et précieux des couvents de l'ancien diocèse de Liège conservés à la bibliothèque du Grand Séminaire de Liège. Catalogue.* (Liège, 1988) p. 5.

[74] C. Verlinden, *Documents pour l'histoire des prix et des salaires en Flandre et en Brabant (XVe–XVIIIe siècles* (Bruges, 1959), vol. 3, p. 199.

[75] Various currencies circulated in the Low Countries in this period. For an explanation of the relative values of each, see P. Spufford, *Monetary Problems and Policies in the Burgundian Netherlands 1433–1496* (Leiden, 1970), pp. 166–9.

[76] A. Dürer, *Diary of his Journey to the Netherlands, 1520–1521* J. A. Goris and G. Marlier (eds), (London, 1971) pp. 69, 71.

[77] NK 2231.

[78] A. F. Mellinck, *Documenta anabaptistica neerlandica*, vol. 2: *Amsterdam (1536–1578)* (Leiden, 1980), p. 232. Another pamphlet probably sold at a low price or even distributed free of charge was the anti-Lutheran tract printed in 1522–23 at the request of the cathedral chapter of Utrecht. Even though the sale price is not known, the printing costs for the 500 copies were only three florins. Alberts, *Bronnen*, p. 582.

[79] NK 1691–1692. The trial documents from Louvain only mention the 'Apostille' but this generic term was also applied to Peeters' sermons, as Jan Beyaerts confirmed when he testified that Joes van Ousberghen said the author was a Franciscan. (Enzinas, *Mémoires*, pp. 406–8).

[80] Enzinas, *Mémoires*, p. 462.

de prekinghe die Christus den twee discipelen dede tot Emaus (353 pages) cost 8 stuivers.[81] In evangelical circles, demand was so strong that those who knew where these books could be obtained were ready to make money from this knowledge. Jan Beyaerts told the inquisitors that when Jan van Ousberghen asked him whether he knew someone who owned Rhegius's *Dialogus*, Beyaerts said yes without divulging the owner's name, as he hoped to make a profit of 2 to 3 stuivers.[82] In other words, Beyaerts hoped to use his knowledge of the book's whereabouts to get more money out of van Ousberghen.

As the Bibles and other important works were relatively expensive, one can assume that they were not purchased by the population at large. R. Gawthorp and G. Strauss built an argument on this fact, criticizing the commonly held view that reading the Bible was a popular activity in Lutheran Germany. They argue that most printed Bibles went to parish churches and clerical libraries, and were bought either by the government or with public funds, following the ecclesiastical ordinances. The cost of the Bibles was so great that the 200 000 or so German Bibles published in the sixteenth century could not all have been absorbed by purchases from the public.[83]

Whether or not these arguments hold true for Lutheran Germany, they cannot be applied to the Low Countries. Between 1520 and 1566, there were around 136 Protestant editions of the Bible and New Testament in Dutch. Added to this were some 56 Catholic editions of the Bible and New Testament in the same period.[84] With an average of 1 000 copies per edition,[85] this means a total of around 200 000 Dutch Bibles and New Testaments printed between 1520 and 1566. As around 2 million people spoke Dutch in the Low Countries,[86] the total number of Dutch-speakers living between 1520 and 1566 would be 5 million. Thus there was approximately one Bible for every 25 Dutch speakers in The Netherlands.[87] Scholars are generally agreed that Catholic versions may have been bought by priests and parish churches, but the Catholic

---

[81] Ibid., pp. 346, 362, 440, 588.

[82] Ibid., p. 440.

[83] Gawthrop and Strauss, 'Protestantism and literacy', p. 40.

[84] These very approximate statistics are taken from W. C. Poortman, *Bijbel en prent* (The Hague, 1983), vol. 1, pp. 201–10.

[85] C. C. de Bruin estimates that the first evangelical Bibles printed in the Low Countries had larger print-runs, around 1 500 to 3 000 copies.

[86] G. Parker estimates the total population of the Low Countries at around 3 000 000: *The Dutch Revolt* (London, 1977). Dutch was spoken by approximately two-thirds of the population.

[87] All the Dutch evangelical Bibles did not remain within the Low Countries. Some were destroyed, while others were used in Dutch settlements elsewhere.

texts only made up a third of total production. The vast majority of Dutch Bibles contained traces of Protestantism, and most of these were banned in the various *Indices Librorum prohibitorum*. Official markets such as the church were closed to these versions, and thus they were bought by the population itself.

Circulation

After examining Protestant printers, books and prices, let us look at distribution. There were several ways of circulating Protestant works in the Low Countries. Firstly, books could be purchased directly from the publisher or printer. If someone became known for printing heretical works, potential buyers could contact him directly. These works were thus supplied 'under the counter'. For instance, Adriaen van Berghen was in the habit of keeping a cache of Lutheran books in his workshop, in all likelihood to sell them to those who made explicit requests for these texts.[88] Some of the members of the Louvain group went to Antwerp to buy books from Matthias Crom.[89] Clearly, this supply method could only help readers who knew printers producing evangelical works.

A second distribution source was that of the peddlers and professional booksellers, who carried Protestant books over highways and byways, selling books acquired directly from the publishers. These traders often brought books to areas remote from the main printing centres, where otherwise this literature would never have had access. Thus in 1526, the writings of Luther and other Reformers clearly found a way to Menno Simons in the remote Frisian village of Pingjum. Some peddlers were discovered in the act of distributing their banned wares. Jan Buidelmaker was banished by Cornelis Cooltuyn in Enkhuisen for having sold books.[90] Another peddler, Aert Aertssen from Schoonhoven, was caught while selling the *Schoone disputatie van ennen evangelisschen schoemaker ende van eenen papistighen coerheere* by Hans Sachs,[91] while on the island of Sud-Beveland in Zeeland, two Anabaptists, Adriaen Carbout and Adriaen Piersen, were caught peddling Bibles and copies of the *Fonteyne des Levens*.[92]

Alongside these professional traders were convinced Protestants, who saw the distribution of Reformation books as a form of evangelisation.

---

[88] *Antwerpsch archievenblad*, 7 (1870), 301.

[89] Enzinas, *Mémoires*, p. 367.

[90] *BRN*, 9, p. 209.

[91] Gouda, Oud recht Archief, 176, 30 April 1547, pp. 208–9.

[92] K. R. Pekelharing, *Bijdragen voor de geschiedenis der hervorming in Zeeland 1524–1572* (Middleburg, 1866), p. 38.

In 1528, for example, a Delft tailor, Gysbrecht Aelbrechtsz was investigated on charges that he distributed heretical books.[93] In certain cases, Protestants were circulating their own works. David Joris, the former glassmaker who became a well-known Anabaptist leader, is a case in point: in July 1528, he was condemned for having written heretical books and making them available to others.[94] Another example of private initiative is that of Cornelis Woutersz, alias Coperpotgen, from Dordrecht. This enterprising shoemaker not only circulated his own writings, but also organised their printing.[95] On the Catholic side, Master 'Luyt' the verger of the Old Church in Amsterdam, was personally responsible for the publication and sale of Johannes Eck's *Declaracie ... teghen zommighe articulen der Lutheranen* (1527).[96]

Authors and texts

Doctrines

The outlook of religious works of the Dutch Reformation between 1520 and 1540 was irresistibly Lutheran. Not only were Luther's works translated many times, but the same was true for many of his lesser-known supporters, like Otto Brunfels, Johannes Bugenhagen, Matthias Bynwalth, Caspar Huberinus, Benedictus Gretzinger, Urbanus Rhegius, Antonius Corvinus, Justus Menius, Heinrich von Kettenbach and Georg Birckmeyer.[97]

Until 1540, Luther was the most influential figure in evangelical circles, except obviously in Anabaptist groups. As noted above, the Reformed current grew stronger beginning in 1545, and the confessional changes in the Netherlands coincided with the move of Protestant printing away from the Low Countries.

The impact of Calvin's influence is equally measurable in the change in the pattern of evangelical writings in this period. Between 1520 and 1550, Dutch writings were generally non-confessional and broadly evangelical. In spite of Luther's prominence, his writings cannot be classed as Lutheran from a confessional standpoint. Two thirds of Luther's

---

[93] *CD*, 5, pp. 352–3.

[94] *CD*, 5, pp. 348–52.

[95] *CD*, 5, pp. 198–203, 209–10. NK 0849 and 01257, see also *CD*, 5, p. 335.

[96] NK 752, see also *CD*, 5, p. 318.

[97] A. G. Johnston, 'The eclectic reformation: vernacular evangelical pamphlet literature in the Dutch-speaking Low Countries, 1520–1565' (Southampton Univ., PhD thesis, 1986), p. 251. The Dutch translations of Luther's writings are presented in detail by C. Ch. G. Visser, *Luther's geschriften*.

works translated into Dutch were written prior to 1525, indicating that the younger Luther was more popular in the Low Countries than confessional Lutheranism.[98] Furthermore, there was a relative lack of biting polemical writings in the Low Countries as compared with Germany. Indeed, polemical works all came from Germany.[99] Dutch evangelical writings were much more irenic in tone, aiming above all to edify and sustain faith rather than fight a verbal war against the enemy.

In the 1550s, these broadly evangelical non-confessional writings were replaced by catechisms, psalters, rituals etc., directly intended for internal use by the Protestant communities.

Literary genres

As in the case of the numerous Lutheran Bibles translated into Dutch, compilations of evangelically-oriented scriptural texts were among the most popular works in the Low Countries. Otto Brunfels's *Precationes biblicae* were translated as *Dat gulden ghebedeboecxken* and were re-published eight times between 1531 and 1564. Another work, this time an original Dutch text, *Der waerheyt onderwijs* was also popular, given its three re-editions following its publication in 1536. However, it seems that the most popular work was the *Fonteyne des levens*, published ten times between 1533 and 1619.[100] Furthermore, the *Fonteyne* also appeared in five other languages: Latin (five editions), French (seven editions), English (two editions), German (one edition), and Italian (one edition). It is not clear how these compilations were used, but it is highly likely that they served as devotional works for those with evangelical sympathies: the readers could be edified without having to go through the entire Bible. Many of the Protestant publications of the Germanic lands were polemical. In Strasbourg, polemic constituted more than a third of total production.[101] Flemish polemical works were much less frequent, around 15 per cent.[102] Furthermore, many of these polemical works were translated from German, like Hans Sachs's *Schoon disputatie van eenen evangelischen schoemaker ende van eenen papistighen Coerheere* (1525),[103] Urbanus Rhegius's *Rechte onderscheyt tusschen die oude ende nyuewe leeringhe* (1527)[104] and the *Daden*

---

[98] A. G. Johnston, 'The sermons of Niclaes Peeters: partially unmasked', *Nederlands archief voor kerkgeschiedenis*, **64** (1984), 124.

[99] Johnston, 'The eclectic reformation', chs 3, 5, 6.

[100] Ibid., p. 120.

[101] Chrisman, *Lay Culture*, p. 156 and below, p. 229.

[102] Johnston, 'The eclectic reformation', p. 71.

[103] NK 3827.

[104] NK 1791.

werken ende leerijnghe ons heeren Ihesu Christi ende des Paus edited by
Philip Melanchthon (*c*.1525).[105] In the 1560s and 1570s, when a clearly
confessional Reformation was established by the Calvinists, polemical
works increased, but in the period 1520–55, the very faint confessional-
ization of the Reformation in the Low Countries only led to a more
discreet polemic than elsewhere.

German influence also manifested itself in catechetical works. Both
Luther's *Kurze Forme der 10 Gebote, des Glaubens und des Vaterunsers*
and his *Kleine Katechismus* were translated.[106] However, most of the
Flemish catechisms did not rely on German sources. Perhaps the most
interesting catechism was Cornelis vander Heyden's 1545 *Corte
instruccye*.[107] Although mainly independent, vander Heyden cleverly
combined his own text with texts by Luther and by a little-known
Lutheran preacher, Matthias Bynwalth of Dantzig.[108]

Some of the most interesting and specific evangelical writings were
works of consolation in times of illness and death. These include Willem
Gnapheus's *Trosst ende spiegel der siecken* (1531),[109] which was reprinted with a more Calvinist theological outlook in 1557[110] and Cornelis
Cooltuyn's *Evangeli der armen*.[111] Cooltuyn began his ecclesiastical
career as a priest in northern Holland, and ended his career as preacher
in the Reformed church in Emden.

German influence was strongest in printed sermons. Apart from
Luther's *Kirchenpostillen*, Antonius Corvinus's and Johannes Spangenberg's
sermons were also translated into Dutch.[112] Furthermore, Niclaes Peeters's
Postillen (*c*.1540), which were thought to be entirely Dutch in origin,
are based at least in part on Luther's sermons.[113]

The plays of the chambers of rhetoric are not pamphlets in a strict
sense, but they are nevertheless an original feature of printed works in
the Reformation in the Low Countries. Not all of the *Rederijker* plays
were Protestant, but some, in particular many of the 19 plays presented
in Ghent in June 1539 and published in the following August, adopted

---

[105] NK 675.

[106] NK 2116, 3458, 3462, 1422.

[107] Machiels, *Catalogus*, H 197. Reprinted in *BRN*, 4, pp. 15–77.

[108] Reprinted in O. Clemen (ed.) *Flugschriften aus den ersten Jahren der Reformation*
(reprint, Nieuwkoop, 1967), vol. 4, pp. 144–57.

[109] *BRN*, 1, pp. 151–245.

[110] Amsterdam, UB, 767 F5.

[111] *BRN*, 1, pp. 217–480.

[112] For Luther, NK 3464; for Corvinus, NK 0323, and for Spangenberg, Wolfenbüttel,
HAB, C 785 8°.

[113] Johnston, 'The sermons', pp. 123–43. The following paragraph deals with this at
greater length.

a clearly evangelical stance. Contemporaries recognized this fact, and the plays were immediately placed on the Index.[114]

Concealed works

Only recently have scholars discovered to what lengths certain writers and printers were willing to go to ensure that the Gospel was proclaimed. Cornelis vander Heyden's *Corte instruccye*, first published by Joos Lambrecht Lettersnijder in Ghent in 1545 was originally considered as orthodox by the Catholic theologians before coming under suspicion and being forbidden by an imperial edict.[115] From then on, the work has been considered as a native Protestant pamphlet. In 1969, however, scholars discovered that parts of the *Corte instruccye* were taken from Luther,[116] and more recently, that major sections of the text were 'borrowed' from Matthias Bynwalth's *Vaterunser* (1525).[117]

Niclaes Peeters's *Sermonen* (1540) present a more complicated case of camouflaged writings. The author or printer of this two-volume collection of sermons took great pains to ensure that the evangelical message would get through without being detected. First, Niclaes Peeters is in all likelihood a pseudonym. Second, on the title-page, the author is described as a devout Franciscan, a deliberate attempt to give the sermons an orthodox appearance. Third, the sermons were antedated. The first volume's colophon states 'printed in the year of our Lord M.D. xx', although the sermons themselves could not have been compiled before 1528, and were probably published around 1540. Finally, the author cleverly blended his own sermons with those of Luther, which had been translated into Dutch in 1528.[118]

Such complex techniques were not specific to publishing in the Low Countries. Protestant works were sometimes inserted into devotional works presenting an innocently Catholic appearance in other areas where the authorities sought to ban the Reformation.[119] However, these tactics seem to have been used on a much greater scale in the Low

---

[114] B. H. Erné and L. M. van Dis (eds), *De gentse spelen van 1539* (The Hague, 1982), p. 27.

[115] *ROPB2*, 5, pp. 174–5.

[116] Visser, *Luther's geschriften*, pp. 127–8.

[117] Johnston, 'The Eclectic Reformation', p. 278.

[118] Ibid., pp. 167–200. See also Johnston, 'Ther Sermons', pp. 123–43.

[119] For instance, the French *Livre de vraye et parfaicte oraison* (1528) included extracts from Luther and Guillaume Farel, and the Italian *Beneficio di Cristo* (1543) included texts by Calvin. See above, p. 135 and below, pp. 321–2; D. Fenlon, *Heresy and Obedience in Tridentine Italy: Cardinal Pole and the Counter Reformation* (Cambridge, 1972), p. 75.

4.3   Niclaes Peeters, *Christelike Sermonen* (*c.*1540)

Countries than elsewhere.[120] This use of camouflage is on the one hand evidence of Dutch authors' and printers' ingenuity and on the other hand, a challenge to researchers, leading them to explore more closely the secrets of Dutch Protestant books.

Reception

Literacy

What was the state of literacy in the Low Countries? What percentage of the population could read the Bible or an evangelical work? The estimates for Germany are that literacy rates ran at between one person in ten and one person in three in the cities, but only at one person in 20 for the population as a whole.[121] Thus, R. W. Scribner affirms that

---

[120] Johnston, 'The Eclectic Reformation', esp. pp. 256–314.
[121] R. W. Scribner, *For the Sake of Simple Folk* (Cambridge, 1981), p. 2.

'access to the printed word was probably reserved for a small cultural elite'.[122] In a partial conclusion to his hypothesis, Scribner firmly underlined the role of visual propaganda in the German Reformation, emphasizing in particular the impact of illustrations on polemic.

As for the Low Countries in the sixteenth century, no one would claim that literacy rates reached modern levels. However, there is evidence to suggest that these rates were higher in the Low Countries than elsewhere in Europe. First, the Low Countries were one of the most heavily urbanized societies in early modern Europe,[123] with 200 cities, and it is generally agreed that here too, literacy rates were higher in the cities than in rural areas.[124] Second, the Italian immigrant Ludovico Guicciardini noted in 1567 that literacy rates in the countryside were particularly high: '[in the Low Countries] there have been and are still many learned people in all areas of science and knowledge. The common people have generally been taught the rudiments of grammar, and most, yes even the peasants and countryfolk, can at least read and write'.[125]

The impact of Protestant books

Being able to read was certainly not an exclusive privilege of the Low Countries' social élite. Lieven de Zomere, a baker, boasted in 1522 that he owned no less than 19 books by Luther.[126] This may have been an exaggeration, but he did own at least three Lutheran works: the *Condemnatio doctrinalis librorum Martini Lutheri per quosdam magistros lovanienses et colonienses facta cum responsione lutheriana ad eandem condemnationem*, the 1520 *Captivitate babilonica ecclesiae*, and an exposition of the Ten Commandments.[127] In 1535, an Anabaptist labourer, Rem Perterssen, was caught with three Protestant books: 'a book done by Johannes Pomeranus', 'the book of the prophets' and 'the Dutch mass by Johannes Oecolampadius'.[128] Finally, Jan van Genk, the

---

122 Ibid.

123 Parker, *The Dutch Revolt*, p. 23.

124 Scribner, *For the Sake*, pp. 1–2.

125 L. Guicciardini, *Beschryvinghe van alle de Nederlanden: anderssins ghenoemt Neder-Duytlandt* (Amsterdam, 1612), p. 27. See also A. Derville, 'L'alphabétisation du peuple à la fin du Moyen Age', *Revue du Nord*, 66 (1984), 761–76.

126 *CD*, 4, p. 110.

127 *CD*, 4, p. 113.

128 G. Grosheide, 'Verhooren en vonnissen der wederdoopers, betrokken bij de aanslagen of Amsterdam', *Bijdragen en mededeelingen van het historisch genootschap*, 41 (1920), p. 163. The book by 'Pomeranus' is probably Bugenhagen's *Souter* (NK 508). The 'book of the prophets' was in all likelihood a translation of Ludwig Haetzer and Hans Denk's *Alle propheten, nach der hebräischen sprache verdeutscht*. The Dutch translation may

son of a Maastricht shoemaker and himself a glassmaker by trade, owned a copy of the *Gulden onderwijsinge om te antwoorden op alle puncten de vyanden der waerheyt bybrenghen moghen* (1525).[129]

However, the illiterate could still have access to these works. Bibles and printed sermons were not only read privately but also aloud, in small groups of Protestants. The members of one of these conventicles meeting in Louvain around 1540 owned nearly 40 books in all. While some of these works were not specifically religious, and others were wholly orthodox, the group possessed a large number of popular evangelical texts. As well as a number of Bibles and New Testaments in the vernacular, they owned some Dutch translations of German Lutheran pamphlets, like Luther's *Christelicke oprechte wt legghinghe des vijfsten boecks Mosi* (c.1530),[130] Caspar Huberinus's *Troostinghe wt der godliker scrift* (1542),[131] Otto Brunfels's *Gulden ghebedeboecxken* (1531)[132] and the *Dialogus van de prekinghe die Christus den twee discipelen dede, tot Emaus* (1538).[133] They also owned native works such as the *Fonteyne des levens* (1533),[134] Niclaes Peeters's *Sermonen*,[135] Willem Gnapheus's *Troost ende spiegel der siecken* (1531),[136] the *Kinderleere: Dat christen gheloove* (1542)[137], *Dat begrijp der gheheelder Bibelen int corte* (c.1535)[138] and the tale of two Augustinians from Antwerp executed in 1523,[139] and the account of the execution of Wendelmoet Claesdochter in 1527.[140] The Bible and Peeters's sermons were read aloud to nurture

---

have been the work of Gerardus Geldenhauer. See C. Augustijn, 'De Vorstermanbijbel van 1528', *Nederlandsarchief voor kerkgeschiedenis*, 56 (1975), 84–5, n. 34. 'The Dutch mass' of Oecolampadius was printed together with the *Summa der godliker scrifturen*, but was also available separately.

[129] NK 1623 and 3631. Kronenberg, *Verboden boeken* p. 44. W. Bax, *Het protestantisme in het bisdom Luik en vooral te Maastricht 1505–1557* (The Hague, 1937) vol. 1, pp. 84–5.

[130] Enzinas, *Mémoires* pp. 392, 410, 460, 462. The *Christelicke oprechte wt legghinghe des vijfsten boecks Mosi* was only recently identified as a translation of Luther's *Deutonomion Mosi cum annotationibus* (1525; LB, 1850–57). See U. Kopp, 'Ein unbekennter und andere niederländische Lutherdruck von ca. 1528 in der Herzog August Bibliothek Wolfenbüttel', *Wolfenbütteler Notizen*, 4 (1979), 46–53.

[131] R. van Santbergen (ed.) *Un procès de religion à Louvain. Paul de Rovere, 1542–1546* (Brussels, 1953), p. 69.

[132] Enzinas, *Mémoires*, pp. 314, 344, 566, 584, 586, 594, 632.

[133] Ibid., pp. 312, 314, 342–4, 346, 352, 356, 440, 458, 506, 552, 588, 594, 632.

[134] Ibid., pp. 310, 506, 552, 530, 600.

[135] Ibid., pp. 314, 318, 326, 348, 350, 352, 364, 392, 408–10, 446, 458, 462, 510, 514, 516, 534, 584, 600, 614.

[136] Ibid., p. 460.

[137] Ibid., pp. 310, 628, 642, 364, 374, 478–80, 506, 560, 632.

[138] Ibid., p. 576.

[139] Ibid., p. 602.

[140] Ibid., p. 602.

the group's spiritual life, thus building a bridge between the literate and illiterate.

Many printed books also circulated among a small group of people in Brussels in the 1520s. Jan de Kinderen, one of the group leaders, owned both an original Dutch work, the *Summa der godliker scrifturen* and works by the leading German and Swiss Reformers. These included six of Luther's writings, Melanchthon's commentary on Romans, Oecolampadius's exegesis of Isaiah and Bugenhagen's commentary on the Psalms.[141] It is not clear whether these works were read aloud, as in Louvain. However, it is likely that the group served as a meeting place for the discussion of the themes developed in these works. Thus, those who could not read could still acquire some 'book-knowledge' through the literate members of the group.

However, Protestant books did not circulate only among lower social groups or evangelical conventicles. They were also read by those belonging to cultured and wealthy circles. Cornelis Grapheus, then city secretary of Antwerp, owned a number of Lutheran books which he was made to burn at his recantation on 6 May 1522.[142] In 1529, Arnoldus Kuyck, the schoolmaster at Doesburg, was caught in possession of a large number of evangelical books. These included Latin works by Johannes Bugenhagen, Otto Brunfels, François Lambert, Philip Melanchthon and Ulrich Hutten as well as Dutch translations of Luther. Thus Kuyck owned *Den Ouden Adam. Een excellente devote godlycke theologie* (1521), *Een excellent boecxken int welcke een kerstemensche leeren mach hoe hi goede ende dueydelicke wercken doen sal* (c.1527), and the Dutch translations of *Von der Freiheit eines Christenmenschen* (1520) and *Eine kurze Form des Paternoster zu verstehen und su beten für die jungen Kinder* (1519). As well, Kuyck also owned a copy of

---

141 Brussels, AGR, Papiers d'Etat et de l'Audience, 1177[6], fol. 6[r], 16[r]. Luther's writings were (1) 'Resolutionis et conclusionis indulgitys cum propositien': *Resolutionis disputationum de indulgentiarum virtute* (1518); (2) 'Die seven psalmen': *Die seven penitencie psalmen* (1520), NK 1426; (3) 'Een schoen bedeboeck etc.': *Een devoet ende zeer schoon bedeboxken wt die heylighe schrifftuer* (c.1525), NK 1419 and 3457; (4) 'Paternoster van Martin Luther': *Van dat heylighe pater noster een verclaringhen* (c.1525), NK 0856; (5) 'Expositie op sint Peters epistelen': *Die ierste epistel S. Peters met een schoone wtlegglinghe* (c.1524), NK 4258 and *Dat ander epistel S. Peters met een schoone wtlegginghe* (1524), NK 0852; (6) 'Een christelike wtlegginghe op die propheet Iona': *Een christelike wtlegginghe op die propheet Iona ende op Habacuc* (pre-1527), NK 01335. Copy in Wolfenbüttel, HAB. For Melanchthon 'Philippien melancton opde epistelen ad Romanos etc.': *Annotationes in epistolas Pauli ad Rhomanos et Corinthios* (1523), NK 4448. For Oecolampadius: 'Ecolampadium op de propheet Ezaiam': *In Iesaiam prophetam hypomnematon* (1525), London, BL 1107. f. 14. For Bugenhagen: 'Pomeranum opden souter': *Die souter. Verclaringhe des gheheelen psalters.*

142 CD, 4, p. 121

Hans Sachs's pamphlet, *Schoone disputatie van eenen evangelisschen schoenmaecker ende van eenen papistighen coorheere* (c.1525).[143]

How Protestant works spread among ecclesiastical circles in the Low Countries remains unclear. Understandably enough, Catholic priests did not publicize their ownership and reading of forbidden heterodox works. However, one can gather together some fragmentary evidence. Nicolaus Christi, a priest from Bergen-op-Zoom in the 1520s, owned a copy of Luther's *Captivitate babylonica* (1520).[144] A canon of the Hasker convent in Friesland, who preached openly against the invocation of the saints, had books by Calvin, Brenz, Luther and Menno Simons in his library.[145] Judging from his *Leken wechwyser* (1554), Johannes Anastasius Veluanus must have read Calvin's *Institutio* (1536) and Melanchthon's *Loci communes* (1521), since he admired them and recommended them as very useful catechisms.[146] It is more than likely that Anastasius had also read works by Luther, Brenz, Bugenhagen and Rhegius.[147] But the Protestant works held by the clergy were normally in Latin rather than in the vernacular. The episcopal visitations of 1559–60 in the Juliers Duchy, for example, made a note of all the books owned by each parish priest, and proved the popularity of Protestant authors in a region which had only recently changed confession. The libraries of various chaplains and priests contained works by Calvin, Bucer, Bullinger, Pellicanus, Luther, Melanchthon, Bugenhagen, Brenz, Corvinus, Jonas, Huberinus, Musculus, Spangenberg and Sarcerius.[148] Barring a few exceptions, these were all in Latin.

Censorship

The writings of Luther and his followers were forbidden by the central government from the very beginning. The first book burnings following the pontifical bull *Exsurge Domine* (15 June 1520) took place in Louvain on 8 October 1520. Later on, book burnings took place in Antwerp, Ghent, Utrecht, Bruges, s'Hertogenbosch and Deventer.[149] In a letter to the pontifical vice-chancellor of Rome, the legate of the Low Countries, Jerome Aleander, boasted of having burnt 400 of

---

[143] A. Gruijs, 'Het inventarium van Doesburg (1529). Een boekarcheologische onderzoek' in *Forty-three studies in bibliography presented to Prof. Dr. Wytze Hellinga* (Amsterdam, 1980), pp. 244, 246–7.

[144] Kronenberg, *Verboden boeken*, p. 40.

[145] J. J. Woltjer, *Friesland in hervormingstijd* (Leiden, 1962), p. 103.

[146] *BRN*, 4, pp. 190, 258.

[147] *BRN*, 4, pp. 198, 202, 224.

[148] See O. R. Redlich (ed.) *Julich-Bergische Kirchenpolitik* (Bonn, 1911).

[149] Kronenberg, *Verboden boeken*, p. 28.

Luther's books, 300 of which were seized in bookshops and 100 from individuals.[150]

The early censorship legislation was rather vague, in the sense that it forbade all of Luther's writings without specifying titles. However, the edict of 23 March 1524 declared it to be a crime to own either the *Summa der godliker scrifturen*, an anonymous pamphlet sometimes falsely ascribed to Hendrik van Bommel (1523)[151] or Johan Pelt's *Evangelie van Matthaeus* (1522). Pelt was a former Franciscan who had adopted the Lutheran cause.[152] Two years later, on 17 July 1526, a more ambitious edict was published at Malines. This edict was a point of reference, as it banned not only Luther's works but those of many of his followers, including Johannes Bugenhagen, Andreas Karlstadt, Philip Melanchthon, Johannes Oecolampadius, François Lambert and Justus Jonas. The edict also condemned all vernacular translations of the Bible which contained Lutheran commentaries or glosses. Anyone found in possession of these works was to be banished from the Low Countries under pain of death and confiscation of property.[153]

The censors' nets widened in 1529 with the publication on 14 October of an edict banning the printing, publishing, sale, purchase, distribution, reading, ownership, preaching, defense and discussion of the books or doctrines of Luther, Wycliffe, Hus, Marsilius of Padua, Oecolampadius, Zwingli, Melanchthon, Lambert, Bugenhagen, Otto Brunfels, Justus Jonas, and Johannes Pupper van Gogh. The edict also forbade the New Testaments printed by Adriaen van Berghen, Christophe van Ruremund and Johannes 'Zel'[154] as well as any other work printed in the preceding decade without the name of the author, printer, date or place of publication. In fact, the importance of this edict lay not in the much broader definition of heresy, but also in that for the first time, culprits were to be executed. Men were to be killed by the sword, women were to be buried alive, and relapsed culprits were to be burnt alive.[155]

These early edicts only dealt partially with the problem of evangelical works, as did the edicts of 10 July and 22 September 1540.[156] There

---

[150] Kronenberg, *Verboden boeken*, p. 32. Let us bear in mind that the first placard forbidding Luther's works was promulgated in Liège already on 17 October 1520, thus preceding the Edict of Worms of May 1521, by which Luther and his writings were banned from the Empire.

[151] J. Trapman, *De Summa der godliker scrifturen (1523)* (Leiden, 1978), pp. 41–52.

[152] Reusch, p. 23.

[153] CD, 5, pp. 142–7.

[154] For the identification of this publisher, see Chapter 6, footnote 68 in this volume.

[155] ROPB2, 2, pp. 578–83.

[156] ROPB2, 4, pp. 210–11, 224–9.

was no systematic Index of forbidden books prior to 1546.[157] The 1546 Index, published on 9 May and compiled by the theological faculty of Louvain, banned 48 editions of the Bible and New Testament, 72 Latin works, 53 Dutch pamphlets, five German and nine French works, as well as all the works already banned by the edict of 22 September 1540.[158] The Index did not claim to be exhaustive. It only listed the works known by the Louvain theologians. However, although it was meant to be limited only to heretical texts, the Index also included writings thought to be dangerous for the unlearned. For instance, the three first titles to be forbidden in the *Duutschboucken* section[159] were *Der Joden biechte*, an anti-semitic text by Jen Pfefferkorn (1543), first published in German in 1508,[160] the *Int paradijs van Venus* (c.1530) an illustrated pornographic pamphlet,[161] and Jean Glapion's anti-evangelical tract, *Tijtcortinghe der pelgrimagien des menschelijcken levens* (c.1540).[162] Glapion had at one time been Charles V's confessor.

Four years later, the 1546 Index was increased and its contents were listed alphabetically. A new document was published in Brussels on 29 April 1550.[163] This Index reversed the order used by the 1546 list, which began with Bibles and New Testaments, and continued with Latin heretical texts. Furthermore, in contrast to the 1546 Index, which only had 72 specific titles, 39 authors, and three condemnations of *opera omnia*, the 1550 Index listed 188 specific titles and 96 authors, 22 of whom saw all their works banned.[164] However, the list of Dutch books is fairly similar in both cases, the only difference being a slight reordering of titles' slots. In 1546, the *Spelen van zinne binnen Gendt vertooght 12–23 juni 1539*[165] was included in the section of works banned in September 1540. In the 1550 Index, these 19 comedies by the chambers of rhetoric were added to the main list of Dutch books.

---

[157] A brief Index was put together in Liège in 1545. See E. Fairon, 'Le premier index de livres prohibés à Liège, 1545', *De gulden passer*, 3 (1925), 1–15.

[158] *ROPB2*, pp. 255–64. It was republished with annotations in *Index 2*.

[159] The 1546 Index also mentioned around seven other books, which cannot strictly be considered heretical.

[160] Machiels, *Catalogus*, p. 290. Pfefferkorn, a former butcher, was a converted Jew. As a Dominican, he zealously worked to eliminate Jews from the world of high finance, and to destroy the *Talmud*. N. Oudejans, 'De jood in de middelnederlandse literatuur', *Literatuur tijdschrift over nederlandse letterkunde*, 1 (1984/85), 250.

[161] NK 1678.

[162] NK 3101.

[163] *ROPB2*, 6, pp. 55–76.

[164] L. A. Kenney, 'The censorship edicts of Emperor Charles V in the Low Countries, 1515–1550' (PhD, 1960), University of Maryland, pp. 172–3. Reprinted in *Index 2*, pp. 298–381.

[165] 'Comédies en vers jouées à Gand du 12 au 23 juin 1539' NK 1926, 1927–1928, 3890.

The 1550 Index acted as a basis for another list of heretical books published in 1558 by Philip II, Charles V's successor.[166] The 1558 edict condemned a large number of books not on the list in 1550, including 77 Latin works, two Dutch New Testaments, 29 Dutch pamphlets and five French books. Yet the most important of the *Indices librorum prohibitorum* in the Low Countries was that approved by the Duke of Alba in 1570.[167] It condemned a total of 334 books which had not appeared in the 1558 Index. These condemned works included not only recently published heterodox works, but also a number of older evangelical pamphlets which had been omitted by mistake in earlier edicts.[168]

Repression

The authorities' concern about reading also surfaced in their attempts to repress all its manifestations. Attacks on heretical conventicles were often linked to their ownership of evangelical works. Even the mere presence of such books was considered as an indication of heresy. Penalties applied to the members of these small groups reflect the hardening of official attitudes towards heresy and heretical writings. In 1527, the discovery of a Brussels group led to fines and banishment for its members.[169] The Louvain conventicle was less fortunate following its discovery in 1543, as its leading members were executed.[170]

Leading printer-booksellers like Adriaen van Berghen and Jacob van Liesvelt, executed because of their printing activities, have already been mentioned. But alongside these were other more minor figures who were persecuted for similar illegal activities. The bookseller Henrick Peters was condemned in February 1525 to a pilgrimage to Cologne for having sold Lutheran books,[171] while committing a similar offence led to Cornelis vander Plassen being banished for a year.[172] In January 1558, the printer Frans Fraet met a much worse fate, as he was decapitated for having printed 'seditious' books.[173]

Authors were also pursued. In fact, these authors were not all clerics and theologians. In March 1545, Joachim Jaestesz was executed for

---

[166] C. Sepp (ed.) *Verboden lectuur* (Leiden, 1889), pp. 101–47. Reprinted in *Index 2*, pp. 298–381.

[167] Sepp, *Verboden lectuur*, pp. 163–261.

[168] For instance *Vanden olden en nieuwen God, geloove ende leere*, first published around 1524 (NK 1013) was not forbidden prior to 1570.

[169] J. Duverger, 'Lutherse predicatie', col. 226.

[170] See Enzinas, *Mémoires*.

[171] *Antweerpsch archievenblad*, 7 (1871), 140.

[172] *Antweerpsch archievenblad*, 7 (1871), 164.

[173] *Antweerpsch archievenblad*, 8 (1871), 441.

heresy. He was condemned for having compiled a book of commonplaces about his faith.[174]

Other home-made heretical works appeared in Anabaptist trials, like that of Otto Berentsz in August 1555.[175] From time to time, those from humble backgrounds were able to have their own works printed, which could lead them into serious difficulties. Cornelis Woutersz, a shoemaker from Dordrecht, encountered such problems when he had seven psalms printed in 1525.[176] He was made to recant and to carry out a public penance because of his writings. Later, he went to Bremen, and remained there for six months. After his return to the Low Countries and the end of his work in the Goslar silver mines in Brunswick, he began to regret his recantation. In spite of his wife's protests, he sent two letters to a printer in Antwerp: one addressed to the city council and the second to the entire city of Dordrecht, retracting his recantation. He was executed in 1529 following the publication of his retraction.[177]

Historians have often noted that the Reformation was the first movement to use printing as propaganda. Some scholars have even hypothesized what impact pre-Reformation heretical groups would have made, had they had printing at their disposal.[178] The large number of investigations undertaken by civil and religious authorities indicates clearly what a significant impact heretical literature could have, at least in the eyes of orthodox Catholics. On the Protestant side, the number of publications, their distribution and sale in spite of the risks, and the printers' activity, which in some cases led to martyrdom, all testify to the awareness of the power of printed books.

Select bibliography

Belgica typographica 1541–1600. Catalogus librorum impressorum ab anno MDLXI ad annum MDC in regionibus quae nunc regni Belgarum partes sunt (Nieuwkoop, 1968–   ), 2 vols to date.

---

[174] Index op de crimineel sententien van het Hof van Holland 1538 tot en met 1572, number 5654, f. 151ᵛ.

[175] Mellink, *Documenta anabaptistica*, p. 255.

[176] NK 0849. Woutersz's humble origins may explain why Nijhoff and Kronenberg translate 'geprent ende gemaect' as 'printed and translated' and that they believe it to be a translation of Luther's *Sieben buszpsalmen* (1517). However, the usual translation is 'printed and written; in the present context, there is no reason to think that the rendering of these psalms was not an original work of Woutersz.

[177] J. G. de Hoop Scheffer, 'Cornelis Woutersz van Dordrecht, een martelaar der Hervorming, 1525–1529', *Kerkhistorisch archief*, 4 (1866), 1–22.

[178] Febvre/Martin, p. 434. E. L. Eisenstein, *The Printing Press as an Agent of Change* (Cambridge, 1979) vol. 1, p. 303.

Bruin, C. C. de, *De Statenbijbel en zijn voorgangers* (Leiden, 1937).

Decavele, J., *De dageraad van de reformatie in Vlaaderen (1520–1565)* (2 vols, Brussels, 1975).

Fontaine Verwey, H. de la, *Uit de wereld van het boek. I. Humanisten, dwepers en rebellen in de zestiende eeuw* (Amsterdam, 1975).

Halkin, L.-E., *La Réforme en Belgique sous Charles-Quint* (Brussels, 1957).

Johnston, A. G., 'The eclectic reformation: vernacular evangelical pamphlet literature in the Dutch-speaking Low Countries, 1520–1565' PhD, Southampton University (1986).

Kronenberg, M. E., *Verboden boeken en opstandige drukken in de hervormingstijd* (Amsterdam, 1948).

Lindenboom, J., *De confessioneele ontwikkeling der Reformatie in de Nederlanden* (The Hague, 1946).

Nijhoff W., and Kronenberg, M. E., *Nederlandsche bibliographie van 1500 tot 1540* (The Hague, 1923–71).

Pont, J. W., *Geschiedenis van het lutheranisme in de Nederlanden tot 1618* (Haarlem, 1911).

Poortman, W. C., *Bijbel en prent* (The Hague, 1983).

Rouzet, A., *Dictionnaire des imprimeurs, libraires et éditeurs des XVe et XVIe siècles dans les limites géographiques de la Belgique actuelle* (Nieuwkoop, 1975).

Visser, C. Ch. G., *Luther's geschriften in de Nederlanden tot 1546* (Assen, 1969).

Wijnman, H. F., 'The mysterious sixteenth-century printer Niclaes van Oldenborch: Antwerp or Emden?', in S. van der Woude (ed.) *Studia bibliographica in honorem Herman de la Fontaine Verwey* (Amsterdam, 1968), pp. 463–72.

CHAPTER FIVE

Three border cities: Antwerp, Strasbourg and Basle

Jean-François Gilmont

Having analysed the main centres of evangelical printing in the sixteenth century, let us turn our attention to a more detailed examination of three chief printing centres located on the border between the Germanic and Roman worlds. Antwerp, Strasbourg and Basle exemplify the profound economic changes which affected urban Europe in the early years of the sixteenth century. The population expansion in Antwerp, part of the Burgundian inheritance, made it into the prototype of a modern metropolis, as it became a vital centre of finance and went from 50 000 inhabitants in 1500 to 100 000 in 1566, prior to its recapture by Philip II. Strasbourg remained a traditional merchant city, averaging between 20 000 and 25 000 inhabitants. The city controlled access to fluvial trade on the upper Rhine, and was the gateway to the north and east. For its part, Basle was an old episcopal city of 10 000 inhabitants, which became a flourishing intellectual centre following the foundation of a university after the Council of Basle. Printing activity in these three cities varied enormously. Basle was a vibrant international centre, maintaining strong links with Italy and France. Strasbourg was a more provincial centre, and its printers supplied works chiefly for more local and more popular markets. For its part, from 1500 onward Antwerp became one of the most important printing centres in Europe, behind Venice and Paris.

Reformation printing followed the paths established in earlier years. Basle printers continued to work with scholars from Italy, The Netherlands and France. In particular, Erasmus acted as a magnet on his contemporaries, thus ensuring the survival of humanist publishing during the Reformation. The presence of these scholars in Basle made it a centre for translation and Bible publications. Prior to 1538, there was no academic centre, nor any similar group of scholars active in Strasbourg. Few printers, therefore, published treatises or documents in Latin. Instead, they preferred German, turning to the educated lay person, able to read in the vernacular. Strasbourg's export markets were in the German Empire, sometimes in its most far-flung areas. During the Reformation, the Strasbourg printers broadened their horizons even further by printing pamphlets and treatises for French and English Protestants.

5.1 The second part of Luther's *Postillen* (Antwerp: Hillenius, 1528)

As for the Antwerp printers, they distributed their works in every European language: Dutch, English, French, Spanish, Italian, Danish, and in Latin, Greek and Hebrew. They dominated markets not only in the Seventeen Provinces, but also in neighbouring lands. When Lutheran writings began to spread, they rapidly disseminated them in Dutch and Latin. The printers' initial enthusiasm was cooled, however, by the condemnation of Luther's writings by Louvain University in 1519, a condemnation soon confirmed by a Papal bull and an Imperial edict. Book burnings in Louvain and Antwerp in 1520 and 1522 conveyed an unequivocal message to those tempted by Protestant publications. Repression pushed Antwerp printers towards clandestine work, especially for the English, Danish and Spanish markets. In spite of the constraints, the presses managed to provide the core texts of the Reformation in these linguistic areas.

Located on the frontiers of the Roman world, the printers in these three cities all ensured that in the early days Luther's key works reached the French-speaking world. In almost every case, the translation of works from German into French operated via Latin editions. The first stage was thus to distribute Latin versions, something which the printers in Basle, Antwerp, and even Strasbourg did. But soon the presses also produced French editions. The censorship carried out by the French authorities only served to encourage the publication of Protestant works just over the border of the kingdom.

However, the catalogue of works in French varied in each of these three cities, depending on politics and the state of the markets. Basle specialized in publishing Bibles, offering a large selection of complete editions of the Bible in Latin, Greek, Hebrew, French and German. Antwerp too could provide many Bibles since, at least at first, these were not prohibited by the censors. Antwerp printers published the Holy Scriptures in Flemish, Latin and French, while English versions of Tyndale's Bible were particularly important. In contrast, there was very little Bible publishing in Strasbourg.

Indeed, the publication of Catholic doctrinal or theological works also came to a rather abrupt end in Strasbourg. In Basle and Antwerp, however, such works continued to appear. But Protestant works, in Strasbourg as in Basle, reflected the views of a wide spectrum of theologians. Given the risks they ran, the Antwerp printers' body of Protestant works show the strength of their beliefs, but also the freedom which artisans had in large commercial cities such as Antwerp or Venice, so long as their actions did not affect trade.

In the end, censorship was the defining factor in the relative length of printing activity in these three cities. In Antwerp, printers were silenced through the resolute will of the monarch, the national governor and local powers. In Basle and Strasbourg, the magistrates only slowly gained control of the printing industry. In spite of the explicit measures of the Edict of Worms in 1521, neither of the two cities published an

Ordinance on the subject prior to 1524. Later legislation appeared in Basle in 1531 and 1542, but in practice in Basle as in Strasbourg, printers themselves policed their profession. In contrast, Antwerp was much nearer to the heart of Catholic power. Charles V was quick to reinforce censorship in his hereditary lands, and his efforts were upheld by papal nuncios. Two Antwerp printers were executed, one in 1542, and the other in 1545, while a third was banished from the city. After 1545 the risks were too great for any printer to publish Protestant works in Antwerp, and production virtually ceased. This example provides ample proof that without the independence allowed in the free cities, the spread of the Reformation would have been very different. The traditional liberties of the free cities enabled the new ideas to spread.

CHAPTER SIX

Printing and the
Reformation in Antwerp

Andrew G. Johnston and Jean-François Gilmont

Antwerp's role in the spread of Protestant books extended well beyond the borders of the Low Countries. This chapter intends to underline Antwerp's importance without repeating what has already been written in the chapters on the Low Countries, England and France. Our intention is not to provide a complete picture of the book in Antwerp, but only to bring to light the specific characteristics of works printed in the city. Only brief references will be made in instances where the Antwerp situation is similar to that of the Netherlands as a whole.

A port open to the world

Lying at the heart of the Low Countries, territories which the Burgundian house, followed by the Habsburgs, had carefully brought together over time, Antwerp by the end of the fifteenth century was a metropolis, channelling the vast majority of economic exchanges. After the Zwin became silted up, cutting Bruges from the sea, Antwerp took the leading role from its rival, thanks to its access to the North Sea. In the second half of the fifteenth century and the first two-thirds of the sixteenth century, Antwerp underwent an unprecedented expansion, growing from 20 000 inhabitants around 1440 to 50 000 at the turn of the century, and reaching 100 000 by 1560.[1] At this point in time, Antwerp was the trade capital of western Europe. The city had no bishop – becoming an active bishopric only in 1570 – nor a university, but was nevertheless a focus of brilliant intellectual life during its 'golden age'. As a commercial city, Antwerp was a cosmopolitan place, where foreigners such as Englishmen, Portuguese, Castilians, Hanseatic men, and South Germans were organized into Nations, thus avoiding local legislation on

---

[1] R. Mois, *Introduction à la démographie historique des villes d'Europe du XIVe siècle au XVIIIe siècle* (Louvain, 1955) vol. 2, p. 520. See E. Coornaert, *Les Français et le commerce international à Anvers, fin du XVe-XVIe siècle* (Paris, 1961) vol. 1, pp. 92–124.

various matters, including religion. Because of their desire to foster trade, the magistrates were very willing to comply with the colonies of foreigners. Indeed, the latter were the motor of the local economy. Although Antwerp was the uncontested trade leader in the North Sea, it could never match the great Mediterranean ports of Genoa and Venice. The magistrates of Antwerp were proud of their autonomy, and sought to control local events, but at the same time, they remained subordinate to their prince. The magistrates were often forced to compromise to reduce the level of intervention of the central authorities, but they still refused to accept the Inquisition or to become the seat of a bishopric.[2]

In the sixteenth century, the city's printing industry was among the leaders of Europe. Antwerp ran a close second to Paris, but both trailed behind Venice, whose domination of the printing industry was unchallenged. However, Antwerp's production level was greater than those of Lyon, Basle, or Strasbourg,[3] and the city had achieved its pre-eminence by the beginning of the sixteenth century. Indeed Antwerp was not the first city in the Low Countries to welcome printers. The new typographical technique only arrived in Antwerp in 1481, while around ten other cities already had functioning workshops since 1473.[4] However, Antwerp rapidly caught up, and soon dominated the printing market in north-west Europe. Between 1500 and 1540, of the 120 printers in the Low Countries, 56 were based in Antwerp; of the 4 600 editions printed during these decades, around 2 500 came from the Antwerp presses.[5]

The first followers of Luther to be spotted by the authorities of the Seventeen Provinces were in fact from Antwerp. Already in 1519, the Augustinian Prior, Jacob Praepositus, was attacked as a supporter of his fellow monk, Luther. The investigations begun in December 1520 led to several recantations or flights into Germany (Jacob Praepositus, Hendrik van Zutphen, Cornelius Grapheus). Two other Antwerp Augustinians, Hendrik Voes and Johannes Esschen, were condemned to death: burnt alive in Brussels because of fears of popular uprisings in Antwerp, they had the misfortune to be the first martyrs of the Reformation.

In a land where the central authorities were firm supporters of the traditional faith, Antwerp was a free area, in which Lutheranism, Anabaptism and Calvinism could successively take root. The vitality of

---

[2] M. Dierickx, *De oprichting der nieuwe bisdommen in de Nederlanden onder Filips II, 1559–1570* (Antwerp, Utrecht, 1950), pp. 168–76.

[3] See the table based on the British Library collections in *HÉF*, p. 442.

[4] *Le cinquième centenaire de l'imprimerie dans les Pays-Bas. Exposition à la Bibliothèque Royale Albert 1er* (Brussels, 1973), pp. 360–61.

[5] M. E. Kronenberg, *Verboden boeken en opstandige drukken in de hervormingstijd* (Amsterdam, 1948), p. 65.

Protestant printing between 1520 and 1545 signals the active life of Luther's supporters. But these followers were never organized into a church community. Thus, they left few traces in the archives. Reformed Protestantism defended an entirely different standpoint, and offered a solid ecclesiastical structure. From the middle of the sixteenth century onwards, Protestantism in the Low Countries moved clearly into the Calvinist camp. By 1550, a Reformed community was set up in Antwerp, around Gaspard van der Heyden.[6] Soon there were two consistories, a Flemish and a Walloon one, the latter exercising great influence over the entire land. In 1561, the *Confessio Belgica* gained its authority from the support of the 'Antwerp brethren'.[7] In the 1560s, as religious tensions rose, Antwerp became the epicentre for the movement. A few surviving fragments of correspondence indicate the openness of the intellectual and religious climate, which fascinated the young Venetian draper Giovanni Zonca, during his stay from 1562 to 1566. In particular, he was able to come into direct contact with forbidden books.[8] After the government troops retook the city in 1567, everything collapsed. But the history of the final decades of the sixteenth century, with the clear decline of Antwerp, extends beyond the scope of our investigations.

Anabaptism is not dealt with in this chapter, despite its importance as a confession in Antwerp. However, this gap is explained by the lack of Antwerp works coming from an Anabaptist context.

A flood of heretical books

In the sixteenth century, Antwerp printers produced works in the main European languages: Dutch, English, French, Spanish, Italian and Danish, as well as Latin, Greek and Hebrew. Antwerp dominated the book market not only in the Seventeen Provinces, but also in neighbouring lands, first and foremost in England.

At a time when Luther's reputation was growing across Europe, Antwerp printers were keen to profit from the interest generated by his writings. For two or three years, they were able to do so without worrying about the condemnations of Luther. The Antwerp printers

---

[6] A. J. Jelsma, *Adriaan van Haemstede en zijn martelaarsboek* (The Hague, 1970), pp. 22–8.

[7] See G. Moreau, *Histoire du protestantisme à Tournai jusqu'à la veille de la Révolution des Pays-Bas* (Paris, 1962), pp. 156–7.

[8] See V. Rossato, 'Religione e moralità in un merciaio veneziano del Cinquecento', *Studi veneziani*, n.s., 13 (1987), pp. 193–253, while waiting for the publication of G. Zonca's Antwerp correspondence, which Rossato is preparing for the *Revue d'Histoire Ecclésiastique*.

published Luther's works in Latin and Dutch, sometimes even with the author's name and their printing address. For his part, Michael Hillenius published writings for and against Luther simultaneously[9] suggesting that his concerns were more commercial than theological. Soon, however, the condemnations by the theological faculty of Louvain (7 November 1519) and by the Pope (15 June 1520) were followed by a placard by the Emperor Charles V (28 September 1520). Heretical works were publicly burnt in Louvain on 8 September 1520. In Antwerp, the first book burnings took place on 13 July 1521. In 1522, the city authorities burnt heretical books on three separate occasions.[10]

Following this warning, printing of Protestant works became a clandestine activity: evangelical authors' names were omitted, and apart from a few exceptions, printers no longer published their typographical address. Printers had more leeway when it came to editions of Scripture, as printers' names often continued to appear on title-pages until the early 1540s. During a quarter-century, a handful of Antwerp printers produced most of the Protestant works in Dutch. Some did so through conviction, others out of self-interest, and some for both reasons.

After 1545, Antwerp was no longer the centre of the evangelical book trade in the Low Countries. This decline was caused above all by repression. The authorities managed to flush out three major heterodox printers in Antwerp, executing Adriaen van Berghen (1542) and Jacob van Liesvelt (1545), and probably forcing Steven Mierdmans into exile (around 1546). But other factors, mentioned below, also help to explain the move of Protestant printing towards other cities.

Prior to 1547, Antwerp was also one of the main production centres of heretical works in English. One must bear in mind that the English presses were not very numerous nor well-equipped at this point in time. Since the beginning of the century, it had been common practice for Englishmen to call upon continental printers, especially those from Rouen and Antwerp. Thus a printer like Christoffel van Ruremund worked primarily for customers in England. It was only natural that these printers who were in touch with English merchants in Antwerp, were asked to produce works forbidden in England. The list of printers involved in this type of production is at least as long as that of those publishing heretical works in Flemish. Furthermore, the Antwerp editions in English were not merely reproductions. After attempts in Cologne and Worms, William Tyndale settled in Antwerp and published

---

[9] Against Luther: John Fisher (NK 0511, 939), Henry VIII (NK 0592, 1045), Jacobus Latomus (NK 1329), Eustachius de Zichenis (NK 885).

[10] Fl. Prims, *Geschiedenis van Antwerpen* (Antwerp, 1940) vol. 7, part 3, p. 292; Moreau (ed.) *Histoire de l'Eglise en Belgique* (Brussels, 1949),vol. 4, p. 251.

his versions of Scripture there, as well as other works. He was arrested in Antwerp and executed in 1536, near Brussels. Ten years later, another leading figure of the English Reformation, John Bale, systematically entrusted his current works to the Antwerp presses.

℄ The sum
me of the holye scripture /
and ordinarye of the Chusten teachyng /
the true Chusten faithe / by the which we
be all iustified. And of the vertue of bap-
tesme / after the teaching of the Gos
pell and of the Apostles / with an informacyon howe
all estates shulde ly
ve / accordynge
to the Gos-
pell.

Anno. M.CCCCC.XXIX.

6.1   English version of *De summa der godliker scrifturen* ([Antwerp], 1529)

The evolution of production in English was shaped more by the situation of the English crown than by that in Antwerp. Until the death of Henry VIII, no radical opinions could be voiced in England. Thus the Reformers turned to continental presses until 1547. Steven Mierdmans, one of the most daring printers of the period, epitomizes this change. After having printed heretical works in English and Flemish from 1543 to 1546 in Antwerp, he went to London in 1547 to continue the same kind of printing there. Mary Tudor's accession made him return to the Continent. However, by this point it was no longer possible to print Protestant works in Antwerp, so he settled in Emden. The same pattern was followed by another Flemish printer from London, Nicholas Hill, who put his original name, vanden Berghe, on his Emden editions.[11]

---

[11] Fr. C. Avis, 'England's use of Antwerp printers, 1500–1540', *GJ* (1973), 234–40; A. Pettegree, *Foreign Protestant Communities in Sixteenth-Century London* (Oxford, 1986), pp. 84–9; H. F. Wijnman, 'The mysterious sixteenth-century printer Niclaes van

To avoid problems, this Antwerp production used false printers' addresses. In the 1520s, several printers paid a heavy price for their daring. Already in 1526, the English consul in Antwerp notified London that two printers were producing heretical works in English in London. In 1527, Hans van Ruremund was arrested in London for having illegally imported copies of Tyndale's New Testament which the latter had printed in Antwerp. In 1530, Ruremund's relative, Christoffel van Ruremund, was imprisoned in Westminster on similar grounds and died in prison in 1531.[12]

Antwerp also produced evangelical writings in French, but these were fewer in number as they were the work of a single figure, Martin Lempereur. Unverifiable tradition states that this Frenchman who worked in Paris for a time, emigrated to the Low Countries on the advice of Jacques Lefèvre d'Étaples. The humanist thought that Lempereur would enjoy greater freedom in Antwerp to publish his French translation of the Bible. And indeed, Lempereur's catalogue illustrates the freedom experienced by the Antwerp printers, so long as they exercised caution. After his death in 1536, his widow kept the business going until 1541. Following this, his successor Antoine Des Gois continued on the same path, but proceeded with increasing caution. In 1544, Des Gois vanished from view, and with his disappearance came the end of the production of French Protestant books in Antwerp.[13]

Danish Protestant works produced by Antwerp printers were few in number, but these were fundamental Reformation texts. They too testify to the welcoming atmosphere of Antwerp. Following the dynastic conflict between Christian II and Frederick I, the canon Christiern Pedersen, one of the main exponents of the Reformation in Denmark, was forced into exile. From 1529 to 1531, he withdrew to the Low Countries, where he toiled ceaselessly to translate Scripture, as well as various works by Luther. He entrusted the printing of these to Willem Vorsterman; around ten Danish works were printed during these two years, especially the translation of the New Testament and of the Psalms. When Pedersen returned to Denmark, he attracted the services of an

---

Oldenborch: Antwerp or Emden?' in S. van der Woude (ed.) *Studia bibliographica in honorem Herman de la Fontaine Verwey* (Amsterdam, 1968) pp. 463–7. The figure of Walter Lynne, highly involved in the Protestant works produced in London between 1548 and 1550, is more enigmatic: was he the same as the Antwerp printer Wouter van Lin? See A. Rouzet, *Dictionnaire des imprimeurs, libraires et éditeurs des XVe et XVIe siècles dans les limites géographiques de la Belgique actuelle* (Nieuwkoop, 1975), p. 130.

[12] All these printer-publishers are described below (pp. 196–205)
[13] See above, p. 109–10.

Antwerp printer, Johannes Hillenius, and made him director of his printing house in Malmö from 1533 to 1535.[14]

Just as Antwerp benefited from its maritime links and from the weakness of local printing to produce works in English, it also took advantage of dynastic links with Spain and the weakness of printing there to produce numerous Spanish books. Production in this area increased throughout the sixteenth century.[15] However, as the chapter on Spain indicates, Protestant books were rare. The first signs of these works appeared in Antwerp. Prior to February 1521, a Spanish translation of Luther was printed in Antwerp, perhaps by Claes de Grave. This work has not been found.[16] In contrast, there are clear traces of Francisco de Enzinas's activity in the 1540s. After having a translation of Melanchthon printed in Ghent, he collated a small doctrinal work based on texts by Luther and Calvin, which he gave to an Antwerp printer, perhaps Matthias Crom, in 1540.[17] Three years later, de Enzinas had Steven Mierdmans print his translation of the New Testament in Spanish, probably with the connivance of Crom. The enterprise, which ended in the imprisonment of de Enzinas, indicates that in 1543, Antwerp had an author and a printer bold enough to distribute such a work openly. Indeed, the printer did not face any major challenges to his activities.[18]

The lack of heterodox Antwerp publications in German is explained by the great freedom experienced by the German printers. The situation for works in Italian was similar, as evangelical circles in the Italian peninsula had access to local production centres or ones in nearby Switzerland, or in Lyon. The only exception is Johannes Grapheus's production of the very first re-edition of the *Nuevo Testamento*, translated by Antonio Brucioli.[19]

After 1546, Protestant books were rarely printed in Antwerp, in any language. Jacob van Liesvelt's widow, together with his son Hans,

---

[14] See below, p. 434. M. E. Kronenberg, 'De drukker van de Deensche boeken te Antwerpen (1529–1531) is Willem Vorsterman', *Het boek*, 8 (1919), 1–8. Pardoned in 1536, Pedersen returned to court and sold off his printing presses. See W. Göbell in *Die Religion in Geschichte und Gegenwart*, 3rd edn, vol. 5 (1961), p. 203; C. S. Petersen in *Danske Biografisk Leksikon*, vol. 18 (1940), pp. 76–82.

[15] J. Peeters-Fontainas, *Bibliographie des impressions espagnoles des Pays-Bas méridionaux* (2 vols, Nieuwkoop, 1965). See below, p. 310.

[16] NK 0860; Peeters-Fontainas, *Bibliographie des impressions*, no. 751.

[17] The work had as address, 'En Topeia por Adamo Corvo'. The suggested identity of the printer is Wijnman's 'The mysterious printer' p. 463. E. Kronenberg attributed the work to Guillaume de Mont (NK 4221).

[18] See F. de Enzinas, *Mémoires* Ch. Al. Campan (ed.), (Brussels, 1862), vol. 1, pp. 643–4 and Wijnman, 'The mysterious printer', pp. 462–3.

[19] NK 422. This was the only Antwerp edition mentioned by A. J. Schutte, *Printed Italian Vernacular Religious Books 1465–1550: A Finding List* (Geneva, 1983).

Dat leſte Ser=
moon D. Martini Lutheri
ſaligher ghedachten / gheſchiet tot Wit-
tenberch/ opten tweeden Sondach naer
Dertiendach den.xvñ.Januarÿ
ſA.D.ende.xlvj.

Euergeſedt in onſer Duyt-
ſcher ſpʒaken
Anno ſAʒ.D.Liiÿ.

Rom.j.
Jch en ſcheme my des Euangeliums
niet.want het is een cracht Gods
tot ſalicheyt allen den ghe-
ven die: gheloouen.

6.2 Martin Luther, *Dat leste Sermoon* … (Antwerp: Gillis Coppens van Diest, c.1566?)

continued to print Bibles containing Lutheran influences. Later, in the 1560s, printers signalled their Protestant sympathies in ambiguous works, like *Eene gheestelijcken A, B, uut de Heylighe Schrift in dichte ghestelt*, printed in 1564 by Willem Silvius and Ameet Tavernier under their own names.[20] Tavernier was famous for his widespread use of script type, often associated with Protestant writings. As well, Christopher Plantin printed a few heterodox pamphlets for the Family of Love.[21] All this remained very sporadic, except in the Wonderyear – *het Wonderjaar* – when the Protestants were able to organize them-selves publicly in Antwerp (April 1566–April 1567). Antwerp's level of printing activity in this period was very high, especially as regards the production of short works on faith or religious and political polemic. During this time, Gilles Coppens produced a remarkable

---

[20] *Belgica typographica 1541–1600* (Nieuwkoop, 1977–80), vol. 2, nos 4988–4989; *Index 2.*

[21] L. Voet, *The Golden Compasses* (Amsterdam, 1969), vol. 1, pp. 21–30. P. Valkema Blouw has retraced various heretical publications which were quietly supported by Plantin. (See the articles mentioned in note 11 in this chapter).

series of clandestine printings.[22] By 1566, penalties were becoming harsher: in October 1566, Jan Mollyns was banished for six years after having published a forbidden book under an assumed address; in August 1567, Gilles Coppens was arrested and then released for lack of evidence; in 1568, Willem Silvius was able to defend himself successfully against charges of heresy; in 1569, Jan Roelants was arrested in May for the sale of banned books, and died in prison in 1570.[23] Antwerp no longer dominated the evangelical book market as it had done during the past quarter century.

A line-up of evangelical printers

A rapid tour of the main printing houses responsible for the production of forbidden works allows one to note the variety of circumstances and levels of commitment in the Antwerp Protestant printing industry. The dozen printers presented in the following section appear in roughly chronological order of their activities in the service of Reformation.[24] The first three were occasional printers active in the early years.

Michael Hillenius van Hoochstraten (1506–46)   This extremely active printer's production was characterized by its great orthodoxy. In 1520 and 1521, he printed under his own name a few small Latin tracts by Luther, Johannes Pupper of Goch, and Johannes Oecolampadius. He had no hesitation in simultaneously publishing works by John Fisher and Henry VIII against Luther.

Claes de Grave (1511–40)   Among his overall production, which was not noted for daring religious attacks, from 1520–22, Claes de Grave published several works by Luther and by a few of his followers. Above all, de Grave offered Dutch translations – and a Spanish one? – which he distributed either using his own name or with Wittenberg as the address. On one occasion, he even used Melchior Lotter's name by reproducing one of his title-borders.

---

[22] P. Valkema Blouw, 'Gilles Coppens van Diest als ondergronds drukker, 1566–67', in *Het oude en de nieuwe bibliotheek: Liber amicorum H. D. L. Vervliet* (Kapellen, 1988), pp. 143–63. More in general, see W. Heijting, 'Protestantse confessies in het Wonderjaar 1566', in *Het oude*, pp. 129–42.

[23] Rouzet, *Dictionnaire des imprimeurs*, pp. 150, 201, 191.

[24] The entries in A. Rouzet's *Dictionnaire des imprimeurs*, especially the bibliographies, are accurate and very thorough. Readers should consult Rouzet's work for the following sections. One can easily obtain an overview of the production of each printer between 1500 and 1540 by consulting NK 3, pp. 139–229 (for Antwerp).

Henrick Eckert van Homberch (1500–21)   Henrick Eckert, who began his trade in 1498 in Delft, settled in Antwerp in 1500. After having printed works of popular devotion in Dutch and in Latin, he offered Flemish translations of Luther in 1521. One of these editions bears his name. He stopped printing in 1521 and died in 1523.

The next printers were more highly committed.

Adriaen van Berghen (1500–41)   After having published many works of piety in Latin and Flemish until 1522, Adriaen van Berghen specialized in producing Lutheran texts in Flemish. He printed translations of Luther, Bucer and Brunfels,[25] as well as original pamphlets such as *Dye pricipaele hooftarticulen van allen dingendye den mensche troostekick zijn* (1533)[26] and the *Profitelic ende troostelic boexken van den gheloove ende hoope* (1534).[27] He was one of the most daring printers, and several forbidden books openly bore his name.

On several occasions, his illicit activities caused him problems, perhaps as early as 1522, but definitely by 1523. In 1533, he managed to extricate himself, but in 1536, he was condemned for selling Lutheran works. The damage was limited to exile and a penitential pilgrimage to Nicosia in Cyprus. In fact, he sought refuge in Holland, while his Antwerp workshop continued to operate at a reduced level. Caught in Delft while trading in forbidden books, he was condemned to death by the court of Holland and executed in The Hague in 1542.

Christoffel van Ruremund (1522–31) and his widow (1532–46)   From the early days of his printing shop onwards, Christoffel van Ruremund preferred to work for England, and specialized in liturgical works. His evangelical production must amount to more than the few Tyndale New Testaments that survive, if we are to believe the accusations of the English Consul in Antwerp in 1526. During a trip to England in 1530, Christoffel was imprisoned in Westminster for having sold banned New Testaments. He died in prison in 1531.

His widow maintained the workshop. She continued to produce works directed preferably towards England at least until around 1540: traditional liturgical works, and, in greater quantity, forbidden works in English, written by native authors (G. Joye, J. Bale) and by foreign writers (Savonarola, Melanchthon, Bullinger, Zwingli). By the end of

---

[25] Luther: NK 3458–3459, 3462. Bucer: NK 2587. Brunfels: NK 502.
[26] NK 3185.
[27] NK 440.

her career, which ended in 1546, she specialized in less dangerous works: ordinances, almanacs and news sheets.

Hans van Ruremund (1522–29)   This printer, probably related to the preceding one, also specialized in English books. His modest production consisted almost entirely of New Testaments in Dutch and English. Already in 1526, he was in trouble with the Antwerp judiciary for having published a Lutheran work. But above all, Hans van Ruremund was a bookseller: in the following year, he was imprisoned in London for having imported 500 Tyndale New Testaments printed in Antwerp. He was able to regain his freedom, and may have ended his career in England.

Johannes Hillenius van Hoochstraten (1525–43)   Johannes Hillenius began work in Antwerp in 1525, and his printing activity was almost entirely focused on heretical works. He was probably related to Michael Hillenius, a printer with whom he worked towards the end of his life. In contrast to van Berghen and the Ruremunds, he was as wise as a serpent, thus avoiding many conflicts with the authorities.

His catalogue and career both testify to his openness on an international scale. He was mainly active in Antwerp (1525–30, 1535–43), but also in Lübeck in 1531–32 and in Malmö between 1533 and 1535.[28]

During his first period of work in Antwerp, Johannes Hillenius published numerous heretical works, both in English and in Dutch. He is known to have produced a Latin edition of François Lambert d'Avignon early in his career.[29] Many more of his publications appeared in Dutch, and from 1528, in English. He produced important works such as the Dutch translation of J. Bugenhagen's psalter (1526) and of Luther's *Postils* (1528). Following this, he worked for the English market, collaborating closely with William Tyndale. He printed another English pamphlet in Malmö in 1535.[30]

All his production appeared anonymously or with a wide variety of pseudonyms, including 'Argentorati [Strasbourg]' (1525), 'te Basel bi mi Adam Anonymus' (1526–28); 'Wittemberch' (1528); 'Marlborow [Marburg] in the Lande of Hesse by my Hans Luft' (1528–35); 'Te Marborch bi mi Steffen Rodt' (1530). His caution enabled him to avoid detection. After his return to Antwerp between 1535 and 1540, until his death in 1543, Johannes Hillenius printed around ten orthodox

---

[28] See p. 434.
[29] Fr. Lambert d'Avignon, *In regulam minoritarum commentarii* 1525 (R. Bodenmann, in P. Fraenkel (ed.) *Pour retrouver Fr. Lambert* (Baden-Baden, 1987) p. 57).
[30] STC 24167.

⁖❧ IN REGV

LAM MINORITARVM COM

mẽtarñ plane aurei, quibus palã fit, quid
tam de ea, quã de alñs monachorum
regulïs & inſtitutis ſentiendũ fit.

Autore Francifco Lamberto, Auenioneñ.
ab eodem recogniti.

Epiſtola commendaticia operis, Anemundi
Cocti equitis,

In authoris præfatione ingentem multarũ
ſectarum perditionis catalogum inuenies.

ARGENTORATI. MDXXV.

6.3   François Lambert d'Avignon, *In Regulam Minoritarum commentarii*
(Strasbourg [Antwerp]: [Johannes Hillenius], 1525)

works under his own name, working in collaboration with Michael
Hillenius.

Martin Lempereur (1525–35) and his widow (1535–41)   A Frenchman, who trained in Paris with his father-in-law Guillaume le Rouge,
Martin Lempereur (De Keysere, Caesar, Lemperowr) settled in Antwerp
in 1525, probably on the advice of Jacques Lefèvre d'Étaples. From
1525 to 1536, he published more than 200 works, mainly in French
and Latin. His 'official' production was focused primarily on humanism, school texts, and historical writings. But at the same time, he
published a series of translations of Luther, Brunfels and Erasmus, thus
providing evidence of regular contacts with publishers in Paris, Lyon
and Alençon. Furthermore, he even dared to put his name on ambiguous writings which were on the borderline of heterodoxy. This was true
for the *Livre de vraye et parfaicte oraison* (1534) to which the editor
added his own very personal touches.[31] His entire production was
shaped by his individualism: he did not merely provide translations and
re-editions, but instead added new elements to the works.

---

[31] F. M. Higman, 'Luther et la piété gallicane: Le livre de vraye et parfaicte oraison',
Revue d'histoire et de philosophie religieuses, 63 (1983), 104–5.

From 1530 onwards, he also became involved in English heterodox production. He printed several psalters and New Testaments, sometimes with his name on them, and also spread Tyndale's writings. He followed Johannes Hillenius in the use of false addresses, pretending that his works were printed *in alma civitate coloniensi* (1527–30), *Tiguri [Zurich] per Iacobum Mazochium* (1527); at *Argentine [Strasbourg] by me Francis Foxe* (1530); *Straszburg by Balthassar Beckent* (1531); *Luneberg [Lunebourg]* (1532).

Following Lempereur's death in 1536, his wife continued in the same vein, but more cautiously, producing New Testaments, English works, writings by Erasmus, and classical texts. It seems that his successor was Antoine des Gois, and that he continued the work until 1544, albeit increasingly discreetly.

Jacob van Liesvelt (1513–44) Although his production included many perfectly orthodox works, Jacob van Liesvelt was actively involved in evangelism. He was famous above all for his Bibles and New Testament editions in Flemish, following the Lutheran versions. On several occasions, Liesvelt was involved in court cases because of his trade in Protestant books. Already in 1526, he produced works of a Lutheran tendency in Dutch. At the same time, he printed his first Flemish Bible, which he continued to print and rework by consulting Luther's German translations as these appeared. Thus he published the 1542 edition, which led to his condemnation to death. He was also responsible for Flemish versions of O. Brunfels, J. Glapion and C. Huberinus. Following trials in 1536 and 1542, he was accused again in 1545 of printing heretical books, especially the Bible. This time, he was condemned and beheaded.

A few 'opportunists' slipped in among these courageous printers:

Willem Vorsterman (1524–43) Vorsterman was one of the printers who had no hesitation in producing both Catholic and Evangelical works. He printed a large number of anti-Lutheran pamphlets, including the Dutch translation of Luther's condemnation by the Sorbonne (1521),[32] the official *Anathematizatio et revocatio* by the prior of the Antwerp Augustinians, Jacob Praepositus (1522)[33] and an anonymous refutation by a few Lutherans of Antwerp, the *Redelijck bewijs der dolinghen van ses prochanien der luterschen secten* (1527–28).[34]

---

[32] NK 706.
[33] NK 1751.
[34] NK 321.

His abundant production in many languages (Flemish, French, Latin, English, Spanish and Danish) included a few texts of suspicious orthodoxy, like the first Antwerp edition of the New Testament translated into French by Lefèvre d'Étaples or, in 1529 and 1531, around ten Danish Protestant pamphlets written by Christian Pedersen.[35]

Vorsterman's opportunism and the ambiguity of his works are clear in the Flemish Bible which he printed for the first time in 1528.[36] This translation of the Vulgate portrayed itself as orthodox in order to satisfy Catholic customers – it had received the approval of the Inquisitor Nicolas Coppin – but the evangelicals found many passages directly derived from Luther in it.[37] The Louvain theologians suspected him of duplicity, and Vorsterman's Bible was banned by the 1546 Index.

Let us now return to more committed printers.

Hendrik Peetersen van Middelburch (1526–49)   Mentioned already in 1520 as an Antwerp printer, Peetersen began publishing books in his own name at the end of 1526. But already in 1525, he was condemned for the sale of heretical books. Amidst a production focused on current events and schooling, he offered Lutheran-inspired religious works, like translations of Brunfels, Campensis's psalter, and of François Lambert d'Avignon. The latest edition of the English *Short Title Catalogue* cautiously attributes a number of English works appearing between 1533 and 1538 to Peetersen.[38]

Towards the end of our period, here are two or perhaps three very productive publishers who served the Reformation cause.

Matthias Crom (1537–43)   He was a well-known heretic: members of evangelical conventicles in Louvain made special trips to Antwerp to buy books from him.[39] His *Kinderleere*, perhaps a translation of Althamer's *Catechismus*, was burnt in Ghent in the year in which it

---

[35] NK 1431–1441.

[36] NK 392.

[37] C. Augustijn, 'De Vorstermanbijbel van 1528', *Nederlands archief voor kerkgeschiedenis*, 56 (1975), 78–94.

[38] STC 2828, 11381, 20193, 24167, 24447 are attributed to Peetersen with a question mark.

[39] Enzinas, *Mémoires*, vol. 1, p. 362.

appeared,[40] while the French version of his catechism was forbidden by an imperial mandate of 13 January 1543.[41] He worked closely with another notorious Protestant, his brother-in-law Steven Mierdmans. In all likelihood, all the works displaying Nicolas van Oldenborch's name were produced by the two brothers-in-law.

Between 1537 and 1543, a half-dozen Dutch New Testaments and eight evangelical pamphlets were printed under the name of Matthias Crom, the Antwerp printer and publisher. He specialized in catechetical works, such as the *Kinder leere, Dat christen gheloove* (1542),[42] the *Christelijcke onderwijsinghe tot de rijcke Gods* (c.1542),[43] *Der Christen reghel* (1543)[44] and *Ghelooven, hope ende liefde* (1543).[45]

He also worked for the English market between 1536 and 1544, but the extent of his production is not easy to define because of the doubtful attribution of several texts: Crom, or Ruremund's widow?[46] Crom, Mierdmans or van Oldenborch?

Steven Mierdmans (1543–59)   Mierdmans began as an apprentice with Matthias Crom, and later became his brother-in-law and collaborator. From 1543, he established his own presses. After three years' work in Antwerp, he settled in London in 1546, probably having been forced into exile. Mierdmans spent the next seven years in London, printing many English pamphlets and a handful in Dutch. After Mary's accession to the throne, he emigrated to Emden, where he published works in his own name and with the pseudonym Magnus van den Merberghe van Osterhout. Mierdmans died in Emden in 1559.[47]

His Antwerp production included many banned English texts, and used imaginary addresses: *Basyll* [Basle] (1543); *Nurenbergh* (1545); *Ausborch, Adam Anonimus* (1545); *Wesel* (1545–46). Mierdmans signed the Spanish translation of the New Testament done by Enzinas in 1543.

Nicolas van Oldenborch (1531–5?)   No other of the post-incunabula period printers causes more confusion than the mysterious Nicolas van Oldenborch. He personified the concealment tactics of all his evangeli-

[40] F. Vander Haeghen, *Bibliotheca belgica, Bibliographie générale des Pays-Bas* (Ghent, Brussels, 1880–1967) K1 file, 2nd edn, vol. 3, (Brussels, 1964) p. 626; *Index* 2, p. 197.

[41] *ROPB2*, 4, p. 423.

[42] NK 3317. J. Machiels (ed.) *Catalogus van de boeken gedrukt voor 1600 aanwezig op de centrale bibliotheek van de rijksuniversiteit Gent* (Ghent, 1979), K 275.

[43] NK 1622. See Machiels, *Catalogus*, p. 295.

[44] Machiels, *Catalogus*, R 85.

[45] Machiels, *Catalogus*, G 147.

[46] See *STC* 2832, 2833, 2834.

[47] Wijnman, 'The mysterious printer', pp. 463–72.

cal colleagues: after several hundred years, historians are still unable to unravel all his subterfuges. Ten works bear his name. Going by the dates on these works, Oldenborch would have published between 1531, the date on Willem Gnapheus's *Troost ende spiegel der siecken* and 1555, in which the anonymous compilation of scriptural texts, *Der waerheyt onderwijs*, appeared. In fact, one cannot rely on the dates printed by Oldenborch on his works. Two of his pamphlets were clearly antedated. Luther's *Uutlegghinghe des 16en capittels van S. Ians evangelie* has a colophon *gheprint van Niclaes van Oldenborch An. 1534*, but the commentary was not printed prior to 1539, when the original work appeared. As well, Luther's *Den 130en psalm uutgheleyt* has in its colophon *ghedruct bi Niclaes van Oldenborch Int jaer ons Heeren MD XXXVI*, while the original work from which the translation was done did not appear before September 1540.[48]

After nineteenth-century bibliographers placed Oldenborch's work-shop in Emden, M. E. Kronenberg suggested that Oldenborch was the leading Protestant printer based in Antwerp. Based on typographical characteristics, she attributed to him no less than 30 heretical works appearing between 1522 and 1540.[49]

Apart from the printer's marks on 11 editions bearing his name, there is only one contemporary reference to Nicolas van Oldenborch's exist-ence. In a 1570 trial, Herman Janssens was charged with the possession of two forbidden works. According to the transcription of the archivist A. Gérard, the trial records described one of the incriminated texts as follows: '*Een medecyne der sielen* [printed] by Claes van Oldenborch in the year 63, the said Claes being *executed* here'.[50] M. E. Kronenberg took the mention of an execution as the proof of the existence of van Oldenborch.[51]

H. F. Wijnman, who reviewed all the evidence, believes that Oldenborch is in fact a pseudonym for Matthias Crom and Steven Mierdmans. His arguments appear to be cogent. Bearing in mind the richness of the Antwerp archives for this period, the total lack of traces of Oldenborch is already suspicious. Furthermore, Janssen's trial records do not mention an execution, but in fact an exile, for it reads *geexcul(e)rt* instead of *geexcuteert*. Wijnman thinks that the expression refers to Mierdmans' departure from Antwerp in 1546. As well, another trial shows that in 1542, Crom sold *Der Kinderen Leere* (1542) to Jan

---

[48] NK 1431, 1434. Wijnman, 'The mysterious printer', p. 449.

[49] See NK 3, pp. 201–3.

[50] *Antwerpsche archievenblad*, 12 (1876), 452. The emphasis is ours.

[51] M. E. Kronenberg, 'Executie te Antwerpen van Niclaes van Oldenborch, drukker', *Het boek*, 10 (1921), 71–2.

Ghedruct by Niclaes van Oldenborch. Anno. 1555.

6.4   Colophon from *Der Waerheyt onderwijs* (Antwerp: 'Niclaes van Oldenborch', '1555')

Schats and a second book, *Dialogus oft t' samen sprekinghe*, dated 1538 and signed by Oldenborch.[52]

Given that the typographical equipment of Oldenborch and Crom was very similar, Wijnman argues that the Oldenborch pseudonym was used prior to 1543 by Matthias Crom, then by Mierdmans from 1543 to 1546 in Antwerp and in 1555 in Emden. This hypothesis goes on to claim that Crom also used other pseudonyms which M. E. Kronenberg attributed to Oldenborch: 'Neurenberg', 'Cornelius Nyenhuys te Marburg', 'Cornelius van Nieuhuys te Straasburg'.

Given the present state of research , this identification of Oldenborch is certainly the least fragile hypothesis. One would still need to specify the origin of some works printed prior to 1537, if one gives credence to the dates of 'Oldenborch'. No conclusions can yet be drawn with certainty, but it is possible that current research will lead to an even more complex picture.

This list of printers brings certain trends to light. Among the artisans who were convinced of the truth of the Gospel as preached by Luther, some were too daring – or too foolhardy – and they paid dearly for their religious propaganda: men like Hans and especially Christoffel van Ruremund, Adriaen van Berghen (executed in 1542) and Jacob van Liesvelt (executed in 1545). Alongside these, others were probably just as committed, but were more careful, as they concentrated on anony-

---

[52] Wijnman, 'The mysterious printer', pp. 455–8 (with a photographic reprint of the register itself).

mous works and, to a greater extent, on pseudonyms: Johannes Hillenius, Martin Lempereur, Matthias Crom and Steven Mierdmans. But the Protestant book market was also used by opportunists, with Willem Vorsterman at their head.

An evangelical spirituality

The heterodox works printed in Antwerp in the first half of the sixteenth century fit into a few main categories. This classification keeps both English works and the more freely distributed editions of Scripture in separate categories. The remainder of this camouflaged production, in Flemish, French and Latin, displayed common features.

Pious works and biblical commentaries

From 1520 to 1550, the 'Lutheran' writings printed in Antwerp reflected a generally non-confessional evangelism. In spite of Luther's major influence, these works did not defend strictly confessional positions. Above all, the works of the younger Luther were circulated, and virulent polemic was rare. Instead, the emphasis lay more on pious works intended for the edification of the faithful.[53] Alongside scriptural commentaries, there were numerous works whose tendencies are reflected in the selection of titles translated here:

- *The old Adam: an excellent and devout divine theology* (1521, Luther's preface to the *Theologia Deutsch*)[54]
- *The Golden book of prayers* (1531, O. Brunfels, *Precationes biblicae*)[55]
- *Consolation and mirror of the sick and those who suffer, taken from Holy Scripture* (1531, G. Gnapheus)[56]
- *A short pious book taken from Holy Scripture including the principal chapters of the ten commandments* (c.1535, Luther)[57]
- *A physic of the soul for those who are in good health and for the sick facing death* (1536, U. Rhegius)[58]

---

[53] This observation ties into the analysis done by J. M. de Bujanda on Flemish books condemned by the Louvain 1546 Index (*Index 2*, p. 50).

[54] NK 2228.

[55] NK 2573; *Index 2*, p. 193.

[56] NK 1010; *Index 2*, pp. 204–5.

[57] NK 3458; *Index 2*, p. 194.

[58] NK 1790; *Index 2*, pp. 203–4.

- *A Christian Instruction regarding the Kingdom of God (c.*1540)[59]
- *A comforting instruction showing how each should willingly bear the cross of Christ* (1543)[60]
- *Brief Instruction and teaching showing how each man is guilty before God and his neighbour, and how he should live* by Cornelis van der Heyden (1545)[61]

More radical English exiles

English works did not conform to the same parameters as the above-mentioned texts. Following Henry VIII's repression, the most radical wing of the English Reformation turned to continental presses. The chapter on England shows that the works of writers such as William Tyndale, Miles Coverdale, John Frith, George Joye and John Bale were much more polemical. This explains the printers' caution and their use of pseudonyms.

The English versions of the Old and New Testaments are also very different from the other editions of Scripture which appeared in Antwerp prior to 1545. Most of the latter group had accurate bibliographical addresses, which was not the case for the English editions. The translations of Tyndale and Coverdale were banned very early on.[62] Thus the Antwerp printers disguised those works, apart from a few exceptions. This was a useful precaution, given that the imprisonment of both van Ruremunds was due to their distribution of Tyndale's New Testament.

The Bible in Flemish and French on the open market

What was the situation for Flemish and French versions of Scripture? Given that the Antwerp printers serenely continued to produce them prior to 1545, it seems that there was no fierce repression. The Catholic authorities' attitude towards vernacular versions of the Bible was not as cut and dried as sometimes claimed. Clearly, some theologians believed that the common people should not read Scripture, and that they should make do with sermons. In spite of its strength, this group did not

---

[59] NK 1622; *Index* 2, pp. 199–200.

[60] *Index* 2, p. 195.

[61] *Index* 2, p. 208.

[62] Already in 1526, the Archbishop of Canterbury denounced certain English translations of the New Testament 'as containing heretical pravity', especially that of Tyndale (Reusch, p. 5). This condemnation was repeated in 1530 (Reusch, p. 10), in 1531 (Reusch, p. 12) etc.

succeed in imposing its views at Trent. But the defenders of vernacular translations were not any more successful in having their position adopted. At this point, it is vital to note that the border between these two positions reflected the linguistic border between Germanic and Romance lands. Charles V's policy in the Low Countries was different to that of the French authorities, and he was convinced of the usefulness of good Bible translations. Barring a small amount of resistance, the theology faculty of Louvain followed his lead. Louvain's path thus separated from that of Paris, without the former's orthodoxy being called into question.[63]

Furthermore, identifying the confessional outlook of a translation is never easy, especially in the early years of the Reformation. After the middle of the century, a few practical characteristics help to establish confessional origins. The Protestants indicated their desire to return to the original Hebrew and Greek sources, while the Catholics turned to the Vulgate. The Protestants placed the Old Testament works written in Greek in the Apocrypha. This division was based on different understandings of Tradition, which for the Catholics was guaranteed by the Vulgate. However, these differences may have been exacerbated by polemic. Indeed, it was Luther who decided to split the Apocrypha from the canonical books, when he began his complete translation of the Bible, and Jacob van Liesvelt was the first to put this plan into practice in his Flemish Bible of 1526. But were they not following St Jerome himself, whose declarations Catholics printed at the head of their editions of the Vulgate?

In the sixteenth century, the 'heretical' nature of a translation had less to do with the version itself than with all that accompanied the sacred text: prefaces and introductions, summary chapter headings, marginal notes and tables as appendices. Indeed, it is not always easy to classify an edition exactly. Thus, one must proceed with caution through this minefield. In the Dutch versions, Liesvelt indicated his clear intention to conform to Luther's model, in terms of the translation, annotations, prefaces and even the illustrations. Adriaen van Berghen, Hans and Christoffel van Ruremund also followed Luther's German versions closely. In contrast, as has been pointed out, Vorsterman followed a *via media* between the two sides. Lefèvre d'Étaples's French translations were forbidden in France, due to the Sorbonne's refusal to authorise a French

---

[63] P.-M. Bogaert and J.-Fr. Gilmont, 'La première Bible française de Louvain (1550)', *Revue théolgique de Louvain*, 11 (1980), 281, 291–7; J.-Fr. Gilmont, 'La Wallonie et la publication des Bibles françaises: XVIe and XVIIe siècles', in *Eglise-Wallonie*, 2, *Jalons pour une histoire religieuse de la Wallonie* (Brussels, 1984), pp. 85–102. See also the conclusion, pp. 469–76.

translation on principle. The venerable humanist had, however, placed faithfulness to the Vulgate above the *veritas graeca*.[64] The first complete edition by Lempereur was duly authorized and never condemned. In fact, it was the modifications in later editions which led to a slow drift towards heterodoxy. From 1534, Lempereur added notes, the source of which should be analysed. If he did borrow some from Robert Estienne's 1532 Latin Bible, the philological and theological commentaries were focused more on pastoral care than on erudition. Furthermore, the notes were more extensive than in the contemporary Flemish Bible of Vorsterman, which contained the same woodcuts.[65]

Throughout the sixteenth century, printing a vernacular Bible was thus not a crime in the Low Countries. Only the editions 'containing or reflecting any false doctrine or error' were banned.[66] In 1526, Charles V issued a first placard condemning all the Bible editions *in Duutsch, Vlaemsch ofte Walsche* containing postils, glosses, prefaces or prologues conveying the errors of Luther or of his supporters. The 1529 edict repeated the overall ban, specifying 'the New Testaments printed by Adrianus de Bergis, Christofferus de Remunda and Joannes Zel[l]'. This was repeated in 1530, 1531 and 1540.[67] Adriaen van Bergen, who reprinted his New Testament in 1533, was arrested in 1535. Christoffel van Ruremund could not reprint the work, as he died in 1531, and his widow prudently decided against reprinting. 'Joannes Zel' probably refers to a minor printer, Jan van Ghelen, who published several Flemish New Testaments between 1519 and 1530.[68]

---

[64] A list of *errata* added after the fact to the first Parisian edition of the Gospels provides evidence of a conflict between Lefèvre d'Etaples and his followers, as the latter tried to force the former's hand. M. A. Screech, 'Histoire des idées et histoire du livre' in P. Aquilon, H.-J. Martin and F. Dupuigrenet Desrousilles, *Le livre dans l'Europe de la Renaissance* (Paris, 1988), pp. 554–6.

[65] The illustrations first used by Lempereur in 1530 were for a large part copied from the Vulgate published in Lyon in 1512 by Jacques Sacon. (J. Strachan, *Early Bible Illustrations* (Cambridge, 1957), p. 63). But the major engraving of the title-page is German inspired, reproducing in particular a theme illustrated by Lucas Cranach the Elder, *Sündenfall und Erlösung* (P.-M. Bogaert, 'La Bible au peuple: Influence de l'iconographie luthérienne sur des Bibles françaises du XVIe siècle' in H. R. Boudin and A. Houssiau (eds), *Luther aujourd'hui* pp. 73–87).

[66] Edicts of 14 October 1529, December 1530, 7 October 1531 (*ROPB2*, 2, pp. 578–83; 3, pp. 67–71, 262–5; Reusch, p. 24).

[67] Edicts of 17 July 1526, 14 October 1529, December 1530, 7 October 1531, and 22 September 1540 (*ROPB2*, 2, pp. 404, 579; 3, pp. 68, 262; 4, p. 225; Reusch, pp. 23–5).

[68] There are three possible interpretations for 'Zel': to suggest that such a printer existed (based only on the imperial condemnation), to identify a Cologne printer, a son of Ulrich Zell (otherwise unknown) or, as does C. C. de Bruin, to suggest a gradual move between the orthographies of Ghelen and Zel (Rouzet, *Dictionnaire des imprimeurs*, pp. 252–3).

From 1537, heretical printing was increasingly prosecuted.[69] The publication of the 1546 Index led to several specific explanations. In his ordinance, Charles V noted, 'and worse still, we have found that several printers have corrupted the Bibles [...] and translated them into many languages, changing the text and words of Holy Scripture in several places, and adding prefaces, summaries or tables and false commentaries'.[70] The dean of Louvain's faculty of Theology reiterated this even more strongly in the preface to the Index. The importance given by the Dean to the justification of the condemnation of certain Bibles reveals a reluctance to forbid these works entirely. Reading between the lines, it seems that there was a certain amount of support for the spread of Scripture in French and Flemish once certain conditions had been met: no corruption of the sacred text, and the use of *biblia vetera*, namely the Vulgate, without wanting to return to the Greek, which would lead to confusion and a dangerous *multiformitas*. Furthermore, the dean attacked commentaries taken from the Lutherans and 'arguments' placed at the head of chapters. Heresy could also penetrate via illustrations and the index, without the words of the sacred text being changed. The Dean's conclusion contains a significant restriction: 'Therefore, we believe that such Bibles should be removed and taken out of the hands of the people, *even though these Bibles are otherwise appropriate*'.[71] Thus even condemned Bibles had some good in them.

As a result, the Louvain theologians banned many Antwerp Bibles and New Testaments. Of the 59 editions specifically mentioned, 34 came from Antwerp: 13 Bibles and 21 New Testaments. The majority of these were Flemish (21) alongside seven Latin and six French versions. The theologians were above all aware of recent publications: 24 of the condemned editions were published between 1540 and 1545. The Scripture editions of W. Vorsterman, J. Liesveld and M. Lempereur were mentioned four times, those of H. Peetersen and J. Steelsius three times. These men were leading publishers, but the first Bibles of Liesvelt escaped the Inquisitors' gaze, as the latter only knew of Liesvelt's 1542 and 1543 editions!

---

[69] Ordinances of 9 February 1537, 10 July 1540, 2 March and 7 April 1543, 19 February and 18 December 1544 and finally of 30 June 1546, establishing the Index drawn up by the Faculty of Louvain. *ROPB2*, 4, pp. 61, 210, 430, 447; 5 pp. 6, 117, 307 etc.

[70] 1546 edition, fol. 5, reprinted in *Index 2*, pp. 390–91.

[71] 'Proinde nos biblia talia, *quamvis alioqui commoda*, iudicavimus auferenda populoque e manibus eripienda'; 'Hier omme eyst, dat wy alzulcke Biblen, *al zijn sy anders oirbaer*, ghejudiceert hebben ghenomen te werden uut de handen des ghemeenen volcs' (emphases ours). The Latin text of the 1546 edition (fols 17ᵛ–22ʳ) is reprinted in *Index 2*, pp. 403–7; see fol. 21ʳ. Dutch text in Reusch, pp. 28–32.

The mid-century situation

The mid-1540s mark a turning-point in the situation of Antwerp printing, as various factors came together. With the support of the emperor,
the more vigilant Inquisition followed the printers' activities closely. As
we have seen, repression became better targeted: criminal proceedings,
executions (Adriaen van Bergen, and Jacob van Liesvelt) and expulsions
(Steven Mierdmans). Furthermore, one of the leading printers, Matthias
Crom, died in 1543. With the accession of Edward VI in 1547, English
Protestants no longer needed to rely on Antwerp's presses. Indeed, the
English welcomed instead those persecuted on the Continent.

Protestantism in the Low Countries changed its nature during this
decade, as the Reformed influence gained the upper hand over Lutheranism. While the earlier model was one of mainly individual piety
without any emphasis on church structure, Bucer, followed quickly by
Calvin offered not only a firmer religious doctrine but also a coherent
ecclesiastical structure and political vision. Calvin offered a radical
choice: Christians could not live among 'Papists'. Refusing all compromise, they had to choose exile or martyrdom. In spite of his unyielding
stance, within a few years, Calvin had brought the majority of
evangelicals in the Low Countries together. In this new religious context, Antwerp's role remained central.

At first glance, it is paradoxical to note that the set-up of a more
structured doctrine led to the almost total disappearance of Protestant
printing in Antwerp. In fact, the increased solidarity between churches
inside and outside the Low Countries encouraged the circulation of
writings. Protestant printing moved outside the Low Countries to work
away from the danger of persecution.

An international group of authors

Without stepping on the various 'national' chapters' territory, one should
note that the Antwerp publishers were inventive in their choice of texts,
in Dutch, English, French or Danish. They translated the leading German works, their choices dictated by the situation of a people living
under Catholic rule. They also found original works, some entirely new,
while others were clever adaptations.

This search for originality sprang into life in the series of small works
of piety in Flemish and French. The Antwerp publishers did not live in a
ghetto cut off from the Protestant centres, nor did they restrict themselves to reprinting works published elsewhere. This tactic was equally
evident in the production of English works. The Antwerp texts include
translations of many writings by the leading Reformers of the first

generation. But they also included original works. Some of these had local origins, like the *Summa der godliker Scrifturen*, reissued by the Antwerp printers in Flemish in 1527, in French in 1528–29, and in English in 1529.[72] In most cases, original works were made up of short anonymous texts.

The Antwerp presses also produced for the first time works written outside the country or by exiled foreigners in Antwerp. This was the case for a significant number of English works as for the Danish works and many French ones. Thus Antwerp was an active and original centre in terms of its printed propaganda in favour of the Reformation.

As noted in Chapter 4, on the Low Countries, Protestant works in this period were generally available in a small format, with only mediocre presentation and almost entirely devoid of illustrations. These were inexpensive booklets, easy to distribute and to conceal. Here too, an exception must be made for Bible editions. Liesvelt's 1526 Bible was not the first complete Bible with illustrations in the Low Countries; indeed, he used the illustrations in Luther's Bible as inspiration.[73] From 1528, Vorsterman too issued abundantly illustrated Bibles.[74]

A Europe-sized market

As an international centre, Antwerp did not limit its book trade to its own inhabitants. Production of evangelical works in Flemish was focused so much on Antwerp that it was clearly undertaken for the entire Seventeen Provinces. Equally clearly, English language production was destined for the export market, and the same held true for the more occasional works in Danish, Spanish and Italian. The foreign merchants' settlements did not provide a large enough market; at most these communities served as relay stations for the books on the way to their homelands. This was equally true for the French book. Lefèvre d'Étaples would never have asked Martin Lempereur to produce his French Bible only to satisfy a few French-speakers in Antwerp! There was only one exception to all this, namely that the Antwerp publishers did not intervene directly in the Germanic world.

This astonishing situation of a Catholic city producing Protestant books only lasted for a quarter-century. Let us summarise briefly the reasons for this paradoxical freedom. A first reason was the political

---

[72] J. Trapman, *De Summa der godliker scrifturen* (1523) (Leiden, 1978).

[73] W. C. Poortman, *Boekzaal van de Nederlandse Bijbels* (The Hague, 1983) vol. 1, pp. 84–5; Strachan, *Early Bible Illustrations*, pp. 66–7.

[74] Poortman, *Boekzaal*, p. 93.

situation of a merchant metropolis, which welcomed many foreigners. The local authorities, keen not to affect trade, tacked from side to side, trying to please everyone, both the emperor and the pope, both Henry VIII and the merchants. One Protestant admitted around 1558, 'Antwerp is like a world: one can hide easily, without having to flee from it'.[75] Although they could not openly refuse to investigate cases, the magistrates attempted to avoid applying severe penalties, apart from the cases of Anabaptists and foreigners. Allowances were made much more readily for Antwerp's own citizens.

The prudence of local magistrates was echoed by the discreet proselytizing of the printers. They circulated among the population small works aimed at increasing piety, away from any virulent controversy, and focusing on the essential elements of Lutheran doctrine. Discussions of Christ's role as the sole mediator did not involve lengthy criticisms of the cult of the saints. Baptism and the Lord's Supper were presented without necessarily criticizing the other sacraments.

The Antwerp printers spread Scripture far and wide in different languages, given that there was little opposition from the authorities in the Low Countries. As their freedom of action was greater, these printers did not hesitate to slip Lutheran-inspired commentaries surreptitiously in editions ostensibly based on the Vulgate.

The religious role played by printing in Antwerp was a unique phenomenon across Europe at the time. Although it formed part of a Catholic state, the city was one of the main relay centres for the spread of the new Gospel, through translations of the leading German Reformation texts into Dutch, English and French and through the publication of more original works by Flemish, English or French authors.

In the 1540s, a sea change occurred. Protestantism in the Low Countries veered towards Calvinism. The reinvigorated Inquisition led to a greater control over heretical books: a first Index was published in 1546. In England, Edward VI's accession to the throne led to a drop in evangelical printing across the channel. In the same period, the French-language Reformation established its printing centre in Geneva.

Thus, a new chapter in Reformation history had begun. The role of Antwerp remained fundamental, but that of its printing diminished.

Select bibliography

(See also the bibliography of Chapter 4 on the Low Countries.)

---

[75] The Protestant was Anton Verdrickt, executed in 1559. His statement is taken from A. van Haemstede's martyrology. See Jelsma *Adriaan van Haemstede*, p. 18.

Estié, P., *Het vluchtige bestaan van de eerste nederlandse lutherse gemeente, Antwerpen, 1566–67* (Amsterdam, 1986).

Nave, Fr. de, 'La Réforme et l'imprimerie à Anvers' in *Bulletin de la Société d'histoire du protestantisme belge*, 10/3 (1985), pp. 85–94.

Prims, Fl., *Geschiedenis van Antwerpen* (2 vols, Antwerp, 1940–43).

Roosbroeck, R. van, *Het wonder jaar te Antwerpen, 1566–1567: inleiding tot de studie der godsdienstonlusten te Antwerpen van 1566 to 1585* (Antwerp, 1930).

The history of Antwerp printing must now take into account the very valuable works by P. Valkema Blouw, in particular 'Predated Protestant works in Nijhoff-Kronenberg', *Quaerendo*, 24 (1994), 163–80; 'Early Protestant publications in Antwerp, 1526–30. The pseudonyms Adam Anonymus in Bazel and Hans Luft in Marlborow', *Quaerendo*, 26 (1996), 94–110. See also W. Heijting, 'Early Reformation literature from the printing shop of Mattheus Crom and Steven Mierdmans', *Nederlands archief voor kerkgeschiedenis*, 74 (1994), 143–61.

CHAPTER SEVEN

Reformation printing in Strasbourg, 1519–60

Miriam Usher Chrisman

In the five decades before the Reformation Strasbourg was an important centre of ecclesiastical publication. From 1508 humanist works, with a particular emphasis on Alsatian authors, became important. These books circulated across the Holy Roman Empire and into Switzerland as well. With the Reformation Strasbourg's printing activity expanded. The city became an international centre for Protestant propaganda. Polemic treatises were printed in French and English as well as in German and several printers specialized, briefly, in publishing Anabaptist theology. The geographic location of the city, close to France and Switzerland, linked to The Netherlands by the Rhine, cannot be ignored as a factor in this development but the decision of individual printers to support the Reform was also crucial in making the city a centre for the diffusion of the new faith. To place it comparatively with other German cities, in the period 1521–25 Strasbourg was fourth in importance in the publication of Luther's polemic works, Wittenberg, Augsburg and Erfurt occupying first, second, and third place respectively.[1]

Reformation printing in Strasbourg took off like a geyser in the 1520s (Figure 7.1), achieving its peak in 1523 (Figure 7.2). Then the geyser subsided. Protestant printing continued but at a level well below that of previous Catholic publication.[2] Since these early years were exceptional, they are discussed separately in the following chapter. They are then placed in context with the later decades. In order to clearly define the books which were printed, Figures 7.1–7.3 include those doctrinal books, sermons and polemic whose author could be identified or had purposely remained anonymous. Liturgical works, service books and anonymous religious songs were not included in these counts. The full Protestant output is shown in Figures 7.4–7.6.

---

[1] M. U. Edwards, *Luther's Last Battles: Politics and Polemics, 1531–1546* (Ithaca, 1983), p. 21.

[2] M. U. Chrisman, *Lay Culture, Learned Culture: Books and Social Change, 1480–1599* (New Haven, 1982), pp. 288–9.

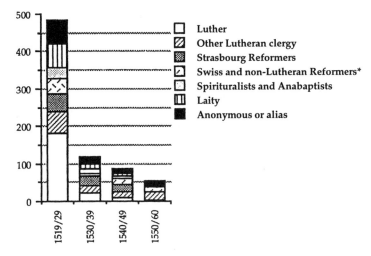

Figure 7.1   Protestant writers published in Strasbourg (1519–60) (apart from liturgical works and hymn-books)

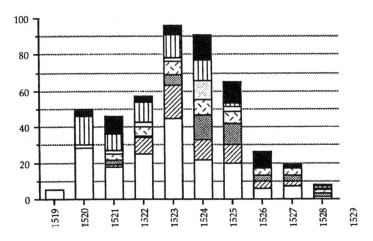

Figure 7.2   Protestant writers published in Strasbourg (1519–29)[†] (apart from liturgical works and hymn-books). Same categories as for the preceding figure

---

* This classification brings together Swiss writers like Joachim Vadian, Oecolampadius and Zwingli, but also authors like Otto Brunfels and Johann Bader, who were non-partisan. This category also includes English and French authors whose works appeared in Strasbourg, like Calvin, Farel and Marot.

† Possible variations in number of Luther editions are due to the different dates ascribed to certain works. Furthermore, for the years 1521–24, the location of the printshop of Matthias Schürer's heirs is uncertain (Strasbourg or Colmar). J. Bensing, who opts for Strasbourg, includes therefore a greater number of editions than in the present figure.

Protestant book production

The printers

On the eve of the Reform, from 1500 to 1517, there were eight large- and medium-scale printing shops in Strasbourg, many of them clustered around the cathedral square and nearby streets. In the period under study, 1517–1560, the number of large and medium shops doubled to a total of 16: five large scale; 11 medium scale.[3] After 1528 many small shops appeared, one-man operations, active for brief periods. This proliferation of printing shops means that throughout the period in question there was economic stress and tension for the printers as well as sharp competition for buyers.

The early Reformation pamphlets in Strasbourg came from the presses of well-established shops, in most cases the master printers were the second generation in the trade, operating large-scale or medium-scale shops. The very first Lutheran pamphlets came off the presses of Matthias Schürer, Johann Knobloch and Martin Flach II in 1519. These men had been established since 1508, 1500 and 1501, respectively. There were close family ties among them, all were tied by kinship or clientage to Martin Flach I, who had founded a press in 1469. Starting as a medium-scale press, by 1489 it had become a large-scale shop, specializing in printing for the Roman church. When Flach I died in 1500 his son Martin II was already a mature man. He maintained the shop at a high level of production for two years. Then his widowed mother married Johann Knobloch, one of the journeymen, and Martin II, was forced to move out and establish his own shop. According to Benzing, Martin II remained on good terms with Knobloch; the latter provided him with type, initial letters and commissions, but Flach never achieved his previous levels of production.[4]

---

[3] Classification of printing shops was achieved by establishing a standard of productivity based on the number of sheets of paper which a printer turned into finished books. The number of printed leaves of each book (which was usually known) was divided by the format of that book (folio or octavo) to create the number of folio sheets which had been placed in the printing forme. Each printer's shop could then be evaluated in terms of the size of its production. Voet's figures for the Plantin press gave the average output of two compositors and a two-man press team. The statistics for the Strasbourg shops revealed a clear pattern of large-scale shops which would have been running at least two presses year-round; medium-scale shops which employed only one press; and one-man shops where the printer did all the work of compositing and running the press himself. See Chrisman, *Lay Culture, Learned Culture*, pp. 4–10.

[4] J. Benzing, *Die Buchdrucker des 16. and 17. Jahrhunderts im Deutschen Sprachgebiet* (Wiesbaden, 1963), p. 412.

At about the same time Matthias Schürer, Martin II's first cousin, was serving as his apprentice. In 1506 Schürer went to work with Knobloch for two years before opening his own shop in 1508.[5] Thus, the three men who began Lutheran printing in the city had familial ties, had all worked with each other and, seemingly, shared religious convictions. They were a major force in Protestant printing in the first decade. Schürer was a dying man in 1519 but the nephews who inherited his press dedicated themselves almost exclusively to Lutheran pamphlets until they moved from the city in 1525.[6] Martin Flach II printed works both by Luther and by his close disciples but the financial problems which had plagued him after opening his own shop forced him to close, also in 1525; Johann Knobloch continued with Protestant tracts and treatises until his death in 1528. Together the Flach–Knobloch–Schürer family were responsible for 32 per cent of the total Protestant publication in the city from 1519 to 1529.[7]

In 1520, Wolfgang Köpfel opened a new printing shop in the city. Born in Hagenau, he had apprenticed with Thomas Wolf in Basle.[8] More important, he was the nephew of Wolfgang Capito, the humanist, who was shortly appointed provost of St Thomas in Strasbourg. Köpfel was already strongly attached to the Reform. He immediately began to publish Luther and embroiled himself locally by printing tracts supporting the actions of the local Reformers. In 1524, he published a tract justifying the marriage of a Strasbourg cleric which pushed the Strasbourg magistrates to establish their first ordinance on censorship. In 1526 he was imprisoned for publishing, anonymously, an account of the colloquy between Oecolampadius and the Catholics.[9] These actions and the consistency of his Protestant publication, reflect strong religious convictions. He was the only printer who produced Protestant books year in, year out, whatever the political climate; 78 per cent of his output was devoted to the cause of the new faith. As late as 1537 and

---

[5] F. Ritter, *Histoire de l'imprimerie alsacienne, au XVe et XVIe siècles* (Strasbourg, 1955), pp. 160–62.

[6] J. Benzing, 'Die Druckerei der Matthias Schürer Erben zu Straßburg, 1520–1525', *AGBr*, 2 (1960), pp. 170–74; id., 'Die Reformationspresse der Matthias Schürer Erben in Straßburg, 1520–1525', *Refugium animæ bibliotheca, Festschrift für Albert Kolb* (Wiesbaden, 1969), pp. 43–55.

[7] All statistical data is taken from my computer study of book publications in Strasbourg, 1480–1599. The figures for this article have been specifically drawn out for the time period of the study, 1519–60. The books from which the figures were calculated are all listed in M. U. Chrisman, *Bibliography of Strasbourg Imprints, 1480–1599* (New Haven, 1982). All the statistics in this article are based on book editions, that is the single printing of a given book title. If there were two editions of the title, it is counted twice. References to a particular author may be checked in this bibliography.

[8] Benzing, *Buchdrucker*, p. 414.

[9] Ritter, *Histoire*, pp. 243–4.

1556 he was printing English polemical treatises, although after 1530 his emphasis was on liturgies, postils and prayer books.

The Prüss family were also driven by strong religious convictions. They took on, almost single-handed, publication of the Spiritualist and Anabaptist leaders. It was a complicated family. Johann Prüss, the founder, had established his printing press in the city in 1480. On his death in 1510 there were two grown children, a son Johann II and a daughter, Margarethe. In 1511 Margarethe married Reinhardt Beck, her father's typographer. At first Beck and Johann II continued to work together in the family shop but after several months they separated. In 1521 Beck died and Margarethe married another printer, Johann Schwan, who died in 1526. Nothing daunted, Margarethe married a third printer, Balthasar Beck (no relation to the first) who survived until 1551. Significantly, Margarethe and her three husbands Beck, Schwan, Beck and her brother were all committed to printing the more heterodox Reformers. It was the Prüss presses that printed the work of Karlstadt, Westerburg, Clement Ziegler and the important Anabaptist leaders.[10] Johann Prüss II was also the first to print the work of French Reformers, Guillaume Dumolin and Wolfgang Schuh. Was there a strong family religious conviction which held them all together despite the problems with the split between the two presses?

Two other men made important contributions in this early decade, Johann Herwagen and Johann Schott. Herwagen arrived in Strasbourg in 1522, as the movement for Reform was beginning to accelerate. Highly educated, apparently well funded, he published much of the biblical commentary which the Reformers prepared to teach and train the new, Reformed pastors. Unlike the other Reformation printers, he published mostly in Latin, encouraging the Reformers to translate their vernacular works to make them more widely read. As Higman points out, these Latin editions made the works of Luther, Melanchthon and Bucer available to the French Reformers.[11] It was an important and distinguished contribution. However, Herwagen left the city before the decade was out to take over the Froben press in Basle.[12] Johann Schott, like Flach and Prüss, was the son of a Strasbourg printing family, his connections went back three generations to Johann Mentelin, the first Alsatian printer. Johann pursued a university education but had to return to Strasbourg in 1500 to take over the family press on the death of his father. For the first 20 years, he ran a humanist press, with a level of production below his father's. In 1520 he became a strong protagonist of the Reform. He

---

[10] Chrisman, *Lay Culture, Learned Culture*, p. 16.
[11] See p. 109.
[12] Ritter, *Histoire*, p. 309.

printed Lutheran works, but more significantly, he published Ulrich von Hutten and Hartmut von Cronberg, including their most vitriolic attacks on the Roman church. He went on to publish Karlstadt and devoted himself for years to the work of his friend, Otto Brunfels, who was never accepted by the inner circle of Strasbourg Reformers.[13] Schott's heterodoxy is further reflected in his printing of the first polemic treatise in English, William Roye's diatribe against Cardinal Wolsey.

To sum up, Protestant publication was undertaken by a core group of six presses. The printers themselves came from well-established printing families, several had important ties to the local Reformers. Other printers printed Protestant work intermittently, but the six presses described were responsible for the majority of the 483 Protestant titles printed from 1519 to 1529. Note that this volume would not be achieved until 1551–64 in Geneva, according to Higman.[14] In contrast to Basle, the majority of these Strasbourg editions were in German. The tendency for a printer to specialize in the work of a particular Reformer or Reformers seems to have reflected his individual religious convictions, but the output as a whole was clearly more radical than the Reformation printing of their Basle colleagues.

By 1525 this group began to break up. Flach II closed his shop; Knobloch died; Herwagen moved away; the number of printers actively producing Protestant works was sharply reduced. Protestant printing fell dramatically by 1526 (Figure 7.2). In part this reflected the smaller number of printers but the promulgation of a censorship edict by the Strasbourg *Magistrat* in 1524 was yet another factor. Like the Basle Council, the *Rat* was slow to establish control of the press. They published the Edict of Worms in 1521 with its provision that all Luther's books were to be destroyed but their only action was to return five Bibles taken from an itinerant peddler. The following year they seized all the copies of Thomas Murner's bitter attack on Luther, *Von dem grossen Lutherischen Narren*, from Johann Grüninger, one of the oldest and most respected printers in the city, and a devout Catholic. In 1524, however, the bishop complained when Köpfel published the sermon justifying the marriage of a Strasbourg cleric. In the same year that the Basle council moved, the Strasbourg *Rat* promulgated an ordinance prohibiting the publication of any book which had not been submitted to the *Magistrat* for censorship. The printer's name was to appear in every book.[15] The drop was also a manifestation of the anxiety and tension growing out of the Peasants' War.

---

[13] Chrisman, *Lay Culture, Learned Culture*, pp. 15–16.
[14] See p. 113.
[15] Ritter, *Histoire*, pp. 240–44.

The following decade saw a proliferation of printers and a consistent decline in production of all types of religious books (Figure 7.1). The printing trade experienced fundamental changes. Schott, Prüss II, Köpfel and Balthasar Beck remained from the original group but Schott shifted almost entirely to scientific publication, much of it the work of his old friend Brunfels, now turned botanist and doctor.[16] Beck chose popular medical texts and classical authors, leaving religious books to others.[17] It is interesting to compare this shift to scientific publication with Higman's similar example of Simon Du Bois from the Meaux group. Most important in Strasbourg, however, was the immigration of six new printers, men who had been established in other cities, Johann Albrecht, Peter Schöffer and Johann Schwintzer were forced to leave Worms because of their Anabaptist leanings. Jacob Cammerlander moved from Mainz to marry a Strasbourg woman. There were two others, Georg Ulricher from Andlau and Matthias Biener (Apiarius), the latter specialized in musical publication.[18] Only two of the six, Cammerlander and Schwintzer, established roots in the city, and Schwintzer gave up printing. The others moved on. The intense competition for the market may have made it impossible for so many men to support themselves. Then, the city itself became less attractive and accommodating to radicals like Schöffer. In mid-decade (1535 and 1536, respectively), two new printers opened shop, Crato Mylius and Wendelin Rihel. Their presses would become two of the most important for the next five decades. Like Köpfel and Schott, Mylius and Rihel were well educated, with close ties of family and friendship to the intellectual community. They worked closely with Jean Sturm and the faculty of the new Gymnasium, which opened in 1538. The Gymnasium with its demand for classical texts became the major market for the printers, religious printing could no longer carry a press.

Despite this, around 1547, four French refugee printers began to print in Strasbourg: Rémy Guédon, Jacques Poulain, Pierre Estiart and Guillotte le Pords. They concentrated on propaganda leaflets and religious treatises for French markets. Whether they brought presses with them or purchased equipment in Strasbourg is not known. It is believed that Rémy Guédon was protected by the eminent local physician Johann Guinther von Andernach. He published two editions of Guinther's treatise on plague and a French edition of Marot's psalms before he followed Bucer into exile in England.[19] By the 1550s the French printers

[16] See Chrisman, *Bibliography*, S3.1.8; S3.1.9; S1.9.44; S1.9.15.
[17] Ibid.; S1.9.16; S1.8.17; S1.10.8; S1.10.9.
[18] Benzing, *Buchdrucker*, pp. 415–17.
[19] R. Peter, 'Les premiers ouvrages français imprimés à Strasbourg', *L'Annuaire des Amis du Vieux Strasbourg*, 4 (1974), 90, n. 77.

Pierre Estiart and François Perrin were undertaking larger works. Estiart, a bookseller with connections in Geneva, Lyon and Basle, purchased citizenship in Strasbourg in 1555 and used the city as a base for his widespread business. He commissioned Perrin to print Francisco de Enzinas' history of The Netherlands, Johann Sleidan's history of the reign of Charles V and a French translation of Bullinger's sermons.[20] Thus, these men were important in disseminating the ideas of the Rhenish and Swiss leaders to French readers. Publication by French refugee printers continued on through the 1560s, and the last French pamphlet was printed in 1587.[21]

The Reformation had a profound impact on the printing trade. In the earliest decade large-scale and medium shops, well established, took on the initial challenge of Protestant printing. After the crisis of the 1520s, however, the majority of them dropped their Protestant work. In the 1530s Protestant printing was mainly in the hands of smaller shops, less stable, less permanent in the community. By the 1540s new large-scale presses, established by a new generation, once again assumed leadership in printing Protestant works. The Protestant printers always remained a minority within the printing trade. Only two men printed Protestant books from decade to decade, Wolfgang Köpfel and Johann Prüss II. Köpfel's last publications before his death in 1556 were treatises by John Ponet, in English. In the 1540s, for his part, Prüss was eclectically printing both Luther and Calvin.[22] The efforts of these two printers to disseminate the new faith in France and England as well as within Germany never wavered.

Production conditions and distribution networks

The format of Protestant and biblical works produced may have reflected the increasing financial difficulties of the printing trade, the need to economize on the cost of production. On the other hand, it may have reflected the fact that the printers saw these works as transient, ephemeral, written for a short period of battle. In the very earliest years most of the Protestant books were quarto in size. This changed and the octavo format became the usual choice. Folio editions were unusual and used mainly for the Luther Old Testament or for service books. Thus, from 1520 to 1524, 84 per cent of Protestant and biblical publication

---

[20] R. Peter, "Les premiers ouvrages français ... (suite)", *L'Annuaire des Amis du Vieux Strasbourg*, 8 (1978), 22–3, n. 58. See also Chrisman, *Bibliography*, V9.1.19; P2.3.14; V9.3.7b; V9.3.8.

[21] Chrisman, *Bibliography*, P3.14.13; L1.7.4.

[22] Ibid., P3.4.16; P7.2.19; P2.1.52; P2.1.49b.

was in quarto, 16 per cent in octavo. There were six folio editions. An abrupt change came in 1525. The printers switched to octavo for 69 per cent of their Protestant and biblical output, with only 31 per cent in quarto. In the later decades the ratio was somewhat closer, but the octavo format remained the most usual. From 1530 to 1539, 49 per cent were in octavo, 40 per cent in quarto, the rest in folio, reflecting the Luther Old Testament editions. From 1540 to 1549, 57 per cent were in octavo, 43 per cent in quarto. In 1550–59, when production was very low and the shops were struggling, 70 per cent of the Protestant and biblical production was in octavo, 30 per cent in quarto. These figures, supported by the fact that only a very few of these books were illustrated, would indicate that the printers brought them out as inexpensively as possible. These were no longer the beautifully illustrated editions of the first decade of the century; they were books for a mass market, printed cheaply, sparing of paper, the major expense.

There is almost no firm evidence with regard to how the books and pamphlets were diffused. Clearly, from the evidence of Herwagen's editions, the French and English editions of Köpfel and Prüss II, Strasbourg books entered the international market. There seems to have been very little effort on the part of the Strasbourg authorities to curb this in any way. When Johann Schott printed William Roy's attack on Cardinal Wolsey the latter asked his friend Hermann Rinck, a Cologne magistrate, to find the printer. Rinck identified the pamphlet as Schott's work and asked the latter how many copies he had printed. Schott told him he had made 1 000 copies and would sell them to the highest bidder. There are no further details on that transaction but Rinck did complain to the Strasbourg *Magistrat* who did not invoke the censorship regulation. Schott may have argued that he did not understand English and did not know what he was printing.[23] But the magistrates also failed to take any action against French refugee printers. The atmosphere was certainly very different from that described by Higman.[24]

Diffusion of German books and pamphlets probably was carried on through established channels: the shops of the printers; booksellers in Strasbourg and other German cities; the Frankfurt book fair. The wide circulation of Strasbourg imprints is reflected in the four Latin editions of Calvin's *Institutes* published by the Rihels, father then son, between 1539 and 1561.[25] Another example of broad dissemination is the Latin edition of Johann Sleidan's history of the reign of Charles V, 14 editions in six years. Both these books would have appealed to Protestants in

---

[23] Ritter, *Histoire*, pp. 183–4.
[24] See pp. 124–6, 150.
[25] Chrisman, *Bibliography*, P1.4.19 a–d.

France, Switzerland and The Netherlands and the Strasbourg printers were clearly playing an important role in these areas.

Protestant books

The authors

The most significant element in terms of the writers of the early Reformation pamphlets was their sheer number and their broad divergence geographically, socially and theologically. Between 1519 and 1529, 81 persons published Protestant treatises on the Strasbourg presses: Luther and his followers accounted for 25 of these; eight were leaders of the Strasbourg Reformation; 12 were Swiss Reformers or men not associated with orthodox Lutheranism; ten were Spiritualists and Anabaptists; 20 were laymen or women, some of these latter were local Strassburgers, but others were from Switzerland or northern and eastern German States. Thus, the very first conclusion is that Protestant writers were not confined to their local area but reached out to the whole Empire. Luther was the major force in the first four years, but few of his disciples at Wittenberg published regularly in Strasbourg. Melanchthon, Johann Lonicer, Stephen Roth, Justus Jonas and Nicolaus Amsdorf had perhaps two or three pamphlets printed in Strasbourg. By contrast, the Lutheran Reformers in Augsburg, Caspar Adler, Michael Keller and Urbanus Rhegius, apparently sent their books to Strasbourg fairly consistently from 1522 to 1526. This may reflect the special tensions which faced the Augsburg group; it may have been safer to have their work published in another city. But the Strasbourg printers also drew from the northern borders of the Empire. Georg Polentz, Bishop of Samland, the first bishop to adopt the Reform publicly, published one of his reforming sermons in Strasbourg in 1524. Kaspar Güttel, the Reformer of Mansfield, had his defense of evangelical teaching printed by the Schürer heirs in 1522. The biblical commentary of Andreas Knopken, the Reformer of Riga, was printed in Strasbourg. In this case the Strasbourg presses drew from a larger area than the Basle presses.

Statistical analysis shows clearly that the Strasbourg printers did not limit themselves to Luther and the local Reformers. From the very beginning they were publishing the work of some of the most radical protagonists of the Reform. In 1520, 13 editions of Ulrich von Hutten's scathing polemic came off the Schott and Knobloch presses, while Martin Flach II published two works by Andreas Karlstadt who had not, however, at that point broken with Luther. The pattern of publication becomes clear in the summary (Figure 7.3). Treatises by Luther and

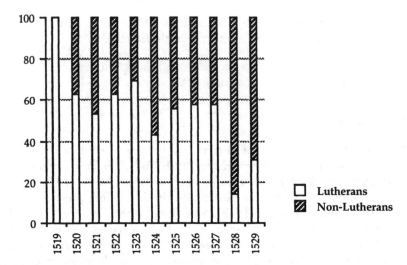

Figure 7.3   Percentage of Lutheran and non-Lutheran Protestant authors in the Strasbourg output (1519–29)

his followers dominated until 1523, but the percentage of publication by non-Lutherans was significant by 1521. In this table the non-Lutherans have been grouped so that the contributions of the Swiss, the Strasbourg Reformers and others, like Brufels, can be compared to the Lutheran output. The Spiritualists, Anabaptists and laymen are shown separately. The percentage figures include all the non-Lutheran writers. The non-Lutherans accounted for 37 per cent of the total Protestant publication in 1520; 47 per cent in 1521; 37 per cent in 1522; dropping to a low of 31 per cent in 1523. Then the ratio became more even, with the non-Lutheran at over 40 per cent. Although the total volume was much lower, the percentage of non-Lutheran writers was greater in 1528 and 1529. These figures raise a series of questions. Why did Lutheran publication fall so quickly and so steeply? There was a similar drop in Basle in 1528. Did the Lutheran writers shift to new printing centres? After the Lutheran publication diminished in Strasbourg there seems to be a surge of publication by the Strasbourg Reformers and their Swiss colleagues, Oecolampadius, Ulrich Zwingli, Johann Schwebel and Ambrosius Blaurer. Was there a similar shift in Augsburg or Nuremberg?

The importance of lay polemic in the earliest years of the Reform is revealed with new clarity (Figure 7.2). Long considered trivial in comparison to the serious polemic treatises of the trained theologians, these figures indicate that from 1520 to 1524, the laity were shouldering a significant share of the responsibility in communicating the new ideas.

In 1520, alone, they wrote 32 per cent of the polemic treatises pub-lished in Strasbourg. This diminished to 25 per cent in 1521 and then to 20 per cent by 1522. The high figures in 1520 and 1521 reflect the stream of Hutten pamphlets which came off the Strasbourg presses. Yet even his death in 1523 did not cut back the lay response. Fifteen laymen and women wrote their own treatises, expounding their own doctrines with regard to confession, penance, the Eucharist, the power of the clergy and the validity of monastic vows. Again, there are unanswered questions. Why were there so many lay treatises in these early years? These figures include only laymen I could identify; there are no anony-mous writers who, posing as laymen, may have been the creation of clerical pens. Rather, the writers were local Strassburgers like the patri-cians Eckhard zum Treubel and Matthias Wurm von Guedertheim; artisans like Stephan Büllheym and Clement Ziegler; Katherina Zell, the wife of the Reformer. Lay people from other regions and cities also had treatises published by the Strasbourg printers, or their work was picked up by the printers. These include Lux Gemmiger, Argula von Grumbach, Hans Sachs and Jacob Schenck. In the early years of the Reform, when the Edict of Worms still created an omnipresent threat, lay men and women were willing to risk the consequences of publicly affirming their religious convictions. This, in and of itself, is significant.

Publication of treatises by radical Reformers, the Spiritualists and Anabaptists, represented a far smaller proportion of the total Stras-bourg output, but it reflects important commitments on the part of those printers who chose to do it, and it reveals a certain tolerance of unorthodoxy (Figures 7.1 and 7.2). As Bietenholz points out, the Basle printers did not pick up Anabaptist work.[26] In 1520 when Martin Flach published two treatises by Andreas Karlstadt attacking externalism in religious worship, these treatises were probably regarded as the work of one of Luther's circle of disciples. It is, perhaps, significant that no other member of this circle was published in Strasbourg until two years later. However, Ronald Sider has emphasized that in 1520 and 1521 Luther and Karlstadt were 'in fundamental theological agreement'.[27] In the early rounds of the unrest in Wittenberg in 1521, Karlstadt took a more conservative stand than Melanchthon and the students, who were eager to offer communion in both kinds. Then, in December of 1521, Karlstadt inaugurated the new communion service, hoping to allay the pressure from the students. The result was his dismissal by the authorities, including Frederick the Wise, and his rejection by Luther.[28] Two of his

---

[26] See pp. 255–6.
[27] R. Sider, *Andreas Bodenstein von Karlstadt* (Leiden, 1974), p. 147.
[28] Ibid., p.177.

Das ander Byechlin
der Geystlichen gsãng/ Von der Erscheinung/ Wandel vñd Leiden Christi vnsers heylandts.

*

7.1 Second part of the *Gsangbuch* edited by Katherina Zell (Strasbourg: Jacob Fröhlich, 1535)

treatises on communion were published by Johann Prüss in Strasbourg in 1522. Challenged by Luther's opposition, forced to define his own thoughts, Karlstadt's theology became increasingly radical. By 1523 he denied the real presence in the Eucharist. His sermons continued to flow from the Strasbourg presses during this period. The intriguing question is why the Strasbourg printers were so open in their support. In the beginning his identification with Luther may have been influential but after February/March 1522 that tie was broken and Luther was overt in his condemnation of his former disciple. Yet ten of Karlstadt's treatises were published in Strasbourg after that date.[29] Furthermore,

---

[29] Chrisman, *Bibliography*, P4.1.6–13; P4.1.15–16.

Johann Schott published Gerhard Westerburg's extremely radical attack on Purgatory in 1523.[30] Westerburg was Karlstadt's follower and brother-in-law. Between 1524 and 1529, as the Anabaptist movement developed, the Strasbourg printers added Andreas Keller (Cellarius), Balthasar Hubmaier, Hans Denck, Johannes Odenbach, Johannes Bünderlin, Melchior Hoffman and Caspar Schwenckfeld to their list of published authors.[31] These men represented the most important leaders of the new movement. Clearly the Strasbourg presses had a reputation in the radical movement as being willing to print unorthodox views. It is significant that the heterodox treatises published in Basle were printed in Latin or French whereas the Strasbourg Anabaptist tracts were in German.

The years 1519 to 1529 marked the apogee of Protestant printing in Strasbourg. Figure 7.1 shows the dramatic decline in the later decades. Sixty-one per cent of the works by self-acknowledged Protestant authors were printed by 1529. Publication of Luther's writings dropped to approximately two a year in the 1530s, one a year in the 1540s and then to a mere four for a whole decade. Works by other Lutheran Reformers followed the same pattern. Publication by the Strasbourg Reformers overtook that of Luther or that of other Lutherans but was consistently less than the two combined. The paucity of work by Swiss Reformers requires some consideration. In view of Bucer's ties with the Swiss and his constant efforts to achieve a concord between them and Luther in the 1520s and after the Marburg Colloquy, why was there so little publication of Swiss theologians? The most important in terms of numbers of editions was Oecolampadius with seven editions.[32] There was only one edition of Zwingli, the articles of the disputation of 1523, published in that same year. In 1539, Wendelin Rihel published Calvin's *Institutes*. These were reprinted three times, along with 11 other works of Calvin.[33] Again the data leads to questions rather than solutions. Bietenholz notes that Zwingli, Gwalther and the other Zurich Reformers were also neglected by the Basle printers. In view of their willingness to publish for the French and English followers of the new faith, the neglect of the Swiss by the Strasbourg printers is difficult to understand, as is the concomitant lack of interest of the Basle printers.

The most noteworthy figure in Figure 7.1 is the 30 treatises by Anabaptists in the decade 1519–29, followed by 14 treatises in 1530–39.

---

[30] Ibid., P1.4.3.

[31] Ibid., see Sections P4.1 and B8.5.

[32] Ibid., B7.6.11; B7.6.12; B7.6.13; Pl.2.6; P1.2.8; P2.3.1; P3.5.5.

[33] Ibid., P1.4.19 a–d; B7.6.16; P1.6.11; P1.6.20; P1.9.5; P3.15.6; P4.2.14–17; P7.2.19–20.

The figure represents the impact of the group of Anabaptist and Spiritualist leaders and theologians gathered in the city and a group of printers who were willing to risk publication of their doctrines. In 1528 Jacob Kautz and Wilhelm Reublin were preaching and teaching in the city. They were joined in 1529 by Caspar Schwenckfeld, Melchior Hoffman, Pilgrim Marbeck and Christian Entfelder. The four last named all published treatises during their stay. Balthasar Beck printed Hoffman's work; Peter Schöffer and Johann Schwintzer both printed Schwenckfeld's treatises.[34] Significantly, despite the *Rat*'s Mandate, five of these Anabaptist books, including all of Marbeck's treatises, bore no printer's signature. This period of Anabaptist activity came to an end with the calling of the synod to organize the Strasbourg church in 1532 and the publication of Sebastian Franck's *Chronica* in 1531. In his history Franck had included Erasmus in a list of men who had been branded as heretics but who had, in Franck's opinion, contributed much to the church and their community. Erasmus failed to recognize the compliment intended and instead wrote to the Strasbourg magistrates demanding they control this dangerous writer and the printer who had published the work. Just as he excluded Vives' works in Basle, Erasmus exercised his influence in Strasbourg. Beck's entire press run was confiscated, a terrible loss for him. The *Rat* also confiscated and destroyed all Beck's copies of Melchior Hoffman's *Prophesy oder weyssagang* and his *Prophetisch gesicht*.[35] The Anabaptists gradually withdrew from the city as the magistrates more rigorously enforced the ordinances of imprisonment and exile. There was a scattering of Anabaptist publication thereafter: two anonymous printings of Schwenckfeld; two religious works by Sebastian Franck. The Anabaptist forces had been routed: the risk to the printers had been proved to be too great.

Literary genres

The publication of biblical materials in Strasbourg was substantially smaller than other areas of Protestant publication. It followed, however, a similar pattern in terms of its production curve (Figure 7.5). The major output was in the first years, 1519–29; production then dropped to a fifth of what it had been; fell again during the next decade; and dwindled to eight editions between 1550 and 1560. These figures for biblical publication were exceptionally low. The Basle figures are far higher and the printers there seem to have specialized in biblical publi-

---

[34] D. Küsser, 'Caspar Schwenkfeld et ses adeptes entre l'église et les sectes à Strasbourg' in *Strasbourg au coeur religieux du xvie siècle* (Strasbourg, 1977), pp. 511–38.

[35] Chrisman, *Lay Culture, Learned Culture*, p. 28.

cation. The Strasbourg ministers and Strasbourg readers may have depended on Basle for their biblical texts. Earlier they had purchased the Nuremburg Bible.

Biblical commentaries were also limited. The Latin commentaries were written by the clergy for other clergy, thus their publication was in the service of the new church. The exception to this was short commentaries by one of the reforming clergy, Luther or Bucer, on a particular psalm or Gospel chapter. These could have been read by the laity and may have been published for them. Only Anabaptist leaders wrote and published major commentaries in German.

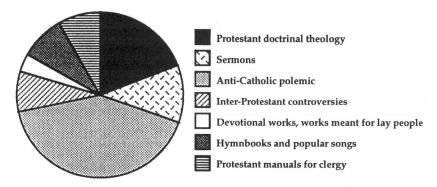

Protestant doctrinal theology

Sermons

Anti-Catholic polemic

Inter-Protestant controversies

Devotional works, works meant for lay people

Hymnbooks and popular songs

Protestant manuals for clergy

Figure 7.4   Types of Protestant works (1519–60). Percentages based on a total of 818 works

The content of Protestant publications is shown in percentages in Figure 7.4. Polemic and controversial works predominated even beyond the combined 49 per cent shown because many of the published sermons, particularly the Luther sermons, were polemic in their thrust. On the other hand, the 19 per cent for doctrine and theology reflects the solid effort of the Reformers, not only Luther but also Bucer, Capito and François Lambert to define and interpret the doctrines of the new church – there were 24 treatises on the question of the Eucharist alone. The other important element of Protestant publication were liturgies and service books. These, together with devotionals for the laity, came to 20 per cent of the total. With 20 different editions of the catechism and the new hymnals and service books, the new churches would seem to have been well supplied.[36]

---

[36] The Protestant books are arranged by 45 subject matter categories in Chrisman, *Bibliography*, pp. 285–358.

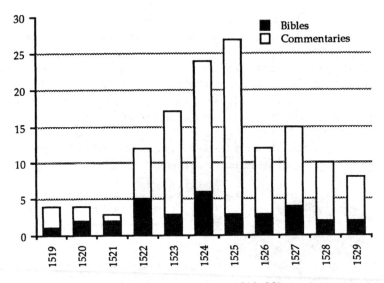

Figure 7.5 Bibles and biblical commentaries (1519–29)

The doctrines published by the Strasbourg printers changed significantly over time, as Higman finds was the case in France.[37] In the earliest years of the Reform, Luther and his Wittenberg followers were the main source of doctrinal writing. Erasmus' Latin New Testament and his commentaries provided the essential biblical texts for the reforming clergy and their educated followers. Thus, the new ideas were introduced originally from outside. Luther's treatises and sermons established the new teachings with regard to penance, the Eucharist, marriage, faith and works. These were printed by Knobloch, Flach II and Prüss II from 1520 to 1524. Martin Bucer arrived in the city in May 1523, a refugee from his former preaching post. Johann Schott published Bucer's summary of the new faith, *Das ym selbs niemant, Sonder anderen leben soll*, in that same year.[38] The following year Schott published Bucer's exposition of the doctrines currently being preached in Strasbourg.[39] From 1523 until 1546 Bucer carried the major responsibility for writing and disseminating the Strasbourg doctrines, publishing some 60 tracts and treatises. While Wolfgang Capito, with Matthias Zell, wrote an important treatise justifying clerical marriage as well as biblical commentaries and Hedio wrote and translated historical works, Bucer outlined the tenets of the faith,[40]

[37] See pp. 135–6.
[38] Chrisman, *Bibliography*, P2.2.1·
[39] Ibid., P1.8.1.
[40] Ibid., P1.8.6; P1.8.14.

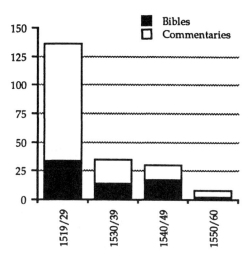

Figure 7.6   Bibles and biblical commentaries by decade (1519–60)

addressed the problem of images,[41] explained the proper ceremonies,[42] and drew up the confession of faith known as the Tetrapolitan.[43]

The Eucharist was the focus of Strasbourg doctrinal publication. Of 80 doctrinal works published after 1525, nearly half of them grappled with the question of the Eucharist. Other theological works devoted a section or sections to the Eucharist. The earliest treatises were written by Luther. A short treatise published in Strasbourg in 1522 established the scriptural basis for communion in both kinds; another dealt with the veneration of the body of Christ.[44] Luther's doctrine affirming the Real Presence was not fully developed until 1525 in his treatise *Against the Heavenly Prophets* written to correct Karlstadt.[45] In that same year the Strasbourg Reformers began to express their particular views, although Capito had formulated a Spiritualist interpretation before it was a matter of controversy.[46] In a treatise published in 1525, Bucer attempted to take a neutral position, asserting that the bread and wine, as material and external elements, had no intrinsic value.[47] By 1526 the question led to a confrontation with Luther, eventually resulting in the

---

[41] Ibid., P1.8.9; P1.8.10.

[42] Ibid., P1.8.14.

[43] Ibid., P1.9.1; P1.9.2.

[44] Ibid., P1.2.1–4.

[45] Ibid., P4.2.3–4.

[46] J. Kittelson, *Wolfgang Capito, from Humanist to Reformer* (Leiden, 1975), p. 145.

[47] H. Eells, *Martin Bucer* (New Haven, 1931), p. 71.

Marburg Colloquy. Whereas before the Colloquy Bucer attempted to reconcile the differences with Luther, the failure at Marburg led to explicit statements of the doctrine of the Eucharist as it was interpreted in Strasbourg. These culminated in the Tetrapolitan and the Articles of Faith drawn up by the Strasbourg Synod of 1533.[48] Bucer was also a leader in the attempt to create a reconciliation with the Catholics. His reports of the conferences held at Haguenau and at Regensburg were published shortly after these events.[49]

After Bucer went into exile in 1549, Strasbourg continued to move in the direction of the Lutheran Confession of Augsburg. Curiously, no attempt was made to publish Luther's major works at this time. Instead Johann Marbach, the head of the Strasbourg church, reaffirmed the Lutheran position in his own treatises published in 1565 and 1567.[50] These doctrines were confirmed by Johann Pappus, who succeeded Marbach, with an explanation of the Formula of Concord in 1591 and the publication of the Lutheran order of service in 1598.[51] In Strasbourg doctrine came full circle over the course of the century. It began with Luther. From 1525 to 1548 it developed its own particular formula. By the end of the century the city had returned to orthodox Lutheran teaching.

Readership

Who was the audience for these publications? The figures on the content of the books would indicate that the major purpose of Protestant publication in Strasbourg was to win people to the new faith, to convert. This is further supported by looking at the language of publication. Of the total 818 Protestant books printed from 1519 to 1560 only 158 (19 per cent) were in Latin, 80 per cent were in German, under 1 per cent were in French. Clearly this means that the main aim of Protestant publication in Strasbourg was to place materials in the hands of the literate laity, those who read the vernacular, in contrast to the Basle printers whose audience was the learned.

During the Reformation Strasbourg extended its importance as a printing centre. Unlike Wittenberg, Erfurt or Geneva, the city presses were open to a wide range of Reformers. This openness meant that it also served as a centre of propaganda for the new faith. Strasbourg

---

[48] Chrisman, *Bibliography*, P1.9.2; P1.5.3.
[49] Ibid., P1.5.8–10
[50] Ibid., P1.2.23–24.
[51] Ibid., P1.9.7; P7.2.25.

printers reached out to the Huguenots fighting for their existence in France, the people of The Netherlands struggling against the Spanish forces, German and Swiss cities beleaguered by the Roman church or the Emperor. The printers responded to the cause wherever it was in jeopardy.

The Reformation printing activity of the two cities, Strasbourg and Basle, shows a remarkable variation given the fact that the cities are geographically so close and that the Reformation experience was not overwhelmingly different in the two places.

The rhythm of publication was crucially different. The Strasbourg printers reached the height of their production of Reformation materials in the decade 1519–29. The Basle printers were active in that period but seem to have reached their height in the 1550s and 1560s when the Strasbourg printers had reduced their religious publication to a trickle. Basle's peak production was three decades after the Strasbourg peak.

The most fundamental difference between the two was linguistic. The Basle printers maintained their tradition of Latin publication; the Strasbourg printers, particularly in mid-century, turned to the vernacular. Basle was dominated by the intellectual community with Erasmus deeply influencing the choice of what was printed: continued publication of the Greek and Latin classics and the church fathers. By contrast, the output of the Strasbourg printers was popular, reflected first in the volume of polemic in the early decades, later in the publication of Anabaptist writers. Basle's printing was for the intellectual community. Strasbourg printers were developing a popular market.

Select bibliography

(See also the bibliography at the end of Chapter 2 on the German world.)

Chrisman, M. U., *Bibliography of Strasbourg Imprints, 1480–1599* (New Haven, 1982).

Chrisman, M. U., *Lay Culture, Learned Culture: Books and Social Change in Strasbourg, 1480–1599* (New Haven, 1982).

Kroon M. de, and Lienhard, M. (eds), *Horizons européens de la Réforme en Alsace: Mélanges offerts à Jean Rott* (Strasbourg, 1960).

Ritter, Fr., *Histoire de l'imprimerie alsacienne, aux xve et xvie siècles* (Strasbourg, 1955).

Ritter, Fr., *Répertoire bibliographique des livres imprimés en Alsace au xvie siècle de la Bibliothèque nationale et universitaire de Strasbourg* (4 vols, Strasbourg, 1937–55).

Schmidt, Ch. G. A., *Histoire littéraire de l'Alsace à la fin du xve siècle et au commencement du xvie siècle* (2 vols, Paris, 1879; reprint, Nieuwkoop, 1966).

Schmidt, Ch. G. A., *Répertoire bibliographique strasbourgeois jusqu'à vers 1530* (9 vols, Strasbourg, 1894).

Livet, G., Rapp F. and Rott J. (eds), *Strasbourg au coeur religieux du xvie siècle. Hommage à Lucien Febvre. Actes du colloque international de Strasbourg (25–29 mai 1975)* (Strasbourg, 1977).

CHAPTER EIGHT

Printing and the
Basle Reformation, 1517–65

Peter G. Bietenholz

The ruling class, the guilds and religion

By 1517 Basle had a population of at least 10 000 and perhaps as many as 12 000.[1] The city was larger than Berne and Zurich, but much inferior in military strength and the size of its territory. Its population was about the equal of Geneva's and about one half that of Strasbourg and Nuremberg. Since the thirteenth century, the citizens had striven to emancipate themselves from the rule of the prince-bishop. Like Strasbourg, Basle claimed the status of a 'free' city; 'free cities' were self-governing, but did not have the privileges and obligations of 'imperial cities'. In 1385 Basle first appointed a *Schultheiss*, and in the following year it obtained the *Reichsvogtei* and thus had far-reaching control over civil and criminal jurisdiction. It also continued to acquire surrounding land and villages from the bishops and thus came gradually to form its own territorial domain. At the same time it had to keep a wary eye on its Habsburg neighbours, who were pursuing the same goal on a much larger scale and assembling a territorial state throughout the Upper Rhine valley. In 1366 Freiburg was incorporated in the Habsburg state; to escape a similar fate, Basle concluded bilateral treaties with its prominent trading partners, Strasbourg and the other Alsatian cities. But whenever pressure mounted, the military muscle of its Swiss neighbours to the south made it imperative for Basle to befriend them. The decisive turn came in 1499. In a bid to strengthen the structures of government in the Empire, the Habsburg emperor Maximilian had tried to impose his reforms on the Alsatian cities and also upon the Swiss. While the Alsatian cities reluctantly conformed with his requests, the Swiss re-

---

[1] For this see H. R. Guggisberg, *Basel in the Sixteenth Century* (St Louis, 1982); E. Bonjour and A. Bruckner, *Basel und die Eidgenossen* (Basle, 1951); P. Burckhardt, *Geschichte der Stadt Basel von der Zeit der Reformation bis zur Gegenwart* (Basle, 1942); H. Füglister, *Handwerksregiment. Untersuchungen und Materialien zur sozialen und politischen Struktur der Stadt Basel in der ersten Hälfte des 16. Jahrhunderts* (Basle, 1981).

sisted. Eventually Maximilian's army, which included the petty nobility of the region but also contingents of the Alsatian cities, met the Swiss in a battle at Dornach near Basle and was soundly defeated. Basle succeeded in remaining neutral until the outcome was decided; then, in 1501, it obtained full membership in the Swiss Confederation.

The noble families of the region kept supplying the bishops of Basle with officials for their curia and territory and with canons for their cathedral chapter, but from the 1380s they were losing influence in the city. In their place patrician burgher families together with the merchant and artisan guilds won control of the civic administration. In 1515 the nobles lost their last privileges. Admission to civic offices fell entirely under the control of the guilds and was subject to their internal election procedures. In growing numbers new names turn up in the registers of office holders, but democracy remained severely curtailed by two factors. The holders of all the most important offices could virtually appoint their own successors, with the result that power was shared by an inner circle of weighty guild leaders who re-elected each other in turns. Moreover, the predominant position of three merchant and professional guilds made it difficult for representatives of the artisan guilds to join that inner circle of power. Soon, however, these ruling citizens split ranks over the question of French annuities for individual magistrates. In October 1521 the defeat of the greedy pension hunters led to a modest advance of the representatives of the artisan guilds, but the government remained oligarchic. However, popular demand for democratic representation soared, and in 1529 a divided and intimidated council was confronted with an ultimatum for drastic reform. As had regularly happened in the German Peasant War of 1525, the civil grievances were accompanied by radical agitation for religious change. This movement also drew strength from the inspiring example of Strasbourg, Zurich and Berne, where the city councils had recently taken control of the parish clergy and the church property. The climax of a decade of verbal battles and provocative pamphlets published on both sides of the religious dispute came on 8 February 1529. Eight hundred guildsmen gathered in the huge Franciscan church located in menacing vicinity of both the city hall and the cathedral surrounded by its chapter mansions. The next day, when the council still procrastinated, the guildsmen underlined their demands with an iconoclastic sweep through the city's churches and chapels. The frightened council promised to fulfil all popular demands, whether religious or political, and expelled 12 dissenting members from its ranks. The exodus of Catholics began, masses ceased to be said throughout Basle's territory, and the city's monasteries were closed. By 1 April new church regulations were in place. The constitutional promises, however, remained unfulfilled. Amazingly the

guildsmen seemed to have lost interest, and the discussions over democratic election procedures for the inner council and the guild executives
soon stalled. By 1533 the government was every bit as oligarchic as it
had been before the Reformation.

In the German Peasant War, popular rebellion had often led to
Staatskirchentum as territorial church ordinances were imposed 'from
above' by the political authorities. On the other hand, advances in
democracy and social justice were rarely significant.[2] For Basle this
meant that by 1529 the political agitation could no longer draw inspiration from the outside, and the city's printers had no incentive to produce political pamphlets. The religious demands, by contrast, brought
Basle in line with a trend that had already conquered her peer cities and
in the judgement of most local publishers merited intensive support.
The members of the government judged the course of events correctly
and saw that their own class was to gain the most from the redistribu-
tion of church property. They also recalled how four years earlier
political concessions were made to Basle's rebelling country folk, and
then ignored with impunity.

The dividing line, which in the 1520s had separated the advocates
and opponents of evangelical reform ever more distinctly, did not extend to foreign relations. In May 1521 Basle, together with all Swiss
cantons except Zurich, signed an alliance with France. The French
crown was guaranteed a liberal supply of mercenaries in exchange for
an equally liberal supply of French gold to the Swiss governments. In
Basle there was considerable opposition, however, and the élite itself
was divided. Among those opposing the French alliance for moral or
political reasons were some leading humanists loyal to the Empire as
well as some magistrates faithful to the papacy. The latter were odd
company for Huldrych Zwingli in Zurich, who also opposed the French
alliance while preaching the new gospel with growing success. In Basle
neither the traditional antagonism between the Swiss and the Habsburgs
nor the Habsburgs' increasingly determined defence of Catholicism
precluded an enduring affection for the Holy Roman Empire of the
German Nation. Basle printing throughout the Reformation period reflected a solid measure of sympathy for the Empire and also the patri-
otic sentiment propagated by the German humanists. For many Basle
intellectuals, the Swiss Confederation and the German Empire evoked
not so much divided as complementary loyalties.

In other ways, too, Basle kept shying away from one-sided commitments. The prosperous citizens continued to own land in, and derive

---

[2] G. Zimmermann, 'Die Einführung des landesherrlichen Kirchenregiments', *ARG*, 76
(1985), 146–68.

substantial portions of their revenues from, the neighbouring Habsburg territories, while the independent Alsatian towns remained Basle's leading trading partners. In the 1530s and 1540s Basle could not help looking with interest and sympathy at the policy of cities like Strasbourg and Constance that laboured to bring about a common creed as well as political co-operation between the Lutheran states of the Empire and the Zwinglian cities of Switzerland. Simon Sulzer, Basle's *Antistes* or head pastor from 1553 to 1585, was also the superintendent of the Lutheran margraviate of Baden. He and others favoured Strasbourg's formula of concord and even the Augsburg Confession over the Second Helvetic Confession of 1566. Basle would never accede to the latter, although by the end of the century it was viewed as fully compatible with Basle's own confession of 1534.[3] Throughout the period under consideration, Basle's progress can best be described as a series of balancing acts. An 'Erasmian' spirit prevailed even before Erasmus came to settle there in 1521 and continued to hold sway long after he had died there in 1536. Catholic leanings were kept alive for decades by some members of the influential families and also by small groups of simple artisans. Even the persecution of Anabaptists abated in the early 1530s, and in the third quarter of the century Basle was a principal centre for dissident Calvinists fiercely critical of Geneva's Venerable Company.

The printing trade, the city council and European outreach

Basle had been an university city since 1459. The university had been created to attract students and professors from adjacent regions as well as distant countries. In the sixteenth century it was at the peak of its international reputation. It could not have flourished as it did without the city opening its gates liberally to foreigners. The printing trade relied heavily on the co-operation of professors and students, including the many short- and long-term visitors to Basle, who registered at the university without any intention of earning a degree. The presses often relied on foreigners to supply them with printer's copy suitable to generate international sales. The printers themselves tended to be immigrants. Cratander, Bebel and Herwagen arrived from Strasbourg; Valentin Curio and Nicolaus Episcopius senior were also Alsatians. Walder was from Zurich. The Froben and Petri dynasties hailed from Hammelburg in Franconia. The Spiritualist Sebastian Franck, who came to Basle in

---

[3] M. Geiger, *Die Basler Kirche und Theologie im Zeitalter der Hochorthodoxie* (Zollikon-Zurich, 1952), pp. 7 ff., and p. 42.

1541 and printed there during the last year of his life, was a Swabian from Donauwörth. Westheimer and Jakob Wolff were from Pforzheim, Faber from Emmerich in Juliers, Parcus from Lyon. Guarinus was from Tournai and had come to Basle by way of Lyon. Perna was from Lucca. Isengrin, Winter and Oporinus, finally, were from Basle. Foreigners were also numerous among the personnel employed by these master printers. French-speakers and to a lesser degree Italians, Flemings and Englishmen, many of them religious refugees, worked alongside native German-speakers, especially as correctors.[4]

Vague rules of preventative censorship were legislated in 1524 and reasserted in 1531 and 1542.[5] New regulations introduced in 1558 were more specific and potentially more costly to the printers, but enforcement remained as lax as before. The intention always was that the trade should police itself. Only when a printer prepared to handle texts that were politically or religiously sensitive was it advisable for him to clear his project with the censors and pay the price in terms of delays, changes and fees. Only when the council felt obliged to respond to pressure, normally from abroad, would it investigate a printer and sometimes punish him with confiscation, fines or imprisonment. It was an arrangement that provided mutual insurance – voluntary on the part of the printers, discretionary on the part of the council.

On 20 April 1550 the council ruled that henceforth no books on religious topics could be printed in languages other than Latin, Greek, Hebrew and German. The regulation was occasioned by a specific project, namely an Italian translation of five sermons on the Antichrist by the Zurich minister Rudolf Gwalther, intended for clandestine export to Italy. No doubt the authorities feared lest the project would jeopardize less sensitive exports. This regulation compelled Francisco de Enzinas to move to Strasbourg in order to realize his plan of a Spanish-language press. It could be enforced at the council's discretion and subsequently was ignored so often that the real signal the council wished to give the printers was probably twofold. Quiet approval of a major

---

[4] In total, we know of 25 printing workers whose mother tongue was not German. Among the French-speakers were Léger Grymoult, Jacques Gète and Ogier Barthol, who all worked on Froben's presses before joining a group of Castellio's followers in the county of Montbéliard. See P. G. Bietenholz, *Basle and France in the Sixteenth Century* (Geneva, 1971), pp. 79–87, 245–6; P. G. Bietenholz, 'Le coeur contre l'esprit. Comparaison entre les exilés français et italiens à Bâle ... ', in Societé de l'histoire du protestantisme français (ed.), *Actes du colloque l'Amiral de Coligny et son temps* (Paris, 1974), p. 211; M. E. Welti, *Der Basler Buchdruck und Britannien* (Basle, 1964), pp. 186–7.

[5] M. Steinmann, *Johannes Oporinus* (Basle, 1966), pp. 22–4; C. Gilly, *Spanien und der Basler Buchdruck bis 1600* (Basle, 1985), pp. 339–41; C. Roth, 'Die Bücherzensur im alten Basel', *Zentralblatt für Bibliothekswesen*, 31 (1914), 49–67.

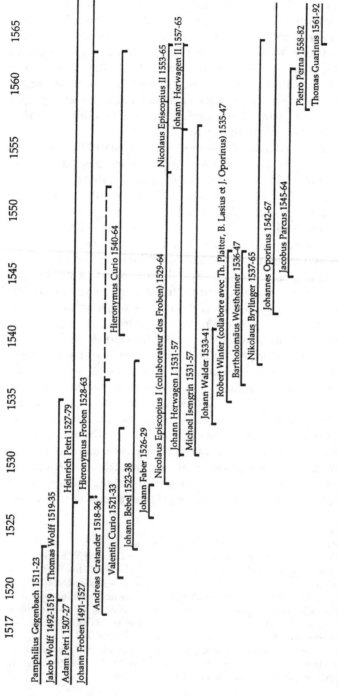

Figure 8.1 Basle printers (1517–65) apart from ephemeral firms

* In 1536, Cratander sold his presses to Winter and his associates, but a few works continued to appear under the name of Cratander's heirs or that of his printshop.

drive to invade vernacular markets, which they had launched in recent years, was combined with a warning that the council might not be able to bail them out if trouble should arise. Despite this basic 'hands off' policy, the council supported individual book men as best it could. In some cases it endeavoured to protect foreign booksellers by granting them nominal rights of citizenship; on another occasion it wrote to the King of France and the Duke of Lorraine in an effort to recover confiscated books.[6]

The authors published in Basle were as international as the markets to which the Basle books were sent. Apart from Swiss, Alsatians and Germans, a significant number of Basle authors were French and Italian. Around ten percent of the books produced in Basle during the Reformation period owed substantial contributions to French-speakers or covered topics related to France, while Italian-speakers and Italian topics accounted for more than 5 per cent.[7] Erasmus, the Dutchman, alone accounted for at least as much. Spanish contributions are likewise impressive; writings by Juan Luis Vives alone figure in 56 Basle editions of this period.[8] England was represented mostly by some Marian exiles.[9] A Basle speciality were the collected works, often in folio volumes, of the classics of Italian humanism, such as Petrarch, Poggio, Valla, Pope Pius II, Pontano, Politian, Ficino, the two Picos, and even Cardinal Bembo.[10] Given the benevolent insouciance of the government, the printers could afford to show little concern for the confessional position of their authors. As long as the subject matter was not religious, Catholic authors who promised sound business could be published just as well as Protestant ones. Even in the field of religious publications, whose share of both the scholarly and popular markets was huge, Catholic authors were not ruled out automatically.

From the 1540s onward the presence of religious refugees in Basle had a noticeable impact on the selection of texts to be printed. In 1546 the council decreed that henceforth residence should be granted only to foreigners who would bring wealth or skills to the city.[11] In view of

---

[6] Bietenholz, *Basle*, pp. 35–6.

[7] Bietenholz, *Basle*, p. 52.

[8] Gilly, *Spanien*, pp. 501–5.

[9] The leading English exiles in Basle were John Foxe, John Bale and Laurence Humphrey. Oporinus published a new edition of Robert Barnes's *Vitae Romanorum Pontificum* in 1555, in 1558 he published the first edition of J. Bale's *Acta Romanorum Pontificum* and in 1559 he produced the enlarged version of Foxe's martyrology: *Rerum in ecclesia gestarum ... pars prima*. See Welti, *Der Basler Buchdruck*, pp. 185–224.

[10] P. G. Bietenholz, *Die italienische Humanismus und die Blütezeit des Buchdrucks in Basel* (Basle, 1959).

[11] Guggisberg, *Basel in the Sixteenth Century*, pp. 39–40.

mounting repression in France, Italy and The Netherlands and the insecure position of the imperial cities there was certainly no shortage of such applicants. Between 1544 and 1546 two exiles arrived who can both be considered dissident Calvinists in that they had given up teaching positions in Geneva and Lausanne, respectively, and departed under a cloud of official suspicion.[12] They were Sebastian Castellio and Celio Secondo Curione, and before long both were teaching the humanities at the University of Basle. A year earlier David Joris had arrived. He was a Dutch Anabaptist leader who, after suffering years of persecution, was glad to find in Basle a safe haven for his retirement. He lived out his days incognito and in discreet wealth, surrounded by his family and chosen collaborators in his clandestine apostolate, for he never relented in his mission. The presence of these men attracted a fluctuating number of immigrants and visitors who held widely differing views in many respects, but were irresistibly drawn together by a common bond of spiritualist leanings and their dislike of all orthodoxies and magisterial churches. Coming and going, they made of Basle a communication centre for like-minded spirits elsewhere – the sort of crucible for heterodoxy that Strasbourg by then had ceased to be. Historians have been justly fascinated by the Basle circles of Italian and French dissidents, but one should not forget that the majority of refugees and visitors were orthodox Calvinists, men like the physician Guglielmo Gratarolo and the jurist François Hotman. Only by some accident was the formal establishment of a French-speaking church in Basle delayed until after the St Bartholomew's Day Massacre.

While the presses and the university were at the peak of their international appeal and the foreigners were bringing a kaleidoscope of religious convictions to Basle, the council, the local intelligentsia and the printers, all displayed a *laissez-faire* attitude worthy of latter-day liberalism. No doubt they were united by a common determination not to let ideology stand in the way of profits and political survival, but there was more to it than that. There was also the common thrill of satisfying one's curiosity, intellectually or otherwise. Thanks to the foreigners the city was saturated with different languages and customs, with rational and spiritual experimentation. Meanwhile the burghers went about their business with the sympathetic but non-committal stance of Londoners hurrying past Speakers' Corner in Hyde Park.

Every Basle printer may from time to time have published a book that could not be expected to sell all that well. He may have done so to

---

[12] For the following section see Guggisberg, *Basel in the Sixteenth Century*, p. 39 ff.; U. Plath, *Calvin und Basel in den Jahren 1552–1556* (Zurich, 1974), pp. 24–35 ff.; Bietenholz, *Basle*, pp. 60, 88–104.

enhance the prestige of his press or, indeed, to defer to his own conviction or to that of a friend. None, however, could afford to act regularly in such a manner. Johann Faber Emmeus, the master of a modest press, was the only printer who in 1529, amid the exodus of Catholic families, left for Freiburg. After his departure, no Basle printer demonstrated an overriding commitment to a specific religious group until the days of Pietro Perna, the friend of the Antitrinitarians Bernardino Ochino and Fausto Sozzini. The large presses in particular were open to publishing books in a wide variety of fields. Hieronymus Curio, who concentrated on the textbook market, and Brylinger, who specialized in Bibles, were exceptional among their Basle colleagues. Some preferences and peculiarities, however, can also be noticed among the output of other presses. Cratander, Adam Petri and Thomas Wolff participated vigorously in the short-lived boom of Luther publications, of which more will be said later. Parcus, Guarinus and Perna showed some natural propensity for the works of French-speaking and Italian authors. Guarinus was also exceptional in his readiness to reprint the work of competitors outside Basle with an aim of surpassing them in the elegance of his rival product. By contrast, Oporinus stands out by the number of books he published from manuscript, among them quite a few that were too daring, or too odd, ever to be reprinted. Similarly, he had personal contacts with many authors and would-be authors of the most varied religious convictions and intellectual interests. He published the writings of uncompromising Lutherans as well as those of Spiritualists and Radical Reformers. Among his numerous Catholic friends was Andreas Vesalius. His splendid edition of Vesalius's epoch-making *Humani corporis fabrica* (1543) stood auspiciously at the beginning of a series of other important scientific editions. With all that, there is not the slightest evidence to suggest that Oporinus was a sceptic or otherwise uncomfortable with the religious practice of the Basle church. In the editorial programme of Heinrich Petri one may discern a general preference for secular scholarship over religious works, whereas the Froben press, when not printing and reprinting Erasmus's own works, followed Erasmus's initiative by paying special attention to the Fathers of the Church. The great Collected Works editions of the classics of Italian and French humanism were due primarily to Petri and Nicolaus Episcopius junior. The Petri and Froben presses also excelled in Hebrew printing. As a rule, vernacular texts and popular tracts were more likely to attract the modest presses such as, for instance, that of Gengenbach.

The production of the Basle presses

As a rough estimate, one might place the total output of the Basle presses in the range of 100 to 120 publications of all sorts annually between 1517 and 1540, rising thereafter to an annual range of 120 to 150. The Basle book production peaked during the second third of the sixteenth century; thereafter – that is to say, after the period considered here – it fell sharply.[13] The share of publications that could broadly be classified as religious may have been as high as one-third of the total.

As for book formats, Basle followed the general trend of the German book production. Octavo sizes gained in popularity, while quarto volumes lost out, especially after the first quarter of the sixteenth century, when the flood of short pamphlets abated. Basle's most notable departure from the norm was no doubt the continuing high proportion of folio sizes. This may be understandable in view of the international markets that the major Basle printers had conquered for themselves. Especially in Germany most printers usually sold their products in a more restricted area. Therefore they could not compete with the Baslers, as it would have taken them too long to recover their capital investment in this category of expensive folio volumes.

Precise information on the shares of various languages in the Basle book production is not available as yet. It is clear, however, that the number of books in vernacular languages other than German was insignificant. To gain some idea of the ratio of German and Latin books, one can turn to Benzing's *Luther-Bibliographie* and its supplements.[14] Basle's share of the publications listed in this work is fairly evenly balanced between German and Latin texts: 76 are in German, 60 in Latin. This may be compared to the share of Strasbourg: 235 publications in German and 67 in Latin. The ratio of the total number of Luther publications is even more lopsided than Strasbourg's share, so that Basle's high proportion of Latin titles is entirely untypical. It seems safe to assume that in Basle throughout our period the number of masterforms set in Latin surpassed those set in German by a considerable margin.

The importance of Latin offers some indication that the Basle presses as a whole endeavoured to supply a scholarly rather than a popular market. Not all vernacular books, however, would primarily appeal to

---

[13] These estimates and much of the following information are taken from the research which I carried out in the Basle Universitätsbibliothek and the Herzog August Bibliothek of Wolfenbüttel; both these libraries have a catalogue in progress dealing with Basle printing in the sixteenth century.

[14] *LB*. The additions by Claus/Pegg (1982) did not substantially change the total number of editions of Luther, which came to 3 692 according to J. Benzing.

a wide readership. Especially when the same text was published both in Latin and in vernacular languages, as was often the case with Luther's writings, the geographical location of a printer's market was probably more decisive in his choice of language than attention to a social class of readers. Thus the needs of an international market still offer the best explanation for Basle's strong commitment to printing in Latin. Basle's share in the production of so-called 'pamphlets' must remain uncertain so long as there is no satisfactory definition of pamphlets as opposed to books. Perhaps the most elusive material in this category was short tracts of religious or political character discreetly printed for one particular customer, who paid for, and took delivery of, the entire edition. Records of legal prosecutions reveal that Basle printers occasionally worked in such a fashion for Anabaptist patrons and even for Spanish agents.[15]

The reputation of the Basle book was enhanced by a high standard of typographical material including illustrations and other book decorations. For its 1513 edition of Erasmus's *Adagia* the Froben press used a new roman type, specifically created for this undertaking. The expense paid off handsomely as the edition was crucial in bringing about the permanent link between Erasmus and the Basle press. The new type continued to be used in six different sizes and aroused great admiration north of the Alps. Oporinus also succeeded in creating books of impressive harmony and simplicity. In Basle as elsewhere the copious use of random book illustrations was phased out after the first quarter of the sixteenth century. However, sophisticated printers' signets, original and elegant series of pictorial initials, and in some cases, title borders continued to be a focus of pride among the major Basle presses. Among the artists employed by the Basle printers were Urs Graf, Hans Holbein the Younger and his brother, Ambrosius, Hans Herbster, the father of Oporinus, and Conrad Schnitt. The famous woodcut depicting Luther as the 'Hercules Germanicus' has repeatedly been attributed to Hans Holbein and clearly issued from a Basle press in the latter part of 1522.[16]

---

[15] For pamphlets by Karlstadt commissioned by Anabaptists, see below, p. 255. There is no firm evidence that David Joris and his disciples printed pamphlets in Basle. In 1557–58, a flood of diplomatic correspondence was caused by the printing of a pamphlet inciting the citizens of Bordeaux to rise up in revolt against the French crown (Bietenholz, *Basle*, pp. 113–14, 208–9).

[16] Fr. Hieronymus in *Oberrheinische Buchillustration 2: Basler Buchillustration 1500–1545* (catalogue of an exhibition in the Basle University Library) (Basle, 1984), pp. iii–xxv, 360–62 ff.

Syß hand zwen schwytzer puren gmracht
Jurwar sy hand es wol berracht.

8.1   *Die göttliche Mühle* (Zurich: Christoph Froschauer, 1521)

Continuity and change in the output of religious books

Erasmus, Bibles and the Fathers   Throughout the Reformation period
no influence was more generally felt in religious printing than that of
Erasmus of Rotterdam. In 1516 Froben printed for the first time
Erasmus's Latin translation of the New Testament, accompanied by the

Greek text that served as a basis for the translation and had never before appeared in print. A separate volume contained copious notes. The revised second edition of 1519 represents Erasmus's chief contribution to the Reformation literature. Three more revised editions and a good many reprints of the Latin text alone appeared during his lifetime. In 1518 Froben began to publish Erasmus's Paraphrases. In due course the Paraphrases would cover all parts of the New Testament except Revelation and achieve more reprints than any other of his works except the New Testament itself.[17]

Erasmus's New Testament provided an important impulse, but Bibles had been printed in Basle well before the Reformation, and Bibles together with parts, commentaries and concordances of the Bible remained the single largest group of books published in Basle throughout the period. In addition to Erasmus and Luther Bibles, one encounters the Latin and French translations of Castellio, but only exceptionally their Genevan rivals translated by Beza and Olivetan. Cratander reprinted in 1526 a Latin version of the Septuagint, which was derived directly or indirectly from the great Complutensian Bible. In 1538, Froben reprinted the entire Vulgate, and Brylinger reprinted in 1544 a Vulgate published previously in Lyon by Servetus. Guarinus copied in 1564 a Lyon edition of the Latin text as arranged by two Catholic scholars, Pagnini and Vatable. Latin and Greek translations were the most numerous, but the Basle Greek and Hebrew Bibles are particularly worthy of note. A Rhaeto-romance New Testament was printed by Parcus in 1560 and a complete Spanish Bible by Guarinus in 1569.

Erasmus had first been brought to Basle to take charge of Froben's great Jerome edition then in progress. Other major editions of the Fathers had preceded his arrival, but it was largely due to his enthusiasm and active co-operation that, throughout the Reformation period, the Fathers maintained a role in Basle printing that was second only to that of the Bible. Apart from Jerome (1516), Erasmus's name is found in Collected Works editions of Cyprian (1520), Arnobius (1522), Hilary (1523), Irenaeus (1526), Ambrose and Athanasius (1527), Augustine (1528/29), John Chrysostom (1530), Basil (1532) and Origen (1536), all published by the Froben press. Other major editions of ancient and medieval Fathers included Tertullian (1521), Theophylact (1524), Prudentius (1527), Salvian (1530), Eucherius of Lyon (1531), Sidonius Apollinaris (1542), Cyril (1546), Gregory of Nazianzus (1550), Pope Gregory I (1551), Bernard of Clairvaux ((1552), Clement of Alexandria (1556), John of Damascus (1559) and Gregory of Nyssa (1562), not to

---

[17] F. Vander Haeghen, *Bibliotheca erasmiana: répertoire des oeuvres d'Érasme* (Ghent, 1893), vol. 1, pp. 142–51; vol. 2, pp. 57–66.

BIBLIA,
Interprete Sebaſtiano Caſtalione.

VNA CVM EIVSDEM
Annotationibus.

TYPOGRAPHVS LECTORI.

In recenti hac translatione, Lector, fideliter expreſſam He-
brææætç Græcç ſentētiæ Veteris ac Noui Teſtamenti ueritatē,
Latini ſermonis puritate & perſpicuitate ſcruata, es habiturus:
id quod ipſe legendo, & cum cæteris editionib. conſerēdo, item
ex Præſatione & Annotationibus, illuſtres rerum diffici-
liorum Imagines habentibus, pleniſſi-
mē cognoſces.

BASILEAE, PER IO-
annem Oporinum.

8.2   Sebastian Castellio's Latin Bible (Basle: Johann Oporinus, 1551)

mention reprints of these, a good many individual texts and also some large collections. What the Basle presses offered to churchmen of all denominations was no less than a corpus of Greek and Latin Fathers, for the most part in folio, more or less critically edited and supplemented by copious indexes, biographies, etc.

As far as Basle printing was concerned, confessional labels simply did not apply to the Fathers of the Church, not even to the medieval ones, as long as they did not share the scholastic preoccupation with Catholic dogmatics. In this line of thinking Erasmus himself could be seen as the most recent Church Father. Between 1538 and 1541 the Froben press published his Collected Works in nine huge folio volumes. There is to date no comprehensive and reliable bibliography of separate editions of his writings in the sixteenth century; it is safe to say, however, that up to 1536 more than 400 titles of his writings and editions were published in Basle,[18] and that afterwards re-editions slowed only gradually, whereas in Strasbourg he practically ceased to be printed after his death.[19]

Erasmus attacked the Reformers in writing and left Basle in protest against the local Reformation, but in 1535 he had returned and it was in Basle that he died on 11/12 July 1536. Earlier that year he had received Bucer and Capito on a courtesy visit.[20] Basle buried him with all due honours and in keeping with its own Reformed rites. Whatever others might think of him, to the Baslers and their friends, Erasmus was not an obedient son of the Church of Rome. He was an *homo sui generis* and an author worthy of as many reprints as the market would bear.

Lutheranism   Late in 1517 Adam Petri reprinted the broadsheet containing Luther's 95 Theses as a quarto pamphlet. He was the first to do so, and his pamphlet was the first of about 120 Luther publications to appear in Basle over the next decade. In October 1518 Froben published in typical Basle fashion the first comprehensive collection of Luther's Latin writings.[21] On 14 February 1519 he excitedly informed Luther that the edition was practically sold out. Never before had he printed a book that moved so fast; 600 copies had gone to France and

---

[18] Fr. Hieronymus, in *Erasmus von Rotterdam ... Austellung zum 450. Todestag* (Historisches Museum Basel) (Basle, 1986), p. 56.

[19] Among the rare exceptions, only a German translation of the *Christiani matrimonii institutio* (B. Beck, 1542) can be described as a religious work. See M. U. Chrisman, *Bibliography of Strasbourg Imprints, 1480–1599* (New Haven, 1982), C5.1.37, H1.4.23, T1.3.4, V8.2.3.

[20] P. G. Bietenholz and T. B. Deutscher (eds), *Contemporaries of Erasmus* (Toronto, 1985–87), vol. 1, pp. 210, 263.

[21] *LB*, nos 3–9, 89.

Spain and a substantial number to Italy.[22] Froben's learned helpers saw
Luther as a shining knight in the phalanx of Christian humanists who
had girded themselves to follow Erasmus, their recognized leader. This
turned out to be an illusion, and the Luther boom that kept the Basle
presses bustling soon ended. Froben was the first to give up Luther, and
he did so in response to an ultimatum by Erasmus.[23] Schürer in Strasbourg and Cratander and Petri in Basle were glad to pick up and
enlarge the collection of Luther's Latin writings. Petri even surpassed
Cratander in his devotion to Luther copy, but Petri died in 1528 and by
then the flood of Luther issues had been reduced to a trickle. At the
same time Cratander had a change of heart and henceforth preferred all
kinds of scholarly subjects to religious topics. Already in 1522 the
Strasbourg printers had overtaken their Basle colleagues in the champi-
onship of Lutherania; moreover, they did not lose interest as quickly as
the Baslers. Where were the Basle printers in February 1529 when the
guildsmen precipitated a forcible end to Catholic worship? The chances
are that they did not stand back; their polemical pamphlets had certainly played their role in motivating and mobilizing the crowd. Only
Faber Emmeus was among the Catholics emigrating to Freiburg. Other
reasons must have dissuaded the Basle and Strasbourg printers from
publishing Luther. The most important reason was perhaps the international character of their clientele. Luther could no longer be exported
freely to France, Spain, Italy, England and even The Netherlands. The
German markets, on the other hand, now belonged to competitors
closer to Wittenberg. The daring booksellers, who now began to organize the clandestine importation of Protestant books from Basle into
France and subsequently into Italy, preferred aggressive or evasive material penned by refugees from these very countries.[24] A good deal of
their market was popular and in need of vernacular publications, but
not suited to the German tracts of Luther.

So Luther waned, but faithful followers of his like Bugenhagen, Brenz,
Johannes Rivius and Erasmus Sarcerius remained favourites of the Basle
presses, as did Melanchthon above all, whose Collected Works were
printed for the first time by Herwagen in 1541 in five folio volumes – a
worthy companion piece to the *Opera omnia* of Erasmus. Hutten's

---

[22] WA Br, vol. 1, no. 146.
[23] P. S. Allen, *Opus epistolarum D. Erasmi* (Oxford, 1913), vol. 3, no. 904; see the
annotation of the *Collected Works of Erasmus* (Toronto, 1974–), vol. 6, no. 904.
[24] Examples of this can be found in Bernardino Ochino's *Prediche ... nomate Laberinti*
(Perna, 1561) published simultaneously as *Prediche del R. Padre Don Serafino da
Piangenza* and in Jacopo Aconcio's *Dialogo* (Perna, 1558); see P. G. Bietenholz, *Der
italienische Humanismus*, pp. 31–3.

Prediche del

R.PADRE DON SE-
RAFINO DA PIAGENZA, DITTE
ᴜᴀʙᴇʀɪɴᴛɪ del libero, o uer feruo Arbitrio, Prefcienza, Predeftinatione, &
Libertà diuina, & del modo
per vfcirne.

*Molto utili alla falute, non mai piu
uifte in luce*

STAMPATE IN PAVIA

8.3 Serafino da Piagenza [=Bernardino Ochino], *Prediche* (Pavia [= Basle]:
[Pietro Perna], 1558)

popularity with the Basle presses peaked between 1518 and 1520, but
here Basle lagged noticeably behind Strasbourg and Paris.[25] The Strasbourg Reformers were printed in Basle only infrequently, no doubt not
for want of interest, but out of respect for the prevalent claims of
Strasbourg colleagues. Among the second generation of Reformation
printers it was Oporinus, in particular, who published such orthodox
Lutherans as Andreas Hyperius and especially Johannes Rivius, whose
Opera omnia theologica he printed in 1562. Three years later, he published a Greek translation of the Augsburg Confession. The same
Oporinus, however, also published Thomas Naogeorgius, a dissident
Lutheran with Karlstadtian leanings, while his most important initiative

---

[25] J. Benzing, *Ulrich von Hutten und seine Drucker* (Wiesbaden, 1956).

in this field led him to the ultra-orthodox Magdeburg Centuriators, Matthias Flacius Illyricus, Matthaeus Judex and Johannes Wigand. Oporinus may have wished to serve scholarship; the first comprehensive Protestant history of the church, the so-called Magdeburg Centuries, which he published between 1556 and 1562, was a much needed undertaking, but it also was one of the most polemical religious works to originate from Basle.[26] Another incident shows how Oporinus valued personal relations, and business prospects, over Lutheran or any other doctrine. In 1563 he began to print a text by the Calvinist Girolamo Zanchi, preacher to the Italian congregation of Strasbourg. Zanchi was embroiled in a dogmatic controversy with the Lutheran-minded Strasbourg pastor Johannes Marbach. The text he had entrusted to Oporinus for anonymous printing presented his case against Marbach. The secret deal was revealed, however, and after diplomatic negotiations Oporinus had to desist. With Zanchi's co-operation the completed masterforms were passed on to Jean Crespin in Geneva, who published them together with additional pieces in 1566 as Zanchi's *Miscellanea theologica*.[27]

Catholic authors and open-minded printers   When Luther first burst upon the scene the old stock-in-trade on the ecclesiastical book list disappeared just as swiftly. Adam Petri, working mainly for German publishing houses, printed his last editions of Petrus Berchorius and Alexander de Villa Dei between 1517 and 1519. In 1518 Nicolaus Lamparter produced for the last time Guido de Monte Rotario's *Manipulus curatorum*, and in 1521 Thomas Wolff printed his last missal for the diocese of Mainz. The change-over was most radical in Petri's press. In 1518 he still printed two sermons by Gabriel Biel, but also half a dozen or more titles by Luther. In 1520 it was Luther and like-minded authors all the way. It was true that some authors of the waning Middle Ages could lend impressive support to the new wave of protest against the Church of Rome; thus the great Conciliarists Pierre d'Ailly, Jean Gerson, Nicolas de Clamanges and Enea Silvio Piccolomini (Pius II) were printed in Basle between 1517 and 1524. The *editio princeps* of Marsilius of Padua appeared there in 1522, and a trickle of Catholic texts *pro causa reformationis* continued, among them the first edition of Dante's *Monarchia* in 1559. In the later 1520s only one printer, Faber Emmeus, supported the doomed cause of Basle's Catholic party with a number of polemical pamphlets before the

---

[26] Steinmann, *Johannes Oporinus*, pp. 69–73.

[27] Steinmann, *Johannes Oporinus*, pp. 102–4; J.-Fr. Gilmont, *Jean Crespin, un éditeur réformé du XVIe siècle* (Geneva, 1981), pp. 133, 256; see also p. 96 in the same volume, where Crespin bought up and distributed the unsold copies of another work produced by Oporinus.

Reformation forced him to move to Freiburg. Until the 1540s statements by contemporary Catholics on religious issues were definitely not welcome. Among the very few exceptions was Bishop Jacobo Sadoleto's *In psalmum xciii interpretatio*, which Froben printed in 1530. This work, however, was bound to displease the hard-line Romanists more than the Protestants. But even Froben, following Erasmus's advice, would not touch Sadoleto's commentary on Romans, which was written to promote reconciliation with the Protestants, but was speedily condemned by the Sorbonne when it appeared in Lyon in 1535.

In the 1540s Catholic authors, including ranking prelates of the Roman church, became more numerous, and quite a number of their works printed in Basle were such as to raise suspicion within their own church and some were headed for the Index, but the majority were orthodox and exportable to territories under Catholic jurisdiction. Almost all of them, however, had one thing in common. They avoided all controversial dogmatic issues such as the sacraments or justification.

One who did so quite deliberately was Vives. In 1522 Froben had printed his monumental and amply commentated edition of Augustine's *De civitate Dei*. After that Vives fell victim to the erratic vindictiveness of Erasmus in his old age, rather than to anti-Catholic sentiment. Not until after Erasmus's death did Basle become the principal place of publication for Vives's many writings. In 1542 Froben reprinted the Augustine commentary twice, and in 1543 Oporinus published Vives's *De veritate fidei christianae* as a companion piece to his Koran edition, which carried a commendatory preface by Luther. A year later he reprinted Vives' work in a more economical size; it was dedicated to Pope Paul III and the second edition contained a prefatory epistle by Oporinus addressed to Ludwig Ber. Ber was a leading figure among Basle's Catholic exile community and subsequently himself became one of Oporinus's authors. In his preface, Oporinus wished Ber a long life *ad … catholicae ecclesiae utilitatem.*[28] The wish caught the spirit of Vives's work; it culminates in a dialogue, in which a Jew and a Muslim, both portrayed as open-minded and reasonable, converse with a Christian, whose faith shows no signs of being subject to partisan divisions. In 1555 Nicolaus Episcopius junior printed the first edition of Vives's Collected Works.

The same spirit animated Joachim Périon, a Paris Benedictine and Aristotelian scholar, whose works appear frequently among Oporinus's offerings. In 1554 Périon wrote to the Protestant printer, expressing confidence that Oporinus would always abide by the holy faith he had

---

[28] Gilly, *Spanien*, pp. 183–5.

imbibed with his mother's milk.[29] In 1556 the ministers of the Basle cathedral engaged in a public debate with a visiting Spanish Jesuit.[30] Although civility prevailed, in real life the religious divisions could not easily be ignored, whereas on the printed page in exchanges across national boundaries the consciousness of the common Christian heritage could always carry the day. In 1557 Parcus printed the first part, dealing with biblical times, of a large dictionary of Catholic saints by Georg Witzel, who was a married man and by then again a Catholic priest in good standing.

Irenicism also was the central message of Guillaume Postel, whose ingenious and bewildering writings were faithfully relayed by Oporinus, regardless of the ire, or laughter, they were bound to arouse in various quarters. They included *De orbis terrae concordia* (1544), a work deemed embarrassing to the French court and therefore suppressed in Paris, but intended to please the Roman Jesuits. Before it could be printed in Basle it had to be thoroughly expurgated. Postel's Πανθενωσια, launched in 1547, appeared two years later on the Index of the Sorbonne.[31] The manuscripts that were printed, however, were outnumbered by others that were left languishing on Oporinus's stacks and are still waiting for a compassionate publisher.

In 1500 Oporinus printed an important collection of letters addressed to Friedrich Nausea, Bishop of Vienna. While this was not considered controversial, the printer was briefly jailed two years later for publishing an apologia for the Council of Trent, written by the same Nausea under a pseudonym.[32] He had broken the unwritten law that Basle authors had to exhibit a catholic spirit, and not a Roman Catholic one. On the other hand, under the auspices of humanistic scholarship and the common Christian heritage the Basle presses were able to produce Collected Works editions of Pope Gregory I (1551), St Bernard and Pope Pius II (1552), Cardinal Pietro Bembo (1556), Guillaume Budé (1557), the Venerable Bede (1561–63), Canon Gilbert Cousin (1562) and Thomas More (1563). The latter was restricted to More's Latin writings; conveniently for the Baslers, More, the Catholic controversialist, had stuck to English.

---

[29] Bietenholz, *Basle*, pp. 203–4.

[30] Gilly, *Spanien*, p. 275.

[31] *Index 1*, pp. 232–3; Bietenholz, *Basle*, pp. 138–9, nos 860–70.

[32] Steinmann, *Johannes Oporinus*, pp. 85–7. The Basle printers participated very actively in the extensive Protestant publicity effort following the Council of Trent. Around 1550 Oporinus or Parcus published an anonymous edition of the famous *Consilium dilectorum cardinalum* proposed by Reginald Pole and his friends.

Religious writings from Reformed Switzerland

Johannes Oecolampadius, the Reformer of Basle, had sermons and polemical pieces printed by the local presses. He was also a prolific scholar; his scriptural commentaries appeared in short succession and continued to be reprinted after his death in 1531. However, Oecolampadius did not set an example for his colleagues and immediate successors. To the end of our period the Basle ministers and theologians, with one exception, produced very little in the way of religious writings. The exception, interestingly, was something of a black sheep. Martin Borrhaus was a Swabian and suspect to many because of his earlier associations with Anabaptists and the Zwickau prophets. In Basle he received the chair of Old Testament and backed the council and the university in a protracted dispute with the ministers. He often acted as a book censor and in this capacity displayed great prudence. He had good reason to be cautious for he was well known to be friendly with the Anabaptist David Joris, who lived incognito in Basle, the Antitrinitarian Servetus and the entire Basle circle of French and Italian dissident Calvinists. The Genevans were fuming. In an early work he had himself shown Antitrinitarian leanings,[33] but in Basle he learned to play it safe. Producing commentaries on the Old Testament, he stuck to the tradition of Oecolampadius and the bearings of his academic office. His predecessor in the Old Testament chair was Andreas Karlstadt, who had an even more embattled past to live down. Between 1522 and 1524 some of his pamphlets had been published in Basle at the expense of admiring Anabaptists, a circumstance that led to the brief imprisonment of the printers Johann Bebel and Thomas Wolff. But when Karlstadt settled in Basle, a turbulent decade later, he had lost all interest in publishing and did what he could to please the government. Between 1520 and 1524 some anti-Roman pamphlets also appeared, written by Ulrich Hugwald, a Basle teacher, and Balthasar Hubmaier, a priest from nearby Waldshut; these predated their authors' subsequent involvement with Anabaptism.

There are no indications that the Basle presses played a role in the clandestine dissemination of early Anabaptist literature; not until the 1550s did some of them acquire a reputation for printing books that in the eyes of the Calvinist leadership were contaminated with shocking heresies. In Strasbourg, by contrast, publications of spiritual and

---

[33] For a comparison between Borrhaus's *De operibus Dei* (Strasbourg, 1527) and Servetus's *De Trinitatis erroribus*, see Gilly, *Spanien*, pp. 292–3. See also Plath, *Calvin und Basel*, p. 30 and following. See also Lucia Felici, *Tra riforma ed eresia. La giovinezza di Martin Borrhaus (1499–1528)* (Florence, 1995).

Anabaptist orientation had been fairly numerous during the 1520s, before they gradually disappeared between 1530 and 1550.[34] Even after 1550 there were limits to Basle's tolerance; in 1552 Servetus's *Christianismi restitutio* could not be printed there. The manuscript had been sent to Borrhaus, but he returned it to the author, pleading with him to appreciate that in this case the risk was unacceptable. Servetus need not have been surprised. Two decades earlier he had failed to have his *De Trinitatis erroribus* accepted by any Basle press despite the ten months he had spent in town. At least his friends in Basle put him in touch with Johann Setzer in Haguenau, who printed the work in 1531.[35]

Other Basle professors deserve at least a mention as serious scholars and authors. Simon Grynaeus, who ended his career as professor of New Testament, published in the field of Greek philology and philosophy, while Sebastian Münster ensured for Basle printing a leading position in Hebrew publishing, which was becoming indispensable to the fledgling Protestant theology. Zwingli, Gwalther and other Zurich ministers were rarely printed in Basle, no doubt for the sake of good relations with Zurich's own Froschauer press. But again there is an exception, and again it concerns a black sheep. The Zurich minister Theodor Bibliander was, like his friend Postel, devoted to eastern languages and the mysteries concealed in their literatures. His encouragement and scholarly assistance were essential when Oporinus produced his great corpus of the Latin Koran and related writings (1543). Among Bibliander's many writings published mostly by Oporinus one contains the texts of a Roman and an Ambrosian Mass.[36] With advancing age he became increasingly embroiled in a dispute with his Zurich colleagues over his Erasmian dislike of predestination. Another Basle author was the clear-sighted and authoritative Wolfgang Musculus, the leading minister of Berne. His many commentaries on books of both the Old and the New Testament were published by the Herwagen press, and some could be reprinted there several times.

In the 1520s religious exiles from France began to arrive in Basle and to importune the presses with requests to print their manuscripts. In all likelihood Cratander printed in 1524 some pamphlets for both François Lambert and Guillaume Farel.[37] Farel's tracts together with his fierce

---

[34] See Figure 7.1 in the previous chapter.

[35] Gilly, *Spanien*, pp. 277–98.

[36] Steinmann, *Johannes Oporinus*, p. 75, also pp. 21–2. On Bibliander, see K. Guggisberg, in *Neue Deutsche Biographie*, vol. 2 (1955), p. 215.

[37] R. Bodenmann, 'Bibliotheca lambertiana' in P. Fraenkel (ed.) *Pour retrouver François Lambert* (Baden-Baden, 1987), p. 48; J.-Fr. Gilmont, 'L'oeuvre imprimée de Guillaume

tirades in public places aroused the ire of Erasmus and the suspicion of the council so that he was soon compelled to move on. It was not until after the Basle Reformation and the Placards affair in Paris that printing history was made in the wake of the visit of another French refugee. John Calvin was in Basle in 1535–36, and soon after his departure Platter and his partners published the first edition of *Christianae religionis instituto*, to be followed in 1537–38 by *Epistolae duae* and the first Latin *Catechismus*. Thereafter Calvin would quite frequently pass through Basle on his journeys, but he was no longer printed there except for an Italian and a German translation of his later catechism in dialogue form (1545, 1556).[38] Other important links between the Basle presses and French authors have a more Erasmian flavour. Cratander reprinted Lefèvre d'Étaples' *Commentarii initiatorii* on the Gospels in 1523 and launched his new commentary on the Epistles of James, Peter, John and Jude in 1527. In 1525 Lefèvre's French translation of the New Testament was reprinted by Bebel for the Écu de Bâle distribution network. In 1533 Nicolas Bourbon corresponded with Erasmus, while Cratander printed an edition of his *Nugae*; in 1540 Cratander's heirs reprinted the enlarged edition of the *Nugae*.

Towards 1550 quite a number of the ingenious and restless refugees from southern countries began to converge upon Basle. Their fiercely individualistic spiritualism might have rendered many of them disagreeable to one another, had not Calvin provided them all with a rallying point. On 27 October 1553 Servetus was burnt in Geneva. Even as his trial was progressing, the dissident Calvinist group in Basle and their friends abroad began to rally in opposition to Geneva's intolerance, whether or not they shared Servetus' Antitrinitarianism to any significant degree. Their protests were resoundingly formulated in the famous *De haereticis, an sint persequendi … sententiae*, directed by Castellio and published by Oporinus in 1554 with a fictitious author's name and printer's address. While most of Castellio's many writings, including his *Defensio suarum translationum Bibliorum* (1562), could be published openly in Basle, not even Oporinus dared touch his rejoinders in the bitter controversy started off by *De haereticis* nor works like his *De arte dubitandi*, where Castellio's rationalist and Antitrinitarian bent found

Farel' in *Actes du colloque Guillaume Farel, Neuchâtel 29 sept.–1er octobre 1980* (Geneva, 1983), vol. 2, pp. 113–16.

38 A. Erichson, *Bibliographia calviniana* (Berlin, 1900), pp. 1–2, 5, 16. The Italian edition, whose preface includes extracts of Juan de Valdès' *Latte spirituale*, is hypothetically attributed to Basle presses by Gilly, *Spanien*, p. 319, no. 642. But other authors attribute this edition to the Genevan presses of J. Girard (J.-Fr. Gilmont, 'Bibliotheca gebennensis: les livres imprimés à Genève de 1535 à 1549', *Genava*, 28 (1980), 45–7).

the most forthright expression.[39] On the other hand, his new plea for toleration in the face of the incipient religious wars in France, *Conseil à la France désolée*, could appear in Oporinus's press (1562), as could his Latin paraphrases of the *Theologia germanica* (1557) and the *Imitatio Christi* (1563), which show that his rationalism did not preclude appreciation of medieval mysticism.

A similar tendency is shown by Bernardino Ochino's sermons and dialogues, of which Perna printed various editions in the early 1560s, both in the Italian original and in Castellio's Latin translation. Although not overtly heretical, they proved sufficiently worrisome to make the author lose his asylum in Zurich and force him to emigrate to Moravia. Giovanni Leonardi was luckier than Ochino. His spiritualism was bordering on mental derangement; in Geneva he announced that he was Moses to Calvin's Aaron. Yet in 1553 Parcus printed his *Tabulae duae legis evangelicae*. Although it seems that the embarrassed council attempted to curtail the circulation of the book, Leonardi continued to live in Basle, for some time actually in Borrhaus's house.[40]

François Bauduin, another dissident, had already antagonized Calvin when Oporinus began to print his legal works. He taught law at Frankfurt and in 1556 published in Basle his *Constantinus Magnus*, a remarkable treatise intended as a lesson for both the Venerable Company of Geneva and the Council Fathers of Trent. In 1562 he arranged, again with Oporinus, for the printing of *De officio pii et publicae tranquillitatis vere amantis viri* by his friend Georg Cassander. The work was a noble appeal to irenicism; as it came off the press, Bauduin took a supply of copies with him to Paris, where preparations for the synod of Poissy were under way.[41] Cassander was an Erasmian Catholic, and Bauduin himself was then preparing to return to the fold of the Church of Rome, but both were held in high esteem by Castellio and his circle. It is true that at the same time Bauduin's professional and personal rival, François

---

[39] Indeed, in 1578, Perna took the risk of publishing Castellio's *Dialogi quatuor* edited by Fausto Sozzini under a false address. The work can be seen as a summary of Castellio's controversial theological views; its publication led to Perna's imprisonment. See Guggisberg, *Basel in the Sixteenth Century*, p. 55 and following; Bietenholz, *Basle*, pp. 122–36; Plath, *Calvin und Basel*, pp. 29–30 and following. Another impressive call for toleration can be found in Jacopo Aconcio's *Stratagemata Satanae*, published by Perna for the first time in 1565, and republished by him in Latin and in a French translation in the same year. Even though he was closely tied to the Basle dissidents, Aconcio was, however, not really heterodox.

[40] Plath, *Calvin und Basel*, pp. 112–19.

[41] Bietenholz, *Basle*, pp. 145–52; M. Erbe, 'François Bauduin und Georg Cassander: Dokumente einer Humanistenfreundschaft', *BHR*, 40 (1978), 537–40. See also M. Erbe, *François Bauduin, 1520–1573: eine Biographie eines Humanisten* (Gütersloh, 1978) and M. Turchetti, *Concordia o Tolleranza? François Bauduin e i 'Moyenneurs'* (Geneva, 1984).

Hotman, had many of his legal works printed in Basle; and Hotman was a pillar of Calvinist orthodoxy. Pier Paolo Vergerio, another Italian exile much printed in Basle, found a new home among German Lutherans. Finally, Curione, the central figure of the Italian community in Basle published many humanistic and anti-Catholic writings there, although his most important, and indeed revealing *De amplitudine beati regni Christi* had to be printed elsewhere.

Markets and readers

All major Basle printers set their sights on international markets. Many are known to have travelled regularly to the Frankfurt book fairs, where a substantial portion of their sales was negotiated and effected, and several of them had outlets elsewhere. The Froben firm maintained close commercial ties with the Écus de Bâle in Lyon and Paris, book-shops which were at the centre of a loosely connected sales organization that seems to have operated until the 1540s. The Birckmann family sold Froben books and no doubt other Basle publications in Cologne, Antwerp and London.[42]

The special significance of foreign markets to the Basle presses is well demonstrated by the Catholic Indexes of prohibited books, and so is the potential threat to their livelihoods that the Basle printers faced from Catholic censors and inquisitors. On the six consecutive Indexes of the University of Paris (1544–56) Basle publications form by far the largest contingent of all condemned titles that are listed with a specific edition (20 out of 77, whereas there are only four Strasbourg books). Likewise of the books condemned without reference to a specific edition as many as 46 had been printed for the first time in Basle, as against only 21 for Strasbourg.[43] Of 282 Latin works condemned by successive Louvain Indexes 87 came from Basle and 30 from Strasbourg. The Louvain Index of 1558, in particular, lists among 74 Latin titles 26 that were published by Oporinus, another 15 from the remaining Basle presses and only five from Strasbourg. The Venice Indexes of 1549 and 1554 add 88 and 89 identifiable titles to those prohibited on earlier lists. Of those 177 titles again 49 were first published in Basle and 24 in Strasbourg.[44] Worst of all

---

[42] Bietenholz, *Basle*, pp. 29–43; Bietenholz and Deutscher (eds), *Contemporaries of Erasmus*, vol. 1, pp. 112–13, 148–50.

[43] *Index 1*, pp. 94–8.

[44] *Index 2*, pp. 57, 76–9; *Index 3*, pp. 84–5, 144–6. The inclusion in the Index of so many works produced by Oporinus may have been facilitated in part by the sales catalogue which Oporinus had published in 1552.

for the Baslers, the Roman Index of 1559 listed in its last section the names of printers, among them no less than 15 from Basle. Any book to be published by these in future was prohibited, and so was any book already published, unless a special exemption was granted. The papal action was seen as a serious blow. The Basle council wrote to Duke Cosimo I of Florence and asked him to intervene in Rome on behalf of the Basle printers.[45]

During the last third of the sixteenth century printing at Basle entered a slow but irreversible decline. This should not be attributed exclusively to Catholic book censorship and the general growth of confessional barriers. The wars in France and The Netherlands were bound to cause disruption in vital markets for the Basle book, although Italy, England and eventually the Dutch provinces were gaining greater political and economic stability. Other factors for the decline of the trade were the lessening demand for Latin books and, most important perhaps, the imponderables of entrepreneurial flair that seemed to forsake the Basle bookmen by the end of the century.

There can be little doubt, however, that the gradual tightening of confessional orthodoxies, both in Basle and abroad, was a significant factor. This is confirmed by what little we know about the precise location of the Basle markets by the end of our period. For the years 1557 to 1563 an account book of the Froben firm has survived.[46] It is incomplete and awaits close scrutiny, but at a glance it will show that retail sales (*Handkauf*) both at Basle and the Frankfurt fairs were unimportant. Commercial buyers accounted for the bulk of the firm's sales, which were effected primarily at Frankfurt. The Birckmann firm of Cologne, with its international network, continued to be the Frobens' single most important customer. Inside Germany sales to Saxony (especially Wittenberg and Leipzig) by far surpassed those to other regions. Sales to Strasbourg bookmen were negligible. Outside Germany, Antwerp was the richest market, followed by Paris and by Venice as a distant third.

No wonder that Catholic censorship hurt the Frobens and presumably other Basle firms of similar orientation. The impact, though, was gradual. In 1554 the Benedictine Joachim Périon purchased in the Paris bookshop of Jacques Dupuys Oporinus's Latin Koran and the *Protevangelion* of James, edited by Guillaume Postel. Neither title was on the Index; however, Périon could not obtain Castellio's Bible, which was prohibited by the Venice Index of 1554, but would not appear on that of Paris until

[45] Steinmann, *Johannes Oporinus*, pp. 97–8.
[46] R. Wackernagel (ed.), *Rechnungsbuch der Froben und Episcopius, Buchdrucker und Buchhändler zu Basel, 1557–1564* (Basle, 1881).

1556.[47] Paris dealers still purchased significant numbers of Basle books in 1562; on the other hand the publishing of French-speaking authors in Basle was then past the peak it had reached in the mid-1550s.[48] In 1570 the Venetian Inquisition drew up an inventory of prohibited titles discovered in the bookshop of Vincenzo Valgrisi (Vaugris), who had personal as well as commercial ties to Basle. There still were major Basle editions such as Erasmus' *Opera omnia* and those of St Basil (edited by Wolfgang Musculus), Oecolampadius's Theophylactus edition and Gilbert Cousin's Lucian, also Postel's Πανθενωσια.[49] And even in 1604 a similar inventory of the huge library of the late Gian Vincenzo Pinelli at Padua listed more books printed in Basle than in any other Protestant centre.[50] Pinelli was a nobleman. While men like him with the right connections could have the books they desired, it was becoming less likely to have to turn to a Basle publisher in order to have them. No general conclusions, however, can be offered here as to the sort of individuals that read Basle books. Suffice it to say that the published correspondences of the Amerbachs, Erasmus, Beatus Rhenanus, Oporinus, and of Luther, Melanchthon, Zwingli and the French Reformers and finally the manuscript treasures of the Basle library offer ample material for further investigation.

It is difficult to subject Basle's output of religious books to statistical classification. Such labels as 'Catholic', 'Lutheran', 'Calvinist', while proving useful elsewhere, often do not make much sense here. Also many Basle books cannot confidently be assigned to either academic or popular and either domestic or international markets. What can be said is that the share of biblical and patristic titles remained exceptionally large throughout the period, that the printing of Luther's books experienced a sudden boom between 1518 and 1525 and that in the middle third of the century religious works of ecumenical and spiritualist tendencies accentuated the Basle publishing programme.

Relations between the presses of Basle and Strasbourg were close and amicable. There is plenty of evidence for collaboration and considerateness. Some bestsellers like individual works by Luther and Erasmus seem to have been a free-for-all, but otherwise pirate reprints were rare. That in itself suggests that the Strasbourg and Basle printers tended to offer a different product to the same market, primarily commercial

---

[47] Bietenholz, *Basle*, pp. 203–4; *Index 1*, pp. 171–2.

[48] Bietenholz, *Basle*, pp. 48–54. For an overview of the remarkable presence of Basle publishers in the sixteenth-century indexes, see *Index 10*, pp. 456–88.

[49] P. F. Grendler, *The Roman Inquisition and the Venetian Press, 1540–1605* (Princeton, 1977), pp. 311–14.

[50] Grendler, *The Roman Inquisition*, pp. 288–9, 321–4.

NOVVM IN

ſtrumentũ omne, diligenter ab ERASMO ROTERODAMO
recognitum & emendatum, nõ ſolum ad græcam ueritatem, ue-
rumetiam ad multorum utriuſq; linguæ codicum, eorumq; ue-
terum ſimul & emendatorum fidem, poſtremo ad pro-
batiſſimorum autorum citationem, emendationem
& interpretationem, præcipue, Origenis, Chry
ſoſtomi, Cyrilli, Vulgarij, Hieronymi, Cy-
priani, Ambroſij, Hilarij, Auguſti/
ni, una cũ Annotationibus, quæ
lectorem doceant, quid qua
ratione mutatum ſit.
Quiſquis igitur
amas ue-
ram
Theolo/
giam, lege, cogno
ſce, ac deinde iudica.
Neq; ſtatim offendere, ſi
quid mutatum offenderis, ſed
expende, num in melius mutatum ſit.

APVD INCLYTAM
GERMANIAE BASILAEAM.

CVM PRIVILEGIO
MAXIMILIANI CAESARIS AVGVSTI,
NE QVIS ALIVS IN SACRA ROMA-
NI IMPERII DITIONE, INTRA QVATV
OR ANNOS EXCVDAT, AVT ALIBI
EXCVSVM IMPORTET.

8.4   Erasmus, *Novum Instrumentum* (Basle: Johann Froben, 1516)

buyers at the Frankfurt fairs. While the publishing programmes differed in orientation and each centre, often each printer, developed individual relationships with specific authors, they also shared a set of common values that resulted from the close economic ties between the two Rhenish cities and the similarity of their positions in political and religious matters.

Summary bibliography

Bietenholz, P. G., *Die italienische Humanismus und die Blütezeit des Buchdrucks in Basel* (Basle, 1959).

Bietenholz, P. G., *Basle and France in the Sixteenth Century* (Geneva, 1971).
Gilly, C., *Spanien und der Basler Buchdruck bis 1600* (Basle, 1985).
Steinmann, M., *Johannes Oporinus* (Basle, 1966).
Welti, M. E., *Der Basler Buchdruck und Britannien* (Basle, 1964).

CHAPTER NINE

Books and the
English Reformation prior to 1558

David Loades

Protestant works

The Lollard inheritance

The use of printing for purposes of religious polemic was a German
innovation. Only after 1520, and the first reports of Lutheran influence in England, did concern begin to be expressed about the influence of the press. Nevertheless, the association between books and
heresy was over a century old by then, and English bishops had long
been accustomed to confronting their subversive influence. The Lollards
had been great writers, and great readers. In 1414, according to the
indictment later preferred against the offenders, 'plures libros Anglicos'
had been seized in Colchester, where they had been read 'both by day
and (night), secretly and openly, sometimes in company, and sometimes individually'.[1] Over 230 manuscripts of the Lollard Bible are
known and about 30 versions of the 'sermon cycle'. Contemporary
evidence also suggests that large quantities of ephemera were produced, usually referred to as *schedulae*, and *quaterni*, although these
now survive only in occasional fragments.[2] The manner and extent of
the interaction between existing Lollard ideas and the new theology
being imported from the Continent in the 1520s are matters of controversy among historians of the English Reformation. It has, however, been established that a number of Lollard tracts, books and
verses were printed in whole or in part by Protestant editors and
publishers. For example *The Lantern of Lyght*, issued in London by
Robert Redman, probably in 1535, also survives in two pre-Reformation

---

[1] Public Record Office [PRO] KB 9 204/1 nos 10–11, cited in A. Hudson, *Lollards and
Their Books*, (London, 1985), p. 182.
[2] *Schedulae* were probably single sheets, like the later printed broadsheets, and none
are known to survive. *Quaterni* were small quires of four or eight leaves. One survives
intact among the Cosin manuscripts in Durham, and portions of others in composite
manuscripts. Hudson, *Lollards*, pp. 183–4.

manuscripts.[3] Similarly *The examinacion of Master William Thorpe*
(Antwerp, 1530) was derived directly from a fifteenth-century source.
At least ten other examples have been identified.[4] There seem to have
been two main reasons for this. One was that their polemical armoury
could be added to with very little effort, given the congruity of the
ideas. The other was that the antiquity of the works themselves served
a useful purpose. As the author of *A proper dyaloge betwene a
gentillman and an husbandman* put it,

> For here agaynst the clergye can not bercke
> Sayenge as they do / thys is a newe werke
> Of heretykes contryved lately.
> And by this treatyse it apperyth playne
> That before oure dayes men dyd compleyne
> Agaynst clerckes ambycion so stately.[5]

Not only could such arguments be used to support the Protestant
historiography of the two churches, they also provided a partial answer
to the Catholic gibe 'where was your church before Luther?'.

There was another continuity in the English situation which could
make the voices of the early fifteenth century speak directly to the
audience of the 1530s, and that was the tendency to look to the royal
authority for redress of religious grievances. The author of *A compendious olde treatyse*, arguing for the vernacular Bible, probably in the
1430s, had written

> And therefore it were good to the Kyng and to the other
> lordes to make some remedy agaynst this constitucyon of
> Antechrist that sayethe it is unlawfull to us englyshe men
> to have in englyshe goddes lawe ...[6]

A hundred years later, when the work was printed by Johannes
Hoochstraten of Antwerp, it was one of a spate of books making the
same point.[7] By 1530 it was generally recognized that the press had
opened up formidable new opportunities to proselytisers of all kinds,
and that those who opposed the traditional order were making the most

---

[3] A.W. Pollard and G. R. Redgrave (eds), revised by W. A. Jackson, F. S. Ferguson and
K. F. Pantzer *A Short Title Catalogue of Books Printed in England, Scotland and Ireland,
... and of English Books Abroad*, (London, 1926, 1976–86) [*STC*], 15225. Hudson,
Lollards, p. 230.

[4] *STC*, 24045. Other examples include *Jack up Lande*, John Gough, 1536? (*STC*,
5098) and *The dore of holy scripture*, John Gough, 1540 (*STC*, 25587.5). Hudson,
Lollards, pp. 230–31.

[5] *STC*, 1462.3, sig. C6^v.

[6] *STC*, 302, sig. A6 and A6^v.

[7] E.g. *An exposition touching al the bokes of holie scripture*, R. Grafton, 1533 (*STC*,
3033.5) and *The summe of the holye scripture*, Antwerp, 1529 (*STC*, 3036).

frequent and effective use of its power. The anonymous Lollard who had originally written the *treatyse* had been over-optimistic in saying 'it lyeth never in Antichristes power to destroye all englyshe books/for as fast as he brennethe/other men shall drawe ... '.

John Foxe, writing in 1563, recognized the relative failure of the Lollards in this respect, despite the goodness of their cause, and contrasted this with the fortunes of the Protestants of his own day, ascribing the reason to the fact that 'God hath opened the press to preach, whose mouth the Pope is never able to stop with all the puissance of his triple crown ... '.[8] In 1408 the Convocation of Canterbury had prohibited the reproduction of English translations of the Scriptures, and in 1414 parliament had confirmed the legal right of ecclesiastical officials to proceed against the makers and writers of heretical books.[9] These simple measures had not prevented the production and circulation of Lollard material, but they had kept the situation under control. It was therefore with an initial sense of false security that Wolsey and his colleagues moved against the first Lutheran writings to come to their attention.

Early infiltrations of Lutheran books

The day-book of the Oxford bookseller John Dorne gives some indication of the identity of these works, which before the end of 1520 included *Operationes ... in Psalmos* and *De captivitate Babylonica*.[10] In Cambridge a lively discussion of Luther's protest had been going on as early as 1518, apparently with reference to his reply to Prierias and the *Resolutiones Disputationum*. The market at this stage was primarily academic, and interest seems to have sprung from existing concerns over ecclesiastical abuses, and from the influence of Colet and Erasmus. There is no suggestion that theological similarities between Luther and the existing Lollard tradition were a factor. The identifiable books were all in Latin, and were part of the common academic currency in western Europe. However, by 1521 the impact of the Lutheran controversy in Germany, and its rapid spread into the vernacular, were well known and the ecclesiastical authorities in England were alerted. On 14 May

---

[8] J. Foxe, *Actes and Monuments of the English Martyrs*, S. R. Cattley and G. Townsend (eds), (London, 1837–41), III, p. 720.

[9] D. Wilkins, *Concilia Magnae Britanniae et Hiberniae*, (London, 1737), III, p. 317; statute 2 Henry V, 1, c.7. This latter confirmed an earlier statute of 1401. Such proceedings were under the common law.

[10] F. Madan (ed.), *The Day Book of John Dorne, Bookseller in Oxford A.D. 1520* (Oxford, 1885).

Cardinal Wolsey issued a legatine commission, directed to all the English and Welsh bishops, and commanded that it be read in every church at the time of mass. This warned its hearers against 'many and diverse pestiferous and pernicious propositions and errors of Martin Luther, setting forth both Greek and Bohemian heresies'.[11] All writings containing such errors (which were promulgated in a separate schedule) were to be surrendered to the bishop or his commissary within 15 days. This was effective enough to enable the cardinal to stage a number of book burnings later in the year, but seems to have done nothing to check the stream of imports. In spite of the reference to 'Bohemian', that is Lollard heresy in the commission, Wolsey was probably more concerned to do his duty in enforcing the papal prohibition within his jurisdiction than to confront an urgent English problem. The controversy was almost exclusively clerical, and there is no indication that any Englishman had yet written on the Lutheran side, either in Latin or in English. Such English involvement as has left any record was, prior to 1525, entirely on the Catholic side.

In 1521 Richard Pynson published the king's *Assertio Septem Sacramentorum*, and in the same year Wynkyn de Worde printed the sermon that John Fisher had preached at the Paul's Cross book burning.[12] 1522 saw a second edition of the *Assertio*, and in 1523 Pynson also published *De Libero arbitrio uersus Melanchthonem* by Alphonsus de Villa Sancta. John Fisher's *Assertionis Lutheranae Confutatio*, which appeared in the same year, was issued from the press of P. Quentell in Cologne, presumably because Fisher rightly saw Germany as the centre of the storm, and still regarded the English problem as marginal.[13]

The evidence for early Lutheran writing in England is slight and circumstantial. In 1524 Cuthbert Tunstall, the Bishop of London, was sufficiently concerned to summon the printers and booksellers of the city to meet him. Having warned them afresh of the consequences of handling heretical books, he then proceeded to issue the first licensing order. No book was to be imported without episcopal permission, and no new work was to be published without the consent of a board of censors consisting of himself, Fisher, Wolsey and the Archbishop of Canterbury.[14] Perhaps this latter regulation was occasioned by the ap-

---

[11] J. Strype, *Ecclesiastical Memorials*, (Oxford, 1822), I, pt. ii, p.21. [*Eccl. Mem.*]

[12] *STC*, 13078. *The sermon of John, the bysshop of Rochester* ... (*STC*, 10894), which was reprinted in 1522, 1527, 1554 and 1556.

[13] *STC*, 24728. Fisher also published two further anti-Protestant works in Cologne, *Defensio Regie assertionis* (1525) and *De veritate corporis et sanguinis Christi* (1527). W. Clebsch, *England's Earliest Protestants, 1520–1535*, (Yale, 1964), pp. 14–19.

[14] P. Took, 'Government and the printing trade, 1540–1560' (PhD, London 1978), p. 67.

pearance of some item, now lost, which was never specifically identified. More likely it was purely a precaution.

In 1526 and 1527 the English printers John Gough, Thomas Berthelet and Robert Redman were briefly in trouble for publishing without episcopal licences, but their offences seem to have been purely technical. The foreign printers, such as Pynson and de Worde, who dominated London publishing at this time, were heavily dependent on royal and ecclesiastical favour to protect them from the jealous hostility of the London Stationers, and were in no mood, or position, to take risks.[15] Controversial lines were not clearly drawn in the 1520s, and it is possible that such books as Erasmus's *Sermon of the exedynge great mercy of god* (Berthelet, 1526)[16] were regarded with suspicion, but no explicitly heretical work can be attributed to an English press until the troubled years of the following decade.

The use of continental presses

Protestant printing in English and for the English market began in 1525, when the first version of Tyndale's translation of the New Testament was attempted in Cologne. In 1526 the better known, and complete edition of P. Schoeffer of Worms followed, and it was this version which soon began to appear in large numbers on the London market. Tunstall responded quickly, and his alarm can be clearly detected in the language of his proclamation of 23 October: 'many children of iniquity, maintainers of Luther's sect, blinded through extreme wickedness and wandering from the way of truth and the catholic faith, craftily have translated the New Testament into our English tongue, intermeddling therewith many heretical articles and erroneous opinions ... '.[17]

All copies were to be surrendered to the archdeacons within 30 days. Ten further editions followed over the next decade, mostly from the Antwerp presses of De Keyser, Cock and Hoochstraten.[18] These editions probably numbered about 1 500 copies each, and the English

---

[15] A statute of 1484 (1 Richard III c.9) had explicitly exempted printers and booksellers from the ban which prohibited other alien craftsmen from working in the city. The Stationers' Company, to which most of the English printers belonged, campaigned assiduously thereafter for the removal of that exemption. C. Blagden, *The Stationers' Company; a History, 1403–1959*, (London, 1960).

[16] *STC*, 10474.

[17] Wilkins *Concilia*, III, p. 705. The Cologne imprint was frustrated by the local authorities, and only a few copies of the Gospels of Matthew and Mark reached England.

[18] *STC*, 2823–2830.5. C. H. Williams, *William Tyndale*, (Stanford, 1969). D. Daniell, *William Tyndale*, (London, 1994).

Thr.prologge.

I haue here translated (brethern and susters moost dere and tenderly beloued in Christ) the newe Testament for youre spirituall edyfyinge / consolacion / and solas: Exhortynge instantly and besechynge those that are better sene in the tonges then y / and that haue hyer giftes of grace to interpret the sence of the scripture / and meanynge of the spyrite / then y / to consydre and pondre my laboure / and that with the spyrite of mekenes. And yf they perceyve in eny places that y haue not attayned the very sence of the tonge / or meanynge of the scripture / or haue not geven the right englysshe worde / that they put to there hande to amende it / remembrynge that so is there duetie to doo. For we haue not receyved the giftes of god for oure selues only / or for to hyde them: but for to bestowe them vnto the honouringe of god and christ / and edyfyinge of the congregacion / which is the body of christ.

The causes that moved me to translate / y thought better that other shulde ymagion / then that y shulde rehearce them. More over y supposed yt superfluous / for who ys so blynde to axe why lyght shulde be shewed to them that walke in derknes / where they cannot but stomble / and where to stomble ys the daunger of eternall dammacion / ether so despyghtfull that he wolde envye eny man (y speake nott his brother) so necessary a thinge / or so bedlem madde to affyrme that good is the naturall cause of yvell / and derknes to procede oute of lyght / and that lyinge shulde be grounded in trougth and veryte / and nott rather clene contrary / that lyght destroyeth derknes / and veritie reproveth all manner lyinge.

A ij

9.1 The beginning of the unfinished publication of William Tyndale's translation of the New Testament ([Cologne]: [H. Fuchs?], 1525)

authorities felt deluged. Tunstall succeeded in seizing some, and arrested one or two of the agents, but was unable or unwilling to exact severe penalties.[19] Even when Sir Thomas More mobilized the royal

---

[19] Humphrey Monmouth, Tyndale's principal financial backer, was arrested and inter-

authority in support of the bishops in 1530, and two of the colporteurs were executed, the traffic continued to grow and diversify. Tyndale followed up his translations with *A compendious introduccion ... to the pistle off Paul to the Romayns* (Schoeffer, 1526); *The parable of the wicked mammon* (Hoochstraten? Antwerp? 1528); *The obedience of a christen man* (Hoochstraten? Antwerp? 1528); and *The practyse of prelates* (Hoochstraten, 1530).[20] In his wake, a number of other Englishmen also began to publish translations or original works of controversy – George Joye, John Frith, William Barlow, Simon Fish and William Roy. The majority of these were also published in Antwerp, which was clearly the main centre, although Barlow's *Rede me and be nott wrothe* came from the press of J. Schott of Strasburg.[21] The importance of Antwerp was partly determined by geographic convenience, and partly by the sympathetic presence of the Merchant Adventurers' headquarters, which provided a periodic refuge and a regular means of access to the trading community. Despite the risks involved, the illicit book trade afforded a healthy profit. Robert Necton, who was arrested in 1530, confessed to buying English books in the Low Countries for an average of 13d. a volume, and selling them all over the south of England at 2s. 4d. or 2s. 8d. each.[22] The demand was strong, and since the purchasers also ran considerable risks it must be presumed that they paid serious attention to what they read. The authorities had good reason to be concerned, because the actual possessors of the forbidden books represented only the tip of the iceberg. As with the earlier Lollard manuscripts, they were passed from hand to hand, and read aloud in company, so that large numbers of the illiterate came within reach of their message. Once Protestant polemic moved from Latin to the vernacular, the whole community was potentially open to its influence.[23]

By 1532, when Thomas More resigned the chancellorship and the climate in England began to change, some 27 or 28 English Protestant books had been printed on the Continent, eight of them translations of Scriptures. Henry VIII's growing dispute with the papacy over his marriage did not make it safe to publish heretical works in England, and

---

rogated in 1528, but his influential friends in the City managed to secure his release. Van Ruremond, one of the main itinerant booksellers, was likewise caught, but released after doing penance. Strype, *Eccl. Mem.* I, pt i, pp. 487–93.

[20] *STC*, 24438; 24454; 24446; 24465.

[21] *STC*, 1462.7. See also B. Cottret, 'Traducteurs et divulgateurs clandestins de la Réforme dans l'Angleterre henricienne', *Revue d'histoire moderne et contemporaine*, **28** (1981), 464–80.

[22] Foxe, *Actes and Monuments*, J. Pratt (ed.), (London, 1853–70), IV, p. 652.

[23] For a full consideration of this point, see Margaret Aston, *Lollards and Reformers: Images and Literacy in Late Medieval Religion*, (London, 1984).

did not affect the king's formal hostility to Lutheranism, but it did reduce pressure on the book trade and complicate the role of the royal authority in censorship. In 1530 the Crown had effectively taken over control of printing and distribution from the Church, issuing its own index and placing supervision in the hands of the council.[24] By 1532 it was clear that this control was going to be used for political rather than doctrinal purposes, and that the king's attitude towards vernacular Scripture in particular was becoming ambivalent. The appearance of John Fisher's *De Causa Matrimonii serenissimi Regis Angliae* in Alcalá in 1530 was suffficient indication of the dangerous cross-currents ahead. During the years of Thomas Cromwell's ascendancy, between 1532 and 1540, 19 translations of portions of Scripture into English were printed on the continent, mostly in Antwerp or Paris, but only 14 other books with Protestant implications. Of the latter, five were editions of two works by Girolamo Savonarola, the fifteenth-century Florentine reformer, *An exposition after the maner of contemplacyon* (Antwerp, Ruremond and Rouen, Le Roux) and *An exposicyon upon the li psalme* (Le Roux and Paris, Reynault).[25] The fates of William Tyndale on the one hand and Sir Thomas More on the other indicate the strict and idiosyncratic path of orthodoxy to which the King of England expected authors to adhere during this period.

After the passage of the Act of Six Articles in 1539, and Cromwell's fall in the following year, the situation of the late 1520s briefly returned. John Bale, John Hooper, Miles Coverdale and a number of others who had enjoyed the patronage, protection or indulgence of the Lord Privy Seal withdrew to the Continent, and the scale of exile publishing again increased.[26] The pattern, however, was different in a number of respects. Vernacular Scripture, which had been the main

---

[24] In May 1530 the king issued a decree in Star Chamber condemning Tyndale's New Testament, and set up a commission from the universities 'to examine certain English books commonly read among the people containing erroneous and pestiferous words, sentences and conclusion', *Letters and Papers of the Reign of Henry VIII*, (London, 1862–1910), IV, 3, no. 2059. A proclamation of June 1530 effectively set up the king as the arbiter of heresy. P. L. Hughes and J. F. Larkin, *Tudor Royal Proclamations*, (London, 1964), I, pp. 193–7.

[25] *STC*, 21789.5; 21789.6; 21790; 21790.5. Three editions of the *Exposition* were also printed in England.

[26] For a consideration of Cromwell's role as patron and protector of radical writers and preachers during this period, see S. Brigden, 'Thomas Cromwell and the Brethren', in C. Cross, D. Loades and J. J. Scarisbrick (eds), *Law and Government under the Tudors: Essays Presented to Sir Geoffrey Elton*, (Cambridge, 1988). On the exiles of this period, see E. F. M. Hildebrandt 'English Protestant exiles in northern Switzerland and Strasbourg, 1539–1547', (PhD, Durham, 1982), *passim*. Also S. Brigden, *London and the Reformation*, (Oxford, 1989).

issue in the earlier period, was no longer contentious because the reaction in England did not extend to the withdrawal of the Great Bible. Nor did old Lollard works any longer feature. Straightforward polemic was much more in evidence, works such as John Bale's *The image of bothe churches after the revelacion of saynt Johan the evangelyst* (Antwerp: Mierdman? 1545?), Henry Brinkelow's *The Complaynt of Roderyke Mors* (Strasbourg: W. Kopfel, 1542?) or William Turner's *Huntyng and fyndyng out of the romishe fox* (Bonn: L. Mylius, 1543).[27] The influence of Switzerland and of Swiss theology was also apparent for the first time. Antwerp was no longer secure, and Lutheran territories less welcoming, so the English exiles went instead to Martin Bucer's Strasbourg or Heinrich Bullinger's Zurich. Bibliander's *Godly consultation* was translated into English in 1542 (Antwerp: M. Crom), Bullinger's *The christen state of matrimonye* in 1541 (same) and *The reckening and declaration of the faith of Zwingly in 1543* (Antwerp: Ruremond).[28] Justus Jonas and Melanchthon also attracted translators, but these were the years in which the Swiss connection, which was to dominate English theology after 1547, became firmly established.[29] Over 40 English titles were published abroad between 1540 and 1547, and less than a quarter of those were Bibles or parts of Bibles. In spite of its general lack of attractiveness to religious exiles, Antwerp was still very much the main publishing centre, 28 English titles coming from its presses during these years. Strasbourg, Wesel, Bonn and Zurich produced the remainder.

The years immediately after Henry VIII's death saw dramatic developments in domestic publishing, as we shall see, but the position and attitude of the exiles changed more slowly. John Hooper, for example, remained in Zurich until 1549, producing three works from the press of Anton Fries – *An answer unto my lord of Wynchesters booke* (1547), *A Declaration of Christe and of his offyce* (1547) and *A declaration of the ten holy commandmentes* (1549).[30] John Bale published two books in Wesel with Van der Straten, and one in Antwerp with Mierdman, before returning in 1548. No more than 11 or 12 English Protestant works were published abroad during Edward VI's six-year reign, plus six new testaments and an edition of the Matthew Bible from Froschauer of Zurich in 1550.[31] By that time the traffic was moving the other way, with Martin Bucer, Peter Martyr and a substantial number of other continental Protestants seeking refuge in England. By 1550 even those Englishmen who

---

[27] *STC*, 1296.5; 3759.5; 24353.
[28] *STC*, 3047, 4045; 26138.
[29] Hildebrandt, 'English Protestant exiles'.
[30] *STC*, 13741; 13745; 13746.
[31] *STC*, 2079.8.

had been most thoroughly imbued with the radical theology of Zurich and Geneva felt that it was safe – and indeed necessary – to go home, and for a short period exile publishing ceased altogether. At this time also Stephen Mierdman, who had already handled a number of English books in Antwerp, was able to set up business in London. Walter Lynne, Thomas Gualthier, Egidius van der Erve and over 50 other foreign printers, stationers and booksellers followed suit, and for a short time the exclusiveness of the London companies was overcome.[32]

However, the days of Josias were short, and by the end of 1553 most of these expatriates had returned from whence they came, spurred on by Queen Mary's council, and the return of the mass to English churches. Over the next five years, English Protestant exiles returned to Germany, Switzerland and the Rhineland in unprecedented numbers – almost 800 have been counted.[33] Of these only a handful became involved in the process of religious polemic, but their impact was out of all proportion to their number. Some 70 works of polemical or pastoral nature were printed abroad during the five years of Mary's reign, and smuggled into England – a source of constant anxiety and unceasing effort on the part of the council.[34] To what extent this was an organized campaign, and to what extent the result of the uncoordinated zeal of groups and individuals remains uncertain. Fifty years ago Christina Garrett argued that a 'committee of sustainers' in England provided the financial backing, and a 'master mind', whom she tentatively identified as Sir John Cheke, organized the actual publication.[35] Close examination has undermined much of this hypothesis, but a few years ago (in an unpublished thesis) Patricia Took revived the idea, suggesting that there were actually several groups operating at different times, a view also supported more recently by Andrew Pettegree.[36]

---

[32] Mierdman was allowed to employ a number of his fellow countrymen, and some of the English printers, particularly Day and Singleton, were hospitable to the foreign workers, thus affording them protection. Took, 'Government and the printing trade', pp. 147, 185. For the connections of the English Protestants with Emden, see also Andrew Pettegree, 'The English Church at Emden', in Andrew Pettegree, Marian Protestantism; Six Studies, (Aldershot, 1996), pp. 10–38.

[33] C. H. Garrett, The Marian Exiles (Cambridge, 1938), p. 32. Also Pettegree, Marian Protestantism, pp. 151–67.

[34] E. J. Baskerville, A Chronological Bibliography of Propaganda and Polemic Published between 1553 and 1558, American Philosophical Society, (Philadelphia, 1979); J. Loach, 'Pamphlets and politics, 1553–1558', Bulletin of the Institute of Historical Research, 68 (1975), 31–45; Took, 'Government and the printing trade'.

[35] Garrett, Marian Exiles, pp. 1–29. Pettegree, Marian Protestantism, pp. 118–28.

[36] Took, 'Government and the printing trade', pp. 225–37, which also suggests that Nicholas Hill, a Dutchman by birth, may have returned to the Continent and been collaborating with Van der Erve at Emden.

The first, consisting of John Day, Hugh Singleton and Anthony Skoloker, all established London printers, produced about 26 books over the first 15 months of the reign until broken up by the arrest of Day and (probably) Singleton in October 1554. According to a theory advanced in 1972 by L. P. Fairfield, Day and Singleton produced the 15 titles bearing the imprint 'Michael Wood, Rouen', and Skoloker those bearing the imprint 'Nicholas Dorcaster'. 'Wood' may have been produced in the Low Countries, or at a secret press in London or East Anglia; 'Dorcaster' most likely in Antwerp. The responsibility of Day for the 'Michael Wood' titles seems to be reasonably well established, but the evidence for the remainder of this thesis is largely circumstantial.[37] What is clear is that over 20 books of non-violent, and largely non-political, Protestant exhortation had been released on to the London market by the summer of 1554. Typical of these works was *A dialogue or familiar talke betweene two neighbours concernyng the chyefest ceremonyes set uppe agayne* (Wood, February 1554).[38] William Cooke, son of the prominent exile Sir Anthony, and brother-in-law of Sir William Cecil was, according to John Foxe, arrested in 1554 for being involved with Day in the publication of the 1553 edition of Stephen Gardiner's *De Vera Obedientia Oratio*.[39] This suggests that the Cooke household may have been behind 'Michael Wood', either as patrons or directors, but the evidence will not sustain a firmer conclusion. Day and Singleton both fled to the continent in the early part of 1555, and the second phase of the exile campaign began. In this phase neither Day nor (apparently) Skoloker played any part, but Singleton went to Wesel, and in collaboration with Johan Lambrecht published 14 titles before returning to England on the accession of Elizabeth.[40] The other main centre of exile printing was the conveniently placed town of Emden, where the press of Van der Erve, the one-time deacon of John a Lasco's London congregation, published 16 titles in 1555 and 1556.[41] Strasbourg, Zurich, and later Geneva also saw the production of exile literature, but on a smaller scale.

---

[37] L. P. Fairfield, 'The mysterious press of "Michael Wood", 1553–4', *The Library* (1972), 221–32.

[38] *STC*, 10383. John Knox, so fiercely polemical later in the reign, was at this stage producing such works as *A faythfull admonition* (*STC*, 15069) and *A percel of the vi psalme expounded* (*STC*, 15074.4).

[39] Foxe, *Actes*, Pratt (ed.), VIII (App.); Took, 'Government and the printing trade', p. 225.

[40] Baskerville, *Chronological Bibliography*, pp. 6–10. For the arguments relating to Skoloker's involvement, see Took, 'Government and the printing trade', pp. 225–6.

[41] Andrew Pettegree, *Emden and the Dutch Revolt*, (Aldershot, 1995).

¶ To the mooste excellent
and vertuoufe Queene, Ma-
rye by the grace of GOD,
Quene of England, Fraunce,
and Irelande, and Defendour
of the fayth, John Chriftofer-
fon her graces Chapleyne, &
daylyoratour wifheth a long,
a quiete, and a profperous
reygne with the daylye
encreafe of al godly
vertue.

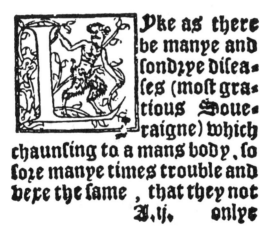

ⱳke as there
be manye and
fondrye difea-
fes (moft gra-
tious Soue-
raigne) which
chaunfing to a mans body, fo
fore manye times trouble and
bere the fame , that they not
A.ij. onlye

9.2   First page of John Christopherson's *An exhortation to all menne to take hede and beware of rebellion* (London: J. Cawood, 1554)

Whether any single mind controlled this activity is uncertain. John Bale was certainly an active author, editor and translator, as well as a tireless controversialist.[42] He travelled widely, and may well have been responsible for a number of anonymous tracts, but only *The vocacyon ... to the bishoprick of Ossorie in Irelande* (Wesel: Lambrecht? 1553)

---

[42] L. P. Fairfield, *John Bale*, (West Lafayette, 1976); Took, 'Government and the printing trade', p.115.

appeared over his own name.[43] Another possible candidate is John Ponet, the Edwardian Bishop of Winchester. He was the highest-ranking ecclesiastical exile, and helped to steer the propaganda campaign on to a more political course with his *Shorte treatise of politike power* (Strasbourg: W. Kopfel, 1556).[44] He published two other controversial works in Strasbourg, but his influence in other centres can only be conjectured. Straightforward religious polemic continued to be the staple diet of the exile propagandists, well aware of the extreme pressure that the English government was bringing to bear on dissidents after March 1555, and of the need to stiffen their perseverance in the faith. Two works by Thomas Becon, under the pseudonym 'Gracious Menewe' were typical of this genre, *A confutacion of that Popishe and Antichristian doctryne whiche mainteineth ... the sacrament under one kind* (Wesel? Singleton? 1555) and *A plaine subversyon of or turnyng up syde down of all the Arguments that the Popecatholykes can make for the maintenaunce of auricular confession* (Wesel? Singleton? 1555).[45] However, after the arrival of Philip in England in July 1554, the revival of papal jurisdiction in December, and the beginning of active persecution in March 1555, exile propaganda began to acquire a more political edge. One new development was the direct celebration of the recent martyrs, works such as *Certein godly learned and comfortable conferences betwene the two Reverende Fathers and the holy martyrs of Christe D.Nicholas Ridley ... and M. Hughe Latimer* (Emden? Van der Erve? 1556) and *A Godly Medytacyon Composed by ... J(ohn) B(radford) Precher who lately was burnte at Smytfelde ...* (1555).[46] A second development consisted of challenging the legitimacy of the queen's government on religious grounds. This was done most notably in books such as Christopher Goodman's *How superior powers oght to be obeyd* (Geneva, J. Crispin, 1558) and John Knox's *First Blast of the Trumpet against the Monstrous Regiment of Women* (Geneva: J. Poullain, 1558).[47] This would have been deeply repugnant to the earlier generation of Protestant leaders, such as Cranmer, and was symptomatic of the extent to which continental, and particularly Calvinist, influences were beginning to transform English thinking. This was a transformation cut short

---

[43] *STC*, 1307.

[44] *STC*, 20178; D. H. Wollman 'The biblical justification for resistance to authority in Ponet's and Goodman's Polemics', *Sixteenth Century Journal*, 13 (1982–83), 29–41. W. S. Hudson, *John Ponet: Advocate of Limited Monarchy*, (Chicago, 1942).

[45] *STC*, 17821, 17822.

[46] *STC*, 21047.3, 3483.

[47] *STC*, 12020; 15070. Wollman, 'Biblical justification'. See also J. E. A. Dawson, 'Christopher Goodman and his Place in the development of English Protestant thought' (PhD, Durham, 1978).

by Elizabeth's accession, but with considerable long-term importance in English puritanism. Some of the exile products, such as *A Warning for England* (Emden? Van der Erve? 1555) or Bartholomew Traheron's 1558 tract with the same title, were so frankly political as scarcely to warrant consideration in this context.[48] Nevertheless, the most influential product of the exile press was not political at all, and harkened back to the days of Tyndale's New Testament. This was the Geneva Bible, set up by Sir Thomas Bodley, and prepared by William Whittingham and Anthony Gilby. By the accidents of fortune, it was not published until after Elizabeth was on the throne, but no discussion of the exile would be complete without reference to it.

The distribution of exile writings in England appears to have been a sophisticated and successful operation, but many things about it are unclear. Foxe is our main source of information, and he was mainly concerned to record the things that went wrong, as when about 60 Londoners were arrested in October 1554 for 'having and selling certain books which were sent into England by the preachers that fled to Germany and other parts ... '.[49] The imprisonment of William Seres for unspecified offences, and his connections with Cecil, may point to another part of the machinery which the authorities succeeded in dismantling, but the books kept on coming. In December 1555 Giovanni Michieli, the Venetian ambassador, reported that 'of late a great quantity of books printed in English have been distributed clandestinely throughout London, concerning the king individually and his mode of government ... '.[50] The Marian council was no more successful than its predecessors had been in checking the illicit import of forbidden books, which continued to be one of the most important features of the English Reformation.

Because of the distinctive manner in which the Reformation developed in England, there was also an intermittent but at times substantial traffic in Catholic literature printed abroad. The largest and most straightforward part of this traffic was not controversial, but arose from the limitations of skill and resources within the home-based industry. Most kinds of service book could be produced more cheaply and efficiently in Antwerp or Paris than in London, and before 1534 the vast majority were imported – 47 different editions of the Sarum Breviary (as against four), and 54 editions of the Sarum Missal (as against six).[51] Only primers were printed in England in any quantity – 37 editions as against

---

[48] *STC*, 10024; *A warning to England to repente*, Wesel, P. de Zuttere? (*STC*, 24174).
[49] Foxe, *Actes*, Pratt (ed.), VI, p. 561.
[50] *Calendar of State Papers, Venetian*, VI, i, pp. 269–70.
[51] Took, 'Government and the printing trade', App. III.

52 imported. However, in 1534 the statute which finally withdrew the special privileges of the foreign printers in London also placed considerable restrictions on the importation of books.[52] The reason offered for both actions was the same – that the skills of the English printers themselves were now adequate to meet all demands. Between 1534 and 1553 no breviaries or missals were imported, but this change probably owed as much to the changing religious climate as it did to the enforcement of the Act. Three breviaries and no missals were produced in England during the same period. Primers were less affected by the 'King's proceedings', and are probably a better measure of the Act's effectiveness. Over the same 19 years 65 primers were printed in England, and 21 imported.[53] After the systematic destruction of such service books during the reign of Edward VI, the restocking required by Mary's council resulted in a sharp upturn of demand, and at first the London Stationers do not seem to have been concerned to enforce the 1534 Act. Of the eight breviaries produced between 1553 and 1558, two were printed in London and six imported; for missals the comparable figures are two and three; while no fewer than 24 primers were issued in England, and ten imported. It was not until 1557 that a test case was brought against a London stationer for having imported 178 bound service books from Rouen, in contravention of the statute;[54] and shortly thereafter the outbreak of war with France finally brought that lucrative trade to an end.

Catholic controversial literature was much less significant in quantity, although the individual items were often important. Henry VIII's divorce was the first incident to drive dissident authors overseas. Apart from Fisher's tract which we have already noticed, in 1532 Thomas Abell resorted to De Keyser's press in Antwerp to print *An answere. That by no maner of lawe maye it be lawfull for King Henry the ayght to be divorsid*,[55] while Reginald Pole's celebrated *Pro ecclesiasticae*

---

[52] Statute 25 Henry VIII c.15. The importation of bound books was prohibited.

[53] Took, 'Government and the printing trade', App. III. For the comparable production of ABCs, catechisms and other elementary works, see P. Tudor, 'Religious instruction for children and adolescents in the early English Reformation', *Journal of Ecclesiastical History*, 35 (1984), 391–413.

[54] It was from the press of Robert Valentin in Rouen that the majority of English service books were imported. Between 1554 and 1557 he published two Manuals, three Missals, nine Primers, one Processional and two Breviaries for the English market. (Took, 'Government and the printing trade', p. 256). By 1556 the demand for these works seems to have been declining, because the expected monastic revival had not materialized. For the case against Francis Sparge, see H. J. Byrom, 'Some exchequer cases involving members of the book trade, 1534–58', *The Library* (1936), 413.

[55] *STC*, 61.

unitatis defensione was published in Rome in 1536. Of these only Abell's could possibly be described as popular polemic, and those Catholic authors who later endeavoured to oppose the Edwardian settlement by similar means retained the same scholarly and somewhat limited appeal. Richard Smith, Maurice Chauncey (an ex-Carthusian), William Rastell, and the printer Robert Caly were among those who fled abroad to escape the Prayer Book. Caly printed a small number of books in Rouen, including Stephen Gardiner's *An explication and assertion of the true catholique fayth* and Smith's tract against the marriage of priests. Chauncey went as far as Mainz to find a printer for his *Historia Aliquot Martyrum* (1550) in defence of the Carthusians, More and Fisher;[56] but the efforts of these exiles can only be described as fragmentary and muted by comparison with those of the Protestants who were to follow them across the Channel in the next reign. It was not to be until the reign of Elizabeth that an effective Catholic press in exile began to develop. The adherents of the traditional faith did not adapt easily to the roles of opposition and evangelism.

The earliest involvement of the London Stationers with heretical printing is, as we have seen, very hard to trace. Apart from Tunstall's warning of 1524, there is no suggestion of their participation before the arrival of the first Tyndale New Testaments. In 1527, however, Robert Wyer appeared before the Vicar General, charged with publishing a work entitled *Symbolum Apostolicum*, which was said to contain many errors, and to have been printed without licence.[57] At the same time, when Tyndale himself was in London, he seems to have had secret discussions with John Rastell for the printing of his *Wicked Mammon* and *Obedience of a Christen man*, discussions which were abandoned owing to the vigilance of the ecclesiastical authorities, and the work transferred to Antwerp.[58] Over the next five years, while the defence of traditional orthodoxy was still unambiguous, no offensive works found their way into print in England, although Thomas Berthelet's two editions of Colet's famous sermon of 1511 (1530 and 1531) must have been sailing fairly close to the wind.[59] The two royal proclamations of 1529 and 1530 were accompanied by schedules of forbidden books, all of which appear to have been either Lollard manuscripts or works

---

[56] *STC*, 11592; Strype, *Eccl. Mem.* II, pt i, p. 307.

[57] Took, 'Government and the printing trade', p. 100.

[58] Ibid., p. 98.

[59] *STC*, 5550; 5550.5. Colet's sermon had originally been published in Latin in 1512, so the reason for its translation and reissue at this stage must be in question. On the significance of Colet see also P. I. Kaufman, 'John Colet's *Opus de Sacramentis* and Clerical Anti-clericalism', *Journal of British Studies*, 22 (i) (1982), 1–22.

printed abroad.[60] But by the end of 1532 the situation had changed sufficiently for Robert Redman to publish *The Lanterne of Lyght*, a well-known Lollard work, bearing his own colophon.[61] Redman, Rastell and Stephen Gough were all strong Protestant sympathizers, and under the patronage and protection of Thomas Cromwell issued a number of reforming works until 1539. In 1536, for example, Redman published Richard Taverner's translation of *The confessyon of the fayth of the Germaynes. To whiche is added the apologie of Melanchthon*.[62] Books by Robert Barnes, Thomas Becon and Johann Bugenhagen were also published in London during the same period, and the changing official attitude towards vernacular Scripture can be seen in the appearance of *Hereafter folowe x certayne places of scrypture* (Wyer, 1533) and *A concordance of the New Testament* (T. Gybson, 1535).[63] Convocation had in 1534 asked the king to approve a translation for general use, and although he did not actually do so until 1537, John Nicholson of Southwark had by then published three editions of Coverdale's version without hindrance.[64] The main driving force behind this campaign was probably Thomas Cranmer, the Archbishop of Canterbury, but it was also consistent with Thomas Cromwell's plans for the promotion of the religious settlement which he had helped to engineer.

Although Henry VIII never relaxed his hostility to sacramental heresy, he was prepared to accept a wide range of reforming measures. The monasteries were dissolved, many saints' days abrogated, and pilgrimage shrines destroyed. *The instituton of a christen man*, published by Thomas Berthelet in 1537, and usually known as the Bishops' Book, marked the most advanced point in the Henrician Reformation.[65] By the following year clerical alarm and the king's own uncertainty had checked the reforming initiative. A proclamation of 16 November 1538 clearly reflected the tensions within the English church. Existing licensing regulations in respect of imported or home-produced books were repeated: 'that no person or persons in this realm shall from henceforth print any book in the English tongue, unless upon examination made by some of his grace's Privy Council, or other such as his highness shall appoint, they shall have licence so to do ... '. Books 'of divine Scripture

---

[60] Hughes and Larkin, *Tudor Royal Proclamations*, I, pp. 185 ff., 194.

[61] *STC*, 15225. This dating follows Took, 'Government and the printing trade', p. 99. *STC*, suggests 1535? Other Lollard works, such as *The praier and complaynte of the ploweman unto Christe* (*STC*, 20036.5) were also printed in London before the end of 1532.

[62] *STC*, 908.

[63] *STC*, 3034.5; 3046.

[64] Strype, *Eccl. Mem.*, I, pt i, p. 472; *STC*, 2063.3, 2064, 2065.

[65] Strype, *Eccl. Mem.*, I, pt i, pp. 485–7; *STC*, 5163–7 (5 edns).

in the English tongue with any annotations in the margin, or any prologue or additions ... ' were to be treated in the same way.[66] Plain translations were not affected, nor works written in the learned tongue. Anabaptists and Sacramentaries were fiercely condemned, and the canon law on clerical marriage upheld. On the other hand the cult of Thomas Becket was denounced, and the use of traditional ceremonies restricted to those 'yet not abrogated by the King's authority'.[67] No fewer than 14 editions of the English Bible were printed between 1535 and 1541, together with several New Testaments, three versions of the Psalms and two of the Proverbs. Despite the apparently draconian regulations in force from 1530, such overtly Protestant tracts as George Joye's *Compendyouse somme of the very christen relygyon*, or the same author's *An apologye made to satisfye ... W. Tindale* (both J. Byddell, 1535) were allowed to circulate freely.[68]

Thomas Cromwell's propaganda campaign on behalf of the royal supremacy, which produced a number of works like Thomas Starkey's *Exhortation to the people* (T. Berthelet, 1536) and Stephen Gardiner's *De Vera Obedienta oratio* (Berthelet, 1535),[69] is a well-known phenomenon which falls outside the scope of this discussion, but should be noticed in passing because of the peculiarly political nature of the religious changes that took place during his ascendancy. With his fall in 1540, effective censorship returned. Although new patents were issued to Cromwell's protégés Grafton, Whitchurch and Mayler, and the Great Bible continued in authorised use, no fresh editions were printed between 1541 and 1547. In the former year Richard Grafton was imprisoned for daring to print so sensitive a work as Melanchthon's tract against the Act of Six Articles, and eight other printers were interrogated by the council and placed under recognizances in 1543.[70] This

---

[66] Hughes and Larkin, *Tudor Royal Proclamations*, I, pp. 270–76. For these marginalia, see also Strype, *Eccl. Mem.*, I, pt i, p. 486.

[67] Hughes and Larkin, *Tudor Royal Proclamations*, I, p. 273.

[68] *STC*, 14821; 14820.

[69] *STC*, 23236; 11584. Another work of equal significance was Edward Fox's *De vera differentia regiae potestatis et ecclesiasticae*, T. Berthelet, 1534 (*STC*, 11218). See also Strype, *Eccl. Mem.*, I, pt i, pp. 263–71. For a recent scholarly discussion of Cromwell's propaganda campaign, see G. R. Elton, *Reform and Renewal*, (Cambridge, 1973).

[70] *Letters and Papers*, XVI, 422. J. R. Dasent (ed.) *Acts of the Privy Council*, (London, 1890–1964), I, pp. 107, 117. The extent to which this development took reformers outside England by surprise can be judged from a letter written by John Butler to Bullinger from Basle in February 1540: 'Barnes and others are preaching the word powerfully in England. Books of every kind may safely be exposed for sale; which fact is so important to my excellent friend Froschauer that I have thought it right to make him acquainted with it.' H. Robinson (ed.) *Original Letters Relative to the English Reformation*, (London, 1847), II, p. 627.

flurry of activity was partly the result of Gardiner's ascendancy in the council, and partly of a rapid upsurge in the output of controversial ephemera. These constituted a new phenomenon in English printing, akin to the German *Flügschriften* of the 1520s. Very few now survive, but they appear to have consisted mostly of scurrilous attacks on the mass or the clergy, lampoons against Gardiner, attacks on Cromwell's memory, and defences of him.[71] Some were handwritten, but most took the form of printed broadsheets and ballads. The appetite of the Londoners for such entertainment was immense, and the temptation irresistible to young printers squeezed by the patent monopolies. At a more serious level the conservative supremacy was seriously undermined by the fall of Catherine Howard in 1543, and by the failure of Gardiner's attempts to destroy Cranmer's influence with the king. There was no dramatic increase in Protestant publishing as the king's life drew to a close, but Richard Grafton was able to print *Praiers of the holi fathers* in 1544 and John Herford (rather more surprisingly) George Joye's *The refutation of the byshop of Winchesters derk declaration* in 1546.[72] At the end of the reign both sides were falling foul of official policy. John Bale complained bitterly of the popularity of the *Genealogy of Heresy*, and of Eck's *Enchiridion*, which he denounced as 'popish', but his own *Actes of the Englysh votaryes* (Antwerp, Mierdman, 1546) was equally unacceptable to authority.[73] Apart from Cromwell's propaganda, the wishes of the government were represented by the Great Bible, by the patents for primers and service books, which endeavoured to bring the whole of that large market under stricter control, and by the *Articles and Injunctions* which came from the press of Thomas Berthelet in numerous editions between 1536 and 1538.[74]

Between 1547 and 1549 the whole situation was transformed by the decision of the minority government of Edward VI, led by the Duke of Somerset, to implement a moderate but fully Protestant ecclesiastical

---

[71] Took, 'Government and the printing trade', pp. 121–9.

[72] *STC*, 20200; 14828.5. The uncertainty of the period is well reflected in the words of one author, written in 1543: 'the laws concerning the wealth, governance and good order of the church, they are now firmly decreed and set forth, and tomorrow unmade and marred again. They are treated and retreated, acted and unacted ... ' *Our Saviour Christ hath not overcharged his chirche* (Antwerp, C. Ruremond) (*STC*, 14556) sig. Aiir.

[73] *STC*, 1270.

[74] *STC*, 10033–87 (nine edns). The council had great difficulty in preserving the precarious balance of enforcement at the end of Henry VIII's reign. As Cox wrote to Paget in 1546: 'Your proclamation (of 8 July) for burning books hath wrought much hurt, for in many places they have burned New Testaments, Bibles not condemend by the proclamation ... They have burned the Kings Majesty's books concerning our religion lately set forth, and his primers ... ' (*Letters and Papers*, XXI, 2, 147). Official policy was not only frequently misunderstood, it was also widely unpopular.

settlement. At the official level this meant the disappearance of missals and breviaries of the Sarum rite, of primers, manuals and processionals. In their place came the reformed Order of Communion (1548) and the Prayer Books of 1549 and 1552. New ABCs for children 'set forthe by the kinges majestie' replaced the old primers, and there was a fresh spate of Bible publishing – 15 full editions in five years, plus innumerable selections of one kind or another. This official programme had behind it an evangelical thrust and sense of purpose which had perforce been lacking from the more equivocal policy of the previous reign, and the terms of the printers' patents reflect that thrust, referring to the 'overcoming of superstition and idolatrye'.[75] At least 20 000 prayerbooks were issued, and imposed on parishes all over the country, while strenuous efforts were made to collect and destroy the earlier liturgies. At the same time the complex restraints under which the printing industry had theoretically been working were swept away. Whether this was done on the idealistic principle that the truth will prevail if it is set free, or from a shrewd judgement that the vast majority of stationers favoured the Reformation, was never made clear. The consequences, however, were immediate and obvious. Explicit works of Protestant theology, such as Heinrich Bullinger's *Two Epystles* (R. Stoughton, 1548) or Calvin's *A faythful and most godly treatyse* (N. Hill, 1548), began to appear in ever increasing numbers,[76] and there was a major explosion of pastoral and polemical treatises. The total number of titles issued went up from about 100 in 1547 to 225 in 1549, and the number of presses from 25 to 39.[77] The enthusiasm of some of the more radical printers, such as John Day and William Seres, began to outrun the government programme, and scurrilous pieces like *The upcheringe of the mass* and *A dyalogue betwene a gentylman and a preest* were published with the bogus colophus of 'H. Lufte, Wittenburg' or 'Hans Hitprick'.[78] As we have seen, foreign printers also began to return to the London scene in numbers, and the refugee congregations were supplied with copies of the Prayer Book translated into their own languages, although it is unlikely that they made much use of them. By 1550 the peak of this euphoria was passed. The council began to reimpose restrictions with an air of disillusionment: 'having caused God's word to be truly and sincerely taught and preached, and a godly order for the administration of the sacraments' the young king was declared to be

---

[75] Took, 'Government and the printing trade', p. 224. Eight patents were issued altogether, forming a coherent policy.
[76] *STC*, 4080; 4409.5.
[77] Took, 'Government and the printing trade', p. 331 and App. II.
[78] *STC*, 17630; 6802.5.

'most sorry, and earnestly from bottom of his heart doth lament ... to hear and see many of his subjects to abuse daily by their vicious living and corrupt conversations that most precious jewel the word of God'.[79]

By 1552 the number of titles issued was back to its 1547 level, at 105, and the foreign workers had begun to drift away again. The Duke of Northumberland, like Cromwell before him, was particularly concerned to suppress criticism of the government, and treated authors much more severely than printers, when both were caught. In 1552 John Lowton the author of 'a seditious ballet' was pilloried, while the printer, William Martin, merely had his stock confiscated.[80] All governments within the period seem to have shared the view that printers were men of commerce rather than propagandists, and to have treated them as accessories rather than principals. In the light of what we now know about some of their views and activities, we may well conclude that such a view was disingenuous.

With the accession of Mary the Protestant press in England was driven underground. In spite of the conciliatory tone of the Queen's first proclamation on religious policy, the last works of Protestant exhortation to be openly published in London were John Bradford's *Sermon of Repentaunce* and *Godlye treatyse of prayer* issued by Stephen Mierdman early in August 1553.[81] Mierdman soon afterwards departed, and although it now appears that far more foreign Protestants remained in London than was once thought,[82] there is no evidence to suggest that any of them were involved in clandestine printing. It seems likely that John Day, operating as 'Michael Wood', was the only substantial publisher of underground Protestant literature, until his arrest in October 1554. Thereafter nothing of any substance can be ascribed with certainty to an English press, although the constant anxiety of the authorities and the frequent references to 'light and seditious' ballads and broadsheets suggests that the Edwardian tradition was to some extent being maintained.[83] Mary's council, like that of Henry VIII between

---

[79] Hughes and Larkin, *Tudor Royal Proclamations*, I, p. 515.

[80] *Acts of the Privy Council*, IV, p. 69.

[81] *STC*, 3496; 17791.

[82] For a full discussion of the extent to which the 'stranger communities' remained underground in London during Mary's reign, and of the nature of the protection afforded to them, see A. Pettegree, *Foreign Protestant Communities in Sixteenth Century London*, (Oxford, 1986), pp. 113–32.

[83] D. M. Loades, *The Reign of Mary Tudor*, (London, 1979), pp. 337–40. A study of the surviving account of one London bookseller for 1553–54 'confirms(s) the view that protestantism maintained its sway unimpeded in London early in Mary's reign'; J. N. King 'The account book of a Marian bookseller, 1553–4', *British Library Journal*, 13 (i) (1987), 334.

1525 and 1532, controlled home-produced heresy with some success, but totally failed to stem the flood from abroad. Mary was the more unfortunate in that the opposition with which she had to deal was larger in scale, better organized, and eventually much more political. After 1532 Thomas Cromwell had brought the situation under control by seizing the political initiative. It could be argued that Mary did not have the time in which to do that, but such an interpretation is hard to sustain in the light of the Edwardian achievement, based on an equally short reign. Mary believed that she had restored normality, and as one scholar has recently put it, left 'market forces' to refurbish and revitalize the Catholic church.[84] Almost nothing of the copious literature of the developing Counter-Reformation was translated into English or adapted for English use. In spite of the return to papal allegiance and the leadership of Cardinal Reginald Pole, the Marian church remained curiously isolated, and fought its war without the aid of its most obvious allies. Its Protestant opponents did not make the same mistake.

Traditional and Catholic works

The weight of medieval tradition

The production of orthodox and traditional religious literature in England began almost as soon as the first printing press was set up in 1477, and had a significant history before the Reformation controversies began. Some of this output was learned, like the *De septem sacramentis* of Gulielmus Parisiensis (R. Pynson, 1516), but most was geared to popular piety – a translation of Bonaventura's *Speculum vitae Christi* (Caxton, 1484) which went through eight further editions by 1530, or *A lytyll treatyse called ars moriendi* (Caxton, 1491) which was reprinted in 1492, 1495, 1497, 1506 and 1532.[85] John Mirk's *Liber Festivalis*, a handy guide for clergy which was first issued by Caxton in 1483, went through 23 further editions thereafter, finishing in 1532. The ending of these popular sequences is at least as significant as their existence. The *Legenda aurea* of Jacques de Voraigne went through 11 editions, the last being in 1527.[86] Individual lives of the saints, reasonably popular

---

[84] Took, 'Government and the printing trade', p. 255. 'No attempt was made by the government of Mary to ensure that the books which it insisted on the churches possessing were in fact available.' For a different view, see Jennifer Loach, 'The Marian establishment and the printing press', *English Historical Review*, 150 (1986), 135–48.

[85] *STC*, 12512.5, 3259, 786–90.

[86] *STC*, 17957–75; 24873–80.5.

until the 1520s, peter out after the *Lyfe of saynt Edwarde confessour* (De Worde, 1533). Only *The wais of god ... unto Elizabeth* (R. Caly) briefly revived the genre in 1557.[87] Initial response to the Lutheran challenge was, as we have seen, very limited, and mostly the work of the king himself. There were two editions of the *Assertio*, and no fewer than six of the *Literarum ... ad quondam epistolam M. Lutheri* (R. Pynson, 1526) including two in English.[88] Eck's *Enchiridion ... adversus Lutheranos* came from the press of H. Pepwell in 1531,[89] but thereafter official policy did its best to impose silence on both sides while Henry established his new, and distinctive, position.

In this connection the growing popularity of Erasmus must be seen as significant. The *Christiani hominis institutum* (De Worde, 1520) appeared in four editions altogether, the last being in 1556. *De misericorde domini* (Berthelet, 1526?), was reissued in 1531, 1533 and 1546; while the *Enchirdion militis christiani* (J. Bydell, 1533) was reprinted eight times at regular intervals until 1552, without regard to the twists and turns of ecclesiastical policy.[90] Richard Whitford, the monk of Syon, had a more limited appeal, but he is particularly interesting in that he represents most aptly the positive theological and pastoral aspects of the precarious Henrician compromise. Although strictly orthodox, he eschewed controversy and became the characteristic voice of the English church during the troubled 1530s. His *Werke of preparacion unto communion* was printed twice by Robert Redman (whose links with the reformers we have already noticed), in 1531 and 1537, and once by John Waylande, also in 1537.[91] *The pomander of prayer* went through four editions between 1528 and 1532; and the most popular of all, *A werke for householders*, appeared seven times between 1530 and 1537.[92] Whitford, like Erasmus, placed great emphasis on simple and practical piety, particularly of a domestic nature, and relatively little on the Sacraments, or on the traditional rites and practices of the Church. Another author whose works were consistently popular was the conformist Bishop of Lincoln, John Longland. In the 11 years from 1527 to 1538 he published five commentaries on the Psalms, a similar number of sermons 'spoken before the king', and an edition of *The paternoster, ye creed and the commaundmentes*, which was reprinted seven times. Sir Thomas More, who enjoyed similar popularity while he was in favour, disap-

---

[87] *STC*, 7500; 7605.5.
[88] *STC*, 13084–7.
[89] *STC*, 7481.4.
[90] *STC*, 10450.2; 10474–6; 10479–86.5.
[91] *STC*, 25412–13.5.
[92] *STC*, 25421.2–22.6; 25421.8–25.5.

peared abruptly from the booksellers' catalogues after 1533, to be replaced by official apologists such as Thomas Lupset, whose *Compendious ... treatyse ... of dyenge well, Exhortation to yonge men* and *Treatise of charitie* all appeared from the press of the Royal Printer Thomas Berthelet between 1533 and 1544.[93] Occasional works of more traditional piety, such as Richard Bonner's *Lytell boke that speketh of purgatorie* (R. Wyer, 1534?) continued to be issued, but the main impression is one of major change in the reading habits of the faithful. Scripture, homiletics and private devotion had by 1540 almost entirely displaced the older style of devotional book based upon familiar rituals or the lives of the saints. How far this was a spontaneous response to changing fashions of piety, and how far the result of official pressure is very hard to say. However, the reformers, Catholic as well as Protestant, had transformed religious publishing in England by the time that the Act of Six Articles appeared to throw the whole process into reverse.

In fact the appearance was temporary, and partly deceptive. The total number of books published in England collapsed from 125 in 1540 to 42 in 1541, because the reformers were briefly silenced, and there was no natural resurgence of the older piety to take their place. As the number of titles began to recover – 62 in 1542, 88 in 1545, 105 in 1546 – the works were of the same kind as those which had filled the catalogues of the previous decade.[94] There were six editions of Queen Catherine Parr's *Prayers stirryng the mynd ...* (T. Berthelet, 1545 etc.), two editions of Bullinger's *Christen state of matrimony* (J. Gough, 1543) and three editions of *The bokes of Solomon* (E. Whitchurche, 1545).[95] By the end of Henry VIII's reign the position had changed to such an extent that the main object of conservative polemic was the defence of the mass, an issue which had scarcely been raised before 1540. Stephen Gardiner, defeated politically by the reformers during 1546, struck back with *A declaration of such true articles ...* (J. Herford) and *A detection of the devil's sophistrie* (Herford); while Richard Smith's *Defence of the blessed masse* (Herford) went through three editions in the same year.[96] Smith and Gardiner were thus naturally among the first to find themselves in trouble with the new government in 1547. Smith was forced to recant 'popish' doctrine at Paul's Cross in May 1547, and to burn copies of his *Defence and Brief treatyse settynge forth divers truthes* (T. Petit, 1547).[97] His own recantation was subsequently pub-

---

[93] *STC*, 16934; 16936; 16939.

[94] The figures are derived from Took, 'Government and the printing trade', App. II.

[95] *STC*, 4818–24a; 404.5, 4047; 2754–6.

[96] *STC*, 11588; 11591; 22820–1.

[97] *STC*, 22818. Strype, *Eccl. Mem.* II, i, pp. 61–3.

lished by the authorities, and he continued his opposition from a safer refuge abroad.[98] Some conservative tracts were published during the period of emancipation, between 1547 and 1551, including Smith's *Of unwryten verytyes*,[99] but they were insignificant in quantity beside the reforming and radical output, and once restrictions began to be reimposed they disappeared altogether.

The restoration of Catholicism by Mary in 1553 was thus a far more traumatic experience for the printing industry than the brief reaction of 1540–42. The number of stationers working in London was halved, from 80 to 41, and a substantial number of presses went out of business. The number of religious works published during the first year of the reign, at about 40 was similar to the equivalent figure for 1547, and well down on the boom years 1548–50.[100] More significantly, 20 of those titles came from just two presses – that of John Cawood the Queen's Printer, and that of Robert Caly, the only Catholic printer to have sought exile in the previous reign. Mary's council controlled its opponents at home with reasonable efficiency, but there are serious doubts about the effectiveness of its counter-attack. Spontaneous tracts and ballads celebrating the queen's triumph, like *A godly psalme of Marye Queene*, were numerous during the first few months,[101] and there were a few works of more substantial polemic, such as Miles Huggarde's *Treatise declaring howe Christ by perverse preachyng was banished out of this realme* (Caly, 1554) and the same author's *Assault of the sacrament of the altar* (Caly, 1554).[102] The only official guidance to appear in print was *A copie of a letter wyth articles, sente from the Queenes Majestie to the Bysshoppe of London* (Cawood, March 1554).[103] Pastoral or devotional works of the Catholic persuasion numbered fewer than half a dozen, and most of those were reissues of old material, such as Fisher's Paul's Cross sermon of 1521 or a translation of *Pro catholicae fide* by St Vincent of Lerins (Richard Tottel, June 1554).[104] A somewhat similar pattern was also followed in the peak year of 1555. The ballads and celebrations had by then disappeared, and a small number of works of political propaganda, such as Proctor's *Historie of Wyates rebellion* (Caly, January 1555), appeared in their

---

[98] *STC*, 22824.
[99] *STC*, 22823.
[100] Took, 'Government and the printing trade', p. 244 and App. II. Baskerville, *Chronological Bibliography*, pp. 6–9.
[101] *STC*, 1655, by T. Brownell.
[102] *STC*, 13560.5; 13556.
[103] *STC*, 9182.
[104] *STC*, 10897; 24754.

place.[105] Religious polemic was represented by two or three tracts, notably *An Exclamation upon the erronious and fantasticall spirite of heresy* (R. Lant) – one of the few pieces to pay the radical Protestants back in their own coin – and popular piety by *A plaine and godlye treatise concernynge the Masse* (J. Wayland).[106]

Thirty-two Catholic works were published during the year, of which 26 came from Caly and Cawood. The most significant achievement, however, was undoubtedly the officially inspired *Profitable and necessarye doctryne with certayne homilies* by Edmund Bonner, the Bishop of London, which went through 15 editions within the year.[107] This was the standard manual of orthodoxy and devotion, and the only serious attempt to explain the full doctrinal position of the church. Although the Great Bible continued in use, there were no fresh scriptural publications, and apart from primers and ABCs most of the new service books required were printed abroad. The Homilies, supported by some 12–15 devotional treatises and aids, absolve the Marian church from the charge of completely neglecting its pastoral responsibilities, but they fell far short of what was needed to re-establish the old faith after a period of such upheaval and change.

After 1555 the publication of all kinds of promotional literature for the Catholic faith declined: 15–20 titles for 1556, less than ten for 1557.[108] A virulent and widespread outbreak of influenza, accompanied by high mortality, may have been partly responsible for this, but if that were so it would only serve to confirm the view that private enterprise had played a larger part than the council in sustaining the higher rates of 1554 and 1555. The nature of the material published did not change greatly. Sermons by prominent divines, John Feckenham, James Brookes and Thomas Watson, remained staple fare, as did expositions of sacramental devotion, such as Watson's *Holsome and catholyke doctrine concerninge the seven sacraments* (Caly, 1558).[109] Translations and para-

---

[105] STC, 20408; also *The copie of a letter sent into Scotlande by John Elder*, a celebration of the queen's marriage (STC, 7552).

[106] STC, 10615; 17629.

[107] This was actually two works. *The Profitable ... doctryne* with the homilies appeared in five editions (STC, 3281.5–83.7. The 13 homilies alone in a further ten editions (STC, 3285.1–5.10).

[108] Baskerville, *Chronological Bibliography*, p. 7.

[109] STC, 25112. Loach, 'Marian establishment' makes the valid point that the priorities of the church under Mary were different from those under Edward, and that the authorities were anxious to ensure that the laity were trained by the clergy, rather than directly by their own reading. As Gardiner put it to one Stephen Gratwick, 'we will use you as we will use the child; for if the child will hurt himself with the knife, we will keep the knife from him. So because you will damn your souls with the word, therefore you

phrases of the Fathers of the church also feature, like *A devout prayer of S.Ambrose, very expedient for all suche as prepare themselves to saye masse* (Cawood, 1555) or *Twelve of S. Augustine's sermons* (Cawood, 1553);[110] and, of course, attacks upon Protestants. Some of these, notably Huggarde's *Displaying of the protestantes*, were witty and hard hitting; others, such as John Gwynneth's *Playne demonstration of John Frithe's lacke of witte* (Powell, 1557) somewhat obsolete in their approach.[111] What was not published is, in some respects, more significant than what was. On the one hand, the literature of the Counter-Reformation was almost totally absent, and hardly any of the effective anti-Protestant polemic produced on the continent over the previous 30 years was called into service. On the other hand, there was no attempt to go back to the popular approach of the *Golden Legend* or the *Fifteen Oes*. The restored Catholicism was also a reformed Catholicism in a distinctively English mould. Erasmus continued to be popular, with 11 editions of various of his works over the five years, and even Catherine Parr achieved a reissue in 1556 (A. Kitson).[112] There was little sign of any revival of the cult of Our Lady, and no works were specifically devoted to the merits of pilgrimages. The literature of the restored Catholic church under Mary reflects the very specific history of the English Reformation; its politics, its frequent and prolonged doctrinal ambiguities, and its detachment from the powerful, papally-led initiatives of the Council of Trent. If we take the year 1558 to mark the end of the first phase of the Reformation in England, we find the paradoxical situation of a Catholic church in power, but uncertain of its orientation and not fully in tune with its majority popular support; whereas the Protestants, in exile and under persecution, are nevertheless well organized, determined, and victorious in the field of literature and published polemic.

Select bibliography

Baskerville, E. J., *A Chronological Bibliography of Propaganda and Polemic Published between 1553 and 1558* (Philadelphia, 1979) (Publications of the American Philosophical Society, 136).

---

shall not have it.' Foxe, *Actes*, Pratt (ed.), VIII, p. 319. There was strong opposition to the continued use of the English Bible, but Pole had supported (vainly) vernacular Scriptures at Trent, and did not change his mind.

[110] *STC*, 548.7; 923.
[111] *STC*, 13557 (R. Caly, 1556); 12560.
[112] *STC*, 4825.

Bennett, H. S., *English Books and Readers, 1475 to 1557, Being a Study in the History of the Book Trade from Caxton to the Incorporation of the Stationer's Company* (Cambridge, 1952).

Blagden, C., *The Stationers' Company: A History, 1403–1959* (London, 1960).

Clebsch, W., *England's Earliest Protestants, 1520–1535* (Yale, 1964).

Hudson, A., *Lollards and their Books* (London, 1985).

Loach, J., 'The Marian establishment and the printing press', *English Historical Review*, **101** (1986), pp. 135–48.

Loades, D. M., 'Illicit presses and clandestine printing in England, 1520–1580', in A. Duke (ed.), *Too Mighty to be Free: Censorship and the Press in Britain and the Netherlands* (Zutphen, 1988), pp. 1–27.

Pollard, A. W. and Redgrave, G. R. (eds), 2nd ed. revised by Jackson, W. A., Ferguson, F. S. and Pantzer, K. F., *A Short Title Catalogue of Books Printed in England ... and of English Books Abroad, 1475–1640* (2 vols, London, 1976–83).

Tudor, P., 'Religious instruction for children and adolescents in the early English Reformation', *Journal of Ecclesiastical History*, 35 (1984), pp. 391–413.

CHAPTER TEN

Printing and
Reformation ideas in Spain[1]

A. Gordon Kinder

Early printing and the beginnings of censorship

Printing was introduced into Spain somewhat later than into Germany, France and Italy, many of the first printers being of Germanic origin, often arriving in Spain after some time in Italy.[2] There is a claim that as early as 1472, Johannes Parix of Heidelberg was active in Segovia. With more certainty, it is alleged that books were printed by Botel, Holtz and Planck in Barcelona in 1473, in Saragossa in 1473 or 1474, and in 1473 by Palmart in Valencia.[3] Clearly dated books, however, begin only in 1475 with Johannes de Salsburga (= Juan Planck or Blanco) and Paulus (Hurus) de Constantia in Barcelona, Matheus Flander in Saragossa, and by an unnamed printer, possibly Lambert Palmart, in Valencia.[4] From the beginning, some books were printed in gothic type, some in roman. Roman had virtually disappeared in most centres by the early sixteenth century; gothic was remarkably resistant in Spain, especially for works in the vernacular and for liturgical books. Theological works tended to be produced in

[1] My thanks are due to various friends and colleagues for reading drafts of this chapter and suggesting improvements, particularly to the editor of the project in French, Jean-François Gilmont, Dr Clive Griffin of Trinity College, Oxford, and Dr Nigel Griffin and Dr Jeremy Lawrance of the University of Manchester. I also gratefully acknowledge grants in various years from the British Academy, especially in 1987, which have facilitated the research that has provided material for this article.

[2] See C. Romero de Lacea, 'Raices romanas de la imprenta hispana' in *Historia de la imprenta hispana* (Madrid, 1982), pp. 9–95. All the other articles in this work are of interest concerning the establishment of presses in Spain, as is P. Bohigas, *El libro español (ensayo histórico)* (Barcelona, 1962), and F. Lopez (ed.) *Histoire du livre et de l'édition dans les pays ibériques. La dépendance* (Bordeaux, 1986).

[3] L. Witten, 'The earliest books printed in Spain', *The Papers of the Bibliographical Society of America*, 53 (1959), 91–113; G. D. Painter, 'The first press at Barcelona', *Gutenberg-Jahrbuch* (1962), 136–49; P. Berger, *Libro et lectura en la Valencia del Renacimiento* (Valencia, 1987).

[4] Witten, 'The earliest books', 91–3; J. Rubió, 'Wurden die ersten Pressen in Barcelona von einem Mann geleitet?', *Gutenberg-Jahrbuch* (1960) 96–100.

the smaller formats, small quarto, octavo and duodecimo, and, unlike the popular romances, few of them had any illustration beyond the title-page and ornamental capitals. At first, there seemed to be no idea that the book trade was anything but advantageous to the country. The Crown seems to have invited two firms to set up their presses in Seville, granting them various privileges and exemptions. One was the 'Compañeros alemanes',[5] and the other was formed by Meinardo Ungut and Stanislao Polono, who had previously worked with Matthias Moravus in Naples.[6] In 1480 books imported into Castile were officially exempted from import duties. The ecclesiastical censorship of theological works enjoined by a bull of Pope Innocent VIII in 1487 appears to have functioned patchily and sporadically in most parts of Spain. However, by the beginning of the sixteenth century the authorities discerned certain disturbing tendencies in the trade, and a licensing system for all books printed or imported into Castile and León was imposed by a royal decree of Ferdinand and Isabella in July 1502. The power to license printing was put into the hands of a motley collection of civil and ecclesiastical authorities, and books were authorized before printing and verified afterwards. Harsh penalties were laid down for failure to comply. The same theoretically rigid but frequently circumvented control does not seem to have existed for the Aragonese realms. Another form of royal intervention, often in response to supplication by interested parties, was the granting of 'privileges' which fixed a number of years during which unauthorized printing of the work concerned was prohibited, as was the import of other editions. Such privileges could be obtained by the author, the publisher, the printer, or, occasionally, the translator. Again, severe penalties were decreed for infractions; even so, such transgressions were commonplace.[7]

When reformist ideas enjoyed a certain vogue and works by Erasmus and his followers were being freely printed, most printers seem to have been motivated exclusively by considerations of profit (although no printer, however altruistic, can completely ignore the financial aspects of his production). Only Miguel de Eguía in Alcalá de Henares and the Crombergers in Seville appear to have felt some affinity with the aims of the movement, and in fact Jacobo Cromberger bought from Eguía

---

[5] These were: Paulus of Cologne, Johannes Pegnitzer of Nuremberg, Magnus Herbst of Fils, and Thomas Glockner.

[6] See N. H. Griffin, 'Spanish Incunabula in the John Rylands University Library of Manchester', *Bulletin of the John Rylands University Library of Manchester*, 70 (1988), 3–141, here p. 68.

[7] F. J. Norton, *Printing in Spain 1501–1520* (Cambridge, 1966), pp. 119–21.

the right to print the first edition of Erasmus's *Enchiridion*. Nevertheless, both also printed works which took the opposing view.[8] No extant work exists to give evidence of categorically Protestant material ever having been printed in Spain.

The Spanish Inquisition

Although Spain was affected by currents of thought common to the rest of Europe in the early sixteenth century, the country had one institution that made the situation there very different from what happened elsewhere. In the run-up to the final reconquest of Spain from the Moors, accomplished by the fall of Granada in 1492, Ferdinand and Isabella were persuaded of the need to set up the Spanish Inquisition as an ecclesiastical court directly responsible to the Crown. Established with papal approval, this differed in certain respects from the medieval inquisition, since its main function at least at first was to supervise the Jewish and Muslim converts produced by various coercive measures. Many of these really never had any intention of leaving their original religion, both faiths having a similar tenet that allowed believers to convert outwardly under duress, provided they remained true in their hearts. The Spanish Catholic interpretation was that once baptism had been accepted, however unwillingly, its obligations could be enforced on the so-called New Christians. The result was a well-organized council of state, such as no other nation in Europe possessed (except Portugal from 1536), with sufficient resources to run a legal system (with its own prisons) parallel to the civil and ecclesiastical courts, to guard the ports and frontiers, and to censor books after they had been printed. Although frequently overstretched, and not efficient by modern standards, it attempted to make its presence felt throughout Spanish territories, and its machinery could be brought to bear against heresy wherever it was suspected. It was soon being used against Old and New Christians alike, and it was ideal for combating the early manifestations of the Reformation. How the intellectual and spiritual life of Spain would have developed without it is a matter for conjecture. What is clear is that by the early 1560s, it had succeeded in imposing an outward conformity on the country: writers had to be circumspect in how they expressed themselves from the beginning of the sixteenth century, and increasingly so as the century advanced. Its retrospective imposition of ever narrower standards meant

---

[8] See J. Goñi Gaztambide, 'El impresor Miguel de Eguía procesado pro la Inquisicíon (c.1485–1546)', *Hispania Sacra*, 1 (1948), 35–54; C. Griffin, *The Crombergers: The History of a Printing and Merchant Dynasty* (Oxford, 1988).

10.1   The Inquisition's crest according to Philippe Limborch's *Historia Inquisitionis* (Amsterdam, 1692)

that there were attempts to destroy some works that had originally passed the censor, and many perished entirely or survive in single or very few copies.[9] This makes the task of assessing the impact of the Reformation

---

[9] See V. Pinto Crespo, *Inquisición y control ideológico en la España del siglo XVI* (Madrid, 1983); V. Pinto Crespo, 'Censorship: a system of control and an instrument of action', in A. Alcalá (ed.) *The Spanish Inquisition and the Inquisitorial Mind* (New York, 1987), pp. 303–20; V. Pinto Crespo, 'El aparato de control censorial y los corrientes doctrinales', *Hispania Sacra*, 36 (1984), 9–41.

through a scrutiny of surviving books extremely difficult, since often the only evidence of a book's existence is that provided by notarial and inquisitorial records, and these are often vague, and survive only in a haphazard fashion; all too frequently even they have been lost.

The first Spanish *Index* (published at Valladolid, Seville, Valencia, and Toledo by the Council of State, but closely controlled by ecclesiastical figures, many of them active as agents or officials of the Inquisition) was not issued until 1551,[10] after which it was updated and reissued at regular intervals. The first version prohibited many editions of Bibles, and in order to mitigate the harm to booksellers and university libraries, the Inquisition ordered an examination of all Bibles in 1552, which was carried out by Domingo de Soto and the universities of Alcalá and Salamanca, and resulted in the publication of an expurgatory *Censura generalis contra errores, quibus recentes haeretici Sacram scripturam asperserunt, edita a supremo senatu inquisitionis* ... (Valladolid: Francisco de Córdoba, 1554). Perusal of the various editions of the *Index*, and of the Inquisition's records reveals how aware the authorities were of developments in intellectual fashions and ideas, and how thorough a control they attempted.

Until comparatively recently, it was common for Spanish writers to express the view that the various measures adopted to reform the Church in Spain during the late fifteenth and the early sixteenth century rendered unnecessary, even impossible, the introduction of ideas of Protestant reform – an absurdity which relies for its credibility on a total disregard of the nature and function of the Inquisition. Menéndez Pelayo even went so far as to say that the Spanish language was not equipped to utter heresies.[11]

Early sixteenth-century scriptural and devotional works

For a long time, the only parts of Scripture in contemporary sixteenth-century vernacular available to Spaniards were to be found either in

---

[10] *Catalogus librorum reprobatum ex indicio Academiae Lovaniensis ... Alius catalogus librorum auctoritate ... D. Ferdinandi de Valdes archiepiscopi Hispalensis inquisitoris generalis ...* (Toledo, Juan de Ayala, 1551) (also issued in other cities mentioned); I. Révah, 'Un Index espagnol inconnu, celui édité par l'Inquisition de Séville en novembre 1551' in *Studia philologica: homenaje ofrecido a Dámaso Alonso* (Madrid, 1963), III, pp. 131–46; reproduced in facsimile in J. M. de Bujanda (ed.) *Index de livres interdits* V, *Index de l'Inquisition espagnole 1551, 1554, 1559* (Geneva, 1984), pp. 595–686; V. Pinto Crespo, 'Los indices de libros prohibidos', *Hispania Sacra*, 35 (1983), 161–91.

[11] M. Menéndez Pelayo, *Historia de los heterodoxos españoles* (Madrid, 1965), p. 46: 'Y es que la lengua de Castilla no se forjó para decir herejías'.

compilations of lectionary passages, such as the *Epistolas y Evangelios, con sus sermones y doctrinas* (Seville: Cromberger, 1506) later revised by Ambrosio Montesino and printed by Coci ([Saragossa, *c.*1515]) with reprints elsewhere, or in Ludolf of Saxony's *Vita Christi*. The Castilian version of the latter made by Ambrosio Montesino, was published in Alcalá de Henares (Stanislao Polono, 1502–03) and again in 1503, and Seville (Cromberger, 1520) – with many reprints until at least the 1550s – though a Catalan version made much earlier by the Valencian poet, Joan Roic de Corella, circulated widely in manuscript and was printed both in Valencia (Costilla, 1513) and Barcelona (Rosembach, 1518). It had a huge popular appeal. Equally popular was the *Imitation of Christ*, attributed to Jean (Charlier de) Gerson and entitled *Contemptus mundi*, published in Spanish translation at Burgos (Basilea, 1495 and 1516), Logroño (Brocar, 1505), Toledo (Gazini and Villaquirán, 1512) and Seville (Cromberger, 1516) – to mention only some of the earlier of many reprints made in different towns – and in the Catalan version of Miquel Perec, *Libre del meyspreu del mon e de la imitacio de Jesuchrist* (Barcelona: Amorós, 1518).

Cardinal Francisco Ximénez de Cisneros, Archbishop of Toledo and Primate of Spain, was the instigator of various measures to reform the Spanish Church during his primacy. Apart from publishing religious stock in trade, such as bulls and missals, he encouraged the production of works of piety both in Latin and Spanish in the hope of raising the level of spirituality amongst both clergy and people. One rather unexpected author whose works were printed in this way was Girolamo Savonarola, whose *Devotissima exposicion sobre el psalmo de Miserere mei Deus* was published several times: Alcalá (Brocar, 1511), Valladolid (Gumiel, [1510–12?]), ([Seville]: Cromberger, 1511–12? and 1513?), and his *Exposicion del psalmo Super flumina* Vallodolid ([Gumiel], 1511). Another such work was Raymundus de Capua's *La vida de sancta Caterina de Sena*, translated by Antonio de la Peña (Alcalá: Brocar, 1511). These were much read by the Alumbrados discussed below, as were Catherine of Sienna's letters, *Obra de las epistolas y oraciones* (Alcalá: Brocar, 1512). But the crowning work of Ximénez as a patron of printing was to gather together in Alcalá the humanist expertise and the necessary manuscripts for the compilation of the great edition of the Bible in six folio volumes with parallel columns of Greek, Hebrew, Latin and Chaldaic, known as the Complutensian Polyglot,[12] in which Erasmus himself was asked to participate, but declined the invitation. The Cardinal expended a great part of his fortune to bring

---

[12] The Latin name for the university city of Alcalá de Henares, where this was produced, is Complutum.

the work to fruition. It was printed in Alcalà by Brocar between 1514 and 1517. The enterprise was for a time upstaged by Erasmus's Greek New Testament of 1516, which received a four-year imperial privilege. This may have been the reason for the delay in the Polyglot's publication, which did not officially occur until after the receipt of the papal privilege in 1520, and probably as late as 1522. Erasmus's work was not only first on the market, but was doubtless more accessibly priced. It seems certain that it was in the possession of many people in Spain affected by reformist tendencies, and there is evidence of its presence in various private humanist libraries there.[13] Erasmus's *Novum instrumentum* of 1522 also found its way into Spain.[14]

Erasmus in Spain

The cultural and political links between Spain and northern Europe ensured that the works of Erasmus in Latin began to arrive in Spain soon after they were published. They had a great effect among certain sections of the educated classes and an Erasmian movement quickly came into being, whose chief intellectual centre was the University of Alcalá de Henares, founded in the humanist spirit in 1498 by Ximénez and functioning from *c.*1508–10. Erasmus became better known as his works were published in vernacular versions, although these were rarely exact translations, and the ideas of Erasmus conveyed by them were filtered through what the various translators felt would prove acceptable to the authorities. The first of these translations seems to have been *Tratado o sermon del niño Jesu y en loor del estado de niñez*, (Seville, Jacobo Cromberger, 1516) – probably the first translation of a work by Erasmus into any vernacular language – although the same year also saw another version of the same work published elsewhere, *Sermon del niño Jesu*, as an appendix to *Contemptus mundi compuesto por Juan Gerson chanciller de Paris* ... (Saragossa: no printer, 1516). Miguel de Eguía, Brocar's successor as printer to the University of Alcalá, brought out a whole series of Erasmian works in both Latin and Spanish between 1525 and 1529, including the *Paraphrases* of the four Gospels

---

[13] A copy was in the library of Cristóbal de Salazar: J.-M. Lasperas, 'La biblioteca de Cristóbal de Salazar, humanista y bibliófilo ejemplar', *Criticón*, 22 (1983), 5–132 (see p. 16).

[14] It was quoted by Pedro Ruiz de Alcaraz, the Alumbrado leader. See also the inventory of Salazar's library made in 1558, (J.-M. Lasperas, 'La biblioteca', where it is clear from later inventories that, although Salazar owned copies of the Index, he did not declare a number of condemned books in his possession right up until his death in 1579).

and the Epistles, and the *Enchiridion*. There was a veritable explosion of Spanish translations of Erasmian works, printed and reprinted in Spain and Antwerp.[15] By far the most popular of these was *Enquiridio o manual del cavallero christiano*, in the translation of Alonso Fernández, with two editions in 1526, the first of which has been lost, and the second, printed by Eguía in Alcalá, was actually dedicated to the Inquisitor General and Archbishop of Seville, Alonso Manrique, who was a friend of the Erasmians in Spain. This achieved something like best seller status in Spain. Bataillon lists 13 different editions of this in the years between 1526 and 1556.[16]

Anti-Erasmians

Erasmus had his opponents in Spain too.[17] Diego López de Zúñiga published *Annotationes contra Erasmum Roterodamum in defensionem tralationis Novi Testamenti* (Alcalá: Brocar, 1520); *Erasmi Roterodami blasphemiae et impietates* (Rome: Blado, 1522); and *Libellus trium illorum voluminum praecursor quibus Erasmicas impietates ac blasphemias redarguit*, (Rome: Blado, 1522). Juan Ginés de Sepúlveda wrote an *Apologia* in favour of Albertus Pius against Erasmus, published in Rome in 1529; Sancho Carranza de Miranda took an anti-

---

[15] Mention of Antwerp renders perhaps necessary a reminder that it was within the Spanish Netherlands. There are reports that in the mid-sixteenth century the Protestant members of the merchant community, many of them of marrano descent, financed the printing and/or export to Spain of quantities of Protestant works in Spanish (*Colección de documentos inéditos para la historia de España* (= CODOIN), V, 519, 529–33).

[16] The list of editions of the many works of Erasmus published in Spanish territory, in Latin or Spanish, is far too lengthy to include in detail in a short article. The interested reader may look in the bibliography to Marcel Bataillon, *Erasmo y España* (Mexico City, 1966), to gain an idea of their variety. Some brief details will show their extent: at least 22 of his religious works were published, of which some 17 were in Spanish, translated by various people (sometimes several different translations of one work exist). They were printed in 14 different peninsular towns (Alcalá de Henares, Barcelona, Burgos, Coimbra, Granada, León, Lisbon, Legroño, Medina del Campo, Saragossa, Seville, Toledo, Valencia, and Valladolid), besides Antwerp, and one originated in Venice. In this production, only Miguel de Eguía and the Crombergers of Seville stand out (see C. Griffin, 'The Crombergers of Seville and the first italic book printed in Spain', in J.-F. Gilmont (ed.), *Palaestra Typographica: aspects de la production du livre humaniste et religieux au XVIe siècle* (Aubel, 1984), pp. 57–96. L. Cuesta Gutiérrez, 'Las impresiones españolas de Erasmo en la época imperial', *Gutenberg-Jahrbuch* (1950), 203–8).

[17] See E. Llamas-Martínez, 'Orientaciones sobre la historia de la teología española en la primera mitad del siglo XVI (1500–1550)' in *Repertorio de historia de las ciencias eclesiásticas en España*, Instituto de Historia de la Teología Española (Salamanca, 1967), I, 95–174.

Erasmian stance in *Opusculum in quo tres Erasmi Annotatione [...]
discutiuntur* (Rome 1518); and Luis de Carvajal first wrote *Apologia
monastica religionis, diluens nugas Erasmi* which was followed by a
defence and reinforcement of it, *Dulcoratio amarulentiarum Erasmicae
responsionis* (Paris: De Colines, 1530). Alfonso de Castro weighed in
with *Loca insuper aliquot in quibus D. Erasmi Rot. libri caute sunt
legendi* (Cologne: Novesanius, 1539). Rather late on the scene came
Antonio Rubio with *Assertiones catholicae adversus Erasmi Rotteradami
pestilentissimos errores* (Salamanca: Cánova, 1567). The beginnings of
the triumph of the anti-Erasmians can be seen in the calling of a
conference in Valladolid in June 1527 with the purpose of determining
the orthodoxy of Erasmus. Although this was to disperse inconclusively
because of an outbreak of plague, with both sides convinced they had
gained the upper hand, and although Charles V's Latin secretary, Alfonso
de Valdés, obtained from the Emperor a brief in favour of Erasmus, this
provided no more than a temporary respite, and in any case it was
conditionally worded, exempting from censure only such works of
Erasmus as were contradictory to Luther.[18]

The Alumbrados of Toledo

During the early part of the century there arose in the region roughly
bounded by Toledo, Salamanca and Alcalá, a movement usually referred to as the Alumbrados or Illuminists. If we accept at face value the
statements of its own adepts, it started before 1517. It is very difficult
to pin down the beliefs of its adherents, because what information we
have comes either from statements made before the Inquisition, in
which circumstance people attempted to play down their beliefs, or
from the Inquisition's own assessments, often made on the basis of
previous known heresies. It seems to have taken its origins among
members of the Franciscan order and tertiaries as a result of reading
various works of piety. Apparently, it quickly divided into two wings,
the *recogidos* (who practised 'recollection') and *dexados* (who 'abandoned' themselves to the love of God); of which the former were approved and the latter eventually suppressed by authority. There was
interaction between the two, cross-fertilization among the various groups
that sprang up, rivalry and friendships between their leaders, and it is
apparent that local groupings were disparate, and that their beliefs
developed with the years.

---

[18] M. Bataillon, *Erasmo y España*, pp. 226–78.

What is more important for our purpose is that it is quite evident that, even though the absolute origins of the movement may have antedated Luther, its reading included Erasmus and what was available of the Bible at the time, and various works of piety, among which Thomas à Kempis's *Imitation of Christ* figured prominently. As time went on, the Alumbrados were at least aware of Luther's ideas (though there seems to be no certain evidence that they actually read his books – only one trial contains unequivocal mention of any work by a Reformer),[19] and the Inquisition often branded someone as 'Alumbrado, Erasmian, and Lutheran' (sc. Protestant) in the same breath. The illuminist movement was condemned by an edict promulgated in Toledo on 23 September 1525, and a systematic prosecution of its leaders by the Inquisition ensued, although for the most part their punishments were relatively mild.

During his service in the household of Diego López Pacheco, Marquis of Villena, Juan de Valdés had been in contact with an Alumbrado leader, Pedro Ruiz de Alcaraz. For years the dictum of Bataillon was accepted without question that Valdés's *Dialogo de doctrina christiana*, published anonymously 'por un religioso' (although Inquisition documents show that its authorship was in doubt from the beginning)[20] and printed by Miguel de Eguía in Alcalá in 1529, was an Erasmian work in which there was no influence from Protestant sources.[21] Recently, however, Carlos Gilly has very credibly established the possibility of such influence as far as publication dates go and displayed what seemed to be conclusive proof of verbal parallels with texts of Luther, Oecolampadius and Melanchthon.[22] Its Protestantism was not, however, overt, so that when the book was officially examined in Alcalá by a panel of theologians, it was approved. Nevertheless, it is surely significant that later every one of these censors was himself brought before the Inquisition, as was the printer.[23] Juan's elder brother Alfonso, a corre-

[19] Madrid, Archivo Histórico Nacional (=AHN), Inquisición de Toledo, 223-12, Proceso de Juan de Vergara, fol. l^v, referring to the library of Gaspar del Castillo.

[20] Ibid., fols 181^r-182^v.

[21] See the introduction by Bataillon in his edition of Juan de Valdés, *Diálogo de doctrina christiana*, facsimile edition of the copy held by the National Library of Lisbon (Alcalá de Henares, 1529) (Coimbra, 1925), pp. 93–114.

[22] C. Gilly, 'Juan de Valdés, traductor y adaptador de escritos de Lutero en su *Diálogo de doctrina christiana*', in *Miscelánea de estudios hispánicos. Homenaje de los hispanistas de Suiza a Ramón Sugranyes de Franch* (Montserrat, 1982), pp. 85–106 (augmented German version in *ARG*, 74 (1983), 257–306).

[23] See J. Goñi Gaztambide, 'El impresor'; E. Asensio, 'El erasmismo y las corrientes espirituales afines' in *Revista de Filologia Española* 36 (1952), 31–99, 78–81. Eguía may have tried to cover his tracks by printing anti-Erasmian material as well, since he was closely associated with the Alcalá Reformists. However, his motives may have been no more than financial.

spondent of Erasmus and Melanchthon, wrote two works in the Erasmian manner that are highly critical of the failings of the Church and of some of its practices, and praise Erasmus. In 1527, Alfonso de Valdés wrote *Dialogo en que particularmente se tratan las cosas acaecidas en Roma: el año de MDXXVII a gloria de Dios y bien universal de la republica christiana* to justify Charles V's part in the Sack of Rome, blaming papal failings, and in the following year the *Dialogo de Mercurio y Caron: en que allende de muchas cosas graciosas de buena doctrina: se cuenta lo que ha acaescido en la guerra desdel año de mill y quinientos y veynte y uno hasta los desafios de los reyes de Francia y Ynglaterra hechos al Emperador el año de MDXXIII* [sic for 1528], continuing much the same argument. Both were published in one volume with no date, printer, or place of origin given. There were four more editions of these works together, also – perhaps significantly – without indication of date, place or printer. Both were translated into various European languages and became extremely popular outside Spain,[24] and both have a strongly Erasmian content, verging on the Protestant. Indeed, since Alfonso escaped interview with the Inquisition by dying of the plague in Vienna in 1532, his orthodoxy was never tested, but there have been suggestions that the strictures against Luther which his books contain were merely there to strengthen the impression of Erasmianism.[25]

The whole Erasmian group at Alcalá came under suspicion, and as the Inquisition began to move in, several people, including the rector of the university, Mateo Pascual, decided that it was prudent to disappear. Fleeing first to Rome and then settling in Naples, Juan de Valdés gathered round himself a group of spiritual reformers. The honour of being the first to translate from the original languages into modern Spanish whole books of both the Old and the New Testaments seems to belong to Juan de Valdés, but these were not published in his lifetime, and indeed only two were published at all in the sixteenth century. Juan Pérez de Pineda brought out Valdés's commentaries on Romans and on I Corinthians, both of which contain full translations, in Geneva with Jean Crespin (although both were given the false imprint of Venice: Juan Philadelpho): *Comentario, o declaracion breve, y compendiosa sobre la epistola de S. Paulo apostol a los Romanos, muy saludable*

---

[24] Seven Italian editions of both together are known, all printed in Venice; only one is dated (1546). Both were printed in German several times in the early seventeenth century. *The Sacke of Roome* appeared in English in London in 1590, and Antonio del Corro edited an adaptation of the Spanish original, printed in Oxford by Joseph Barnes in 1586, to serve as a reader to his Spanish grammar. This edition also appears with a false imprint spuriously implying that it was printed in Paris.

[25] J. C. Nieto, 'Luther's ghost and Erasmus' masks in Spain', *BHR*, 39 (1977), 33–49.

para todo Christiano, 1556, and *Comentario o declaracion familiar, y compendiosa sobre la primera epistola de San Paulo apostol a los Corinthios, muy util para todos los amadores de la piedad Christiana,* 1557.[26] There is evidence that these reached Spain.[27] The versions of Psalms and of Matthew's Gospel had to wait for several centuries before their publication.[28] Juan wrote a considerable number of other works, but in Italian, and these fall outside the scope of this article. There is evidence that at least one manuscript copy of his *Las ciento y diez divinas consideraciones* in Spanish was in the hands of Juan Sánchez, a member of the Valladolid Protestant conventicle in 1558, but in printed form this is known only in Italian.[29]

The Seville evangelicals

The migration of a number of theologians trained at Alcalá to Seville gave rise to an evangelical movement there in the 1540s and 1550s. Francisco de Vargas seems to have been an influence, but he apparently wrote nothing, and died without having to face the Inquisition, although there is some suggestion that he was marked for investigation. His library reveals nothing by Protestant Reformers, although there is a fair amount of biblical material, and works by Erasmus.[30] The sermons of the cathedral preacher, Juan Gil (Dr Egidio), appointed in 1537, gave rise to conventicles in the city, and eventually led to his being brought before the Inquisition and required to retract in 1552.[31] It does not seem that he ever published anything either, although it is reported that

---

[26] Crespin was by far the most prolific printer of Spanish Protestant works. See J.-F. Gilmont, *Jean Crespin, un éditeur réformé du XVIe siècle* (Geneva, 1981), pp. 134–7.

[27] Both were among the books carried to Spain by Julián Hernández in 1557, the misdelivery of which made the Inquisition aware of the spread of Protestant ideas in that city, and triggered the general move against Protestants all over Spain. They are two of the titles of those listed as seized for destruction in Seville and Valladolid, and they also occur in inventories of private libraries of the day.

[28] E. Boehmer (ed.), *El Salterio traduzido del hebreo en romance castellano por Juan de Valdés, ahora por primera vez impreso* (Bonn, 1880); T. Fliedner (ed.), *El evangelio de San Mateo declarado por Juan de Valdés, ahora por primera vez publicado* (Madrid, 1880).

[29] J. de Valdés, *Las ciento y diez divinas consideraciones, recensión inédita del manuscrito de Juan Sánchez (1558),* J. I. Tellechea (ed.), (Salamanca, 1975).

[30] K. Wagner, 'La biblioteca del doctor Francisco de Vargas', *Bulletin Hispanique,* 78 (1976), 313–24.

[31] Text in German translation in E. H. J. Schäfer, *Beiträge zur Geschichte des spanischen Protestantismus und der Inquisition im sechzehnten Jahrhundert* (Gütersloh, 1902) II, pp. 342–53.

manuscripts of various commentaries on books of the Bible written by him existed at his death. These have since disappeared. He died in 1556 shortly after he had returned from an exhausting journey to confer with Agustin Cazalla, the leader of the evangelical conventicle in Valladolid. Four years later, however, Egidio's followers were being harassed, he himself was tried posthumously and condemned, and his bones were disinterred and burnt with his effigy. He was succeeded in his office of cathedral preacher in 1556 by Constantino Ponce de la Fuente, who continued the same trend.

In 1530 Constantino became a correspondent of Erasmus when he wrote a reply (apparently never printed) to Luis de Carvajal's anti-Erasmian *Dulcoratio*. He had already had an earlier period of service at the cathedral from 1533 to 1548, followed by a tour of duty with the court as royal chaplain and had written a number of works. His *Summa de doctrina christiana en que se contiene todo lo principal y necessario que el hombre christiano deve saber y obrar* came out on the Cromberger press in Seville in 1543. It is in the form of a dialogue, and draws heavily on Juan de Valdés's *Dialogo de doctrina*.[32] There were other editions printed in Seville by the Crombergers in 1544, by Juan de León in 1545, and by Cristóbal Alvarez in 1551, and an undated Antwerp edition by Martin Nuntius. In 1546 the *Exposicion del primer Psalmo de David cuyo principio es Beatus vir, dividida en seis sermones* appeared in Seville, probably on the presses of Juan de León. Other Seville editions of 1547 and 1548 (printers unknown) are known, as is an Antwerp edition of 1556 by Martin Nuntius. Constantino's *Catecismo* is now represented only by an edition of 1556 in Antwerp, but it originally appeared in Seville in 1547, and in the following year Juan Canalla printed at Seville his *Doctrina Christiana. En que esta comprehendida toda la informacion que pertenence al hombre que quiere servir a Dios. Por el Dr. Constantino. Parte primera. De los articulos de la fe.* This last edition was copied in Antwerp in 1554 by Jan Steelsius and in 1554–55 by Martin Nuntius. In the inquisitional censure of this work, certain passages are condemned as 'Alumbrado doctrine'.[33] *Confission delante de Jesu Christo redemptor y juez de los hombres* (Seville: no printer, 1547), was also reprinted in Évora in 1554 as *Confession de un pecador penitente* by Andrés de Burgos, probably the same printer who had moved there from Seville, where he had printed a translation of Erasmus, *Tratado de la oracion* in 1546. Constantino's *Catecismo christiano* together with his *Confession d'un*

---

[32] See M. Bataillon, introduction to J. de Valdés, *Diálogo de doctrina christiana* pp. 198, 234, 237, 260, 265–6, 269–70, 296, 309–13.

[33] AHN, Inq. lib 323; fol. 233^v; Inq. leg. 4444–5, and 49.

pecador was reprinted in Antwerp by Guillaume Simon in 1556, and his *Sermon de Christo nuestro Redemptor en el Monte* came out in Seville as an appendix to the *Suma* in 1545 and 1551, and in Antwerp in 1550.

Constantino was eventually imprisoned by the Inquisition, and died in 1560 before coming to trial. His works were placed on the *Index* after he was tried *post mortem* and his bones burnt with his effigy in 1560. He is also reported to have written several other books of biblical commentary, which were taken in manuscript to Germany, where the pseudonymous Reginaldus Gonsalvius Montanus stated his intention of publishing them. None the less, they do not seem ever to have been printed.[34] Other manuscripts, described as anti-papal, were discovered after his imprisonment concealed in the home of one of his followers,

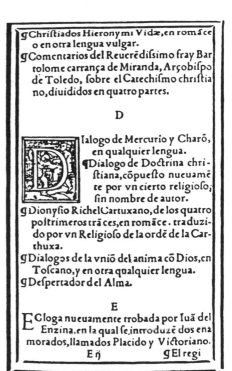

> Iuan Philadelfo,año de.1556.conpuesto por Iuan Valdesio.
> ¶Commentario en romance, sobre la epistola primera de sant Pablo ad Corinthios,traduzida de Griego en romance, sin autor ni impressor.
> ¶Confessionario,o manera de confessar,de Erasmo,en romance.
> ¶Colloquios de Erasmo,en romãce, y ē Latin,y en otra qualquier lengua vulgar.
> ¶Combite gracioso de las gracias del sãcto Sacramento.
> ¶Cõtemplaciones del Idiota, en qualquier lengua vulgar.
> ¶Comedia llamada Iacinta: conpuesta & imp. essa con vna epistola familiar.
> ¶Comedia llamada Aquilana, hecha por Bartolome de Torres Naharro.
> ¶Comedia llamada Theforina,hecha nueuamente por Iayme de Huete.
> ¶Comedia llãmada Tidea, compuesta por Francisco de las Natas.
> ¶Colloquio de damas.
> ¶Circe de Iuan Baptista, en qualquier lengua vulgar.
> ¶Chronica de Ioan Carriõ,en romãce,y en latin,o otra qualquier lēgua vulgar.
> ¶Christianos.

> ¶Christiados Hieronymi Vidæ,en romãce o en otra lengua vulgar.
> ¶Comentarios del Reuerēdifsimo fray Bartolome carrança de Miranda,Arçobispo de Toledo, sobre el Catechismo christiano,diuididos en quatro partes.
>
> D
>
> Ialogo de Mercurio y Charõ, en qualquier lengua.
> ¶Dialogo de Doctrina christiana,cõpuesto nueuamēte por vn cierto religioso, sin nombre de autor.
> ¶Dionysio RichelCartuxano,de los quatro poltrimeros trãces,en romãce. traduzido por vn Religioso de la ordē de la Carthuxa.
> ¶Dialogos de la vniõ del anima cõ Dios,en Toscano,y en otra qualquier lengua.
> ¶Despertador del Alma.
>
> E
>
> ECloga nueuamente trobada por Iuã del Enzina,en la qual se.introduzē dos enamorados,llamados Placido y Victoriano.
> E ij   ¶El regi

10.2 *Cathalogus librorum qui prohibentur* (Valladolid: Sebastian Martinez, 1559). These two pages contain condemnations of works by Erasmus and comedies alongside Protestant texts

---

[34] M. Menéndez Pelayo, *Heterodoxos*, II, 61; R. Gonsalvius Montanus, *Sanctae Inquisitionis hispanicae artes detectae ac palam traductae* ... (Heidelberg, 1567), pp. 283–4.

and there are contemporary claims that this cache also included prohibited works. Although the inventory of Constantino's library reveals much biblical, Erasmian, and reformist literature, it contained little clearly Protestant material, except a harmony of the Gospels by Osiander and possibly two volumes of Zwingli's works; and it did contain four works against Luther, two each against Bucer and Melanchthon, and one each against the Anabaptists, Oecolampadius and Musculus.[35] The libraries of other members of this same Seville group yield little in the way of condemned material: Gaspar Baptista Vilar had two Bibles listed on the *Index* and various books by Erasmus; Gil de Fuentes possessed a considerable number of works of Erasmus and one edited by Oecolampadius; and Alonso de Escobar had the complete works of Erasmus in nine volumes.[36]

Infiltration of Protestant works

The entry into Spain of foreign editions of Protestant works is well documented. Pope Leo X issued briefs on 21 March 1521 to the Constable and Admiral of Castile, then Regents of Castile during the absence of Charles V on his first imperial tour, requiring them to adopt measures to prevent the introduction into Spain of the writings of Luther and his sympathizers;[37] the grandees of Spain assembled in Tordesillas to express their dissatisfaction with Charles in the presence of his mother, Joan the Mad, pointed out to the Emperor on 12 April of the same year, soon after his accession, that such 'tares' were being sown among the 'wheat' of Spain,[38] and the Royal Council sent a

---

[35] K. Wagner, *El doctor Constantino Ponce de la Fuente. El Hombre y su biblioteca* (Seville, 1979). This scholar notes that the discovery by the Inquisition of several hundred books belonging to Constantino walled up in the house of one of his disciples probably provides a fair explanation as to why his own library did not contain any condemned books: they had all been taken away and hidden.

[36] K. Wagner, 'Gaspar Baptista Vilar, "herege luterano", amigo de Constantino y de Egidio', in *Archivo Hispalense*, 187 (1978) 107–18; K. Wagner, 'Los maestros Gil de Fuentes y Alonso de Escobar', *Hispania Sacra*, 55/56 (1976), 239–47.

[37] AHN, Inq. lib. 317, fol. 182[r–v]; T. McCrie, *History of the Progress and Supression of the Reformation in Spain in the Sixteenth century* (Edinburgh, 1829), p. 61; Augustin Redondo, 'Luther et l'Espagne de 1520 à 1536', *Mélanges de la Casa de Velázquez*, 1 (1965), p. 121; J. Simón Díaz, *El libro español antiguo: análisis de su estructura, Texto* [sic] *del Siglo de Oro, Bibliografías y catálogos* (Cassel, 1983) vol. I, p. 23: 'La provisión del cardenal Adriano, Inquisidor general dada en Tordesillas a 7 de abril de 1521, para recoger las obras de Lutero, y las cartas a diversos inquisidores en 1523 sobre lo mismo'.

[38] Archivo General de Simancas (AGS), Estado 8–91; Redondo, 'Luther et l'Espagne', p. 122.

similar letter from Burgos to the Emperor the following day[39] – all of these clear indications that some infiltration had begun quite early. The wording of these letters makes it clear that Lutheran works were being translated into Spanish and introduced into Spain. Later that year the Headquarters (Suprema) of the Inquisition alerted provincial branches that there was a danger that books were being brought into Spain, and a letter of 27 September congratulated the Inquisition of Valencia for having detected and burnt 'Lutheran' books.[40] In 1523, the Inquisition of Navarre was thanked for its vigilance in the ports and along the border with France. Books were seized and destroyed in Aragon too.[41] In February 1525, Charles V was informed that three Venetian galleys loaded with 'Lutheran' books had been detected in a port in the kingdom of Granada.[42] Inquisition visitations of 1552 and 1554 in Seville produced many Bibles, of which many were in forbidden editions,[43] and when, after 1557, the Inquisition came to move savagely against all expression of heterodox ideas, the harvest of forbidden books listed as being in its headquarters in Seville makes impressive reading: around 1563 it housed confiscated works by Erasmus, Constantino Ponce de la Fuente, Juan de Valdés, Alfonso de Valdés, Juan Pérez de Pineda, Bucer, Bullinger, Oecolampadius, Viret, Melanchthon, Zwingli and many other Reformers, some of them not mainstream, such as Ochino, Osiander, Celio Secondo Curione, and Sebastian Castellio.[44] Surprisingly there were none by either Luther or Calvin. A list of books burnt in Valladolid in 1558 includes all Constantino's works, most of Juan Pérez's production in Geneva, a harmony of the Gospels by Osiander, a commentary of Erasmus, Castellio's *Dialogi sacri* and a Latin Bible printed by Robert Estienne.[45] Books are mentioned in trials of those accused of heresy, but they are often difficult to identify. Nevertheless it is clear that works produced abroad in Spanish did achieve a certain dissemination. There are various claims that books by Protestant authors were even published in Spain in Spanish versions: that for instance, Luther's *Commentary on Galatians* was translated into Spanish in 1520,[46] and that

---

[39] AGS, Estado 9–1; Redondo, 'Luther et l'Espagne', p. 125.

[40] AHN, Inq. lib. 319, fol 13ᵛ; Redondo, 'Luther et l'Espagne', p. 127.

[41] AHN, Inq. lib. 319, fol 13ᵛ; Redondo, 'Luther et l'Espagne', p. 127; J. I. Tellechea, *Tiempos recios: Inquisición y heterodoxias* (Salamanca, 1977), p. 25.

[42] A. Rodríguez Villa, *El emperador Carlos V y su Corte (1522–1539)* (Madrid, 1903–05), p. 255.

[43] J. I. Tellechea, 'La censura inquisicional de Biblias de 1554', *Anthologica Annua*, 10 (1962), 89–142; J. I. Tellechea, 'Biblias publicadas fuera de España secuestradas por la Inquisición de Sevilla en 1552', *Bulletin Hispanique*, 64 (1962), 236–47.

[44] Schäfer, *Beiträge* vol. 2, pp. 392–400.

[45] Schäfer, *Beiträge* vol. 3, pp. 101–3.

[46] J. Stoughton, *The Spanish Reformers* (London, 1883), p. 36.

Calvin's *Institutes* were published in Saragossa.[47] Alarm was expressed in 1532 when it was suggested that a 'Lutheran' book had been printed in Valencia.[48] As no documentary references are given, and the books themselves are not extant, it is difficult to substantiate such allegations. There is no doubt, however, that definitely Protestant doctrines took root briefly in two major centres, Seville and Valladolid, and in at least one minor centre in Aragon, and in scattered individuals elsewhere. The spectacular autos da fe held between 1559 and 1562 in the two first-named cities and in Saragossa, together with various individuals fleeing to safety abroad, eradicated them completely. There is no evidence of these people publishing anything within Spain.[49]

Spanish opponents of Protestantism

Of course there were opponents of Protestant ideas in Spain, and books were written to confute such views. The first appears to be the unpublished tract of Jaime de Olesa, and sent to Pope Leo X (d. 1522), *jacobi de Olesia contra erroris Martini Luteri*. The first printed work against Luther's ideas by an Iberian seems to have been Jerónimo Pérez's *Monoctium, sive unius noctis opusculum* (Naples, 1525). A book, *Adversus Lutherum*, which has since disappeared, is mentioned in a letter of Leo X dated June 1522 to its author Diego de Muros. The well-known Spanish humanist, Juan Ginés de Sepúlveda, wrote his *De fato et libero arbitrio libri tres: quo in opere dogma nefarium Martini Lutheri de cunctorum actiorum eventorumque necessitate* ... (Rome: Mazzolini, 1526), and a catalogue of the library of Alcalá University dated 1523 reveals two Latin works against Luther, one evidently by a Spaniard named Pérez (possibly *Monoctium* above); and another list of 1526 gives three further Latin titles.[50] Alfonso de Castro wrote *Adversus*

---

[47] *CODOIN*, vol. 5, p. 400.

[48] R. Garcia Cárcel, *Herejia y sociedad en el siglo XVI. La Inquisición en Valencia 1530–1609* (Barcelona, 1980), pp. 22–5.

[49] See J. I. Tellechea, 'Perfil teológico del protestantismo castellano del siglo XVI. Un memorial inédito de la Inquisición (1559)', *Diálogo Ecuménico* 17 (1982) 315–73; J. I. Tellechea, 'Profil théologique du protestantisme castillan du XVIe siècle', *Revue d'Histoire et de Philosophie Religieuses*, 63 (1983), 125–40; J. I. Tellechea, 'Don Carlos de Seso, luterano en Castilla, Sentencia inédita de su proceso inquisitorial', in *Homenaje a Pedro Sáinz Rodriguez* (Madrid, 1986), vol. 1, pp. 295–307; A. G. Kinder, 'A hitherto unknown centre of Protestantism in sixteenth-century Aragon', *Cuadernos de Historia de Jerónimo Zurita*, 51/52 (1985), 131–60. For Seville, the many documents published by Schäfer, and the subsequent careers of those who fled, provide sufficient evidence.

[50] A. Redondo, 'Luther et l'Espagne', p. 129.

omnes haereses lib. XIII (Paris: J. Bodía and Jean Roigny, 1534), and this went through 12 editions in as many years, most of them outside Spanish territory, although one did appear in Salamanca (Portonariis, 1541): it contains sections on Wycliffe and Hus, and a long denunciation of Luther. The translator of Erasmus, Alonso de Virués, composed *Philippicae disputationes vigenti adversus Lutherana dogmata per Philippum Melancthonem defensa* (Antwerp: Crinitius, 1541). In his *De justificatione doctrina universa libri XV, absolute tradita et contra omnes omnium errores juxta germanam sententiam orthodoxae veritatis et sacri Concilii Tridentini praeclare defensa*, Venice (1546), Alcalá (Angulo, 1564), Cologne (Calenius, 1572), Andrés Vega concentrated his attacks on justification by faith and the merit of good works, and Gaspar Cardillo de Villalpando wrote a treatise, *De traditionibus Ecclesiae*, and a book, *Disputationes adversus protestationem trigintaquattuor haereticorum Augustanae Confessionis* (Venice: Bertellus, 1564), both of them containing refutations of Luther and his followers. Martín Pérez de Alaya had Protestantism as his main target in *De divinis Apostolicis atque ecclesiasticis traditionibus* (Cologne: Gennepeus, 1549).

Spanish Protestant books produced abroad

Apart possibly from the few Protestant works about which assertions are made, perhaps apocryphally, that they were printed in Spain, all overtly Reformation-minded publications by Spaniards seem to have been produced outside Spain. In 1556 a Spaniard flirting with Protestantism in the Low Countries, Fadrique Furió Ceriol, published in Basle *Bononia, sive de Libris sacris in vernaculam linguam convertendis, Libro duo* (Oporinus), and it is obvious that he had manuscripts of other books of a similar or more Protestant slant, when his desire to return to Spain led him to hand the manuscripts of these over as part of a deal which would bring him a pardon and prepare the way for his restoration to favour in Spain.[51]

The first translation into Spanish of the complete New Testament made directly from the original Greek was the work of Francisco de Enzinas (or Dryander), *El nuevo testamento de nuestro redemptor y*

---

[51] This is revealed by an interesting document in AGS, Consejo y Juntas de Hacienda 37/55–174, discussed in R. W. Truman and A. G. Kinder, 'The pursuit of Spanish heretics in the Low Countries: the activities of Alonso del Canto, 1561–1564', *Journal of Ecclesiastical History*, 30 (1979), 65–93. On Furió Ceriol in Louvain, see P. Bogaert and J.-F. Gilmont, 'La première bible française de Louvain', *Revue théologique de Louvain*, 11 (1980), 294–6.

salvador Jesu Christo, traduzido de griego en lengua castellana (Antwerp: Mierdmann, 1543), an edition dedicated and presented personally to Charles V. After this was examined by the emperor's confessor, the translator found himself imprisoned in Brussels, although he was to escape two years later. Dryander also published pseudonymously in 1540 a small work which turns out to be a compilation from Luther and Calvin, with his own introduction, *Breve i compendiosa institución de la religion christiana, necessaria para todos aquellos que con justo titulo quieren usurpar el nombre de Christo.*[52] After lodging some time in Wittenberg at the home of Melanchthon, the same author published in 1546 a commentary on the proceedings of the Council of Trent, *Acta Concilii Tridentini, anno MDXLVI celebrati: una cum annotationibus piis, et lectu dignissimis*, printed by Oporinus in Basle, and in 1558 his posthumous *Histoire de l'estat du Pais Bas, et de la religion d'Espagne* (Ste Marie [=Strasbourg]: Perrin), gives an account of the first definitely Protestant martyr of Spain, Francisco de San Román, who died in Valladolid in 1542. Dryander's brother, Jaime de Enzinas, is said to have translated a catechism into Spanish. This was printed in Antwerp in 1541, but all trace of it has been lost.[53] An associate of Enzinas, Juan Díaz, wrote *Christianae religionis summa. Ad illustrissimum principem dominum Ottonem Henricum Palatinum Rheni, & utriusque Bavariae Ducem &c* (Neuburg: Johannes Kilian, 1546). The author's murder in the same year by his own brother for sectarian reasons, gave rise to several books.[54]

Since nearly all the copies of Enzinas's New Testament had been destroyed, Juan Pérez de Pineda used a copy of that work to produce a new Spanish version. It was printed by Jean Crespin in Geneva in 1556: *El Testamento nuevo de nuestro señor y salvator Jesu Christo* as was his version of the Psalms in 1557, *Psalmos de David con sus sumarios en que se declara con brevedad lo contenido en cada Psalmo*, with the

---

[52] The place is given as 'Topeia', the printer as 'Adam Corvo'. Bataillon suggests Antwerp or Ghent as the place of printing: see M. Bataillon, *El hispanismo y los problemas de la historia de la espiritualidad española (a propósito de un libro protestante olvidado)* (Madrid, 1977).

[53] Ed. Boehmer, *Bibliotheca Wiffeniana: Spanish Reformers of two centuries from 1520* (3 vols, London, 1874–1904) vol. 1, p. 168.

[54] *Ein erbermlich geschicht, wie ein Spaniölischer, und römischer Doctor, umb des Evangelions willen seinen leiblichen bruder ermordt hat* (Erfurt: Marten von Dolgen, 1546); Claudius Senarclaeus, *Historia vera de morte sancti viri Joannis Diazii Hispani, quem eius frater germanus Alphonsus Diazius, exemplum sequutus primi parricidae Cain, velut alterum Abelem, nefarié interfecit* ([Basle: Oporinus], 1546), with a preface by Bucer; *Histoire d'un meurtre execrable commis en la personne de Iehan Dias* (Geneva: J. Girard, 1546).

BREVE

Y COMPENDIOSA
*inſtituçion de la religion Chriſtia
na,neçeſſaria para todos aquellos
que con iuſto titulo quieren uſur
par el nombre de Chriſto.Eſcripta
por el docto uaron Francifco
de Elao a ruego de un
amigo y hermano ſuio
en Chriſto.*

*☙Impreſſa en Topeia por Adamo
Coruo el Anno de. 1540.*

10.3   Francisco de Enzinas, *Breve y compendiosa institucion* ([Antwerp]: [M. Crom], 1540)

same concealment of origin, except that the printer is now stated to be Pietro Daniel. Juan Pérez also produced several other books in Geneva: *Sumario de la doctrina Christiana hecha por via de pregunta, y respuesta, en manera de coloquio* (Venice [=Geneva]: Pietro Daniel [=Jean Crespin], 1556), an adaptation of Calvin's Catechism (but differing in many respects from an earlier Spanish translation of that work, *Catechismo. A saber es formulario para instruyr los mochachos en la Christianidad,* published in Geneva in 1550 ([Jean Girard]), of which copies were sent in 1551 in sealed covers to many Spanish notables including the Admiral of Castile);[55] *Carta embiada a nuestro augustissimo Senor [sic] Principe Don Philippe, Rey de España* (Geneva: [Crespin], 1558); an adaptation of a work by John Sleidanus, *Dos informaciones muy utiles, la una dirigida a la Magestad del Emperador Carlos quinto [...] Con una suplicacion a la Magestad del Rey* (Geneva: [Crespin]); a Spanish translation of Calvin's Catechism, *Catechismo, que significa forma de*

---

[55] AHN, Inq. lib. 323, fol. 154ᵛ, 156ᵛ; Boehmer, *Bibliotheca Wiffeniana*, vol. 2, pp. 43–8; Bataillon, *Erasmo y España*, p. 704.

instrucion (Geneva: [Crespin], 1559); an expansion of a free translation of Urbanus Rhegius's *Novae doctrinae ad veterem collatio* (Geneva: [Durand], 1560); and *Epistola para consolar a los fieles de Jesu Christo, que padecen persecucion por la confession de su Nombre* (Geneva: no printer, 1560).

EL SANCTISSIMO PADRE

De fu padre el diablo recibe el Antechrifto las leyes,
Con que tiraniza cófciencias de vaffallos y Reyes.
1. a Timotheo. 4.

10.4   Bernardino Ochino, *Imagen del Antechristo* ([Geneva]: [Jean Crespin], [1557]), f. A^v

It is not entirely clear just how much connection Juan Pérez had with another Spanish publication produced at this time in Geneva – there were after all other Spaniards in Geneva – but the translation of a pamphlet, *Breve sumario de Indulgencias y gracias*, without place, printer or date, but certainly printed by Crespin, is very much in his style. It is printed to look like an indulgence of the traditional Catholic kind, but carrying a strongly Protestant message. Still less certain is the connection of Pérez with another pamphlet, this time robustly anti-papal and not in his style at all, *Imagen del Antechristo*, which claims to be (and demonstrably is) translated from the Italian of Bernardino Ochino by an unidentified 'Alonso de Peñafuerte'. It is illustrated with a series of dramatic woodcuts.[56] Copies of both these pamphlets were carried overland to Spain by Julián Hernández on the eve of the savage eradica-

---

[56] E. Droz, 'Note sur les impressions genevoises transportées par Hernández', *BHR*, 22 (1960), 126–31; A. G. Kinder and E. M. Wilson, 'The Cambridge copy of the *Imagen del Antechristo*', *Transactions of the Cambridge Bibliographical Society*, 6 (1974), 188–94.

tion of Protestant ideas that occurred there in the late 1550s and early 1560s;[57] and Peter Veller of Antwerp, an employee of Steelsius, had been engaged in the shipment of quantities of them to Seville.[58]

The first complete Spanish Bible (including the books of the Apocrypha printed as part of the Old Testament) was published in Basle in 1569. Its translator-compiler, Casiodoro de Reina, had hoped to have this printed by Crespin in Geneva, but the latter's experience of setting works in Spanish was offset by inconveniences produced by distance, politics, and Reina's personal circumstances.[59] In the end, he contracted its printing with J. Oporinus, who began it, but it was completed after the latter's death by Samuel Biener for Thomas Guarin.[60] As he acknowledges in his preface, Reina used several other Spanish versions of parts of the Bible to help him, but it has recently been noted that the last five or six books of the New Testament were copied almost word-for-word from Juan Pérez's version, even though Reina does not say so.[61] Extant correspondence shows that Reina had tried unsuccessfully to obtain from Paris a copy of the reprint of Pérez's New Testament that was being prepared there at the same time as his Bible was being printed in Basle; he was not to know that Spanish spies had informed the French authorities of what was afoot, that one of the printers had fled and the other was in prison, and that the whole printing had been destroyed.[62] The Pérez New Testament and a number of other books which were being printed at the same time

---

[57] AGS, E121–165; *CODOIN*, vol. 90, p. 220. See also J. E. Longhurst, 'Julián Hernández, Protestant Martyr', *BHR*, 22 (1960), 90–118.

[58] *CODOIN*, vol. 5, pp. 529–33; J. Pérez de Pineda, *Dos informaziones* ... (San Sebastian, 1857), pp. 3–4 (Reformistas antiguos españoles, vol. 12); Boehmer, *Bibliotheca Wiffeniana*, vol. 2, pp. 64–5.

[59] See Reina's letter to Beza from Strasbourg, 9 April 1567, in Théodore de Bèze, *Correspondance* (Geneva, 1976), vol. 8, p. 109.

[60] This is the generally accepted view, although C. Gilly, *Spanien und der Basler Buchdruck bis 1600* (Basle, 1985), pp. 393–4, argues that the work was wholly carried out by Guarin, and that the woodcut of Biener on the title-page, which gives the Bible its name of 'Bear Bible', was nothing more than a borrowing because of the aptness of its illustration for a vernacular Bible.

[61] C. Capó, 'Une Bible espagnole et son traducteur sur les chemins de l'Europe au XVIe siècle', unpublished mémoire de licence, Faculté autonome de théologie Protestante, Geneva, 1985.

[62] A. G. Kinder, *Casiodoro de Reina, Spanish Reformer of the Sixteenth Century* (London, 1975), pp. 47–50; strictly speaking, one copy escaped destruction by being sent to Spain, but even that seems to have disappeared; see the correspondence of the Ambassador to France, AGS, E K1508–7, K1509–10, 20, 25, 36, 60, 80, K1510–4, 7, 16, 52, K1511–33, 60, 69, K1514–68 (this last document reports the burning of 800 New Testaments, catechisms and hymn-books). Money for this enterprise had been provided by the rich Antwerp financier of Spanish marrano descent, Marcos Pérez (AGS, E 526–125), who, having fled the 'Spanish Fury', was to help Casiodoro to survive in Basle as he saw his Bible through the press.

had doubtless been intended as part of the French Huguenot ideological offensive against Spain, carried on but with no long-term success during the 1560s and 1570s. The fact that Reina's Bible was being produced was also known to the Inquisition many months before it eventually appeared, and a close watch was kept to forestall all attempts to introduce copies into Spain. When Reina travelled to England in 1578, the Spanish ambassador reported that he had brought with him copies of his Bible to be sent to Spain. In Frankfurt in 1576 he published for the first time a printed version of the confession of faith he had written in London in 1561, and it was evident from the editorial material that he intended it for export to Spain. The fact that only one copy of this work has ever been recorded (and that was lost during the bombardments of 1939–45) may indicate that the Inquisition blockade proved successful and that most of the copies eventually perished in the flames.[63] There is no doubt, as the records of the Strasbourg Council demonstrate,[64] that Reina also had something to do with the production of the book by the fictitiously named Reginaldus Gonsalvius Montanus, *Sanctae Inquisitionis hispanicae artes detectae ac palam traductae* (Heidelberg: Schirat, 1567), which was responsible almost single-handed for the rise of the so-called Black Legend.[65] Indeed, one modern scholar has stated categorically that Reina was its author,[66] a view strongly contested by B. A. Vermaseren who believes it to be the work of one of Reina's fellow monks in exile, Antonio del Corro.[67] Both views are plausible, and neither is totally convincing. Corro himself was the author of a number of works, published in French, Latin or English, and unlikely therefore to have been intended for export to Spain as instruments of popular evangelization. The most polemical of

---

[63] Boehmer, *Bibliotheca Wiffeniana*, vol. 2, pp. 232–3. Fortunately, the text is known from a bilingual reprint (German and Spanish) made in Cassel (Eberhardt von Redrodt, 1601). However, more recently still, another copy has come to light in the British Library (see A. G. Kinder, 'The Spanish confession of faith of London, 1560/1561', *BHR*, 56 (1994), 745–50).

[64] Strasbourg, Archives Municipales, Protocoles XXI number 45 (1567) fols 37ᵛ, 60ᵛ.

[65] A second Latin edition was printed in Amberg (Schönfeld, 1611), and an abridged Latin version had already been published in Heidelberg (Voegelin, 1603). It was early translated into various languages: English, (London, J. Day, 1568 and again in 1569) (London: Bellamy, 1625); French (no place or printer, 1568); Dutch taken from the French (no place or printer, 1569), and Dutch taken from the Latin (London: Day, 1569), and a different translation (no place or printer, 1569) and The Hague (Meuris: 1621): various German versions, Heidelberg (Mayer, 1569), Amberg (Schönfeld, 1611–12), Eisleben (Petri, 1569): and a Hungarian adaptation in 1570; not to mention many versions of the martyrology taken from it.

[66] C. Gilly, *Spanien und der Basler Buchdruck*, pp. 373–85.

[67] B. A. Vermaseren, 'Who was Reginaldus Gonsalvius Montanus?', *BHR*, 47 (1985), 47–77.

Corro's works was, however, aimed at a Spanish target: the *Lettre envoyée à la maiesté du roy des Espaignes* (Antwerp: no printer, 1567), explained to King Philip II the author's reasons for leaving the Roman Catholic Church for the Protestant camp, and argued strongly in favour of religious toleration in the King's dominions. The rest indicate his efforts to assimilate himself into the society in which he was living, at which he was successful, finally becoming *censor theologicus* of Christ Church, Oxford, and a prebendary of both Lichfield Cathedral and St Paul's, London.[68]

A fellow exile of Reina and Corro, Cipriano de Valera, began to publish virulently anti-papal works in 1588, the year of the defeat of the Armada. These were largely funded by semi-official sources, and they earned for him the title in the Spanish *Index* of 'el herege español'. It is evident that they were intended for shipment in quantity to Spain as an ideological component in the hostilities between England and Spain. First to appear was *Dos tratados: el primero es del Papa [...] el segundo de la misa* (London: Hatfield, 1588). It was followed in quick succession by a series of others till Valera's death soon after 1602. The year 1594 saw *Tratado para confirmar los pobres cativos de Bervería en la catolica y antigua fe y religion Christiana* (London: Short) – clearly modelled on Juan Pérez's *Epistola consolatoria* – to ome copies of which is appended *Enxambre de los falsos milagros con que María de la Visitacion priora de la Anunciada de Lisboa engaño a muy muchos, y de como fue descubierta y condenada, año de 1588*. In 1596 Valera published his revision of Reina's version of the New Testament, *El testamento nuevo de nuestro señor Jesu Christo* (London: Field), and in the same year he edited a new edition of Juan Pérez's *Catecismo* of 1559 (Field). One year later came Valera's translation of Calvin's *Institutes: Institucion de la religion christiana* (London: Field), altered subtly in various places to make it more applicable to the Spanish situation, and in 1599 Valera wrote the preface to the Spanish version of a work by William Perkins, translated by Guillermo Massan, *Catholico reformado, o una declaracion que muestra cuanto nos podamos conformar con la Iglesia Romana* (London: Field). The same year also saw a second edition, much enlarged, of *Dos tratados*, with the *Enxambre* as an appendix (London: Field), and the next year he published, anonymously, his *Aviso a los de la Iglesia Romana sobre la indiccion del Jubileo por la bulla del Papa Clemente octavo* (London: Allde for Wolfe), a translation of a French pamphlet. Aged 70, Valera travelled to Amsterdam to

---

[68] For Corro, see A. G. Kinder, 'Antonio del Corro', *Bibliotheca Dissidentium*, 6 (1986), 121–76.

supervise the printing of his revision of Reina's Bible (changes are few, the main one being that the Apocrypha is printed as a unit between the Old and the New Testaments) in 1602, *Los sacros libros del viejo y nuevo testamento, segunda edicion* (Jacobi), the cost of that edition being borne by Prince Christian I of Anhalt Bernberg (although it is by no means clear why it had to be printed in Holland rather than England). There is no evidence that more than isolated copies of any of these, together with Inquisition 'file-copies', ever got through to Spain, although there are records of concerted efforts to introduce in quantity the version of Calvin's *Institutes* and of the Bible.[69]

Primate of Spain accused of heterodoxy

J. I. Tellechea has demonstrated that the Archbishop of Toledo, Bartolomé Carranza, used Melanchthon's works to prepare a number of texts to present at the Council of Trent, evidence of the penetration of at least one Protestant writer's work into the possession of Spain's highest ecclesiastic.[70] These texts were later used against Carranza in his lengthy trial for heterodoxy from 1559 onwards, during which it was made clear that opponents of reform clearly recognized their Protestant content. Carranza's *Comentarios [...] sobre el catechismo christiano* (Antwerp: Nuntius, 1558), dedicated to Philip II, was also considered suspect in the censure by Melchor Cano and used in the trial, Cano even accusing it of an illuminist tendency.[71] These accusations against the Primate of Spain were part of the exemplary crackdown on all forms of heterodoxy enjoined by the dying Charles V on his son and ordered by Philip II with the backing of papal approval from Paul IV.[72] The inventory of Carranza's library reveals many foreign editions of the Bible, one work each by Luther and Calvin, and a large number of works by Erasmus in both Latin and Spanish.[73]

---

[69] A. G. Kinder, *Casiodoro de Reina* p. 39; Kinder, 'Cipriano de Valera (?1530–?1602)', *Bulletin of Hispanic Studies*, 46 (1969), 109–19; Kinder, 'Religious literature as an offensive weapon: Cipriano de Valera's part in England's war with Spain', *Sixteenth Century Journal*, 19 (1988), 223–5.

[70] J. I. Tellechea, *Melanchton y Carranza: préstamos y afinidades* (Salamanca, 1979).

[71] See the introduction to the modern edition, *Comentarios sobre el Catechismo christiano*, edición crítica y estudio histórico por J. I. Tellechea (Madrid, 1972), pp. 75–81.

[72] It is debatable whether this episode would have happened at all but for the animosity of the Inquisitor General, Fernando de Valdés, who took advantage of the King's absence from the country to make his move against the Archbishop.

[73] J. I. Tellechea, 'La biblioteca del arzobispo Carranza', *Hispania Sacra*, 16 (1963), 409–99.

America

The Erasmian reformist influence was taken to the New World by the first bishop of Mexico, Juan de Zumárraga, who had works of Erasmus shipped to him, along with the *Suma* of Constantino. In 1544 he published in Mexico City *Doctrina breve muy provechosa de las cosas que pertenecen a la fe catholica y a nuestra cristiandad* (printed in the Cromberger branch office, the first press of the New World), a work which reproduces considerable parts of Erasmus's *Enchiridion* and *Paraclesis*. In 1545–46, there appeared also in Mexico City his *Doctrina cristiana: mas cierta y verdadera para gente sin erudicion y letras: en que se contiene el catecismo o informacion para indios con todo lo principal y necessario que el cristiano deve saber y obrar* ('Cromberger'), which is more or less a reprint of the *Suma* without the dialogue form, and in 1547 his *Regla christiana breve*, Mexico City ('Cromberger').[74]

Spain, then, is a case apart when we consider the introduction and spread of Reformation ideas through the printed word. Although there was some penetration from outside by Erasmian and more definitely Protestant literature, and although for a short time Erasmus's works were printed enthusiastically inside Spain, the printing of overtly Protestant works in the country was almost, if not entirely, nil. Whatever reformist ideas were published in Spain were carefully presented in a devotional context (except the two works of Alfonso de Valdés, where the concern is political); Protestant propaganda was all written and printed outside the country. After the purge against Protestantism of the late 1550s, the extreme vigilance exercised in the ports and along the frontiers, and the ideological straitjacket imposed by the Inquisition meant that all attempts to reintroduce such ideas proved vain.

Select bibliography

The classic works on the Reformation in Spain are those by Ed. Boehmer, *Bibliotheca Wiffeniana: Spanish Reformers of two centuries from 1520* (3 vols, London, 1874–1904; reprint, New York, 1969); by E. H. J. Schäfer, *Beiträge zur Geschichte des spanischen Protestantismus und der Inquisition im sechzehnten Jahrhundert* (Gütersloh, 1902); and by M. Menéndez Pelayo, *Historia de los heterodoxos españoles* (Madrid,

---

[74] Joaquín García Icazbalceta, *Don Fray Juan de Zumárraga* (4 vols, Mexico City, 1947), vol. 2, pp. 17–28, 36, 46–60; Joaquín García Icazbalceta *Bibliografia mexicana del siglo XVI* (revised by A. Millares Carlo) (Mexico City, 1954), pp. 62–80; M. Bataillon, *Erasmo y España*, pp. 540–41, 823–7.

1880–82). These works are old, but they contain valuable information, to be completed by my volumes, A. G. Kinder, *Spanish Protestants and Reformers: a Bibliography* (London, 1983); *Spanish Protestants and Reformers, Supplement 1* (London, 1994) (second supplement in preparation).

The sources gathered in the bibliographies of the four progressively expanded editions by M. Bataillon are information goldmines: *Erasme et l'Espagne* (Geneva, 1937, 1991); *Erasmo y España* (Mexico, 1950, 1966). The same is true for the chapters dealing with the sixteenth century in J. L. González Novalín (ed.) *Historia de la Iglesia en España* (Madrid, 1980) volume 3; M. Andrés Martín, *La teologia española en el siglo xvi* (2 vols, Madrid, 1976).

More specific bibliographical information can be found in A. G. Kinder, 'Juan de Valdés', in A. Séguenny (ed.), *Bibliotheca dissidentium: Répertoire des non-conformistes religieux des seizième et dix-septième siècles* (Baden Baden, 1988) vol. 9, pp. 111–95; A. G. Kinder, 'Casiodoro de Reina', in *Bibliotheca dissidentium*, vol. 4, pp. 99–153; A. G. Kinder, 'Antonio del Corro', in *Bibliotheca dissidentium*, vol. 6, pp. 121–76; A. G. Kinder, 'Michael Servetus', in *Bibliotheca dissidentium*, vol. 10; A. G. Kinder, 'The Alumbrados of Toledo', in *Bibliotheca dissidentium*, vol. 16, pp. 7–53.

CHAPTER ELEVEN

The book and the Reformation in Italy

Ugo Rozzo and Silvana Seidel Menchi

Our intention is not to define in detail the characteristics of the Italian Reformation. Suffice it to say that this country, which remained Catholic, had a different history as compared with other countries with a Roman culture. Italy differed from Spain, where the civil and religious authorities blocked any attempt at religious innovation, and from France, where the Catholic majority could not ignore Huguenot power. The end of this chapter will show the particular significance of the concept of Reformation for the Italian context.

The overall political situation in Italy can be described as *policentrismo*, that is, a political organization with many power bases. Spain dominated the scene in Lombardy, Naples and Sicily, while a few regional states like Venice and Savoy jealously guarded their relative autonomy, but the presence of the papal states and the Roman curia still had a strong impact. The curia made its moral and doctrinal authority felt, apart from brief periods in Venice and Lucca, which alone managed to withstand these pressures.

While the Italian Reformation pursued its own path, the sources available also offer unique features. The history of Italian Protestant publishing was directly affected by the clandestine nature of production, through the use of pseudonyms and camouflaged titles. This situation made the identification of authors and topics difficult for the Inquisitor at the time, and continues to cause difficulties for present-day scholars. As most heterodox works are not what they seem at first sight, they probably escaped the Inquisitor's checks more than once, not to mention their owners' talents at hiding these books. Present-day research has to deal with some of the same problems, but at the same time, the scope for new discoveries is vast, although scholars in the field work amid many uncertainties. Not only must one decode documents which have been more or less camouflaged, but many of the works were systematically destroyed by the forces of censorship. Today, there are only 378 Luther texts (452 copies) published between 1518 and 1546 and held in Italian libraries.[1] Only the remnants of a much larger 'library' survive today.

While these gaps have a serious impact on any study of book production, they are counterbalanced by the exceptionally rich sources collected by the Inquisition trials, which, as was suggested at the start of the third paragraph, provide very specific information on the spread of evangelical and Reformed ideas in Italy. Many historians of other European countries can only dream of such an abundance of material.

From the historiographical point of view, the central question of this book is a new one. Relatively little research has been done on the books which provoked and then fed the need for religious reform in Italy.[2] In fact, whether for practical editorial reasons or on ideological grounds historians have virtually ignored both those who printed works and their motivations.

Given that the collections of Inquisition material available today have only been accessible for the last 20 years or so, research in this area is also only beginning. The following remarks constitute the first overall summary of this new field of research, and therefore anticipate the tentative steps of the new enquiry. The bibliography outlined in the following pages can also only offer examples of situations or particular figures, rather than conclusions drawn from systematic analyses.

The production and circulation of books

When the Reformation sprang into life in Germany, Italian publishing was in full swing, perfectly equipped to help inform and reflect on the ideological debate which had opened up across Europe. There were more Italian presses than in any other European state, and in Venice alone, for instance, there were more than 500 printers and publishers at work.[3] These men were firmly at the forefront in the technical domain,

---

[1] G. Mazzetti, *Le prime edizioni di Lutero (1518–1546) nelle Biblioteche italiane* (Florence, 1984). Many of these texts came into Italy after the period we are interested in.

[2] On the general context, see C. De Frede, *Ricerche per la storia della stampa e la diffusione delle idee riformate nell'Italia del Cinquecento* (Naples, 1985); for the bibliography of sixteenth century Italian editions, see L. Sereni (ed.) *Arte tipographica del sec. XVI in Italia. Bibliografia italiana (1800–1983)* (Rome, 1984). Another useful work is P. Chiminelli, *Bibliografia della storia della Riforma in Italia* (Rome, 1921). See also U. Rozzo, *Linee per una storia dell'editoria religiosa in Italia (1465–1600)* (Udine, 1993).

[3] P. F. Grendler, *L'Inquisizione romana e l'editoria a Venezia, 1540–1603* (Rome, 1983), p. 23; G. Borsa, *Clavis typographorum librariorumque Italiae, (1465–1600)* (Baden-Baden, 1980).

in typesetting, in their knowledge of the markets and in their organization of trade. A growth in the number of customers and thus a division of interests in the world of printing led to a diversification in production. *In forma enchiridii* volumes were joined by heavy folio tomes, while small popular editions, poorly executed and inexpensive, were put up for sale alongside weighty commentaries and 'scientific' works complete with illustrations.

The printed book acquired its final aspect and functional role in the first two decades of the sixteenth century, as it became an everyday object, even in houses where literacy was a recent phenomenon. Evidence of this lies in the paintings of the period in which books appear even in the most humble setting. They are also portrayed without fail in the hands of the Virgin at the Annunciation, or on the study bookshelves of St Jerome or St Augustine.

Camouflaged production

Yet from its inception, Italian printing did not participate much in the production of books connected with the 'religious revolution' of the sixteenth century, or of works providing information on such topics. Only one volume printed in Italy bears the name of Martin Luther on its cover page, and it was published in 1518. The book was a Venetian reprint by Bernardino Stagnino of the *Appellatio ad Concilium*, which had appeared in Wittenberg in the same year. After the *Exsurge Domine* Bull of 15 June 1520 and the *Decet Romanum Pontificem* of 3 January 1521, in which Pope Leo X excommunicated the German monk and consigned all his present and future books to the fire, no Italian printer or bookseller dared to print or sell any texts of the 'Saxon monster' in broad daylight, nor even works favourable to his cause. After this point, therefore, there were no further overtly Protestant publications. As one could not allow oneself to be seen to be in agreement with a German monk solemnly anathematized by the Pope, 'Lutheran' works took on a clandestine nature.

One of the major difficulties of this research lies in the very definition of 'heretical' books. Among the works denounced by the Inquisition, apart from foreign imports, one finds works written by Italian reformers and crypto-reformers. The latter went from translations reasonably faithful to the original to all manner of transformations. As it was impossible to offer openly complete works coming from the other side of the Alps, writers summarized, transformed, or made interpolations into various works. Certain publishers offered both more or less heterodox works and books of devotion, or even Catholic apologetical works. This practice, undoubtedly in response to market pressures, was moti-

vated in more than one instance by the need for justification or preventative camouflage. Otherwise, how can one explain the clever request for printing privileges for works such as Rhegius's *Medecina dell
'anima* (Comin da Trino in 1543) or the *Alphabeto Christiano* of J. de
Valdes (with an introduction by the translator Marcantonio Magno in
1544)? In the same way, Valgrisi, who published the Index of Venice in
1549, did not hesitate when invoking a probably non-existent privilege
to justify the translation of the Koran in 1547.

However, the spread of Reformation ideas in Italy was not only due
to the works of authentic national or foreign Protestants, but also to
'evangelical' works. Defining the characteristic features of the evangelical movement is difficult, as calls for profound spiritual renewal were
made alongside hopes for a limited transformation of church structures
and for a reform of morals. To a large extent, historians have been
responsible for the unification of these divergent tendencies into a single
movement.[4]

Furthermore, apart from clearly 'well-placed' theological writings,
others had a subversive effect, going sometimes well beyond their authors' expectations, as these works' themes and viewpoints prepared
the way for or supported Protestant questioning. Romantic literature
from Boccacio to Bandello[5] exercised an incontrovertible influence, as
did certain works of drama and political history, from the Aretin to
Guicchardini and Machiavelli. These works are among the best in terms
of raising doubts and therefore weakening respect for religious institutions and their representatives at various levels. A large section of
popular or street literature, including the lampoons and the cultured
poems of Caravia,[6] prepared the way for new theological messages.
Erasmus's writings played a significant role in this context, as they were
often read as a clever satire of religious behaviour.[7] For these reasons,

---

[4] The breadth of this movement is illustrated by the extreme positions of two of its
protagonists, the Spaniard Juan de Valdès on the one hand and the Bishop of Verona,
Gian Matteo Giberti on the other. A. Prosperi, *Tra Evangelismo e Controriforma, G. M.
Giberti (1495–1543)* (Rome, 1969); P. Simoncelli, *Evangelismo italiano del Cinquecento.
Questione religiosa e nicodemismo politico* (Rome, 1979); A. Aubert, 'Valdesianesimo
ed evangelismo italiano. Alcuni casi recenti', *Rivista di Storia della Chiesa in Italia*, 41
(1987), 152–75.

[5] U. Rozzo, 'Bandello, Lutero e la censura', in U. Rozzo (ed.), *Gli uomini, le città e i
tempi di Matteo Bandello: Il Convegno internazionale di studi* (Tortona, 1985), pp. 275–
300.

[6] V. Marucci, A. Marzo and A. Romano (eds), *Pasquinate romane del Cinquecento*
(Rome, 1983); E. Benini Clementi, 'Il processo del gioielliere veneziano Alessandro
Caravia', *Nuova Rivista Storica*, 65 (1981), 628–52.

[7] S. Seidel Menchi, *Erasmo in Italia (1520–1580)* (Turin, 1987).

such texts were noted, pursued and condemned with the same ferocity as were openly heterodox works.

The Italian production centres

The 'Reformed' books circulating in Italy not only offered an assortment of theological perspectives but also stemmed from different locations. Two groups of works can be examined, those produced in Italy and those imported from outside the country. Although imported books made up the most important group chronologically, theologically, and also perhaps numerically, the discussion will focus first on national production.

The first evidence of local underground printing activity favouring Protestantism was in 1525, when an anonymous work, *Uno libretto volgare con la dechiaratione de li dieci commandamenti* was published in Venice. Containing several texts in dialogue form including two by Luther, it was reprinted again in Venice in the following year, but under a different title and with Erasmus as author, a strategy which had been used before to conceal the true nature of such works. But already in 1533, the translation of the appeal to the Christian nobility of the German nation was printed in Strasbourg, entitled *Libro de la emendatione et correctione dil stato Christiano.*[8]

One cannot measure the size of the national production of evangelical books in Italy, although it does seem that the production was always sporadic even in the years 1530 to 1560, and thus played only a minor role as compared with imports. The largest production effort by Italian Reformers and reformists occurred between 1540 and 1550, during the decade which saw the colloquy at Regensburg and the first sessions of the Council of Trent, as long as hopes of agreement survived and repression had not yet come into full effect. This period also saw the greatest interest in religious matters on the part of the general population, coinciding with an increase in cultural interests in society. This production effort was profoundly affected by the first real index of prohibited books issued by the nuncio Della Casa in Venice in May 1549. Production finally ceased in the early 1560s, as the doctrinal statements of Trent were definitive from then on, and the first Roman Index of 1559 coupled with the repressive power of the Inquisition took away any desire whether imagined or real to create ambiguous titles or authors' names. From this point onwards, no one could print anything outside official control. And yet because of the lack of knowledge and at times the lack of competence of the censors, who had problems

---

[8] See the list of Italian translations below, numbers 1, 2, and 5.

countering the imitative or obsfuscating ability of their adversaries, certain works were able to circulate more or less freely for approximately 40 years, before being spotted as dangerous bases for doctrinal infection.[9]

The international language used in the spread of the Reformation was Latin, but at the time when Protestant ideas were introduced into Italy, the vernacular had acquired a definite place in cultural and social life. Italian Reformers soon realized that they needed to use the language of the people in order to attract new and more numerous adherents. For this reason, books produced locally were almost always in the vernacular. Translations of the works of leading foreign figures from the Latin or the original language were thus essential and urgent. Translators, completely ignored until now by historians, thus played a fundamental role in the spread of the Reformation message. By identifying those who carried out such work, one could establish both editorial strategies and doctrinal allegiances. Translators included professionals, linguists who carried out such work perhaps for more than economic reasons, and finally converted intellectuals, for whom translation was an educational and confessional duty. Apart from Antonio Brucioli's specific and onerous task of translating the Bible and adding commentaries, a task which was finally felt to be clearly contaminated by works of Calvin and other foreign masters,[10] other translators' names emerged. Pietro Lauro, from Modena, included in his vast output a translation of Erasmus's *Colloquia* (Venice, 1544, 1545 and 1549) and of the *Chronica* of Johann Carion (Venice, 1543 and 1548). Lodovico Domenichi, another professional, translated Calvin's *Nicodemiana*[11] and Cornelius Agrippa's *De incertitudine et vanitate scientiarum* into Italian in 1550. Lodovico Castelvetro, a scholar who favoured Protestantism translated Melanchthon's *Loci Communes* from his *Principii* perhaps before 1535,[12] while Bernardino Tomitano dealt with Erasmus's *Parafrasi a Matteo* published in 1547. But the works of the Rotterdam humanist were published in Italian at a later date as well. The *Moria* was translated by A. Pellegrini in 1539, while Emilio dei Migli's translation of the *Enchiridion* was published in Brescia in 1531 and 1540 and in Venice in 1539, 1542 and 1543. Stefano Pinelli translated *Il divotissimo libro de la preparatione alla morte* (Venice, 1539) and *Della institutione de'*

---

[9] U. Rozzo, 'Dieci anni di censura libraria (1596–1605)', *Libri e documenti*, 9 (1983), pp. 43–61.

[10] G. Spini, 'Bibliografia delle opere di Antonio Brucioli', *La Bibliofilia*, 42 (1940), 138–63.

[11] See below, footnote 17.

[12] See number 6 on the list of Italian translations, below.

Fanciulli (Venice 1545 and 1547). In 1546, Fausto da Longiano provided an Italian version of the *Apoftegmi*, while Lelio Carani's translation of *I proverbi* appeared in 1550. Marco Antonio Magna put Juan
de Valdès's *Alfabeto Christiano* into Italian, a work which was printed
in Venice in 1545, and an anonymous Italian Protestant translated
Alfonso de Valdès's *Due Dialoghi*, adding many anti-Roman features to
it. This last work was published at least seven times between 1545 and
1555.[13] As for non-professional translators, there were some clerics,
such as Bartholomeo Fanzio, a Franciscan who translated *An den
Christlichen Adel*, and certain Augustinian hermits who probably translated the *Sommario della Santa Scrittura* and the *Dottrina vecchia et
nuova* into Italian. The translation of the latter work is ascribed to
Niccolò da Verona.[14] This list reflects only a small part of religious
works, be they ancient or modern, translated into Italian to contribute
to the theological debate. In future, it may be possible to identify others
engaged in translation, and thus to expand the list of translated works
attributed to specific individuals.

The situation of manuscript books is even less well known, both in
terms of the identification of manuscript works in circulation or of their
number. Some data suggests that manuscripts played an important role,
but in certain cases, manuscripts were sometimes kept for future possible publication. The copying workshop set up in Naples by Mario
Galeota to transcribe works by Juan de Valdes was certainly no isolated
event.[15]

The contribution of Venice to heterodox printing

During the first half of the sixteenth century, Venice remained the centre
of European printing. On its own, Venice produced 70 per cent of
printed books in Italy, or 15 000 titles in the course of the century, for
an average of 50 new works or re-editions each year. Given that it
would certainly be difficult to exercise any control over such an output,
it is not surprising that the majority of printshops working for the
Reformation were located in Venice. There were very few Italian heterodox works published outside Venice, and in most cases these were
sporadic occurrences. In a few cases, the works had been given false
places of publication: certain Basle editions were ostensibly published in

[13] A. de Valdès, *Due dialoghi*, G. De Gennaro (ed.), (Naples, 1968).

[14] S. Peyronel Rambaldi, 'Itinerari italiani di un libretto riformato: il "Sommario della
Sacra Scrittura"', *BSSV*, 160 (1987), 3–18.

[15] P. Lopez, *Il movimento valdesiano a Napoli: Mario Galeota e le sue vicende col
Sant'Uffizio* (Naples, 1976), pp. 27–50.

Rome, a choice made on humorous and polemical grounds. Those who chose Trent clearly upheld anti-Tridentine views, but in other cases the grounds for such choices are less clear, as for books supposedly brought out in Milan or Plaisance.[16] The Genevan printer Jean Crespin used Venice for some of his Spanish editions of the work of Juan de Valdès. In contrast, there is no evidence of Italian books being published under foreign place names: even the *Dottrina Vecchia e nuova* of Urbanus Rhegius, published between 1539 and 1545, and the *Nicodemiana* of 1550–51,[17] may in fact have been published in the Swiss lands, in spite of a few indications to the contrary. Certain works were published outside Venice in a search for greater tranquility and less pressure from the Inquisitors. For instance Juan de Valdès' *Lacte spirituale* appeared in Pavia in 1550 with Francesco Moscheni as printer. In the light of these examples, the information regarding Neapolitan printing of popular works like the *Beneficio di Cristo* and the *Sommario della Sacra Scrittura* seems possible.

As the history of Venetian printing largely remains to be written, the absence of works on contacts between publishers and the Reformation is understandable. By putting together the information presently at our disposal, the most one can hope for is to draw out certain general conclusions. One must bear in mind that the state of current knowledge is so minimal that a study of heretical printing can transform the image of a publisher like Zoppino: although in the past he had been generally perceived as a specialist in romantic and poetic literature, he now appears to have been one of the main distributors of the new theology.

Among the major Venetian printers who began their work in the first two decades of the sixteenth century, only a few were linked to the new religious developments, and some had only minor connections with it. For instance, members of the Bindoni family, and Alessandro in particular, worked together with Matteo Pasini from 1523. Bernardino Viani, who began as a printer in 1520, and the aforementioned Niccolò Zoppino,

---

[16] Only a part of the reported cases appear in M. Parenti, *Dizionario dei luoghi di stampa falsi, inventati o supposti* (Florence, 1951).

[17] For these two cases, Italian sources mention printing done in Verona and Florence respectively, with Basle as the false place of printing appearing on the title page (S. Cavazza, 'Libri in volgare e propaganda eterodossa: Venezia 1543–1547', in A. Prosperi and A. Biondi (eds), *Libri, idee e sentimenti religiosi nel Cinquecento italiano* (Ferrare, 1987), p. 27; A. D'Alessandro, 'Prime ricerche su Lodovico Domenichi', in A. Quondam (ed.), *Le Corti farnesiane di Parma e Piacenza, 1545–1622* (Rome, 1978), pp. 182–4. See also D. Cantimori, *Prospettive di storia ereticale italiana del Cinquecento* (Bari, 1960), p. 38 and especially F. Bonaini, 'Dell'imprigionamento per opinioni religiose di Renata d'Este e di Lodovico Domenichi ... ', *Giornale storico degli archivi toscani*, 3 (1859), 268–81.

La declaratione delli dieci comandaméti:
del Credo:del Pater noster:con vna breue an
notatione del viuere christiano p Erasmo
Rotherodamo vtile z neceffaria a cia
scuno fidele christiano. Historiata.

11.1   Writings of Luther published under Erasmus's name: *La declaratione delli dieci commandamenti* (Venice: Niccolò Zoppino, 1526)

active in Venice since 1507, all had links with the new religious outlook. Printers who appeared between the 1530s and 1540s were even more active in Reformation printing: Andrea Arrivabene from 1534,

Bartholomeo Zanetti since 1535, Comin da Trino beginning in 1539, and the Brucioli brothers, Michele Tramezzino, and Vincenzo Valgrisi since 1540. At the same time, around 1540, the large printing firms which had opened in the first decades of the century closed their doors.

The relative freedom in Venice progressively shrank beginning at the end of the 1540s. Some heterodox works were still being published in the 1550s, like Erasmus's Latin treatises or volumes of vernacular correspondence containing clearly evangelically-inspired texts, as for example the letters of Orazio Brunetto.[18] Some later reprints of biblical translations by Brucioli can be found up until 1556.

Given the state of present research, it is difficult to establish the motives of all these printers. As it was unlikely that any of them expected to make a profit investing in this type of book, and as the works were aimed at a relatively small clientele, the printers must have been committed to the cause of Reform or been given an order large enough to cover the economic risks of seizure and potential criminal proceedings. Once a certain frequency of heterodox publications was established, one can exclude the filling of an order for mercenary reasons alone. But any analysis of motives must also examine the theological consistency between the published works.

At times, especially during the first years, partial or total ignorance of the subversive content of certain works was possible. Once denunciations and trials began, it is inconceivable that the talented and often well-educated entrepreneurs in Venice, for instance, had no knowledge of the content of their publications. Even though they might not have had any real sympathy for heterodoxy, at the very least they were confessionally indifferent. In no way were they innocent printers fooled by interested parties or rash advisers. This is proved by the fact that no printer, publisher or bookseller accused by the Inquisition placed their editorial responsibility on others. Instead, they blamed the need to hurry, their good faith, and their own incompetence. The frequent omission of the place of printing confirms that printers were aware of the daring doctrines contained in their works. Neutral-looking volumes, often anonymous, made up a large percentage of production.

Among the above-mentioned printers, the Brucioli brothers seem to be the only ones who published works which tended towards the Refor-

---

18 A. J. Schutte, 'The "Lettere volgari" and the crisis of Evangelism in Italy', *Renaissance Quarterly*, 28 (1975), 639–88; A. Del Col, 'Note sull'eterodossia di fra Sisto da Siena e i suoi rapporti con Orazio Brunetto e un gruppo veneziano di "spirituali"', *Collectanea franciscana*, 47 (1977), 27–64; G. Moro (ed.), *Novo libro di lettere scritte da i più rari auttori e professori della lingua volgare italiana*, reprint of Gherardo's edition of 1544 and 1545 (Sala Bolognese, 1987), pp. lxxvii–lxxxvi.

mation because of their own confessional allegiance. Francesco Brucioli was in fact the only Italian printer whose complete body of work was condemned by the Roman Index of 1559. Andrea Arrivabene and Vincenzo Valgrisi also adopted the new religious ideas, but it is much more difficult to make any overall judgements regarding the other printers who occasionally brought out heterodox works. Once the names of printers can be attached to previously anonymously printed works, the catalogue of forbidden works will likely be enriched once again by works from previously mentioned authors and from new ones.

A strong printing network beyond the Alps

As has been noted, books printed outside Italy made up the greater part of Italian heterodox books. This includes not only works of foreign Reformers imported into Italy, but also works by Italian theologians, who chose to have their works printed abroad because of more or less well-founded fears. Thus Aonio Paleario's work appeared in Lyon in 1536 and Giovan Battista Folengo's in Basle in 1540. Nevertheless, these writers clearly bore the Italian scene and debates in mind. This publishing presence beyond Italy's borders increased greatly and changed significantly when a number of leading dissenters fled Italy over the Alps. Between 1542 and 1549, leading figures like Agostino Mainardi, Bernardino Ochino, Pietro Martire Vermigli, Celio Secondo Curione, Camillo Renato, Francesco Negri, Guilio della Rovere (or da Milano) and Pier Paolo Vergerio all left Italy behind. A body of work mainly written in Italian then surfaced especially in the Swiss lands, in Basle, Poschiavo, Geneva and Zurich, but also in Lyon and London. These works were aimed not only at fellow exiles, but also at the large number of sympathizers still in Italy. This movement died down after 1560, as that generation of exiled Italian theologians died. Ochino, Mainardi, Vermigli and Vergerio as well as two famous radical Reformers, Gribaldi Mofa and Lelio Sozzini died between 1562 and 1565, followed by Aconcio, and then Curione in 1569, although the last had been absent from the heart of the debate for many years.

Italian printers' presence was most strongly felt in Geneva, where twenty or so were active especially in the first half of the century. Their most famous member was Giovanni Girard or Gérard, who came from Suse in 1536, and was talented enough to become Calvin and Farel's most trusted publisher. Between 1542 and 1545 he produced the vast Genevan works of Bernardino Ochino.[19] The Italian Reformed

---

[19] J.-Fr. Gilmont, 'Bibliotheca gebennensis: les livres imprimés à Genève de 1535 à 1549', *Genava*, 28 (1980), 229–51.

community's concern for the faithful who remained in Italy can be seen in the production of some 45 works in Italian between 1550 and 1600, of which slightly less than half was produced by printers of Italian origin. But of the 16 printers involved in the work, only four were Italian.[20] Beginning in 1545, with Ochino's *Expositione sopra la Epistola alli Romani*, they made certain works available without an author's name or a printer's address, in order to introduce them more easily into Italy.

Basle was another crucial printing centre for Italian Protestants. Several dissident authors benefited from its more tolerant atmosphere to publish important texts though these were often debatable in doctrine and of doubtful orthodoxy. Besides original editions and reprints of Ochino's writings, Basle was the printing centre for C. S. Curione's *Araneus*, Peter Martyr's *Una semplice dichiaratione sopra gli XII articoli della fede christiana*, both in 1544, and for two editions of Francesco Negri's *Tragedia del libero arbitrio* in 1546 and 1550. In 1547, Francesco Stancaro published his *Opera nova della reformatione*. In 1550, Curione organized the publication of Juan de Valdès' *Le cento e dieci divine considerazioni*, in 1553, his *Selectarum epistolarum libri duo* and his famous *De amplitudine beati Regni Dei* in the following year. Aonio Paleario's *Opera Omnia* were also published in Basle in 1552 and 1556.[21]

Oporinus published many of these texts, but Basle also housed the shop of Pietro Perna, from Lucca.[22] As a bookseller, he began an intense activity in book trafficking to Italy from 1545, and then, from 1558 at least, he printed numerous works of Italian 'heretics'. Among the most well-known authors and texts he published were Peter Martyr's commentary on the Letter to The Romans (1558) and his *Defensio* (1559);

---

[20] E. Balmas, 'L'activité des imprimeurs italiens réfugiés à Genève dans la deuxième moitié du XVIe siècle', in J.-D. Candaux and B. Lescaze (eds), *Cinq siècles d'imprimerie genevoise: Actes du Colloque international sur l'histoire de l'imprimerie et du livre à Genève, 27–30 avril 1978* (Geneva, 1980), pp. 109–31. See also U. Rozzo, 'Editori e tipografi italiani operanti all'estero "religionis causa"', in M. Santoro (ed.), *La stampa in Italia nel Cinquecento* (Rome, 1992), vol. 1, pp. 89–116.

[21] P. G. Bietenholz, *Der italienische Humanismus und die Blütezeit des Buchdrucks in Basel: Die Basler Drucke italienischer Autoren von 1530 bis zum Ende des 16. Jahrhunderts* (Basle, 1959), pp. 19–37. See Chapter 8 above.

[22] L. Perini, 'Note e documenti su Pietro Perna libraio-tipografo di Basilea', *Nuova Rivista Storica*, 50 (1966), 145–91; Perini, 'Ancora sul libraio-tipografo Pietro Perna e su alcune figure di eretici italiani in rapporto con lui negli anni 1549–1555', *Nuova Rivista Storica*, 51 (1967), 363–404; A. Rotondò, *Studi e ricerche di storia ereticale italiana del Cinquecento* (Turin, 1974), vol. 1, pp. 273–391. See also L. Perini, 'Amoenitates typographicae', in S. Rota Ghibaudi and F. Barcia (eds), *Studi politici in onore di Luigi Firpo* (Milan, 1990), pp. 873–971.

the *Catechismo* (1561), the *Disputa* (1561), the *Labyrinthi* (1561) and especially the renowned *Dialogi XXX* (1563), all by Bernardino Ochino, and Jacobo Aconcio's *Dialogo di Giacopo Riccamati Ossanese*, his *Somma brevissima della dottrina Christiana* and his *De methodo* (all in 1558) as well as his *Satanae Stratagemata* (1565). In 1558, Perna also published the *Mundi constitutionum et tempestatum praedictiones certae ac perpetuae* by Guiglielmo Grataroli and Olimpia Morato's *Opera Omnia*, which Perna reprinted in 1562. Still in Basle, Pier Paolo Vergerio used the presses of Jacques Parcus to publish his many anti-Catholic polemical works, while at the same time making use of Froschauer's Zurich presses.

In Poschiavo in the Grisons, Dolfino Landolfi had been at work as a printer since the end of 1547. Directed first by the former hermit Guilio Della Rovere, the Reformed minister in the town, and then by Vergerio, Landolfi published a series of small volumes containing Italian texts by these two theologians, and then by Agostino Mainardi and Francesco Negri.[23] This explains why the Roman Index of 1559 lists Genevan names among the 61 publishers whose entire body of work was condemned. The Genevan names (Italian in origin) were Girard, Paschale and Pinerolio, as well as Landolfi from Poschiavo.

As for Lyon, the dozen Italian printers and publishers who worked there never seemed to have been involved in heterodox publications, apart from Sebastian Onorati (Honorat) beginning in 1563.[24] And yet books written by 'reformed' Italians, and destined essentially for Italy were not lacking. Certain editions put out by Sebastian Gryphe's presses especially between 1530 and 1540 merit closer scrutiny: they were written by Ortensio Lando, Aonio Paleario and Gaudenzio Merula, all linked to movements of dissent and religious protests.[25] Many anonymous works published in Lyon in 1551 were of great theological importance, as was the translation of the New Testament by the Florentine benedictine Massimo Teofilo (reprinted in Lyon in 1556), the *Semenze de l'intelligenza del Nuovo Testamento* by the same author (republished in 1552 and 1554), the Calvin text *Come Christo è il fine de la Legge*, and finally *Le Parafrasi* of St Paul's Epistles by Cornelio Donzellino. (*Le Parafrasi* and Calvin's preface were reprinted in Geneva by Giovan

---

[23] R. Bornatico, *L'arte tipografica nelle Tre Leghe (1547–1803) e nei Grigioni (1803–1975)* (Chur, 1976), pp. 39–55. See also U. Rozzo, 'L'"Esortazione al martirio" di Giulio da Milano', in A. Pastore (ed.), *Riforma e società nei Grigioni Valtellina e Valchiavenna tra '500 e '600* (Milan, 1991), pp. 63–88.

[24] E. Balmas, 'Librai italiani a Lione', in U. Rozzo, *Gli uomini*, pp. 261–74.

[25] U. Rozzo, 'La cultura italiana nelle edizioni lionesi di Sébastien Gryphe (1531–1541)', *La Bibliofilia*, 90 (1988), 161–95.

Luigi Paschale in 1555, while the Florentine Sebastian Onorati re-printed the four Italian works of 1551 in Lyon in 1565).[26] As it is difficult, even today, to locate these editions even in foreign archives, it is probable that a large part of the print-run was sent to Italy and that the Inquisition destroyed it. Finally, one must bear in mind that as far as one can tell, none of the printer-publishers active outside Italy seems to have been in the profession in Italy. Italian printers did not flee for religious reasons, unlike the massive departures from France to Geneva.

A small, portable and economical book

Protestant or crypto-Protestant works printed in or for Italy adopted formats making them harder to detect: the volumes were small and without relief characters even in the choice of fonts for the title-page, in the use of illustrations or other decorative elements. Clearly, affordability was not the chief concern, as much as the need to go unnoticed. This was manifest in the attempt to follow a specific and widespread model of publishing, namely that of works of piety and edification. This disguise is reflected in the frequent absence of the author's name or of the printer's address, as well as in the choice of titles. The same holds true for translations of famous works, which too use neutral terms like *libro, libretto, sommario, dottrina, trattato*, almost always accompa-nied by reassuring adjectives like *devoto, devotissimo, pio, Christiano*, etc. It is equally possible that these adaptations were meant as a subver-sive attack on devotional literature, where the *Miracoli della Madonna* or other *Legende dei santi* proliferated, all of which were condemned by Protestants as leading to superstitious and magical religiosity.

The preference for small-sized books was due to several factors: less paper was used, transport over long distances to a scattered readership was made easier, and finally, the books could be hidden more easily both during transport and afterwards. All of these needs led to pocket-sized, rather than 'bag-sized' books. The only exception was Brucioli's large folio volumes of translation and commentary on Scripture. Here too, the choice of format may have been dictated by current custom, for though another format may not have attracted the censors' attention, it might also have been ignored by readers.

The number of typographical errors in these booklets and the use of multi-purpose fonts indicate how rapidly these works were often printed,

---

[26] E. Droz, 'Propagande italienne (1551–1565)' in E. Droz, *Chemins de l'hérésie. Textes et documents* (Geneva, 1971), vol. 2, pp. 228–89; A. Del Col, 'Il Nuovo Testa-mento tradotto da Massimo Teofilo e altre opere stampate a Lione nel 1551', *Critica Storica*, 15 (1978), 642–75.

but also how incompetent certain second-rate printers were, to whom controversial works were sometimes entrusted, as these printers did cheap work, and were often uninterested or badly prepared. Books were printed as often in roman as in italic type, while gothic type, still used in certain works of the 1520s, disappeared completely after 1520, in another sign of the appeal to general tastes.

Illustrations were rare, but are often of great interest. A limited study showed that alongside well-known and traditional woodcuts intended to reinforce the familiar, were ideological reinterpretations of iconology. For example, the blood of Christ flowing in the chalice would become the symbol of communion in two kinds.[27] In certain exceptional cases, one must not exclude the possibility that new scenes were created to reflect new values, as when Tobias seems to be dragging the angel along, rather than being led by him.[28] There is one case of a theological message being transmitted through a picture. Though the example is unique, it had a major impact, as it was done by one of the great painters of the century. It is the frontispiece of Brucioli's *Bibbia* (1532), created by Lorenzo Lotto's very refined figurative inspiration. The anti-Roman nature of the symbolism borrowed from Lucas Cranach is especially evident in a few illustrations of the Apocalypse: the Saint Ange castle is represented in the picture of the apocalyptic Babylon destroyed by fire, and the triple papal tiara is placed on the head of the whore of Babylon.[29] Unfortunately there are very few sources and studies on iconographical themes presented in the rare but still extant tracts and in booklets of religious polemic, where illustrations were vital in the search for a new audience beyond the literate.[30]

Lacking explicit information, we assume that the print-runs were always small or very small – a few hundred or a few dozen copies[31] –

---

[27] U. Rozzo, 'Antonio da Pinerolo e Bernardino Ochino', *Rivista di storia e letteratura religiosa*, 19 (1982), 355–7.

[28] B. Ochino, I *"Dialogi sette" e altri scritti del tempo della fuga*, U. Rozzo (ed.), (Turin, 1985), pp. 177–8.

[29] G. Romano, 'La Bibbia di Lotto', *Paragone*, 317–19 (1976), 82–91; M. Cali, 'Ancora sulla "religione" di Lorenzo Lotto', *Ricerche di storia dell'arte*, 19 (1983), 37–60.

[30] L. Perini, 'Ancora sul libraio-tipografo Pietro Perna' p. 389, no. 30; p. 391, nos 26–30; A. Del Col, 'Lucio Paolo Rosello e la vita religiosa veneziana verso la metà del secolo XVI', in *Rivista di Storia della Chiesa in Italia*, 32 (1978), 439–40; O. Niccoli, 'Un aspetto della propaganda religiosa nell'Italia del Cinquecento: opuscoli e fogli volanti', Prosperi and Biondi, *Libri, idee*, pp. 29–37.

[31] Print-runs of 12 copies have been mentioned for occasional works (weddings, princely entries, …); it is equally possible that such low print-runs were also done for forbidden texts slipped in between two official works. (see Grendler, *L'Inquisizione romana*, p. 28).

despite certain outstanding examples like the extraordinary *Trattato utilissimo del Beneficio di Cristo*. According to the almost unbelievable testimony of Pier Paolo Vergerio, approximately 40 000 copies were sold between 1543 and 1549.[32] Like so many other books published in Italy, only a few or a single copy of this work remains in existence, in most cases in foreign collections. There is no way, therefore, to calculate the initial print-run based on surviving copies. The number of copies was tied, naturally enough, to the absorption capacity of the market.

The purchase price of these works is even more difficult to establish. On the one hand, market forces dictated a similar cost for similar works (one or two lire maximum). But once censorship and persecution appeared, these books became dangerous, and thus rare, and thus expensive. Clearly they were much sought after by the 'faithful' who remained in Italy, and for whom these books were the only sustenance for their faith.

The circulation of forbidden books

A study of the edicts of condemnation and seizure of books shows how rapid and important the penetration of foreign Protestant works into Italy was. Between 1520 and 1523, works by Luther, Zwingli and Melanchthon were denounced to the authorities in Venice, Bologna, Naples, Turin and Milan. In 1538, among its 41 forbidden works, the Milan index listed alongside Luther and Melanchthon Calvin's Catechism, recently printed in Basle, Brunfels's *Pandectae*, Erasmus Sarcerius's works on four occasions as well as all the other leaders of the Reformation in Europe, including Zwingli, even though his name has not been identified. The only work in the vernacular was *El Summario de la Sacra Scriptura*.[33] This index was not in fact intended as a general condemnation of abstract doctrines, but was an attempt to affect and if possible destroy the bases of theological infection which were in fact present in the Duchy of Milan.

The penetration of Protestant works from outside Italy reached its peak around 1540. At that time, Melanchthon spoke of entire libraries sent to Italy through Savoy, the Milan Duchy, and the Venetian lands. In spite of the large number of condemnations of those possessing forbidden books, and of various appeals from Rome, the Venetian Republic only slowly adopted measures to control the importation of books. However, large numbers of works were arriving, and to keep

---

[32] P. P. Vergerio, *Il catalogo dei libri li quali nuovamente nel mese di maggio nell'anno presente MDXLVIIII sono stati condannati* (Poschiavo, Landolfi, 1549), fol. g5r.

[33] E. Balmas, 'In margine al centenario luterano', *BSSV*, 155 (1984), 24–37.

watch over works sent from outside Italy was no easy task. But Venice only enacted legislation on the subject in 1547.

The Venetian index published by the Nuncio Della Casa in May 1549 confirms both the variety and the vast amount of imports: in terms of isolated works, 73 were published abroad, as against only as few as 13 editions which were definitely Italian, all in the vernacular.[34] For the most part, the list indicated works which were circulating in Venice, some quite freely as the author's name was not as well known. The large number of books in circulation is confirmed by the burning of some 1 400 books on 18 July 1548 and 10 000 to 12 000 burnt in March 1559.

Books printed in Germany, Switzerland or France could easily be in Italy in less than a month: There were multiple means of circulation in Italy, but these became more and more risky, as the censorship measures took effect. Already in February 1519, Pavia's bookseller, Francesco Calvó, purchased from Froben the Lutheran pamphlets recently translated into Latin.[35] This trade continued to be uneven at least until 1570, without even coming to a complete stop after that. The reissuing of censorship measures and repressive actions well beyond the chronological limits of this study confirm the importance of the book trade.

The circulation channels of the book trade were naturally very varied. Often illegal, they partly managed to escape any institutional structures. This can be shown by the very limited number and late date of trials of booksellers for selling forbidden works, as compared with the massive presence of these books in Italy at the time. During the entire sixteenth century, but especially from 1520 to 1540, when checks were rare and the Inquisition less powerful, the circulation of books was carried out in large part by isolated individuals like the many foreign students who attended Italian universities, Italian and foreign merchants travelling across Europe, or even the clergy who in obedience to their duties or their rule travelled from one monastery to another. Others active in the book trade included itinerant traders, or finally the foreign armies that passed through the peninsula or were based there, and often included soldier-students. The major German and French fairs also enabled Italian visitors to discover new publications.

Although the number of booksellers involved in trials for the sale of forbidden literature was small, as far as the state of present research can tell, their effective role may have been a determining factor in the spread of such books. They did not work merely for mercenary reasons,

---

[34] See *Index 3*.

[35] See F. Barberi, 'Calvo, Francesco Guilio', *Dizionario biografico degli Italiani*, 17 (1974), 38–41.

even if in 1559 Cardinal Ghislieri, the future Pope Pius V, believed that this was the prime motivation behind the *tempestas et ruina maxima* of the Reformation, disseminated throughout the world by booksellers. Men like Francesco Calvó from Pavia changed their line of work and their place of residence, as he went to Rome and became a publisher there, but his brother Andrea seemingly replaced him, and continued to import banned books into Lombardy until 1541.[36] Apart from a few anonymous betrayals across Italy, the only trials were those of Cristoforo Dossena, Tommaso Linguardo and Giordano [Ziletti] in 1548 in Bologna,[37] and in the same year another major bookseller was investigated in Siena.[38] Again in 1548, speaking on behalf of the Venetian booksellers, Tommaso Giunta presented to the magistrates a strongly worded document upholding the freedom of trade and opposing the growing pressure of censorship. His action clearly indicates the presence of a large number of this type of book in city shops. These works were still widely available in 1555, as evidenced by four lists of works under investigation or sequestered from booksellers in that year, three of whom were well known: Tommaso Giunta, Marchio Sessa and Gabriele Giolito.[39] Publishers of heretical works who were also booksellers, like Andrea Arrivabene in Venice or Antonio Gadaldino in Modena had a better opportunity to distribute their works. In some instances, a printer who showed no particular sympathy for the Reformation, like Gabriele Giolito in Naples in 1565, nevertheless held a large quantity of forbidden literature in his own library, in Giolito's case 150 titles, with sometimes more than one copy of each.[40] Two publisher booksellers of Venice, Paolo Avanzo and Francesco Rocca engaged in such activities from 1550 to 1570, while in 1558, their colleague Pietro Longo was condemned to death.[41]

Besides itinerant traders operating more or less undercover, and merchants transporting various goods, slowly but surely private individuals also brought these dangerous works lent by friends and acquaintances into Italy. The importance of book-lending, a frequent occurrence, should

---

[36] See F. Barberi, 'Calvo, Andrea', *Dizionario biografico degli Italiani*, 17 (1974), 34–5.

[37] L. Carcereri, 'Cristoforo Dossena, Francesco Linguardo et un Giordano librai processati per eresia a Bologna (1548)', *L'Archiginnasio*, 5 (1910), 177–92.

[38] G. Catoni, 'Processi a librai senesi del Cinquecento', in *Studi di storia medievale e moderna per E. Sestan* (Florence, 1980), vol. 2, pp. 519–28.

[39] A. Del Col, 'Il controllo della stampa a Venezia e i processi di Antonio Brucioli (1548–1559)', *Critica storica*, 17 (1980), 498–503.

[40] P. Pironti, *Un processo dell'Inquisizione a Napoli (Gabriele Giolito e Giovan Battista Cappello* (Naples, n. d.).

[41] Grendler, *L'Inquisizione Romana*, pp. 156–8, 263–5.

be measured on the basis of frequent references to such activities in Inquisitorial court records and private correspondence.

Catholic theologians' need to know what their adversaries believed in order to launch polemical attacks against them also meant that Protestant works were imported into Italy, at least for a number of years. This dissemination had dangerous consequences, not only, as it happened, for authorized readers, but also for occasional and accidental ones. Luther's 95 Theses were known in Italy through a work by the Master of the Sacred Palace, the Dominican Silvestro Mazzolini da Prierio who had his *In praesumtuosas Martini Lutheri conclusiones de potestate papae dialogus* printed in the summer of 1518. But soon even the briefest 'heretical' quotation was banned, even when used to refute arguments, as was the traditional practice in theological polemic.

Authors and works

The literary production of the Reformation circulating in Italy until 1565 can be divided into three categories: writings of foreign Reformers in their original languages, the same works translated into Italian and finally those of Italian writers who joined the Reformation.

The spread of Reformation works in their original languages

The first category consists of essential Reformation texts, treatises of systematic theology or exegesis circulating in Italy in their original language, which in almost every case was Latin.[42] This group consisted almost entirely of works imported over the Alps via merchants or through private initiative. The two copies of the Lutheran treatise *De Captivitate Babylonica Ecclesiae* discussed in 1521 by the Milan jurist Bernardino Arluno and a senator identified only by the initials A. F., as well as the *Resolutio de potestate papae* also by Luther, already read by A. F. and which Bernardino Arluno managed to find in a Milan bookshop in spite of the *Exsurge Domine* Bull, were all printed outside Italy. The same was true for the *De libertate Christiana* treatise which the humanist Christophe of Longueil read in Padua in the same year. Another unspecified work by Luther was located by the Venetian chronicler Marino Sanuto during the summer of 1520, in spite of the

---

[42] One exception was a few works of Luther, which circulated in German. See S. Seidel Menchi, '"Certo Martino è stato terribil homo". L'immagine di Lutero e la sua efficacia secondo i processi italiani dell'Inquisizione', in L. Perrone (ed.) *Lutero in Italia* (Casale Monferrato, 1983), pp. 119, 126, 129.

confiscation of all the Reformer's works by the Venetian senate, works which had been for sale in the shop of 'Zordan Todesco merchande di libri', probably Jordan von Dinslaken. The *Enarrationes in sacra quatuor Evangelia* and the other works of Martin Bucer read by the medical student Giovanni Angelo Odoni, in Bologna in 1533 were printed in Strasbourg. Luther's 'postils', *Enarrationes quas Postillas vocant* or *Postillae maiores* which Pier Francesco Riccio, the secretary of the Duke of Florence, awaited with impatience from a Venetian bookseller in 1544, were published by a northern press.[43] Even the polemicists reviewed by Friedrich Lauchert in his list of Italians writing against Luther, came into contact with their opponent's ideas through books produced beyond the Alps: *Resolutio de potestate papae, De abroganda missa privata, De captivitate Babylonica Ecclesiae, Resolutiones disputationum de indulgentiarum virtute, De libertate Christiana*, etc.[44] Only very exceptionally were Protestants' works reprinted in Italy in their original language.[45]

Until 1535, Luther's works unquestionably dominated the imported 'heretical' works. Following this date, Luther was predominant only in certain limited areas of the peninsula, in the north-east. Book collections like the one assembled between 1550 and 1557 by Dionisio de Rizardis, the notary and grain merchant, were typical of the strong presence of Lutheran works in the philo-Protestant conventicles of the Frioul. The Gemona merchant's collection included the *Declamationes in Genesis*, the *Enarrationes quas Postillas vocant seu Postillae maiores* (or *Enarrationes epistolarum et evangeliorum quas postillas vocant)*, the *Commentarius in epistolam Pauli ad Galatas* and the *Commentarius in Oseam prophetam, Das 17. Kapitel Johannis von dem Gebet Christi* (or maybe *Das 16. Kapitel S. Johannis*), all by Luther, the psalter translated and introduced by Luther, as well as Melanchthon's *Loci Communes*, a copy of the Zurich Bible, an edition of Bernardino Ochino's

---

[43] S. Seidel Menchi, 'Le traduzioni italiane di Lutero nella prima metà del Cinquecento', *Rinascimento*, 17 (1978), 36–40; A. Biondi, 'Il ciceroniano e l'eversore. Una lettura politica di Lutero nell'orazione di Christoforo Longolio "Ad Luterianos quosdam iam damnatos" (1521)', in *Lutero*, pp. 29–46; P. F. Grendler, 'Introduction historique', in *Index 3*; S. Seidel Menchi, 'Sulla fortuna di Erasmo in Italia: Ortensio Lando e altri eterodossi della prima metà del Cinquecento', *Rivista Storica Svizzera*, 24 (1974), 627; S. Caponetto, 'Lutero nella letteratura italiana della prima metà del Cinquecento: Francesco Berni', in *Lutero* [see note 64 below], p. 50.

[44] Fr. Lauchert, *Die italienischen literarischen Gegner Luthers* (Freiburg am Breisgau, 1912) (Erläuterungen und Ergänzungen zu Janssens Geschichte des deutschen Volkes, 8).

[45] The only exception of note that I am aware of is the edition of the *Unio dissidentium* by the mysterious Hermannus Bodius, printed in Venice in 1532 by Agostino Bindoni and Giovan Battista Pederzani (*Index aureliensis*, vol. 1/4, p. 412).

Prediche and a work by Pier Paolo Vergerio. The ease with which this Frioul merchant obtained so many forbidden books was the result of particularly favourable circumstances, such as the proximity of Habsburg lands, where Luther's books circulated freely and in great numbers, and Rizardis's occupation, which gave him ample opportunities to cross the border.[46]

Though Frioul offered other cases similar to that of Rizardis – for instance that of Guilio Passavolante, also from Gemona[47] – outside the area, beyond Trieste and the Istria, from the middle of the century onwards Luther was no longer well represented in Italian clandestine libraries. The Swiss Reformers – including Calvin and his Genevan followers to simplify matters – and those of the Rhineland caught up to Luther in popularity in the 1530s, and pulled ahead in the next decade. This trend is mirrored in the list of forbidden books which the Augustinian preacher Guilio da Milano or della Rovere, imprisoned in Venice on suspicion of heresy admitted having read, some of which were found in his possession. Reformed Swiss and Palatine theology was represented on the list by the *Enarrationes perpetuae in sacra quatuor Evangelia* of Martin Bucer, by Heinrich Bullinger's 'homilies' on the Pauline Epistles (clearly one of the volumes of the *Commentarii* which the Zurich Reformer wrote on the various letters of Saint Paul), by Bullinger's 'homilies' on the Acts of the Apostles (*In acta apostolorum commentarii*), by the *Pandectae Veteris et Novi Testamenti* of Otto Brunfels and by Conradus Pellicanus' *Repertorium Bibliae*.

In contrast, Lutheran evangelical theology was only represented by two works, 'Martin's homilies on three or four chapters of Saint Matthew' (*Enarrationes in quintum, sextum et septimum capita Matthaei*, Haguenau: J Setzer, 1533) and by Melanchthon's *Loci Communes*. The preference for Swiss and Palatine works of Reformed theology is even more clearly visible in the library of the Dominican Giovanni Rubeo, also known as Savorgnan, assembled in 1558 in his Udine monastery: Martin Bucer's *Enarrationes perpetuae in sacra quatuor Evangelia*, a work which was much appreciated by Italian dissidents, Bullinger's *Homiliae super epistolis Pauli* once again, Zwingli's *Commentarii super prophetis* (*Annotationes in Genesim, Exodum, Esaiam et Jeremiam prophetas?*) and Calvin's 'Controversies' (the *Institutio christianae religionis?*) besides works by Italian writers, such as the sermons of Bernardino Ochino and Guilio da Milano.

In both these cases, the works influenced more people than their reader alone. Indeed the sermons of the two monks who owned the

---

[46] See Seidel Menchi, '"Certo Martino"', pp. 117–21.
[47] Udine, AA, SU, b. 1, fasc. 42, 'Contra Iulium Passavolante de Glemona'.

books reflected the contents of these works, and their message circulated orally afterwards. This picture of dissemination through concentric circles was often found in Italy. One eye-witness testified that the Dominican Giovanni Rubeo had the habit of copying passages, sometimes entire pages from books by Bucer, Bullinger, Zwingli and Calvin, books which he 'kept hidden and locked away in a box in his cell'. He then inserted these extracts into his sermons. A colleague of Guilio da Milano testified that many listeners followed his sermons in Bologna in 1538 with the help of Hermannus Bodius's *Unio dissidentium*, since Fra Guilio 'preached his maxims *ad ungem*'. The texts used in this oral dissemination were obviously not the most theologically sophisticated, nor the most radical and clear-cut. Preference was given to conciliatory works, like those of Bodius, flexible passages like those used by fra Giovanni Rubeo – passages 'with more than one meaning, and which could be upheld by one or other party', so that the preacher had a way out in case of reports to the authorities.[48]

The same doctrinal path illustrated by the libraries of these two monks is found in that of Cremona's priest, Ombono Asperti, regent of the parish of Tomba near Verona, who proclaimed that he was a disciple of 'Zwingli, Bucer, Bullinger, Oecolampadius'. A list of his books established in 1550 in fact included Heinrich Bullinger's *Commentarii* on the Gospels and the Acts of the Apostles, which were four large folio volumes, matching in number and size Johann Brenz's *Homiliae in Evangelion quod inscribitur secundum Lucam*, his *Homiliae in Acta apostolica*, Andreas Osiander's *Coniecturae de Ultimis temporibus ac de fine mundi*, and Hermannus Bodius' *Unio dissidentium*.[49] A similar example can be found in the surviving 1549 inventory of the library of the lawyer Francesco Stella from Portobuffole. His book collection included alongside Luther's *De captivitate babylonica Ecclesiae* treatise, Melanchthon's *Acta Concilii Tridentini una cum annotationibus*, Erasmus Sarcerius's *Nova methodus in praecipuos Scripturae divinae locos* and his *Locorum communium ex consensu divinae Scripturae et sanctorum patrum clarissima confirmatio*, Heinrich Bullinger's *Commentarii in Novum Testamentum*, Otto Brunfels's *Pandectae Veteris et Novi Testamenti*, Johannes Oecolampadius' *Adnotationes in epistolam Pauli ad Romanos*, Theodor Bibliander's *Propheta Nahum iuxta veritatem hebraicam latine redditus*, as well as the

---

[48] For Guilio da Milano, see Venice, AS, SU, b. 1, 'Processus magistri Julii Mediolanensis', fols 46ᵛ–49ʳ and fol. 22ʳ, as well as the list of books found in Guilio da Milano's room, dated 19 April 1541. For G. Rubeo, see Udine, AA, SU, b. 1, fasc. 13, 'Contra fratrem Joannem Rubeum seu Savornianum', the testimony of fra Bernardino da Colloredo, 22 November 1558.

[49] Venice, AS, SU, b. 8, 'Contra Bartholomeum dalla Barba' 1550, fols 35ʳ⁻ᵛ.

work of an author who rarely appeared in this type of inventory, Sebastian Meyer's *Commentarius in Apocalypsim Johannis.*[50] The doctrinal tendency guiding Francesco Stella's choice of books was reflected in the library of the Paduan priest Lucio Paolo Rosello, as described in a 1551 inventory there. Luther was only present in the treatise *De abroganda missa privata*, of which Rosello seems only to have possessed the first page, and as the preface writer for Urbanus Rhegius's collection of the *Prophetiae Veteris Testamenti de Christo.* The Lutheran current of Reformation theology was more strongly represented by Erasmus Sarcerius's *Locorum communium ex consensu divinae scripturae et sanctorum patrum clarissima confirmatio*, by Johann Spangenberg's *Postilla*, by Antonius Corvinus's *Postilla in epistolas et evangelia totius anni* and by the second volume of Johann Brenz's *Homiliae in Evangelium lucae.* In contrast, Swiss and Palatine Reformed theology was represented by a greater range of texts, from Otto Brunfels's *Pandectae Veteris et Novi Testamenti*, to Calvin's *Institutio christianae religionis*, from Heinrich Bullinger's *Paraenesis quo pacto cum aegrotantibus ac morientibus agendum sit* to Johannes Oecolampadius's *Homiliae in epistolam Joannis apostoli Catholicam primam*, from Zwingli's *Responsio brevis ad epistolam satis longam in qua de Eucharistia quaestio tractatur* to Martin Bucer's *Disputata Ratisbonae in colloquio anno 1546.*[51] This brief enumeration will usefully conclude with an examination of the book collection brought together by the priest Francesco Bertholdo of Oderzo around 1550. Among the books which this cleric, the chancellor of lay governors in the Venetian territories, and a friend of Rosello, gathered together were works by Zwingli, Bullinger, and Brenz, alongside a copy of 'all Martin Luther's works, with his portrait'.[52]

The make-up of the four aforementioned book collections owed much to the activities of Pietro Perna, a bookseller and itinerant trader originally from Lucca but who emigrated to Basle for religious reasons. He zealously distributed books in a series of cities in central and northern Italy (Venice, Bologna, Bergamo, Padua, Milan and Lucca), acting as an agent of the Basle printer Johann Oporinus, but also introducing works printed in Strasbourg and Zurich into Italy. Thus, for example, Bucer's *Disputata Ratisbonae in colloquio anno 1546*, found in Lucio Paolo Rosello's library, was in all likelihood one of the 200 copies of the work which Perna brought into Italy in 1547.[53] The Italian dissidents' in-

---

[50] Perini, 'Ancora', pp. 392–4.

[51] Perini, 'Ancora', pp. 387–9.

[52] Venice, AS, SU, b. 26, fasc. 'Vincenzo Bertoldi', testimony of pre Leonardo da Refrontolo given on 8 August 1569 at Ceneda.

[53] Perini, 'Note', p. 147. On Perna, see above, p. 330–31.

creasing interest in the Swiss and Palatine Reformers is also confirmed by the admittedly rarer and more vague information from Italian regions untouched by Perna's activities. This holds true for the 1558 description of the library of Jacopo Chierici alias Malchiavelli of Modena, which included alongside Luther's *Enchiridion piarum precationum* and a work by Erasmus Sarcerius, Bartolomaeus Westheimer's *Conciliatio Scripturarum*, also known as the *Farrago concordantium insignium totius sacrae Bibliae*, Johannes Oecolampadius's *De eucharistica* treatise – *De dignitate Eucharistiae Sermones duo* – and Hermannus Bodius's *Unio dissidentium*. The book collection (around 1556) of Annibale Salato of Amalfi, monk, then schoolmaster, should also be noted, as its most striking theological presence is that of Oecolampadius. The books of the notary Fabio Cioni from Grosseto included a work by Calvin, and the library of the conventual Franciscan Tommaso Fabiani from Mileto (prior to 1564) brought together Antonius Corvinus, Erasmus Sarcerius and Martin Bucer and Johannes Oecolampadius.[54]

Calvin's *Institutio christianae religionis* was held in particularly high esteem among the Reformers' works available in Italy in their original languages. The presence of Calvin's book, or an insistent demand for it is suggested or evidenced in Bologna in 1541, in Florence in 1541, in Vicenze over a three-year period 1545–48, in Venice in 1551, in Modena in 1555, in Siena in 1556 and 1560, in Bologna again in 1567 and in the Padua diocese between 1566 and 1569, to mention only a few of the numerous testimonies on this subject, scattered throughout Inquisition records.[55] On the basis of this evidence, it seems possible to conclude that from around 1540, Italian pressure for religious change was centred around Calvin, especially since as well as his *Institutes*, Bibles with Calvin-inspired commentaries were circulating in vast numbers in Italy, and since influential nobles collaborated with rich merchants in organ-

[54] Modena, AS, Inquisizione, b. 3, 'Contra Jacobum de Clericis alias de Malchiavelis 1558'; P. Lopez, *Inquisizione, stampa e censura nel regno di Napoli tra Cinquecento e Seicento* (Naples, 1974), pp. 74–7; V. Marchetti, *Gruppi ereticali senesi del Cinquecento* (Florence, 1975), pp. 77–8; Dublin, Trinity College, ms. 1224, sentence passed on 16 December 1564 against Tommaso Fabiani from Mileto.

[55] 'Processus magistri Julii Mediolanensis', fol. 72^r; M. Firpo, 'Valdesianesimo ed evangelismo: alle origini dell'"Ecclesia Viterbensis" (1541)', in Prosperi and Biondi, *Libri*, p. 61; A. Olivieri, 'Alessandro Trissino e il movimento calvinista vicentino del Cinquecento', *Rivista di Storia della Chiesa in Italia*, 21 (1967), 56; Perini, 'Ancora', p. 388; Modena, AS, Inquisizione, b. 7, accusation against Francesco Maria Busello; Seidel Menchi, *Erasmo*, p. 91; Marchetti, *Gruppi ereticali*, p. 77; Dublin, Trinity College, ms. 1224, 5 July 1567, sentence 'Contra Julium Placentinum' of Bologna; 16 September 1567, sentence 'Contra Petrum Cephalot Lotharingum', 20 September 1567, sentence against Antonio di Bonfiolo dei Severi of Bologna; Seidel Menchi, *Erasmo*, pp. 97–8.

ising trips to Geneva 'to bring back barrel-loads of sermons'.[56] One must, however, bear in mind that the confessional allegiance of readers did not depend solely on what they read. Even though a heretical library may have contained mostly works by Luther, this did not necessarily mean that its owner was Lutheran, and certain Italians' preference for Genevan catechisms in the 1550s[57] does not mean that the readers of these works were confessionally at one with Geneva's inhabitants.

The examples of dissidents' book collections given above tended more towards an evangelical syncretism, in which a curiously organized and varied reception of Reformation writers could be as much the cause as the consequence of a diversity of doctrine either accepted or chosen as a permanent state. In Stella or Rosello's libraries, theologians divided by violent polemic or irreconcilable hatred in the historic reality of the Reformation, coexisted peacefully side by side. This peaceful cohabitation in areas still under the yoke of the one known as the Antichrist, illustrates the Italian interpretation of the Reformation, leaving aside the bitter confessional divisions within Protestantism. The Italian perspective did not share the fondness for anathemas, and attributed a greater role to basic doctrinal tendencies than to a rigorous definition of particular dogma.

Versions of foreign Reformers' works, and their camouflage

Had the works discussed in the previous section been the main point of contact between the Italians and the Reformation, the spread of Reformation ideas in Italy would have had a very limited impact. Indeed, Reformers' works in their original language were rather inaccessible. The main obstacle in the dissemination of these works was a linguistic one. If in the second half of the sixteenth century, in 1587 in a cultured city like Venice, the percentage of boys and girls attending school, and therefore through a reasonable extrapolation, the percentage of literacy in the population as a whole was 14 to 26 per cent of boys and not even 1 per cent of girls,[58] the percentage of those able to read Latin in Italy must have been around 5 per cent. The thorough knowledge of Latin

---

[56] Olivieri, 'Alessandro Trissino', p. 63.

[57] One example was the Milanese group of Antonio da Limito and the Neapolitan Ascanio (Venice, AS, SU, b. 13, fasc. 'Antonio da Limito', interrogation of Domenico della Selva on 29 November 1556). The popularity of the Calvinist catechism is also evident in the list of Italian translations of Reformation texts given below.

[58] P. F. Grendler, 'The organization of primary and secondary education in the Italian Renaissance', *The Catholic Historical Review*, 71 (1985), 204.

EL SVMMARIO
DE LA SANTA SCRITTVRA ET LOR
dinario de Chriftiani ilqual demonftra la
vera Fede Chriftiana mediante laqua,
le fiamo giuftificati. Et della virtu
del battifmo fecondo la dottrina
de l'Euangelio,& delli Apofto,
li,con vna informatione co,
me tutti gli ftati debbono
viuere fecondo lo
Euangelio.
¶ La tauola trouera nel fine del libretto.

11.2   *El Summario de la santa Scrittura* ([Venice], [*c*.1543])

needed to read works by Luther or Zwingli for instance is one which a
large section of the clergy itself admitted lacking.[59] Another obstacle to

---

[59] Venice, AS, SU, b. 8, fasc. 11, 'Inquisitione fatta per il reverendo ... Annibal
Grisonio sopra la vita et costumi delli canonici e preti di Chioggia ... dell'anno 1549'

the circulation of the works detailed above was their cost. The cost of paper, typesetting, and printing fonts meant that Reformers' works printed in Basle, Strasbourg and in Zurich were expensive goods, made even more costly for Italian markets by the price of transport. In 1534, according to a witness, the Italian translation of Luther's *An den Christlichen Adel deutscher Nation* was priced prohibitively at 4 silver marcelli, or a gold half-ecu in Bologna.[60] The large size of the volumes also had a negative effect on price: the big dogmatic or exegetical treatises, which often appeared in the lists of 'heretical' libraries mentioned above were ambitious printing projects, folio volumes illustrated with masterly engravings of eye-catching beauty. The aforementioned clandestine library of the priest Francesco Bertholdo included works described by a witness as 'beautifully printed and bound books from Basle'.[61] These works were beyond the reach of an artisan or a small merchant, even if he knew Latin or had some hope of learning it.

The impact of the books in the first group was further reduced by the openness with which they announced the identity of their authors. The Reformers' texts printed beyond the Alps and primarily destined for those markets were the first to disappear from circulation in Italy, because they were hidden by frightened owners who could not plead ignorance, since such works were being officially confiscated by inquisitors or even being spontaneously handed in to the tribunals. This was particularly true as the states began to reinforce ecclesiastical ordinances regarding forbidden books with their own legislation: Milan in 1538, Lucca in 1545, Siena in 1548, etc.[62] The relatively small number of major works of evangelical doctrine and reformed exegesis listed in the inventories of books confiscated and burnt in 1559 and in the following years, once Paul IV's Index had come into force, was because such works had already been eliminated.

Although the field of action of printed Protestant propaganda was very limited in terms of the large works circulating in their original language, the introduction of Italian translations printed in Italy or beyond the Alps, particularly in Geneva, helped to make a greater impact. Their spread through Italy was helped not only by the language factor, but also by their modest cost. For example, Benedetto Morello, a

---

(many of the canons who were asked to give testimony admitted having a poor knowledge of Latin); Rovigo, Archivio Storico Diocesano, Cause criminali, b. 1, 'Contra Dominum Antonium Mariam Turolam, 1560' and 'Contra presbiterum Julium de Virgilio, 1560' (illiterate priests).

[60] Seidel Menchi, 'Sulla fortuna', p. 629.

[61] Quotation taken from Seidel Menchi, 'Sulla fortuna', n. 52.

[62] Grendler, in *Index 3*, pp. 33, 38–9.

shoemaker, sold the *Sommario della Santa Scriptura* to Antonio Filipello of Montagnana for seven pence in 1540.[63]

Here are the Italian translations of the writings of foreign Reformers. Certain specific abbreviations appear in the list.[64] A number followed by an asterisk indicates that one or more copies of the work have survived:

1525

1*   [Martin Luther/Nikolaus von Amsdorf], *Uno libretto volgare, con la dechiaratione deli dieci comandamenti, del Credo, del Pater Noster, con una breve annotatione del vivere christiano* Venice: Niccolò Zoppino, 1525, 8°.

        Translation, probably from the German (by Jakob Ziegler?) of a short catechetical work by Luther, *Eine kurze Form der zehn Gebote, eine kurze Form des Glaubens, eine kurze Form des Vaterunsers*, linked to a work by Nikolaus von Amsdorf, *Eine christliche Vorbetrachtung, so man will beten das heilige Vaterunser*, the third text, *Breve annotatione come se debbe havere et exercitare lo vero christiano verso Dio et lo proximo suo* is probably also by Luther (*Lutero*, p. 41; Claus/Pegg, no. 18a; Florence, BNC).

1526

2*   [Martin Luther/Nikolas von Amsdorf], *La declaratione delli dieci commandamenti, del Credo, del Pater Noster, con una breve annotatione del vivere christiano per Erasmo Rotherdamo* Venice: Niccolò Zoppino, 1526, 8°.

        Work 1, this time printed under Erasmus's name (*Lutero*, p. 61; Claus/Pegg, no. 18b.; The Hague, KB).

1530

3   [Martin Luther/Nikolas von Amsdorf], *Uno libretto volgare, con la delaratione de li dieci comandamenti, del Credo, del Pater Noster* [Venice?]: no publisher, [c.1530].

---

[63] Modena, AS, Inquisizione, b. 2, 'Contra Magistrum Antonium Filipellum da Montagnana 1540'. In Gadaldino's bookshop, a new copy of the *Sommario* cost eight pence (Cesare Bianco (ed.), *Il Sommario della Santa Scrittura e l'ordinario dei cristiani* (Turin, 1988), p. 28).

[64] *Catechismo* = Valdo Vinay, 'Il piccolo catechismo di Lutero come strumento di evangelizzazione fra gli italiani dal XVI al XX secolo', *Protestantismo*, 25 (1970), 69–71. CDM = P. Chaix, A. Dufour and G. Moeckli, *Les livres imprimés à Genève de 1550 à 1600* (Geneva, 1966). *Lutero* = Seidel Menchi, 'Le traduzioni'. Trapman = J. Trapman, 'Überlegungen zu einer unbekannten Ausgabe des Summario de la Santa Scrittura', *Nederlands Archief voor Kergeschiedenis*, 67 (1987), 143–55. *Venezia* = Cavazza, 'Libri in volgare'.

Works 1 and 2, anonymous printing (*Lutero*, p. 41; *LB*, no. 19).

1532

4*   [Martin Luther/Nikolas von Amsdorf], *La dechiaratione delli dieci commandamenti, del Credo, del Paternostro ... per Erasmo Rotherodamo* Venice: Niccolò Zoppino, 1532, 8°.

Works 1 to 3, printed under Erasmus's name for the second time (*Lutero*, p. 61; Ghent, UB).

1533

5*   [Martin Luther], *Libro de la emendatione et correctione dil stato christiano* [Strasbourg: Georg Ulricher], 1533, 8°.

Translation attributed to the Venetian Franciscan Bartolomeo Fonzio, of Luther's *An den christlichen Adel deutscher Nation von des christlichen Standes Besserung*, with important polemical additions (*Lutero*, p. 64; *LB*, no. 698; Florence, BNC).

6*   [Philipp Melanchthon], *I principii de la theologia di Ippophilo da Terra Negra* [Venice: no publisher, 1530/34? *c*.1540?] 8°.

Translation, attributed to the Modena humanist Ludovico Castelvetro, of the second edition (1522) of the *Loci communes* (S. Caponetto, 'Due opere di Melantone tradotte da Ludovico Castelvetro: "I principi de la theologia di Ippophilo da Terra Negra" e "Dell'autorità della Chiesa e degli scritti degli antichi"', *Nuova Rivista Storica*, 70 (1986), pp. 253–7; Florence, BNC).

1534

7*   *El Summario dela sancta Scriptura et l'ordinario deli cristiani, qual demonstra la vera fede christiana, mediante la quale siamo iustificati, et dela virtù del baptismo secondo la doctrina del evangelio et deli apostoli, cum una informatione come tutti li stati debbono vivere secondo lo evangelio* [Venice]: no publisher (printer's mark: Peter and Paul) [*c*.1534?], 8°.

Translation of the French version of the short evangelical tract, *De summa der godliker scrifturen* published in Leiden in 1523, which itself was a reworked translation of the Latin tract, *Oeconomica christiana* (Trapman, pp. 145–6, no. 3, and pp. 148–9; Wolfenbüttel, HAB). Around 150 at least, the Peter and Paul mark was used by Pietro da Fino (Del Col, 'Il Nuovo Testamento' p. 157).

1540

8   *Il Sommario della santa Scrittura* [?], [1540?].

Work 7, reprinted on the initiative of Giovan Matteo Giberti, bishop of Verona (Trapman, p. 145, no. 2).

9*   [Martin Luther/Nikolaus von Amsdorf], *La dechiaratione de i dieci commandamenti, dil Credo e dil Pater Noster ... per Erasmo Roterodamo ...* Venice: Niccolò Zoppino, 1540, 8°

Works 1 to 4, printed for the third time in Erasmus's name (*Lutero* pp. 61–2; Claus/Pegg, no. 19a; Florence, BNC).

10   *Il summario de la sacra scrittura* [Venice]: Comin da Trino's printer's mark?, [*c*.1540?], 16°.

Works 7–8 (Trapman, pp. 144–5, no. 1).

11*   [Martin Luther], *Opera divina della christiana vita* [Venice?: no publisher, *c*.1540?], 16°.

Translation of the tract *De libertate christiana* (*Lutero*, pp. 89–90; Wolfenbüttel, HAB).

12*   [Martin Luther], *Opera divina della christiana vita* n. p., no printer [*c*.1540?], 8°.

Reprint of work 11. (*Venezia*, n. 54; Florence, BNC).

1542

13   [Martin Luther], *I tre muri* [?], [1540/1543?].

Reprint of work 5 under a different title (*Venezia*, n. 53).

14   *Il Sommario della santa Scrittura* [?]. [Naples?, *c*.1542?].

Works 7, 8, 10 (C. Bianco (ed.) *Il Sommario della Santa Scrittura e l'ordinario dei cristiani* (Turin, 1988), p. 40).

1543

15*   Antonio Brucioli, *Compendio di tutte l'orationi de Santi Padri, Patriarchi, Propheti, et Apostoli, raccolte da sacri libri del vecchio et nuovo Testamento et tradotte in lingua Toscana* Venice: Aurelio Pinzi, 1543.

Free adaptation of Otto Brunfels, *Precationes biblicae sanctorum Patrum, illustrium virorum et mulierum utriusque Testamenti* Strasbourg: J. Schott, 1528 (C. Ginzburg, *Il nicodemismo: Simulazione e dissimulazione religiosa nell'Europa del Cinquecento* (Turin, 1970), p. 101 n.).

16*   *El Summario dela santa Scrittura* [Venice]: no printer (printer's mark: Peter and Paul), [*c*.1543?].

Works 7, 8, 10, 14 (Trapman, p. 147, version A; Zurich, ZB).

17*   [Martin Luther/Nikolaus von Amsdorf], *La dechiaratione de li dieci commandamenti, del Credo, del Pater nostro … per Erasmo Roterodamo* Venice: Bernardino de' Viani, 1543, 8°.

Works 1–4, 9, printed for the fourth time in Erasmus' name (*Lutero*, p. 62; Claus/Pegg, no. 19b; Lucca, BC).

18*   [Urbanus Rhegius], *Opera utilissima intitolata dottrina vecchia et nuova*, n. p., no printer [1540/1545], 16°.

Translation of the *Nova doctrina* (*Venezia*, n. 59).

1544

19*   [Urbanus Rhegius], *Medicina dell'anima, tanto per quelli che sono amalati, tanto per quelli che sono sani* Venice: Comin da Trino, 1544, 16°.

Translation of the tract *Seelen Artzney für Gesund und Kranken* via a Latin version (*Venezia*, n. 62).

20* [Johann Sleidan], *Il Capo finto, nuovamente dalla lingua tedesca nella italiana tradotto* "Rome: heirs of Marco Antonio di Prati" [= Venice], 1544, 8°.

Translation of the *Oration an alle Stende des Reichs vom Römischen Nebenhaupt im Keyserthumb erwachsen* (*Venezia*, n. 21; Florence, BNC).

1545

21* [Martin Luther], *Prefatione del reverendiss. Cardinal di santa Chiesa M. Federico Fregoso nella Pistola di san Paolo a'Romani* Venice: Comin da Trino, 1545, 16°.

Translation of Luther's *Praefatio methodica totius Scripturae in epistolam Pauli ad Romanos* printed in the name of Cardinal Federico Fregoso (*Lutero*, p. 81; Claus/Pegg, no. 1814a; Vienna, ÖNB).

22* [Urbanus Rhegius], *Simolachri, historie e figure de la morte, ove si contiene la medicina de l'anima* ... Venice: Vincenzo Valgrisi, 1545, 8°.

Reprint of work 19, with engravings inspired by Hans Holbein's *Totentanz* (*Venezia*, p. 22; G. Franz, *Huberinus-Rhegius-Holbein* (Nieuwkoop, 1973), p. 137).

23* *Il desordine della Chiesa dove si vedino le perverse tradizioni de suoi menistri esser contra le sante leggi di Christo, e de gl'antichi Padri* [Venice, no printer, 1545], 16°.

Probably the translation of a work coming from the Protestant lands, but the original text has not yet been identified (*Venezia*, n. 34).

24* [Urbanus Rhegius], *Libretto consolatorio a li perseguitati per la confessione de la verità evangelica* "Milan" [= Venice] no printer, 1545, 8°.

Translation, probably from the Latin, of *Trostbrief an alle Christen zu Hildesheim, die um des Evangeliums willen jetzt Schmach und Verfolgung leiden* or *Libellus consolatorius ad eos qui patiuntur persecutionem propter iusticiam* (*Venezia*, n. 65).

25* [Jean Calvin], *Catechismo cio è formulario per ammaestrare i fanciulli ne la religione Christiana fatto in modo di dialogo, dove il Ministro della Chiesa dimanda et il fanciullo risponde* [Geneva: J. Girard], 1545, 8°.

Translation of *Le catéchisme de l'Eglise de Genève* ... *c'est à dire le formulaire d'instruire les enfants en la chrétienté* (Gilmont, 'Bibliotheca gebennensis', p. 242).

1547

26*   [Urbanus Rhegius], *Dottrina verissima et hora nuovamente venuta in luce tolta dal capitolo IV a' Romani a consolare fermamente le afflitte coscientie dal peso de' peccati gravate. Aggiuntovi uno dialogo fra Satan et il peccatore, ove si manifesta dove debbe ricorrere l'afflitta coscientia* n. p., no publisher, 1547, 16°.

Translation of *Gewisse Lehre und unüberwindlicher Trost wider Verzweiflung der Sünden halben* and the *Dialogus oder Gesprech zwischen dem Teuffel und einem biessenden Sunder* (*Venezia*, n. 68).

1549

27*   [Urbanus Rhegius], *Simolachri, historie e figure de la morte. La medecina de l'anima. Il modo, e la via di consolar gl'infermi ...* Lyon: Jean Frellon, 1549, 8°.

Reprint of work 19, but with the set-up of work 22 (*Venezia*, p. 22).

1550

28*   Rudolf Gwalther, *L'Antichristo* [Zurich? Cremona?: no printer, *c.*1550] 8°.

Translation of the *Antichristus* (Schutte, *Printed Italian Vernacular*, p. 198, with a date suggested by S. Cavazza in a letter of 5 June 1988, based on the evidence of P. P. Vergerio). See also the reactions of the Basle council (above, p. 241).

1551

29*   Jean Calvin, *Catechismo*. Geneva: Adam and Jean Rivery, 1551, 8°.

Translation of Calvin's catechism by Giulio Domenico Gallo (CDM, p. 17).

30*   [Urbanus Rhegius], *Simolachri, historie e figure de la morte. La medecina de l'anima. Il modo, e la via di consolar gl'infermi ...* Venice: Vincenzo Valgrisi, 1551, 8°.

Work 19, following the form of works 22 and 27 (*Venezia*, p. 22).

31*   [Jean Calvin], *Come Christo è il fine de la legge* [Lyon: Jean Frellon?, Philibert Rollet?], 1551, 8°.

Translation of the preface added by Calvin to Olivétan's Bible, combined with *Le dotte e pie parafrasi, sopra le Pistole de Paolo a Romani, Galati et Hebrei di Gian Francesco Virginio Bresciano* (Del Col, 'Il Nuovo Testamento', pp. 146–7).

32*   [Jean Calvin], *La forma delle preghiere ecclesiastiche, con la maniera d'amministrare i sagramenti et celebrare il matrimonio, et la visitation degl'infermi* Geneva, Adam and Jean Rivery: 1551, 8°.

Translation by Guilio Domenico Gallo of *La forme des prieres ecclesiastiques, avec la maniere d'administrer les sacremens, et celebrer le mariage et la visitation des malades* (CDM, p. 18).

33   Heinrich Bullinger, *Demonstratione, che il concilio di Trento non sia ordinato per haver a cercare ed illustrare la verità con la Sacra Scrittura ma per sovertirla e per istabelire gl'errori della sedia Romana* n. p., no printer, 1551, 8°.
Translation by Pier Paolo Vergerio (J. Staedtke, *Heinrich Bullinger Bibliographie* (Zurich, 1972), vol. 1, p. 113).

1553

34*   Gio[vanni] Cal[vino], *Del fuggir le superstitioni che ripugnano a la vera e sincera confession de la fede. Opera ... ne la qual si contiene: Il modo de bene e piamente governarsi tra gl'infedeli e idolatri. Segue poi vn'Escusatione de l'Autore ai Nicodemiti, che si dogliono de la sua troppa rigidezza. E più, un suo Consiglio e due Epistole a due suoi amici sopra la medisime materie ... Sonvi poi aggiunti quattro Sermoni del medesimo Autore* [Geneva: J. Crespin] 1553, 8°.
Translation of several antinicodemite tracts (Cantimori, *Prospettive di storia*, p. 37; T. Bozza, 'Italia calvinista: Traduzioni italiane di Calvino nel secolo xvi', in *Miscellanea in onore di Ruggero Moscati* (Naples, 1985), pp. 245–6; CDM, p. 21; J.-Fr. Gilmont, *Bibliographie de Jean Crespin 1550–1572* (Verviers, 1981) vol. 1, pp. 36–7).

1554

35*   [Jean Calvin], *Catechismo* [Geneva]: Jean Crespin, 1554, 8°.
Reprint of work 29, printed as the third part of the *XX Salmi di David tradotti in rime volgari Italiane* ...; see also work 36 (CDM, pp. 22–3; J.-Fr. Gilmont, *Bibliographie*, vol. 1, pp. 41–2).

36*   [Jean Calvin], *La forma de l'orationi ecclesiastiche* [Geneva]: Jean Crespin, 1554, 8°.
Reprint of work 32, printed as the second part of the *XX Salmi di David* ... see work 35 (CDM, p. 126).

1556

37*   [Martin Luther], *I dieci commandamenti dati da Dio nel Monte Sinai, dechiarati in volgare ad utilità et commodo di ciascheduno fedele Christiano. La dechiaratione del Credo diviso in tre parte, secondo le tre persone de la Santissima Trinità. Il Pater noster insegnato dal nostro Signor Misser Giesù Christo, con la dechiaratione delle sette dimande in quello contenute* Venice: Agostino Bindoni, 1556, 8°.
The first of the three texts in works 1–4, 9, 17. (*Lutero*, p. 42; Florence, BNC).

38*   Pierre Viret, *De fatti de veri successori di Giesù Christo et de suoi Apostoli et de gli Apostati della Chiesa Papale* [Geneva]: Giovan Luigi Paschali, 1556, 8°.

      Translation of the tract *Des actes des vrais successeurs de Jésus Christ et de ses apostres et des apostats de l'Eglise papale* (CDM, p. 30).

1557

39*   [Jean Calvin], *Institutione della Religion Christiana* Geneva: Jacques Bourgeois, Antoine Davodeau and François Jaquy, 1557, 8°.

      Translation of the *Institutio christianae religionis* by Giulio Cesare Paschali (CDM, p. 31.).

40*   Johann Sleidan, *Commentarii, o vero historie* [Geneva: François Jaquy, Antoine Davodeau and Jacques Bourgeois], 1557, 8°.

      Translation of the *De Statu religionis et reipublicae Carolo Quinto Caesare commentarii* (D. Rhodes, 'La traduzione italiana dei "Commentarii" di Giovanni Sleidano', *La Bibliofilia*, 68, 1966, pp. 283–7; CDM, p. 33).

1560

41*   [Jean Calvin], *Il catechismo* [Geneva]: Giovan Battista Pinerolio, 1560, 8°.

      Translation of works 29 and 35, making up the third part of the *Sessanta Salmi di David, tradotti in rime volgari italiane* ... (CDM, p. 42).

42*   [Jean Calvin], *La forma de le orationi ecclesiastiche* [Geneva]: Giovan Battista Pinerolio, 1560, 8°.

      Translation of works 32 and 36, making up the third part of the *Sessanta Salmi di David, tradotti in rime volgari italiane* ... (CDM, p. 43).

43*   Théodore de Bèze, *Confessione della fede christiana ... nella quale è confermata la verità e sono rifiutate le superstitioni contrarie* [Geneva]: Fabio Todesco, 1560, 8°.

      Translation of *Confessio christianae fidei, et eiusdem collatio cum papisticis haeresibus* (F. Gardy, *Bibliographie des oeuvres ... de Théodore de Bèze* (Geneva, 1960), p. 79; CDM, p. 41).

1561

44*   Jean Calvin, *Il vero modo della pacificazione christiana e de la riformatione de la Chiesa* [Geneva]: François Duron, 1561, 8°.

      Translation of Calvin's treatise against the Interim (CDM, p. 48; R. Peter, 'Oeuvres de Calvin publiées à Genève entre 1550 et 1560', *BHR*, 31 (1969), p. 183).

45*   Jean Calvin, *Breve et utile trattato de la vita de l'homo christiano, nuovamente riveduto et ampliato da l'autore* [Geneva]: Fabio Todesco, 1561, 8°.

Reprint of chapter XXI of the *Institutio christianaem religionis* in Guilio Cesare Paschali's version (CDM, p. 47).

46* Gio[vanni] Cal[vino], *Breve e risoluto trattato de la cena del Signore* [Geneva]: François Duron, 1561, 8°.

Translation of the *Petit traicté de la Sainte Cène de nostre Seigneur* (CDM, p. 47).

47* *Confessione di fede fatta di comun consentimento da le chiese che sono disperse per la Francia, e s'astengono da le idolatrie papistice, con una prefatione, la quale contiene la risposta e difensione contra le calunnie che gli sono imputate* [Geneva]: Jacques Bourgeois, 1561, 8°.

Translation of the *Confession de foy, faicte d'un commun accord par les Eglises qui sont dispersées en France*, a collective work which however owed much to Calvin (CDM, p. 48).

48* Théodore de Bèze, *Parlamento de protestanti del regno di Francia, proposto da M. Theod. Bez.* [Geneva]: no printer, 1561, 8°.

Translation of *La première harangue faicte en l'assemblée de Poissy le mardi 9e jour de septembre 1561* (CDM, p. 46).

1562

49* Martin Luther, *Catechismo picciolo verso dal latino in lingua italiana per gli fanciugli* Tübingen: [Ulrich Morhart]; [Urach]: Hans von Ungnad, 1561, 8°.

Translation of the *Kleiner Catechismus* by Alessandro Dalmata and Stefano Consul (*Catechismo*; Wolfenbüttel, HAB).

50* *La confessione della fede data all'Invitissimo Carolo V. nella dieta di Augusta del M.D. XXX. novamente versa dal latino in lingua italiana per alcuni fideli Christiani amatori d'Italia. Aggiontovi la Defesa della istesa Confessione et la confessione della dottrina delle Chiese di Sassonia scritta del M.D. LI* Tübingen: [Morhart], 1562, 8°.

Translation of the *Confessio Augustana* in its 1542 version. The title-page offers Melanchthon's *Apologia*, which was printed in 1563, as well as the *Confessio Saxonica* which never appeared. The *Confessione* was printed in Tübingen by Morhart. The translation is attributed to Pietro Lauro, who also translated Erasmus's *Colloquia* (W. H. Neuser, *Bibliographie der Confessio Augustana und Apologie, 1530–1580* (Nieuwkoop, 1987), pp. 35, 95; R. Vorndran, *Südslavische Reformationsdrucke in der Universitätsbibliothek Tübingen* (Tübingen, 1977), pp. 52–4; Wolfenbüttel, HAB).

1563

51* [Philipp Melanchthon], *La Defesa della confessione, detta Apologia. Versa dal latino in lingua italiana, revista et corretta con* *diligenza per Antonion Dalmata et Stephano Istriano* [= Antonio Dalmata and Stefano Consul] Tübingen; [Urach: Hans von Ungnad], 1563, 8º.

Translation of the *Apologia Confessionis Augustanae* together with the edition of the *Confessio Augustana* of 1562. This edition was printed by von Ungnad in Urach, in spite of the mention of Tübingen (*Catechismo*; Neuser, *Bibliographie der Confessio*, p. 95; Vorndran, *Südslavische Reformationsdrucke*, pp. 55–6; Berlin SB; Tübingen, UB).

1564

52*   Martin Luther, *Espositione nel Salmo LI Habbi misericordia di me Signore. Et nel Salmo CXXX. Dal profondo gridai a te Signore ... pur hora tradotti di Latino in lingua Italiana. Revisti et corretti con diligenza per Antonio Dalmata et Stephano Istriano* Tübingen; [Urach: Hans von Ungnad], 1564, 8º.

Translation of the *Enarratio psalmorum LI. Miserere mei Deus et CXXX. De profundis clamavi ...* done by the two translators mentioned for works 49 and 50. This edition was printed by von Ungnad at Urach, in spite of the mention of Tübingen (*Catechismo;* Munich, UB; Tübingen, UB).

53*   [Jean Calvin], *La forma de le orationi ecclesiastiche* [Geneva]: Giovan Battista Pinerolio, 1564, 16º.

Works 32, 36, 42, added once again to the *Sessanta salmi* but without a separate title-page. (CDM, p. 58).

1566

54*   Jean Calvin, *Il catechismo* [Geneva]: Giovan Battista Pinerolio, 1566, 16º.

Translation by Niccolò Balbani (CDM, p. 63).

Without trying to do more than reflect the state of present research, this list is long enough to allow certain general conclusions to be drawn, regarding three aspects of this phenomenon: the preferred authors, the printing chronology, and the criteria used in selecting the works to be translated.

As regards the authors, the list shows the Italian preference for Luther: 14 works out of 54 are translations of his works, without counting the fact that the twenty-sixth chapter of the *Sommario della Santa Scrittura* is literally based on Luther's treatise, *Von weltlicher Obrigkeit.*[65] The Italian interest in Calvin is equally strong, comprising 15 works, not counting a *confessione di fede* which owed much to him. For Italian readers of vernacular religious literature, Luther was the preferred Re-

---

[65] J. Trapman, *De summa der Godliker Scrifturen (1523)* (Leiden, 1978), pp. 33–4.

P REFATIONE
DEL REVERENDISS.
Cardinal di santa Chiesa.
M. FEDERICO FRE-
goso nella Pistola di san
Paolo à Romani.

IN VENETIA M. D. XLV.
Con Gratia & Priuilegio.

11.3 Frederigo Fregoso [=Martin Luther], *Prefazione alla lettera ai Romani*
(Venice: Comin da Trino, 1545)

former during the first phase of the spread of Protestant ideas into Italy, between 1525 and 1545; after 1545, Calvin took the lead. One must, however, bear in mind that Calvin's works in translation were almost all printed in Geneva, and were not only intended for circulation in Italy but also in Geneva's Italian colony. In terms of the interests and outlook of the philo-Protestant movement south of the Alps therefore, the ten clandestinely produced translations of Luther printed in Italy between 1525 and 1545 had a greater documentary weight than the 14 translations of Calvin's work printed in Geneva.

Chronologically speaking, the publication of Reformation texts in the vernacular peaked between 1540 and 1550, during which 20 of the 54 works listed above appeared. This adds weight to the recently accepted time-scale of the Italian movement.[66]

Finally, the selection criteria used in choosing works to be translated can be reduced to four, based on the list described above:

---

[66] A. J. Schutte, 'Periodization of sixteenth-century Italian religious history: the post-Cantimori paradigm shift', *Journal of Modern History*, 61 (1989), 269–84.

1. Brevity – with a marked preference for small or very small books.
2. Practical theological discourse – works with catechetical tendencies were preferred for translation.
3. Doctrinal moderation – the most daring theological works were avoided. Therefore the publishing and sales success of the *Sommario della Santa Scrittura* can be considered as symptomatic of the Italian preference for texts which were rather conservative in their approach, as compared with the general body of evangelical theological works.[67]
4. Possible integration of the work into the Italian context – the need for works answering the specific experiences and psychological hopes held by Italian dissidents explains why works relatively unknown in Germany, like Urbanus Rhegius's *Libretto consolatorio a li perseguitati per la confessione de la verità evangelica* (number 24) were part of the context of persecution.[68]

Local works

The third category of works favouring the Reformation and circulating in Italy was that of the writings of Italian authors who joined the ideological movement or were close enough to it to have their works included in this group. The works most closely read by Italian dissidents and most often found in the hands of those accused in Inquisition trials were in this third category. Helped by their local knowledge, led by their personal experience in their choice of tone and polemical objectives, and moved by a desire to provide Italians with a new religious vocabulary, the authors who dared to produce works in this genre created a few jewels of national literature, from Benedetto da Mantova and Marcantonio Flaminio's *Beneficio di Cristo* to Federico Fregoso's *Trattato dell' orazione*. This is in spite of problems of national religious identity which kept Italians from fully accepting this aspect of their cultural tradition for centuries. Among the most common works in this group, alongside the *Beneficio di Cristo* and the *Trattato dell' oratione*, one must include Celio Secondo Curione's *Pasquino in estasi*, in its second edition, Bernardino Ochino's *Sermoni*, *Prediche*, and *Dialoghi* in their many editions, Francesco Negri's *Tragedia del libero arbitrio* (printed several times, both in Italian and in Latin), Pier Paolo Vergerio's production of pamphlets and Guilio da Milano's *Prediche*.[69]

---

[67] Trapman, *Summa*, p. 39.

[68] Cavazza, 'Libri in volgare', p. 22.

[69] List and summary description of these works in A. J. Schutte, *Printed Italian Vernacular Religious Books: A Finding List* (Geneva, 1983); see also Cavazza, 'Libri in volgare'.

DIALOGI SETTE DEL
REVERENDO PADRE FRATE
Bernardino Occhino Senefe Generale di frati
Capuzzini,doue fi côtiene.Nel primo dell'ina≠
morarfi di Dio nel fecôdo il modo di diuetar feli
ce,nel terzo di conofcer fe fteffo,nel quarto del la
trone buono, nel quinto del pelegrinaggio p an
dar al paradifo,nel fefto de la difputa di Chrifto
cô l'anima,nel fettimo,& vltimo della diuina
profeffione con vn fpûale teftaméto,Nuo≠
uamente Stampata, & hiftoriata.
Con il Priuilegio.

M. D.   XLIL

11.4   Bernardino Ochino, *Dialogi sette* (Venice: Niccolò Zoppino, 1542)

Antonio Brucioli's biblical studies, his translation of scriptures and his New Testament commentaries should be included as well as Massimo Teofilo's translation of the New Testament. Indeed, in the context of the Reformation, vernacular translations of the Bible played such a vital role that they can be classed as original work.[70] Furthermore, Biblical translations were among the most sought after works by Italian dissidents. If in the future one were able to count the number of heterodox works in circulation, Brucioli's Bible would probably be in close competition with the *Beneficio di Cristo* for first place as the most widely read book.[71] Other works by Italian Protestants, such as those of Peter Martyr Vermigli or Galateo were much less common.[72]

In terms of content, this category of works can be divided into two groups: those intended to edify and those intended to challenge. The first section contains works which focused on developing the positive aspects of Reformation theology, and on the message of peace and comfort, while leaving aside subversive comments and carefully avoiding any polemical tone. Readers could even come to the end of such a work, and even reread it several times without noticing the break it represented as against traditional pious texts. The prime example in this section is the *Beneficio di Cristo*, which was not only accepted by many sixteenth-century Catholics as a work of great piety and a source of comfort, but which even today major historians also place in the tradition of Benedictine piety.[73] In contrast, the works intended to fight Catholicism included works which attacked Catholic theology, the tradition of the Church, ecclesiastical organization and discipline directly, openly, and sometimes crudely. These texts made indiscriminate use of insult and sarcasm as weapons, and vehemently took up the theme of the Antichrist, leaving readers in no doubt from the first page onwards of the subversive programme outlined in these books. This section includes Curione's *Pasquino in estasi* and Francesco Negri's *Tragedia del libero arbitrio*.

Authors, too, can be divided into two groups, matching the division of their works into two categories. The authors of works intended for edification most often were supporters of the *status quo*. Writing a work with more or less clearly 'heretical' tendencies – on two occasions in the case of Federico Fregoso – did not lead to a perceptible conversion in their lives, nor did it create any great conflicts leaving traces in the sources. This calm may have been due to wide enough margins of

---

[70] On this subject, see A. Del Col, 'Appunti per una indagine sulle traduzioni in volgare della Bibbia nel Cinquecento italiano', in *Libri*, pp. 165–88.

[71] This is an empirical conclusion based on years of study of the Italian inquisitorial documents. A scientific demonstration of this will only be possible once all the documents have been systematically analysed.

[72] For Vermigli, see Schutte, *Printed Italian Vernacular*, p. 373. For Galateo, see S. Peyronel Rambaldi, *Speranze e crisi nel Cinquecento modenese* (Milan, 1979), p. 256.

[73] C. Ginzburg and A. Prosperi, *Giochi di pazienza: Un Seminario sul 'Beneficio di Cristo'* (Turin, 1975).

tolerance of disagreements at the time, or to the influence of powerful patrons inside the system, patrons who recognized their own aspirations for reform in these incriminated works, and thus protected the authors through their authority. Polemical works, in contrast, were written by authors whose lives had been dramatically affected by persecution and exile, like Celio Secondo Curione, Francesco Negri and Pier Paolo Vergerio. Their books, normally written and printed outside Italy, were intended to challenge readers, to confront them with an 'either/or' scenario, and to prove that any compromise solution was impossible. One example of this approach is Celio Secondo Curione's *Pasquino in estasi*, with its very harsh attack on Erasmus, condemning his flexibility in doctrine and his conciliatory confessional approach.[74]

There is often a correlation between reading done in a dissident group and the religious approach of its members. The circulation and collective reading of books which we have classified as polemical took place mainly in groups who lived their religious experience in organised clandestinity, and who were conscious of the definite rift between themselves and society at large. Thus, such groups felt themselves to be in permanent danger: in 1557, the Venetian group of the *muschiaro* Antonio da Limito owned the *Pasquino in Estasi* and the *Tragedia del libero arbitrio*, as did that of the Neapolitan glazier Ascanio in the same year, while the merchant group centred around Battista and Giovanni Catinari in Forlì in 1567 possessed the *Tragedia del libero arbitrio*, etc.[75] In contrast the circulation and reading of books classified as works of edification were signs of a form of religious dissidence in which profound fervour and an open attitude were united, along with an ardent wish for dialogue with adversaries and much flexibility in matters of doctrine. Thus the *Beneficio di Cristo* and Fregoso's *Trattato dell'orazione* appeared in groups like the one in Asolo, centred around Antonio and Benedetto dal Borgo in 1547 or the one led by the grocer of Vincence, Giovanni Donato della Columbina, in the same year, etc.[76]

To complete the overview of Reformation literature available in Italy, one must add a fourth category to the first three, that of hybrid books. These are ones in which the Italian authors covertly inserted into their own text more or less lengthy and significant passages by Reformation

---

[74] [C. S. Curione], *Pasquino in estasi, nuovo e molto più pieno ch'el primo ... Stampato a Roma* [= Basle]: nella botega di Pasquino, a l'istanza di papa Paulo Farnese, [1546?], pp. 191–2.

[75] Venice, AS, SU, b. 13, fasc. 'Antonio da Limito'; Dublin, Trinity College, ms. 1224, sentence passed 20 September 1567.

[76] Venice, AS, SU, b.6, 'Contra hereticos de Asyllo 1547' and, in the same dossier, 'Contra Joannem Donatum della Columbina 1547'. However, polemical works like the *Tragedia del libero arbitrio* also circulated in these two groups.

authors who had definitely been condemned. In order to evade censorship more effectively, these 'inlaid works' were sometimes camouflaged behind vague or misleading book titles. Antonio Brucioli created hybrid works, taking sections of Calvin's *Institutio Christianae religionis*, as did Ortensio Lando, taking from Otto Brunfels's *Pandectae*, Bartholomäus Westheimer's *Collectanea troporum Bibliorum*, and Martin Bucer's *Enarrationes perpetuae in sacra quatuor Evangelia*, and Celio Secondo Curione, integrating passages from the *Sommario della Santa Scrittura*.[77] The first Italian translation of Calvin's catechism offered in its preface large sections of Juan de Valdés's *Qual maniera si devrebbe tenere a informare insino della fanciulleza ...* .[78] Hybrid texts are the most difficult to identify, and therefore research in this area is only beginning.

The reception

Twelve archival collections have survived, providing information on the attitude of the Inquisition tribunals in 11 different cities – Venice, Modena, Rome, Naples, Bologna, Udine, Siena, Rovigo, Pisa, Imola and Belluno – as well as an indeterminate number of isolated trials.[79] These remnants give a particular tone to the situation of sources in Italy in terms of the reception of Reformation ideas, and distinguish the Italian situation from that of other European or even Mediterranean lands. While Spanish Inquisition trials dealing with the spread of Reformation ideas – in its most general sense – only accounted for a minimal proportion of the cases dealt with by these tribunals – less than 10 per cent in Galicia, and in most cases the accused were foreigners – in Italy, around 80 per cent of suspects called before the tribunals prior to 1580 in the north were thought to be Protestants, or admitted that charge.[80]

---

[77] On Brucioli's use of Calvin, see T. Bozza, 'Calvino in Italia', in *Miscellanea in memoria di Giorgio Cencetti* (Turin, 1973), pp. 410 and following. For Ortensio Lando's use of Bucer, Brunfels and Westheimer, see Seidel Menchi, 'Sulla fortuna' pp. 594–7 and Seidel Menchi, 'Spiritualismo radicale nelle opere de Ortensio Lando attorno al 1550', *ARG*, 65 (1974), 210–77. For C. S. Curione's use of the *Sommario della Santa Scrittura*, see Peyronel Rambaldi, 'Itinerari', pp. 7–9.

[78] A. G. Kinder, 'Juan de Valdés' in Séguenny (ed.) *Bibliotheca dissidentium: Répertoire des non-conformistes religieux des seizième et dix-septième siècles* (Baden-Baden, 1988), vol. 9, pp. 111–195, esp. p. 180.

[79] The most famous tribunal was that of Cardinal Giovanni Morone: M. Firpo and D. Marcatto, *Il processo inquisitoriale del cardinal Giovanni Morone. Edizione critica* (Rome, 1981–89).

[80] For Galicia, see J. Contreras, *El Santo Oficio de la Inquisición de Galicia* (Madrid, 1982), pp. 588, 609–20; for Italy, see E. W. Monter and J. Tedeschi, 'Towards a statistical profile of the Italian Inquisitions, sixteenth to eighteenth centuries', in G.

A significant proportion of the thousands of sympathizers of the Reformation preserved in these records came into contact with the new religious ideas through books, or at the very least their beliefs were reinforced by their readings. A very approximative and hypothetical calculation suggests that roughly half of the Inquisition trials dealing with heresy prior to 1580 furnish information on the books read by Italian dissidents, on their distribution networks, and on the ways and means of reading. These sources are sufficiently rich and geographically diverse to provide representative data for all of Italy, except Sicily and Sardinia. But because a general analysis still remains to be done, the following observations should be taken as fragmentary foretastes of a work which is only in its project stages.

Heretical works present everywhere

In Italian society supporters of the Reformation were seen as voracious readers, who always had books to hand. For example, Pietro Vagnola, the *Petrus lutheranus* who moved to Grignano Polesine to spread Reformation ideas among the peasantry 'is always studying heretical or Lutheran books, which he owns and always carries around with him' (1547). Francesco Garzotto, a Franciscan from Udine went around 'always with Saint Paul's Epistles in his hands' (1543) and the shoemaker Niccolò dalle Monache from Conegliano owned a book which he kept in his workshop, and invited passersby in to hear him read from it (1549), etc.[81] Whenever a heterodox group gathered around an itinerant preacher to hear his doctrine, or even when holding internal discussions, books formed a constant part of the decor: 'and there were many books on the table' (1543) 'and they owned certain books' (1547), etc.[82]

The Bible's central role in this indoctrination ritual is not surprising. However, it is more surprising to realize that the works of edification accompanying the Bible and using it as their base should take on the status of the Book itself, and the Bible's own authority. For instance, when an inhabitant of Grignano invoked the authority of tradition in support of the Mass – 'I found it very strange that [the heretic Pietro

---

Henningsen, J. Tedeschi and Ch. Amiel (eds), *The Inquisition in Early Modern Europe* (Dekalb [Illinois], 1986), pp. 133 ff.

[81] Venice, AS, SU, b. 6, 'Contra Petrum Vagnola senesem', deposition of 8 March 1547; b. 1, fasc. 'Girolamo Venier, Alvise Cavallo e altri', fol. 21ᵛ; b. 7, 'Contra Ricardo pittor e Nicolò dalle Monache'.

[82] Venice, AS, SU, b. 1, fasc. 'Girolamo Venier, Alvise Cavallo e altri' fol. 27ᵛ; b. 6, 'Processus contra Joannem Donatum della Columbina', fol. 10ʳ.

Vagnola] should condemn the Mass which has always been praised by all' – his philo-Protestant interlocutor opposed the authority of the printed page to that of the Mass. 'What can one do? If [the heretic] proves his argument with books, one must be patient', in other words, one must accept the unquestionable authority of the written word.[83] Religious dissidents turned spontaneously to the authority of the book whenever opponents placed them in an awkward position in the course of a religious discussion: 'I cannot discuss this [freely] but I have a book' (1543); 'He would take a book from under his jacket and would want to show it to me' (1547); 'He wanted to show me something or other in that book' (1547), 'He picked up a small book' (1547), etc.[84]

In the same way as the repercussions of the Bible went well beyond literate groups, the works of the Reformation were not stopped by the barrier of illiteracy. Through group reading, one of the fundamental means of proselytizing, 'heretical' books reached an audience made up of all socio-cultural sections of society. The source of Protestant communities was often sociologically mixed groups. Artisans' workshops, private dwellings, and even churches were the setting for such readings. Certain testimonies suggest that philo-Protestant reading circles grew out of pre-existing meditation or prayer groups-confraternities – or even out of groups dedicated to reading traditional edifying works, such as the lives of saints or controversial ones, like Savonarola's works.[85]

Reading as a choice

What do Inquisition documents reveal concerning reading as a means of acquiring knowledge, as an interaction between book and reader? The most explicit testimonies provide a picture of reading as a vertical topical model, as opposed to the more familiar transversal/dianoetic model. Instead of following a logical line of argument through the book, readers tended to focus on a particular theme of high semantic density. They then took such themes out of their context and spread them orally. One can assume that these central themes emerged from the collective reading of works as the focal points of the group's perception.

The following are some examples of topical reading, referring to Francesco Negri's above-mentioned *Tragedia del libero arbitrio*, one of

---

[83] Venice, AS, SU, b. 6, 'Contra Petrum Vagnola senesem', deposition of 29 December 1547.

[84] Venice, AS, SU, b. 1, fasc. 'Girolamo Venier, Alvise Cavallo e altri', fols 3ᵛ–4ʳ; b. 6, 'Processus contra Joannem Donatum della Columbina', fols 10ᵛ–11ʳ, 10ʳ, 14ʳ.

[85] There are indications to this effect in the two trials mentioned in the previous footnote.

the works which circulated most among philo-Protestant groups. During the Inquisitorial trial of the conventual Franciscan Stefano Boscaia, who had joined in the group reading of the *Tragedia* in a fellow monk's cell at Asolo, he was asked, 'What is the subject of this tragedy?' He answered 'that Grace cut off Free Will's head' (1547). A highly complex theological argument, laboriously transported into a dramatic setting, was thus condensed into a single sentence.[86] Another example of the same procedure was the success of the Augustinian adage, 'He who created you without your help will not justify you without you'. In the *Tragedia del libero arbitrio*, this axiom was presented to the reader in two different readings: a negative one put by Francesco Negri in the mouths of traditional theology's defenders, and a questioning reading – 'He who created you without your help, will he justify you without you?' Negri argued that the second version was the more ancient one, thus recommending it indirectly as against the authentic version, but turning the original meaning upside-down. Leaving this philological argument aside, readers took the Augustinian lemma in its interrogative form from the *Tragedia* and began to transmit it orally. Its presence was attested to in Chiogga in 1549, in Arbe in 1558, etc.[87] The use of works for purposes of display led to a clearly established formula which carried such persuasive power that it needed no further proof. A third example confirms this practice. During a discussion of the cult of saints and the veneration of relics, one of the characters in the *Tragedia del libero arbitrio* quoted the statement 'Many bodies are venerated upon earth, while their souls are tormented in Hell', Niccolò Guidozzo, a chancellor investigated for heresy in Parenzo and Venice in 1575–76 repeated the same statement in an apodictic form, needing no proof, and even better, rejecting the cult of saints in one simple phrase.[88] A similar statement was circulating in Udine in 1543 ('Saint Augustine said that there are many bodies venerated on earth who are tormented in Hell'), the source of which cannot have been the *Tragedia*, first

---

[86] Venice, AS, SU, b. 6, 'Exemplum processus contra hereticos de Asyllo de anno 1547', account of the interrogation of Stefano Boscaia held on 6 June 1547, fol. 22^{r-v}.

[87] Fr. Negri, *Della tragedia intitolata Libero arbitrio* (2nd. edn, Basle: J. Oporinus, 1550) fol. E4^r. The quotation from Augustine occurs in the *Sermon 169*, *Patrologia latina*, vol. 38, col. 923. For the reception in Chiogga and Arbe, see Seidel Menchi, *Erasmo*, p. 419, n. 20. One should note, however, that the spread of Augustine's adage may have been helped by a sermon of Bernardino Ochino (see Seidel Menchi, *Erasmo*, p. 202).

[88] Fr. Negri, *Della tragedia* fol. G^v. For its reception, see Venice, AS, SU, b. 40, fasc. 'Niccolò Guidozzo', fol. 41^r: 'Saint Paul said: "on earth, we venerate many saints' bodies, whose souls are in Hell" and I learned this from certain Paduan students who came here from Padua by boat'.

published in 1546.[89] This coincidence deserves closer scrutiny: it suggests that Italian readers in different surroundings and at different times tended to draw out the same adages from different works.[90]

Another constant feature of the Italian reception of Reformation works is illustrated by a Venetian testimony, ending our series of examples. In 1568, the schoolmaster Zuane from Naples confessed to the Inquisition tribunal in Venice:

> In 1539, I married a poor girl. Everything we owned did not even amount to six marcelli. Every morning ... we went to Mass together, except when she was pregnant. And every day I would recite the seven penitential psalms and the Virgin's mass as my personal devotions, as well as the Rosary ... And in 1552 I began to run an arithmetic school in Treviso, and continued my devotions every day for ten years. And ... when I was house-bound for fifty days because of illness, I paid a lady to go do these devotions for me. In 1562 or maybe in 1561, someone brought a book to the school. It was God's will that the book was brought there, so that I would undergo these tribulations. The work was in the vernacular, and contained the Creed, the Ten Commandments and other similar things from the New Testament. The book condemned long prayers in particular, and called those who prayed at length hypocrites. The booklet had no title, place of printing, or author's name. And after having read it for ten, fifteen or twenty days, I became so indifferent when praying, that I stopped saying the seven penitential psalms, I completely stopped telling the Rosary, and I rarely went to Mass, and when I did go, I did so reluctantly. And my poor wife reproached me bitterly, seeing that everything we did was going badly. And having read in this booklet that what enters the mouth of a man does not make him unclean, but rather what comes out of his mouth, I began to eat meat carelessly during Lent and vigils. And because I had read in this book that the use of sacred images was condemned, I stopped honoring them, and worse than that, I hated and despised those who honoured them.[91]

This document has been quoted at length in order to show how Italian readers tended to select the parts of the Reformation discourse which had to do with daily religious practice, rather than the fundamental theological ideas. The book which had such a disturbing effect on the life of Zuane of Naples is not easily identifiable. One can reasonably suppose that it was the *Pia expositione ne' dieci precetti, nel Symbolo Apostolico et nella oratione Dominica, dove si ha quello che ci comandi*

---

[89] Venice, AS, SU, b. 1, fasc. 'Girolamo Venier, Alvise Cavallo e altri', fol. 2ʳ.

[90] One must bear in mind the possibility that in the case of Udine, the source was Curione's *Pasquino in estasi*, which did circulate among this group. See *Pasquino in estasi*, p. 117: 'How many are there on the altars, whose souls are in Hell!'.

[91] Venice, AS, SU, b. 24, 'Contra Adream quondam Merchioris Gambararum', confession of Zuane of Naples, 20 June 1568.

Iddio, quello che si debba credere, et come si debba orare. Ostensibly, the work was by Antonio Brucioli, but in fact it was a free reworking of the first three chapters of Calvin's *Institutio christianae religionis* in its 1536 edition.[92] Zuane of Naples thus probably read a text which communicated its message very effectively, in which the fundamental categories of systematic theology – the dichotomies of law/Gospel, faith/works, merit/grace and human nature's inability to do good, etc. – were presented to readers in formulations, the strength of which was only equalled by the excellence of the language. But these themes, considered to be the fundamental basis of Calvin's system are not those which troubled the conscience of this reader and transformed his life. Instead, a greater impact was caused by what may seem to us to be peripheral corollaries of Protestant doctrine, matters of minor theological importance: the times and ways of prayer, dietary rules, and the worship of images.

Thus in the Italian book, theological brilliance and doctrinal systematizing seem to have been less effective, less able to make an impact than features relating to real life and a message applicable to day-to-day activities.

A Reformation going beyond the Reformation

In the European context, the Italian reception of 'heretical' books leads to a general reassessment of the very concept of Reformation. The picture of the reader emerging from Italian sources gives to the Reformation, as an ideological movement, wider borders than those given to it today. This growth of the Reformation's domain is further confirmed by the Catholic Church itself through the Indices of forbidden books. Sixteenth-century Italy thus reintroduced into the Reformation area three names which have generally been left aside by current historical criticism. These are: Erasmus of Rotterdam, and following him Alfonso de Valdès with his *Dialogo di Mercurio e Caronte* and his *Dialogo di Lattanzio et di un arcidiacono*, as well as Federico Fregoso's *Trattato dell 'orazione*, and one further name whose adherence to the Reforma-

---

[92] Schutte, *Printed Italian Vernacular*, p. 108; Bozza, 'Calvino in Italia'. The book which Zuane of Naples read could not have been Luther's *Dichiarazione de dieci commandamenti* (see nos 1–4, 9, and 17 from the list of Italian translations) because this work did not adopt a polemical approach regarding long prayers, prohibited foods, or the veneration of images. Identifying Zuane's book with the *Pia expositione* can be countered by the fact that the work was published under Brucioli's name, with the place and date of printing indicated on the book, but Zuane of Naples may have had a copy without the title page, given that Brucioli was among those whose entire works were placed on the Index.

tion is still controversial – Juan de Valdès. These four authors' inclusion in the Reformation domain is both logical and of long standing, especially if one considers the success of another author whose works were often printed, and were read with fervour during these years, namely Girolamo Savonarola. Even though certain of Savonarola's works and subsidiary writings like the *Oracolo della renovazione della Chiesa* contributed a substantial source to the Italian religious revolt,[93] sources known at present do not allow us to conclude that the work of the Dominican of Ferrare was in fact co-opted into the Reformation domain, in contrast to the case of Erasmus,[94] Fregoso, and the Valdès brothers, and Juan in particular.[95] Italians who evaluated this genre of writings seem to have taken as their basic presupposition that a book could be given a theological role beyond what the author himself had been willing to consider.

Select bibliography

Balmas, E., 'L'activité des imprimeurs italiens réfugiés à Genève dans la deuxième moitié du xvie siècle', in J.-D. Candaux and B. Lescaze (eds), *Cinq siècles d'imprimerie genevoise: Actes du Colloque international sur l'histoire de l'imprimerie et du livre à Genève, 27–30 avril 1978* (Geneva, 1980), pp. 109–31.

Balmas, E., 'Sulla fortuna editoriale di Lutero in Francia e in Italia nel xvi secolo', in A. Agnoletto (ed.) *Martin Luther e il Protestantesimo in Italia* (Milan, 1984), pp. 39–76.

Cavazza, S., 'Libri in volgare e propaganda eterodossa: Venezia 1543–1547', in A. Prosperi and A. Biondi (eds), *Libri, idee e sentimenti religiosi nel Cinquecento italiano* (Ferrare, 1987), pp. 9–28.

De Frede, C., *Ricerche per la storia della stampa e la diffusione delle idee riformate nell'Italia del Cinquecento* (Naples, 1985).

---

[93] There is a list of the editions of Savonarola's works up to 1550 in Schutte, *Printed Italian Vernacular*. That Protestant groups read the work of the Dominican Luca Bettini, *Oracolo della renovatione della Chiesa secondo la dottrina del reverendo Padre Hieronimo Savonarola* is evidenced by the trial 'Contra Martial di Clemente' (Venice, AS, SU, b. 25).

[94] Seidel Menchi, *Erasmo*.

[95] The religious stance of Jean de Valdès and the success of his thought are closely analysed by M. Firpo, 'Juan de Valdès e l'evangelismo italiano. Appunti e problemi di una ricerca in corso', *Studi storici*, 24 (1985), 733–54, and Firpo, 'Valdesianismo', pp. 53071. For a more complete bibliography on Juan de Valdès and the circulation of his books in Italy, see the studies mentioned above, Lopez, *Il movimento* and Kinder, 'Juan de Valdès'.

Del Col, A., 'Il Nuovo Testamento tradotto da Massimo Teofilo e altre opere stampate a Lione nel 1551', *Critica Storica*, **15** (1978), 642–75.

Del Col, A., 'Il controllo della stampa a Venezia e i processi di Antonio Brucioli', *Critica Storica*, **17** (1980), 457–510.

Grendler, P. F., *L'Inquisizione romana e l'editoria a Venezia, 1540–1603* (Rome, 1983).

Rotondò, A., *Studi e ricerche di storia ereticale italiana del Cinquecento* (Turin, 1974), vol. 1.

Rozzo, U., 'Dieci anni di censura libraria (1596–1605)', *Libri e documenti*, **9** (1983), 43–61.

Rozzo, U., 'La cultura italiana nelle edizioni lionesi di Sébastien Gryphe (1531–1541)', *La Bibliofilia*, **90** (1988), 161–95.

Schutte, A. J., *Printed Italian Vernacular Religious Books: A Finding List* (Geneva, 1983).

S. Seidel Menchi, 'Le traduzioni italiane di Lutero nella prima metà del Cinquecento', *Rinascimento*, **17** (1978), 36–40.

S. Seidel Menchi, *Erasmo in Italia (1520–1580)* (Turin, 1987).

P. Simoncelli, *Evangelismo italiano del Cinquecento. Questione religiosa e nicodemismo politico* (Rome, 1979).

CHAPTER TWELVE

The book and the beginnings of the Reformation in Hungary

Gedeon Borsa

The arrival of Hungarians into Europe was one of the last migratory waves. At the end of the ninth century, coming from the east, they arrived in the Carpathian basin. Their progress halted by German armies at Lechfeld in 955, these nomadic herdsmen settled along the Danube. Their choice of settlement was influenced by two factors: the favourable agricultural location, and the political situation, as the territory they chose stretched between the Holy Roman Empire and the Byzantine Empire. Saint Stephen (d. 1038) firmly brought the Hungarian people to Christianity. The crown which Sylvester II offered him in 1001 became the symbol of Hungarian independence. At the time of the great schism (1054) the country decisively joined the Roman side, but the Byzantine presence along Hungary's southern frontier remained an important long-term condition.

The country was a colourful mix of languages: besides the Slavs who were already there, (Slovaks in the north and Croats in the south), the first arrivals were German immigrants coming from the west, followed later by Romanian shepherds coming from the south, who settled on the periphery of inhabited lands. Thus, from the thirteenth century onwards the representatives of three principal groups of Indo-European languages coexisted there: several Slav languages, German (Germanic) and Romanian (Romane). But the most numerically important people in the Carpathian basin still speak Hungarian today, a language which is not part of the Indo-European family of languages, but of the finno-ugrian group of languages from the Urals.

Following this brief historical and linguistic preface, let us now turn to the two themes of this essay: printing and the Reformation. Gutenberg's invention made a remarkably rapid appearance in these areas. On 5 June 1473, the *Chronica Hungarorum* came out of the presses of Andreas Hess in Buda, Hungary's capital, preceding many other countries such as Bohemia, Poland, Spain and England. Only one other work is known to have been published by the Buda press. The second Hungarian printing house named after its first production, *Confessionale*, had an equally short life span, as it was active only between 1477 and 1480. During the next decades, no printing activity took place in Hungary. Around 60 works printed in Latin for Hungary between 1488 to 1526 are presently known. For the most part, they were ordered by Buda's dozen or so publishers – and were generally printed in Venice.

1526 marked a historical turning point for Hungary. The defeat at Mohács by the Turks had long-lasting consequences. A few decades of turmoil led to a tripartite division of the country, as the Turks dominated the centre and the south, the Habsburgs, who considered themselves as the legitimate successors of the king killed in battle at Mohács, dominated the west and north, and ruled over royal Hungary, while the principality of Transylvania was created in the east. Transylvania acted as a buffer zone between the two great powers: the German Empire and the Ottoman Turk Empire, and remained in this role while neither of the two was able to predominate (1541–1711). One interesting observation is that while Latin remained the official language in Hungary until the nineteenth century because of its linguistically diverse population, Hungarian played the same role in Transylvania.

The tripartite division of the country, which continued for more than a century and a half after 1526, is fundamental for our topic. In spite of the major differences in the evolution of printing and in the progress of the Reformation in the three parts of the country, evidence of reciprocal influence show how unstable and permeable the borders were.

One of the main objectives of the Reformation begun by Luther was to make the Bible directly accessible to the people, by eliminating the intermediary role played until then by the clergy. This objective called for two preconditions – on the one hand, that people be able to read, and on the other, that the Bible be available to them in their mother tongue. Schooling and the vernacular are therefore the two aspects which best allow for a study of the revival of printing in Hungary in the sixteenth century.

Book production

No book is known to have been printed in the Hungarian territories under Turkish occupation. Printing activity was limited more by permanent insecurity and general impoverishment than by administrative prohibitions.

The principality of Transylvania was quite isolated, since the normal communication routes towards the west – first and foremost the Danube via Buda, the centre of communications – were not safe enough for regular travel. The other possible route through the Carpathian mountains to Cracow and Breslau (present-day Wrocław) was much longer, and the dangers of the road made the transport of goods difficult and expensive as well. The small principality was thus condemned to self-sufficiency. In fact, it was thanks to this inward-looking economy that Transylvania became the centre of the first Hungarian printing presses operating after Mohács, as well as that of the paper mills which were closely linked to the presses.

In the so-called Royal Hungary, that is to the west and north, printing began more slowly, for relations with the Austrian provinces and with Bohemia remained on an even keel. These areas could thus supply the modest demand for books from the kingdom. Supplies continued to come in even when the vernacular became more important in publishing, as the Germans in the west turned to Austria while the Slovaks in the north looked to Bohemia, which used the same literary language at the time. Although a few works were printed in Hungarian, this did not lead to the creation of indigenous printshops in this period. Instead, such works were printed only and without exception in the two nearest centres possessing permanent printing presses, Vienna and Cracow. Hungarian students in these two university cities were able to proofread the works in Hungarian, a language which was completely isolated within an Indo-European setting.

In the Carpathian basin, the Germans were among the Reformation's first adherents. Their principal city, Nagyszeben (in German, Hermannstadt, today Sibiu) housed the first sixteenth-century printing press. No books produced by this workshop have survived, but ancient manuscript sources describe in detail an elementary Latin grammar completed in 1529, and medical advice against the plague, published in German in the following year. These works did not yet show any influence of the Reformation.

Johann Honter and Valentin Wagner in Brassó

Ten years later, a printing press began to operate in the other major city of Transylvanian Saxons, Brassó (Kronstadt in German, Braşov today). The press was run by Johann Honter, a native of the city. This high-calibre humanist had come into contact with the Reformation during a stay in Basle, and his interest, combined with Transylvania's economic isolation, had led to the start of a more lasting printing house in the Carpathian basin around 1539. Nine editions published in its first year of operation have survived. These indicate that Honter's printing press was primarily intended to produce school books. After many years spent in foreign lands, he started a school in his native city. Though his school was founded in the spirit of the Reformation, the first products of his press showed no traces of this, but then again the classical works for schools, both in Latin and in Greek (Aristotle, Cato, Seneca, etc.) did not provide much scope for Reformation influences.

However, even from the first years there were certain traces of this new religious approach. In Saint Augustine's *Haeresion catalogus*,[1] Honter, whose philological skills were very good, indicated by the use of asterisks – without any other explanation – the sections of the text in which he was making cuts, seemingly explained by his religious beliefs. The Brassó publications in the following years were again exclusively school-books, for the most part written or rewritten by Honter. Some of these works aimed to develop the teaching of history, civil law, etc, following Lutheran views. These were decorated or illustrated with woodcuts produced by Honter himself.

In 1541, the Turks occupied Buda, the Hungarian capital, shortly after the death of King János Szapolyai. The already weak central authority thus had practically no impact in Brassó from then on. Therefore, 1543 was a turning-point in the life of its printing house, with the publication of the *Reformatio ecclesiae Coronensis ac totius Barcensis provinciae*.[2] The book was written by Honter, and was modelled on German works. In a letter dated 1 September 1543, Luther expressed his satisfaction with the work, which was then republished in Wittenberg at the end of the same year, complete with a preface by Melanchthon. This first Reformation text to be printed in the Carpathian basin was thus linked to Honter and the city of Brassó. Its influence extended from the city throughout the region of Barcaság, in which a large proportion of the inhabitants spoke German.

Another work produced during this year in the Brassó workshop also merits attention, namely the *Geistliche lieder* by Andreas Moldner,[3] the local preacher, containing six hymns and two Biblical stories in verse. This work was Honter's first production in German. The development of the vernacular was a logical outcome, in Transylvania as elsewhere. However, Honter had not counted on this move when he acquired his printing equipment on his departure from Basle. Hence his workshop did not possess the appropriate character fonts for printing in German. In this period, therefore, he used roman characters (antiqua), a most unusual procedure.

In 1547, Honter's presses published three works which were highly significant for the Transylvanian Reformation: the *Kirchenordnung aller Deutschen in Sybembürgen*[4] and its Latin version *Reformatio ecclesiarum*

---

[1] *RMNy*, no. 29.
[2] *RMNy*, no. 52.
[3] *RMNy*, no. 53.
[4] *RMNy*, no. 68.

Saxonicarum in Transylvania[5] as well as the *Agenda für die Seelsorger und Kirchendiener in Sybembürgen*.[6] These works were intended for the entire Saxon community in Transylvania, offering it the basic documents for a new ecclesiastical organisation. Thus Honter was continuing his pioneering task begun four years before with the *Reformatio*: a new version of it, reworked by Honter and two of his companions, Valentin Wagner and Mathias Glatz, was immediately translated and published in German. In 1550, the 'Universitas Saxonum Transylvaniae', the Transylvanian Saxons' autonomous governing body, based on privileges granted hundreds of years before by the Hungarian kings, made the *Kirchenordnung* into law.

Inside the geographical area of Transylvania, the spread of the new religious outlook was shaped by the different linguistic communities. Furthermore, the new church organized itself in the same setting, thanks to the above-mentioned privileges. The Brassó printing press, originally equipped only for the production of Latin and Greek school-books, and Honter himself were at the forefront of the movement. In 1547, Honter obtained the necessary fonts for the publication of works in German, which had become the official language.

Transylvanian Saxons who joined the evangelical church often believed that Honter had established his printing presses to further the Lutheran Reformation, and thus that Luther's shorter German catechism had been one of his first publications. In contrast to this pious tradition, this central work for the Reformation was only published in Brassó in 1548. This catechism, modelled on the Wittenberg editions of 1543, also had original features. Even its title differed from the original: *Der Kleine Catechismus für die Pfarherr und Hausväter*. The liturgical section of the confession was eliminated in Honter's version, as were the sections on marriage and baptism in the appendix. On the other hand, a translation of Manasseh's prayer was added.[7]

After Honter's death, his disciple Valentin Wagner (1549–57) took over the leadership of Brassó's printing press. In 1550, he prepared and published a catechism in which the fundamental Lutheran teachings were presented in Greek, in dialogue form.[8] Wagner thus brought together in a highly original manner both Greek and evangelical religious education.

---

[5] *RMNy*, no. 69.
[6] *RMNy*, no. 67.
[7] *RMNy*, no. 72. *Das Gebet Manasse* does not appear in any German edition of Luther's catechism; the text does appear in Luther's *Betbüchlein* of 1539 and in various editions of 1543 (see J. Sólyom, 'Zur Überlieferung des Gebetes Manasse: Zugleich ein Beitrag zur Geschichte der Siebenbürger Katechismusausgaben', in *Zeitschrift für Kirchengeschichte*, 75 (1964), 339–46).
[8] *RMNy*, no. 82.

Georg Hoffgreff and Gáspár Heltai in Kolozsvár

The first printing press systematically producing Hungarian works in the Carpathian basin was also established in Transylvania, this time in the city of Kolozsvár (Klausenburg in German, Cluj-Napoca today) in 1550. From the very start, it worked for the Reformation. Between 1539 and 1541, another printing press operated in Sárvár in western Hungary, and printed the New Testament in Hungarian.[9] But the latter workshop was only ephemeral, and there is no evidence that it was founded to help the Reformation. Instead, it seems to have been created to publish the writings of Erasmus and other humanists. In contrast Kolozsvár's presses published several works with clearly evangelical tendencies from its inception onwards, among others Luther's small catechism translated into Hungarian by Gáspár Heltai.[10] Latin works by Martin Bucer and Johann Brenz, defending the Lutheran view of the Lord's Supper, were published at the same time.[11] A Hungarian satire fiercely ridiculing Catholic priests was also published by the Kolozsvár presses, but under the false printing address of Craców.[12] In this period, the Transylvanian principality was actually ruled by the bishop, György Martinuzzi, in the name of the underage prince. Because of fear of reprisals from the bishop, the actual place of origin of this strongly anti-Catholic work had to be camouflaged. However, objective expressions of the Lutheran viewpoint found from the very start an unhindered place among the publications of the city, as had been the case in Brassó some years before.

The Kolozsvár presses were founded in 1550 by Georg Hoffgreff, using equipment acquired in Nuremberg. From 1550 to 1558, Hoffgreff directed the workshop jointly with the German-speaking minister of the local Lutheran community, Kaspar Helt. The two men worked both separately and together, but always from a Lutheran perspective. But the unanimity of the Reformation is a myth, as the movement split into multiple approaches which continued to grow in number and in diversity, and which fought against each other, also in the Carpathian basin. One of Ferenc Dávid's works of 1555 provides a good example of this, as in the book, Dávid attacks a work with Unitarian tendencies by Francesco Stancaro.[13] Two years later, Dávid defended the Lutheran position against the Calvinists, who were constantly growing in

---

[9] *RMNy*, no. 49.
[10] *RMNy*, no. 86.
[11] *RMNy*, no. 84.
[12] *RMNy*, no. 88.
[13] *RMNy*, no. 127.

strength.[14] Hoffgreff died in 1558, and from then on the presses of Kolozsvár were taken over exclusively by his associate. Adopting Gáspár Heltai as a Hungarian name, Kaspar Helt ministered to Hungarian-speaking as well as German-speaking Lutherans.

In 1559, Heltai and Dávid accepted the Calvinist doctrine of the Lord's Supper. Immediately, Calvinist works began to appear in Kolozsvár, in Latin for theological works, like those of Dávid[15] and of Bullinger,[16] and in Hungarian otherwise. Thus a text favouring the Reformed approach by Péter Melius Juhász appeared in the course of the same year.[17] This minister, active in Debrecen, to the east of the central Hungarian plain, was the source of Heltai and Dávid's changed religious outlook.

The publication of parts of the Bible in Hungarian began in the year after the establishment of the printing presses in Kolozsvár (1551).[18] The task continued under Heltai's direction in spite of more or less lengthy interruptions, even in his 'Reformed' period: the complete New Testament was finished in 1561.[19] Even though major sections of the Old Testament were printed in Kolozsvár, a complete version was never achieved. The first full Bible in Hungarian was finished only much later, in 1590 in Vizsoly in northern Hungary, translated by the Reformed Protestant Gáspár Károlyi.[20]

In 1563, the strictly Lutheran Transylvanian Saxons parted company with Heltai, their former fellow believer and fellow citizen. The ensuing polemic had repercussions in print: the chief minister of Nagyszeben, Mathias Hebler, published a work in Brassó summarizing the views of many Lutherans and German universities on the Lord's Supper. These works, dating from 1560 to 1561 reinforced the Lutheran position, and criticized that of Calvin.[21] The Transylvanian Saxons also mobilised those with greater authority by publishing, also in Brassó, writings of Luther, Melanchthon and Bugenhagen from 1543 under the title *Approbatio reformationis ecclesiae Coronensis ac totius Barcensis provinciae*, all of which supported unanimously the Lutheran-inspired religious reforms carried out by Honter.[22]

The break between Heltai and his former associates made itself felt not only in print, but also in the distribution of paper. This shows how

---

14 *RMNy*, no. 143.
15 *RMNy*, no. 153.
16 *RMNy*, no. 152.
17 *RMNy*, no. 155.
18 *RMNy*, no. 90.
19 *RMNy*, no. 186.
20 *RMNy*, no. 652.
21 *RMNy*, no. 189.
22 *RMNy*, no. 190.

far religious controversies impinged upon all areas of life. Transylvania was forced to be economically self-reliant, leading to difficulties for the Brassó presses established in 1539, in terms of their paper supplies, since they were dependent on the outside world for paper. In 1546, a papermill was founded in Brassó, creating a firm foundation from then on for the functioning of local printing. As long as the Kolozsvár presses worked in a Lutheran perspective, they could rely on paper from Brassó, but when its managers turned towards Calvinism, paper stopped coming from Brassó, creating serious shortages in Heltai's work-shop. With the help of the city, Heltai immediately turned to the crea-tion of a papermill in Kolozsvár. From 1564 onwards, he printed on self-produced paper.

Transylvania was being constantly swayed by new currents of reli-gious beliefs. The radical movement of Unitarians, propagated by Giorgio Biandrata, became increasingly successful, and was joined by the above-mentioned Ferenc Dávid and then, influenced by Dávid, the prince of Transylvania himself, János Zsigmond. In the course of several public disputations organized by this prince, an attempt was made to clarify religious doctrines, sometimes by stark reiterations of differing under-standings, and sometimes by softening stances in a search for compro-mise. Such gatherings took place in 1566, and led to the publication in Kolozsvár of a *Catechismus ecclesiarum Dei in natione Hungarica per Transilvaniam* and of the *Sententia concors pastorum et ministrorum ecclesiae Dei nationis Hungaricae in Transylvania*.[23] The first work was an adaptation along Unitarian lines of the Heidelberg catechism, while the second reflects a compromise reached in the presence of the prince between the Reformed led by Melius Juhász and the Unitarians with Biandrata and Dávid at their head. Discussions on the Holy Trinity were also published in Kolozsvár in 1566. As these were published in Hungarian, they were not intended only for theologians, but also for the public at large.[24]

During these years, Heltai's reaction to Unitarian doctrine was a hesitant one, and he was not alone in this. Indeed, the Unitarian posi-tion was a very radical one, particularly in its rejection of the Trinity. Heltai's uncertainty was apparent in his publication of the religious disputation which took place in 1568 in Gyulafehérvár. The account was published in 1568 in Kolozsvár at Melius Juhász's request. He was one of the major Calvinist figures, and the edition of the disputation has one of his letters to Heltai as its preface.[25] Two years later, the same

---

[23] *RMNy*, no. 215.
[24] *RMNy*, no. 220.
[25] *RMNy*, no. 256.

work was republished with a new preface, this time containing a statement of faith from Heltai, supporting the Unitarians.[26] In between times, a jointly written work by Dávid and Biandrata was completed in 1569. Brought out without any indication as to the place of printing, and thus more or less camouflaged, the work was published to counter Georg Mayer (Maior) of Wittenberg's writings on the Trinity.[27] In 1570, Heltai openly supported the Unitarians, mirroring from then on the religious views of the prince, and published several works by Dávid from a Unitarian perspective. At the same time, Heltai published *Háló* (the Net), a critique of the Spanish Inquisition, which he had reworked and put into Hungarian. This work, the original version of which had been published a short time before under the pseudonym Reginaldus Gonsalvius Montanus, contained the most virulent attack on the Catholic Church ever published by a printing house in the Carpathian basin.[28]

In 1570, a specifically Anabaptist work was published in Hungarian and German in the Kolozsvár workshop, presumably through the efforts of Ferenc Dávid.[29] The religious radicalization had thus progressed a step further and the already colourful religious kaleidoscope of Transylvania had become even more diverse.

Gál Huszár in Óvár, Kassa, and Debrecen

The third area of Hungary, in the west and north, beside the Turkish-held territories and the Transylvanian principality, had been ruled by the Habsburgs who had worn the Hungarian crown since the middle of the sixteenth century. We have already noted that in this area, of all the linguistic groups Hungarians were those who most lacked works in their mother tongue. This reality remained the prime motivating factor in the foundation of new printing houses for decades. The printing house at Sárvár, where the first Hungarian New Testament was printed in 1541, has already been mentioned. The Protestant preacher Gál Huszár lived in Óvár (Mosonmagyaróvár today, Ung. Altenburg in German), also in the west, on lands belonging to Archduke Maximilian, a Reformation sympathizer. Conscious of the power of printing as well as its possibilities for the development of religion, Gál Huszár learned about 'the art of artificial writing' in 1557 in the Viennese printing house of Rafael Hoffhalter. Having acquired printing equipment in that workshop, he began work in Óvár in the following year. He published

---

[26] *RMNy*, no. 287.
[27] *RMNy*, no. 272.
[28] *RMNy*, no. 288.
[29] *RMNy*, nos 284 and 292.

his own Hungarian sermons, which he dedicated to Archduke Maximilian, the future emperor Maximilian II.[30] In 1559, the publication of a satirical comedy by Mihály Sztárai mocking Catholic ecclesiastical institutions in dialogue form was a particularly significant event in the history of Hungarian literature.[31]

In the first weeks of 1560, Huszár began printing in Óvár the first book of Hungarian Protestant hymns.[32] During that year, he moved his presses to Kassa (Košice today), still in northern Royal Hungary, as he was invited there as the Hungarian city preacher. But before the end of the year, the persecution carried out by the Bishop of Eger made him flee to Debrecen. The chief minister of Debrecen was at the time the most effective exponent of Calvinism in Hungary, Péter Melius Juhász, already mentioned in connection with the Kolozsvár presses. Debrecen was at the crossroads of the three sections of Hungary at that time. The conflicting ambitions of the Turks, the Habsburgs and of Transylvania cancelled each other more or less, and created a relatively neutral zone. This simplified Melius's work, as he came closer to Calvin's perspective, and spread such views freely and very effectively. His influence progressively stretched over large sections of the Hungarian-speaking population in all three parts of the country. Even today, the Calvinists in the Carpathian basin are almost all Hungarian-speaking. In the first months of 1561 in Debrecen, Huszár finally finished the printing of the hymn-book begun in Óvár, and enriched it with over 200 lines of music. This work remained the ancestor of all Hungarian Protestant hymn-books, even up until now, both for evangelicals and for the Reformed. The work consists of an original compilation of hymns used in worship. Most are of Hungarian origin, though some are foreign, and the hymns are classified according to their use: one particular section of the volume contains the paraphrases of the Psalms, almost all written by Hungarians.

Melius, who had known Huszár for a long time immediately took advantage of the possibilities offered by the printing press operating in Debrecen. During the next few years, he published his sermons, his teachings on religion, his religious polemic, etc. But as Huszár wished to distribute Lutheran writings, he soon left to return to Royal Hungary. A large part of his printing equipment, however, remained in Debrecen.

---

[30] *RMNy*, no. 151.
[31] *RMNy*, no. 158.
[32] *RMNy*, no. 160.

Rafael Hoffhalter in Debrecen and in Gyulafehérvár

The abandoned press acquired a new lease of life in 1563, with the arrival of Rafael Hoffhalter, one of the most important Viennese printers. Hoffhalter, a member of a noble Polish family (Skrzetusky), established himself in Vienna after stays in The Netherlands and in Zurich. Later, in all likelihood because of his religious beliefs, he emigrated to Debrecen, and at the time probably shared the Calvinist views of Melius, and in 1565 he printed in his own name the entire output of the Debrecen presses, in particular Melius's works.[33] He did so by using the equipment he had brought with him from Vienna to salvage Huszár's press, and to which he added more. However, the paths of the printer and the minister soon separated, and Hoffhalter moved his workshop to Nagyvárad (Grosswardein in German, Oradea today) on the eastern border of the great plain of Hungary (*Alföld*). There he printed a book of sermons by Melius, but abandoned its production, which was brought to fruition in 1568 by Török, the director of the Debrecen printing presses at the time.[34]

This abrupt abandonment on Hoffhalter's part is explained by the growing radicalization of his views, as he too became a partisan of Unitarianism which was then flourishing under the leadership of the prince. Hoffhalter settled in the capital of the principality, Gyulafehérvár (Karlsburg in German, Alba Iulia today). There, in 1566–67, he prepared Unitarian works for publication, first and foremost the writings of Ferenc Dávid. His former Calvinist colleagues were so angered by this that, according to contemporary rumours, they had him killed in the street. The anger of Unitarianism's opponents was particularly due to the woodcuts done by Hoffhalter, which made fun of the Holy Trinity (three heads on the neck of one man, etc.).[35] After his death, the Gyulafehérvár workshop continued at a high level of activity until 1569, under the direction of his widow, bringing out over a dozen Hungarian and Latin works. In these books the representatives of Unitarianism, and Dávid and Biandrata in particular, directed polemical attacks against the leaders of other confessions, and especially against the most influential figure, the Reformed Melius Juhász. The printing presses of Hoffhalter in Gyulafehérvár ceased their operations in 1570.

---

[33] *RMNy*, no. 205.

[34] *RMNy*, no. 259.

[35] The *De falsa et vera unius Dei Patris, Filii et Spiritus Sancti cognitione libri duo*, put together by Biandrata and Dávid, and printed in 1568 (*RMNy*, no. 254) was republished in a facsimile edition with a lengthy English introduction by Antal Pirnát (Utrecht, 1988) (Bibliotheca Unitariorum, 2).

DE FALSA

ET VERA VNIVS DEI PATRIS, FILII, ET SPIRITVS SANCTI COGNITI- ONE, LIBRI DVO.

Authoribus miniftris Ecclefiarum confentienti- um in Sarmatia, & Tranfyluania.

1. Theffalonicenfium 5.
Omnia probate, quod bonum eft, tenete.

ALBAE IVLIAE.

12.1 *De falsa et vera unius dei patris, filii et spiritus sancti cognitione* (Gyulafehérvár: Hoffhalter's widow, 1568)

Other Protestant workshops

Also in Transylvania, but in Pál Karádi's workshop in Abrudbánya, a Hungarian play was printed in 1569.[36] Karádi then moved to Simánd, in the Great Plain in Turkish territory, and then to Temesvár where he

---

[36] *RMNy*, no. 260.

became a Unitarian preacher in 1572. No other book published by him has survived. If such works had existed, they would be the only printed works produced in Turkish-held Hungary.

One further aspect of confessional diversity was the Romanian publications using the cyrillic alphabet and intended to help convert the Romanian Orthodox population of Transylvania to the Reformation. Indeed, between 1544 and 1588, a series of works primarily for liturgical use appeared in Romanian and Ancient Slav in Transylvania. These publications aimed to fulfil the needs of Romanian and Bulgarian Orthodox churches, in lands where there was no printing activity at this time, apart from in one monastery in Bucharest, where a single book was produced. These Transylvanian publications from time to time included a work spreading the Reformation message. For instance, around 1561 an evangelical catechism in Romanian appeared thanks to cyrillic character printing in Brassó. Around 1567, another similar volume came off the presses, offering Reformed sermons and a Protestant liturgy.[37] The latter work was modelled on one produced by Heltai in his Lutheran period. However, the Reformation had as little influence on the Romanian Orthodox as in the next decades on Croatian Catholics. These two first Reformation works in Romanian only survive in very incomplete form. It is thus possible that other such works have completely vanished.

Catholic works

Caught up in the turmoil of the Orthodox, Calvinist, evangelical and Unitarian confessions in the Carpathian basin in the second half of the sixteenth century, previously dominant Catholicism found it difficult to make its mark. Small groups which stayed faithful to Rome only survived in the peripheral areas of the country: in the extreme west, close to the Habsburg lands, and in the isolated valleys of extreme east Transylvania, among the Szekler population (Székely). Until 1578, these communities did not even have the support of a printing press in Hungary itself. Thus Hungarian Catholic works, which were few and far between, appeared outside Hungary, primarily in Vienna. Hence for example the translation of the Jesuit Canisius's catechism was published in 1562 by the Viennese printing press of Hoffhalter.

The multi-faceted nature of the Hungarian Reformation as mirrored by printing became more uniform from 1571 onwards. In that year, the Unitarian Transylvanian prince died. The Catholic István Báthori, elected as his successor, shortly afterwards occupied the Polish throne. Given

---

[37] *RMNy*, no. 239.

that the weakness of the Transylvanian Catholics meant they were unable to impose their religious beliefs, in the name of pacification, in September 1571, Báthori forbade the publication of any work on a religious topic likely to cause controversy. From the point of view of printing, this marked the end of the first phase of the Reformation in the Carpathian basin.

The content and the authors

The preceding account described Hungarian typographical production, from printing press to printing press, in the chronological order of their appearance. The following is an analysis of the same information from a different angle.

More than half of the 250 publications or so produced in the Carpathian basin prior to 1571 can be attributed to a specific confessional current: Orthodox, Catholic, Lutheran, Calvinist, Unitarian or even Anabaptist. To these one must add Biblical texts, which represent approximately 15 per cent of the total. The proportion of works having a direct religious link was thus more than two-thirds of the total book production, the rest being for the most part school-books and calendars.

The largest group of works with a religious subject matter (49 works) were polemical writings, broken down as follows: one Catholic, seven Lutheran, 17 Reformed and 24 Unitarian. The most radical groups thus produced the greatest number of such works. The publications of presses in Kolozsvár, Debrecen and Gyulafehérvár towards the end of the 1560s dealt principally with discussions between Reformed and Unitarians.

While the Unitarians mainly published polemical works, those which provided a calm exposition of the doctrines held by a confessional group were mostly written by the Reformed (17 works) and the evangelicals (17 works) as the Unitarians only produced three such works, and the Anabaptists two. The Lutherans headed the list in terms of catechisms, producing Luther's small catechism and occasionally that of Brenz (17 editions), well ahead of the Reformed, who produced those of Gergely Molnár (inspired by Melanchthon's *Examen Ordinandorum*) Péter Melius and Calvin (three editions) and of the Catholics, who published that of Canisius (two editions). The other confessional groups did not publish such works.

In Hungary in the middle of the sixteenth century, the propagation of religious doctrines was often carried out through drama or comedy (seven editions) or through Biblical stories (four editions). In 1558, Gál Huszár was the first to print one of his sermons preached in Hungarian.

Shortly afterwards, the Reformed Melius Juhász followed suit (six editions), and then the Unitarian Ferenc Dávid also exploited the possibilities inherent in this genre (one edition).

In chronological order, the list of the most prolific authors of works printed prior to 1571 in the Carpathian basin opens with the Transylvanian Saxons, Johann Honter and Valentin Wagner, followed by Gál Huszár (evangelical) Péter Melius Juhász (Reformed), then Gáspar Heltai and Ferenc Dávid (evangelical, Reformed and Unitarian in turn) who published mainly in Hungarian. It is no coincidence that all those listed above, apart from Melius and Dávid, had a printing press, placing them in a favourable position to publish their own writings.

The location of the presses shows that Reformation printing took place mainly in the cities, although the Hungarian bourgeoisie was much weaker, both numerically and in terms of its economic power, than its counterparts in lands to the west. Because of the feudal regime which flourished in the country at the time, Reformation printers had to rely on the moral and material support provided by certain sections of the upper nobility, especially during the last decades of the sixteenth century when a number of printers worked in these noblemen's castles.

The printers' motivations were very diverse. Honter and Wagner certainly had a basic pedagogical aim, which then merged into the wish to establish and strengthen the Reformation. As for the Kolozsvár presses, from the start these produced both lay and religious publications. This lay aspect of production was put aside during the religiously turbulent 1560s, but became predominant again after the 1571 edict forbidding any religious publication, and Heltai for instance became an entrepreneur seeking to make a profit. Huszár saw the presses only as a means of propagating his faith, and only used them for this purpose, without abandoning the preaching of the Word. Hoffhalter, who for years worked as a professional printer in Vienna, working to order, even for the Jesuits, threw himself into the production of religious works from his arrival in Hungary onwards. He solely produced works which matched his beliefs at the time.

Few books published in Hungary before 1571 were illustrated. The most important of these came from the Brassó presses. Among the works produced in the context of the Reformation, particular mention should be made of the woodcuts illustrating Unitarian polemical writings of the 1560s, which sought to demonstrate the irrationality of the Trinity (in Kolozsvár as in Gyulafehérvár). This was a unique phenomenon in Europe at the time.

Several types of printing fonts were used during the first half of the sixteenth century in the production of Hungarian language books, chiefly in Vienna and Cracow (roman characters [antiqua], gothic ones

12.2 Two caricatures taken from *De falsa et vera unius dei patris, filii et spiritus sancti cognitione* (Gyulafehérvár: Hoffhalter's widow, 1568)

[schwabacher], etc.) The modest equipment in the Kolozsvár workshop and the resulting practice had a unifying effect: from 1550, nearly all Hungarian works were composed in roman and italic fonts.

Reading and the circulation of books

The tripartite division of Hungary by the middle of the sixteenth century had such a weakening effect on the central power that no systematic censorship was possible, either by the State or by the Church. In Royal Hungary, some of the leading dignitaries of the Catholic Church led a fierce rearguard campaign – with increasing Habsburg support – against the various Reformation movements which were spreading so widely and so fast. In Transylvania, however, up until 1571, religious toleration flourished, which was unheard of in other areas at that time, and which encouraged the development of the different Reformation currents. Later, princely power was again strong enough to make itself felt, and to apply edicts of censorship.

We do not have sufficient quantitative data regarding the circulation of the first works to be printed in Hungary, as only a few copies of each often existed. The discussion of censorship probably holds equally true for any discussion of the sale of books. The works produced in the Carpathian basin in general only satisfied local needs. In most cases, the book-buying circle was so small that Hungarian books printed in Transylvania only rarely made it to Royal Hungary. The only exception was liturgical works printed in Ancient Slav or Romanian and in cyrillic: these works were specifically meant for export to the Romanian and Bulgarian Orthodox faithful, who lived for centuries under Turkish domination.

Select bibliography

Borsa, G., 'Johannes Honterus als Buchillustrator', *GJ* (1986), pp. 35–56.

Borsa, G., et al. (eds), *Régi Magyarországi Nyomtatványok 1473–1600 = Res litteraria Hungariae vetus operum impressorum 1473–1600* (Budapest, 1971) (cited in *RMNy*). Bibliographical work containing the detailed description of all works printed in Hungary prior to 1601.

Fitz, J., *A magyarországi nyomdászat, könyvkiadás és könyvkereskedelem története* [The History of Printing, Publishing and the Book-Trade in Hungary] (Budapest, 1967) vol. 2: summary of the period 1526–1600.

Soltész, Z., *A magyarországi könyvdíszítés a XVI. században* (Budapest, 1961). Summary in German: 'Buckschmuck in Ungarn im XVI. Jahrhundert' (pp. 151–72).

Botta, I., 'A reformáció és nyomdászat Magyarországon', *Magyar Könyvszemle*, 89 (1973), pp. 270–89. With a summary in German: 'Reformation und Buchdruckerei in Ungarn'.

On the history of Hungary in general, western readers should consult:

Bak J. M. and Király, B. M., *From Hunyadi to Rákóczi. War and Society in Eastern Central Europe* (vol. 3, Brooklyn, 1982) (Eastern European Monographs, 104).

Histoire de la Hongrie des origines à nos jours (Budapest, 1961).

Tihany, L., *A History of Middle Europe* (New Brunswick, NJ, 1976).

CHAPTER THIRTEEN

The book and the Reformation in Bohemia and Moravia

Mirjam Bohatcová

When the first phase of the Bohemian Reformation ended with the execution of Jan Hus in 1415 in Constance, printing did not yet exist. However, it is worth outlining some of the political and doctrinal aspects of the religious movement which sprang into existence at the time, in order to establish firmly the basis of the relationship between the Czech printed book and the development of the Reformation in Bohemia in the sixteenth century.

Religious attitudes in the Bohemian lands

The Hussite movement, born around 1419–20, shaped the nation during a relatively complex period of its history. In 1420, the Hussites stated their demands in the four Articles of Prague (*Čtyři artikule pražské*):

1. The free preaching of the Word of God.
2. The distribution of the Lord's Supper in two kinds to all believers (*sub utraque specie*).
3. The ban on priests exercising any form of civil power.
4. Severe sanctions in all the states of the Kingdom of Bohemia, both civil and ecclesiastical, against mortal sins and the infringement of divine laws.[1]

The movement rather rapidly divided into a moderate wing linked to the wealthier levels of the nobility and the patricians of Prague, which

---

[1] Published by F. Palacký in *Archiv český*, 3 (1844), 213–16. New critical edition with commentary by R. Říčan, *Čtyři vyznání. Vyznání augsburské, bratrské, helvetské a české. Se čtyřmi vyznáními staré církve a se čtyřmi články pražskými* [Four Confessions: that of Augsburg, the Bohemian Brethren, the Helvetic confession and that of Bohemia, with four confessions of the ancient church and the Four Articles of Prague] (Prague, 1951), pp. 35–52.

worked above all for a pacification of the country even to the point of a doctrinal compromise with the Catholic Church, and the 'Taborite' wing, more radical theologically and more aggressive militarily.

A string of Hussite military victories in the 1420s led the Council of Basle in 1431 to discussions with the heretics about their return to the Catholic Church. But by exploiting the internal strife in the movement, and by making use of its more moderate supporters, the Council diplomats managed to reverse the situation and proposed the *Kompaktáta* as the basis for agreement. This document undoubtedly looked to the Four Articles of Prague, but it changed their original meaning through new formulations, leading to diametrically opposed reactions on the part of the moderates and the radicals. The latter took up arms once more, but they were crushed in 1434 near Lipany by a coalition of moderate Hussites and Catholics.

Thus the reconciliation with the Catholic Church was officially sealed. A series of compromises and ambiguities meant that this agreement was never fundamentally challenged. In 1435, the Utraquist Czech states elected the conciliatory Jan Rokycana (d. 1471) as Archbishop of Prague, but the Catholic Church refused to recognize him. The *Kompaktáta*, published in 1436 in Jihlava, became the official agreement between the Council of Basle and the Hussites of Bohemia.[2] Sigismund of Luxemburg was elected King of Bohemia after having agreed to a limitation of the royal powers, without, however, considering the arrangement as permanent. But he died in 1437.

After a number of brief interregna, a member of the Czech Utraquist upper nobility, Jiří of Poděbrady, was elected king in 1458. He swore to respect national liberties and the *Kompaktáta*. But at the same time he made a secret oath to obey the pontifical legate and repress heresy. Indeed, Jiří used the sects which began to separate themselves from legal Utraquism as support, which led to a conflict in which the Catholic nobility of Bohemia united against Jiří, and in which the Pope abolished the *Kompaktáta* and deposed the king in 1466. Shortly thereafter, the country was drawn into war. After Jiří's death in 1471, the son of the Polish king Wladislaw Jagiełło was elected king of Bohemia, while his rival Matthias Corvinus who was king of Hungary and Jiří's son-in-law maintained his power in the neighbouring lands of Moravia, Silesia and Lusatia.

---

[2] The *Kompaktáta* were printed in Prague on Severin's presses around 1500, and again in 1513. F. Palacký has produced a modern edition in *Archiv český*, 3 (1844), 401–3. Jan Mantuan-Fencl, the humanist of Plzeň published the *Kompaktáta* in Latin in Nuremberg in 1518.

The apparent reconciliation between the Council and the Hussites did not, however, mean that the Utraquist church was at peace, for it was being undermined from within, as lay people sought religious and moral renewal in a simple and fraternal life, away from the world. The Unity of Brethren, founded in 1457–58, declared that it only accepted the authority of Scripture. It was sharply critical of contemporary society and its lack of religious fervour and scandalous practices. Beginning in humble settings, the Unity of Brethren slowly began to recruit more widely. In 1530, 20 nobles were even officially welcomed as members. However, the Brethren were persecuted from the start, because they went beyond the *Kompaktáta*. They were accused of being 'Waldensians' or 'Picards' who believed that the sacrifice of the Mass was only a symbol. The Brethren differed from the Utraquists in other beliefs as well, especially regarding the effectiveness of sacraments done by corrupt priests. The Unity of Brethren believed that compelling people in matters of faith was against the Gospel;[3] that civil authorities could hold no powers in the spiritual sphere and that their Unity was only a part of the Christian church struggling in the world. Their doctrine made distinctions between the necessary elements of salvation – God's grace, the merits of Jesus Christ and the gifts of the Holy Spirit, alongside human faith, charity and hope; the useful elements – Scripture, the Church and sacraments; and the accidental or suitable elements – church ordinances. The Unity of Brethren imposed strict discipline on all its members, including nobles; certain occupations leading to dishonour or to an excessive thirst for profits were forbidden, and leadership of communities was given to priests and their lay assistants. Finally the Brethren established their own presbytery system, with elders, priests and bishops elected following the model of the apostolic church, independently of any consecration by the powers of Rome (1467).

The theologians of the Unity of Brethren sought above all to provide the Unity with original theological works. Their bishop Lukáš Pražský (d. 1528), an educated man, played a pre-eminent role in this regard. Besides pastoral letters, he wrote over a hundred doctrinal works,[4]

---

[3] M. Bohatcová, 'Nález dalších litomyšlských tisků z počátku 16. století' [A discovery of a new printing of Litomyšl at the beginning of the sixteenth century] in *Časopis Národního muzea v Praze, Hist. řada*, 150 (1981), 138–52. This deals with a previously unknown work by Prokop of Jindřichův Hradec in 1508 on this theme and on the first confessions of the Bohemian Brethren. Edited by A. Molnár in *Husitský Tábor*, 6/7 (1983/84), 423–48; see also 10 (1988/91), 219–20.

[4] J. Th. Müller, *Geschichte der Böhmischen Brüder* (3 vols, Herrnhut, 1922–31); A. Molnár, *Boleslavští Bratří* [The Bohemian Brethren of Mladá Boleslav] (Prague, 1952). R. Říčan, *Dějiny Jednoty bratrské* (Prague, 1957) (in the conclusion, A. Molnár discusses the theology of the Bohemian Brethren); German translation: *Die Böhmischen Brüder* (Berlin, 1961).

approximately 36 of which were printed in Litomyšl, Bělá and especially in Mladá Boleslav. Lukáš himself divided his works between polemical or more precisely apologetical writings destined for the outside world, and writings meant to answer internal needs in the Unity of Brethren: the training and education of its members, the creation of a liturgy and the organization of the Unity. Finally, there were also writings (confessions of faith) against the power of the secular authority held by the king and the Estates.

The religious peace settlement of 1485 between the Bohemian Utraquists and the Catholics guaranteed equal rights to both parties, leading to a climate of religious toleration unparalleled in Europe. But this peace agreement did not include the Unity of Brethren, and legally their position was horrendous. The royal edict of St James published against them in 1508 and approved by the Bohemian diet decided on the total extermination of the 'Picards': they could not gather together in public or in private, the dissemination and printing of their works was forbidden, and any such works were to be consigned to the flames, and the priests of the Unity of Brethren were forbidden to administer the sacraments. All the Estates, the nobility and the bourgeois were personally responsible for seeing this edict put into practice, as the 'Picards' in the general population had to be brought back into the Utraquist or Catholic Church. But in reality, the authorities, especially in Moravia, had no wish to persecute hard-working subjects, so that the mandate was not efficiently applied.

Royal power, which had diminished considerably since the beginnings of the Hussite movement, continued to shrink under the Catholic successors of Jiří of Poděbrady, Wladislaw Jagiełło, and, after 1526, the Habsburgs. These monarchs had to take into account the power of the Bohemian nobility, as well as the fact that Utraquism, the majority confession in Bohemia, rejected all religious oppression. This was particularly the case in Bohemia, for neighbouring lands did not always follow the same political evolution. In 1471, when he was enthroned as king of Bohemia, Wladislaw Jagiełło swore to respect the *Kompaktáta*, to have them approved by Rome and to have an archbishop appointed for the Utraquist church. The Habsburg Ferdinand I also swore to respect the *Kompaktáta*, which seemed acceptable to him following the old Utraquist model of compromise, but he refused their reinterpretation as proposed under the influence of the German Reformation, and objected even more strongly to the renewal begun by the Unity of Brethren with the support of the Bohemian Estates.

Thus the Hussite movement led to major changes in the country's organization, what with the weakening of the authority of the Church and the king. The position of the Czech language had strengthened, as it became the democratic means of communication in civil and religious administration. A growing audience had access to the entire Bible, already considered as the sole criterion of Christian life, and could participate actively in the liturgy, chiefly through choral singing. As for the Unity of Brethren, its policy of sending its theology students in the early 1530s to complete their training in Europe's evangelical universities, and encounter the Reformation directly, together with Biblical studies, literature and humanist philology, led to an improvement in the Unity of Brethren's image and increased its cultural impact on the entire nation.

Thus, once printing was introduced, the written works of two groups were legally produced, that of the Utraquists and that of the Roman Catholic minority – in the regions which had remained Catholic, especially the city of Plzeň and the entire south. Already in the fifteenth century, the works printed in Bohemia[5] were largely in Czech: of 44 incunabula, only five were in Latin, whereas in Moravia, in all likelihood led by the diocese of Olomouc, foreign printers were at work producing mainly Latin texts: of 25 incunabula or so, two were in German, and one was bilingual Latin and German. Until the 1540s, national printers produced Czech works almost exclusively, while later publications were at times done in humanist Latin, alongside Czech works and in conjunction with these. German was used in works appearing in northern and western border areas of Bohemia, which were directly in contact with Lutheranism. Indeed these works were produced outside Bohemia,[6] and sections of these publications were only translated into Czech quite late, in the 1570s. Jáchymov (Joachimsthal) was an important economic and cultural centre for the effort to spread Latin, and in the sixteenth century it also had a major Latin school complete with a well-stocked library.[7]

A similar evolution from Catholicism to Lutheranism was also evident in Silesia and Lusatia. During the sixteenth century, Bohemian humanists also published many Latin works abroad. Furthermore, even

---

[5] The register of all the works in Czech, together with a list of the copies currently known and a detailed description of each can be found alphabetically by author in the national bibliography, Zd. V. Tobolka and F. Horák (eds) *Knihopis českých a slovenských tisků od doby nejstarší až do konce XVIII. století* (Prague, 1925–67).

[6] R. Wolkan, *Böhmens Anteil an der deutschen Literatur des XVI. Jahrhunderts* (3 vols, Prague, 1890–94); A. Eckert, *Die Deutschen evangelischen Pfarrer der Reformationszeit in Westböhmen* (Bad Rappenau-Obergimpern, 1974–76); Eckert, *Die deutschen evangelischen Pfarrer der Reformationszeit in Nord- und Ostböhmen* (Bad Rappenau-Obergimpern, 1977).

[7] H. Sturm, *Die St. Joachimsthaler Lateinschulbibliothek aus dem 16. Jahrhundert* (Stuttgart, 1964) (with a catalogue).

in the first half of the century non-Catholic and anti-Roman religious works were printed in Czech outside Bohemia, particularly in Nuremberg, and then imported into Bohemia in spite of all the prohibitions.

Sixteenth-century printed works

Thanks to current bibliographical research,[8] the surviving printed works in Czech have almost entirely been examined, and fairly accurate estimates can be made for foreign language production. In the sixteenth century Bohemia and Moravia printed more than 2 000 works in Czech, more than 1 400 in Latin (among which were almost 1 170 smaller booklets of humanist poetry[9]) and more than 200 in German and other foreign languages. In total, more than 4 000 titles are known about, not including administrative printing and Hebrew works, mainly produced in Prague from 1512. Among these works, the typographical place of origin of some 440 works without a printer's name has not yet been identified.

The surviving output can be divided into four 25–year periods, based on the political and cultural situation of the States of Bohemia. Under the rule of Jagieło (1501–25), approximately 5 per cent of the total output was produced. In the period 1526–50, during which printing came to a sudden stop in Bohemia due to a ban on printing after the Schmalkalden War, around 10 per cent of the entire century's production appeared. In the third stage, 1551 to 1575, until the reception of the Bohemian Confession, the production of books reached 15 per cent of the total. Finally, the fourth period under Rudolf II produced on its own 70 per cent of the total number of books in the century. The disproportionate production between periods was thus great: the first half of the century produced 15 per cent of surviving works, whereas 85 per cent appeared in the second half. The reason for this lies not only in

---

[8] For the sake of conciseness, see my list of current syntheses and monographs on this subject: M. Bohatcová, 'Der gegenwärtige Bearbeitungsstand der Druckproduction vom 15.–18. Jahrhundert in den böhmischen Ländern', *GJ* (1987), 265–78. From now on, I will only indicate bibliographical additions to this article. See also A. Bad'urová, M. Bohatcová, J. Hejnic, 'Frekvence tištěné literatury 16. století v Čechách a na Moravě' [The frequency of sixteenth-century printed works in Bohemia and Moravia], *Folia Historica Bohemica*, 11 (1987), 321–43.

[9] J. Hejnic and J. Martínek, *Rukověť humanistického básnictví (Enchiridion renatae poesis Latinae in Bohemia et Moravia cultae*, 1–5 (Prague, 1966–82). See also J. Hejnic and V. Bok, 'Gesners europäische Bibliographie und ihre Beziehung zum Späthumanismus in Böhmen und Mähren' in *Rozpravy Československé akademie věd řada, společenských věd*, 98 (1988) 3.

the natural progress of printing in Bohemia, but also in the considerable losses due to the short print-runs of works. Indeed, the outlook of a large number of the first printers of Bohemia in the sixteenth century, many of them university members, was often more ideological than commercial. Furthermore until the 1540s hardly any foreign-language literature was produced in Bohemia: contemporary Latin poems chiefly appeared during Rudolf's reign. In short, the figures presented above for the output of printing in Bohemia are minimums, for among the losses one must take into account the systematic destruction of Czech religious books by the Catholic Counter-Reformation of the seventeenth and eighteenth centuries.

As the greater part of book production in Bohemia was not Catholic, and thus in part illegal, printing did not establish itself only in the major urban centres which had economically and culturally developed hinterlands, such as in Prague throughout the century, in Plzeň until 1533, in Olomouc in Moravia, where fifteenth century production continued between 1501 and 1504, and then restarted in 1538, while in Brno, almost nothing was printed in the sixteenth century. Printing also took place in provincial towns where Reformed groups or sects had established themselves. In Bohemia, certain individuals made outstanding contributions to printing: in Litomyšl Pavel Olivetský (1504/06–31) and his son-in-law Alexandr Oujezdecký (1534–45), in Mladá Boleslav the doctor Mikuláš Klaudyan (1518–19) and the printer of the Unity of Brethren Jiřík Štyrsa (1521–33), in Bělá pod Bezdězem the humanist Oldřich Velenský of Mnichov (1519–21), translator of Erasmus and Luther. All of these were supporters of the Unity of Brethren. In Moravia, Simprecht Sorg-Froschauer operated a German press for Anabaptist refugees in Mikulov (1526–27)[10] while a Czech printing press worked for the Zwinglian sect of the Habrovany Brethren in Luleč (1530–36), and Beneš Optát and Petr Gzel, two Utraquist philological humanists, ran a press in Náměšť (1533–35). In the last two cities, one must also note the contribution of the printer Kašpar Aorgus, from Prostějov. While these printing presses generally only produced works over a short period of time and had small outputs, they made books of remarkably high quality, which showed how hard the printers tried to match the appearance of the books to their important, often religious contents. It is true that in many cases, the printers were also the authors or translators of the works produced.

In the first half of the sixteenth century, the presses in the large urban centres also had an ideological perspective which was stronger than

---

[10] Zd. V. Tobolka, 'Knihtiskař Simprecht Sorg-Froschauer' [The printer Simprecht Sorg-Froschauer], *Časopis Matice moravské*, 53 (1929), 501–8.

13.1 Lukáš Pražský, *Spis tento o pokání* [*On Penitence*] (Mladá Boleslav: Jiřík Štyrsa, 1523). Border based on a model by Urs Graf, using a favourite illustrative device of the Hussites

commercial interests. The Catholic city of Plzeň produced unobjection-able theological works: the Slovakian Mikuláš Bakalář who had attended university in Cracow, printed in Plzeň between 1498 and 1513, followed by Jan Pekk of Nuremberg, who became part of the local population (1526–31). Once his presses closed in 1533, no further printing took place in Plzeň. In Prague, the major printing house of the Utraquist Severin family continued its activities begun in 1488.[11] Pavel Severin of Kapí Hora (1520–41) was an active neo-Utraquist, one of the first pub-lishers of Luther in Czech, while his relative Jan Severin the younger (1538–46) took a more professional approach. Pavel's son-in-law and successor, Jan Kosořský of Kosoř (1546–57) worked first for the rebel states of Bohemia during the Schmalkalden Wars, and ended his career with the publication of the biggest Czech book of the sixteenth century, the translation of the *Cosmography* of S. Münster, *Kozmografia česká*, a work suggested by King Ferdinand I and carried out at the expense of the administrator of the Catholic archbishopric, in order to counter the tendency of the Czech public to consult the Bible alone for information. Mikuláš Konáč of Hodiškov, an ardent defender of ancient Utraquism and an active writer, was part of the Prague book world from 1506 to 1528. Jan Had (Coluber) worked in Prague from 1536 to 1543 and his successor in this prosperous printing press was his widow's second hus-band, Jan Kantor Had (1544–73), and finally his wife herself, widowed for the second time (1578–79).[12] Bartoloměj Netolický deserves a special mention among the Prague printers (1540–52, 1561–62):[13] having begun as a councillor and court recorder in Little Town of Prague, he strongly supported Ferdinand I's policies, and after the Schmalkalden War, he was considered by some as the court printer.

In total, in the first half of the sixteenth century, 15 printers worked more or less permanently in Prague, and 11 outside Bohemia's large urban centres. From 1550 onwards, printing began to be concentrated in Prague, something which the monarch wished, and which censorship helped to accomplish. Later, when Prague became the imperial seat in 1583, this also had an impact on the concentration of printing in the

---

[11] M. Bohatcová 'Otázky nad publikační činností pražských Severinů' [Questions regarding the activity of a Prague printing family, the Severins], *Listy filologické*, 109 (1986), 97–115 (with an overview of their production).

[12] M. Bohatcová, 'Hayd-Haden-Had: drei Namen eines und desselben Druckers?', *GJ* (1990), 118–42. This article deals with the identification of Jan Had's wife as the daughter of the Nuremberg printer Friedrich Peypus, and with the rare Nuremberg New Testament and its Prague reprints.

[13] P. Mašek, 'Význam Bartoloměje Netolického pro český knihtisk 16. století' [The significance of Bartoloměj Netolický for the sixteenth century Czech book] in *Příspěvky ke Knihopisu*, 4 (1987).

city. From the 1550s until the end of the sixteenth century, no less than 43 printers worked in Prague – only five of whom had already begun before 1550 – while elsewhere in Bohemia there were only four printers at work. These were Šebestián Olivetský intermittently in Litomyšl in 1556, then the Catholic Ondřej Graudenc at greater length (1573–1611), and in Eger (Cheb) two German printers were at work between 1572 and 1574: Johannes Bürger and Michael Muhlmarckart.

In Prague the Utraquist printing presses of the graduate Jiří Melantrich of Aventin (1547–49, 1553–80) were the most important, with some 230 works, 80 in foreign languages. His son-in-law Daniel Adam of Veleslavín's workshop (1582–99) followed suit. Adam was a very methodical publisher, a former professor of Prague University, a historian, and a supporter of the Unity of Brethren. His son and successor, Samuel Adam of Veleslavín, used his presses solely to support the anti-Habsburg opposition of the non-Catholic Bohemian Estates. After the defeat of the White Mountain (1620) he was condemned to death, and only escaped by fleeing the country. The members of the Adam of Veleslavín families printed a total of some 370 editions. In the second half of the sixteenth century, most of the Prague printing houses became more professional: for instance, the most productive printer during Rudolf's reign, Jiřík Nigrin (Černý, Schwarz), who published around 600 works from 1571 to 1609, among them many sheets of music and of drawings, nevertheless worked for writers of different confessions. However, the printing houses of Prague were divided into categories by buyers and authors, according to the type of work produced: religious, literary, humanist, or works of information. Among the professional printers with a large output, mention must be made of Jiří Jakubův Dačický (1568–1613), Daniel Sedlčanský (1582–1613) and the Šuman family (1588–1617).

In Moravia, the situation was different. Throughout the century, it was a place of refuge for the illegal production of non-Catholic works, under the sovereign protection of the nobility. This publishing activity reached its peak with the secret presses of the Unity of Brethren in Ivančice near Brno (1563–1577), then transferred to a discreet village citadel in Kralice nad Oslavou, close to the castle of Náměšť (1579–1619). The founder of the first printing press in the episcopal city of Olomouc, Jan Olivetský, son of Pavel the printer in Litomyšl, held clearly non-conformist religious and political views, and thus his career came to an abrupt end: in 1547, he was condemned to death for the printing of an anti-Habsburg pamphlet, which has not survived. The Moravian city of Prostějov where a short-lived press was set up in 1527, was home to the printer Jan Günther (1544–53), originally from Nuremberg. His partner and successor in Prostějov, Kašpar Aorgus, printed in his own name from 1554 until around 1562. Their book-list was Utraquist. In 1554, Günther moved to Olomouc, founding a new press there, but died in 1567. The press continued to operate in Olomouc until 1609 in the name of his son-in-law Fridrich Milchtaler of Nuremberg and his heirs. Overall, at least 25 printers worked in Moravia during the sixteenth century, 13 in Olomouc and four in the presses of the Unity of Brethren in Ivančice and Kralice, namely Václav Solín, Zachariáš Solín Slavkovský, Samuel Silvestr and Václav Elam.

13.2   Closing vignette of the Jan Blahoslavs New Testament (Ivančice, 1568). Note the cryptogram: Finitum in insula hortensi 1568 Pridie Calen. Augusti

The Jesuits, the most active Catholic group and the most pro-Habsburg, arrived in Bohemia in 1556, settling in Prague, and in 1566 in Olomouc in Moravia. They established colleges and an academy for higher studies, but their use of printing in Bohemia was sporadic for many years. This can be seen from the list of foreign authors whose works were translated and published in Bohemian lands from the fifteenth century until 1621: out of a total of 264 authors, 50 were classical and medieval writers, and the rest lived in the fifteenth to the seventeenth centuries. Only 13 foreign Jesuits' works were produced.[14]

---

[14] M. Bohatcová, 'Das Verhältnis der tschechischen und fremdsprachigen Drucke in Böhmen und Mähren vom 15. Jahrhundert bis zum Jahre 1621', *GJ*, (1988), 108–16.

The content of religious works

As the general overview of Bohemian printing has shown, the spread of Reformation literature began in the first half of the sixteenth century, but non-Catholic works only increased significantly in number later in the century. And the main work of the Bohemian Reformation, the translation and commentary of the Bible from its original languages, was published for the first time only in 1579–94 by the Unity of Brethren press in Kralice. The end of the first phase of the Bohemian Reformation thus cannot have the so-called Bohemian Confession of 1575 as its conclusion, even though it marked the agreement between the main currents of the Reformation: the neo-Utraquists inspired by Luther and the Unity of Brethren. Religious freedom only appeared following the *Majestát* edict of Rudolf II in 1609. However, the infringement of its measures (among other factors) led to the revolt in 1618 and the beginning of the Thirty Years' War.

The Czech books published in the sixteenth century focused more on doctrine than on literature. This included religious and moral works, which held enduring interest for authors, readers and printers as well. Czech-language works in this category numbered about 960 titles. One can be even more specific as regards the themes dealt with. Biblical texts were the most numerous. The first complete translation of the Bible into Czech was done in the second half of the fourteenth century.[15] The next century saw the production of other manuscript copies of the Czech Bible, some of which were superbly illustrated. These works did not give their patrons an opportunity to show off, but they did demonstrate the great respect in which the Bible was held during the Hussite period, as the only theological authority.[16] This tradition continued after the introduction of printing: among the small number of Czech incunabula were three New Testaments (after 1476 and 1497/98), two collections of psalms (1487 and 1499) and two complete Bibles. The production of printed Bibles continued in the sixteenth century, mostly due to urban initiatives. The text was based on the Vulgate, although the evolution of humanist philology led to certain textual changes. Here

---

[15] V. Kyas (ed.) *Staročeská Bible drážd'anská a olomoucká. Biblia palaeobohema codicis Dresdensis ac Olomucensis. Editio critica bibliae Bohemae versionis antiquissimae XIV. saeculi 1. Evangelia. 2. Epistolae. Actus Apostolorum, Apocalypsis. 3. Genesis - Esdras.* (Prague, 1981–88). Facsimile: 'Die alttschechische Dresdener Bibel' in *Biblia Slavica* (Paderborn, 1993) series I (Tschechische Bibeln) vol. 1, with a commentary by Vladimír Kyas, Jaroslava Pečírková, Karel Stejskal.

[16] Vladimír Kyas, 'Die alttschechische Bibelübersetzung des 14. Jahrhunderts und ihre Entwicklung im 15. Jahrhundert' in R. Olesch, H. Rothe and F. Scholz (eds), *Biblia Slavica* (Paderborn, 1989), series I, vol. 2 (Kuttenberg Bibel), pp. 9–32.

is an overview of complete editions of the Bible, known in Czech as *Biblí česká*:[17]

1488	First printed Bible, the 'Prague Bible' without illustrations, produced by the print-shop of Severin in Prague.
1489	The 'Kutná Hora Bible' whose text and illustrations were produced twice, often described as two editions in the same year. The Bible was printed by Martin of Tišnov in Kutná Hora, with illustrations taken from a Nuremberg model. Facsimile: 'Kuttenberger Bibel' in *Biblia Slavica* series I (Tschechische Bibeln), volume 2 (Kuttenberg Bibel); companion volume by Vladimír Kyas, Karel Stejskal, Emma Urbánková (Paderborn, 1989).
1506	The 'Venice Bible' printed at the expense of three Prague citizens in Venice by Peter Liechtenstein, with decorative motifs and illustrations taken from local models.
1529	Bible printed in Prague by Pavel Severin of Kapí Hora, with illustrations based on Nuremberg examples.
1537	Second edition of Pavel Severin's Bible, with an illustration mainly based on Luther's Wittenberg Bible of 1534.
1540	Bible produced in Nuremberg, by Linhart Milchtaler at the expense of Melchior Koberger, with illustrations done by various local artists.
1549	In Prague, in the printing house and at the expense of Bartholoměj Netolický and his young companion Jiřík Melantrich Rožďalovský, with the intellectual collaboration of Sixt d'Ottersdorf – whose work continued beyond this date – with illustrations based on Severin's Bible and augmented by those in Luther'sWittenberg Bible. In practice, this 1549 edition is considered as Melantrich's first edition.
1556/57	In Prague, Melantrich's second edition, with illustrations; in 1552 Melantrich bought up Netolický's printing presses.
1560/61	In Prague, Melantrich's third edition, with illustrations. The publisher did not consider this as a new edition, and did not mention it in the preface to his 1577 edition, even though it

[17] M. Bohatcová, 'Die tschechischen gedruckten Bibeln des 15. bis 18. Jahrhunderts', in R. Olesch, H. Rothe and F. Scholz (eds), *Biblia Slavica* (Paderborn, 1995), series I, vol. 3 (Kralitzer Bibel), Kommentare, pp. 1–182.

contained a number of variants in both the text and the illustrations.

1570   In Prague, Melantrich's fourth edition, printed in a new type, with a new page set-up and a series of new and improved engravings, especially those bearing the initials FA and FT, probably the monograms of the painters Florian Abel from Cologne and Francesco Terzio, the painters of the Prague royal court..

1577   In Prague, fifth edition by Melantrich, fully identical to the 1570 edition in terms of typography and illustration.

1613   In Prague, by Samuel Adam of Veleslavín, an edition essentially identical to the 1570 version. One significant novel feature, however, was the division of the text into numbered verses following the model of the Kralice Bible, as well as the separation of the two text columns with vertical lines. Copies of Samuel's extensive introduction are rather rare today, as it had been ripped out from most copies and destroyed at the Counter-Reformation, because of its contentious political and ideological contents.

The second series of complete Bibles – representing the culmination of Bohemian Reformation exegesis – was the product of the Unity of Brethren's presses.[18] These versions were translated from the original languages and took into account existing Czech versions, foreign translations, and philological and exegetical tools. The translators' group from Kralice included theologians and philologists whose expertise contributed to each other's work. They had at hand a fine library containing around 835 printed books and 62 manuscripts. Besides examples of classical literature there were 200 copies of contemporary foreign exegetical works and textual editions, as well as theological, pedagogical, philosophical, rhetorical, poetical, historical and biological studies, in Latin, Greek, Hebrew, Aramaic, German, French, Polish and Czech.[19] As narrative or interpretative illustrations were unacceptable in the eyes

---

[18] M. Daňková, 'Bratrské tisky ivančické a kralické' [Publications of the Unity of Brethren in Ivančice and Kralice], *Sborník Národního muzea v Praze*, A series, 5 (1951), no. 1. Vl. Fialová, 'Persönlichkeiten und Schicksale der berühmten Druckerei der Böhmischen Brüder', *GJ* (1967), 138–43. Fialová, 'Ein Letternfund aus dem XVI. Jahrhundert in Kralice nad Oslavou', *GJ* (1959), 85–91. Fialová, 'Bronzennadeln aus einer Buchdruckerei des XVI. Jahrhunderts', *GJ* (1961), 136–41.

[19] M. Bohatcová, 'Schriftsteller der europäischen Reformation in der Bibliothek der Böhmischen Brüder', *GJ* (1970), 218–24. A complete edition of the catalogue can be found in *Slavia*, 39 (1970), 591–610.

13.3 The page of the fourth section of the Kralice Bible (1587). Note the set-up of text and commentary

of the Unity of Brethren, their Bibles only had sober decorative draw-ings. Each of the three editions they published had been revised:

1579–94 The 'Kralice Bible' in six volumes (*Biblí česká*), containing lengthy marginal commentaries and considered by the clergy of the Brethren communities as equivalent to the similar foreign exegetical texts, which were much more difficult to obtain. The sixth part, the New Testament, appeared a second time in 1601. Facsimile: 'Kralitzer Bibel' in *Biblia Slavica*, series I, volume 3. Commentary volume by M. Bohatcová, E. Michálek, Jan Heller and M. Balabán (Paderborn, 1995).

1596   The 'Kralice Bible' in one volume (*Biblí svatá*) without commentaries, in a small format.

1613   The 'Kralice Bible' in one volume (*Biblí svatá*) without commentaries, in a larger format.[20]

Apart from complete Bibles, there were many partial editions of the Bible in the sixteenth century, especially of the New Testament (*Nový zákon*), the book of Psalms (*Žaltář*) and liturgical pericopes (*Evangelia a epištoly*). Certain individual books were also published, like the popular apocryphal book of Ecclesiasticus (*Kniha Jezusa Siracha*). At least a few of these works deserve special mention: the New Testament printed by Jiřík Štyrsa in Mladá Boleslav for the Unity of Brethren in 1525; the New Testament published in Plzeň in 1527 by Jan Pekk for a Catholic readership; the New Testament translated and edited in 1533 by the Utraquist philologists Beneš Optát and Petr Gzel in Náměšť in Moravia on the basis of Erasmus's Latin texts, and the Old Testament translated from the Hebrew by Jan Vartovský of Varta, the Prague philologist who died young. His manuscript, which was never printed, was lost already in the sixteenth century. Other works of note include the New Testament translated from the Greek by the Bishop of the Unity of Brethren, Jan Blahoslav (1523–71), published in Ivančice in 1564 and 1568. As translator, he founded the Unity of Brethren's exegetical approach and his work served as a later basis for the sixth part of the Kralice Bible. The Book of Psalms was printed in Kralice in 1579, and republished in 1581: it was second in popularity among works published, and in this instance was translated by Izaiáš Cibulka (Caepola) and also appeared immediately after the Pentateuch of the Kralice Bible.

The Bible which was completely revised by learned Jesuits, *Biblí česká*, known as the 'Bible of Saint Wenceslas' appeared for the first time in 1677 (New Testament) and in 1712 and 1715 (Old Testament in two volumes), and was reprinted from 1769 to 1771. The New Testament was published first because 'the heretical evil bases itself particu-

---

[20] M. Bohatcová, 'Die Kralitzer Bibel (1579–94) – die Bibel der böhmischen Reformation', *GJ* (1992), 238–53.

13.4   Illuminated letter showing the Brethren's school. Hymn-book edited by
Jan Blahoslav (Ivancice, 1564)

larly on the falsifications of the New Testament, and finds in it the
sources of its doctrinal errors'.

In the sixteenth century, Czech hymn-books had as great an impact as
Biblical works. Lay singing in the vernacular during worship was in any
case a traditional phenomenon. Once again, the Unity of Brethren's role
was a determining one in this domain, as it provided successive editions
of hymn-books throughout the century from small pocket-sized books
to large annotated editions – the 1564 Ivančice edition, *Písně duchovní
evanjelistské*, edited by Jan Blahoslav, was the culminating work of
this kind. The hymns did not appear in the order of the church year,
but were divided into three categories, based on the dogmatic difference between things essential, useful and accidental, for the hymn-
books were also designed for family singing. They acted as a communal
focus in times of persecution, by providing theological teaching. This
was in fact the way these works were used, as evidenced by the bitter
remark of one of the Unity of Brethren's staunchest opponents. The
theologian Václav Šturm (1533–1601), educated in Rome by Ignatius
of Loyola, wrote concerning the Brethren's annotated hymn-book of
1576:

> Everyone, nobles and peasants, rich and poor have this book at
> home. Because they all sing these hymns at their meetings and in

> their homes, those who can barely read also use the texts of the hymn books as the basis for a sermon for the people, and present commentaries on the hymns to them. (*Rozsouzení*, 1588)

The other non-Catholic groups also printed hymn-books with a characteristic collection of old and new hymns.

Even though the martyr Jan Hus[21] and his friend Jerome of Prague burnt in Constance in 1415 and 1416 were immediately entered into the community of saints by the Utraquist church and though Hus's execution day – 6 July – entered the calendar as a feast day, their writings were rarely published. Between 1509 and 1547 only nine Czech treatises of Hus were published, mainly minor ones, edited by P. Olivetský, M. Konáč, J. Kantor and V. Oustský. Hus's Czech *Postilla*, including also his few minor works, appeared for the first time in Nuremberg printed by Johann vom Berg (Montanus) and Ulrich Neuber in 1563, and a second time in an anonymous publication in the following year together with the sermon collections of Jakoubek of Stříbro. This delay was not only due to the weight of censorship, but also to the new contacts between the Bohemian and European Reformations, and not only with Luther.

Among the Reformation writers of Bohemia whose works were published individually, mention should be made of the great lay thinker of the lower nobility of southern Bohemia, Petr Chelčický (d. *c*.1460), whose thoughts had a great influence on the early Unity of Brethren. His collection of sermons (*Kniha výkladuov spasitedlných*) was published in 1522 and 1532, while his penetrating treatise on the 'Net of the Faith' (*Siet viery*) was published even earlier, in 1521. The work was decorated with a symbolical woodcut, in which a net 'made from many truths of Holy Scripture' was torn by two whales, the Pope and the emperor, accompanied by various groups of evil-doers, both ecclesiastical and lay.[22]

---

[21] F. M. Bartoš, *Literární činnost M. J. Husi* [The literary activity of Master J. Hus] (Prague, 1948). Additional information in F. M. Bartoš and P. Spunar, *Soupis pramenů k literární činnosti M. Jana Husa a M. Jeronýma Pražského* [Sources on the literary activity of M. J. Hus and M. Jerome of Prague] (Prague, 1965). See also the very thorough bibliography of the important works in Czech and other languages by Amedeo Molnár, dealing with patristics, Valdeism, the Reformation in Bohemia and Europe, and the history of biblical exegesis, in the *Festschrift*: N. Rejchrtová (ed.) *Směřování* [Orientations] (Prague, 1983). See also J. Macek, *Jean Hus et les traditions hussites* (Paris, 1984).

[22] Facsimile in Zd. V. Tobolka (ed.) *Monumenta Bohemiae typographica* (vol. 1, Prague, 1926). P. Cheltschizki, *Das Netz des Glaubens* translated from Czech into German by C. Vogl, introduction by A. Molnár (Hildesheim, New York, 1970).

13.5 Illustration taken from the first Luther translation, *Kázaní na desatero*
[*Sermon on the Ten Commandments*] (Prague: Pavel Severin, 1520)

The first and strongest wave of interest in Luther's work in Bohemia
occurred between 1520 and 1523. This led to intense theological activity in the ranks of the Utraquist Church, not only because of Luther's
evident knowledge of Hus, but also because of the rapid translations of
Luther's recent treatises into Czech, published by O. Velenský, P. Olivetský
and P. Severin, as well as because of the warm and personal contacts
between the Bohemian intellectuals and Luther and his colleagues, and

with Melanchthon in particular.[23] Those who looked to Luther are known by the modern term, neo-Utraquists. This group and the conservative Utraquists quarrelled violently in Prague in 1523 and 1524 over ecclesiastical ordinances and liturgical customs, and naturally enough the debate also turned to ecclesiastical structures which had existed until then. The neo-Utraquists shaped their articles of faith, *Artikule víry* during the Candlemas meeting (Prague, 29 January 1524) and on 2 May 1524 they published their 'Writings on necessary Christian things', *Spis o potřebných věcech křesťanských*. This document was aimed against the practice of exposing the body of Christ in the monstrance, 'For Christ is present in good men through his grace as in the sacrament of the altar', and against processions: it explained that the Mass was not a sacrifice, and that the consecration of the body and blood of Christ had to take place in a language understood by all. The neo-Utraquists were, however, defeated and, lacking support, left the city. This temporary lack of success does not make these articles any less interesting. The later attempts in the 1540s to have an autonomous neo-Utraquism legally recognized and to create a Protestant church of Bohemia following the Lutheran model were based on these 'articles of faith'. The same held true for the preliminary work on the 'Bohemian Confession' of 1575. While Ferdinand I maintained the *Kompaktáta* as the sole basis for relations between the Roman and Utraquist churches, the neo-Utraquists believed that the *Kompaktáta* were no longer enough to ensure the development of the Reformation and actually hindered its advance. Following the installation of Maximilian II, the *Kompaktáta* no longer formed part of the ratification of national privileges by the king, at the request of the Bohemian Diet (1567), but with the royal clause that no heretical sect could be allowed into the country other than confessions which recognized communion in one or two kinds.

In 1561, after a 129–year vacancy since 1432, the Pope finally filled the Archbishopric of Prague, by nominating an influential member of the Council of Trent, Antonín Brus of Mohelnice.[24] In 1571, on his own authority, the king removed control of the Utraquist consistory from the

[23] R. Říčan, 'Tschechische Übersetzungen von Luthers Schriften bis zum Schmalkaldischen Krieg', *Vierhundertfünfzig Jahre lutherische Reformation* (Berlin, 1967), pp. 282–301. A. Molnár, 'Luther und die böhmischen Brüder', *Communio viatorum*, 24 (1981), 47–67. R. Říčan, 'Melanchthon und die böhmischen Länder', in *Philipp Melanchthon, Humanist, Reformator, Praeceptor Germaniae* (vol. 1, Berlin, 1973) pp. 237–60. M. Bohatcová, *Sborník Narodniho muzea u Praze*, C series, 11 (1966), no. 4, pp. 121–39.

[24] A. Skýbová, 'Knihovna arcibiskupa Antonína Bruse z Mohelnice' [The library of the Archbishop A. Brus of Mohelnice], in F. Šmahel (ed.) *Knihtisk a kniha v českých zemích od husitsví do Bílé hory* [Printing and the book in the Bohemian lands from the Hussite movement to the Battle of the White Mountain] (Prague, 1970), pp. 239–56.

Estates. Through this procedure, he sought to provoke a total split between the neo-Utraquist majority and the consistory, and to bring together the former and the Unity of Brethren into an ecclesiastical organization based on the Augsburg Confession of 1530. Thus he aimed to transform and complete the fundamental articles of Bohemian Reformation doctrine, articles which went back to the Hussite tradition. In 1575, when the non-Catholic Estates submitted their deliberations to the king on the compromise of the Diet, the so-called Bohemian confession *Vyznání víry*,[25] which only loosely included the Unity of Brethren, the Unity did not give up its own confession and ecclesiastical ordinances. Impelled by financial and diplomatic pressures, Maximilian gave an oral promise that the neo-Utraquist confession would be accepted, but only for nobles and their subjects, thus excluding the royal cities, and he renewed the principal measures of the Edict of Saint James against the Unity of Brethren.

Apart from Luther's writings, other European Reformers' works also appeared in translation in Bohemia, firstly Erasmus (1519 onwards), then Martin Bucer (1540 onwards), Heinrich Bullinger (1540) and Philipp Melanchthon. Melanchthon was particularly admired in Bohemia: apart from numerous extracts and quotations included in other editions, his Latin–Czech grammar also went through numerous editions. Christoph Gutknecht printed the translation of *Die Fürnemisten unterscheid zwischen reiner Christlicher Lere und der Abgöttischen Papistischen Lere* of Melanchthon, *Největší a najpřednější rozdílové*, as well as the first Czech translations of Calvin, the *Epistolae duae, Dvě epištoly*, and the *Supplex exhortatio ad Caesarem, Pokorné a ponížené napomínání* in Nuremberg in 1546. Calvin's *Institutio* appeared in Czech for the first time in 1612–17, *Sklad velikého zboží moudrosti nebeské*. Translations of works by Anton Corvinus (1539 onwards), Urbanus Rhegius (1539 onwards), Johannes Spangenberg (1545 onwards) and individual works by Kaspar Schwenckfeld (1540) and Georg Major (1561), all of which appeared in bookshops in Bohemia, were also widely read.

Apart from postils or sermon collections, prayer-books and works of consolation, funeral orations and other sermons, one must also mention the whole range of religious works by Czech authors. Naturally enough among these were many polemical works primarily directed against the neo-Utraquists and the Unity of Brethren.

---

[25] R. Říčan, 'Die Böhmische Konfession vom Jahre 1575. Ihre Entstehung und geschichtliche Bedeutung', in *Die Reformation, ihr geschichtlicher Ablauf und ihre Bedeutung für die Theologie der Gegenwart* (Halle an der Saale, 1969), pp. 55–64. A. Eckert, *Böhmische Konfession 1575* (Jubiläumsausgabe zum 400. Bestehen des Unionsbekentnisses) (Amberg, 1975).

The distribution and reading of non-Catholic works

The vast majority of Czech books printed in the sixteenth century, whether religious or not, were destined for national markets. This was linked to the situation of the Czech language, which was shaped by Bohemian scholars' wish to encourage a national literature through the printed book. Foreign markets were sometimes interested in foreign-language works of scientific, specialist or artistic interest, produced by a few great printers of Prague: Melantrich, Nigrin, Peterle or Šuman. As for the works of non-Catholic minorities, apart from confessions of faith and most of the polemical works, they were intended not even for the country as a whole, but for their fellow believers alone. This was evident in the publications of the Unity of Brethren, which were sold in closed markets, making it difficult for their opponents even to obtain copies of the works. Concrete evidence confirms these statements.

Information regarding the relations between authors and printers, who often organized the sale of the books they produced, is rare, as is any evidence of the size of output and the prices of these works. Any information still available survives in archival sources: sales contracts, wills, trial records, inventories made after printers' deaths, etc., but also in the prefaces and dedications of books. The systematic analysis of this scattered data has not yet been done. As for patronage, it was not uncommon for nobles to decide that a certain book should be published, and for instance to give to a middle-ranking cleric the task of translating a foreign book.

Due to the political situation in the Bohemian lands, no regional index of forbidden books was put in place, in spite of the efforts of the Council of Trent, the repeated censures of the Habsburgs and of both the Catholic and Utraquist churches, the Archbishop of Prague's interdicts (from 1561) and those of the Bishop of Olomouc (since 1567), and finally, in spite of the Jesuits' efforts. The celebrated *Clavis haeresim claudens et aperiens. Klíč ...* by the Jesuit missionary Antonín Koniáš appeared for the first time in the canonization year of Jan Nepomucký in 1729, when the Counter-Reformation practice of destroying heretical books had been in place for a century at least.

From the first half of the sixteenth century, public interest in printed books, and primarily in their religious content was based on relatively high literacy levels, even among the bourgeoisie. The traditional Hussite encouragement of lay Bible reading was rapidly extended by the ongoing creation of municipal schools, which helped pupils gain a good knowledge of Latin. However, one must not ignore group reading, which enabled even illiterate people to access the content of books. The Czech writers of the first half of the sixteenth century often addressed themselves to 'those who read or who are read to', a formula which gained the status of a stock phrase. In 1540, the sermon of Jan Augusta, the Bishop of the Unity of Brethren, on election to the ministry in the Unity of Brethren had an extraordinary impact, so much so that he had to have it printed, because his secretary was unable to keep up with the demand for copies. This example shows how useful printing was even in situations where there had been no thought of using it in the first instance. We also know that readers sought new editions of works which were out of print, particularly of the Bible.

Until the first decades of the nineteenth century, Czech books were printed in gothic characters, but the *antiqua* font was used for Latin texts. The technique for illustration and decoration in the sixteenth century was primarily the use of narrative woodcuts, with some exceptional use of copper engraving in the second half of the century. Illustration of religious texts was primarily important in Utraquist editions of the Bible and of sermon collections. Otherwise, any illustration was placed on the front cover or in the first pages of the book. Saints' pictures were popular, as in the Catholic prayer-book, *Hortulus animae*, *Zahrádka duše* (Nuremberg, 1520 and Plzeň, 1533). An engraved border, figurative or decorative, often appeared on the title-page. Pavel Olivetský and Jiřík Štyrsa's work for the Unity of Brethren were especially known for this type of Renaissance decoration.

The Unity of Brethren was especially aware of the importance of a proper integration of any iconographical elements in the social role of these publications. From the beginning the Brethren were convinced that the exterior aspect of the book should match the quality of its contents. This belief had an impact on the functional, rather than formal aspect of their books. They limited the use of biblical motifs in their work. For example, in the six-volume Kralice Bible, biblical motifs only appeared on the title-page of the sixth section, that of the New Testament. They used illuminated initials with biblical themes especially in hymn-books destined for large groups of lay people. These illustrations were not tied to the text, but reminded readers of the main biblical themes. The decorated borders in works printed for the Unity of Brethren also served as a location for symbols understandable only by the initiated. The Kralice editors quietly went against their readers when the third edition of the Bible was published, and justified it not only by the lack of copies of earlier editions, but also by the intentional choice of a larger format. According to the editors, the second edition had been printed 'in too small a format' which 'could not be used by those who were elderly or had poor eyesight, because of its small print'.

In short the printed book in the sixteenth century was not only fundamental for Reformation movements in Bohemia because of its

13.6   Coat of arms of the old city of Prague on the title-page of a book by
Luther for the neo-Utraquists (Prague: Pavel Severin, 1523)

impact on contemporaries' inner life, and on the world at large. Furthermore, the presence of printed books forced the various confessions
to make comparisons, and thus to undertake fundamental searches for
publications which reflected the spiritual characteristics of each group.

Select bibliography

Bohatcová, M., 'Schriftsteller der europäischen Reformation in der
    Bibliothek der Böhmischen Brüder', *GJ* (1970), 218–24.
Bohatcová, M., 'Der gegenwärtige Bearbeitungsstand der Druck-
    produktion vom 15.–18. Jahrhundert in den böhmischen Ländern',
    GJ (1987), 265–78.
Bohatcová, M., 'Das Verhältnis der tschechischen und fremdsprachigen
    Drucke in Böhmen und Mähren vom 15. Jahrhundert bis zum Jahre
    1621', *GJ* (1988), 108–16.
Bohatcová, M., 'Die Tschechischen gedruckten Bibeln des 15. bis 18.
    Jahrhunderts', in H. Rothe, et al. (eds), *Biblia Slavica* (Paderborn,
    1995), series I (Tschechische Bibeln), vol. 3 (Kralitzer Bibel 1–6).
    Commentary volume by M. Bohatcová, E. Michálek, J. Heller, M.
    Balabán (Paderborn, 1995), pp. 1–182.
Eckert, A., *Böhmische Konfession 1575*, Jubiläumsausgabe zum 400.
    Bestehen des Unionsbekentnisses (Amberg, 1975).
Fialová, Vl., 'Ein Letternfund aus dem XVI. Jahrhundert in Kralice nad
    Oslavou', *GJ* (1959), 85–91.
Fialová, Vl., 'Persönlichkeiten und Schicksale der berühmten Druckerei
    der Böhmischen Brüder', *GJ* (1967), 138–43.

Fialová, Vl., 'Bronzennadeln aus einer Buchdruckerei des XVI. Jahrhunderts', *GJ* (1961), 136–41.

Hejnic J. and Martínek, J., *Rukověť' humanistického básnictvi (Enchiridion renatae poesis Latinae in Bohemia et Moravia cultae)*, vols 1–5 (Prague, 1966–82).

Molnár, A., 'Luther und die Böhmischen Brüder', *Communio viatorum*, 24 (1981), 47–67. For the bibliography of A. Molnár's works, see note 21 in this chapter.

Müller, J. Th., *Geschichte der Böhmischen Brüder* (3 vols, Herrnhut, 1922–31).

Říčan, R., *Die Böhmischen Brüder* (Berlin, 1961).

Říčan, R., 'Tschechische Übersetzungen von Luthers Schriften bis zum Schmalkaldischen Krieg', in *Vierhundertfünfzig Jahre lutherische Reformation* (Berlin, 1967), pp. 282–301.

Říčan, R., 'Die Böhmische Konfession vom Jahre 1575. Ihre Entstehung und geschichtliche Bedeutung', in *Die Reformation, ihr geschichtlicher Ablauf und ihre Bedeutung für die Theologie der Gegenwart* (Halle an der Saale, 1969), pp. 55–64.

Říčan, R., 'Melanchthon und die böhmischen Länder', in *Philipp Melanchthon, Humanist, Reformator, Praeceptor Germaniae* (vol. 1, Berlin, 1973), pp. 237–60.

Tobolka Zd. V. and Horák, Fr., *Knihopis českých a slovenských tisků od doby nejstarší až do konce XVIII. století* [National bibliography of Czech printed works of the fifteenth to eighteenth centuries, with detailed descriptions and information on the surviving copies] (Prague, 1925–67).

Urbánková, E., 'Prvotisky' [Incunabula] in *Dodatky ke Knihopisu* [Supplements to *Knihopis*], part 1 (Prague, 1994).

Wiżd'álková, B., 'Tisky z let 1501–1800' [Prints of 1501–1800] in *Dodatky*, part 2 [this time, 1–3=A–J] (Prague, 1994–96).

CHAPTER FOURTEEN

The book and the Reformation in Poland

Alodia Kawecka-Gryczowa and Janusz Tazbir

From the start, one must briefly outline the geopolitical situation in sixteenth-century Poland to understand clearly how the Protestant movement developed there. The Polish state at the time was made up of two political entities united by a freely established treaty: the 'Crown' (Poland) and Lithuania, which included a part of Ruthenian territory. The Poland–Lithuania union had the prince of Prussia as vassal. His state, founded by the Teutonic Knights, was secularized in the sixteenth century by Prince Albert of Hohenzollern. In 1525, Albert swore an oath of vassalage to his uncle Sigismund I, the Old, King of Poland. This did not keep Albert from becoming a fervent and effective supporter of Lutheranism. He spread this confession beyond the borders of his principality, and naturally it penetrated into Poland. All the evidence suggests that his religious fervour was coupled with political ambitions. At the time, Poland was surrounded by Prussia to the north, Germany and Silesia to the west, and Bohemia and Hungary to the south. All these lands were either ruled by the Habsburgs or were under that family's influence, as the Habsburgs were related to the Jagiellons who ruled in Poland. It appears that this situation facilitated the penetration of ideological movements from Central Europe, and particularly from Germany, the cradle of Lutheranism.

The first contacts with the 'new faith' quickly followed the appearance of Luther's theses. Although the king enacted a decree in Toruń already on 24 July 1520 forbidding entry to Luther's works into Poland, Protestant works arrived rapidly, using the traditional trade routes of Wrocław and Poznań. These writings were particularly popular at the university of Cracow, where both students and professors showed increasing interest in them, until the promulgation of the bull of Leo X, which limited somewhat the fervour for the new faith. Poland's southern cities were even more easily supplied with the writings of Luther and other German theologians. In the port city of Gdańsk in 1522, religious and social problems led to riots.

The production of books

Prussia

In the capital city of his principality, Königsberg (Królewiec in Polish, Kaliningrad today) Prince Albert organized an entire propaganda centre for the new faith aimed at his subjects, who included a large and homogeneous group of Poles. The printers which he brought in from Germany did not, however, manage to fulfil the tasks which the prince set for them. His projects became more specific with the arrival of Polish and Lithuanian refugees threatened by the clergy in their countries of origin. Thanks to the foundation of the Academy in 1544, where Lithuanian professors taught among others, Königsberg became a scientific and publishing centre.

From 1544, the initiator and main supplier of Polish texts was a refugee from Poznań, Jan Seklucjan. Thanks to him, the German press of Johannes Weinreich acquired Polish and Latin characters. Already at the end of 1544, Seklucjan published a small catechism, though it is not known whether it was Luther's or Melanchthon's. By 1547 he had published the *Greater Catechism* and the *Spiritual and Pious Hymns*, as well as other religious works. In total, between 1543 and 1549, Weinreich printed 15 works totalling 80 sheets.[1]

However, Seklucjan's ambitions and those of his prince were much greater: to print the Bible in a Polish and Lithuanian translation. Although the Lithuanian version never appeared, the Polish translation was carried out thanks to Seklucjan's inexhaustible energy. Then it was thought that Königsberg should have a printing press able to produce Polish works on a greater scale than the modest presses of Weinreich could. Aleksander Augezdecki (Oujezdecky), who came from Moravia, adapted Czech characters for Polish orthography, but his presses lacked orders. Without the firm support of Prince Albert, Augezdecki left the city in 1549. In that year, he published dialogues and a tragedy, *The Merchant*, by the eminent Polish writer Mikołaj Rej.

Augezdecki returned rather rapidly to Königsberg. In the years 1550–56, his presses published several important works, in particular the first Polish translation of the New Testament, done by Stanisław Murzynowski. Seklucjan seemingly edited Luther's *Small Catechism* at this time. The publications of this highly dynamic militant also included the first Polish collection of sermons, by Grzegorz Orszak. The greatest work of Augezdecki's presses was a splendid folio volume, a translation

---

[1] To measure the activity of a press, we add up the number of sheets in each edition, regardless of the book's format.

by Walenty of Brzozòw of the hymn-book of the Czech Brethren, *Piesni chwal Boskich* (1554). The title-page was decorated with a beautiful woodcut showing the faithful singing in the temple, which, with the illuminated initials, made it a stunning edition.

Augezdecki probably left Königsberg towards the end of 1556. He had published approximately 20 works in Polish in the city (around 600 sheets out of a total of 700). A part of the Czech's typographical equipment was acquired by the Franconian Wolfgang Dietmar, who ran a press in Elbląg in northern Poland from 1558 to 1563.

Turning our attention back to Albert of Hohenzollern's province, Seklucjan, the principal publisher of Polish Protestant literature, had a rival in the territory of the Prussian principality itself, namely Jan Sandecki-Malecki, who had already been a printer in Cracow. The two publishers engaged in cut-throat competition by publishing similar works, such as Luther's *Catechism* (printed by Weinreich in Königsberg in 1546) or the New Testament. Malecki founded a small press in Ełk in Mazuria, where he managed to print a proof sheet of a *New Testament* translated into Polish from the text established by Erasmus (1552). He may also have produced in this small printing house the work (now lost) of one of the first who propagated Antitrinitarianism, Piotr of Goniądz (Gonesius). In any event, it was in Ełk that a Polish *Catechism* was published (1558), of which no copy survives.

While Polish works continued to appear there from time to time, the city of Königsberg, like the entire Lutheran movement in fact ceased to play a significant role in the development of Polish Protestantism. Lutheranism, however, held an unquestionable sway in the north of Poland, notably among the largely German-speaking merchant classes. A translation of the Augsburg Confession was published for Polish readers by Jan Busz Krakowczyk, a pastor in Toruń, entitled, *Schmalcaldici articuli, to jest Artykuły krześcijańskiej nauki* (1566). Jan Seklucjan, an astute observer of the book trade in Poland, described acutely in 1555 the decline of Prusso-Lutheran influence: 'I made some profit from my Polish books, but now, not only my booklets, but also the entire doctrine of the Saxon churches has been rejected by sacramentarians [Calvinists] in Poland, Lithuania, Russia, Moravia and Podolia. Everywhere, sacramentarian works proliferate.' Indeed, as Calvinism anchored itself in central Poland, it opened its own printing presses there.

Poland

In Poland, the doctrine of Zurich and Geneva proved more attractive than that of Wittenberg, as it resembled noble democracy more closely. Lutheranism remained more a confession held by the city-dwellers in the north of Poland. Therefore, it is not surprising that the presses created by Calvinism appeared especially in the most intellectually active region of Poland, namely Little Poland. These printing presses also multiplied in Lithuania thanks to the support of powerful local magnates.

Before Calvinism took root, Erasmian philosophy had a profound impact on large sections of the Polish intellectual élite. Interest in his thought went from the royal court to scholars via lay and ecclesiastical hierarchies.

The strength of the enthusiasm for the great Dutchman can be measured by the 40 editions of his work published in Cracow between 1518 and 1550. The first edition of *Querela Pacis* was produced in 1518 by Hieronim Wietor, responsible for a total of 24 editions of Erasmus. Two works, *Precatio dominica* and *Lingua* were translated into Polish. The Basle edition of *Lingua* (Froben, August 1525) was reprinted in Poland already at the beginning of 1526. This general enthusiasm declined, however, during the 1540s.

Favourable conditions for the expansion of the Reformation in Little Poland and Lithuania appeared at the death of Sigismund I (1548). His young successor Sigismund II Augustus was known for his tolerance. Many in his entourage had studied in Italy or Wittenberg, or had spent time in the Swiss cities. Thus it was a propitious period in which to promote the renewal of the Church and to transmit new ideas. Protestant works began to flood into the country, while at the same time such works were also being published in Poland itself.

Before dissidents set up their own presses, from the 1540s the Cracow presses began to carry out embryonic activities favouring the new confessional stream. Hieronim Wietor, whose presses were very active in the development of humanism, produced some of these early works. Originally Silesian, and trained at Cracow University, he worked in Vienna between 1510 and 1517. In Vienna, Wietor worked for local humanists. In Cracow, where he began printing in 1518, he immediately made contact with the humanists. His presses produced the first book in Greek and the Polish translation of Erasmus' *Lingua*. Wietor did not remain aloof from the new religious currents. In 1536, he was even arrested for having imported and distributed books and images considered as 'scandalous' in the eyes of the Catholic Church. His printing house also welcomed Hungarian dissidents and printed their works, including the *Hymnbook* by Istvan Galszecsi and Benedict Komjathy's *Letters of Saint Paul*. In 1549, Wietor published a Polish adaptation of Luther's hymn, *ein Kinderlied*. By producing in-octavo hymn sheets, Wietor began a presentation which became characteristic in later Protestant hymnology. These hymn sheets, often with music, were republished by other printers and led to contemporary collectors' books, in which sheets were added in order thanks to page numbering. Two such works survived, that of Pulawy (1556) and Zamość (1558).

Lazarz Andrysowic, Wietor's successor, continued to publish hymns. He also printed a few Protestant books but only anonymously. But these were only small orders, carried out for financial reasons.

Lithuania and Little Poland

The consolidation of Calvinism in Poland led to the creation of confessional printing houses. The first was founded by prince Mikołaj Radziwiłł, known as the Black, in Lithuania in Brest Litovsk, and directed by the writer Bernard Wojewódka, in partnership with the famous poet Andrzej Trzecieski. Three works printed in 1553–54 have survived (24 sheets). A few years later, and in the same city Mikołaj Radziwiłł founded a new printing press. Among his publications was the first *Kancjonal* printed in central Poland, by Stanisław Zaremba with musical scores by Cyprian Bazylik. From 1558 to 1561, the workshop produced a total of 16 works (approximately 147 sheets). In 1563, although the name of its owner is not known, the press recorded a major achievement with the printing of the first full translation of the Bible into Polish. It came out as an impressively large folio volume, and had been produced by a large number of translators centred around the Calvinist community of Pińczów. This was one of the greatest successes of the dissident camp. Mikołaj Radziwiłł, the real overseer, bragged about it throughout Europe. In the following year, a quarto psalm-book was produced in a more portable format. From 1562 to 1567 the Brest presses published 12 works entirely in Polish (887 sheets).

In fact the Lithuanian production in the field of printing postdated the set-up of Calvinist structures in Poland. At the beginning Calvinism's 'capital' was the small city of Pińczów, and it was here that the first Protestant service was held in 1551. A year later, a school based on Swiss models was also founded in the same city. In 1558, a printing press directed until 1562 by Daniel z Łęczycy opened its doors. 1562 was the date of the schism between the Major Church (Calvinist) and the Minor Church (Antitrinitarian).

Alongside supporters of Calvin, Pińczów also housed foreign newcomers who brought ideological turmoil with them, as did Francesco Stancaro in particular. Antitrinitarian ideas grew up from debates of Stancaro's ideas on the mediation of Christ. His book *Collatio doctrinae Arii et Melanchtonis et sequacium* was even burnt in 1558. This was the first occurrence of Protestant censorship.

Thirty works printed in Pińczów in the course of five years are known of today, and the majority were published in Polish (332 sheets in total).

Antitrinitarian tendencies found support in other areas of the Polish states, mainly in Lithuania. At Brest Litovsk the works of Grzegorz Paweł, the leader of Polish Antitrinitarianism, were published among others. Paweł's *Tabula de Trinitate* provoked a reaction from Calvin himself in 1563 in his *Brevis admonitio ad Fratres Polonos ne triplicem in Deo essentiam pro tribus personis imaginando, tres sibi deos fabricant*. However, the principal spokesman of Lithuanian Unitarianism was Szymon Budny. Two printing presses on Lithuanian territory spread his ideas: one in Nieśwież, and the other in Losk. The printing house of Nieśwież published the first Antitrinitarian version of the *Kancjonał* written by Marcin Czechowic and began the publication of the Bible in Szymon Budny's translation.

Among the Antitrinitarian militants who also fought infant baptism was one of the main leaders of the movement from the start, Piotr of Goniądz. Some of his writings have disappeared; four others were published in the town of Węgrów (1570). It is worth noting that all of the above-mentioned dissident printing presses were founded and financed by landed magnates. Only the Pińczów press operated thanks to funds provided by the members of Calvinist communities.

Great Poland

Leaving Little Poland and Lithuania aside for the moment, let us examine another printing press established with the support of nobles from Great Poland. In 1548, the arrival of a large group of Czech Brethren from Bohemia and Moravia led to a curious situation of conflict and collaboration between the two communities of Lutherans and Czech Brethren. The latter found support at Szamotuły, in the castle of Łukasz Górka. This magnate founded a printing press in 1557, directed by Aleksander Augezdecki, after his return from Bohemia. The printing house did produce Lutheran works, but essentially served the Brethren. The latter also kept in touch with the group which remained in Moravia, led by Bishop Blahoslav. Of the works produced by the Szamotuły presses until 1568, 11 works remain, in Polish, Latin, and Czech (269 sheets). The primary work produced by this press was the Czech hymn-book, *Pisne duchownj Ewangelitske*, a large folio edition, illustrated with woodcuts including a portrait of Hus (1561). This work was a reprint of the Roh *Kancjonał* prepared by Blahoslav. The printing, carried out with typographical equipment from Bohemia was controlled by Vaclav Solin, a Czech, although the existence of this press was only a brief one.[2]

---

[2] The Lutherans tried to establish another printing press in Great Poland, but their activity takes us beyond the chronological boundaries of this study.

Cracow

After this very short overview of the territories of the old Polish Republic, let us now return to Cracow, to the centre. The small and often clandestine services rendered by a few printers supporting the new religious currents have already been discussed. Maciej Wirzbięta's presses, however, openly produced Calvinist works, and he was in fact the main distributor of such works. In contrast to the presses established by magnates, his press was noteworthy for its relatively long-running operation: 1555/57–1605. Its foundation was in all likelihood supported by a renowned Polish writer, the wealthy nobleman Mikołaj Rej. The inaugural work produced by the press was a luxurious, richly illustrated folio edition of Rej's *Postylla*. Other works of his followed, in particular the *Apocalypsis*, inspired by Bullinger. Artistically speaking, the *Zwierciadło albo kształt w którym każdy stan snadnie się może swym sprawom jako w zwierciadle przypatrzeć*, magnificently illustrated, was a great success, as a form of celebration of everyday life in a Polish village. Approximately ten years later, after the death of his first patron, Wirzbięta became the printer for the Calvinist community of Little Poland. Furthermore, after Augezdecki's departure from Szamotuły, Wirzbięta offered his services to the Czech Brethren of Great Poland. Among other works, he printed a new revised version of their *Kancjonal*.

The high-quality printing in Wirzbięta's works gained the general respect of Polish humanists and even that of the royal courts, who sought his services. Thus he gained a place as one of the foremost Polish printers in the sixteenth century. The *Postylla* and *Mirror* by Rej are thought to be among the most beautiful books of Renaissance Poland. One should note that when the sermon collection was republished, it included three new illustrations, of which two were definitely anti-Catholic. Even now, the origin of the woodcuts' models is unknown, but masters of Cracow definitely carved the wood models.

Until the death of its founder, the printing press produced 175 works (at least 3 750 sheets), although it is highly unlikely that this was the sum total of his publications. The Wirzbięta press was the most productive and most representative of Polish Protestantism in the sixteenth century.[3]

---

[3] The printing house which began in Cracow and was transferred to Raków at the beginning of the seventeenth century, holds a special place in the history of Polish dissident printing. The history of this press, which goes beyond the chronological limits of this study, is well known thanks to the monograph of A. Kawecka-Gryczowa, published in Polish and French: *Les imprimeurs des antitrinitaires polonais: Rodecki et Sternacki, Histoire et bibliographie* (Wrocław, 1974).

Ku temuß to Krześćiáńskye=
mu Rycerzowi nápomináníe.

Cóż chceß czynić moy miły człowiecze/
Gdyż wieß żeć czás iáko wodá cyecze/
A co bliżey to do kresu byeżyß/
Przecz nic nie dbaß á beśpyecznye leżyß.
Jeśteś práwye on co go Lew gonił/
Vpadł s skáły gáłaski sie chwyćił/
Pozrzał ná dół Smok sye k niemu scyaga/
Ledwye że mu iuż nog nie dosiaga.
Pozrzał wzgore á gáłaski one/
Myßy gryza iuż ná druga strone/
Z yednej strony czarna z drugyey byała/
Ták iż iey iuż máła część zostáłá.

Aa   Vzrzał

14.1 [Mikołaj Rej], *Postylla* (Cracow: Maciej Wirzbięta, 1557), f. Aa1

The typographical format of the works

The typographical specifications of Reformation works matched those applied more generally in Polish presses at the time. Latin texts were composed in roman fonts (*antiqua*) and italic ones brought in from Italy in the first decades of the sixteenth century. The influence of French and Dutch models only grew after 1560. Books in Polish were mainly printed in gothic (*schwabach*). The gothic *Fraktur* font was rarely used for texts (for instance in the hymn sheets printed by Lazarz Andrysowic in 1556) but rather in titles and headings. The few publications in Cyrillic printed in Lithuania to spread Antitrinitarianism among bielo-Russian populations were an exception: they were due to the work of Szymon Budny (Nieśwież, 1562) and Bazyl Ciapiński (Ciapin, 1570?).

Reformation polemical and propaganda works were principally produced in small formats, generally quarto. Works intended for daily use (hymn-books and prayer-books) were normally octavo, except the folio hymn-books (*Kancjonal*) printed by Augezdecki (Königsberg, 1554 and Szamotuly, 1561). The folio format was meant above all for complete editions of the Bible, as well as sermon collections (Grzegorz Orszak, Mikołaj Rej, Grzegorz z Żarnowca).

As has been noted above, the richly decorated works of Mikołaj Rej printed by Wirzbięta in Cracow were famous examples of non-Catholic Polish printing. The woodcuts were carved by an artist who signed his initials on the title-page as ICB 1556. Only two illustrations of foreign origin were anti-Catholic. One must note that these two were omitted from Grzegorz z Żarnowca's Protestant sermon collection, which was then republished with the same woodcuts. The monumental Bible of Radziwiłł (Brześć 1563) only had illustrations in Exodus, with woodcuts depicting the Temple. In contrast, the engravings in Luther's Bible (Wittenberg, 1534) were reprinted in Jan Leopolita's Catholic Bible of 1561.[4] It is worth pointing out that the first three-quarter length authentic portrait of Luther was displayed in a historical work, whose author supported the Reformation: Marcin Bielski's *Kronika polska* (2nd edn, Cracow, 1564). The hymn sheets printed by Lazarz Andrysowic around 1556 and later by Mateusz Siebeneycher in 1558 were decorated with Catholic-style engravings which came from the old material formerly produced by the two presses.

---

[4] E. Chojecka, *Deutsche Bibelserien in der Holzstocksammlung der Jagellonischen Universität in Krakau* (Baden-Baden, 1961).

Authors and texts

A doctrinal kaleidoscope

The overview of printing houses has shown the doctrinal diversity of sixteenth-century Polish religious publications. Lutheran and Calvinist movements, but also more minor confessions, such as the Antitrinitarians or the Czech Brethren, all had access to printing.

Those who spread the Polish Reformation rarely published original works before the middle of the sixteenth century, but they made abundant use of imported publications – the works of Luther – or ones printed in the nearby city of Königsberg (Królewiec). These texts coming from outside were mainly in Latin, more rarely in German, while Prussia also produced Polish works. For the most part, the last were translations and adaptations. In any event, the contribution of Polish authors was minimal. However, after 1552, the number of original works increased, written by Poles who supported different confessional groups in the Reformation: Lutherans, Calvinists, or Antitrinitarians. At the height of religious polemic, in the third quarter of the sixteenth century, these indigenous works made up approximately two-thirds of all printed texts. At the same time, a considerable increase in the number of Polish texts being printed took place. From 1550 to 1580, Polish works constituted approximately 60 per cent of total production, and even reached 70 to 80 per cent in certain years. Towards the end of the century, there was a marked decrease in the production of Polish Protestant works. One must add that few Polish Protestants published their works outside the country in the sixteenth century. Jan Laski was an exception, printing in Dutch. A few other Polish Protestant works were translated, primarily into German.

Such a variegated confessional printing scene was difficult to find elsewhere in Europe. The phenomenon was due to the fact that currents of every confessional shade swept through the republic, from Lutheranism to semi-Judaism, through all the forms of Antitrinitarianism. Furthermore, in a state in which an important proportion of the population was Orthodox, and also included Jews and Muslims, the variety of Christian confessions only managed to survive in the 'Golden Age' of Polish culture thanks to the famous Polish tolerance. Tolerance was enshrined in the 1573 Warsaw confederation, while the unifying tendencies of the major Protestant confessions were expressed in the Sandomir Consensus of 1570.

Literary genres and styles

Polish Protestant groups published a range of publications specific to each confession: Bibles, sermon collections, creeds, catechisms, hymn-books and prayer-books and liturgies. In order to hold worship services, not only in churches but also in private homes, hymn-books and catechisms were the indispensable companions to Bibles. This return to the sources, this interest in reading the Bible, manifested in the annual production of hundreds of copies of scripture at relatively low prices, also worried the 'Papists'.

Every confessional group, both Catholic and Protestant, engaged in printed polemic: Calvinists (Andrzej Wolan, Grzegorz of Żarnowiec, Cyprian Bazylik), Lutherans (Erazm Gliczner) and Antitrinitarians (Grzegorz Paweł of Brzeziny, Marcin Czechowic, Szymon Budny and Jan Niemojewski). The most talented polemicists even included authors who changed confessional camps (Stanisław Orzechowski) or who tried to 'shorten the distance' between confessions (Andrzej Frycz Modrzewski).

The Reformation also used dialogues in verse form – a literary genre which had never been employed on such a scale – religious dramas and finally satirical pamphlets. Many of these genres had appeared on a large scale in Poland prior to the birth of the Reformation. Pamphlets and satirical writings accompanied juridical and economic debates, anti-royalist conflicts during the reign of Sigismund I – known as the 1537 'hens' war' – and the passionate debate over the marriage of his son to Barbara Radziwiłłowna. Confessional themes were simply inserted into traditional literary forms which already had a loyal readership. But any interest in these works was only secondary in comparison with the passion displayed by nobles in discussions over national political power.

Reformation drama drew heavily on Biblical sources, as in Mikołaj Rej's *Life of Joseph* or on western Protestant works, as in Trepka's translation of Bernardino Ochino's *Tragedy of the Mass*. In many cases, the style was closer to rhyming dialogue than to classical forms of drama. These works were often performed in schools, particularly Lutheran ones. Reformed satire on the one hand brought the conflicts between nobles and clerics to light (*A short discussion between a nobleman, a mayor and a presbyter*), and on the other hand attacked Catholic liturgy and teachings (*A brief and sharp discussion of certain ceremonies and practices of the church*, often attributed to Jan Seklucjan). Reformation writers did not stray far from epigram and pamphlet style.

Polish Protestant books, especially polemical ones, remain little known. Many works were never read in their entirety, while some were burnt by their opponents. The destruction of Protestant books or even of entire libraries occurred mainly in the seventeenth century when the Polish nobility sought to erase even the memory of 'heretical' ancestors.

In spite of the abundance of polemical works, no trace has been found of Polish *Flugschriften*. This characteristically German form of pamphlet thus seems not to have penetrated into Poland, except in the Prussian principality. The disappearance of a large number of Protestant books leads us to further paths of enquiry in this regard, rather than definitive statements.

The reception

The readership

Certain scholars believe that the Reformation's zone of influence corresponds more or less with areas of higher literacy. The new faith was welcomed more readily in areas where the majority could read and write. Thus Mazovia, an area with probably the highest percentage of illiteracy remained unmoved by the appeal of the Reformation, while the nobility and city patricians, richer and more cultured, were more receptive to it. A. Wyczański and W. Urban established that 90 per cent of noblemen and half their wives were able to read. For patricians, percentages oscillated between 70 to 90 per cent of men and around 25 per cent of women. More than half the nobility was made up of gentry, who owned smallholdings, or were even landless. Sixty per cent of these could hardly sign, 25 per cent could not even do that, while 15 per cent could read and write a little. This evidence shows that 'heretical' printing was not sufficient on its own to spread reforming ideas, for printing presupposed the ability to read. Thus Protestants were particularly insistent on the need for reading to be taught.

Illiteracy did not, however, constitute an impetrenable barrier to the influence of writing, for 'reading' was associated first and foremost with reading out loud, as in the Middle Ages. Many contemporary paintings show a reader in the midst of a group of listeners. In Poland, the Reformation spread through reading the Scriptures aloud, followed by group discussions and through reading polemical pamphlets. This was not uncommon at a time when the urban authorities had official decisions read out in public. Thus the Reformation enabled religious debate to penetrate into wide sections of the population. As the supporters of Rome ironically commented, 'tailors, shoemakers and executioners are allowed' to discuss questions of faith. Protestant books which spread through society also found their way into women's hands, women to whom Protestants dedicated some of their works.

Censorship

It is no coincidence that for a long time, the struggle against the new faith in Poland was limited to the repression of 'heretical' printers, rather than to the persecution of Protestant preachers and the betrayal of those who criticized the priests. The discovery of religious books during searches of itinerant book traders' baggage or in citizens' houses – the nobility escaped due to their privileges – led to grave suspicions on the part of civil and ecclesiastical authorities. Owning religious books meant that one wished to examine questions of faith on one's own, without the clergy as intermediary. Thus, it meant that the living word transmitted in Catholic preaching or in the confessional was no longer enough for those who possessed such books.

Already in 1487, the papal bull of Innocent VIII made the bishops responsible for the censorship of printed books, but in practice, they passed this task on to priests in their service. In Poland, this mission was mainly given to the professors of Cracow's academy. From 1523, its rector was charged with preventative censorship. But the first case of ecclesiastical involvement in the spread of printed books in Cracow went back to 1492, when the printer Szwajpolt Fiol was suspected of heresy after printing schismatic books in Cyrillic. However, the accused managed to get off reasonably lightly.

In Sigismund I Jagiellon's decrees published in the 1520s against Lutheranism, the penalties for introducing the writings of Wittenberg's Reformer became gradually more harsh. In 1520, pushed by the papal legate Zaccaria Ferreri, the king threatened to confiscate goods and banish transgressors. Three years later, influenced by another legate, Tommaso Negri, he introduced the death penalty and the confiscation of all possessions if Protestant writings were introduced, read, or distributed. The king gave the bishops of Cracow the right to conduct searches, not only in booksellers' and printers' workshops, but also in private book collections.

However, Protestant works must have been hidden for a certain time, as, in 1524, the chancellor Krzysztof Szydłowiecki triumphantly announced to Leo X that Cracow was totally free from the Lutheran 'infection'. As stringent decrees were renewed in the following years, they seem to have had little effect. In 1540, Sigismund I threatened those who sent their children away to foreign Protestant schools with infamy, confiscation of property, and death. The same penalties were intended for those who introduced or distributed works by Luther and other heretics in Poland. Ecclesiastical tribunals or the Inquisition applied these penalties. Once again, the king made it compulsory for bishops to hand in the names of parents who sent their children outside Poland and to punish those who brought back heretical books.

Any overview of the matriculation registers of Wittenberg, Königsberg and Leipzig universities in the 1550s will show that the Poles ignored the prohibition to matriculate in foreign universities. At the same time, a growing number of Protestant books ended up in increasing numbers of families. When these were discovered, the owners of 'heretical' books defended themselves by claiming that they never read the books, or that they had no idea which books they actually owned. Jan Schnitzer, a Cracow bookseller, in whose house a Luther Bible was discovered in 1544, explained that he did not keep it to read it, but because of Albrecht Dürer's magnificent illustrations. This type of explanation seems to have been taken at face value. In the first half of the sixteenth century, in Cracow alone, 30 trials took place for book offences, and in most cases, the trials ended in a simple reprimand. No accused was harmed, even though certain publishers were briefly put in prison. We have already described the case of Hieronim Wietor in 1536. In 1585, an Antitrinitarian printer, Aleksander Rodecki was imprisoned for having printed a pamphlet by Christian Francken. However, after a few weeks King Stephen Bathory ordered his release. On this occasion, the king declared that he would never shed blood in the cause of religion, since he did not want to force consciences. However, heretical presses were sometimes destroyed during anti-Protestant pogroms. In 1578, the Poznań bishop Lukasž Kościelecki reacted against the printer Melchior Nehring who had published an anti-Jesuit pamphlet, *Diatribe*, by the Calvinist Jakub Niemojewski. The bishop had the printer's books burned, and condemned him to a whipping and a period in the stocks.

The lack of serious action against printing and the sale of Protestant books was due in part to the nobility's resistance. Already in 1534, nobles strongly opposed censorship of printing. At the Środa Wielkopolska diet, the delegates demanded not only the freedom to publish chronicles and edicts in Polish without prohibitions from the priests, but also the freedom to publish the Scriptures in their own tongue. There was, however, some delay before the national production of Protestant books could take over from imports. In 1543, the ecclesiastical censors still forbade the printing of Jan Ostroróg's *Monumentum ... pro Republicae ordinatione*. The first version of this work was written in the middle of the previous century. Supporters of the Reformation probably made amendments to strengthen their position regarding Poland's independence from the Pope and a reduction in clerical privileges.

In 1551, Catholic censors confiscated the book *Of the Church* as it came off the presses, one of five sections of *De Republica emendanda* by Andrzej Frycz Modrzewski (Modrevius). The religious authorities feared that 'religion would suffer' because of this work. However, a complete version was published in Basle in 1554 and thus it reached Poland. Indeed, the author dedicated his work to King Sigismund Augustus, who for his part clearly expressed his wish that Frycz Modrzewski not be punished in any way for the publication of the *Emendanda*. It was not the only work of this type in the king's library, which housed many books warmly dedicated to the king, but considered as 'heretical' by the Catholic clergy. The decisions of the synod of Piotrków of 1551 indicate that numerous dissident writings in Polish had entered the country. In 1560, the Italian Nuncio, Bernardo Bongiovanni wrote that all these books 'freely enter Poland, are sold before the royal palace gates, and as everyone knows who authorises this, no one is challenged'.

In spite of the proliferation of Protestant presses, the ecclesiastical authorities did not abandon their struggle against heretical books. They invented new procedures, such as the one known by historians as 'literary execution'. This involved burning confiscated books in public, but this practice was rarely carried out by civil powers. One should only bear in mind the case of Christian Francken's books, burnt in 1585 on the orders of Stephen Bathory. In 1554, Marcin Krowicki's *Christian Remonstrances* were burnt in front of Przemyśl Cathedral. The 'literary execution' which took place in 1581 in Vilna by the order of the bishop, Jerzy Radziwiłł, had a particularly large impact, although the books which were burnt had been bought, not confiscated. Around 1551, the Płock Chapter confiscated the dissident books of a nobleman, Paweł Dąbrowski, but afterwards, the cost of the books was repaid to him, so that he would not demand restitution.

Although the ecclesiastical synods of 1542 and 1564 recommended burning works which had been established as being harmful for the Church, confiscations were uncommon. Apart from books bought for that purpose, those which were burnt came from libraries of converted Catholics, or from those of dead Protestants, whose Catholic heirs wanted to get rid of the works.

Calvinists rather rapidly began to use the Catholic methods to fight against heretical works, although on a much more modest scale. Already in 1558, the first official printer of the Pińczów community, Daniel of Łęczyca, could not print anything without prior permission from the ecclesiastical authorities. The burning of Stancaro's book, published in Pińczów, is mentioned above. In 1556, Prince Mikołaj Radziwiłł bought up a large part of the print-run of Piotr of Goniądz's *De filio Dei homine Jesu Christo*, in order to burn it. The work is now known only through its title. However, these were relatively rare events

Kommentharz/ albo

wykład na Prorocżthwo Hożeaßa Prozoká/ktorego piſmá/ku dziſieyßym czá= ſom oſtátecżnym / właſnie ſie przydáć á przytrefić moga. Teraz nowo po Polſku vczyniony.

Actuum íx.
Durum eſt contra ſtimulum recalcítrare &cæt.

Quícumcp agnita vcrítate conculcauerít ſanguinem
Ieſu Chriſti, huíc non remíttetur peccatum íllud,
necp in hoc nec ín futuro ſæculo &cæt.

14.2 [Martin Luther], *Kommentarz albo wyklad na proroctwo Hozeasza* [*In Hoseam prophetam enarratio*] (Brześć [Cracow: Maciej Wirzbięta, 1559)

in Poland. Books were burned, rather than their authors or printers, while in western Europe people often perished with their works.

The influence of Protestant books

The effects of Protestant printing on the cultural and religious life of Poland are difficult to measure. However, its influence can be charted in different directions. The development of polemic led to a better mastery of language, both in terms of form and of argument, since the main aim was to convince a large circle of readers. This was the first time that Polish had been used on such a scale in religious controversies and in liturgical and theological writings. As the Reformation led to discussions of abstract issues (theology, ethics, philosophy), it contributed to the development of Polish as a vehicle for the expression of intellectual topics (Konrad Górski). Instead of Latin treatises intended for a small circle of specialists, shorter works were now produced, like sermon collections and parenetic literature (which included all forms of 'images', 'mirrors' and 'imitations'.)

The creation of a new translation theory was significant for the later history of the genre. Abandoning the technique of freely adapting literary works – Lukasz Górnicki's *Courtisan*, an adaptation of Castiglione's *Il Cortegiano* is a case in point – the translation of theological texts, and especially of the Bible, moved towards a greater emphasis on fidelity, especially as each translation could lead to new doctrinal disputes. This evolution also had an impact on terminology, whether the Protestants used older words with new meanings (penitence), or whether they introduced new words or created new meanings (minister, assembly). Antitrinitarians even created words which were specific to their group.

The struggle against the weight of Latin and the aspirations of independence from the Church of Rome on the part of the state encouraged particularism and national pride. The first national anthem, *Prayer for the State and the King*, was a creation of the Reformation camp and was written by the Calvinist Andrzej Trzecieski. Furthermore, the exaggeration of odious foreign intrigues which 'portrayed Polish good nature to be Spanish cruelty' prepared the way for a later increase in xenophobia. The Antitrinitarians, who kept in permanent contact with foreign lands and who included many foreigners, did not, however, join in this distrust.

The most characteristic feature of polemic was its 'laicizing argumentation'. In its most acute phase, polemic developed more and more around the following theme: does the Reformation really lead to disorder, both in the church and in the state? Does it really lead people to revolt and to a breakdown of social structures?

The view of the Christian world widened thanks to controversy surrounding missions. As they wanted to condemn Rome and not the entire Church, Protestants pointed to the fact that eastern Europe had been free from papal authority for some time, and that few people had converted to Catholicism in a New World which had been conquered by violence and force.

The Act of the Warsaw Confederation (1573) led to a major debate over the significance and need for toleration. This situation was probably similar to that of Germany, with its debates over the Peace of Augsburg and that of France, with the Edict of Nantes. Polemical works provided the opportunity to discuss every aspect of theological, historical, sociological or psychological arguments, whether they favoured the Act of 1573 or not. The Act did not lead to notions of freedom of conscience and full toleration, but at least reflected the desire for coexistence in one state which allowed for a confessional minority alongside the dominant church. In the eyes of Protestants, this Act preserved the noble Republic of the wars of religion.

Polish readers' interest in Reformation works reporting on European events was fuelled by the belief that these events could recur in Poland. This view shows the growth of the belief that Poland and Europe were following the same historical path. In the sixteenth century, the belief in the specific destiny of the Estates, which was so powerful later, had not yet taken root. The satisfaction in having avoided religious wars was always tempered by the fear of seeing Poland torn by peasant revolts inextricably tied to the progress of the Reformation. In 1574, a spokesman for the nobility wrote 'You have seen how German lands reddened abundantly, fed by internal conflicts [...], you have seen the peasants' wars in Swiss lands, you have seen the peasants fighting against the nobility, the nobles against their prince, the prince against an evil emperor and miserable people in revolt'. By bringing up events occurring in Poland's neighbouring lands, Catholic propaganda could be sure of its readers' interest and of the success of its discourse.

Discussions on the Peasants' War in Germany or the Anabaptist 'kingdom' of Münster led (probably for the first time in Poland) to a more general debate on the influence of religious ideologies on the stability of social structures. In the light of the German experience, it seems that religious propaganda can shake social equilibrium. The debates provided the opportunity to teach readers certain stereotypes. By claiming that Lutheranism was akin to Anabaptism and that the latter was the cause of the Peasants' War, associations of ideas were made which were then often used in later political propaganda. Short-cuts were used to remind readers of certain events, such as 'The German fire' or the hope that 'things would not go the French way' in Poland, phrases which expressed the nobles' fear of religious wars in Poland. It was probably in this period that one began to alter the image of the past on a regular basis for propaganda purposes, without later scholars being able to determine whether these were conscious errors or not.

The Reformation books influenced not only the level of historical consciousness and socio-political ideas, but also played a role in inter-ethnic relations. By encouraging Polish publications in Ducal and Royal Prussia, Lutheranism helped in the development of Polish culture and language. On the other hand, Lutheranism had assimilation difficulties in Poland, due to its links with Leipzig and Wittenberg universities and to its use of German sermons and writings. But Aleksander Brückner's view is untenable, as he argues that in the sixteenth century, the Refor-mation revived a dying German feeling in the territory of Royal Prussia. In reality, this German sentiment was far from dead, especially as the minority Polish bourgeoisie could only count on itself in its struggle to preserve its language. Local authorities and the royal power had no interest in Polonization, not even in Cracow or Poznań. The monarchs were indifferent to the language spoken in Gdańsk, Toruń or Elbląg. Overall, indications are that reciprocal links existed between language and religion in Royal Prussia: the citizens of Gdańsk or Toruń, using German, adopted Lutheranism which was closer to them culturally and geographically, and in turn this reinforced their own national con-sciousness.

It is no coincidence that the confessional allegiance of Reformation works is dealt with last in this study. These are the most difficult ones to trace. Evaluating the number of people who joined the new faith influ-enced by books is problematic. Outside Royal Prussia, there was, how-ever, a striking parallel between the number of Protestant works entering Poland, including those edited there, and the growing sphere of influ-ence of Protestantism. In the Polish-Lithuanian territory, Protestants made up 16 to 20 per cent of the nobility, a smaller proportion of city-dwellers, and a very small proportion of peasants.

Protestant publications also influenced the work of Catholic theolo-gians. Through time, the latter began to be aware of the impact of printing on public opinion and to overcome their lack of interest for Polish, although this was a slow process. In the second half of the sixteenth century, the Jesuits still had to resist conservative opposition, which claimed that the publication of polemical works brought more inconveniences than advantages. In 1582, Alfonso de Pisa, a Spanish professor in the Jesuit college of Poznań attempted to convince General Claudio Aquaviva that the sponsorship of polemical works was the best financial investment. He wrote that the Jesuits had many preachers, 'but a single book means more than thousands of sermons, above all in

Poland, where the nobility does not normally live in the cities but in the countryside, and nobles can be reached more easily through books than through preachers'.

Among other factors, the influence of Protestant books led Catholics to show a greater degree of interest in the Old Testament. The excellent Polish translation of the Bible by the Jesuit Jakub Wujek borrowed heavily from the Antitrinitarian translation of the New Testament done by Marcin Czechowic. The censorship commission for Wujek's work, scenting 'heresy', radically modified his original text, which had been a fine translation, according to contemporary sources.

Finally, one should remember that later claims for freedom of expression stemmed from the struggle for freedom of printing and for the circulation of Reformation texts. Sixteenth-century Polish nobles easily brought the two together. The freedom of Reformation propaganda was closely linked to the general freedom of printing and of expression enjoyed by this social class thanks to its privileges. It is striking to note that in the seventeenth century, around 30 per cent of printers published panegyrics or other laudatory works, praising wholeheartedly the organization of the state as a noble republic.

In short, confessional polemics which stemmed above all from the Reformation brought a creative spark to sixteenth-century Polish culture, fuelled by opposition and criticism. The invention of printing preceded the start of the Reformation by more than half a century. Very rapidly, the printed book became a powerful means of propaganda in the hands of Protestants. The reciprocal links between Protestants and printing were so strong that it is impossible to determine which of Calvin and Luther's supporters or Gutenberg's adherents owed the most to the other. For the first time, alongside older means of communication – speech, art and music – religion put printing to use. It is true that both early Italian humanism and late Czech Hussites did without, but the upholders of the Reformation enthusiastically made use of the new technique. While Martin Luther was convinced that the truth of the Gospel was primarily heard – *Solae aures sunt organa Christiani* – Calvin proclaimed that if everyone learned to read, no one would pay any attention to 'pagan images'.

What did Protestantism bring to the culture of the Polish 'Golden Age' and to the greater transmission of books? As in every place penetrated by this movement, often following the ideas of the Renaissance, Protestantism contributed to the spread and the enrichment of the Polish language. The extent of religious debates also led to an increase in the demand for books. Furthermore, the Reformation pushed the production of books outside cities like Cracow and Poznań, by expanding the number of non-urban presses. Leaving aside the presses of

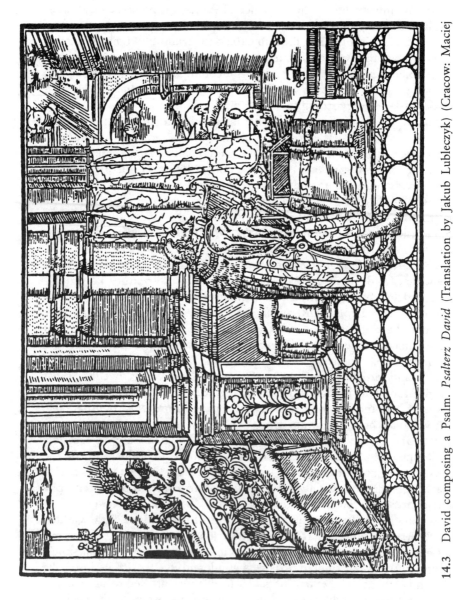

14.3　David composing a Psalm. *Psalterz David* (Translation by Jakub Lubleczyk) (Cracow: Maciej Wirzbięta, 1558)

Königsberg and Gdańsk, in a 20–year period there were nine printing houses serving the Reformation. The total number of these even doubled in 1560, and were naturally surrounded by a literary and cultural milieu. However, these presses did have one weakness, namely their dependence on a local patron, rendering their existence precarious. If the patron died or changed confessions, the press could disappear. But, the rapid progress of Protestantism could not have taken place without the fundamental tools of the book and printing.

Select bibliography

Buchwald-Pelcowa, P. (ed.) *Polonia typographica saeculi sedecimi*, VIII, *Aleksander Augezdecki. Królewiec-Szamotuły, 1549–1561*, IX–X; A. Kawecka-Gryczowa (ed.) *Maciej Wirzbięta. Kraków, 1555/7–1605*, XI; A. Kawecka-Gryczowa (ed.) *Maciej i Paweł Wirzbiętowie. Kraków 1555/7–1609* (Wrocław, 1972–81).

Górski, K., 'Zagadnienie słownictwa reformacji polskiej', *Odrodzenie w Polsce*, III/2, *Historia języka* (Warsaw, 1962).

Jobert, A., *De Luther à Mohila: La Pologne dans la crise de la chrétienté, 1517–1648* (Paris, 1974).

Kawecka-Gryczowa, A., *Drukarze dawnej Polski od XV do XVIII wieku*, I/1 *Małopolska: wiek XV–XVI*, III/1 *Wielkopolska*, IV *Pomorze* (Wrocław, 1962–83).

Kawecka-Gryczowa, A., 'Rola drukarstwa poškiego w dobie Odrodzenia', in *Z dziejów polskiej ksiazki w okresie Renesansu. Studia i materiały* (Wrocław, 1975), pp. 7–163.

Kawecka-Gryczowa, A., 'Miejsce książki w kulturze polskiej XVI wieku', in A. Wyczański (ed.) *Polska w epoce Odrodzenia państwo-spoleczeństwo-kultura* (Warsaw, 1986).

Kot, S., 'Le mouvement antitrinitaire au XVIe et au XVIIe siècles', *Humanisme et Renaissance*, 4 (1937), pp. 16–58, 109–56.

Kot, S., 'Szymon Budny. Der grösste Häretiker Litauens im 16 Jahrhundert', in *Wiener Archiv für Geschichte des Slaventums und Osteuropas, Festschrift für H. F. Schmid* (Vienna, 1956), vol. 2.

Nadolski, B., 'Zapomniany toruński tłumacz Lutra Jan Krakowczyk', *Pamiętnik Literacki*, 53 (1965), 139–47.

Szelińska, W., 'Książka różnowiercza na uniwersytecie krakowskim w początkach reformacji', *Roczniki Biblioteczne*, 29 (1985), 85–114.

Tazbir, J., *A State without Stakes. Polish Religious Toleration in the Sixteenth and Seventeenth Centuries* (Warsaw, 1973).

Wyczański, A., 'Alphabétisation et structure sociale en Pologne au XVIe siècle', *Annales, économies, société, civilisations*, 29 (1974), 259–69.

CHAPTER FIFTEEN

The book and the Reformation in Denmark and Norway, 1523–40

Anne Riising

In 1521/23 after Sweden's breach of the Nordic Union, the Danish monarchy reigned from then onwards over Denmark, Norway, Iceland, the now Swedish provinces of Scania, Halland, Blekinge and the island of Gotland. The Duchy of Schleswig, united to that of Holstein, was a Danish fief, overseen by the Archbishop of Lund. The Reformation quickly affected Schleswig, a vital area for Denmark in many respects, though these inroads had little effect on printed books. Given that Norway played no role in the Reformation and that Iceland remained more or less Catholic until 1550, the centres of the movement were in Denmark and Scania.

During his reign, King Christian II (1513–23) sought to break the power of the Church and the nobility and to create a national reformed Catholic Church. But he met with no success and was forced to leave the kingdom. Although he was removed for political reasons, his departure was justified by supposedly 'heretical' sympathies. Indeed, Christian II had had direct contacts with Wittenberg, calling a court preacher briefly to Denmark from there. But during his reign, there were no schismatic Lutherans in Denmark. Henrik Smid's preface to the *Hortulus synonymorum* (Copenhagen, 1520) mentioned Luther for the first time in a Danish book, in which he was praised only as a great humanist, and his Reformation work was not even mentioned.

The new king Frederick I (1523–33) was totally dependent on the prelates and nobles: he promised to them that he would maintain the Church's allegiance to Rome and would fight Lutheran heresy. In spite of these declarations of intent, the king soon began to favour the Reformation. The new preaching swept through the countryside and in particular the cities, where many people hoped for the return of Christian II, who had become a Lutheran.

Through royal letters, the king put the preachers outside episcopal jurisdiction, and took them under his protection. In 1526, the ties with Rome were severed. In 1527, the king declared in highly Lutheran terms that as the monarch, he could command bodies and goods, but not souls. From then on, everyone could preach the Gospel, as long as they avoided political propaganda. This toleration continued until the king's death, which was followed by an interregnum and a civil war, ended by the victory of Frederick's son, Christian III. After Christian, a fervent Lutheran, had deposed and imprisoned the bishops in 1536, the Lutheran Church was established. The Ecclesiastical Discipline, mainly written by Johannes Bugenhagen in 1537–39, put the seal on the Reformation. There was certainly much to be written in Danish, Latin and Icelandic before the Church could be firmly established and the clergy and people be properly taught. But the aim was to become strictly Lutheran, and the time for discussion was definitely past. Without the help of printing, all this would barely have been possible.

Printers and books

The *Breviarium ottiniense*, the first Danish book, was printed in Odense in 1482 by Johan Snell, a printer from Lübeck who later settled in Sweden. Lauritz Nielsen has counted more than 300 works appearing prior to 1550, taking into account Denmark's production, books written outside Denmark by Danes, for Danes, or in Danish. Many of these works are, however, only known via old catalogues or manuscript copies. A certain proportion of these works is probably lost.

Until 1520, there were only itinerant German or Dutch printers, working wherever they obtained orders. From 1523 to 1528 there was still no printing press at work in Denmark. The first Danish printer, Povl Reff, was also itinerant. After having been vice-chancellor of Copenhagen University, Reff, a canon, became a printer in the city from 1512 to 1519. In 1522, he published a few works in Nyborg. In 1530/31, he was called to Aarhus by its bishop to open a printing workshop in a recently abandoned Carmelite monastery. He only published Catholic works, but his press was closed in 1533. The task was continued by Hans Barth, a German, who established the printing workshop in Roskilde from 1534 to 1540; he printed Catholic works until 1536, as well as some Protestant texts. Another German, Hans Vingaard, became the official Reformation printer in Viborg from 1528 to 1531, then in Copenhagen until 1559. The great Reformer Hans Tausen may have called him to Viborg. Indeed, Tausen published his heartfelt thanks to God for having granted them a printer, to spread His Word to the people. And when Tausen went to Copenhagen, Vingaard followed soon afterwards.

Malmö can take credit for two printing presses, one of which belonged to a Swede, Olof Ulrichsson (1528–56) who worked for a number of years for the Swedish Bishop of Söderköping until King Gustav

closed down the workshop to avoid any Catholic propaganda.[1] But the
most remarkable printer/publisher was Christiern Pedersen, a canon of
Lund; he graduated as master of arts in Paris where he lived for a
number of years, writing and publishing many books from 1508 to
1515, and generally entrusting the printing to Josse Bade. In particular,
Pedersen published the *Gesta danorum* by Saxo Grammaticus and a
collection of Danish sermons with the Epistles and the Gospels (Paris,
1515; 2nd edn, Leipzig, 1518). He returned to Denmark, but in 1523
he followed Christian II into exile, and became his chaplain in Holland.
There, he translated, compiled and edited many books which Vorsterman
printed in Antwerp, and then acquired equipment there, enabling him
to open a printing house in Malmö in 1532, managed by the Flemish
Johannes Hillenius van Hoochstraten. After several fruitful years, the
workshop was closed in 1535.[2]

No printing press operated in Norway until 1643. In Iceland, the
bishop Jón Arason employed a Swedish priest Jón Matthiason, who
printed a breviary in 1534, but after 1536, Icelandic works were imported from Denmark. After 1556, Copenhagen thus held the monopoly on printing.

Most printers only had very modest equipment, often transferred
from one to another. Beginning with simple gothic characters, sometimes even without engraved initials, they gradually acquired fonts,
typographical decorations, and other gothic characters (*schwabacher*
and *fraktur*); roman characters did not appear prior to 1538. The rare
woodcuts seem to have been imported. Apparently, printers generally
worked to order, and only published at their own risk small easily sold
works, such as school-books, novels and medical books, often bound
and sold by the printers themselves. Thus Vingaard had a bookshop in
Malmö. Polemical works were normally small quarto or octavo volumes of four to 80 pages, easily skimmed, copied or read out loud.
Probably because of the haste in production, typographical errors were
rampant, and punctuation was used without order or consistency. Local
printers, the evidence suggests, played an essential role in giving polemicists the opportunity for rapid attacks and counter-attacks, but they did
not have the resources of the great foreign printing houses. As late as
1548, Ludwig Dietz was called from Rostock to Copenhagen to print
the first complete Danish Bible: its publication was finished in 1550.
However, Danes who left Denmark like Christiern Pedersen often published in other countries: in Lübeck, Paris, Rostock, Magdeburg, Cologne and Wittenberg. This practice continued and grew after 1536,

[1] See p. 450.
[2] See pp. 193–4, 198.

when Denmark became a recognized part of Protestant Europe. By publishing in Wittenberg in Latin, the Danish authors could benefit from large distribution networks.

Books were sold in the markets, by German booksellers, and by all and sundry at the Sund Straits Fair. Christiern Pedersen was the only large-scale publisher, and even though there is no information on how he distributed his books from Paris and Antwerp, it seems certain that he came into Denmark with a large number of copies of his works.

In 1532, Knud Gyldenstjerne printed a translation of Luther's *Small Catechism* rendered by Jörgen Jensen Sadolin. Gyldenstjerne was a Catholic bishop, while Sadolin was a committed Lutheran, imposed on the bishop by a royal edict. The translation was Sadolin's idea, and Gyldenstjerne's name may have been put on the title-page as a courtesy. But it is also possible that the bishop paid for the publication, as it was destined for the diocesan clergy.

The Danish New Testament, published at Christian II's instigation, was printed by Melchior Lotter. The title-page gave Leipzig as place of publication, but Lotter had a printing press in Wittenberg, in Cranach's house where the exiled king lived. Leipzig was mentioned on the title-page because it was considered to be more neutral than Wittenberg. The book was distributed in Scandinavia partly through Antwerp, but mainly directly from Wittenberg by German booksellers.

In Denmark, there were no booksellers nor professional publishers before 1551. In that year, a German immigrant, Claus Föerd, founded a firm in Copenhagen. At the same time, Poul Knobloch published a number of Danish books in Lübeck, produced by various German printers. The print-runs and costs are unfortunately not known, apart from those of the 1550 Bible, which cost 5 marks, and 2 000 of the approximately 3 000 copies were distributed to Danish and Norwegian churches.

During the years of confessional strife, nearly all Danish books were printed in Danish, sometimes even in a slightly dialect form. Thus the intended readership was clearly Scandinavian. By chance, a Scottish work was also published in Denmark, by a Scottish evangelical, John Gau, who fled his country after the death of Patrick Hamilton. He settled in Malmö where there were a number of other Scots, and in 1533 he published *The Richt Way to the Kingdom of Heuine*, a translation of a book by Pedersen published in 1531 with the same title.

Original Danish works were usually ones of controversy, and a survey of these can quickly be done. Translations, or more commonly free adaptations played an important role in transmitting Protestant ideas. These works were generally popular and were widely available in numerous editions. Only painstaking studies can show – and have shown in many cases – which edition formed the basis for which translation. In most cases, the translations were done from German or Low German. There is one case of a German book, Johann Toltz's *Handbüchlein für junge Christen* which was first translated into Swedish by Olaus Petri,[3] and then from Swedish into Danish (Malmö, 1529; Viborg, 1530).

Apart from translations, the importing of original works was clearly crucial, but there is no means of measuring such a phenomenon. However, it is at least clear that Luther's German and Latin works were well known.

Authors and translators

Leading figures

On the Catholic side, bishops were administrators rather than theologians, and they limited themselves to writing a few unpublished letters warning against heresy. Although certain canons, particularly in Lund, took an active part in disputations against Lutherans, they wrote little, or what they did write has been lost. In 1530, the king asked both Catholic prelates and Protestant preachers to write down their views. The bishops called in some German theologians for assistance. The Protestant preachers insisted on the use of Danish, since public opinion was being sought. In contrast, the bishops offered a Latin *Confutatio*, tightly argued, logical and well structured; they may have wished to present it before an ecumenical council or an ecclesiastical court. This very traditional text has never been printed, perhaps because of the lack of royal support.

Apart from this, Catholic production stemmed from a single author, the Carmelite Povl Helgesen. This child of Danish and Swedish parents may have been an oblate. Learned, talented, and profoundly shaped by humanism, he taught at the university for a time. He passionately sought to rid the Church of its abuses, but through internal reform without any lay intervention. Because of his humanism and his zeal for reform, he was not popular with the bishops, and was even suspected of heresy for a time. Indeed in 1524 he translated Luther's *Betbüchlein*, and distributed manuscript copies of it. In his edition (Rostock: Michaelis, 1526), he clearly stated that there was no salvation outside the church, that only in the Church could the means of grace be found, as well as the only true interpretation of Scripture. Here as elsewhere, he made

---

[3] See p. 457.

reference to the Bible and to the Church Fathers. In general, he saw the cause of the Church's decline in priestly ignorance, primarily of patristics, but he hoped that with the invention of printing, this ignorance would be defeated. He agreed with Luther in denouncing the sale of indulgences and other spiritual goods. Apart from suppressing the criticisms of the Ave Maria and adding certain passages on the Mass and on Purgatory, he made no changes in Luther's prayer-book. In 1528, he tried to influence the course of events in Sweden by printing a letter to King Gustav.[4] He seems to have died in 1534.

Among the Protestants, there were two former Carmelites, disciples of Helgesen, trained in their monastery and at the University of Copenhagen. Frands Vormodsen was Dutch, and a great friend of Helgesen, but in 1529, he went to Malmö and became a preacher and professor in a school for evangelical preachers. After 1536, Vormodsen was appointed as superintendent of Lund. Peder Laurentsen was Danish. He lived for a time in the Carmelite monastery in Assens, then left the order and went to Malmö. Another leading Protestant was Hans Tausen, a minor nobleman, who was a member of the order of the Knights of St John. He studied in Wittenberg and in other universities, and thus had a better level of education than his peers. In 1525/26 he was sent to Viborg in Jutland, but was soon expelled from the order because of his sermons. Protected by the king and looked after by the citizens of Viborg, he continued to preach, in all likelihood with the support of his future brother-in-law, Jörgen Jensen Sadolin. As for Sadolin, the events of his life are only known from 1526, when equipped with a masters of arts degree and a royal letter, he opened another school for evangelical preachers in Viborg. In 1529, the king called Tausen to Copenhagen. In 1532, Sadolin became the Bishop of Funen's assistant, and later succeeded him as superintendent. These four men were the main Protestant leaders in the following years. Their actions were supported by a growing number of preachers, almost all former monks or priests, protected by the king and in close contact with urban councils.

Polemic

Controversies began around the New Testament. In 1524, rumours began to circulate that the exiled King Christian II intended to send thousands of heretical books to Denmark. In that year, Luther's works were banned, but the Scriptures could still be distributed freely. In fact, Christian II sent in the New Testament discussed above, with introduc-

---

[4] See p. 459.

15.1   First page of the New Testament (Leipzig [Wittenberg?]: Melchior Lotter, 1524)

tions (by Luther, but published anonymously) which were polemical in their interpretation of Scripture, of the priesthood of all believers and of justification by faith. However, these introductions were much less polemical than the letter of the former mayor of Malmö, Hans Mikkelsen, which was inserted before the Epistle to the Romans. Mikkelsen passionately pleaded for a Lutheran interpretation of the Epistle, attacked the church, indulgences, pilgrimages, etc. and criticized the clergy for having sinned against God by deposing the king. This highly political letter was often cut out of books and distributed covertly for fear of later censorship. The first edition was seized by the authorities in Denmark and Sweden, but a second edition rapidly followed. As this did not yet satisfy demand, Christiern Pedersen published his own revised translation in Antwerp in 1529, with a few prefaces by Luther. However, Pedersen did not reject the Epistle of James. His interpretation of Scripture was conservative without, however, being Catholic. He rejoiced that everyone could now read and understand the Word of God, since in fact the common man understood it much better than the wise scholars. The first Antwerp edition was anonymous, perhaps because of the regent, Margaret of Austria, an intransigent Catholic. After her death in 1530, the second edition bore Pedersen's name and the title-page was decorated with the three nordic royal coats of arms – a clear reference to Christian II. Once Pedersen focused on publishing, he must have found a secure niche, as the call for Danish Bibles seems to have been great. In any event, these publications were important for discussions in the following years, as polemicists took their arguments from Scripture and directed them at lay people highly familiar with the Bible.

The letter-preface by Hans Mikkelsen provoked a *Response to Hans Mikkelsen* by Helgesen (Rostock: Michaelis, 1527). He spoke clearly in favour of the Church, as an official spokesman of the bishops, and claimed in particular that if laymen tried to interpret Scripture without the direction of the Church, only opposition and heresy would be the outcome. He also justified the rebellion against Christian II, in which he himself also took part, as the king had not acted as a truly God-fearing monarch. Thus from the first publications onward, one of the Reformation's central questions was raised, that of Scriptural interpretation. Everyone, both Protestant and Catholic, agreed that faith should be based on Scripture, but who could be its interpreter?

The preachers always presented a united front against the bishops, but there was no apparent co-ordination in their opposition. Geographic reasons easily explain why two translations of the anonymous work, *Eine tröstliche Disputation* were published in 1530, one in Antwerp by Pedersen, and the other in Viborg. But it is rather surprising that both Sadolin and Laurentsen published reports of their meeting with the bishops in 1530. Clearly the factors which united them were stronger than that which divided them, but there were visible differences of opinion between Viborg and Malmö.

As everywhere else, the Danish Reformation had its stronghold in the cities. The peasants revolted against economic exploitation and priestly absenteeism, but as far as we know, they did not oppose doctrines, unlike in the cities. Malmö was actively in contact with northern German cities, and through these, with more southern cities such as Nuremberg, but not with Saxony and Wittenberg. The Stettin and Stralsund preachers turned up at the fairs along the Sund straits. Thus, the Malmö Protestants were influenced much more strongly by a radical biblicism and by pamphlets than by Luther. Social unrest, often clearly anti-clerical and linked to religion opened the way for more radical ideas such as, for example, the project to make Malmö and Copenhagen into independent free cities united with Lübeck.

Already in 1528, a purely Danish liturgy was printed in Malmö. Even though certain sections came from Luther's *Deutsche Messe*, the greater part was influenced by the *Nürnberger Messe*. In 1529, the Reformation took hold in several northern German cities. Inspired by this situation,

Malmö city council organized an evangelical church, secularized ecclesiastical possessions, and was strongly intolerant of Catholics. In the *Book of Malmö*, Laurentsen justified and defended the Reformation. It was clearly the duty of civil authorities to reform the Church, even though the communities also had something to say about this. His work was not a reasoned argument, but rather an accumulation of Scriptural quotations. He insisted that the divine Word was God's Law, and that everyone could and should learn and follow it. Everything that was not based on Scripture in the Church was to be abolished as a sinful human invention and money given for Masses was to be used for schools, hospitals, and other charitable works. Clearly, his attitude was one of opposition to hierarchy, and was almost revolutionary in a social sense. Catholic liturgies, ornate and costly, and masses for cattle, for headaches, etc. were entirely worthless, and done only for money. As a contrast, he depicted the common man, sitting on a dung-cart, and glorifying God. Clearly, Laurentsen wished to abolish Church Latin. His rather superficial remarks on the sacraments indicate a Zwinglian faith.

Many of his ideas may have come from Urbanus Rhegius's *Erklärung der Zwölff Artikel*, translated into Danish in 1528 (Rostock: Michaelis), but omitting Rhegius's original and rather polemical introduction, and reorienting the work slightly in a more humanist than Lutheran vein. The translator may have been Helgesen, who at the time still hoped for a reform of the Catholic Church. He also composed an answer to the *Book of Malmö*, only known in manuscript form and which may never have been printed, or the printed version has been lost. But the precentor of Lund, Adser Pedersen, published an attack against the city council and defended the worth of the Catholic Mass, though this work has not survived. For him, priests could bear witness to the faith without preaching. The mayor, Jep Nielsen, responded with Zwinglian views of the Eucharist, and declared coldly that the priest was a preacher, and was paid to preach. Everyone could at all times bear witness through their way of life.

In 1533, Laurentsen published two small works, in which he repeated the usual attacks against the stupidity, avarice, laziness, adultery etc. of the clergy and vigorously defended the right and even the duty of priests to marry. He noted that Scripture made no mention of celibacy and that the councils and Church Fathers did not know of it. He freely quoted from these last two sources, even giving them the same weight as Scripture. In fact, he never explained his views coherently. His works were purely polemical and were even nothing more than acid commentaries on Catholic texts.

Vordmodsen offered the same Scriptural interpretation, but in general he held more radical opinions. In two works, he sought to explain the differences between evangelical and Catholic teaching, first in 1531 then in 1534 in *Twenty-One excellent Articles*. In this work, everything rests on the antitheses between truth and falsehood, God and the Devil, etc. The usual attacks against good works, monks, mendicant orders, bishops, saints, purgatory, indulgences, the Mass, etc. were combined with a defence of clerical marriage. Vormodsen appealed to the mayor and council of Malmö as his natural judges in this conflict.

Christiern Skrok, a former priest, also devoted many pages to a justification of married priests. The slightly comical preoccupation with this issue was not only a personal justification, but also a counter-attack against a work of Helgesen which has not survived, distributed in all the dioceses, defending celibacy and seeking to discredit married priests publicly as oath-breakers. Neither Laurentsen nor Vormodsen cited contemporary sources, but they did not oppose the practice of married priests.

In 1529, Oluf Chrysostemos gave a solemn speech in Latin hexameters, the *Lamentatio Ecclesiae*, at the university. He belonged to Helgesen's circle, and at the time was hesitating whether to take the step and become a Protestant. He lamented the general decline of society. Studies were neglected, the saints attacked, the old heresies were reappearing, etc., but he also criticized the lazy shepherds who sheared their sheep, the bishops whose lives were unedifying, ignorant priests, etc. He only saw a pale glimmer of hope in the poor but sober men who dedicated their lives to their studies, and were ready to undergo anything in the hope of better days. His speech was a sign of the humanists' aristocratic assurance, and of their confidence in being as far away from the noble bishops as from the proletarian priests. This was probably a major reason why humanism could not become a popular movement. Chrysostemos sent his poem to Vormodsen and left him to deal with it as he saw fit. Vormodsen and Laurentsen published it in 1529, with a preface and a conclusion and added marginal notes so that the critique originally directed against Lutheranism was redirected against the Anabaptists. In the conclusion, Vormodsen explained that the numerous typographical errors were not his fault but that of the printer Ulrichssön. As an example, Vormodsen pointed out that in the introduction, hypocrites and *imposturas ipsorum* were mentioned but that the printer had composed *imposturas episcoporum* and could not or would not change it in spite of Vormodsen's numerous complaints.

While radical Biblicism held sway in Malmö, Viborg, and later Copenhagen were the centres of Lutheranism, ever since Tausen had become aware of Luther's ideas and had adopted them. Following a letter warning against heresy from the Bishop of Funen, Tausen printed a *Brief Response to the Bishop's letter* (1529). He began, like Laurentsen

Edt kozt antſwoz till biſpeſſ ſendhæ‑
bzeff aff Othenſe huilcketh handtil‑
ſkzeeff the bozgheræ ı wıbozg och Olbozg/
raadhendheſſ theunũ ath bluffwæ wbewozedhæ
mz thenñe Euangeliſche lerdom/ Fom gudh haff‑
wer nu aff ſyn beſøndhezligh naadhæ ſeend oſſ/
aff Hans Tawſſen pzedickeræ ı wıbozg.

Chzıſtus Matth. rrıij
We ether i ſchrifftkloghæ och phariſeer/ i øghō
næſchalckæ/ Fom lycke hymerngſſruighe fozjmē‑
neſkenæ/ ſielff wille i icke ther md/ och ey ladhç
ı indgoo thm̄ Fom ghierñæ wilphç.

15.2   Hans Tausen, *Edt kort antswor till bispenss sendhaebreff* [*Brief response to the Bishop's letter*] (Viborg: Hans Vingaard, 1529)

and Vormodsen, by showing the contrast between God's Word and man's word, and he attacked the ways in which the bishops exploited and tormented the people. In his scriptural interpretation, Tausen was closer to Luther and he made a distinction between the dead letter and the living Word of God. The ability to interpret Scripture was not a learned privilege, but a gift of the Holy Spirit. Tausen's arguments used biblical quotations, without citing them at random. Even though in his eyes, as for many others, Christ was a master whose example should be followed, he was also concerned about personal sin, salvation, and justification by faith. In Malmö, the Reformation was perceived as a rediscovery of the Word and as freedom from clerical tyranny. Only Tausen noted Luther's importance, clearly supported by Sadolin, who translated Luther's *Bekenntnis* in 1529, his *Kleiner Katechismus* and Johannes Bugenhagen's *Summa der Seligkeit* in 1532, and the *Confessio Augustana* in 1533.

The Mass was probably the most debated question, after the interpretation of Scripture. It provided the grounds for a debate between Tausen and Helgesen, which proved the importance of local printers as well. In the autumn of 1530, Helgesen wrote a book on the Mass and sent the manuscript to the city council of Copenhagen, hoping to provoke a response by Tausen. Tausen completed his answer on 8 December 1530 and sent it to Helgesen, who added a postscript to his original book and published it on 21 April 1531. Angered at Helgesen's unwillingness to publish his answer, Tausen hurriedly gave it to a printer who published it on 1 July 1531. Helgesen accused Tausen of Zwinglianism, but the latter fiercely refuted the allegation. They may have been the only two polemicists able to engage in a truly theological discussion.

For many others, the question of the Mass revolved around the right of lay people to receive communion in both kinds as well as the issue of votive Masses, which were continually criticized and ridiculed. The unceasing condemnation of the Church's avarice in this area made the Mass a welcome subject for satire. In 1533, Christiern Pedersen translated two of the best known satires: Nicolaus Manuel's *Dialogus* – published in verse, unlike the original, perhaps for a dramatic performance – and *Vigilies*, a coarse parody of the Mass, only teaching the common people that priests invented the Mass for money, in order to commit adultery. In 1530, foreign Catholic theologians were ridiculed in satirical ballads, and it is probable that many other such works were lost.

Already in 1528, Tausen translated Nicolaus Hermann's *Ein Mandat Jesu Christi*. He may have attributed it to Luther, because of the letters M[elchior] L[otter] on the title-page. But the Lutheran features of this work were added by Tausen himself, and thus he modified the meaning of the prophecies somewhat. Another popular work was the anonymous *Ein Gespräch zwischen vier Personen* translated in 1529/30. The two works were so effectively rewritten to take into account the local conditions and people of Jutland that they were believed to be original Danish writings until recently. These satires and other similar works did not present any theological arguments, but only bitter and savage criticism of abuses. They clearly held a wide popular appeal.

Both parties remained in entrenched positions throughout the period, and publishing their opinions doubtlessly contributed to their rigidity. Any small movement was purely tactical, caused by political changes. Helgesen's pessimism increased: in 1532 he published a book on Luther, directed at the Danish nobility. He had not altered his view of Luther, but pleaded for toleration for Catholics and rejected Protestant persecution. In 1533, he translated and edited a section of the 1530 *Confutatio*, with an introduction giving it a new direction. He left aside the project for an ecumenical council or ecclesiastical court which would resolve the controversy, as the king had shown that he could not be relied upon. The only solution remaining was an appeal to public opinion. After Helgesen's death in 1534 no more Catholic works were published. During the civil war, some pamphlets appeared linking the Catholic party with the nobility, the Protestants with the cities, and violently criticizing the preachers. In fact, these pamphlets were more political than religious, and in any event, the civil war divided two Protestant parties.

Style

In polemical works, and in most other texts, the style was kept simple and direct. Arguments were often presented in an easy to follow question and answer form. Nicknames and imaginative epithets were freely used on both sides. In fact, they were no more numerous, nor worse than in St Bernard's writings or than in contemporary sermons. In the heat of the debate, problems were simplified in the extreme, and slogans were designed more for popular appeal than to present deeply reasoned arguments. Often, the work had as its basis, 'They say that we are liars, but we say that they are the liars'. The cementing of positions meant that controversy could not become a dialogue, and no one could admit the truth of any criticism from opponents. Helgesen saw very clearly the inconsistencies among preachers' opinions: they may have decided how to put their ideas into practice only after 1536. In their enthusiasm for everyone's right to interpret Scripture, they forgot that the general population might not be in agreement with their aims. The Protestants' view of the Church as a community of true believers was a beautiful construct, but they did not take into account the fact that some people did not wish to become true believers, and refused to be educated. The question of ecclesiastical discipline required much more thought. Indeed Helgesen made a point of noting that the Protestant areas of Europe were not exactly an ideal model of love and fraternal concord.

Prayer-books and catechisms

Polemical writings, offering controversy alone, suddenly disappeared after 1536. Readers looking for instruction and comfort had access to a number of translations, generally done by Christiern Pedersen. Luther's

Betbüchlein was published several times, among others in a vast compilation, *The New Book of Prayers* (Magdeburg, 1531) where the *Betbüchlein* translated by Helgesen was joined by various prayers by Otto Brunfels, Georg Schmaltzing, Johann Slüter, by the first Danish translation of Luther, *Die deutsch Litanei*, and by Oecolampadius's *Testament Jesu Christi*. Pedersen translated many small edifying and catechetical works by Luther. Even though he was a sincere Protestant, Pedersen never understood nor accepted the Lutheran opposition between the Law and the Gospel. In 1531, he published a translation of Luther's *Sermon vom Leiden und Creuz*, but added to it a series of chapters from Thomas à Kempis's *Imitatio Christi*, which clashed with Luther's ideas. In the same way, he translated Agricola's *Hundertunddreissig Fragestücken*, adapting it to a theology of imitation, and seemingly remained oblivious to Agricola's completely opposite views.

Catechetical works like the *Handbüchlein* and Johann Toltz's *Eine tröstliche Disputation* were relatively well distributed, but Luther's *Kleiner Katechismus* outstripped them both. It was translated into Danish in 1532 and 1537 by two different people, and was often republished later.

After 1536, as every cleric had to preach, the less talented needed sermon collections. Tausen's collection was published first, and then those of Anton Corvinus.

The unrestricted development of Protestant communities inevitably led to liturgical chaos. Tausen composed a liturgy for Vespers, which has not survived. In 1528, both Viborg and Malmö had Danish Masses. Malmö's Mass was published in different versions in 1528, 1535 and 1539, while the Copenhagen manuals appeared in 1535 and 1538. The publication of hymns, whether in translation or original compositions accompanied the printing of the liturgy. The hymns were rapidly adopted everywhere, both to teach the faithful, and for propaganda. Helgesen hated all church singing, especially because of the high-pitched women's voices.

Claus Mortensen, a preacher in Malmö, published a now lost hymn-book through Ludwig Dietz in Rostock. In total, 12 hymn-books are known about prior to 1568, but six of these are lost, two are incomplete, and one is known only in a later edition. Thus only three original and complete hymn-books survived. These hymn-books generally included the liturgy.

The Ecclesiastical Discipline was intended to end the liturgical chaos by following Wittenberg's model. It expressly forbade the publication of liturgical works without the approval of the university and the superintendents, and specifically forbade the use of Danish words in the

Gregorian chant 'like Münster does'. This interdiction was probably directed against Vormodsen who, together with Claus Mortensen published the 1539 Malmö Mass with hymns of this kind, but otherwise had no intention of imitating Münster. For the Reformers as for the humanists, the use of the vernacular was self-evident, but Luther, and thus Tausen as well, wanted to keep parts of the liturgy in Latin for the sake of continuity, while the Malmö preachers wanted the liturgy only in Danish. The Ecclesiastical Discipline followed the Wittenberg model, and authorized services in Latin, especially in order to maintain Latin as a living language and to have schoolboys able to sing. In fact, Latin services continued on feast days until 1685.

Ecclesiastical Discipline: the Ordinatio ecclesiastica, 1537/39

In 1536, the Reformation was fully established and the Church became a national church under the king's authority, following the Lutheran model. A system of independent communities closely collaborating with local civil authorities was possible in the cities, but was not suited to a primarily rural society. Above all, it did not suit the king, who clearly saw the advantages of a Lutheran *Landeskirche*. Tausen had always asked the king for a reform of the Church, not as an emergency measure, but by virtue of the monarch's divine right, similar to that of Old Testament rulers. Christian III, a fervent Lutheran passionately interested in theological questions, immediately took on the direction of the Church, even in doctrinal questions. His closest adviser was not one of the pioneers but Peder Palladius who after six years' stay in Wittenberg was a solid Lutheran, in no way involved in the struggles of previous years. The Ecclesiastical Discipline insisted on the now definitive order of God and the true faith as expressed in the *Confessio Augustana*. These features could not be altered nor discussed, while royal decisions regarding practical organization could be modified in the light of changed circumstances.

The readers

No estimate of the literate population is possible, but there were certainly more readers in the cities than in the countryside, as councillors, merchants, artisans and many others could read, including many women. The actual existence of printed works probably stimulated many to read. The use of Danish clearly indicates that the intended readership is not one which understood Latin, but rather Danish. Even though in their books the preachers addressed themselves generally to the man of the people, it is doubtful whether such simple men on their dung-carts, as in Laurentsen's favourite image, actually read at all. Readers were more likely to be found among educated lay people, mainly in the cities. Nobles clearly read as well, but they were mainly Catholic, and in any case would not have appreciated being linked with the general population. A few of Helgesen's writings were addressed directly or indirectly to the nobility. The leading polemicists frequently addressed each other through the medium of printed works, but their actual objective must have been the undecided reader, who could still be influenced.

For the illiterate, woodcuts in pamphlets and satires generally spoke for themselves. Pedersen's translation of Luther's *Passional*, with woodcuts illustrating the biblical quotations, was an excellent primer. As for hymns and songs, these could rapidly be learned off by heart.

Censorship

Luther's books were banned in 1524, but the measure was rarely put into practice, as Helgesen distributed copies of his translation of the *Betbüchlein* in the same year. In any event, the prohibition disappeared during the period of toleration, although the king complained about works which, under cover of Scripture, contained propaganda for Christian II; he probably had Hans Mikkelsen's letter in mind. The Ecclesiastical Discipline explicitly stated that in future, any book dealing with theology or politics, in Danish, German or Latin, could not be printed or imported without the authorization of the university and the superintendents. Concretely, a close eye could be kept on Danish printers, but the prohibition on imports, repeated on several occasions, was almost impossible to police. Furthermore, there was no question of controlling the reading of the increasing number of Danes travelling and studying abroad, nor what they brought back with them.

The Reformation was established without bloodshed. There may have been a few black eyes and bruises here and there, but not a single martyrdom took place on one side or the other. The remaining chapters, together with several monasteries and convents, were allowed to die away naturally, and bishops and abbots were quietly put into retirement. They had to live quietly and to conform to certain practices such as attendance at sermons. Public disputations which learned people could attend took place between canons and Lutherans, but naturally no Catholic books were permitted to appear. The Ecclesiastical Discipline asked priests to treat gently those who remained Catholic, but Peder Palladius insisted on attacking Catholicism. However, attention gradually moved away from Catholics to members of different Protestant groups, considered by the strictly Lutheran Church as abominable heretics.

Select bibliography

Andersen, N. K., *Confessio Hafniensis* (Copenhagen, 1954).

Bogvennen 1982 (Copenhagen, 1982).

Den danske kirkes historie (Copenhagen, 1959, 1965) vols 3–4.

Dunkley, E., *The Reformation in Denmark* (London, 1948).

Gierow, K., *Den evangeliska bönelitteraturen in Danmark 1526–1575* (Lund, 1948).

Nielsen, L., *Dansk bibliografi 1482–1550* (Copenhagen, 1919).

Nielsen, L., *Dansk bibliografisk atlas 1482–1600* (Copenhagen, 1919).

Poulsen S. H., (ed.), *Danske Messebøger fra reformationstiden* (Copenhagen, 1959).

Reformations-perspektiver (Aarhus, 1987) (*Acta Jutlandica*, **62/3**; Teol. series 14).

Schwaiger, G., *Die Reformation in den nordischen Ländern* (Munich, 1962).

Schwarz Lausten, M., *Christian den 3. og kirken 1537–1559* (Copenhagen, 1987).

CHAPTER SIXTEEN

The book and the Reformation in the Kingdom of Sweden, 1526–71

Remi Kick

The kingdom of Sweden became independent in 1521. The geo-political entity which then freed itself from Danish domination matched the Swedish ecclesiastical province. The Archbishop of Uppsala oversaw seven dioceses: Uppsala, Linköping, Skara, Strängnäs, Västerås, Växjö and in Finland, Turku. Indeed until the nineteenth century, Finland was part of Sweden. The dates chosen for this chapter are those marking two significant events: the first Swedish work on the Reformation appeared in 1526, and the Ecclesiastical Ordinance which gave the Swedish Church its definitive structure was published in 1571.

The dissolution of the Union of Calmar of 1397, which had united the nordic lands under a single crown occurred in the midst of violent tensions, in which the Church, its political role and its wealth played an important role. Indeed, the Church was a third power, united in turn with the national party and with the union party, in an attempt to preserve its power and independence. Christian II, who acceded to the Danish throne in 1515, managed to be crowned in Sweden in 1520. Soon afterwards, a brief war of liberation carried out with the support of Lübeck led to his total eviction. Gustav Vasa (1496–1560), the leader of the national party, was elected king in 1523. His iron control made him a strong power, even over the Church. As a large proportion of the episcopal seats were vacant, he took the opportunity to choose bishops loyal to him. Furthermore, financial pressures led him to take an interest in ecclesiastical wealth. Within this political context, his attention was drawn to the new doctrine which had begun to be broadcast in Scandinavia, beginning in German merchant circles. Soon two clerics

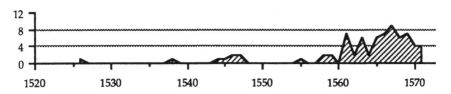

Figure 16.1 Religious works (number of titles)

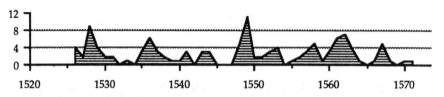

Figure 16.2   Secular works (number of titles)

began to play a leading role, namely Laurentius Andreae and Olavus Petri.

The book, a manufactured product[1]

Books were first printed in Sweden in 1483. In the following years, production remained low, especially as many printing presses only had an ephemeral existence: the 16 Swedish incunabula were all produced in Stockholm. The first book in Swedish appeared in 1495, and the next one only in 1514. Both were translations of works by Jean Gerson. From 1510 to 1519, Uppsala also had a printing press, directed by Paul Grijs. Uppsala's presses, re-established by Bartholomäus Fabri in 1525, were rapidly handed on to Georg Richolff. Furthermore, in 1523 the Bishop of Linköping, Hans Brask, installed a printing press in Söderköping, and appointed Olof Ulrichssön as its manager, in an effort to support the traditional church.

But from 1526 and throughout the period under discussion, Sweden only had a single press capable of producing books, as a result of a royal decision. In November 1526, Gustav Vasa ordered the closure of the Söderköping press, and seized the equipment of the printing press of the Uppsala diocese to transfer it to Stockholm. The Uppsala printer, Georg Richolff was put in charge of the royal printing press, and was entirely dependent on the royal administration. The Crown owned the equipment, and gave the Stockholm printer a workshop. It also granted him the income of a fief, and later at least, provided funding in kind for the manager of the press. For his part, the printer was to pay the salaries of the press's workforce and had to provide a part of the print-run to the Crown for free. This monopoly over book production as set

---

[1] For this section, see especially A. Adell, *Nya Testamentet på svenska 1526, till frågan om dess tillkomst och karaktär* (Lund, 1936); I. Collijn, *Sveriges bibliografi intill år 1600* (Uppsala, 1927–28), vols 1–2; G. E. Klemming and J. G. Nordin, *Svensk Boktryckeri-Histtoria 1483–1883, Jubileumsutgåva med tillägg 1983* (Stockholm, 1983), pp. 150–52; H. Schuck, *Den svenska förlagsbokhandels historia* (Stockholm, 1923), pp. 51–96.

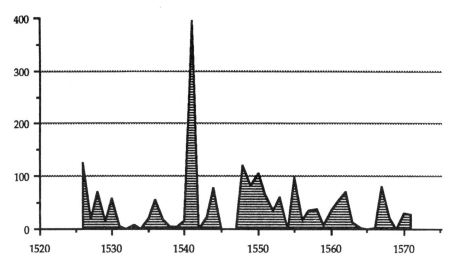

Figure 16.3   Religious works (number of sheets)

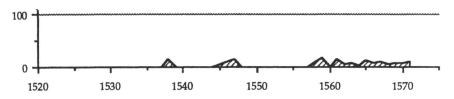

Figure 16.4   Secular works (number of sheets)

up by Gustav Vasa continued until the first decade of the seventeenth century.

The Swedish printing industry remained highly dependent on other countries, as printing equipment was imported. This was particularly true for the woodcuts which decorated Swedish works of the time, as these were all borrowed from continental, mainly German, editions. This may explain the limited use of illustrations in the products of the Swedish presses, as no engravings illustrated the few polemical works of our period, all of which appeared prior to 1540. Similarly, only in the seventeenth century did the Swedish printers benefit from locally produced paper: throughout the sixteenth century paper was imported as and when it was needed.

The first director of the royal printing house, Georg or Jürgen Richolff, only put his printer's mark in the 1526 edition of *A useful teaching*. The Swedish New Testament which appeared in the same year was also his work. Soon afterwards, he returned to Germany, to Hamburg and then to Lübeck. Those responsible for the royal presses from 1527 to 1539 are little known. Only Claes Pederson's name appeared once as the printer of the 1530 *Collection of Sermons*. Only when the complete Bible appeared in 1541 did a printer's name reappear on a work, and once again, it was Georg Richolff. Indeed, he was recalled for this work, but he returned to Lübeck after its completion in 1542. The royal presses were particularly productive under Richolff's leadership (1526, 1539–41), as well as around 1530, when Pederson's name appeared. Otherwise, no information about Pederson survives. Apart from these periods, the royal press's activities were very irregular, if not sporadic.

From 1543 to 1575, Amund Laurentsson was responsible for book production in Sweden. His name appeared on many works produced by the royal presses, for a total output during these years of around a hundred books and 70 royal ordinances. He also provided the first Finnish editions. His production levels, which did vary considerably, were of a modest level, even for a small printing house, averaging forty sheets or so (or 80 forms) composed annually.[2]

Thanks to the information provided by the account books on the importation of paper, one could determine the print-runs of editions and confirm the existence of works which have been partially or totally lost. Unfortunately, these sources, though incomplete, have not yet been exploited from this perspective.

As far as I am aware, the Swedish kingdom's book market has never been studied. Swedish book production was to a large extent dependent on decisions taken as much by the synods as by the diet, and thus reflected the need for books as perceived by these authorities. The Swedish New Testament of 1526, for example, was financed by a subscription imposed on the 1 700 parishes of the ecclesiastical province of Sweden and Finland.

The authors and the texts[3]

Until the end of the seventeenth century, the Church remained the largest book 'producer' in Sweden. The first non-religious work of the period, a Latin–Swedish lexicon, only appeared in 1538, and was in fact the largest secular work. Apart from royal mandates or ordinances, other secular works had a maximum length of 30 sheets. The only exception was Peder Svart's 1558 chronicle, which ran to 80 sheets in-octavo. Besides political works, educational texts and volumes of po-

---

[2] For this calculation per sheet, see above, pp. 17–18.

[3] All the bibliographical information is from I. Collijn's work as cited in note 1.

etry were also produced.[4] But secular works began to expand only after 1560. This statement takes into account the size of editions, as most secular works were only single-sheet placards.

Thus the relatively strict governmental control gave rather unique characteristics to printing production as compared with the rest of Europe: few polemical works, and instead texts intended to serve the policies of civil and ecclesiastical powers, together with a strong concern for the population's religious instruction. The lack of a pamphlet war in Sweden similar to that in various continental countries is a good example of its uniqueness.

Prior to the official establishment of Protestant worship (1526–39)

Between 1526 and 1540, the Reformation slowly spread through the country. The king was particularly anxious for a peaceful evolution, well prepared for by teaching and preaching. The king brought in from Strängnäs an archdeacon who was full of zeal in announcing the new doctrines, Laurentius Andreae (1470–1552) and his secretary Olavus Petri (1493–1552), and the king supported their actions to promote the Reformation in Stockholm. The preaching of the Word of God alone had already been made a requirement by the royal council in Vadstena in October 1524, although it was an ambiguous formula, and was repeated in the Diet of Västerås in June 1527 and at the Synod of Örebro in 1529. But the religious question was tied to political concerns, for the royal power was forced to appropriate some of the Church's wealth in order to repay the debt to Lübeck, incurred through the latter's assistance during the war of liberation. The reduction in the Church's goods as well as the first changes in the liturgy led to a popular revolt. Olavus Petri's brother, Laurentius (1499–1573), who had studied for three years in Wittenberg, was elected Archbishop of Uppsala at the end of August 1531, by an assembly of representatives of the entire ecclesiastical province. On 22 September, he was consecrated Archbishop in Stockholm.[5] In a letter dated 24 April 1533, the king urged the archbishop not to make any changes without his consent. The synod for central Sweden, meeting in Uppsala in October 1536 decided to impose the Swedish Ritual and asked that the Swedish mass be celebrated in the cathedrals, and as far as possible in the main churches. The synod also eliminated the vow of celibacy for priests, giving them a

---

[4] A first volume appeared in 1559 (Henricus Mollerus, *Epithalamion Esardo et Catharinae*), two in 1561, two further volumes in 1562 and one in 1564. The first volume is the longest one.

[5] See L.-M. Dewailly, 'Petri (Olaus et Laurentius)', *Catholicisme* 11, (1986), cols 93–5.

choice between marriage or effectual chastity. From October 1536, all three dioceses of central Sweden had a bishop who favoured the Reformation. In a letter dated 24 April 1539, Gustav reminded the archbishop that bishops no longer held temporal power. The king wanted the Reformation to be carried out first of all by the preaching of the faith and the fruits of this preaching, and only afterwards by the transformation of customs. The archbishop was responsible for the training and recruitment of priests able to preach the Gospel, and this responsibility was not limited to the archdiocese. This, then, was the setting for the first Protestant works to be printed in Sweden.

Almost every publication coming off the royal presses prior to 1540 dealt with religious matters. Hardly any polemical works appeared in

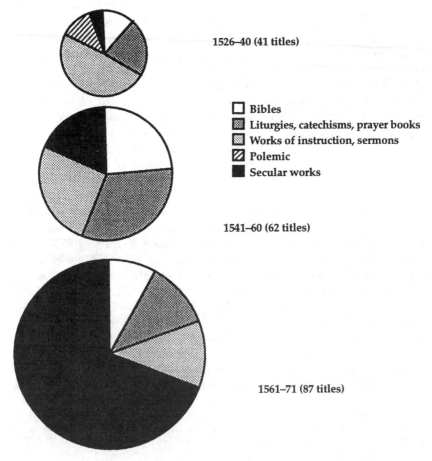

1526–40 (41 titles)

☐ Bibles
▨ Liturgies, catechisms, prayer books
▨ Works of instruction, sermons
▨ Polemic
■ Secular works

1541–60 (62 titles)

1561–71 (87 titles)

Figure 16.5   Swedish printing by type (number of titles)

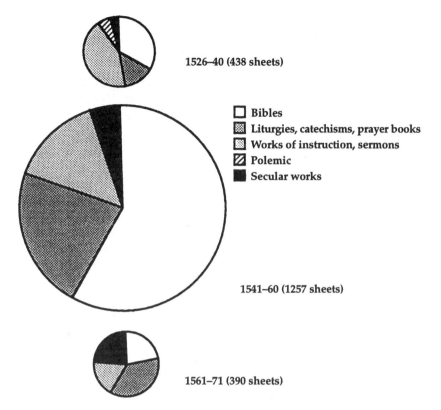

1526–40 (438 sheets)

☐ Bibles
▨ Liturgies, catechisms, prayer books
▨ Works of instruction, sermons
▨ Polemic
■ Secular works

1541–60 (1257 sheets)

1561–71 (390 sheets)

Figure 16.6   Swedish printing by type (number of sheets)

the context of a peaceful establishment of the Reformation, but many works of religious instruction and sermons were published instead. The desire to restore the Church was clear in the gradual production of works which were indispensable for its internal existence: translations of Scripture, liturgical works and prayer-books. The actual importance of Bible editions and sermon collections was greater than indicated by the number of editions. Indeed, these were the only large volumes, representing 33.5 per cent and 22.4 per cent respectively of the total production in terms of the number of sheets.

Almost all the works of these two decades came from a single author, Olavus Petri, and his role in establishing the Reformation in his country was a fundamental one. After studying in Uppsala and Leipzig, he matriculated in Wittenberg, and became *magister artium* there in February 1518. When he returned to Sweden in 1518, Laurentius Andreae, Sweden's first Protestant preacher, took him on as his secretary. When Gustav called them both to Stockholm, Olavus became the city secre-

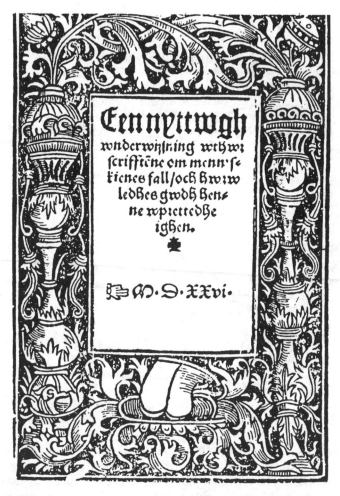

16.1   Olavus Petri, *Een nyttwgh wnderwijsning* (Stockholm: G. Richolff, 1526)

tary. In 1527 he was appointed as the king's secretary and from 1531 to 1533 was chancellor of the kingdom.[6]

On 14 February 1526, the royal presses in Stockholm printed *A useful teaching*, an adaptation of Luther's *Betbüchlein* attributed to Olavus Petri. This work, reprinted in the same year, was the first in a long series of small works of instruction. During the same year, the

---

[6] See Dewailly, 'Petri'. For Olavus Petri's works, see S. Ingebrand, *Olavus Petris reformatoriska åskådning*, Acta Universitatis Upsaliensis, Studia Doctrinae Christianae Upsalensiae, **1** (Lund, 1964)

presses produced *A very useful teaching*, a more aggressive work, translated from a Lutheran adaptation of a Hussite catechism.[7] Olavus Petri was particularly productive in 1528. First, on the occasion of the coronation of Gustav Vasa on 12 January 1528 at Uppsala, he published *A Christian Exhortation to the inhabitants of Sweden*. This sermon set out the reciprocal duties of the Christian prince and his subjects. In advance of the diocesan synods of Uppsala, Strängnäs and Västerås, Olavus produced on 12 June *A Christian Exhortation to the clergy explaining the reciprocal obligations of the clergy and the laity*. *A small book on the sacraments, their nature and their legitimate use*, was published on 14 August, and focused more on continuity than on radical shifts in sacramental discipline. It was an adaptation of Osiander's Nuremberg–Brandenburg Ecclesiastical Discipline. On 27 August, Olavus published *An Instruction on marriage, demonstrating that priests can be married*[8] and on 13 November *An Explanation of monastic vows, showing the damage they have caused*. Olavus dealt with the validity of God's word and human ordinances in the spiritual realm in a work which appeared on 18 December. During 1528, he also published an incomplete translation of Luther's *Auslegung der Evangelien von Ostern bis aufs Advent* of 1526.[9]

Also in 1528, Laurentius Andreae's *Instruction on faith and good works* appeared. In it, he affirmed justification by faith alone. This was the only work which appeared with Andreae's name on it. Along with Olavus Petri, Andreae was later known as the co-Reformer of Sweden.

During 1529, Olavus Petri published *A short introduction to Holy Scripture*, a translation of Johann Toltz's *Eyn korth hantboek vor yunge Christen* (Rostock: L Dietz, 1526), and the work was republished in 1538. At the end of 1530, Olavus Petri's *Sermon Collection* appeared, an original work which brought together 72 *de tempore* and 18 *de sancto* sermons, all in a simple and popular style. In contrast to the smaller works previously published, this was a respectable quarto volume of 230 sheets. An adaptation of Luther's greater catechism was included at the end of the *Sermon Collection* as a response both to Olavus Petri's catechetical concerns and to the demands of the Örebro Synod. Georg Richolff republished the *Sermon Collection* in Lübeck

---

[7] Translation with additions by Joachim Slüter (?), *Eyne schöne vnnd ser nutte Christlike vnder wysynge allen Christgelouigen mynschen (nicht allene dennn kynderen vnde jungen luden/synder och den ollen wol antomarkende/ na der wyse eyner vrage vnd antwordt* (Rostock: Ludwig Dietz, 1525)

[8] This work was republished in 1529.

[9] This was a relatively faithful translation of M. Luther's works with a *Summa* taken from J. Bugenhagen's *Indices in evangelia dominicalia* (Wittenberg, 1524). See Ingebrand, *Olavus Petris reformatoriska åskådning*, p. 41.

twice in a very short space of time (1537–38). This edition provided the opportunity to test the characters to be used in the complete Bible edition of 1541.

Two other writings by Olavus were published in 1535: *A small book explaining how man receives eternal salvation; whether by his own merits or the grace and mercy of God alone*, and *An exhortation for all evangelical preachers*. The latter work, which only survives in a defective copy, provides a line of conduct in case of persecution because of God's word; and was a 16–section commentary on Matthew 10.

The famous consolatory work, the *Seelenarztnei* published by Urbanus Rhegius in Augsburg in 1529 and distributed throughout Europe, was translated into Swedish by Olavus Petri. After a first edition was published in 1537, the work was reprinted three times before 1571.

In 1539, Olavus Petri's sermon *Against the curses and blasphemies commonly used today* was published, in which he did not hesitate to criticize the authorities for failing to set a good example.[10] The king, who frequently swore, felt that the work was directed at him and in a letter to the archbishop dated 24 April 1539, he indicated that from then on nothing was to be published without his consent.

At the very end of this first period, in 1538, the Archbishop of Uppsala, Laurentius Petri, published his first work: *An Explanation of Holy Water*. This was intended to prepare the way for the suppression of ceremonies and practices thought to be idolatrous, like the use of holy water.

The pioneers of the Reformation were obviously aware of the importance of the transmission and translation of the Scriptures. But in this first period, only the first steps were made towards a complete translation of the Bible. On 15 August 1526, the Swedish New Testament appeared. It was an imposing folio volume of nearly 200 sheets, complete with eight engravings. The royal coats of arms printed on the last sheet gave an official cachet to the entire work. It has already been noted that funding for the work was provided by a subscription imposed on all the parishes. Translations of other books of the Bible only appeared in 1536: the Book of Psalms, Proverbs, the Wisdom of Solomon and Ecclesiasticus. These partial works paved the way for the complete version which appeared in 1541. One should note that a version of Erasmus's New Testament appeared in 1530 printed by Ludwig Dietz in Rostock with the Swedish royal coat of arms on the title-page, and was thus destined for use in Sweden.

As for the Swedish liturgy, once again Olavus Petri was responsible for the first editions. On 28 April 1529 he published a Swedish ritual,

---

[10] The re-edited version of 1560 provided a censored text.

reprinted twice before 1541, when the Swedish Mass and liturgy were made official. On 10 May 1531, Olavus published again *The Reasons for which the Mass must be celebrated in the language understood by the people*, a work which preceded his *Swedish Mass as now celebrated in Stockholm*. The two re-editions of the Swedish Mass which appeared prior to the imposition of the new rite, in 1535 and 1537, included Olavus Petri's manifesto for a vernacular Mass in their prefaces. In 1530, the first Swedish hymn-book appeared, but unfortunately only an incomplete version has survived. Four other editions of similar works, produced slightly later, still exist. Besides these categories of books – instructions, sermons, Bibles, liturgies and hymns – other genres were much less well represented.

The Synod of Örebro met in February 1529 in the presence of three of the five bishops of the Swedish ecclesiastical province. Its decisions were signed on 7 February and published in a quarto format. Bishops had to ensure that priests preached the Gospel or had someone do it in their place. The schools run by cathedral chapters had to have at least one daily lesson on Scripture, to which all clergy had to be able to attend. Schoolboys had to be able to use the Latin New Testament and they too had to have a daily Bible lesson.

As for polemical works, these were few and far between. On 28 March 1527, Olavus Petri published his *Response to a non Christian Letter sent by a Lying Monk named Paul Helie against the Holy Gospel which has now appeared in the light of day by God's grace*. In this first work in which his name appeared as author, Olavus violently attacked a letter which has since been lost from the Danish Carmelite, Paul Helie or Poul Helgesen (1485?–1535?), an Erasmian who supported the Reformation until the break between Erasmus and Luther. On 14 May Petri then published the *Answer to 12 questions on points where the evangelical doctrine and the Papist doctrine are in disagreement, rejecting Doctor Peder Galle's own responses*. In this work, Petri printed and rejected the answers given by his former Uppsala teacher, Peder Galle (died 1537/38?) to each of the questions which the king had asked both sides to answer. This work, which was more serene in tone than the previous one, was not the result of an oral theological debate. Indeed this confrontation only took place later at the Västerås Diet of June 1527. Olavus's *Brief response to Paul Helie*, which appeared on 27 May 1528, was an echo of this meeting, for Paul Helie had reacted to the previous work. Petri's 1528 text showed a good understanding of Luther's writings and of the Catholic polemicists' works, Eck, Faber, Hieronymus Emser and John Fisher. *A Few Songs about the Antichrist*, four polemical and anti-papist works appeared in 1536, and were attributed to Stockholm's city secretary Olof Svensson.

In the period under review, one work was printed in Sweden for export. From the summer of 1526 to the winter of 1527, the German Reformer Melchior Hoffman lived in Stockholm, where he preached until January 1527 in the German community of the city. This community, which was probably the first centre of Lutheran ideas, lost its dominant political role under Gustav Vasa. Hoffman's apocalyptic preaching led to disturbances and to his expulsion, but nevertheless he managed to have his commentary on Daniel 12 printed in Stockholm, with the help of the city's German merchants.[11] Finally, in 1535 one must note the publication of a synodal circular from the Uppsala canons, which was in fact a 'pirate' edition.[12]

The official establishment of Reformation worship (1540–60)

In his role as 'Defender of the holy Christian faith throughout the kingdom', Gustav Vasa appointed the German Georg Norman as *ordinator et superattendens* for the entire Swedish church on 8 December 1539. Gustav had previously called Norman into his service as ecclesiastical councillor, and had similarly appointed Konrad von Pyhy as chancellor. The independence of thought of the two Swedish reformers irritated the king so much that Olavus Petri and Laurentius Andreae were accused of high treason in early 1540. The tribunal, which included Archbishop Laurentius Petri, condemned the two to death, but the king pardoned them immediately. Although Olavus Petri, appointed as priest in Stockholm, gradually regained the king's confidence, his literary activities diminished significantly from this date. At the same time his brother the archbishop was also temporarily eclipsed by Norman the superintendent, whose mission was in fact the obedience of the Church to the king's will.

A royal edict of 1540 imposed evangelical worship in Swedish throughout the kingdom. From this point on, the Swedish Mass and Ritual were official documents, and appeared three times between 1541 and 1571. The years 1542 to 1544 were shaped by Nils Dacke's revolt in the south of the country. Opposed to the Reformation, the revolt had no support outside Sweden and was crushed. Once his power had been strengthened, the king blamed certain prelates considered to be lukewarm in their suppression of papist offices, and pushed them aside. The Västerås Diet of 1544 proclaimed the victory of the Reformation in

---

[11] See Kl. Depperman, *Melchior Hoffman, Soziale Unruhen und apokalytische Visionen im Zeitalter der Reformation* (Göttingen, 1979) p. 346. On his stay in Stockholm in general see pp. 79–83.

[12] It was an 18-line sheet (150 × 183 mm). Both the composition and the printing were not the work of a professional.

Sweden. It also established a hereditary monarchy beginning with Gustav Vasa. All Swedish dioceses supported the Reformation, or at least their leaders did. The assurances given by the estates of the kingdom to the king in 1550 tend to show that the Reformation held large popular support. In 1557, the king divided the seven former dioceses into 15 smaller administrative units, seemingly wanting to suppress the classical episcopal system in Sweden. After his death on 29 September 1560, he was succeeded by his eldest son, Erik (1533–77).

The official establishment of Protestant worship explains why during the next two decades, religious publishing moved more towards works designed to support religious life: bibles, liturgical and catechetical works. The Bible, produced in many different partial editions following the complete edition in Swedish in 1541, made up 59.2 per cent of the total production volume in the period. Liturgical works, prayer-books and catechisms together accounted for 21.7 percent. Works of religious instruction retained their favoured position, however, especially through the number of titles published. Olavus Petri's disgrace broadened the range of authors, with works by Archbishop Laurentius Petri and especially those of Michael Agricola, who inaugurated the publication of works in Finnish.

The list of religious works in this period opened at the start of 1541 with the translation of the entire Bible in Swedish, carried out by Georg Richolff. Called back from Lübeck for this purpose, he established the royal presses at Uppsala. This Bible contained a number of engravings done by Georg Lemberger. The translation, which followed the model of Luther's 1539 Bible owed much to Laurentius Petri, to his brother Olavus, and probably also to Laurentius Andreae. Publication was funded by the king, which meant that each parish in the kingdom had to purchase a copy. Clearly, this marked an important date in the history of the Swedish Reformation.

Partial re-editions of the Swedish Bible appeared in subsequent years. Ecclesiasticus was first republished in 1543, after having been included in the 1541 Bible. 1549 was a particularly fertile year for the production of religious texts, as several Old Testament works appeared: Ecclesiasticus – in its third edition – Proverbs, Ecclesiastes, the Wisdom of Solomon, Job, Judith and Esther. The first three seem to have been very popular, given the number of times they were republished. In 1550, a quarto edition of the New Testament in Swedish appeared, and the Book of Psalms was reprinted in 1560. The Scriptures were also published in Finnish, as detailed below.

Besides the Rituals and Mass books already mentioned, many hymn-books, prayer-books and catechisms also came off the presses. In 1544, the first edition of the volume containing the hymn-book, the catechism,

Abckiria.

Michael Agricola
Christiano Sa-
lutem.

Oppe nyt wanha/ia noori /
joilla ombi Sydhen toori.
Jumalan kesKyt / ia mielen/
iotca taidhat Somen kielen.
Laki / se Sielun hirmutta /
mutt Cristus sen tas lodhutta.
Lue sijs hyue Lapsi teste /
Alcu oppi ilman este.
Nijte muista Elemes aina /
nin Jesus sinun Armons laina

16.2   Michael Agricola: *Abc-kiria* (2nd ed. [Stockholm: A. Laurentsson, 1548])

the Gospels and the story of the Passion appeared, and was re-edited three times in the period. Isolated elements have also survived: a hymn fragment, dated 1549, and a Passion narrative of 1556, reprinted in 1561. A prayer-book in Swedish, with a catechism and passion narrative was published in 1552, and was reprinted with the addition of an almanac in 1553. *A few Prayers from Scripture* appeared in 1559.

Works of religious instruction continued to be printed on a regular basis. In a short work dated 1548, Olavus Petri warned the faithful against disregarding the signs of the times, in particular that of the plague in his treatise, *On the greatest changes and the age of the world*.[13] In 1550, he wrote a Biblical drama, *Tobit*, which survives in

---

[13] A second edition appeared in 1558.

three editions. Archbishop Laurentius Petri produced a treatise in 1557, *Against drunkenness*, a translation of Matthaeus Friderich's *Wider den Sauffteuffel* (1552). Petri's translation was reprinted already in 1560. Two other works by Laurentius Petri appeared in 1558, an *Exhortation to the priests and people to become penitent*[14] and his translation of Luther's *Vermahnung zum Sakrament des Leibes und Blutes unseres Herrn* (1530). The Bishop of Skara, Erik Falck (151?–67) published an adaptation of Johannes Spangenberg's *Margerita theologica* (1540) based on Melanchthon's *Loci* of 1535. The longest work produced under Laurentius Petri's name – a nearly 800-sheet octavo volume – was a *Sermon Collection* which appeared in 1555 and offered sermons translated from German. In fact, it was the only work of its type to appear in these two decades.

The main feature of these years was the beginnings of religious printing in Finnish. Michael Agricola (1508/12–57) was its instigator. After having studied in Wittenberg from 1536 to 1539, he began the Finnish Reformation, and was also the father of written Finnish. During the last seven years of his life he held the bishop's seat in Turku.[15] His first book in Finnish was a *Primer*, joined by a short catechism published in 1543. Neither of the two editions of this work in the period have survived intact. In 1544, Michael Agricola published a book of prayers for use in the parishes, containing both general information and a series of collects and prayers from the Bible. The Finnish New Testament appeared in 1548. In the following year, he produced a Ritual and Mass in Finnish, as well as a Passion narrative. In 1551, Michael Agricola published his translations of the Psalms and the *Songs and Prophecies from the Pentateuch*. The Finnish translation of the prophets Haggai, Zechariah, and Malachi appeared in the following year.

Waiting for the Kyrkoordning (1561–71)

From the moment of his accession to the throne, Erik XIV seemed to want to eliminate all traces of 'papism'. At the Arboga Diet in April 1561, the answers to his questions on liturgy and ecclesiastical legislation showed him how conservative the clergy's views were. Influenced by his former tutor, the Calvinist Denis Beurreus (1507?–67), from March 1561 the king offered asylum in Sweden to French and Dutch Protestants. In the following years, Erik was torn by the conflicting influences of his two mentors: the Melanchthonian Gregor Norman and

---

[14] The work was published simultaneously in a folio and octavo volume.

[15] See J. Gummerus, *Michael Agricola, der Reformator Finnlands*, Schriften der Luther-Agricola Gesellschaft in Finnland, 2 (Helsinki, 1941).

the Calvinist Denis Beurreus. At the 1562 Stockholm Diet, he opened a debate between Calvinist and Lutheran doctrines, won by Laurentius Petri. However, Petri failed to obtain the king's consent for his proposed ecclesiastical ordinances finalized in 1561. Scholars have pointed to Calvinist influence as a factor in the monarch's refusal, but it is more likely to be explained by the king's desire to preserve his initiative in religious matters as well as by the advice of the Melanchthonians.

Confessional disputes had not ended, and a violent quarrel broke out from 1562 to 1565 around Calvinism.[16] The Nordic Seven Years' War which began in 1563 distracted the king from church matters and led to a deterioration in the religious climate. Until 1562, theological discussions had focused on liturgical practices, but from 1563, these turned to 'sacramentarian' theology. The lack of wine due to the war led to a 'liquorist' quarrel in 1564 over the use of wine in the Lord's Supper. Erik XIV slowly began to distance himself from the Calvinists. Two mandates in 1563 and 1565 forbade any propaganda on their part, while still respecting the principle of freedom of conscience.

Erik XIV's reign ended tragically. In conflict with his brothers ever since his accession to the throne, the king became insane and was deposed in 1568. The new ruler, John III (1537–92), crowned by Laurentius Petri on 10 July 1569, stated in his installation oath that he wished to restore the episcopate in Sweden. John had gained solid theological learning during his house arrest in Gripsholm Castle following his marriage with the Polish princess Catherine Jagellon (1526–83). He wished to restore the Church on the model of the first six centuries. John III eliminated the division imposed by his father Gustav on the dioceses of the Swedish ecclesiastical provinces. The Peace of Stettin, signed in 1570, ensured Sweden's long-term independence.

The main feature of printed works produced by the royal presses in this decade was the sharp rise in secular works, which accounted for more than two-thirds of the titles produced and slightly less than a quarter of the number of sheets (23.6 per cent). To a large extent this was the consequence of the political situation which led to the publication of many mandates and placards. In the religious domain, increasing numbers of prayer-books and catechisms were produced (35.9 per cent of sheets). However, works of religious instruction remained numerous. In every domain, previously published works were often reprinted.

As for Biblical texts, the Swedish presses produced re-editions of Ecclesiasticus, the Wisdom of Solomon and Proverbs, and in 1563 a

---

[16] For this period see S. Kjöllström, *Striden Kring kalvinismen i Sverige under Erik XIV, En Kyrkohistorisk Studie*, Lunds universitets årsskrift, NF, avd 1, 31, 5 (Lund, 1935).

reprinting of the book of Job, while a new translation of Isaiah appeared in 1568.

Among works dealing with liturgies and prayers, one should note two re-editions of the volume containing the hymns, the catechism, the Gospels and the Passion narrative, in 1562 and 1567.[17] In 1567, Martin Olai Helsingus published a volume of prayers of 'doctors' of the Church, entitled *A Useful and Christian book of prayers*, with a second edition in 1570. In the following year, a prayer for use in times of war also appeared.

New works which appeared were primarily ones of religious instruction and sermons. The archbishop's sermon at the coronation of Erik XIV on 29 June 1561 was printed shortly after the event. 1562 was marked by the publication of two works by Laurentius Petri on worship, his translation of Justus Menius' defense of baptismal exorcism and his *Dialogue on the Lord's Supper*, which attacked sacramentarians as fiercely as it did the Papists. The next stages of this controversy remained in manuscript form. The archbishop's sermon on the fifth commandment also came off the presses in 1562. Three pastoral letters from Laurentius Petri appeared between 1563 and 1566,[18] in a context shaped by the Nordic Seven Years War (1563–70) and religious conflict centred around Calvinism. In 1563, the presses brought out *A prayer in preparation for Communion* and a translation by Veit Dietrich, *A Short explanation of the Lord's Prayer*.

After promulgation by John III, Laurentius Petri's ecclesiastical ordinance was published in 1571 and established the Swedish Reformation through an officially printed text.[19] Inspired by the German examples of Johann Brenz and Melanchthon, the text was finally approved by a

---

[17] The editions of 1562, which are not mentioned by I. Collijn, are known through an incomplete edition, preserved in Reykjavik: *Then Swenska Psalmeboken förbätrat och medh flere Songer förmerat och Kalendarium* (Stockholm: A. Laurentsson, 1562. 8°, 102 fols, 8 plates. Royal arms on title-page); *Catechismus eller Christeligh kennedom för yngt och eenfoldigt folck ganska nyttigh. Jtem een liten Bönebook* (Stockholm: A. Laurentsson, 1562. 8o, 54 fols, 26 plates); *Evangelia och Epistler/som effter sedwenion läsas eller siungas j Tiderna på alla Söndagar och på the förnemligesta Högtijder och Helgedaghar om året. Jtem Collecterna öffuer hela året/Och een bön effter hwart Euangelium* (Stockholm: [A. Laurentsson], 1562. 8°, 172 fols, 59 plates. Royal arms on title-page); *Passio* (Stockholm: A. Laurentsson, 1562, 8°).

[18] These were a circular letter urging prayers for victory, a pastoral letter on the wine shortage, and a letter to the ministers on the plague and the war.

[19] The text of the ordinance is presented and translated by L.-M. Dewailly in *Istina*, 30 (1985), 246–320. For its early versions in manuscript form, see S. Kjöllerström, *Svenska förarbeten till kyrkoordningen av år 1571*, Samlingar och studier till Svenska kyrkans historia, 2 (Lund, 1940)

general synod in Uppsala on 22 August 1572. Finally, in 1571, three pedagogical works appeared alongside the ecclesiastical ordinance.[20]

The reception of the texts

There is very little information on the reception of Swedish works. Reprints could be the sign of a positive welcome and of readers' demands. It seems clear that the bourgeoisie and the members of the royal administration had access to German works. Reformation literature seems to have reached Sweden already in 1524. A systematic study of lists of books bought abroad for princes and other Swedish notables, in so far as such lists have survived, still remains to be done.

Printed works, like manuscripts of the period which still survive, probably had a mainly mediating effect, as Swedish imprints of the period made an impact not through direct reading but through sermons, lectures and reading in public. Texts were read collectively, with ministers and schoolteachers ensuring that the printed message was broadcast. The insistence of the Reformers on the preaching obligation of ministers was striking. And the editions of the New Testament in 1526 and the Bible in 1541 were meant first and foremost for the kingdom's parishes.

Ecclesiastical censorship was unknown during this period, as both production and market forces operated in such a way that only works which were judged to be useful and necessary could have a chance to be printed. Civil censorship was also unknown. Gustav Vasa's annoyance at Olavus Petri's *Sermon against Curses* published in 1539 certainly led him to express his desire to control the production of the Swedish presses in a letter dated 24 April 1539. But the only known case was in fact that of the second edition of the *Sermon against Swearing* in 1560, which shows signs of 'censorship'. Censorship only became 'necessary' when printing had acquired the means of production in a fully independent fashion.

---

[20] [O. Brunfels], *Disciplina et institvtio pverorvm ex optimis quibusque autoribus collecta* (Stockholm: A. Laurentsson, 1571); D. Erasmus, *De civilitate morvm pverillvm libellus nvnc primvm & conditvs aeditus* (Stockholm: A. Laurentsson, 1571); [P. M. Fecht], *De naturali, simplici et grammatico verborvm ordine* (Stockholm: A. Laurentsson, 1571).

Note to the English edition

In the light of research carried out since the publication of the French version of this chapter, I now would prefer to be more circumspect in stating that Swedish titles were translations of German books. The exact nature of these works seems to be far more complicated to assess, as the extent of the translator's relative freedom or dependence on the original text can hardly be measured at this point in time, given that we do not know which originals were used. In my research for my doctoral thesis on the ecclesiology of Archbishop Laurentius Petri,[21] I have noted that although some of his writings remained in manuscript form, they appeared to have been highly influential, as in the case of the church ordinance of 1561. A similar observation could be made when examining the anxious reaction of King Gustav Vasa when he learned of Olavus Petri's chronicle, which was, however, only published several hundred years later.

The information available on sixteenth-century Swedish libraries seems very limited. The books owned by the Petri brothers were probably lost together with the greater part of the Royal Library when Stockholm Castle was destroyed by a fire in 1697. Some evidence of the Swedish book market can be collected from inventories and wills. I was able to see the inventory of the possessions of Sveno Jacobi, who was Bishop of Skara from 1531 to 1540 and died in 1554. The list of his books comprises some 40 entries which show that he possessed some exemplars of the writings of the Church Fathers, two editions of Melanchthon's *Loci communes* and some of his exegetical works, Bible commentaries and other works of Erasmus. Bishop Jacobi also owned a Latin–Greek New Testament and the New Testament in Swedish, but there is no information on which editions he had. Most entries are extremely short, and would not help in the search for the source of the imports.[22]

Select bibliography

Collijn, I., *Sveriges bibliografi intill år 1600* (3 vols, Uppsala, 1927–38).
Dewailly, L.-M., 'Aux origines de l'Eglise suédoise, l'Ordonnance ecclésiastique de 1571', *Istina*, 30 (1985), pp. 228–320.

---

[21] R. Kick, 'Tel un navire sur la mer déchaînée la communauté chrétienne dans l'oeuvre de Laurentius Petri, archevêque d'Uppsala (1531–1573)', *Studia Theologica Lundensia*, 52 (Lund, 1997).

[22] Royal Archives Stockholm RA E 5702.

Dewailly, L.-M., 'Petri (Olaus et Laurentius)', *Catholicisme*, II, (49), (1986), cols 93–5.

Hoffmann, J. G. H., *La Réforme en Suède, 1523–1572 et la succession apostolique* (Neuchâtel, 1945) (L'Actualité protestante).

Holmquist, H., *Die schwedische Reformation 1523–1531* (Leipzig, 1925).

Ingebrand, S., *Olavus Petris reformatoriska åskådning*, Acta Universitatis Upsaliensis, *Studia Doctrinae Christianae Upsaliensia*, 1 (Lund, 1964), with summary in German, pp. 347–70.

Metclaf, M. F., 'Scandinavia 1397–1560', in T. A. Brady, H. A. Oberman and J. D. Tracy (eds), *Handbook of European History 1400–1600: Late Middle Ages, Renaissance and Reformation*, Volume II: *Visions, Programs and Outcomes* (Leiden, 1995) pp. 523–50.

Montgomery, I., 'Die cura religionis als Aufgabe des Fürsten: Perspektiven der Zweiten Reformation in Schweden', *Die reformierte Konfessionalisierung in Deutschland: Das Problem der 'Zweiten Reformation'*, Schriften des Vereins für Reformationsgeschichte, 195 (Gütersloh, 1986) pp. 266–90.

Montgomery, I., 'La Réforme en Suède, une Libération nationale et politique', *Revue d'histoire et de philosophie religieuses*, 63 (1983), 113–24.

Schwaiger, G., *Die Reformation in den nordischen Ländern* (Munich, 1962).

Yelverton, E. E., *An Archbishop of the Reformation, Laurentius Petri Nericius Archbishop of Uppsala 1531–1573* (London, 1958).

Conclusion

Jean-François Gilmont

At the end of this long journey across Europe, it is worth returning to our original two-fold question: on the one hand, what influence did printing have on the success of the Reformation? On the other hand, did the rise of Protestantism have an impact on printing, on the circulation of printed books, and in the end on reading practices? After attempting to answer these two questions, we shall present some methodological and historiographical considerations suggested by this research.

The influence of the book on the Reformation

From the sixteenth century onwards, the question of the origins of the Reformation has been an ongoing topic of discussion. Indeed, the problem is highly complex, and the various explanations proposed have at least brought to light the multiple crises undergone by society at the time of Luther's 'tower experience'. Some of these changes occurred in the theological or spiritual realm alone. Because of the slow death of scholasticism, the Reformers could not enter into a dialogue with the thirteenth-century masters, but instead confronted a system without substance. In the same period, exegetical practices were re-examined thanks to the use of the philological methods advocated by humanism. The breadth of this transformation can be measured by names like Erasmus, Sante Pagnini, Sebastian Münster and the Polyglot Bible of Alcalá. But these religious and intellectual changes do not explain everything. The Reformation's success also had its roots in social factors. The end of the Middle Ages was shaped by the rise of the bourgeoisie. Having mastered new economical and commercial sectors, this social group was intent on participating in political decisions affecting its activities. At the same time, it wanted to display its social success by paying more attention to culture, though potentially shaping culture to fit its own concerns. The Reformation had yet other causes. The disorder in ecclesiastical circles certainly provided a powerful weapon to those who wished to reform the Church of their day. This moral crisis also had socio-economic ramifications.

These changes coincided with a dual revolution in the means of communication: the discovery of a new technique of reproducing writings and the increasing use of vernacular languages. Gutenberg's invention modified the conditions under which ideas circulated by rapidly and inexpensively expanding the number of texts. This acceleration in the spread of works occurred simultaneously with an increasing use of national languages in numerous areas of social life. The following analysis examines in turn the new conditions in the spread of the Bible, the use of national languages, and the attitude of political powers towards printing.

Should the Gospel be transmitted orally or in writing?

It was certainly no coincidence that the central concepts of Christian theology used terms borrowed from means of communication. Indeed, Christianity was the religion of the Word – λογος – and the religion of the Book – Βιβλος. Christians went back and forth without sensing any potential opposition between the two. However, the main features of these means of communication were very distinct and non-identical! But Christianity aimed precisely at cumulating the properties of each, the living and spontaneous presence of the Word and the intangible eternity of the Book.

In reality, the unchanging nature of doctrine was an unattainable ideal. Throughout the centuries the transmission of the Gospel's message regularly led to schisms and anathemas. There were also various and at times contradictory levels of awareness in the Church, over oral versus written transmission. This debate came into full force around the Bible.

Two opposing views resurfaced time and time again. Some, like Erasmus, felt that the Bible should be distributed widely.

> I am therefore not at all in agreement with those who would keep the Holy Scriptures from being read by the unlearned and translated into the vernacular, as though Christ had taught such complicated things that not even a quarter of theologians could understand, or as if Christian religion could only be defended by the bulwarks of ignorance. Therefore, I would wish that the humblest women read the Gospel and that they read the Epistles of St Paul. And would to Heaven that our holy books were translated in every language![1]

But this viewpoint frightened certain clergy, who refused to cast pearls before swine. At the start of the Reformation, the rigid defenders of orthodoxy regularly condemned Luther's disciples for having spread the Gospels among the artisans and women. Jean Gachy wrote ironically:

---

[1] P. Mesnard: 'La paraclesis d'Érasme', *BHR*, 13 (1951), 37.

Dames, dames, prenez aguille, ...
Meslés vous de faire vos mesnaiges
Lessés Luther, et serez saiges;
Et devenez devocieuses,
Femmes sont toujours curieuses.[2]

The result of the debate was fundamental as it affected the very conditions of transmission of Biblical truth. On the one side, were the defenders of the professionals' monopoly, namely priests and theologians: 'What use will the apostles, priests and doctors of the Church be', asked Florimond de Rémond, [...]

> if the distribution and interpretation of the Holy Scriptures or the use of the Holy Books was done by artisans and women as well as them? God gave heralds and ambassadors to his church. Those are the only voices we should listen to, and not these bastard, foreign and unknown voices.[3]

On the other side, the representatives of the opposing party reminded them that Christ addressed himself to all, and particularly to the simple and the humble. Lefèvre D'Étaples offered his New Testament translation 'so that the simple members of Christ's body, having this [book] in their own tongue, can be as certain of the Gospel truths as those who read it in Latin'.[4] In their eyes, promoting the written word did not go against the oral one. In one of his colloquies, Erasmus stated his preference for a sermon, but if the preaching was intolerable or there was no sermon, he read instead. 'I feel, said one of his characters, that I have not been entirely deprived of a sermon, if I have heard Chrysostom or Jerome speak to me in writing.'[5]

Thus, this question concerns the very nature of access to the biblical message: should one encourage reading which could technically lead to a personal interpretation of Scripture or should one preserve the primacy and even exclusiveness of the transmission of the Gospel truths to clergy alone? Whenever Judaism and Christianity have had confidence in the written word, at the start they had only one characteristic of these texts in mind, namely their ability to establish a message perma-

---

[2] J. Gachy, *Trialogue nouveau* n.p., 1524, fol. g3ᵛ, quoted by Cl. Longeon, in *La Farce des théologastres* (Geneva, 1989), p. 91. In the same footnote, Cl. Longeon lists other witnesses speaking for and against women's access to Scripture. See also B. Roussel, 'Des lecteurs' in G. Bédouelle and B. Roussel (eds), *Le temps des Réformes et la Bible* (Paris, 1989), pp. 286–7 (Bible de tous les temps, 5).

[3] Florimond de Rémond, *Histoire de la naissance, progrez et decadence de l'heresie de ce siecle*, bk 7, ch. 7, para. 4 (Rouen, 1623), p. 875.

[4] *Nouveau Testament* Paris: S. de Colines, 1523, fol. a.2.

[5] *Confabulatio pia (Pietas puerilis)* cited by A. Godin, 'La Bible et la "philosophie chrétienne"', in Bédouelle and Roussel, *Le temps*, p. 571.

nently. In these distant periods, there was no question of considering the written text as a mode of communication accessible to all. The problem of more general access through the written word probably did not surface before the early Middle Ages, as a result of heresies which demanded a more widespread reading of the Bible.[6] The invention of printing made the problem an even more pressing one.

Already at the end of the fifteenth century, ecclesiastical authorities were alerted by the danger of bibles circulating among untrained laity. The unlearned were in danger of no longer wanting to hear the Word preached by the priests, but of wanting to interpret it themselves. Johannes Cochlaeus echoed the authorities when he deplored that tailors and shoemakers and even 'women and some simple idiots' were reading the Gospels.[7] In his 1533 treatise, *An expediat laicis legere novi Testamenti libros lingua vernacula*, Cochlaeus made a distinction between the educated laity of a high social standing, who were allowed to read the Scriptures, and the simple and uncultivated people – *idiotas, populum rudem, homines contentiosos*.[8] This classification of Christians into several categories was extended by Henry VIII. When he allowed the distribution of the Bible in English in 1543, he carefully made distinctions between three categories of people and three ways of reading the Bible. Nobles and the gentry could not only read the Scriptures in English, but could have them read aloud for themselves and all those under their roof. At the other end of the scale, reading the Bible in English was completely forbidden to 'women, artisans, apprentices and companions working for those of an equal or inferior rank to yeomen, farmers and manual labourers'. Those situated between these two categories, namely the bourgeois as well as noble women, 'could read for themselves but for no one else, any text from the Bible and the New Testament'.[9]

On the Catholic side, prohibitions simply took the form of edicts.[10] However, one should not over-simplify the case. The Spanish Inquisi-

---

[6] See V. Coletti, *L'éloquence de la chaire: victoires et défaites du latin entre moyen âge et Renaissance* (Paris, 1987), pp. 29–51. The Italian original of this fine work, *Parole dal pulpito* was written in 1983.

[7] See p. 93.

[8] Cited by Coletti, *L'éloquence de la chaire*, p. 191.

[9] *The Statutes of the Realm* (London, 1817), vol. 3, p. 896: 34 and 35 Henry VIII, c. 1, ss. 10–13.

[10] The clearest decision was the condemnation by the Paris faculty of theology in July 1529 of the above-mentioned text by Erasmus. (C. Du Plessis d'Argentré, *Collectio judiciorum de novis erroribus* (Paris, 1728), vol. 2, pp. 60–62.). A decree by the Scottish bishops forbidding the reading of the Gospels in the vernacular led to a disputation in 1533 between Alexander Alesius and Cochlaeus. (See Coletti, *L'éloquence de la chaire*, p. 191). The councils of the ecclesiastical provinces of Bourges and Sens meeting in 1528

tion, one of the most conservative as regards Bible translations, published a *Censura generalis bibliorum* in 1554, the details and severity of which, with 65 censored editions, shows by its gaps that there was still a place for authorised works.[11]

In fact, the debate over the transmission of God's Word did not oppose Catholics and Protestants, but divided Christians of every confession. As regards access to the Bible, there was no unanimity on the Protestant or Catholic side. As Guy Bedouelle shows, the arguments upheld by Esprit Rotier on one side and Furió Ceriol on the other, echoing the views expressed at Trent, illustrated the positions well.[12] To justify his refusal to translate the Bible, Rotier noted that the best guarantee of orthodoxy was to leave the transmission of the divine message exclusively to preaching. In contrast, Furió emphasised the importance of individual reading, which allowed Christians to nourish their faith. He went quite far along these lines: as for the argument regarding the indispensable monopoly of the clergy, he noted that the absence of good ministers made it imperative to turn to the written word: given the lack of authentic preaching, the faithful at least had the support of Scripture in the vernacular. The passionate debates at the Council of Trent over the translation of the Bible used the same arguments.[13] Alonso de Castro and Ambrogio Catarino feared that new heresies would crop up if just anyone was allowed to read and interpret the divine message, and thus they refused any translation of the Bible. The opposite viewpoint was defended by Cardinal Cristoforo Madruzzo: instead of invoking with disgust the *idiotas* who could not understand Scripture, the Cardinal pleaded for the holy books to be put in the hands of the 'holy people of God'.[14] Similarly, Gentian Hervet remarked

---

wanted to limit the reading of the Bible in the vernacular, but did not ban it permanently (J. D. Mansi, *Sacrorum Conciliorum nova et amplissima collectio* (Paris, 1902), vol. 32, col. 1142, 1197–8; see Ch.-J. Hefele and H. Leclerq, *Histoire des Conciles* (Paris, 1921), vol. 8/2, pp. 1067, 1080). See also Ph. Denis, 'La Bible et l'action pastorale', in Bédouelle and Roussel, *Le temps*, pp. 534–7.

[11] *Index 5*, pp. 619 24.

[12] G. Bédouelle, 'Le débat catholique sur la traduction de la Bible en langue vulgaire', in I. Backus and F. Higman (eds), *Théorie et pratique de l'exégèse. Actes du 3e colloque international d'histoire de l'exégèse biblique au XVIe siècle (Genève 31 août–2 septembre 1988)* (Geneva, 1990), pp. 39–59. See also G. Bédouelle and B. Roussel, 'l'Écriture et ses traductions, éloge et réticences', in Bédouelle and Roussel, *Le temps*, pp. 471–6.

[13] F. Cavallera, 'La Bible en langue vulgaire au concile de Trente (IVe Session)', in Facultés Catholiques (eds), *Mélanges E. Podechard* (Lyon, 1945), pp. 37–56; P. G. Duncker, 'La Chiesa e le versioni della S. Scrittura in lingua vulgare', *Angelicum*, 24 (1947), 140–67; R. E. McNally, 'The council of Trent and vernacular bibles', *Theological Studies*, 27 (1966), 204–27.

[14] Soc. Goerresiana, *Concilium Tridentinum* (Freiburg im Breisgau, 1930), vol. 12, p. 528; Coletti, *L'éloquence*, p. 208.

THE REFORMATION AND THE BOOK

that the Biblical image of casting pearls before swine could not be upheld, because one could not call swine those whom Christ had purchased with his blood.[15] While the refusal to translate the Bible into the vernacular was regularly repeated on the Catholic side, especially in the Romance language countries, the Bible was still regularly printed and distributed in many European languages with the official authorization of the Catholic Church. Thus not everyone among its representatives followed the hard-liners in their refusal to publish the sacred texts. G. Bedouelle ably discerned that behind the arguments on one side or the other lay a social conflict between oral and written communication; on the one side, the message was transmitted through the spoken word, whereas on the other side it based itself on the written text.

The lack of agreement among Catholics was reflected in the Protestant camp, where there were similar reservations as to the merits of putting any religious text into any hands. One must not forget that the principle of 'free examination' was introduced in the eighteenth century by liberal Protestantism.[16] In the heat of the first battles, Luther probably hoped 'that each Christian could study for himself both Scriptures and the pure Word of God'.[17] But the Reformer had no confidence in democracy, as shown by his comment that if his writings pleased everyone, then he must have done poor work![18] When he invited magistrates to build up good libraries, Luther had two purposes in mind: to preserve books and to allow spiritual and secular leaders to study. There was no question of popular reading.[19] He had no wish to put Scriptures in everyone's hands: his early enthusiasm was seriously tempered later

---

[15] Soc. Goerresiana, *Concilium*, p. 535; Coletti, *L'éloquence*, p. 213.

[16] J. Lecler, 'Protestantisme et "libre examen": les étapes et le vocabulaire d'une controverse', *Recherches de science religieuse*, 57 (1969), 321–74.

[17] WA, vol. 10/1–1, p. 728.

[18] WA, vol. 51, p. 264. However, he did not despise *Herr Omnes*, as seen by his reaction regarding the edition of his *Opera omnia*: 'It is better to print individual works; they then remain within reach of the common man' (WA, vol. 48, p. 706). Elsewhere, he bemoaned the lack of readers (WA Tisch., vol. 4, no. 5168, p. 691).

[19] WA, vol. 15, p. 49. I do not know the source for a comment which A. G. Dickens attributes to Luther. In reply to Bucer, who had been urging the Wittenberg theologians to go out into the world to preach, Luther was to have said, 'this is precisely what we do with our books' (A. G. Dickens, *La Réforme et la société du XVIe siècle* (Paris, 1969), p. 86; Dickens, *The German Nation and Martin Luther* (London, 1974), p. 109). I am doubtful of the authenticity of this plea on behalf of books. A passage from a letter of 1520 provides better picture of the general thought of the Reformer: after regretting the excessive spread of his books, Luther added, 'From my point of view, it would be much better to increase the number of living books, that is, the number of preachers' (WA Br., vol. 2, p. 191); see also P. Veit, 'Le chant, la Réforme et la Bible', in Bédouelle and Roussel, *Le temps*, p. 661, n. 10.

on. He insisted vigorously on the mediation of the community as regards access to the Bible. His view of education confirms this perspective. For Luther, the goal of schooling was not universal access to the Bible but rather the creation of an élite intended to direct both religious and lay society. This has been brilliantly shown by R. Gawthrop and G. Strauss.[20]

In the same way, the Calvinist policy as regards the transmission of Scripture needs to be clarified. Indeed, accumulating quotations such as those of Antoine Marcourt, who in 1534 invited the readers of his *Declaration on the Mass* to judge everything by the rule of Scripture 'through which everything must be regulated, valued and weighed' is not sufficient.[21] Thus affirming that the Word of God is the sole norm of the faith does not mean that each Christian, without restrictions, can invoke Scripture every which way. Around 1557, when Barthélemy Causse responded to Nicole Grenier in *The Very True Shield and Buckler of Faith*, his praise for printing included praise for sermons. He wrote that when the apostles preached the Gospel, 'they printed it in their hearers' hearts, through the power of the Holy Spirit', at a time when printing had not yet been invented. Arguing against those who believed that translations of the Bible were sources of heresy, he stated that the lack of ministers was the cause of the faithful's disarray. Implicitly, therefore, he upheld the complementary relations between reading the Bible and preaching.[22] Calvin did not believe that the Bible was accessible to all. To feed his flock, God wants 'the bread to be cut for us, the pieces to be put in our mouths, and the chewing to be done for us'.[23] Reformed ecclesiastical structures demonstrated the desire to keep power in the hands of an enlightened minority. In the dedication to the French translation of his *Christian questions and answers*, Beza expressed the Calvinist theologians' aversion to using French in doctrinal debates. He reluctantly accepted that his treatise be translated, in response to the public's curiosity, which on occasion would lead it into the 'labyrinths' of obscure questions. Beza was not commenting on the reading of Scripture, but he did state that theology

---

[20] R. Gawthrop and G. Strauss, 'Protestantism and literacy in early modern Germany', *Past and Present*, 104 (1984), 31–55, especially 32–43. See also R. Engelsing, *Der Bürger als Leser: Lesergeschichte in Deutschland, 1500–1800* (Stuttgart, 1974), p. 37.

[21] [A. Marcourt], *Declaration de la messe* [Neuchâtel, 1534], f. A^v. Quoted by G. Berthoud, *Antoine Marcourt, Réformateur et pamphlétaire: du "Livre des marchans" aux Placards de 1534* (Geneva, 1973), p. 236.

[22] Quoted by E. Droz, 'Bibles françaises après le concile de Trente, 1546', *Journal of the Warburg and Courtauld Institutes*, 28 (1965), 215.

[23] J. Calvin, *Opera quae supersunt omnia* (Berlin, 1863–1900), vol. 55, p. 151; Ph. Denis, 'Bible', p. 517–18.

was a closed-off area, which required theologians 'to know all the routes and passages through which one should enter and return' to settle certain debates.[24]

As for the left wing of the Reformation their view on the use of Scripture was closely tied to their conviction of the Spirit's priority over the text. As a matter of principle, the Spiritualists rejected mediation from any ecclesiastical body at all. Christians could go to the Bible on their own. In *Die Rechte Weis, auffs kürtzist lesen zu lernen* (n.p., 1527) Valentin Ickelsammer praised the ability to read which opens access to God's Word, and even better, 'to be a judge of it oneself'. Thus, this Spiritualist believed that 'the Spirit gives us the freedom to believe and the power to judge'.[25] But the questioning stance of a Caspar Schwenkfeld did not stop at comments from ministers, but went as far as to minimise the importance of the Bible itself. This then led to the principle of 'free examination'.[26]

Distinguishing reading practices

Michel de Certeau noted that 'the text only has a significance through its readers'.[27] We must pay careful attention to the ways in which these texts were actually assimilated. The first problem encountered is the ambiguous notion of illiteracy and thus of reading. Indeed in the past as in the present, there were very different levels of ability in deciphering a written work. Basic literacy did not automatically lead to silent reading.[28]

In the still deeply oral world of the sixteenth century, the irruption of the printed word did not lead to any immediate radical changes, and very mixed reading practices remained.[29] Besides silent reading where an intimate contact took place between reader and book, other ways also existed to gain access to written works: reading softly to oneself, group readings in narrow circles which could also welcome the illiter-

---

[24] T. Beza, *Questions et responses chrestiennes ...* (Genève, 1572). Reprinted in Beza, *Correspondance* (Geneva, 1988), vol. 13, pp. 19–21. See p. 22, n. 5, for more evidence of Beza's reluctance to engage in certain theological debates in public.

[25] Gawthrop and Strauss, 'Protestantism and literacy', p. 42. The second quotation comes from a pamphlet by Ickelsammer dated 1525.

[26] A few Spiritualist positions are analysed by B. Roussel, 'Des protestants', in Bédouelle and Roussel, *Le temps*, pp. 314–22.

[27] M. de Certeau, *L'invention du quotidien*, vol. 1, *Arts de faire* (Paris, 1980), p. 287.

[28] R. S. Schofield, 'The measurement of literacy in pre-industrial England', in J. Goody (ed.), *Literacy in Traditional Societies* (Cambridge, 1975), pp. 311–25.

[29] R. Chartier, 'Les pratiques de l'écrit' in Ph. Ariès and G. Duby (eds), *Histoire de la vie privée*, vol. 3, *De la Renaissance aux Lumières* (Paris, 1986), p. 113.

ate, and collective reading in a liturgical context, where at certain points the minister read for all, and at other times everyone followed the text of the hymns in their own booklets.

Individual reading could have an impact which went beyond the reader if he or she, convinced by the text, then spread the ideas which it contained. Italy provides several such examples dealing with heretical works.[30] For his part, Luther believed that theological works were not intended for the common people, but in order that 'the theologian and the bishop be learned and well-taught, so as to make them capable of expounding the doctrine of piety'.[31]

The assimilation of a text by a reader is a particularly personal work as regards the choice and restructuring of the book's contents. As M. de Certeau noted, reading is 'poaching'.[32] While the texts appear as a succession of words, lines and pages to work through in a linear fashion from start to finish, readers are still free to explore this space as they please. Furthermore, readers are not passive recipients of the text, and do not necessarily accept its values and ideas. This is proved by polemical works, which in fact spread the heretical ideas they were meant to be refuting.[33]

Is there a way to shed light on a few main features of this diversity of possible readings? Any answers must obviously be carefully nuanced ones. First, one should distinguish specific literary genres, for certain types of work seem linked to certain forms of reading, sometimes works to be read only out loud, sometimes to oneself. However, other works were probably read alternately collectively and privately. This is at least our working hypothesis, stemming from our overview by country.

Polemical works were a category with a prototype provided by the extraordinary popularity of the *Flugschriften* which flooded Germany especially between 1520 and 1525. This kind of 'press campaign' was repeated later elsewhere in Europe: in France during the religious wars or in The Netherlands after 1565. This publishing phenomenon was primarily based on reading aloud: as its oral structure, its impact on a largely illiterate population, and the frequent use of images, if not caricatures, all point to an oral transmission. The abundance of sixteenth-century pamphlets should not be seen as direct communication in written form, but above all as an indirect transmission. As R. W.

---

[30] See p. 339–40.

[31] WA, vol. 54, p. 179.

[32] M. de Certeau, 'Lire: braconnage et poétique de consommateurs', *Projet*, 124 (1978), 447–57, reprinted with the title 'Lire: un braconnage', in M. de Certeau, *L'invention du quotidien*, pp. 279–96.

[33] Examples are given for Italy (p. 337).

Scribner noted, 'the multiplying effect often attributed to the written word was much more the result of the spoken word'.[34]

Another type of work, namely catechisms, flourished during the Reformation and Counter-Reformation. In any case, this was the type of text which Luther preferred to see in everyone's hands, rather than the Bible.[35] However, catechism classes were primarily an oral activity. The book was certainly indispensible, as the text read aloud by the catechism leader was followed silently by the listening children in their books, a continuation of the medieval university practice where students followed the professor's lecture in their individual books. Indeed, it was common for reading to be learned only after the catechism had been taught.[36] In this use of writing,

> books were used as mnemonic aids; and had to be memorised before being considered as read. Thus, the early stages of schooling focused more on the repetition of books' contents than on acquiring a skill. In these circumstances, learning to read led to a rigidity which was the complete opposite of the curiosity of mind which literacy led to elsewhere.[37]

Other books meant to be used, like liturgical works and psalm-books, were read in a similar fashion. They served as a reminder, rather than as a means of direct communication. Indeed, a Czech Catholic noted that the hymn-books of the Unity of Brethren had a pernicious effect, as the printed works helped the memory of those with poor reading skills.[38]

However, other works were explored primarily in the silence of individual reading. These were technical works aimed at the specialists whom Beza defined as 'those already versed and trained in these subjects'.[39] These exegetical, theological or polemical works, normally in Latin, were published for readers who could understand a printed message without intermediaries. Indeed, this type of work may only have had a limited appeal. The real impact of the doctrinal controversies which divided Lutherans and Calvinists from the 1540s onwards

---

[34] R. W. Scribner, *Popular Culture and Popular Movements in Reformation Germany* (London, 1987), p. 65 and pp. 54–60. See p. 85.

[35] Gawthrop and Strauss, 'Protestantism and literacy', pp. 36–8.

[36] O. Henrivaux in P. Colin et al. (eds), *Aux origines du catéchisme en France* (Paris, 1989), p. 297 (many of the contributions in this volume shed light on this theme); Chartier, 'Les pratiques de l'écrit', p. 120; Gawthrop and Strauss, 'Protestantism and litercy', p. 38.

[37] J. Goody, in his introduction to *Literacy in Traditional Societies* (Cambridge, 1968), p. 14.

[38] See p. 401–2.

[39] Beza, *Correspondance* (Geneva, 1988) vol. 13, p. 19.

was probably much smaller than the reactions of the debating theologians would suggest.[40]

Other works were probably read simultaneously in different ways. This was certainly the case for the Bible. Indeed one must re-examine the question of the use of these Bibles produced in every language by the Protestants. R. Engelsing denounced the myth of the Bible as popular reading.[41] In 1552 in Lyon, when Pierre Navihères tried to justify access to Scripture for all in the presence of his Catholic judges, he made explicit links between reading and preaching. He used the holy ancient fathers as examples, who believed that 'before coming to the sermon, one should read what was being preached on, so that one would understand more'.[42] R. Gawthrop and G. Strauss have shown that the sixteenth-century German Bibles were mainly intended for parishes and clergy.[43] In the case of Denmark and Sweden, the evidence clearly shows that Bibles were systematically and almost exclusively distributed to parishes.[44] Did the same situation hold true in The Netherlands? Johnston does not think so.[45] It is quite likely that the attitude of Calvinism, more firmly based in urban and bourgeois settings, was different in this regard to that of Lutheranism. In any case, the comparison of formats used by each indicates differences. The Calvinist Reformation preferred small formats, suggesting a more frequent private use, whereas Lutheran printers chose the folio format more often, aimed at a collective, liturgical or familial reading.

Works of piety and spiritual comfort also seem to me to be a category of books with multiple uses. One should include in this group all works with a deliberately ambiguous presentation, and with discreetly heterodox contents which served as vehicles for religious opposition where open combat was too dangerous, as in Italy, The Netherlands, and France.[46] By their very nature, they were intended for individual reading, following the model of the pious works of the *Devotio Moderna*. But the few testimonies regarding their influence point to collective readings in small groups, followed by discussions.

---

[40] It is this specific kind of technical polemical works which forms the basis for my remarks on those of Crespin's works which did not sell well (J.-Fr. Gilmont, *Jean Crespin, un éditeur réformé du XVIe siècle* (Geneva, 1981), p. 205). I should add that my point of view on the limited impact of this form of theological debate is controversial.

[41] Engelsing, *Der Bürger*, p. 37.

[42] J. Crespin, *Histoire des martyrs* (Toulouse, 1885) vol. 1, p. 647. This document was published for the first time in *Les actes des martyrs* (Geneva, 1564), pp. 381–2.

[43] Gawthrop and Strauss, 'Protestantism and literacy', p. 40.

[44] See pp. 435 and 461.

[45] See p. 168.

[46] See pp. 135, 149, 173, 321, 356–8.

In this section regarding multi-purpose works, one should perhaps add a category of works mentioned very rarely, namely collections of edifying stories intended to help preachers. Indeed these works, which divide the stories by theme as edifying or terrifying ones, were, on the evidence of their titles, intended as much for the help of preachers as for the edification of individuals and families.[47]

The consequences of silent reading, which was a limited practice in the early stages of the Reformation, were fundamental, in the sense that over the long term, this access to books led to new forms of behaviour. 'Reading done in a private space takes one away from the community, and allows for solitary reflection'. R. Chartier was correct in seeing it as 'one of the major cultural evolutions of modernity'.[48] The fears of many Catholic leaders regarding reading were not baseless. The control of the church over the interpretation of Scripture risked being questioned once individual reading became more generalized.

Early Reformation writings thus circulated in a changing society, which was in the process of discovering new uses for books thanks to their rapid and less expensive reproduction. However, praise for the new technique was not unanimous. Some traditionalists remained unconvinced of its merits,[49] while others who could read and write with ease, aristocratically rejected a technique which 'opened' a field of knowledge, thus putting an end to this group's monopoly.[50] The advent of printing did not, one must remember, stop manuscript copying.[51] But history moved inexorably onwards: 'modernity is writing'.[52]

This advance was supported by other factors, not directly tied to reading. Writings acquired a new authority, impressing both those who could read and those who could not.[53] Furthermore, the call for *Sola Scriptura* naturally meant that theological positions had to be reinforced by texts. While Protestantism was opposed to medieval scholasticism which produced multiple commentaries and preferred to work on

---

[47] For this literary genre, see W. Brückner (ed.) *Volkserzählung und Reformation: ein Handbuch zur Tradierung und Funktion von Erzählstoffen und Erzählliteratur im Protestantismus* (Berlin, 1974), in particular part 3, 'Kanzelwort und geistlicher Hausschatz', pp. 579–756.

[48] Chartier, 'Les pratiques de l'écrit', p. 126.

[49] See above, pp. 25–6.

[50] Chartier, 'Les pratiques de l'écrit', pp. 124–5; Coletti, *L'éloquence de la chaire*, pp. 114–15, 157.

[51] See p. 325. For a slightly earlier period, see also A. Derolez, 'The copying of printed books for humanistic bibliophiles in the fifteenth century', in H. Bekker-Nielsen, M. Børch and B. Algot Sørensen (eds), *From Script to Book: A Symposion* (Odense, 1986), pp. 140–60.

[52] Certeau, *L'invention du quotidien*, p. 283.

[53] See p. 362.

chains of quotations, Protestantism was not always consistent in its return to the authentic text. Indeed, bible annotations were more a feature of Protestant works than Catholic versions.

The persistence of printing's role was also apparent at the end of the period in the insistence of central European dissident sects to establish their own presses. These sects felt the need for presses as much to furnish their fellow believers with liturgical, catechetical or spiritual works as to carry out propaganda or counter-propaganda directed at the surrounding society.[54]

The explosion of national languages

The beginnings of the modern era coincided with a sharp rise in vernacular languages. Evidence of this has been shown in the preceding chapters, in particular in Bohemia, Italy, France, England and the German Empire. In the religious domain – although this phenomenon is not limited to religion alone – the choice of a language which was understood by all the faithful had repercussions on liturgy,[55] pastoral care, theological discourse, and especially on the Bible. This evolution had several consequences which occurred at very different levels.

From the outset, a question arises as to the dignity of vernacular languages, and their ability to serve in the sacred domain. Certain people felt that the religious language should retain an aura of mystery, a distance which made an impression on the faithful. This perspective was similar to the refusal to allow free access to Scripture, for fear of mistaken interpretations by the population. Maintaining Latin also provided the security of stability: as the Vulgate text was unchangeable, so the prayers of the Latin liturgy should preserve a feeling of eternity. This view had its weaknesses, as the rediscovery of classical Latin by the humanists put the quality of ecclesiastical Latin into question, as well as the quality of Saint Jerome's translation. The use of vernacular languages was advocated by those who sought a broader-based communication in the Church and an easy access for all to the riches of the evangelical message.[56] This group

---

[54] See pp. 375, 391, 412–14.

[55] See H. A. P. Schmidt, *Liturgie et langue vulgaire: le problème de la langue liturgique chez les premiers Réformateurs et au concile de Trente* (Rome, 1950) (Analecta gregoriana, 53); L. Lentner, *Volkssprache und Sakralsprache: Geschichte einer Lebensfrage bis zum Ende des Konzils von Trient* (Vienna, 1964) (Wiener Beiträge zur Theologie, 5). See also Coletti, *L'éloquence de la chaire*.

[56] This problem is analysed effectively by V. Coletti, *L'éloquence de la chaire* for the Italian context; see in particular pp. 21–8 and 147–69. See the works of Schmidt and Lentner cited in the previous footnote. For Strasbourg, see R. Bornert, *La réforme protestante du culte à Strasbourg au XVIe siècle, 1523–1598* (Leiden, 1981).

included Catholics as well, even if they did not follow Luther in his ironical comment on the Mass: 'they hid the words of the Sacrament from us, and told us that laypeople were not to be taught what they meant'.[57] On a more positive note, Luther stated 'I do not blush to preach and write in the vernacular languages for the untaught laity', emphasizing that the use of vernacular languages would bring to Christianity a benefit 'which would be greater than the big and famous books on questions dealt with in the schools between scholars alone'.[58]

But these popular languages were evolving rapidly. It was difficult to express in these idioms concepts which had been shaped and reshaped in classical languages. As Olivétan stated at the beginning of his Bible translation, 'to make Hebrew and Greek eloquence speak French' was to want to 'teach the gentle lark to sing the song of the croaking raven'. He was echoing Luther's comment to Wenceslaus Linck:

> I am sweating blood to put the Prophets in the vernacular. Dear God, it is such hard work and so difficult to make the Hebrew writers speak German! As they refuse to abandon their Hebrew style, they balk at flowing into this German barbarity. It is as though the lark, having lost its sweet melody, had to imitate the cuckoo and its monotonous note.[59]

A few decades later, Robert Estienne's assessment was quite different. For him, 'there is no question that French expresses and represents Greek and also Hebrew better than Latin does'.[60] Difficulties grew, almost over each word. In 1548 Esprit Rotier asked how one was to translate *verbum* from *In principio erat verbum*: 'In the beginning was the Word'? This translation brought Saint John's phrase down to the level of an external concept, while in fact it was meant to be internal to the Trinity. Thus the Dominican believed that one should paraphrase the word *Verbum*.[61] In his 1552 *Monotessaron*, Benjamin Beausport also took this verse as an example of the impossibility of a translation without a gloss.

> What would be the problem if for *Verbum*, *In principio erat verbum*, we translated Son of God, given that there is no proper French word apart from that? Some called it the Word, which was not well-chosen. Others tried the speech, yet others the sermon,

---

[57] WA, vol. 6, p. 362.

[58] WA, vol. 6, p. 203.

[59] WA Br., vol. 4, p. 484.

[60] Preface to the Latin–French *Nouveau Testament* of 1552. This passage is quoted by E. Armstrong, *Robert Estienne, royal printer* (revd edn, London, 1986), p. 228, n. 6.

[61] E. Rotier, *De non vertenda Scriptura sacra in vulgarem linguam dissertatio* (Toulouse, 1548) in *Collectio quorundam authorum qui ... in vulgarem linguam translationes damnarunt* (Paris, 1661), vol. 2, p. 71 (following G. Bédouelle, 'Le débat catholique', pp. 46–7).

and neither one nor the other is right for *verbum* if they are taken in their everyday sense. If I say the Word, I am only massacring the Latin, as if I said the vulners for *vulnera* or ubers for *ubera*.[62]

Beza also noted the deficiencies in the vernacular, 'the poverty of our language', to justify his reluctance to translate one of his theological treatises. 'It could be, he added, that the French translation is less clear in certain places, especially for the common people, than is my original Latin.'[63]

In spite of these technical reservations, printing probably encouraged the use of vernacular languages. The economic operation of the new technique meant a growth in the reading public and thus the search for new markets. Together with the great German, English and Dutch translations of the Bible, the *ars artificialiter scribendi* accustomed the readers to a uniform vernacular language. Furthermore, by bringing theological debates to public attention through books, the Reformation increased the use of the vernacular.[64]

At the end of the Middle Ages, while the Catholics were willing to distribute works of piety and books of hours in the vernacular, they held to Latin for theological and liturgical works. We have seen how the Reformation transformed these habits. One can add to this a futher instance of Catholic reluctance to abandon Latin. In the following centuries, teaching took place in Latin in Catholic lands and in the national languages in Protestant areas.[65] Thus the Catholics participated only half-heartedly in theological debates in the vernacular. When they did do so, they emphasised the need to counter the Protestants on their own territory. To defend his version of the Bible, René Benoist noted in 1568 'Heretics have almost persuaded everybody that they should own and read this holy book [the Bible]'.[66] And certain Italian humanists, like Girolamo Muzio, after having called for a wider use of the language of the people, were forced by the effects of the Counter Reformation to reduce drastically the cultural space of the vernacular.[67] In the same way as when confronting the Bible, the general attitude on the Catholic side was a rather negative one.

---

[62] Quoted by Droz, 'Bibles', p. 219.

[63] Beza, *Correspondance* (Geneva, 1988) vol. 13, p. 19.

[64] Coletti, *L'éloquence de la chaire*, pp. 137–8; Febvre/Martin, pp. 477–96.

[65] R. Engelsing, *Analphabetentum und Lektüre: Zur Sozialgeschichte des Lesens in Deutschland zwischen feudaler und industrieller Gesellschaft* (Stuttgart, 1973), pp. 40–41.

[66] *La Sainte Bible* Paris: S. Nivelle, 1568, fol. *4ᵛ; see also the reaction of Guido da Fano in 1532 and that of Cardinal Madruzzo in Trent (Coletti, *L'éloquence de la chaire*, p. 143 and 208).

[67] See Coletti, *L'éloquence de la chaire*, pp. 168–9.

As for use in the liturgy, the Catholic position remained unchanged, strictly faithful to Latin. For his part, Luther abandoned Latin only progressively, under pressure from his most radical disciples. However, he never totally rejected the liturgical use of Latin.[68] For Catholics as for Protestants, Latin was certainly the technical language for theological debate, holding unparalleled advantages for international communication.

A certain broadening of written discourse should have brought to light a question which has seemingly not yet been discussed. Anyone who has put an oral presentation into writing knows the distance separating the spoken discourse from its written version. When they entered into polemical debates, from the pulpits or in the market places or on pages covered with small typographical marks, were the Reformers aware of the specificity of the different means of communication? One would have to gather evidence together systematically to provide at least a preliminary answer to this question. Thus for example what were the real reasons for Calvin's reluctance to publish his sermons? Even though the texts of many of his sermons were carefully saved, Calvin only rarely authorized their publication. In his preface to the edition of a few sermons, Jacques Roux admitted that he had obtained Calvin's consent to have his sermons published 'only with difficulty, as all who know him privately will readily believe'. Roux's explanation for Calvin's reticence probably does not go to the very heart of the matter: those close to him 'are well aware that he only wanted to serve the flock that God entrusted to him, by teaching it in a familiar fashion, and not to create sermons at his leisure to be paraded before everyone'.[69] Is it not the case that this master of the language felt that the sermon was not a literary form suited to printing?

The conditions of book production

This work has shown widely diverse situations of printing in sixteenth-century Europe. Germany saw the multiplication and spread of presses, without any city taking a leading role. In France, Italy and The Netherlands, production was focused in Paris, Venice and Antwerp respec-

---

[68] M. Lienhard, *Martin Luther, un temps, une vie, un message* (Paris, Geneva, 1983), pp. 188–95.

[69] J. Calvin, *Opera quae extant omnia* (Brunswick, Berlin, 1863–1900), vol. 35, cols 521–4. Calvin's influence on the development of the French language is a central feature of F. M. Higman's work (see for instance, 'Theology in French: religious pamphlets from the Counter-Reformation', in *Renaissance and Modern Studies*, 23 (1979), 128). On Calvin and the book, see J.-Fr. Gilmont, *Jean Calvin et le livre* (Geneva, 1997).

tively. Other lands progressively acquired a measure of relative autonomy in this domain. They did so either by establishing a single press,
as in Sweden, or by multiplying the number of small printing houses
with the support of local magnates, as in Poland, Bohemia, or Hungary.
Indeed, political reasons explain why certain presses established themselves in villages in Central Europe.

The impact of the political situation in the establishment of a printing
press was thus crucial. Freedom, and possibly the active support of
ruling powers were very favourable factors, but were not strictly indispensable for the smooth running of a printing house. The production of
forbidden books was carried out in very different circumstances in
different locations. Certain presses which operated openly with the
support of local rulers could camouflage a part of their production to
facilitate its entry into Catholic lands. This was Geneva's speciality in
the period under discussion. As for clandestine presses, the situation
varied. In some places, the authorities turned a blind eye, as long as the
printers did not go beyond certain limits, as in Antwerp before 1545 or
in Basle throughout the century. Elsewhere, presses did brave every
prohibition. This was generally the case for evangelical and Reformed
printing houses in Catholic lands; and in Protestant lands for printers
sympathetic to the radical ideas of the Spiritualists or the Anabaptists.[70]
Indeed, the efforts of these marginal groups on the Reformation's left
wing deserve more attention. They were welcomed for a few years in
Strasbourg, and then in Basle, especially at Oporinus's shop. Other
printers did freelance work at their own risks, including Sebastian
Franck and Étienne Dolet.

Printing presses could not operate without financial support. This
rule was universal, even though the profession attracted both idealists
and canny businessmen. If no profits were to be had, then a wealthy
backer was indispensable. Indeed, political and religious powers had no
hesitation in imposing the purchase of certain works when they wanted
more copies to be distributed. This was the case in Sweden with the
large version of the Bible of 1541, which all the parishes of the kingdom
were compelled to buy. This was a rather simple model of authoritarian
financing. The movement of reprints and of more or less pirated copies,
and the conflicts between publishers and between booksellers reflect the
importance of the financial stakes. Then as now, the religious book
could be profitable for the publisher. But errors of judgement could also
occur, as evidenced by bankruptcies and crises.

Many chapters emphasized the role of individuals in the establishment of the presses. These chapters showed in particular the range of

[70] See pp. 32–3.

motivations which led to the publication of religious books, from a personal calling to straightforward professional work.[71] This is, however, a delicate area. If one were to judge the editors by the catalogue of their publications, one must not neglect the prudent gestures designed to gain the support of the ruling powers nor the profit-seeking ventures designed to balance the budgets. Furthermore, the protestations in the prefaces are a literary genre needing careful interpretation. In any case it is interesting to note that often in sixteenth-century minds, the printer remained a negligible factor, whose responsibility for the production of forbidden books was only secondary.[72] Catholic authorities should, however, have been alerted by the rapid Protestantisation of the printing workers.

Indeed, the publishers' role was even greater in that the rights of authors over their texts were not yet recognized. How many works were in fact taken from previous texts, and modified, amplified and reoriented in a way that was more or less faithful to the original? The obligatory discretion in clandestine productions was not only due to a reflex of prudence but also mirrored ambiguous relations vis-à-vis the text itself. And – especially in the case of Italy – the very definition of a 'Protestant' text was a matter for debate. When readers' reactions could be measured thanks to the Inquisition trials, it was clear that texts considered by modern critics as perfectly orthodox were read as corrosive messages radically challenging traditional religion.[73]

The study of the circulation of printed works brought the existence of several production models to light. Some were happy to respond to local consumption, while others aimed at larger markets. Exports alone explain how small cities like Basle or Geneva welcomed such a large number of printers. In the former case, the printers focused on producing scholarly works for the international humanist community, while in the latter case, at least in the 1550s and 1560s, the presses primarily supported the spread of the Reformation in French-speaking lands. However, the expansion into a wider market called for the development of commercial trade links. Wittenberg's situation demonstrates this a contrario. Given Luther's presence, the city could have massively dominated the German evangelical production. This did not occur, as the city lacked an effective distribution network. It is possible that the political structures of Germany, as well as its linguistic diversity were unfavourable.[74] In contrast, the Genevan organization was impressively

[71] See pp. 110, 158.
[72] See p. 284.
[73] See pp. 365–6.
[74] See p. 46.

efficient, at least before the start of a certain amount of competition based in France itself. This vast project called both for the production of books more or less camouflaged in terms of content and for the existence of a very strong itinerant book trade.[75]

Protestants and Catholics confronting printed works

Can one simply conclude that Protestants trusted books and Catholics feared them? To avoid simplification, one must first distinguish literary genres. Traditional views for the spread of the Reformation through books are based above all on the famous pamphlet war that shook the German States between 1520 and 1525. And it is in fact clear that the Protestants were innovators in the field of printed religious polemic. They showed themselves to be past masters at it, while Catholics followed only reluctantly, being constrained and compelled to do so. Indeed the latter often allowed favourable opportunities for intervening to escape. This was the case in Germany: when a few Catholics discovered pamphlets in 1529, 'it was a bit too late'.[76]

In contrast, in the traditional areas of liturgy[77] and piety, Catholics continued to turn to the presses, following a tradition established already in the fifteenth century. The Reformation appears to have made no impact on production in this sector. There were no visible changes in the content of these pious works.[78]

As for the Bible, as we have seen, the unenthusiastic Catholic attitude was not monolithic. For their part, the Protestants made full use of printing for catechetical instruction, liturgy, and hymn-singing. Access to a printing press was indispensable from this point on for each Protestant church.

The Catholic authorities' fears of the dangers of printing were expressed in the generalized practice of censorship, over which the Catholics held no monopoly. For both religious and political reasons, every civil and ecclesiastical power sought to control more or less closely the output of the presses.[79] Faced with the new invention, the Catholic Church used the stick more often than the carrot, doing more to forbid

---

[75] See pp. 125–6.

[76] R. W. Scribner, *For the Sake of Simple Folk. Popular Propaganda for the German Reformation* (Cambridge, 1981), p. 233.

[77] This is verifiable despite the reservations of certain manuscript lovers, as Flood points out (Chapter 2, footnote 9, above).

[78] See p. 117.

[79] See the complaints regarding the Protestant authorities' interventions voiced by M. Judex in his book cited in the Introduction (footnote 8).

488 THE REFORMATION AND THE BOOK

the circulation of heretical books than to promote attractive orthodox works. The establishment of efficient controls was, however, a long time in coming. Throughout most of Europe, it was only by the middle of the century that the authorities were able to halt efficiently the infiltration of new ideas through the book. Spain is a unique example of a country in which an immense machinery not only controlled internal production, but especially impeded any importation of dangerous books. Elsewhere, as in France, Italy, or England under Henry VIII and Mary Tudor, the authorities were generally able to close down presses under their jurisdiction, but not so the book trade: forbidden works ceaselessly crossed borders. For its part, the German empire with its political divisions provided a large amount of typographical freedom, similar to that found in Central Europe. Some of the large merchant cities, like Antwerp and Venice until the 1550s, were also places where the local authorities would turn a blind eye, so long as a certain amount of discretion was maintained.

While Protestantism clearly felt more confident about printing, one should not simply take it for granted that all Catholics rejected the new technique. Often goaded by the Protestants, certain Catholics saw that the use of printing would help their cause. They too sought a broad-based communication, both in oral and written forms, in a language understood by all. At the same time, the clerical reflex of reserving the monopoly of the sacred science to one caste was not unknown in the Protestant world. The dividing line between the supporters and opponents of written culture split the Christian confessions, with the proviso that Catholics who advocated printing and popular languages were a minority in their own camp and in society. Indeed, the Protestantization of the typographers contributed to the slow entry of Catholics into the printing establishments. The difficulties encountered by the Catholic polemicists in Germany bear witness to this,[80] as were the problems encountered by French translators of the Bible.

The Influence of the Reformation on the book

The reverse question remains: did the Reformation movement have an impact on the evolution of printing? A measured response, it seems to me, calls for a distinction to be made between the short- and longer-term effects of the Reformation on printing.

[80] See pp. 25, 41–2.

Visible changes in the short term

The religious debate opened by Luther certainly led to an increase in printed production. The first real 'press campaigns' were brought into existence by the Reformation. The German *Flugschrift* phenomenon, with its ups and downs after 1525, manifested itself in different forms in England,[81] France[82] and The Netherlands. This use of printing was begun and popularized by the Reformation.[83]

The Reformation led not only to a clear acceleration in the printed production of polemical works, but also of other texts used on a daily basis, such as Bibles, liturgical works, catechisms, psalters etc. Wittenberg and Geneva were extreme cases of cities where printing made an extraordinary leap forwards, due to the presence of a great Reformer and author. The impulse provided by the Reformation led to the creation of an industrial tool which in the final third of the century faltered because of the decrease in demand. Almost everywhere, the end of the sixteenth century was a difficult time for printing presses, which seems to indicate that the effects of the Reformation's influence on printing were not always uniformly positive.

Conclusions as to cause and effect in other changes at the beginning of the modern era are harder to draw. The content of books evolved, with the disappearance of many medieval best sellers still sold in the fifteenth century, with a completely renewed approach to the authors of classical antiquity and patristics, but especially with the increasing welcome for contemporary authors. Indeed, these writers saw their situation change, as the success of certain works led to a real dialogue between authors and readers. Erasmus clearly forged the path in this domain.[84] But what were the links between these changes and the Reformation? Was there a causal link or merely coincidental development? In my opinion, no solid argument has been made until now to establish the Reformation's direct influence in this matter. Would it not be more prudent to conclude that these two phenomena occurred side by side, and that any changes in the content of books and the

---

[81] See pp. 281, 284.

[82] See R. M. Kingdon, 'Pamphlet literature of the French Reformation', in S. Ozment (ed.) *Reformation Europe: A Guide to Research* (St. Louis, 1982), pp. 233–48.

[83] There are no real precedents for the production of information in this form by the printing presses. See B. Moeller, 'Flugschriften der Reformationszeit', in *Theologische Realenzyklopädie* (Berlin, New York, 1983) vol. 11, p. 240; J.-P. Seguin, *L'information en France de Louis XII à Henri II* (Geneva, 1961).

[84] N. Z. Davis, 'Printing and the people', in N. Z. Davis, *Society and Culture in Early Modern France* (Stanford, 1975), pp. 213–14; J. Lough, *Writer and Public in France* (Oxford, 1978) ch. 2.

status of authors derived rather naturally from the development of printing?

However, the generalized use of national languages in the religious domain was largely due to the Reformation. The comments made regarding the use of Low German show that in spite of the support of the Evangelical Church for the dialect, its use decreased. In such a situation, where diverse factors pulled in different directions, evangelism was on the side of the language of the people.[85]

Protestantism was also linked to certain forms of research and innovation in graphical arts. The civility characters are the most unusual case: all the printers who joined the search for a new font were linked more or less closely to Protestantism.[86] While the Reformation played no role in the introduction of roman and italic characters into France, it did play a part in England via the Genevan Bible of Rowland Hall.[87] However, when the German and Dutch printers attempted to print in roman or italic fonts, they failed.[88] But these details are only really relevant to the anecdotal history of the book.

A different assessment of the book over the long term

Any examination of the facts which tries to ignore the evolution of the book in later centuries seemingly does not end up with a real division between Protestants and Catholics in terms of their relations with printing. Certain clear tendencies do emerge, but in essential matters, such as the relation between preaching and individual reading, between the use of Latin and that of national languages, the borderlines went right through the confessions.

Indeed, it is normal that the evolution of fundamental phenomena such as the links with writing should be felt only over the long term.[89] Should one establish a link between confessional phenomena and the present-day gap between countries with a Protestant tradition and Catholic ones regarding books and reading? Clear hints of this divide can be found in the respective situation of libraries[90] or in the print quality of

---

[85] See p. 48.

[86] See pp. 123–4, 162–3.

[87] St Morison, *The Geneva Bible* (Zurich, 1954), and its French version, *La Bible anglaise de Genève, 1560* (Geneva, Berne, 1972).

[88] See pp. 48, 161–2.

[89] Chartier, 'Les pratiques de l'écrit', pp. 121–2.

[90] A recent study by the European Community Commission indicates the great disparities in the Common Market in terms of library policy. While the differences do not tally exactly with previously dominant confessional borders, there is, however, a certain amount of evidence to this effect. (Ph. Ramsdale, *A Study of Library Economics in the European Communities* (Luxemburg, 1988)).

publications. Can one in fact give a religious explanation to these contrasting attitudes *vis-à-vis* the book?

In order to do this effectively, one would have to increase the number of comparative analyses like those carried out for Metz at the end of the seventeenth century: while 70 per cent of Protestant inventories recorded books, only 25 per cent did so on the Catholic side.[91] In the Lutheran world, as shown by R. Gawthorp and G. Strauss, it was only in a later period, that of pietism, that the habit of reading the Bible on one's own became more general. At that point, the seeds of cultural revolution sown by Luther began to grow. The encouragement of reading led to individual reading with all its ramifications in terms of the growth of privacy and autonomy in relation to the text and even the sacred text.[92] In the same way, one must note that the Reformed ministers were partly responsible for the growing literacy rate in the French rural areas. The evidence gathered by N. Z. Davis is generally convincing. The clergy's religious zeal led them to distribute printed works and to encourage reading in rural areas in spite of insufficient economic justification for such a project.[93]

A fruitful field for further research

Our work is not intended as the final say in the matter. On the contrary, we hope to suggest new lines of research. A first point seems to come from the links between the different essays, namely the usefulness of comparing central issues and research techniques. Differing sensitivities and national traditions led researchers towards different aspects of the book's past and towards varied sources. Thus each had an interest in learning from the others.

Our authors all agreed that a good contribution stemmed from as complete a knowledge as possible of early printing production. This was the primary source for researchers to work on. Any analysis of typographical production, whether carried out with authors or publishers as the main focus, calls for good bibliographies. In this regard, the situation from country to country is very uneven, although those countries whose bibliographies are not as complete have almost all begun to fill the gap.

---

[91] P. Benedict, 'Bibliothèques protestantes et catholiques à Metz au XVIIe siècle', *Annales, Économies, Sociétés, Civilisations* 40 (1985) 343–70. See Chartier, 'Les pratiques de l'écrit', pp. 131–5.

[92] Gawthrop and Strauss, 'Protestantism and literacy', pp. 43–55.

[93] Davis, 'Printing', p. 205.

The history of the book can be approached from a variety of angles, and the contributions in this book are evidence of this. Traditionally the history of doctrines and ideas has been given priority, and has generally been examined most carefully. Naturally enough, older works have been read for their contents. But it is equally fruitful to examine their aspect, to inquire about those who produced these books, and about the routes they took before ending up in readers' hands. This approach, which goes beyond that of cataloguing and bibliography, gives a new depth to the texts.

But the newest, most fruitful, and also most difficult approach is to examine reading practices. At this point one must go beyond a purely literary perspective, which would limit the problem to the reception of texts by famous authors.[94] Instead, one must determine how average readers used books. The possibilities provided by the archives of the Italian Inquisition are doubtlessly exceptional, but research on the *Flugschriften* has shown that there are many indications as to reading practices. Because their attention was not drawn to the existence of these levels of literacy, historians probably did not realize what could be drawn from the sources.

The book is a means of communication. The new feature in the sixteenth century was its multiplication in a world in which most links were oral. Indeed, at this time information circulated through many channels, as underlined by N. Z. Davis: 'rumors, street singers, private letters, the announcements of town criers, fireworks, bell-ringing and penitential processions'.[95] One must thus put aside the twentieth-century situation and never lose sight of the omnipresence of oral communication.

In the same way, one should not neglect the firm links between printed works and illustrations.[96] The role of printing was in fact much more revolutionary as regards images than for texts. In spite of its slowness, the copying of texts by scribes had been an effective technique since antiquity. In contrast, one had to wait for printed engravings before being able to reproduce images that were faithful to their original. This was the most radical change in communications.[97]

For Johann Brenz, there were three forms of preaching. The most important one was done from the pulpit, but it was complemented by

---

[94] See S. Seidel Menchi, *Erasmo in Italia, 1520–1580* (Turin, 1987), pp. 12–13.

[95] Davis, 'Printing', p. 219.

[96] Scribner, *For the Sake*; R. C. Cole, 'Pamphlet woodcuts in the communication process of Reformation Germany', in K. C. Sessions and P. N. Bebb (eds), *Pietas et Societas: New Trends in Reformation Social History, Essays in Memory of Harold J. Grimm* (Kirksville, 1985), pp. 103–22. See also p. 164–5.

[97] W. M. Ivins Jr, *Prints and Visual Communication* (Cambridge, Mass., 1953).

reading on the one hand and singing on the other.[98] The links between printing and singing also merit attention, not only because the printed aid allowed generations of Protestants to participate actively in worship, but also because of the role which each confession assigned to text and music. Zwingli, though himself a fine musician, rejected music in worship; Calvin and Bucer favoured an austere sound: 'one must always beware that the ears are not more attentive to the harmony of the singing than the mind is to the spiritual meaning of the words';[99] and Luther, equally concerned about the balance between texts and melodies, highlighted the delights of polyphony.[100]

Finally, theatre could also encourage reading or at least could disseminate ideas carried by the texts. In 1585, the biblical sketches carried out by the chambers of rhetoric in Lille worried the authorities, for 'through these, both the participants and the populace end up buying and leafing through French Bibles'.[101] La Farce des théologastres, a text which was performed well before it was published, also acted as a relay for Reformation and humanist ideas spread by printing.[102] Thus the book cannot be detached from an entire gamut of human relations, in which oral culture often played a major role.

---

[98] See P. Veit, 'Le chant', p. 661.

[99] J. Calvin, Institution de la religion chrestienne, J.-D. Benoit (ed.), (Paris, 1957–63), l. 3, ch. 20, para. 32, p. 375; see W. S. Reid, 'The battle hymns of the Lord: Calvinist psalmody of the sixteenth century', in Sixteenth Century Essays and Studies, 2 (1971), pp. 36–54. For Bucer, see R. Bornert, La Réforme protestante du culte à Strasbourg au XVIe siècle, 1523–1598 (Leiden, 1981), pp. 469–84.

[100] P. Veit, 'Martin Luther, chantre de la Réforme. Sa conception de la musique et du chant d'église', in Positions luthériennes, 30 (1982), 47–66. On communication via singing, see Scribner, Popular, pp. 60–62.

[101] R. Lebègue, La tragédie religieuse en France: Les débuts, 1514–1573 (Paris, 1929), p. 58.

[102] Cl. Longeon (ed.), La Farce des théologastres (Geneva, 1989). See also the section 'Le théâtre et la polémique', in M. Gravier, Luther et l'opinion publique (Paris, 1942), pp. 175–89.

Index